MINE DISASTERS AND MINE RESCUE

THIRD EDITION

MINE DISASTERS AND MINE RESCUE

THIRD EDITION

M A Ramlu

B.Sc., (Madras University), B.Sc. (Min.Engg.), (B.H.U.),
Dr.-Ing. (Clausthal), F.R.G., M.G.M.I., F.I.E., MEAI

Formerly,
Professor and Head, Department of Mining Engineering
Deputy Director and Acting Director, IIT Kharagpur

&

UGC Visiting Professor Indian School of Mines, Dhanbad

Universities Press

MINE DISASTERS AND MINE RESCUE (THIRD EDITION)

UNIVERSITIES PRESS (INDIA) PRIVATE LIMITED

Registered Office
3-6-747/1/A & 3-6-754/1, Himayatnagar, Hyderabad 500 029, Telangana, India
info@universitiespress.com, www.universitiespress.com

Distributed by
Orient Blackswan Private Limited

Registered Office
3-6-752 Himayatnagar, Hyderabad 500 029, Telangana, India

Other Offices
Bengaluru, Chennai, Guwahati, Hyderabad, Kolkata,
Mumbai, New Delhi, Noida, Patna

Second Edition 2006
Third Edition 2018
Reprinted 2022, 2025

ISBN 978 93 86235 58 9

502248

Cover and book design

Typeset in Times New Roman 10.5/12.5 *by*
Orient BlackSwan

Printed in India by
Replika Press Pvt. Ltd., Kundli Sonepat 131 028, Haryana

Published by
Universities Press (India) Private Limited
3-6-747/1/A & 3-6-754/1, Himayatnagar
Hyderabad 500 029, Telangana, India

To

my wife, Saroja,

for her encouragement and enduring patience

Contents

Preface to the Third Edition

This edition of Mine Disasters and Mine Rescue has significant additions of importance to mine functioning and mine safety. A description of the leaky feeder digital radio communication system for operating in deep mining conditions, the role of predictive dust modelling at the mine planning stage, the use of explosibility diagrams, including U.S.B.M., for interpreting samples of mine atmospheres, and the problem of acid mine drainage and the prevention and control of the same are some of the topics that have been newly added. Besides this, the text has been improved considerably with the elimination of few inadvertent errors and the inclusion of essential descriptions in many places. It is my sincere hope that this edition will continue to contribute to the cause of improving mine safety and mine environment in the Indian mining industry, and that teachers, students and practitioners of mining engineering will benefit from it.

M.A. Ramlu
2018

Preface to the Second Edition

This edition of *Mine Disasters and Mine Rescue* has been brought out in the hope that it will continue to further the important cause of improving mine safety and mine environment in the Indian mining industry. While preparing this edition, steps have been taken to bring the material on mine fires, mine explosions and mine rescue has been re-written to accommodate the recent developments in mine rescue apparatus abroad and in India.

Although the book will be of great value to practising mining engineers and students of mining engineering, it is not really intended for specialists. Research has been continuously producing vast scientific and technical literature on the mechanisms of spontaneous heating of coal and sulphide ores as well as of other mine fires and explosions, all of which are easily available to the interested scholar. This book provides a basic though comprehensive treatment of the subject of mine disasters and mine rescue.

I wish to acknowledge the invaluable help provided by Mr. Nicholas Kyriazi of the US Bureau of Mines, Pittsburg research Centre, who generously sent me product information and the latest reports of investigations on self-contained breathing apparatus and self-rescuers. I am also very grateful to Mr. William R. Flynn of Biomarine Inc, USA for making available to me useful drawings for inclusion in the book. I would like to acknowledge the generosity of Auergesellschaft mbH, Berlin; National Draeger Inc., Pittsburg; CSE Corp. Monroeville and Ocenco Inc., Kenosha, USA who provided me product catalogues on their mine rescue equipment. I am grateful for the encouragement given to me by Universities Press Pvt. Ltd. Last but not least I must thank my wife, Saroja, for her encouragement and enduring patience.

M.A. Ramlu
2006

Preface to the First Edition

Disasters occur in mines as a result of large mine fires, powerful mine explosions violent rock gas outbursts, and water inundations. All operating mines have to contend with the real danger of being overtaken by one or more disasters at some points of time during their life. Plans for disaster management are, therefore, drawn by the mine managements and, therefore, the mining industry.

This book is a completely revised edition of an earlier work by the author *Mine Fires, Explosions, Rescue, Recovery and Inundations* which at once became a standard textbook on mine safety for all students of mining engineering in India. Owing to the rapid advances that have been made in mining research for further promotion of mine safety and the pressing demand for the book as it went out of market, the author undertook the arduous task of updating the book with new techniques, instruments, equipment, research findings, and experiences accumulated over the past decade. The subject of spontaneous combustion received an enlarged treatment. The inclusion of the subject of mine environmental monitoring and control which has become an important production tool and outbursts of coal and gas have added to the usefulness of the book.

Thanks are due to the following manufacturers of gas measuring instruments, environmental monitoring and control equipment, and mine rescue apparatus, who have generously supplied at different time points technical information with illustrations and schematic diagram for illustrating the text:

Drägerwork AG, Lübeck, Germany.
Auergesellschaft GmbH, Berlin, Germany.
Mine Safety Appliances Company, Pittsburg, USA
CSE Corporation, Monroeville, USA
J & S Sieger Ltd., Poole, UK
Hawker Siddley Dynamics Engineering Ltd., Welwyn Garden City, UK.
Oldham France SA, Arras, France.
Riken Keiki Instrument Co. Ltd., Tokyo, Japan.
Sabre Safety Ltd., Aldershot, UK.

Special thanks are also due to the Superintendent, Doncaster Mine Rescue Station, UK, and the Head of the Central Rescue Station, Essen, Germany who provided useful material for inclusion in the book.

Acknowledgement to the authors/information source is made in the appropriate places in the text.

The author wishes to express his gratitude to his son, M. Avanindra, an electronics engineer, who co-authored with him in writing the section on Environmental Monitoring & Control.

Appreciation is expressed to S.P. Hazra and Sri A.K.M. Burman of the Department of Mining Engineering IIT Kharagput, for preparing the drawings with great care, ingenuity, and skill. Finally, the author express deep appreciation to his wife without whose driving force, the revision work would have taken much longer.

M.A. Ramlu
1991

CHAPTER 1

Mine Fires

1.1 Underground Fires

Fires constitute an ever-present hazard in coal mines. They occur whenever and wherever combustible materials are present in mine workings. They endanger not only the valuable lives of men in a mine but also cause considerable economic losses to the organization affected by them. The losses incurred are both direct and indirect. The direct losses include loss of coal reserves and valuable mining equipment and the cost of fire-fighting and recovery of sealed-off areas. The indirect losses arise out of a fall in production from the affected section resulting in a fall in productivity and subsequent increase in operating costs. These costs are usually higher than the direct ones. It is well-nigh impossible to make an accurate assessment of the full cost of a serious mine fire. To those engaged in fire-fighting or in the unsealing of the fires, mine fires are far more hazardous than explosions.

Fires also occur in underground metal mines mining reactive sulphide ores.

Most mine fires start very small and can be extinguished, if detected in time, with a bucket of water or a bag of stone dust. It is only when a fire is discovered late or improper fire-fighting procedures are adopted that it gets out of control.

For a mine fire to break out, the following three conditions must be fulfilled:

(1) Combustible material must be available in sufficient quantity;
(2) Sufficient supply of oxygen must be available; and
(3) A source of ignition of adequate energy must be present.

If any of these conditions is not fulfilled, a mine fire will not break out.

There are two distinct types of mine fires:

(1) Incipient fires or fires due to spontaneous combustion; and
(2) Open fires.

Incipient fires, also called seam fires, are fires which originate in abandoned and discontinued mine workings, in goaves of seams being worked, in falls of roof coal, in fractured coal pillars, and in the vicinity of geological disturbances. They account for up to 75 to 90 per cent of all underground coal and 20 per cent of all underground metal mine fires, and are difficult to detect in their early stages.

Open fires are fires which originate in open mine workings such as shafts, roadways, and coal faces due to a variety of causes including spontaneous combustion and are characterized by visible active combustion or flame. They spread quickly in the direction of ventilation, the rate being dependent upon the kind and quantity of the combustible material, the amount of air reaching it, and the velocity of the air current. In any case, they develop much faster than incipient fires and spread quickly in the direction of ventilation if they are not suppressed within one or two hours after their outbreak. Fire in hard-rock metal mines occur, though infrequently, due to decaying timber supports in stopes and burning of mining equipment.

Coal mine fires have a century-long history in Indian coalfields. The first fire was reported in the Raniganj Coalfield in 1865 and in the Jharia Coalfield in 1916.

1.1.1 Causes and prevention of coal mine fires

The various causes of coal mine fires may be grouped under the following main headings:

(i) Open flames
(ii) Spontaneous combustion
(iii) Electricity
(iv) Friction
(v) Blasting
(vi) Explosions
(vii) Miscellaneous.

The relative importance of these causes varies from district to district in the same mine and depends to a great extent on the equipment and supplies used, on the training and discipline among the workmen, and on the liability of the coal to spontaneous combustion.

1.1.1.1 Open flames

In naked-lamp mines, in which naked or open lights are used, fires may originate through careless handling of lamps and carrying matches or other flame-making devices.

1.1.1.2 Spontaneous combustion

By the term 'spontaneous combustion', one understands self-heating of coal or of any easily oxdizable substance due to auto-oxidation at ordinary atmospheric temperatures. The oxidation process is a catalytic, exothermic and self-sustaining reaction.

Spontaneous combustion as an unwelcome feature had accompanied mining right from the days mining began up to the present day. There are several instances of fires due to spontaneous combustion in the history of mining which continued to burn for several decades and centuries. A well-known Indian example is the Jharia Fire consisting of several fires which has continued to burn since 1925. In reports of the shipping industry of the 19th century, cases of a number of coal cargo ships catching fire and sometimes causing explosions have been mentioned.

Today, storage of run-of-mine or prepared sizes of coal has become an integral part of coal-handling systems at mines, power plants, and metallurgical coking plants. The undesirable aspects of storage of coal, however, are spontaneous combustion and coal deterioration. Proper protection of coal storage piles is afforded by the prevention of oxidation of coal, which will prevent not only spontaneous combustion but also deterioration of coal.

The subject of spontaneous combustion has attracted the attention of several research workers since the beginning of the 19th century. It is still being worked upon today in many countries.

Most of the researchers have investigated the subject from chemical as well as physical considerations under isothermal and adiabatic conditions. The most important theories of spontaneous combustion that had been advanced are the pyrite theory (Plot), the bacterium theory (Potter), the phenol theory (Fischer), the coal–oxygen complex theory (Rhead and Wheeler), and the electrochemical theory (Kamneva and Aleksandrov). These theories do not hold good under all conditions and are applicable only under certain conditions because of the complex compositions of the coals and the lack of a full understanding of the mechanism of auto-oxidation. The generally accepted theory at present is the Coal–Oxygen Complex Theory, which, according to a simplified consensus, considers that following an initial physical adsorption of oxygen, a variety of more or less stable coal–oxygen complexes are formed at different temperatures with release of gaseous products of oxidation.

The oxygen absorption reaction is considered to take place as follows:

$$\text{Coal} + \text{Oxygen} \longrightarrow \text{Coal–oxygen complex} \longrightarrow \text{Oxidized coal} + CO,\ CO_2,\ H_2O$$

The oxygen fixed on the coal is believed to be in carboxyl (–COOH), carbonyl (>CO) and other functional groups.

The common view, however, generally held by mining engineers is that the main causes of spontaneous heating are the sorption and oxidation properties of the coal substance itself at low temperatures. The following description is, therefore, suggested as a working hypothesis which fits the known facts.

Freshly exposed coal has, at ambient atmospheric temperatures, affinity for the oxygen of the air in contact with it. At first, the oxygen is adsorbed by a purely physical process, depending on the temperature, which, however, rapidly gives place to a chemical chain reaction resulting in the oxidation of certain constituents of coal with the production of a small quantity of heat.

A rise in the temperature of the coal, in consequence, takes place, which has the effect of further increasing the rate of absorption of oxygen and production of heat. If the heat produced cannot be dissipated by radiation or conduction or both at a rate faster than it is produced, a further rise in temperature takes place which accelerates further the rate of oxygen sorption and production of heat until, finally, the ignition point of coal is reached. It is evident from what has been stated above that the existence of a weak leakage air current is an important condition for spontaneous combustion to take place in mines. Such a condition exists in goaves of coal seams being worked by the bord and pillar method with open caving of the goaf or in the vicinity of faulted or geologically disturbed zones.

1.1.1.2.1 Factors affecting liability of coal to spontaneous combustion

Auto-oxidation of coal is a complex physico-chemical process in which concurrent and overlapping reactions take place which are difficult to separate out. The rate of oxidation of coal in air gives a measure of the liability of coal to spontaneous combustion.

The most important factors bearing on the liability of coal to spontaneous combustion are:

(1) *Surface area of coal* The rate of oxidation of coal and, hence, the amount of heat liberated depends on the total surface area of the coal including the internal surface area due to its pore structure. Pores are present in coal in abundance, so that the entire pore surface which, for different coals, is more than 80 m^2/g, forms the reaction site. According to Peters [1], free diffusion takes place in macropores below 10^{-5} mm in size, their velocities differing by a factor of 10^9. Münzner and Peters [2] found that, at low temperatures, the oxidation rates were practically the same for particles less than 0.3 mm in size and that above 0.5 mm, the deviations were significant. Kuchta *et.al.*, [3] found from exploratory experiments that self-heating of most U.S. bituminous coals could be obtained with a maximum particle size of about 50 to 70 mesh (270 to 297) at an air flow rate of about 50 cm^3/min.

(2) *Coal rank* The lower rank coals which are generally higher in moisture, oxygen, and volatile contents are more reactive and, hence, more susceptible to spontaneous heating than higher rank coals. The oxidation rate of coals of the same rank may, however, vary within a wide range.

(3) *Volatile content* It was found by several investigators that medium- to high-volatile coals (VM greater than about 18 per cent) oxidize faster than low-volatile coals and that high-volatile coals are more susceptible to spontaneous heating than are medium-volatile coals.

(4) *Petrographic composition of coal* Opinions were divided for a long time on the influence of petrographic composition of coal on the susceptibility to undergo spontaneous combustion. It is now generally accepted that the ease of oxidation of coal decreases with the macro constituents in the order: vitrain, clarain, durain, and fusain.

(5) *Oxygen content* The increased reactivity of low-rank coals is attributed to their higher inherent oxygen content, and hence, the oxidation rate decreases with decreasing oxygen content, although the heating tendency is not in all cases proportional to the oxygen content.

(6) *Moisture content* The oxidation of coal in air at ambient temperatures takes place practically always in the presence of moisture in the surrounding oxidizing atmosphere, inherent in the coal itself, which should be less than that of the environment, or formed through oxidation. As the ability of coal to absorb moisture is considerably higher than that for oxygen or nitrogen, the H_2O formed due to the oxidation reaction is mostly absorbed in the coal, affecting its ability to absorb oxygen by hindering its diffusion and hence its oxidation rate. But a high inherent moisture and oxygen content,

as found in low-rank coals and humidity in the surrounding atmosphere have been reported to be indicative of a tendency to spontaneous heating. Field experience has shown that the coal piles of Raniganj Coals (India) are more liable to spontaneous heating when the moisture content lies between 5 and 7 per cent. The exact mechanism of the action of moisture on the oxidation process in the early stages of oxidation, however, is not clear.

It is apparent that the presence of moisture would tend to reduce the tendency to spontaneous heating because of the latent heat of vaporization and high specific heat of water.

Studies conducted by the US Bureau of Mine on North Dakota lignite [4] have shown that the rates of oxidation were found to be maximum at 20 per cent moisture content and lower at either above or below this value.

(7) *Presence of pyrite* Iron pyrite (FeS_2), which frequently occurs in coal seams as discrete particles in a wide variety of shapes and sizes, distributed through the coal matrix, oxidizes easily at ordinary temperatures in moist air through a combination of reactions leading to the formation of ferrous sulphate and sulphuric acid besides other products, increasing in volume and liberating heat, in turn leading to accelerated oxidation and self-heating of coal.

The effect of pyrite on coal has been investigated by many workers with conflicting results. According to Münzner [5], the heat change caused by oxidation is the same for coal and pyrite in dry state and the reactivity of coal is only doubled when wet, whilst the reactivity of finely dispersed pyrite (below 0.06 mm size) is raised 10-fold. The oxidation of pyrite in the presence of free moisture has only a promoting effect on auto-oxidation of coal when present in concentrations higher than 3%.

(8) *Ash content* Oxidation occurs chiefly on the organic portions of the coal and only slightly on mineral constituents. Ash in coal generally decreases the oxidation rate but may be influenced to some extent by the mineral composition of the ash, which is reported to have both accelerating and inhibiting effects on oxidation.

(9) *Temperature* Temperature exercises a great influence on the oxidation rate. Below ~ 70°C, the relationship between them is described by the Arrhenius equation. The rate of oxidation increases about two times for every 10°C rise in temperature. At a constant temperature, the oxidation rate will decrease with time and the oxidized products will accumulate on the coal. Lower temperatures favour accumulation of oxygen on the coal, whereas, at higher temperatures > 70°C, gaseous oxidation products are released.

(10) *Freshness of exposed coal surface* Freshly exposed surfaces of coal as when it is first mined consume oxygen at a relatively high rate which falls off continuously with time during the progress of oxidation for a given set of constant conditions.

(11) *Concentration of oxygen in contact* At any point on a coal surface, the oxidation rate is directly proportional to the oxygen concentration, that is, the partial pressure of oxygen surrounding the particles. For an atmosphere devoid of oxygen, the oxidation rate is zero regardless of all other factors.

Coal may be stored in water indefinitely as without air there is no oxidation From laboratory studies conducted, the minimum oxygen concentration to develop spontaneous combustion has been found to be 7 per cent [6].

(12) *Methane content of coal* The desorption of methane from coal creates an inert atmosphere in the macropores and micropores and may retard low-temperature oxidation, particularly in highly gassy coals. However, as the desorption of methane falls sharply with time, more and more of the coal surface becomes exposed to oxidation by air. The residual methane content of coal is reported to be the best indicator for predicting the hazard in a mine due to spontaneous combustion [7]. (Coals containing less than 5 m^3 of CH_4/t coal show high oxidation rates and are, hence, more liable to spontaneous combustion, while coals containing above 8 m^3 of CH_4 $/t$ are not oxidized.)

(13) *Inhibitors* The rate of oxidation of coals and, hence, their tendency to spontaneous heating can be reduced by treatment with inhibitors or antipyrogenes which act in one or more of the following ways:

   (1) Formation of a protective surface coating both on the macropore and micropore surface coal particles, resulting in the formation of a heat insulating layer;
   (2) Formation of a layer which increases the thermal conductivity of the coal and thereby enhances the rate of removal of heat from local hot spots;
   (3) Formation of a layer which consumes heat during its decomposition while the coal is in the process of oxidation before reaching the critical temperature range;
   (4) Formation of a layer, preferably gaseous, which acts as a diluent and removes heat;
   (5) Chain-breaking reaction which retards oxidation.

Many kinds of inhibitors – solid, liquid, and gaseous – have been tried by many investigators in the erstwhile USSR, Czechoslovakia, Germany, India, and a few other countries for fighting incipient and open fires in underground coal mines and coal-stack fires on the surface with a fair amount of success. Special mention may be made of $Ca(OH)_2$, $CaCO_3$, $Ca(HCO_3)_2$, NH_4Cl, Na_2SiO_3, $CaCl_2$, Montan Powder, NaH_2PO_4, $NH_4HB_4O_7$ and H_3BO_3.

1.1.1.2.2 Contributing factors for spontaneous combustion of coal in mines

Besides the intrinsic properties of the coal, there are several other factors which contribute to spontaneous heating of coal in mines. These can be grouped under two main heads: geological and technical.

Geological factors

(1) Coal seams greater than 3 m thick pose the greatest hazard due to crushing of coal under rock pressure, high losses of coal during extraction, higher geothermic gradients in deep mines, and occurrence of bands of inferior coal.

(2) In zones of tectonic disturbances such as faults, the coal is in a crushed state, and leakage of water and air takes place along the fault planes when intersected by mine workings.
(3) Carbonaceous shales associated with the coal seams in the roof are a potential source of fires. The irregular bands of coal and unworkable seams occurring in the immediate roof and floor of a seam being worked may pose a danger, especially at great depths.
(4) Contiguous seams The geological factors cannot be controlled.

Technical factors
Mining itself disturbs the coal seam and adjacent strata and can produce conditions that are favourable for self-heating.

The mining practices which contribute to the spontaneous combustion hazard are as follows:

(1) Extensive development within the seam (s) will expose a large area of the coal surface to oxidation as well as increase leakage of air currents.
(2) The winning technology will determine the intensity of working of coal faces and the percentage recovery. A high rate of extraction is the best guarantee against the incidence of fires due to spontaneous combustion.
(3) The caving method of roof control and the orientation of fracture lines especially with bord and pillar or room and pillar workings control the stress concentration on the coal faces, pillars, and adjacent galleries and their crushing under pressure. Depending on the seam thickness, its depth, and nature of adjacent roof rocks, caving may develop cracks in the overlying seams unworked for whatsoever reason, in coal bands, and in left-over coals in the already extracted seams, creating conditions favourable for development of seam fires. Caving under shallow overburden cover may produce cracks reaching up to the surface, inducing leakage air currents from the surface to the underground.
(4) Unduly high ventilating pressure differentials between mine workings and across panels will cause air leakages through the coal and defective fire-stoppings, which might supply air just sufficient for oxidation but not sufficient for dissipating the heat produced. A good rule to be observed by mining men would be 'No ventilation at all is better than a deficient ventilation'.
(5) Mining of contiguous seams and thick seams in slices with danger of air leakage between goaves in the same seam and/or contiguous seams
(6) Mining of seams liable to coal outbursts with the system of shockblasting, which creates conditions conducive to spontaneous heating through air leakage.

1.1.1.2.3 Stages of oxidation and spontaneous combustion of coal

The oxidation of different coals has been extensively investigated using thermogravimetric and thermovolumetric oxidation tests at low and high temperatures under isothermal conditions, but because of the diversity in coal substances and experimental conditions, one could draw only a few general conclusions out of the quite contradictory results which some of the studies have yielded.

According to the generally accepted simplified view of the complex low-temperature oxidation reactions, all coals react in the same basic manner, and that following an initial phase of physical adsorption of oxygen, a variety of solid coal–oxygen complexes are formed at different temperatures as a result of saturation at these temperatures of the unsaturated constituents of coal with the release of some gaseous products. A major proportion of the oxygen consumed is absorbed by most coals within the first hour. Physical adsorption of oxygen releases much less heat than does chemical oxidation of coal. Both CO and CO_2 are evolved at ambient temperatures immediately after the start of the oxidation, though with a slight delay interval between their liberation. Much more carbon dioxide is produced in the reaction than carbon monoxide. As the absorption of oxygen and temperature increase, CO increases slowly and gradually up to a certain temperature of about 40°C, beyond which it is evolved at an increasingly rapid rate.

At and beyond some elevated temperature between 50° and 100°C, the oxidation rate accelerates greatly due to a sustained exothermic reaction and ultimately produces smouldering or flaming combustion or ignition within the temperature range 327° to 420°C for bituminous coals. This temperature, usually 60°C to 85°C, identifies the limit of low-temperature oxidation and the beginning of normal combustion under adiabatic conditions and is called the minimum or critical temperature or self-heating temperature. Hydrogen and hydrocarbons occur at temperatures above the critical temperature but their proportion in the oxidation products decreases with increasing oxidation.

1.1.1.2.4 Stages of spontaneous combustion of coal in mines

One recognizes three distinct stages of combustion of coal in coal mines:

(1) The incubation period;
(2) The indication period; and
(3) Open fire.

The incubation period is the period between the onset of first oxidation and the particular time at which one can detect it by the senses. From a practical point of view, the term, however, is used in a broader sense to denote the period between the first roof fall after beginning of coal extraction in a district or panel and the appearance of the first signs of heating which may take 90 to 120 days after the coal is mined. The incubation period varies widely, depending on the seam thickness, nature of the immediate roof, method of working, method of roof control, regularity and continuity of working, and liability of coal to undergo spontaneous heating. It usually varies between 3 and 18 months, higher rank coals having longer periods. During this period, one does not detect heating during one's passage through mine workings.

The end of the incubation period marks the beginning of the indication period which is marked by 'sweating' and haze in the air, caused by the warmed-up air from a fire coming into contact with the cooler coal, rock, and metallic surfaces and depositing moisture. The indication period is often of very small duration lasting sometimes only a few hours. It comes to an end with the appearance of 'fire stink' when an open fire with visible active combustion breaks out at 70°C. The fire stink can be easily recognized by the characteristic petrolic smell. Seams seldom burn with a bright flame but glow, developing bluish-white clouds of smoke.

1.1.1.2.5 Experimental methods for the study of spontaneous combustion of coal

Various methods have been used in the laboratory for studying the relative tendencies of coals to heat spontaneously. Most of the methods are based on the measurement of the oxidation rate and ignition temperature. The various methods may be broadly classified under the following heads:

(1) Isothermal method
(2) Adiabatic method
(3) Chemical method
(4) Temperature differential method
  (a) Crossing point method and
  (b) Differential thermal analysis (DTA).

Isothermal method (isothermal calorimetry)

In this method, the coal sample is heated in a bath or furnace at constant temperature, with oxygen or air passing through it at a predetermined rate. The oxidation rate is determined, which can be used as an indicator of the coal's potential for spontaneous heating.

Adiabatic method (adiabatic calorimetry)

The coal sample is placed in an insulated bath or oven chamber designed to maintain the coal and its immediate surrounding medium at the same temperature automatically so that no heat is lost or gained. During an experiment, the temperature of the sample is brought to a preselected value (starting temperature) in a stream of flowing nitrogen and after the system has attained thermal equilibrium, the apparatus is put into an automatic control mode, the nitrogen is shut off, and the sample is exposed to a flowing stream of preheated oxygen or air (dry or moist) when the temperature of the coal rises above its surroundings. The temperature of the bath/oven chamber automatically rises to coincide with the coal temperature. The experiment is run over a period of several hours up to 100 hours depending on the starting temperature and oxygen concentration till ignition occurs, which is determined as the minimum temperature at which there is a steep rise in the temperature on the temperature–time curve (Fig. 1.1). Coals may also be characterized by their 'adiabatic self-heating time', which is the time interval between the starting of the experiment and ignition of the sample [8]. By incorporating an automatic oxygen feed regulating system, oxidation rate–adiabatic self-heating time curves can be drawn.

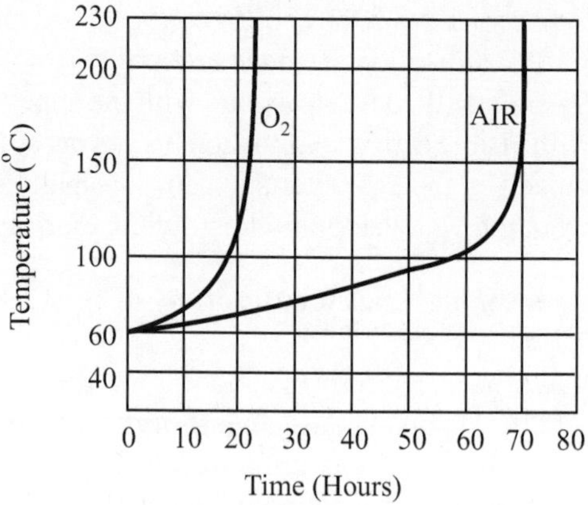

Fig. 1.1 Adiabatic heating curve of coal.

Chemical method

This method [9] has been used in Eastern Europe for determining the relative tendencies of coals to undergo spontaneous combustion. It is based on the fact that the ignition point of coal is lowered due to oxidation. By measuring the ignition temperature (puff or explosion temperature) of coal in the as-mined/as-received state *(T)*, fully oxidized state (T_0) and fully reduced state (the original in-situ state) (T_R), the degree of oxidation and liability index are calculated from the lowering of ignition temperatures as follows:

$$\text{Degree of oxidation} = \frac{T_R - T}{T_R - T_0} \times 100\%$$

Liability index $\Delta T_R = T_R - T_0$

When		
	$\Delta T_R < 10$	no danger of self-heating
	$10 < \Delta T_R < 25$	less liable to self-heating
	$\Delta T_R > 25$	very liable to self-heating

Investigations conducted in the erstwhile USSR showed that the lowering of ignition temperature through oxidation is independent of the coal rank and that for coals of the same rank, it may vary significantly.

With this method, though the degree of oxidation of coal can be determined, there is some uncertainty regarding the link up of the puff temperatures with the ignition temperatures obtained by other methods.

The apparatus consists of a cylindrical copper block furnace with six holes for introducing quartz reaction tubes and a central hole for inserting a thermocouple which measures the temperature of the copper block and reaction tubes. This design ensures the same rate of heating for both the reaction tubes and the copper block. The open ends of the reaction tubes outside the furnace are connected through three-way cocks to six audiometer tubes placed in a trough filled with water. The audiometer tubes end in a common manifold at the top one end of which is provided with an aspirator bulb.

Two of the reaction tubes are filled with the original sample, another two are filled with fully reduced Samples (treated with benzidene or p-phenylene-diamine) and the remaining two are filled with fully oxidized samples by treating, with perhydrol. Sodium nitrite is added to each of the samples and intimately mixed before filling into the reaction tubes. The furnace is switched on and the heating rate maintained at 4.5°C per minute. The water in the eudiometer tubes is raised to a certain level by means of the aspiration bulb, and the eudiometer tubes are then put in line with the reaction tubes. The temperatures at which a sudden fall in the water columns occurs due to rapid evolution of the reaction products are noted and the liability index calculated.

Crossing-point temperature method

In this method, the coal sample (4 g) is heated in a reaction tube in a furnace or bath at constant or rising temperature, with oxygen or air passing through it at a predetermined rate till the coal temperature crosses the furnace or bath temperature (Fig. 1.2). The temperature at which the temperature of the coal and the furnace/bath coincide is called the crossing point temperature. It is also called the relative

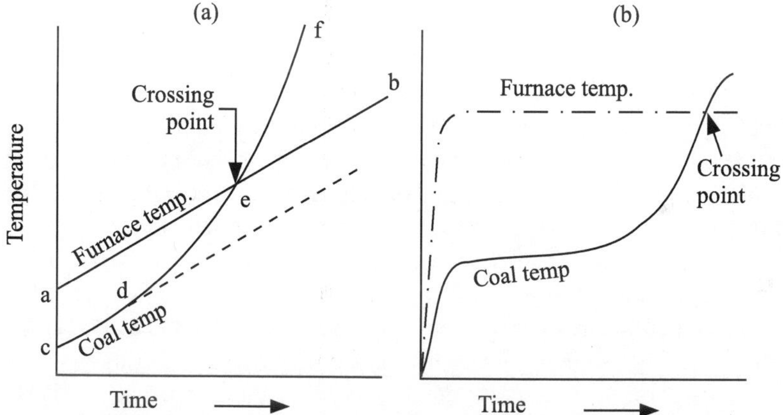

Figure 1.2 Determination of crossing point temperature coal: (a) with increasing furnace/bath temperature, (b) with constant furnace/bath temperature.

ignition temperature. The heating rate, the air-flow rate, and the particle size must be optimized.

Figure 1.3 gives a schematic diagram of the crossing point apparatus used by Raju et al. [10] with manual and automatic control using a temperature programmer for their studies on crossing point temperatures of Indian coals.

Some researchers consider the point *d* in Fig. 1.2(a) to be more important than the crossing point for the simple reason that the temperature of the sample can overtake the furnace or bath temperature only after the process of perceptible self-heating has set in without additional heat. The heating curve can, therefore, be divided into three zones c-d, d-e, and e-f. The third zone starts from the crossing point to active combustion.

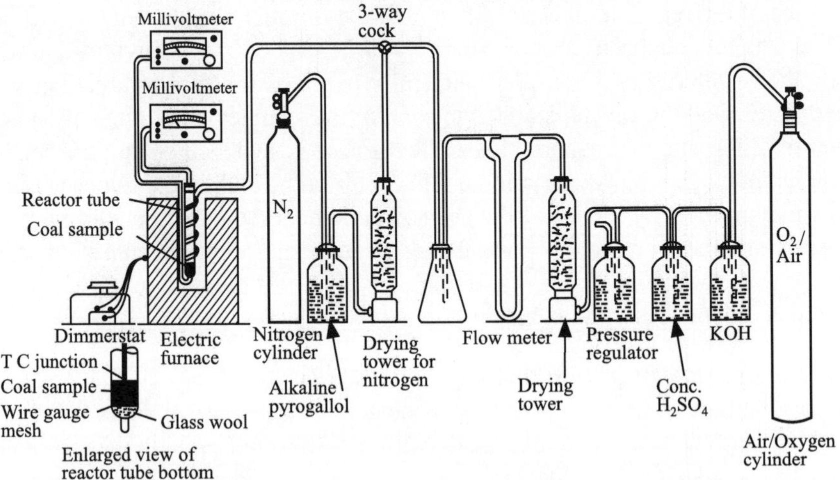

Figure 1.3 Schematic diagram of crossing point temperature apparatus.

The crossing point temperature of Jharia coals lies between 130–185°C and Raniganj coals between 130–140°C.

Differential thermal analysis (DTA)

Thermal analysis is a technique in which some physical or chemical changes of a substance are measured as a function of temperature as the substance is subjected to a controlled heating rate. Differential thermal analysis is one of the seven thermal analysis techniques used for the study of spontaneous heating of coals. In this technique, the difference in temperature (Δt) between a substance and a thermally-inert reference material is recorded against temperature as the two specimens are subjected to identical temperature changes in a block which is heated at a linear heating rate. If the sample undergoes no thermal change, and the temperature difference is zero, a so-called baseline parallel to the temperature axis (that is $\Delta T = 0$) is given by the recording instrument. However, if the sample undergoes a thermal decomposition reaction with loss or gain of heat, the temperature gradient with respect to the inert material will change, producing a negative or positive ΔT, depending on whether the transformation taking place in the sample is endothermic or exothermic. The curve recorded with ΔT plotted on the ordinate and temperature or time on the abscissa is called the DTA curve or thermogram.

The DTA method is being increasingly applied over the last three decades for the study of coals and coal products.

Typical thermograms for coal are shown in Fig. 1.4. There is first the endothermic region due to evaporation of water with the curve going below the baseline and subsequently returning to the baseline after an endothermic peak. As the temperature rises due to oxidation, the curve rises steeply. The steeper the rise of the curve, the faster is the heat evolution. A slow rise after the endothermic region indicates a higher ignition temperature. The curve then attains a single peak

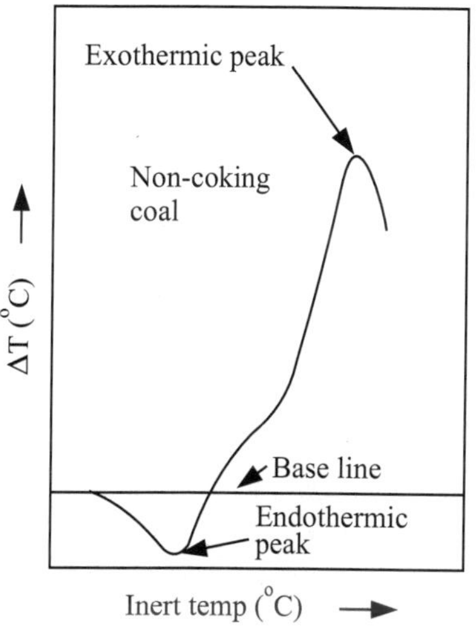

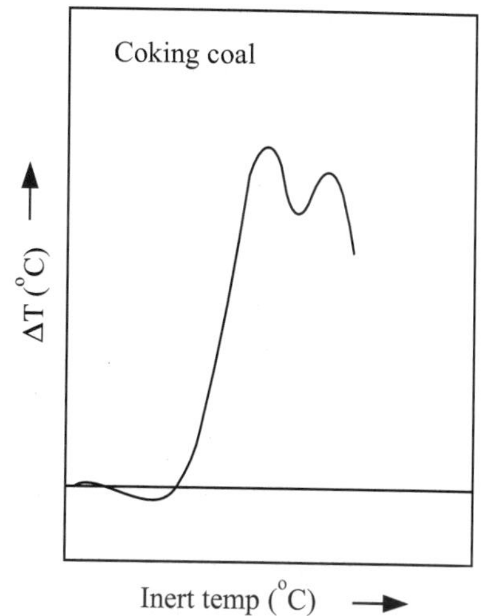

Figure 1.4 Typical thermograms for coals.

and falls, unlike with coking coals, in which two peaks with a valley in between are observed. It is known that low-rank coals have lower ignition temperatures and higher susceptibility to spontaneous heating compared to higher-rank coals. A comparison of DTA curves would help in determining the relative liability to spontaneous heating of coals.

1.1.1.2.6 Relative liability of coals to spontaneous heating

Although the occurrence of a fire in a mine due to spontaneous heating of coal is the result of the interplay of a large number of factors, a knowledge of the relative liability of coal seams would be useful in making important decisions when planning mining operations in a new seam. There is no single accepted method of evaluating the liability of a coal to spontaneous combustion. There are several methods which utilize correlations existing between known properties or characteristics of coal and susceptibility to spontaneous combustion. Different methods have thrown out various indices, the comparison of which would, however, be inaccurate and possibly misleading owing to the diversity of experimental conditions. For a laboratory comparison of the relative heating tendencies, only one method may be used under standard conditions, and adiabatic calorimetry is the preferred choice, although it is time-consuming and laborious. The DTA technique may also be used for fast, accurate, and reproducible results. The crossing point method offers a cheap, though not quite accurate method of determining the crossing point temperatures. In many instances, past experience with the working of given seam(s) in other mines and storage of coal on the surface is the most commonly used indicator of hazard due to spontaneous heating.

The most common indices that may be, used are the following :

Heating rate: It is the temperature increase under controlled conditions in °C/h g

Heat release: It is the quantity of heat released per gram (ΔH) in cal/g.

Crossing point temperature: It is the temperature value at which the temperature of coal coincides with that of the heating furnace or bath in °C.

Ignition temperature: It is the minimum temperature at which the coal ignites without an additional external source of heat on account of the exothermic reaction with oxygen. It is determined by observation.

Oxidation rate: It is the consumption of the oxygen given in mg per kg coal per minute, (mg O_2 / kg min) or in mg per g coal per hour, (mg O_2 / g h).

Adiabatic self-heating time: It is the time interval between the starting temperature of the experiment and ignition of coal.

Ignitibility or liability index with chemical method

It is the difference in puff or 'explosion' temperatures of coal in the fully reduced and fully oxidized states.

Liability index proposed by Feng et al.[11]

$$\text{Index} = \frac{\text{average heating rate between } 100° \text{ and } 220°\text{C}}{\text{relative ignition temperature}} \times 100$$

This is based on the assumption that the average heating rate between 110° and 220°C is only slightly influenced by the evaporation of moisture and the exit of volatile matter from the coal in this temperature range. Coals were classified as follows:

Index	Liability to spontaneous combustion
0-5	Low
5-10	Medium
> 10	High

Liability indices proposed by Mahadevan and Ramlu [12]
Susceptibility potential using the chemical method is defined as the difference in puff temperatures of coal in fully reduced and as-mined/as-received states (T_R – T) the extreme limit of which is $T_R - T_O$, where T_O is the puff temperature in fully oxidized state.

Liability index: It is derived from the crossing point temperature heating curve of coal (Fig. 1.5). It is defined as

$$\frac{\text{Average heating rate between the inflection and crossing points}}{\text{Time to reach the inflection point}} \times \frac{\text{Time to reach the crossing point}}{\text{heating rate at the crossing point}} \times 10$$

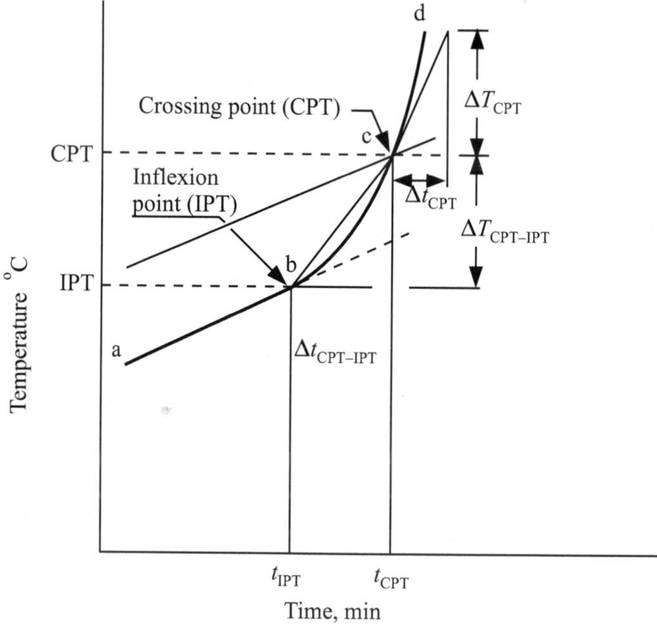

Figure 1.5 Heating curve analysis of coal.

$$= \frac{\left(\frac{\Delta T}{\Delta t}\right)_{CPT-IPT}}{t_{IPT}} \times \frac{t_{CPT}}{\left(\frac{\Delta T}{\Delta t}\right)_{CPT}} \times 10$$

This index which increases with the increasing tendency of coal to spontaneous combustion takes into account the entire heat-up history of the coal right from the ambient temperature. It is only necessary that the experiments are conducted under standard conditions.

1.1.1.2.7 Fire-risk rating of coal mines due to spontaneous combustion

Attempts were made by some research workers to evaluate the tire risk rating of coal mines on the basis of the possible fire hazard from working of seams liable spontaneous combustion. Feng et al. [11] proposed a method in which a risk index is obtained for a mine as a product of the liability index as determined by them from the crossing point temperature heating curve for coal and the mine environmental index estimated as a function of coal loss in extraction, and fissuration of the coal mass and strata as a result of mining and ventilating pressure differentials all of which are governed by geological and technical factors.

Risk index = Liability index × Mine environmental index

Table 1. 1 gives the various indices and ratings proposed which may help in categorizing different coal mines.

Banerjee [13] suggested a methodology for computing the total fire-risk inherent in a particular situation obtained in a mine taking into account the amount of risk involved in each of the different mining operations being carried out under different conditions in the mine. Mahadevan and Ramlu [12] utilized the method of Feng et al. to estimate the mine environment index based on Indian conditions. They, however, used a new liability index derived by them from the crossing point temperature heating curve.

Table 1.1 Liability index–Environmental index–Risk index

Liability index for coal	Rating
0–5	Low
5–10	Medium
>10	High

Mine environmental index

Coal loss	Fissuration	Ventilation pressure differential	Environmental index	Rating
Normal	Natural	Normal	1	Low
High	Natural	Normal		
Normal	High/induced	Normal	2	Medium
Normal	Natural	High		
Normal	High/induced	High		
High	Natural	High	3	High
High	High/induced	Normal		
High	High/induced	High	4	Very high

Risk index for mine (Liability index × Mine environment index)

Index	Rating
0–1	Low
10–20	Medium
20–40	High

1.1.1.2.8 Detection of spontaneous combustion

Early detection of spontaneous combustion is of utmost importance as experience has shown that late discovery of a heating may prove to be very costly to the mine.

The spontaneous combustion of coal in mine workings may be detected by the physical and chemical indications given by the heating itself.

Physical indications

The traditional physical examination for physical indications consists of combustion in detecting the presence of warmth, sweating, and smell of fire in the district return airway or in the path of air coming from a suspected area. In practice the first sign that a heating has developed is the characteristic smell of fire stink or 'gob stink' due to the gases distilled from coal and products of sulphur if the coal contains a high percentage of sulphur. In the initial stages of heating, the smell resembles that of petrol, but as the heating progresses, it changes to the odour of kerosene, and later to the odour of tar. A strong smell is often an indication that the heating has made sufficient headway. In mines, it is difficult to find personnel who are experienced in the detection of a heating by smell. Sniffing should be restricted to the general body of air currents and not be practised with gases issuing from gateside packs of longwall faces and cracks in the strata. The smell may not be detected where oxidation products have to travel long distances through caved rock in the goaf before reaching an airway or where a heating is deep seated or is near an intake airway. Although, in practice, most fires are first detected by mine personnel by seeing and smelling smoke or seeing the fire start, too much reliance should not be placed on it. An air analysis is always more reliable to provide the first warning.

Chemical indications

As coal passes through different stages of spontaneous combustion, gaseous products such as CO, CO_2, CH_4, C_2H_6, C_n,H_{2n}, and H_2O are liberated, the composition of the gaseous products depending on the stage of oxidation. CO and CO_2 are evolved at low ambient temperatures to 100°C. Whereas CO is produced in measurable quantities even at temperatures of 30°C, the concentration of the hydrocarbons at temperatures not greatly above the ambient cannot be measured by the present-day sampling techniques. As the concentration of CO increases consistently with temperature during the low-temperature stage of the oxidation process, it has been used as the most sensitive indicator of the onset as well as progress of the spontaneous combustion of coal. CO_2 may be produced from other sources or may be lost due to sorption by coal or by solution in water. As CO may be produced from shotfiring or from the use of diesel haulage equipment, its concentration must be determined at carefully selected sampling points at times when contamination of air will not take place from these sources. CO entering the mine from the surface along with the downcast air due to nearness of the downcast shafts to the boiler house, carbonisation plants, etc., cannot, of course, be eliminated. To detect any increase in CO content, one must, therefore, know the, content normal for a district or a seam under given conditions so that any increase above it may be viewed with suspicion and immediately investigated.

Today, computerized CO monitoring and control systems have been adopted for early detection of spontaneous combustion in several coal mines throughout the world.

Graham developed in the 1920s, a ratio called the Graham index or Graham ratio, given as the ratio between the actual concentration of CO produced and the deficiency of O_2 compared with fresh air. This ratio, which is also called the carbon monoxide/oxygen deficiency ratio or carbon monoxide index, has stood the test of time and is extensively used throughout the world for predicting the presence and development of spontaneous heating. It is usually multiplied by 100 to give a convenient number.

With the natural oxygen–nitrogen ratio of 0.265 in intake air,

$$\text{CO Index} = \frac{100\ CO}{0.265\ N_2 - O_2}$$

$$N_2 = 100 - CH_4 - CO - CO_2 - O_2 - H_2$$

where CH_4, CO, CO_2, H_2, and O_2, are the percentages of the gases present at any given time in a sample of air coming from a suspected area in a mine. Mine air may contain small traces of CO up to 0.005 per cent even when there is no fire, and as CO may also enter the mine from the surface, the background $CO/\Delta O_2$ ratio in the return air of every district must be established.

$$\text{CO Index} = \frac{\text{final CO} - \text{initial CO}}{\text{initial } O_2 - \text{final } O_2}$$

The normal value of the CO index is usually 0.4 or less. In German hard coal mines, values up to 30 with incipient fires and up to 90 with open fires have been obtained [14].

When an inert gas is introduced into a fire area without closing the ventilation tunnel or pipe in the stopping on the return side,

$$\text{CO Index} = \frac{100\ CO}{\left(\frac{O'_2}{N'_2}\right) N_2 - O_2}$$

where O'_2 and N'_2 are the percentages of the gases in the intake air samples and O_2 and N_2 the percentages in the return air samples.

One should, however, bear in mind that the CO index is reduced by dilution with blackdamp and that the ratio can be used only when ΔO_2 is not less than 0.5 per cent by volume due to an accuracy of ± 0. 1 per cent that is obtained in measuring the oxygen concentration. Also, an error in the calculation of the index increases with a decrease in CO and an increase in O_2

Monitoring mine air for CO and O_2 will enable determination of the CO index.

1.1.1.2.9 Prevention of spontaneous combustion of coal in coal mines

The best safeguards against mine fires due to spontaneous combustion consist in conducting mine operations carefully and systematically. The following points should be observed when working seams liable to spontaneous combustion:

Development

(1) Main shafts should be properly located, lined, and equipped so that there is less pressure loss.

(2) Development within the coal seam should be kept to a minimum. All coal surfaces not being directly worked on must be protected against absorption of oxygen by stonedusting, guniting, or coating with an antipyrogene (a fire-proofing composition).

(3) When working seams by the bord and pillar method:
   (a) the dimensions and shape of the pillars must be such that no crushing of the pillars takes place before or during their extraction which will increase the air permeability of the fractured coal;
   (b) panels with independent ventilation should be formed as far as practicable;
   (c) the panels must be laid so that severe crushing of coal during extraction is minimized;
   (d) the panels formed must be of a size which would permit complete extraction within the incubation period; and
   (e) the development work should be kept out of abutment areas.

(4) When designing longwall face layouts, face lengths should be selected so that good closure and compaction of the goaf are assured. Face lengths smaller than 60 to 65 m are generally not recommended.

(5) The roof of roadways in coal should be well-supported and the sides (ribs) well-lagged.

(6) When traversing seams with cross-cuts, coal should be removed to an adequate depth and the cavities so formed should be filled or packed with clay, pulverized ash with Portland cement, or other incombustible material.

(7) Side-by-side intakes and returns must be avoided as far as practicable. The main intake and return airways and the main haulage roadways should be driven in stone as far as practicable. In thick and inclined seams, the main roadways should be driven in the floor of the seams with cross-cuts driven to the seams.

(8) The maximum air travel distance from surface to surface (which ranges from 1 to 20 km) must be kept low so that the number of stoppings and the leakage that takes place are reduced.

Coal winning

(1) The coal should be won as completely as practicable using an efficient extraction method, especially in disturbed zones, thick seams, and strongly folded steep seams.

(2) The working faces should be worked intensively as a high rate of extraction is the best means of preventing fires due to spontaneous combustion. The advance or retreat of a coal face should never be interrupted and, if any local fall of roof or a fault is encountered, immediate steps should be taken to get over the obstacle or minimize its effect on the face advance.

(3) When mining a group of seams or mining thick seams by longwall slicing, the workings in an upper seam should be in advance of those in a lower seam and the coal of the upper seam should be extracted as completely as practicable.

(4) The best methods of working seams are the longwall and stall methods.

(5) When working a seam by longwall mining, the retreating longwall should be preferred as it eliminates stray leakage currents through the goaf behind the face if regular caving of overlying strata behind the face is accomplished. Retreating is the best method if there is a goaf above the seam. It is the only method for working thick inclined seams by sub-level caving with inertization of the goaves behind faces using liquid nitrogen or nitrogen foam to combat the high spontaneous combustion risk.

(6) As it is not always possible to avoid coal remains in the goaves of long wall faces even when powered supports are used for extracting a seam by longwall advancing with caving, the gateside packs should be airtight in order to increase the airflow resistance of the goaf; also one must balance the pressure on all sides of the goaf. When extracting a seam by retreating longwall, the tail gate and the main gate behind the face line must be stowed as tight as possible or they should be sealed off at regular intervals. When starting a new face from solid, the gate pack must be well tied into the barrier pillar

(7) Worked-out areas should be effectively. sealed off as soon as possible or ventilated. Stowed seals should be preferred to other forms of seals. If the worked-out areas are ventilated, as they are in most American coal mines, a system of bleeder entries must be planned.

(8) Blasting in coal must be restricted as much as possible.

(9) Loose coal and other combustible material such as oily or greasy waste, and decaying timber should be cleaned up and not be permitted to accumulate.

(10) In bord and pillar workings, the pillars should be mined as fast as practicable at an even rate after their formation.

(11) Partially-built seals or preparatory stoppings should be erected in the entries of panel fire barriers before extraction is commenced.

(1 2) When extracting folded seams, the limbs of a synclinal or anticlinal fold must be extracted, as far as possible, simultaneously and uniformly with stowing.

(13) When working seam outcrops with shallow overburden, barrier pillars of sufficient size should be left to the surface so that air leakage or water seepages through fissures is avoided.

Roof control

(1) Solid stowing is the best method of roof control for working seams liable to spontaneous heating. Pneumatic and hydraulic stowing are eminently suitable as stowing methods.

(2) Where advancing longwall mining with caving is practised, the gate roads should be supported with tight roadside packs.

(3) In bord and pillar workings with open caving of goaf, a straight line of fracture should be maintained. The fracture line should be oriented to the natural fracture system of the roof so that caving is promoted and long roof spans projecting over the goaves are prevented. The extraction must also be planned so that points formed by converging fracture lines are avoided as far as is practicable.

(4) Oxidizable waste materials, native or foreign, should not be discarded into the goaves.
(5) Washery dirt, if used for stowing, should be admixed with crushed rock so that, when in place, it does not constitute a fire risk.

Ventilation

(1) All active mine workings must be adequately ventilated.
(2) The mine ventilating pressure should not be unduly large so that air leakages through crushed roadway pillars or defective stoppings or seals of sealed-off areas do not take place.
(3) Short-circuiting of air as well as its uncontrolled circulation must be eliminated. Systematic air leakage test should be conducted in workings of high-risk seams by quantity surveys and smoke tube tests.
(4) All roadways in coal should be ventilated and unused roadways sealed off.
(5) Roadways in coal should not be wide and high, so that the air currents flowing through them have sufficient velocities to facilitate heat dissipation.
(6) Ventilation stoppings, doors, and regulators should be correctly placed.
(7) Air-crossings should be airtight and be constructed of fireproof material.
(8) Mine ventilation should be efficiently supervised. The ventilating air current in the return of each ventilating district where coal is liable to spontaneous combustion must be checked for CO concentration at least once per day.

Inspections

(1) Every underground working place should be inspected by a supervisory official or competent person at least once during each working shift. During inspections, attention should be paid to the presence of and means of eliminating fire risks arising from spontaneous combustion and other causes.
(2) On idle days, all districts liable to spontaneous combustion should be inspected at least once by competent persons.

1.1.1.3 Electricity

The advantageous electrification of mines has brought in its wake numerous hazards of short-circuiting and sparking due to improper methods of installation, use, repair and maintenance of electrical equipment most of which are constantly on the move as mining advances or retreats. Short-circuits and sparks may ignite any combustible material present in the immediate vicinity if proper safeguards and preventive measures are not installed.

1.1.1.4 Friction

Fires due to frictional causes occur in roadways and inclined shafts/inclines in which rope haulages and belt conveyors are installed; in staple shafts which are supported with timber; and at coal faces which are cut by coal-cutting machines, continuous miners, or shearer leaders. Belt conveyor fires form the largest percentage of these fires.

Belt conveyor fires

Nearly all belt conveyor fires result from frictional heating. The chief causes are:

(1) Overheating at the drive pulleys due to their continuing to rotate against a stalled or slipping belt;
(2) Overheating at the carrying and return idlers with rolls rotating against obstructions; and
(3) Overheating of brakes and gears.

Fires associated with belt conveyors can be minimized by adopting the following preventive measures:

(1) Using fire-resistant belting of neoprene (a trade name for polychloroprene), PVC (polyvinyl chloride), and styrene butadiene;
(2) Using fireproof roadway support at the drive and tail-end units;
(3) Selecting suitable electrical equipment and installing it properly;
(4) Installing the conveyor so that there are adequate clearances between it and the roadway floor and sides;
(5) Installing an automatic fire sensor system at the beginning and end of each belt flight, at the belt drive and along the belt flight that will stop the drive automatically should dangerous overheating develop and provide an automatic warning, both audible and visual. It may be used to actuate a deluge-type water system, foam generator system, multipurpose dry powder system, or other equivalent automatic fire suppression system. Of the various types of fire detectors successfully developed and used for mine conveyor belt applications, the thermal point-type detector using a thermistor sensor has been found to be adequately sensitive for early fire detection, rugged to withstand the mine environment, simple and economical to use, and not actuated by combustion products from areas other than belt haulage roads. The point-type sensors should be closely spaced in the roadway as the hot gases from the fire cool rapidly when mixed with the ventilating current;
(6) Installing, safety devices that will automatically stop the conveyor drive should the belt break, jam, slip excessively, or fall below its normal speed;
(7) Preventing accumulation of dangerous electrostatic charges;
(8) Inspecting at frequent intervals while conveyors are working and at suitable times on idle days;
(9) Maintaining correct alignment and tension of the belt;
(10) Checking constantly the running condition of the idler rolls and bearings;
(11) Keeping the idler rolls clear of coal dust and all obstructions that might cause friction;
(12) Repairing the belt promptly and preventing exposure of the belt carcass;
(13) Making and maintaining belt joints as tight as possible;
(14) Clearing, at frequent intervals, coal falling on the cover plates and on the roadway floor under the belt;

(15) Cleaning transfer points at regular intervals;
(16) Providing a good communication system that will provide contact along the main points on the conveyor system and other parts of the mine;
(17) Providing fire protection by installing water lines along belt lines with fire hose outlets at 100 m intervals, multi-purpose dry powder extinguishers, automatic sprinklers, or automatic foam generators at all drives and electrical controls;
(18) The roadway support at conveyor drives and transfer points should be fireproof; and
(19) Providing proper ventilation.

Staple shaft fires

Fires in staple shafts by friction may occur through an unattended hoist starting up of its own accord while its brakes are in the 'On' position. Frictional sparks may be produced at the brake rim which may ignite coal dust settling upon it. Where a friction hoist is used, hot abraded particles of the rope tread, if of aluminium alloy, may ignite a pile of fine coal dust immediately beneath and the fire may spread to the support of the engine room and finally to the shaft. Fires in staple shafts may be prevented by using brake lining and rope tread of fire-resistant materials, constructing fireproof engine rooms, and providing fire protection in engine rooms and shafts by means of an automatic sprinkler system.

Fires in rope-haulage roadways and inclined shafts

Fires in rope-haulage roadways and inclined shafts may result from haulage ropes rubbing on frozen rollers or coming into contact with surfaces of combustible materials such as coal and timber, and from overheated bearings of mine cars. They may be prevented by proper selection, installation, and maintenance of rollers, pulleys, and car axle bearings. The shaft rollers may be rubber-faced. Coal or other carbonaceous materials should not be utilised as packing material in track-laying.

Fires in machine-cut and power-loaded faces

Fires may occur on machine-cut dry coal faces from frictional sparking, during orthodox coal-cutting operations in thin seams which have a hard sandstone roof or floor or intrusions of quartzitic or pyrite rock at the cutting horizon. The frictional sparks produced by the travelling picks can ignite a flammable mixture of firedamp or dust, causing burning or an explosion which may start a fire (Fig. 1.6). The most effective method known at present to prevent formation of flammable mixtures near the cutting picks is to provide additional ventilation in the cut to dilute the mixtures below the lower flammable limit.

Figure 1.6 Fire in undercut.

Fires may occur on power-loaded faces from frictional ignition of firedamp during the coal-cutting operation. The firedamp may burn into or spread along, the surface of the small coal which is left in the track behind the machine and through which firedamp filters at a rate which will be maximum immediately after the coal has been cut [15].

1.1.1.5 Blasting

Blown-out shots in coal especially when coal dust is present in shotholes may cause mine fires through ejected glowing particles igniting coal dust or loose coal near the face. Inducer shotfiring in solid coal when working seams subject to coal and gas outbursts creates conditions for spontaneous heating of coal despite its low liability to spontaneous combustion. Blasting can also ignite an unknown methane blower which in turn may set an entire coal face on fire. Blasting is definitely a minor cause of fire.

1.1.1.6 Explosions

Firedamp and coal-dust explosions leave in their wake smouldering and active fires. The explosion flame, explosion gases, and coal dust taking part in an explosion may set on fire wooden doors, paper, non-fireproof brattice line, pieces of clothing, unburnt coal dust and loose coal, and ultimately coal faces. The danger of fires from explosions increases in the colder months.

1.1.1.7 Miscellaneous

Welding, cutting, and soldering operations with an arc or open flame underground may result in mine fires. As a precaution against such files, these operations should be performed only by competent persons under the constant supervision of a qualified person at places free from danger due to firedamp or coal dust and where adequate fire-extinguishing appliances and stone dust are immediately available.

Methane blowers may catch fire and the gas flame may start a fire.

Static or frictional electricity may also cause fires indirectly from flammable firedamp–air or coal dust–air mixtures.

Friction of belts against pulleys and passing of dust-laden air through ducting may generate charges sufficient to produce sparks. The danger can be greatly minimised by installing all machinery so as to secure a safe discharge of static electricity.

Diesel-powered equipment, if not maintained properly, may become a cause of fire due to the risk of malfunctioning of the equipment. Diesel oil can also feed a fire. Their maintenance facilities should, wherever possible, be located in return airways.

Fires following coal-dust explosions resulting from deephole blasting in coal may occur when opencasting, shallow seams which were earlier laid out on the bord and pillar system for underground mining.

Glow fires may originate on electric face lights due to ignition of fine coal dust deposited on them by undissipated heat of radiation.

Fires may occur on compressors, which can be controlled through proper maintenance.

Surface fires may communicate with underground workings.

1.1.2 Detection of open fires

For the detection of open fires which, in general, evolve much larger quantities of CO than incipient fires, CO recorders can be installed in main return airways and at upcast shafts on the surface.

1.1.3 Localization of mine fires

Mine fires can be localized or confined to the place of their origin. Localization may be effected by using fireproof or fire-resistant building or construction materials for the support of mine workings or for fighting a fire either directly by fire-extinguishing means or quickly controlling the air supply to it.

Roadway fires can be localized by one or more of the following measures:

(1) Forming fire-resistant or fire-arresting zones of incombustible support at least 75 m long at distances of 500 m from one another in the case of long roadways or less in the case of short ones;
(2) Forming fire-protected zones by applying a fire-proofing coating of calcium chloride, calcium chloride clay, sodium silicate-clay, vermiculite-portland cement, magnesium-oxysulphate cement, steel fibre-reinforced concrete, gypsum-fibre glass, and foamed plastic (Isoschaum) on roadway sides, roof, and floor. Polyurethane foam should not be used as it burns away at temperature of 150°C producing a thick black smoke containing ammonia, poisonous cyanate, amines, carbon dioxide, carbon monoxide, and other complex gases;
(3) Installing automatic sprinkler systems which will form deluge-type water spray barriers about 10 m long (Fig. 1.7) to cool hot gases from the fire and prevent the latter from spreading;
(4) Lining roadway crossings and junctions with fireproof material such as brick or concrete especially in mines where a considerable fire hazard exists;
(5) Constructing fire-resistant fire doors in the pit bottoms of all shafts at all working levels so as to isolate shafts from the levels in case of fire.

Staple shaft fires can be localized by the following measures:

(1) Sinking the staple shafts a little away from the cross-cuts and laterals in flat measures laid out on the horizon mining system so that the shafts may be reliably cut off from air currents in the roadways in the event of fire;
(2) Using fireproof shaft lining;
(3). Constructing the engine rooms and tops of shafts fireproof; and
(4) Providing steel fire doors at the bottom, top, and any intermediate landings.

Fires in substations, rectifier rooms, battery-charging stations, oil storage rooms or chambers, pump chambers, and repair and maintenance shops can be localized

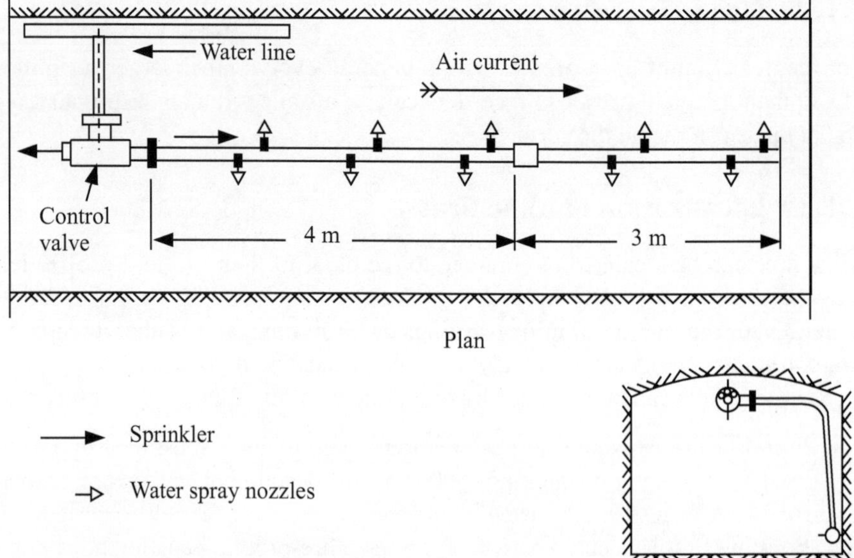

Figure 1.7 Automatic sprinkler system in roadway

by constructing them fireproof and equipping them with automatic fire doors and fire-fighting equipment.

Where compressed-air supply is available, the compressed air may be used to build up pressure of fresh air inside the hoist and pump chambers, in addition to protection by fire doors, to counteract entry of fire gases to a large extent.

Fires due to spontaneous combustion can be localized and extinguished in the incipient stage by direct attack with water, sand, stone dust, or chemicals, but when they have gained such headway that it is impossible to fight them directly, they require to be cut off from air reaching them.

1.1.4 Fighting mine fires

The common methods of fighting mine fires are:

(i) Fighting by direct attack;
(ii) Fighting by indirect attack:
  (a) Isolation of the fire;
  (b) Sealing the fire area or the entire mine;
(iii) Flooding the fire area or the entire mine;
(iv) Flushing the fire area with sand or other suitable solid materials conveyed with water;
(v) Introducing an inert gas into the fire area; and
(vi) Special methods of fire-fighting.

There can be no fixed rules for the application of one or the other method for dealing with mine fires as each fire presents a problem of its own which requires careful thinking. The position, intensity and extent of a fire, depth and layout of the workings, degree of gassiness of the mine, and immediate availability of firefighting facilities govern the selection of a method. In any method of extinguishing a fire, safety should be given the utmost consideration. However, it frequently happens in mines that, in order to prevent loss of production or damage to property, improper methods of fire-fighting, at great risk to life, are followed. Fighting fires in confined spaces may be attended by serious consequences.

1.1.4.1 Fighting by direct attack

Many mine fires, especially the open ones, can be checked and extinguished in their early stages by direct attack if they can be reached by digging out the heated or burning material into cars for sending out of the mine after covering it with stone dust or by attacking them with water, sand, stone dust, chemicals, or other smothering materials. Failure to extinguish fires by direct attack is usually due to late discovery, lack of fire-fighting means, or following improper fire-fighting procedures, so that the fire gets beyond control and a chain of events may follow that may result in extensive damage to property and loss of life.

When digging out a fire pocket, the resulting cavity should be immediately filled with an incombustible material such as clay, screened boiler ash mixed with Portland cement, broken rock or brickwork, or an approved sealant. This method is less frequently used due to the probable risk of ignition of firedamp, spreading of the fire while transporting the hot material outbye, or increasing the intensity of the fire by providing free access of air to it.

When fighting fires directly, the quantity of air reaching the fire must be controlled so that the fire does not intensify or propagate unnecessarily in the direction of the air current. With ascensional ventilation, an increase in the ventilating air occurs due to natural ventilation as a result of fire, which may cause reversal of air current in a parallel airway, while with descensional ventilation a decrease in ventilating air or reversal of air current may take place. The air quantity should, however, be controlled to be sufficient enough to prevent backing up of smoke and gases against the air current due to convection effects (Fig. 1.8) or reversal of air current. The backing up of smoke and gases against the ventilating current seriously affects the visibility and access to the fire. The smoke and gases backing out from a fire in an airway flow adjacent to the roof of the airway has a thickness which is related to the air velocity, the temperature, and heat radiated from the fire. Control of air current reaching a fire is not easy as it may affect the safe working of the rest of the mine, from which samples of air must be continuously collected for evaluation.

To obtain access to a fire where the smoke and gases have already backed out from it, it is necessary to use hurdle cloths which will cause the incoming intake air current to be carried up to the roof level, where it meets the warm air and gases tending to flow outbye, thereby cooling them and causing them, under the ventilating pressure, to flow back in the normal direction of the ventilation. As the smoke and gases are cleared in the immediate vicinity of the hurdle cloth, the

Figure 1.8 Backing up of firegases

latter can be shifted forward to clear the roadway, section by section, until the fire is accessible. The height at which a hurdle cloth is effective must be found by trial. It should be such that it will clear the smoke but not reduce the ventilation.

Fundamentally, a fire should be attacked from the fresh-air side in the direction of its propagation and not against it. If a fire cannot be extinguished within a few hours of starting fire-fighting operations, it would be advisable to resort to some other method, sealing off in all probability, as prolongation of the fire-fighting efforts might prove disastrous.

1.1.4.1.1 Fire-fighting facilities

Every mine should be provided with suitable and adequate fire-fighting facilities so that different classes of fires (fires from solid combustible materials, fires from flammable liquids, and fires from energized electrical equipment) may be quickly controlled. The minimum fire-fighting facilities that should be made available at a mine depend on the hazardous character of the mine, number of men employed, daily output, and size of the mine.

The standard fire-fighting facilities which are considered when planning fire protection in mines are:

(a) Water mains or water lines;
(b) Sprinkler systems;
(c) Truck-mounted water tanks;
(d) Fire extinguishers;
(e) Stone dust, sand, or dry chemical; and
(f) Miscellaneous fire-fighting materials and tools.

1.1.4.1.1.1 Water mains

Water, without any doubt, is an excellent fire-extinguishing agent for fire at any stage. It can be used as a solid stream or as a spray, depending on the nature and location of the fire. It usually works by cooling the surface of the burning material. The only conditions for its efficacy are that it should be available in sufficient quantity and that adequate means for distribution are available. The water mains should be capable of giving at least 400 litres per minute of water at a minimum flowing pressure of 1.5 bar(g). They should preferably be connected, where practicable, to a covered steel or reinforced concrete static water reservoir/tank on the surface (Fig. 1.9) rather than to the conventional public water system. The tank should have a storage capacity of at least 100 m^3 and should preferably not be used for any other purposes. In mines which are located so that a constant adequate supply of fresh water is not available from streams, lakes or ponds, water stored

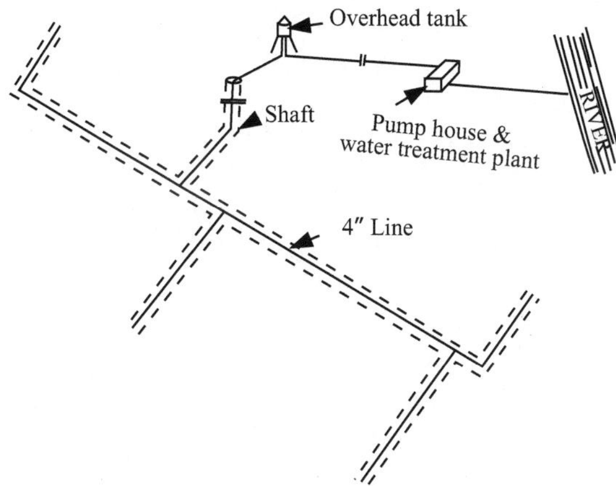

Figure 1.9 Water supply for fire fighting.

in underground sumps or suitably worked-out areas may constitute a supply for fire-fighting. In such cases, connections, bypasses and valves must be installed on the discharge line at the pumping station to supply water under sufficient pressure to the working sections along the main and panel haulage roadways. In deep mines, in order to prevent excessive pressures at hydrants or hose taps, cascade dams or break-pressure tanks with ball float valves or pressure-reducing valves are provided at different insets (Fig. 1. 10).

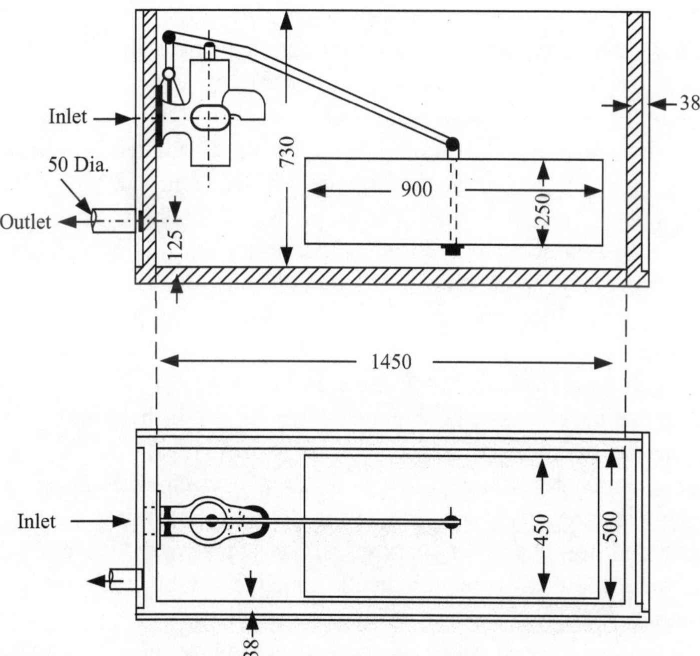

Figure 1.10 Break-pressure tank

Water mains should be provided at all mines, not naturally wet throughout, at the top and bottom of the main shafts, in main and secondary haulage roadways, and in staple shafts. They should extend to all working sections of a mine with section control and isolating valves. They should be at least 50 mm in diameter (usually 100 mm) and be fitted with hydrants near the pitbottoms and at intervals not exceeding 100 m in the main roadways, 50 m in gate roads, 25 m in conveyor haulage roadways, and 20 to 25 m on the intake side of main junctions, engine rooms, fan houses and substations, and at suitable central points in bord and pillar workings. The hydrants should be installed in such a way that they are protected against damage and are easily accessible and clearly visible. To prevent bursting of a fire-hose where the pressure at a hydrant exceeds 7 bar(g), a reducing valve or a pressure relief valve in the hydrant control valve should be used. The fire hose should be at least 38 mm (1.5 inches) in diameter (usually 2.5 inches or 2.75 inches for use from pressure pumps or water mains) and be quickly available in suitable lengths in coils stored in containers, recesses, or compartments especially provided for that purpose, or stored on reels at suitably located fire-hose stations. It should be fitted with instantaneous couplings with male inlet and female outlet. To obtain effective streams for fire-fighting purposes, the proper size and type of nozzle or nozzles should be selected for use with the standard size of hose used. Owing to the restricted space in roadways and the desirability of using the minimum quantity of water necessary, nozzles of 13 mm (0.5 inch) and 16 mm (0.625 inch) are usually used. Adjustable-type nozzles can also be used but they must be provided with a positive stop so that they cannot be closed to an extent which will cause bursting of the hose. A combination adjustable fog-and firestream type may also be advantageously used, which will produce either a fire-fighting stream or the heavy fog for approaching the fire. It is claimed that water under pressure in the form of fog will effectively control the backing out of smoke and fumes, will reduce the danger of hydrogen explosion or steam scalds, and will reduce the temperature to a level that will permit directing fire-fighting streams of water by adjusting the nozzle after the fire has been reached.

In mines using compressed air, the air pipes or lines must be interconnected through pressure-reducing valves where necessary so that they can be quickly converted into water mains in an emergency.

The laying out of an efficient water main system can at times be a difficult problem. Consideration must be given to the quantity of water required at the farthest possible inbye point in the mine and the method of mine development followed so that the contour of the pipe-range is below the hydraulic gradient and does not intersect it.

To ensure reliable functioning of the water supply system, tests and examinations should be made at regular intervals to ensure that the water-supply at all hydrants is adequate and hoses, couplings, nozzles, etc. are in operating condition. The quality of water should also be periodically tested to see if it gives rise to corrosion or incrustation.

The underground use of water as a fire-extinguishing agent may be associated with certain hazards. The water may cause a damaging physical effect on materials which have been subjected to intense heat from fire. If a jet of it is directed full on to the centre of a deep-seated large open fire of coal or coal face instead of attacking the fire from its fringes towards the centre it may bring about an explosion due to water gas. In deep mines, wet-bulb, temperatures may be raised to such an extent that working conditions may become unbearable.

1.1.4.1.1.2 Sprinkler systems

Where they can be applied, sprinkler systems, automatic or manually operated, are efficient fire-protection devices. Automatic sprinkler systems as fixed fire-extinguisher systems, are advantageous because of their economy, reliability, good suppression capability, and minimum maintenance. They are particularly suitable for controlling fires in belt conveyor roadways, in timbered main and staple shafts, and in underground hoisting engine rooms (Fig. 1.11). In timbered shafts, the sprinkler devices installed should sprinkle every square metre of shaft section and be controlled from the landings or insets and shaft top. The amount of water required is at least 500 litres per minute per square metre of cross-section for main shafts and 400 litres per minute per square metre cross-section in the case of staple shafts. Each water sprinkler system should be examined weekly and a functional test of the complete system should be conducted at least once a year.

The automatic sprinkler head usually used has a sealed frangible bulb operating element. The small bulb of special glass contains a low boiling point liquid which does not completely fill the bulb as a small air bubble is left entrapped in it. As the liquid expands due to heat, the bubble is compressed and finally absorbed by the liquid. As soon as the bubble disappears, the pressure rises rapidly and the glass bulb shatters at a temperature of about 55°C actuating a water control valve and the water-spray nozzles. The exact actuation temperature may, however, be regulated by adjusting the amount of liquid and the size of the bubble when the bulb is sealed.

Sprinkler heads may also be equipped with a fusible link that will actuate at a temperature of 74°C or higher. Sprinkler systems have the disadvantage that their installation, care, and maintenance are somewhat complicated.

1.1.4.1.1.3 Truck-mounted water tanks, portable water cars

In mines not equipped with water mains or when used as auxiliary equipment in large mines having water mains, mobile truck-mounted water tanks or fire cars should be provided. A truck-mounted water tank should have sufficient capacity, at least 4 to 5 m^3, and be equipped with a pump or a compressed-air cylinder, fire hose, Siamese coupling, hydrant connection and nozzles. The pump should be capable of delivering at least 200 litres of water per minute through a 50 m long, 38 mm diameter hose fitted with 13-mm nozzle at a nozzle pressure of 3.4 bar. The truck-mounted water tank should be stationed within 1500 m of each working section. In mines where such tanks are adopted as principal fire-fighting means, each unit should be stationed near the shaft-bottom, at intervals not exceeding 1500 m along the main and secondary haulage roadways, and within 800 m of each working section. However, the use of truck-mounted water tanks is limited in

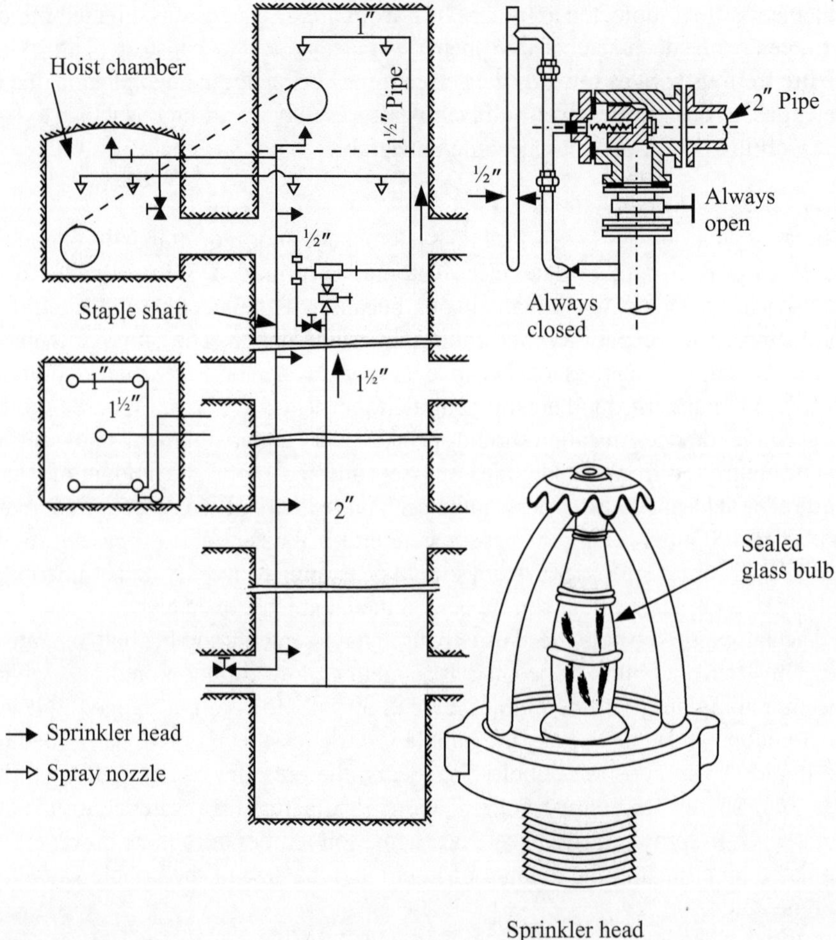

Figure 1.11 Automatic sprinkler system in staple shaft.

many mines as difficulties may be experienced in moving them from the place of storage to the place of a fire due to obstructions such as is offered by loaded and empty cars and other equipment. To increase the extinguishing ability of the water, sodium bicarbonate (8 per cent by weight) may be added in the water tanks.

1.1.4.1.1.4 Portable fire extinguishers

Most mine fires are small when they first start and they can often be easily controlled by the use of suitable hand-held portable fire extinguishers which are 'first-aid' fire-fighting appliances. When the fires assume larger proportions, they may still be fought successfully by large truck-mounted fire extinguishers or chemical fire-fighting trucks (chemical cars). When the gross weight of an extinguisher exceeds about 25 kg, it is usually placed on wheels.

Fire extinguishers are extremely handy when fighting fires at places which are not connected with water mains. They have greater extinguishing ability than water but suffer from a limited supply of the extinguishing agent. The maximum extinguishing effect is achieved when it is possible to cover or blanket the fire completely with the extinguishing medium. About 20 to 25 per cent of the workforce underground must be trained in the use of fire extinguishers.

The principles on which fire extinguishers suitable for use in mines function are:

(1) the cooling, effect of water;
(2) the fire-extinguishing effect of carbon dioxide;
(3) the blanketing or shutting-off effect of foam;
(4) the smothering effect of solid substance; and
(5) the combination of more than one effect.

The smothering effect of halogenated hydrocarbons or Halon (Halon 1211 and Halon 1301) by dilution of the oxygen content of the air surrounding a fire and interfering with the chemical reactions in the fire zone is not utilised for fire-fighting underground because many of them are toxic and produce extremely toxic decomposition products at the elevated temperatures prevalent in fires.

The different types of hand fire extinguishers used in mines can be classified as follows:

(1) Soda-acid extinguishers;
(2) Foam extinguishers
    (a) Chemical foam extinguishers and
    (b) Mechanical or air-foam extinguishers;
(3) Carbon dioxide snow extinguishers;
(4) Dry chemical (dry powder) extinguishers; and
(5) Multipurpose dry chemical (dry powder) extinguishers.

Fire extinguishers are not all equally effective on different classes of fire. Only fire extinguishers certified by an approving authority, carrying appropriate labels as to size, type and rating and the classes of fires on which they can to be used, should be used underground. Hand fire extinguishers are generally designed with 5 to 10 kg capacity.

The various extinguishers described here are the common standard types. Basically, a fire extinguisher consists of a container, the extinguishing agent, a pressure-producing device or agent or the vapour of the liquid extinguishing agent itself, and a discharge orifice or a hose, and nozzle.

Soda-acid extinguishers

This type of extinguisher depends for its action on the cooling effect of a jet of liquid. The extinguisher consists of a conical or cylindrical sheet steel container (Fig. 1.12) charged with basic sodium bicarbonate solution, a siphon or discharge tube, a nozzle, a hermetically-sealed acid phial or bottle, a perforated acid bottle metal cage, and a plunger knob assembly. The nozzle is closed with a protection disc which ruptures at a pressure of 2 bar(g) and has the object of preventing the stopping of the nozzle besides protecting the solution against the action of

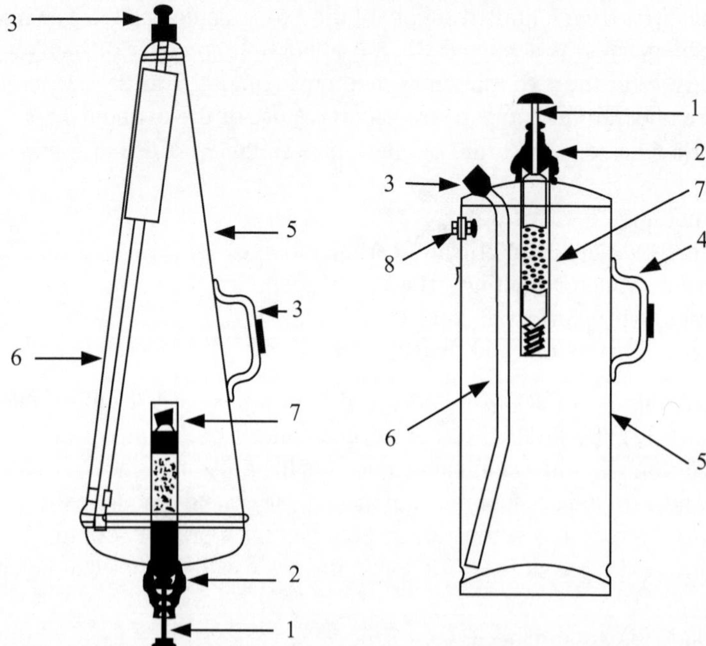

Figure 1.12 Minimax soda-acid extinguisher, 1–plunger knob; 2–plunger assembly; 3–nozzle; 4–handle; 5–container; 6–siphon tube; 7–metal cage with acid bottle; 8–safety valve.

the surrounding atmosphere. The rupture disc, furthermore, builds up a pressure inside the extinguisher when the latter is operated, which is sufficient to force the extinguishing liquid out of the nozzle in a powerful jet after breaking the disc.

The extinguisher is operated by breaking the acid phial with the plunger knob, permitting the acid and soda solutions to mix, and directing the nozzle at the same time towards the fire with the extinguisher held almost horizontally. The chemical reaction produces carbon dioxide in such a quantity that a pressure of about 6.5 bar(g) is developed which forces the whole of the contents of the extinguisher to discharge on to the fire.

A 10-litre capacity soda-acid extinguisher has a horizontal covering range of up to 14 m and a discharge time of 90 seconds. Soda-acid fire extinguishers are suitable for fires of solid combustible materials. They cannot be used for electrical fires or fires involving burning oils or flammable liquids. The extinguishing ability is practically the same as that of an equal quantity of water. The carbon dioxide evolved with the liquid is not produced for such an effect. Soda-acid extinguishers have ceased to be approved for firefighting underground as well as on surface due to their wetting characteristics.

Foam extinguishers

This type of extinguisher produces, when operated, a thick foamy fluid either by reaction between two chemical solutions (chemical-foam type) or by powerfully stirring an aqueous solution of a foam-forming compound by means of compressed air (mechanical or air-foam type). When directed against a fire, the foam spreads over the entire fire, covering or blanketing it, and thus cutting off the oxygen supply. The wet foam layer also produces a cooling effect which assists in extinguishing the fire. Foam is an extremely bad conductor of heat. It is to this fact that it owes its value. The topmost layer of foam has a temperature which is little above that of the surrounding atmosphere. All foams are capable of flowing and self-levelling over horizontal liquid or solid surfaces and adhering to vertical surfaces.

Foam extinguishers are especially used for fighting fires involving combustible and flammable liquids. They are not recommended for use in fighting electrical fires where the foam could come into contact with energized equipment.

Chemical foam extinguishers

A chemical foam extinguisher consists of a cylindrical outer container filled with an aqueous solution of sodium bicarbonate containing a special foam-forming compound and a stabilizer, a cylindrical inner container containing an acid solution of aluminium sulphate, and a nozzle fitted to the outer container.

The extinguisher is operated by inverting it, permitting the acid and basic solutions to mix, and directing the nozzle, which may be fitted with a short length of hose, on to the fire to be extinguished. The chemical reaction produces gelatinous aluminium hydroxide and carbon dioxide according to the equation

$$6NaHCO_3 + Al_2(SO_4)_3 = 3Na_2SO_4 + 2Al(OH)_3 + 6CO_2$$

The carbon dioxide is liberated in a state of very fine bubbles which are maintained in that state by the foam-forming compound. The light gelatinous precipitate has the effect of making the bubbles more tenacious and permanent, thereby giving a very stable foam. The excess carbon dioxide under pressure serves to force the foam in a stream out of the nozzle. For the acid and basic solutions to thoroughly mix and form foam in the shortest time, a mixing chamber is provided before the nozzle.

Chemical foam extinguishers have been increasingly displaced by mechanical foam extinguishers in mines.

Mechanical or air-foam extinguishers

This type of extinguisher produces a foam somewhat similar to that produced by a chemical foam extinguisher. A great advantage is that it can be readily charged underground and contains less amount of dissolved solids in the charge.

The Minimax air-foam extinguisher (Fig. 1.13) consists of a cylindrical container filled with an aqueous solution of a foam-forming compound or foam concentrate, a siphon tube, a mixing chamber, a discharge hose, a nozzle, a safety valve, and a compressed-air cylinder fitted with a cylinder valve of the handwheel type and accommodated in the centre of the container.

The extinguisher is operated by turning on compressed air by means of a handwheel. The compressed air which is at a pressure of 150 bar(g) is reduced to a pressure of 8 bar(g) by a reducing valve before it exerts pressure on the top of the solution forcing it up the siphon tube and the mixing chamber. A part of the

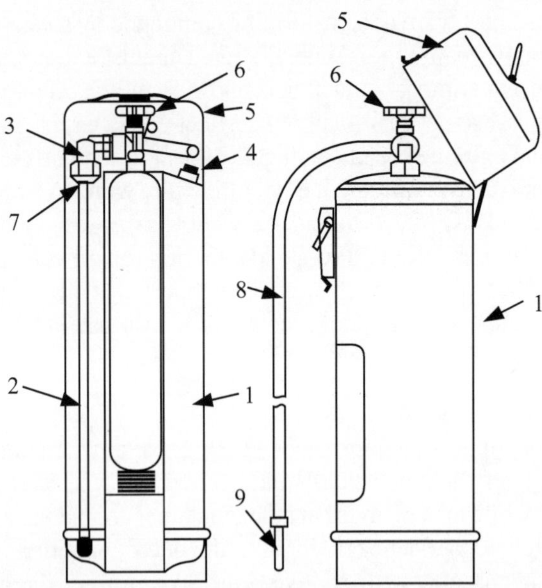

Figure 1.13 Minimax mechanical (air) foam extinguisher: 1–container; 2–siphon tube; 3–headpiece; 4–safety valve; 5–protective lid; 6–handwheel; 7–air inlet hole; 8–discharge tube; 9–nozzle.

compressed air flowing through a hole in the siphon tube at its top mixes with the solution in the mixing chamber and the resulting mixture is converted into a very fine-bubbled air foam in the discharge hose and forced out of the nozzle.

A 10-litre air-foam extinguisher produces with one filling about 120 to 140 litres air foam and has a discharge range of about 5 m. Two other sizes, 15 and 50 litres, are also manufactured for use in mines. Instead of compressed air, compressed carbon dioxide gas may also be used, but a jet pipe, a specialized discharge appliance, must be used which will suck the required quantity of air for foam formation and discharge it.

For continuous production of air foam, portable air-foam equipment, foam inductors, can be used in which the foam concentrate is continuously inducted into a water stream by means of an admixer or in-line proportioner located between a source of pressure water and an air-foam jet pipe or a foam-making branch. Figure 1. 14 shows the Minimax portable air-foam equipment.

The foam compounds now in general use with mechanical foam apparatus are of the hydrolyzed protein-type manufactured from horn and hoof meal or animal blood.

Carbon dioxide snow extinguishers

A carbon dioxide snow extinguisher essentially consists of a light-steel cylinder of about 8 litre capacity filled with a charge of 6 kg liquid carbon dioxide under a pressure of 56 to 63 bar(absolute). The cylinder valve which may be of handwheel, lever, or handlegrip type is fitted with a tube that nearly reaches the bottom of the

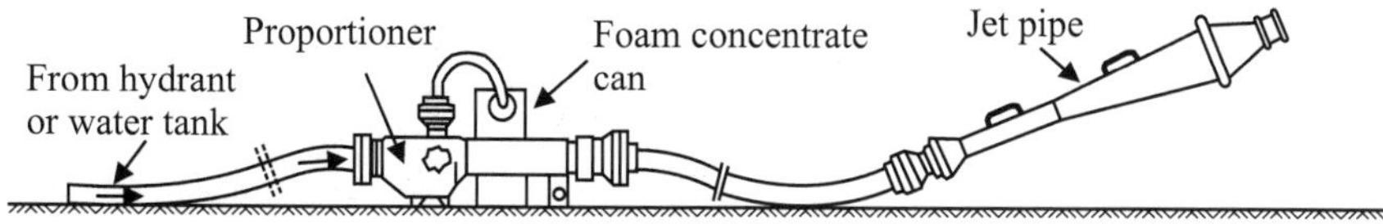

Figure 1.14 Minimax portable air-foam equipment.

cylinder and is also connected by means of a short length of high-pressure hose (about 1 m long) either directly or through an extension pipe to a snow pipe or discharge horn.

When the valve is opened, a portion of the liquid carbon dioxide evaporates at an orifice at the closed end of the horn by expansion to gas. This chills the horn to low temperatures. When the gaseous carbon dioxide further expands by streaming through the horn to atmospheric pressure, the remaining carbon dioxide is converted into loose snow due to intense cooling (–79°C) in the horn.

Thus, the extinguishing stream consists of an undercooled carbon dioxide gas with finely divided snow. A safety device on the cylinder valve prevents undue excess pressure in the steel cylinder.

The extinguisher has a discharge range of about 1.5 m. The best extinguishing results are obtained by applying the discharge as close to the fire as possible, first at the near edge of the fire moving the discharge horn slowly from side to side, and slowly progressing forward as the flames are extinguished. Carbon dioxide is essentially a non-conductor of electricity and leaves no residue. It is effective as an extinguishing agent primarily due to its ability to cover the burning material when released on it and reduce the oxygen content of the air to a point where it will no longer support combustion. The extinguisher is specially suitable for use on fires which cannot be fought by water or are only fought with damage, such as electrical fires and fires above flammable liquids. Figure 1.15 shows Minimax carbon dioxide snow fire extinguishers with different types of cylinder valves.

Dry chemical powder extinguishers

This type of extinguisher uses a fire-quenching chemical powder with a bicarbonate base for its action. The dry chemical commercially available is made up of one or more of five basic powders–sodium bicarbonate, potassium bicarbonate, urea potassium bicarbonate, potassium chloride, and monoammonium phosphate with various additives to improve their storage and flow characteristics. Chief among the additives are metallic stearates and tricalcium phosphate. When used on a fire, the dry chemical causes the flame to go out at once. The exact mechanism and chemistry of the extinguishing action are not definitely known. Smothering, cooling, radiation shielding, and chain-breaking reactions in the combustion zone are conjointly responsible for the extinguishing action of the dry chemical. Potassium bicarbonate-base dry chemical has a faster extinguishing action than the sodium bicarbonate-base type.

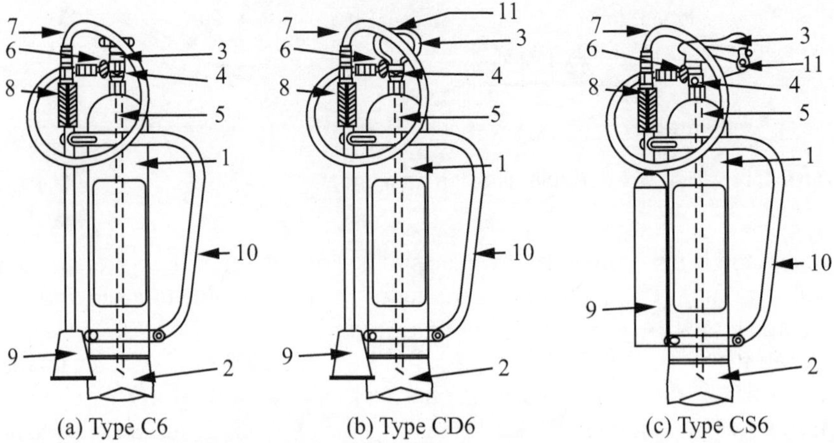

Figure 1.15 Minimax carbon dioxide snow extinguisher; 1–CO_2 cylinder; 2–standing base 3–cylinder value 4–safety device with rupture disc and indicator; 5–tube; 6–gasket; 7–high-pressure house; 8–hand grip; 9–discharge horn; 10–carrying handle; 11–safety pin.

Dry chemical powder extinguishers are primarily used for extinguishing flammable liquid fires, fires on diesel mining vehicles, fires in electrical equipment subject to flammable liquid fires such as oil-filled transformers and circuit-breakers, and flaming mine fires. They can also be used against fires in ordinary combustible materials. They are, however, less effective in extinguishing glow fires and fires that get beneath the surface. Figure 1.16 shows the construction of a Minimax dry chemical extinguisher using a sodium bicarbonate-base dry chemical. It consists of a container with a fixed nozzle at its bottom, a liquid carbon dioxide steel cylinder outside the container fitted with a cylinder valve, and a tube extending from the cylinder valve down to the bottom of the container. The nozzle is provided with a protection disc to prevent the action of the surrounding atmosphere upon the charge in the cylindrical container. When the cylinder valve is opened, carbon dioxide gas is released which, when sufficient pressure is developed in the container, expels the dry chemical out of the nozzle in a cloud after rupturing the nozzle protection disc.

Under very low temperature conditions, nitrogen is preferred as the expellant since the vapour pressure of carbon dioxide at such temperatures is too low to permit proper functioning of the extinguishers. There are other methods by which the expellant gas is released to provide pressure for expelling the dry chemical.

Multipurpose dry chemical (dry powder) Powder extinguishers

Multipurpose dry chemical is a mixture of chemicals consisting of ammonium sulphate and monoammonium phosphate and additives which improve storage and flow characteristics. It has little cooling effect on the fire but its extinguishing action is considerable as due to the inhibiting effect of the liberated ammonia and the formation of an adhering glassy crust of metaphosphoric acid over the fire in

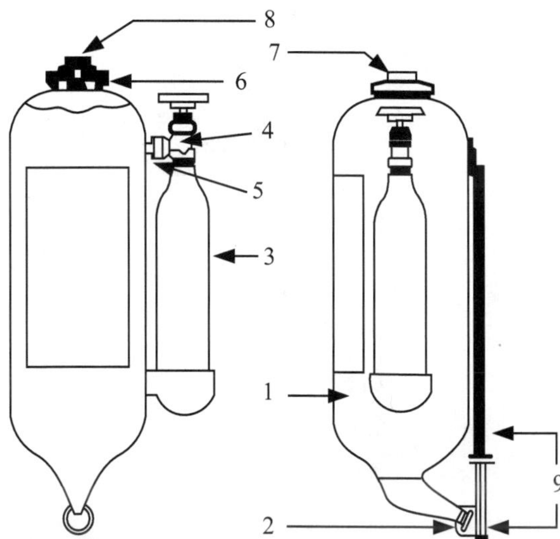

Figure 1.16 Minimax dry chemical extinguisher: 1-container; 2–nozzle; 3–steel cylinder; 4–cylinder valve; 5–nut; 6–filling opening; 7–screw-on type lid; 8–safety device.

ordinary combustible materials, which tends to retard further combustion. The mechanism causing a flammable liquid fire to go out is believed to be a chain-breaking reaction.

The extinguishers may be either of the stored-pressure type (the charge under constant pressure of the expellant gas) or of the cylinder or cartridge-operated type. The working pressure of the stored-pressure extinguishers at ordinary temperatures using carbon dioxide expellant is 21 bar(g).

The extinguishers are effective against glow fires, flaming fires, flammable liquid fires, and electrical fires. Tests had shown that multipurpose dry chemical is at least as effective as water on kg-for-kg basis when used against fires in ordinary combustible materials and is slightly more effective than the bicarbonate-base type dry chemical. Their disadvantages are: increased maintenance and potential re-ignition of fire because of limited cooling capability. Figure 1.17 shows a Minimax multipurpose dry chemical extinguisher using carbon dioxide as the propellant gas.

Maintenance of fire extinguishers

The following general rules are applicable to all types of portable fire extinguishers:

(a) All extinguishers must be properly charged, maintained and operated according to the instructions of the manufacturer;
(b) All extinguishers should be examined at least once in six months to determine that they are in an operating condition;
(c) Frequent inspections should be made to determine that the extinguishers are in their designated places, are readily accessible, have not been tampered

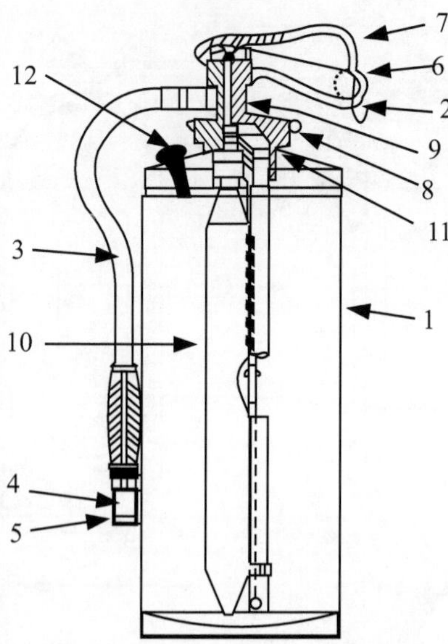

Figure 1.17 Minimax multipurpose dry chemical extinguisher: 1–container; 2_carrying handle; 3–hose; 4–nozzle rest; 6–safety pin; 7–valve trigger; 8–screwed connection; 9–valve unit (lever valve); 10–CO_2 gas cylinder; 11–spring-type safety value.

with, and that the nozzles are not clogged;

(d) Extinguishers should be recharged immediately after use or a replacement unit should be provided; and

(e) Periodic hydraulic testing or air testing under water should be conducted in accordance with the standards laid down.

Selection of fire extinguishers

Proper selection and location of the correct type and size of extinguishers are very important if mine fires are to be effectively and quickly put out while still small. Although the different types of extinguishers are best suited to certain classes of fires, it should not be assumed that they are valueless when used on other classes of fires.

For fires in substations, rectifier stations, battery-charging stations, pump chambers, and underground shops with electric-driven machinery, carbon dioxide snow extinguishers are the best. But dry chemical and multipurpose dry chemical extinguishers can also be used although they leave a residue.

For fires in oil-storage areas, belt conveyor roadways and diesel mining vehicles, air-foam, dry chemical, and multipurpose dry chemical extinguishers may be used. Carbon dioxide snow extinguishers may also be used.

For smouldering fires and fires in ordinary combustible materials, air-foam and multipurpose dry chemical extinguishers may be used. For fires on self-propelled electrical machinery, dry chemical and multipurpose dry chemical extinguishers are the best.

For fixed automatic fire extinguisher systems which are necessary where fire hazards require immediate response, dry-chemical and multipurpose dry-chemical extinguishers will be suitable. Carbon dioxide gas is used in closed systems containing flammable diesel fuel oil. Halogenated extinguishing agents are normally used only in relatively small areas that can be totally flooded.

1.1.4.1.1.5 Stone dust, sand or dry chemical

Inert dust (limestone, dolomite, or anhydrite dust) or sand can be successfully used in smothering many heatings in their incipiency. A sufficient supply of stone dust in sacks and suitable equipment for conveying and using it should be provided at suitable places along main haulage roads, at the entrance of each district, at the entrances of pump rooms, and at rectifier stations in the mine. When the relative humidity at places of dust storage is high, a plan should be adopted for renewal at regular intervals as dictated by experience.

Dry chemical stored in moisture-resistant sacks on mobile mining equipment can be used successfully for putting out any fires occurring during their operation.

1.1.4.1.1.6 Miscellaneous fire-fighting materials and tools

On every haulage roadway in each mine, a fire depot or fire station should be established at suitable places which should be conspicuously marked. At such stations, fire extinguishers (air-foam hand fire extinguishers, portable air-foam admixers or proportioners with discharge devices), dry chemical, sand and/or stone dust, fire- extinguishing cars or trailers equipped with equipment and accessories for fighting with water and tools, foam generators, materials and equipment for sealing off fires, a high-pressure stonedusting machine, brattice boards, and brattice cloth should be stored.

1.1.4.2 Fighting by indirect attack

When it is no more possible or is useless to extinguish an open or incipient fire by direct attack within a reasonable time, one takes recourse to indirect fire-fighting by isolating or sealing off the area from the rest of the mine workings and air currents so that the fire does not spread further but gets extinguished due to lack of oxygen.

1.1.4.2.1 Isolation of fire

Isolation of a fire by preventing air from gaining access to it depends on the location of the fire, the rate and direction of advance of the fire, and the nature of the combustible material. Isolation of a fire is easy in mines which are well-sectionalized, that is, divided into suitable fire sections by means of steel fire doors and preparatory stoppings at strategic locations. Each of the fire sections may be further subdivided into smaller sections. In laying out fire sections on the mine plans and sections, advantage should be taken of the presence of want or barren areas and large dykes.

Steel fire doors offer a safe, quick and easy means of isolating fires. They must be designed so that the door frames are as large as possible to reduce air resistance to a minimum when the doors are open and form an airtight seal. They must be provided with a mechanical means of assisting opening and closing against high pressures without difficulty, and must be capable of being locked in the open position. Their number must be kept to a minimum and be installed in suitable ground. All fire doors must be numbered and be provided with a water trap where considered necessary. The fire doors can, however, also be used for reducing air quantities and redirecting air flow.

Hydraulic filling may also be used for isolation of a fire area. The method of isolation of fire, however, suffers from the following disadvantages:

(1) The isolated area is a temporary loss to the mine;
(2) There is danger of explosion from firedamp in gassy mines and from fire gases in non-gassy mines; and
(3) Complete isolation may be difficult, if not impossible, to achieve.

Isolation of engine chambers or transformer rooms in the event of a fire is done by means of hermetically-closed steel doors which are automatically operated.

Where the fire is near enough to the surface to be reached by a trench, a trench barrier may be used to halt the fire. An open trench is excavated by a (dragline across the fire area in order to cut it off from the remaining coal and is backfilled with earth, fly ash, or granulated slag (Fig. 1.18). The base of the trench must extend below the bottom of the seam. Trenching, however, is an expensive operation. Another serious drawback is that the fire may jump across the trench as found from experience.

1.1.4.2.2 Sealing off the fire area

Mine fires that originate from explosion are usually very difficult to fight due to uncertain ventilation. The objective of sealing off a fire area is to control and eventually extinguish the fire by cutting off oxygen supply so that the oxygen content in the area is below that which will support combustion; it also minimizes or eliminates the explosion hazard. A decision to seal off a fire area or an entire mine must be taken when it is no longer reasonably safe or feasible to fight the fire by direct attack due to the danger of build-up of flammable gases, bad roof conditions due to heat, insufficient fighting materials available, too large an area affected etc. With every fire, one should anticipate sealing off from the very beginning, and, along with the initial fire-fighting operations, certain preparatory measures should be undertaken. The most important of these measures are:

(1) Withdrawal of endangered workmen;
(2) Selection of sites for the erection of permanent stoppings;
(3) Preparation for inert gas injection where necessary infrastructure is available to deliver sufficient quantities of an inert gas to the point of application in the mine;
(4) Determination of the type and construction of stoppings, their order, and duration of erection;

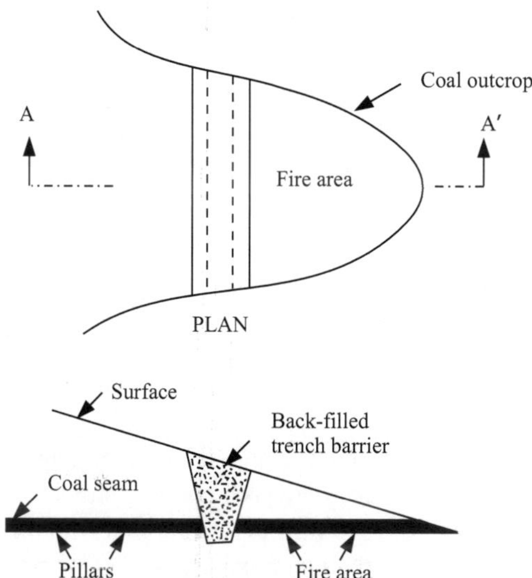

Figure 1.18 Trench barrier

(5) Preparation of the sites selected for permanent stoppings;
(6) Supply of necessary building materials; and
(7) Analysis of gases.

Some of the above measures necessitate inspection or exploration work by rescue-trained men to define the extent of the affected area, the number of working districts that could be directly affected by the fire, and the temperatures that may be experienced. One should bear in mind that early sealing will limit the extent of the damage and reduce the time necessary to re-establish production. Once a plan has been drawn up, it must be strictly implemented.

The selection of sites for permanent stoppings or, in other words, determining the distance at which the stoppings should be constructed will depend on the nature of the ground, whether unsettled (or moving), fractured, or settled, the number of openings to be sealed, the intensity of the fire, the condition of the air in the fire area, the system of ventilation, the likelihood of formation of flammable gas mixtures, the coal dust hazard, the gradients in the area, the difficulty of transporting the materials of construction, balancing of pressures after sealing, and access to communication facilities. In general, the stoppings should be erected in sound (firm and unbroken) ground free of geological disturbances such as dykes, faults and burnt coal, as near to the fire seat as practical without, however, sacrificing mine safety. Alternative plans for re-siting the stoppings should also be prepared, should this be found necessary.

The type and construction of stoppings are governed by the condition of the ground, size of opening, rock pressure, availability of construction materials, danger of explosion, occurrence of acid mine water and necessity to hold back water.

The sites for the stoppings should be prepared by digging hitches in the sides, roof, and floor (at least 0.5 m in rock and 1 m in coal), so that the stoppings are well-sealed to the surrounding ground and air-leakage around the stoppings is avoided. The sides, roof, and floor should be cleaned to remove as much loose material as possible and sprayed with a fireproofing plaster for a distance of 3 m on either side of the stoppings.

Where inertization of mine fires by injection of an inert gas is practised, the location of the stoppings loses its importance. Necessary materials in sufficient quantities must be stored at suitable places. The materials usually required are sand bags, sand, stone dust, bricks, cement, clay, screened dirt or ash, timber, slurry injection pumps, materials for the construction of emergency stone-dust barriers, fireproof clothing, etc.

Analysis of air from a fire area must be undertaken at regular intervals of time. The laboratory at the mine or mobile gas analysis laboratory should work day and night to supply the man in-charge of the fire-fighting operations with the results for judging the status of fire, danger due to carbon monoxide, and explosion hazard. The presence of high quantities of carbon monoxide (0.25 to 1.5 per cent) usually indicates an active fire and a high oxygen content in the fire area (10 to 15 per cent)

Where firedamp drainage pipelines run through a fire area, the drainage must be allowed to continue but with the following precautions:

(1) The percentage of methane in the drainage line must be monitored continuously;
(2) The condition of the pipelines must be checked if possible breakage(s) may pose problems; and
(3) Alternative routes for pipelines bypassing the fire area be examined.

The manner of sealing off a fire area depends on whether any explosion hazard exists till the time of completion of the stopping and also on whether the area to be sealed would be re-opened at a later date.

1.1.4.2.2.1 Sealing off without explosion hazard

When it is known from the knowledge of firedamp emission that there is no explosion hazard during the sealing-off operations, one restricts the air supply so that little oxygen reaches the fire. Temporary stoppings are then erected on the intake and return sides of the fire followed by permanent or main stoppings at selected places for final sealing off. Experience had always shown that it is convenient to erect temporary stoppings first on the intake side instead of on both intake and return sides of the fire simultaneously as respiratory protective equipment will be necessary when men work in the return air. The temporary stoppings are erected with any available materials normally used within the mine that will require minimum time for construction with reasonable airtightness such as brattice line, sand bags, stone-dust bags, rockwool, boards, clay, light-gauge sheet metal and concrete or fly-ash blocks. It is advisable to seal off as small an area as possible so that the fire will reduce the oxygen quickly. Sealing off the return airways requires considerable experience and should not be undertaken lightly.

1.1.4.2.2.1.1 Temporary stoppings

Temporary stoppings may simply be constructed of brattice line (jute, jute-plastic, nylon-plastic, propylene) if they are to be erected quickly and air leakage is not very important. Where a stopping has to withstand considerable pressure, a more substantial one (heavy-duty brattice) in which the brattice line is nailed to boards covering the entire roadway cross-section should be used. A brattice line covered with wire-netting may be sprayed over with a mine sealant to decrease the air leakage. Whatever the material used, the edges should be sealed with a sealant to make them as air-tight as possible.

Wooden stoppings

They are more substantial than brattice line stoppings. They may be of single- or double-boarded type. Usually, rough boards of varying width and about 25 mm thickness are used.

A single-boarded stopping (Fig. 1.19) usually consists of several boards which are horizontally nailed to wooden posts (three to five in number depending on the width of the opening) firmly set in hitches (0.3 to 0.5 m) deep in the roof and floor. The boards must be nailed in such a manner that the upper edge of each board overlaps the bottom edge of the board above. The stopping is rendered air-tight by covering its entire surface with a fairly thick coating of mud plaster, mud-and-cement plaster, calcium chloride-and-clay paste, Hardstop (a gypsum compound) or a permitted sealant. The overlap of the boards helps in holding the plaster in place. The calcium chloride-and-clay paste is much more effective than mud or mud-and-cement plaster as it remains plastic for a long time, has good adhering characteristics and can seal off small openings around the edges of the stopping. Vermiculite-cement-water mixture is also an excellent material for covering the boards.

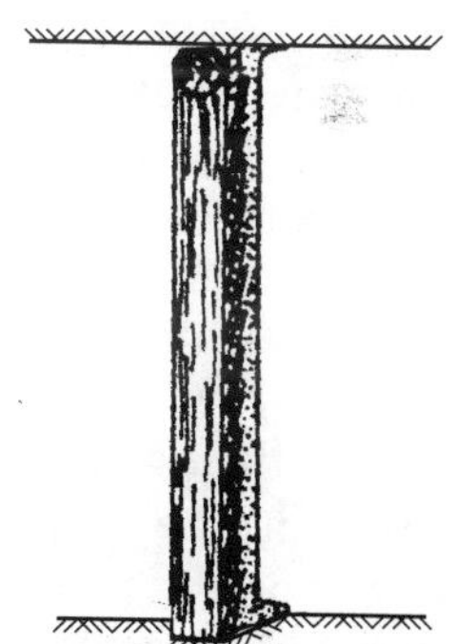

Figure 1.19 Single-boarded stopping.

A double-boarded stopping (Fig. 1.20) consists of two single-boarded stoppings erected 0.5 to 1.2 m apart, the space between them being filled with sand, loam, stone dust, screened boiler ash or broken rock which should be well tamped. The outbye face of the stopping is plastered or sprayed with a sealant to make the stopping as tight as possible.

The disadvantages of wooden stoppings are that they cannot withstand excessive rock pressure, are combustible and are affected by mine water. They are normally erected in pillar and stall panels where speed of construction is an absolute necessity and pressures are minimum.

Rockwool stoppings (Fig. 1.21)

They can be quickly erected and are also called 'quick-build stoppings'. They should not be less than 4 to 6 m thick. The glasswool or rockwool is used in the form of bales enclosed in chicken wire-netting for ease of handling. The stoppings get

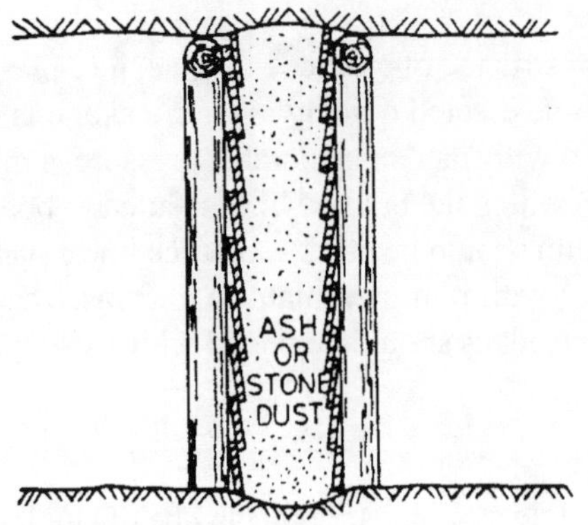

Figure 1.20 Double-boarded stopping.

Figure 1.21 Rockwool stopping.

compressed under rock pressure and, in consequence, become tighter with time. They are absolutely incombustible and act as heat insulators. The wool fibres, however, have been found to be carcinogenic and the use of such stoppings should be discouraged.

Sand-bag stoppings (Fig. 1.22)

They have proved themselves to be very useful in practice. They should not be less than 4 to 6 m thick and they must be embedded in stone dust. They should not be completely filled with sand in order that they snugly rest over one another. To prevent their possible sliding down, particularly on the fireside, wooden or steel posts should be firmly anchored between the roof and floor over the entire roadway cross-section and boards placed between them and the sand bags. Sand bag stoppings, however, suffer from the following disadvantages: the sand bags cannot be stored as such underground; they may be burnt out by the fire, resulting in the running-off of the sand; they shrink in course of time causing leakage of air along the roof; a large number of bags will be required.

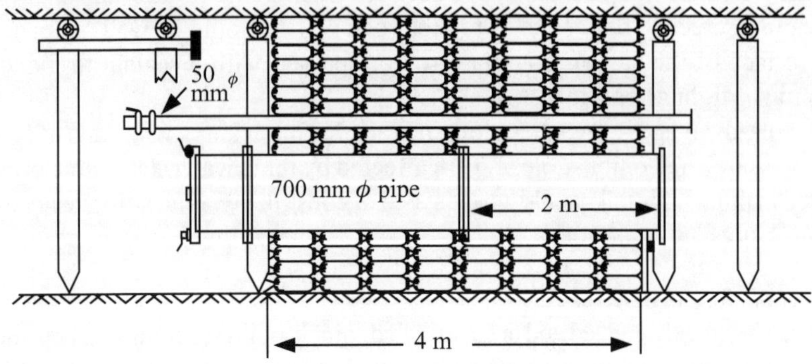

Figure 1.22 Sand-bag stopping,

Concrete and fly-ash block stoppings
These can be built in a short time. A single or two courses of blocks are laid without mortar or with a weak mortar. The stopping is not hitched into the sides, roof, or floor. Its fireside is covered with a cement-sand plaster and the perimeter is caulked with cement mortar

1.1.4.2.2.1.2 Permanent stoppings

Work on the construction of the permanent stoppings commences half to one hour after the completion of the temporary stoppings. The stoppings should be well-hitched in the sides, roof, and floor so that hot gases or air do not 'jump' the stopping by travelling through fissures in the roof, sides, or floor. The stoppings may be built of bricks, cement concrete or fly-ash blocks, monolithic concrete, gypsum, or packwalls of various kinds for long-term ventilation control.

Brick stoppings
They are most commonly used. They should be 0.5 to 3 m thick. They may be constructed as single or double stoppings (Figs. 1.23 and 1.24).

A double stopping may be used in unsettled or broken ground. It consists of two walls 2½ to 3 bricks thick and 0.8 to 1 m apart. The space between the walls is filled with broken rock or screened dirt which is injected after completion of the second wall with cement-stone dust-water slurry by an injection pump (Fig. 1.25). In gate roadways of longwall faces, the distance between the two walls should be assumed not less than 20 m and the space filled with broken rock and injected. Carbonaceous material should not be used as filling. After a stopping has been completed, the entire face of the stopping should be plastered with a strong cement mortar or sprayed with a cement-stone dust-water mixture by a slurry stone dust distributor. Brushing mortar on the stopping face is more effective in reducing leakage than trowelling. Figure 1.26 shows a combined brick- and-sand bag stopping that may be used in badly broken ground.

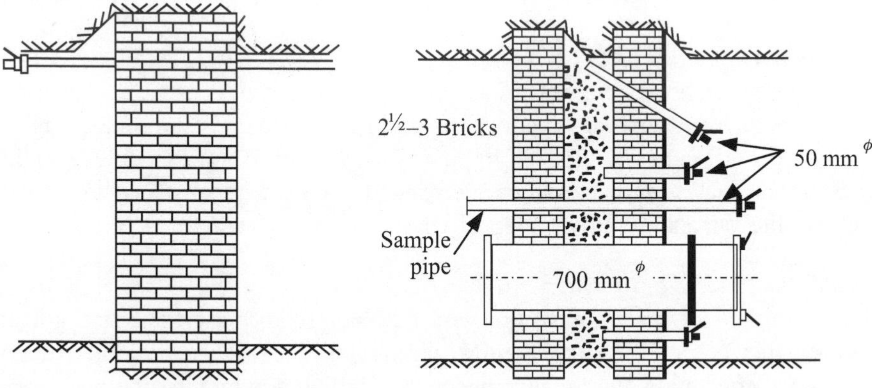

Figure 1.23 Single-brick stopping.

Figure 1.24 Double-brick stopping.

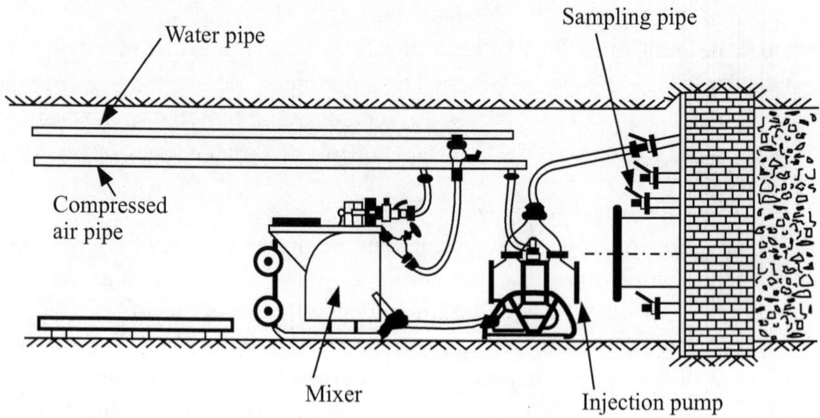

Figure 1.25 Slury injection pump

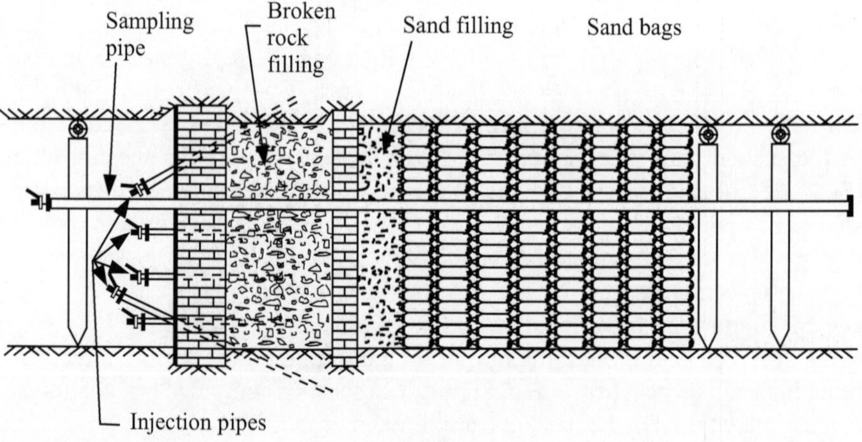

Figure 1.26 Combined brick- and-sand-bag stopping.

Concrete and fly-ash block stoppings

Like bricks, precast concrete or fly-ash blocks laid in cement mortar may be used to erect permanent stoppings. They are easier to erect than brick stoppings. 'Light-weight' precast concrete blocks (46 cm × 23 cm × 15 cm) using light- weight aggregates such as furnace clinker, expanded clay, sintered fly ash, expanded vermiculite can also be advantageously used.

Monolithic concrete stoppings

Monolithic concrete stoppings are very durable. To increase their strength in tension, they are reinforced with old steel rails (Fig. 1.28). The chief objection to the use of concrete is the inconvenience in handling and moving the necessary ingredients to the site of the stopping.

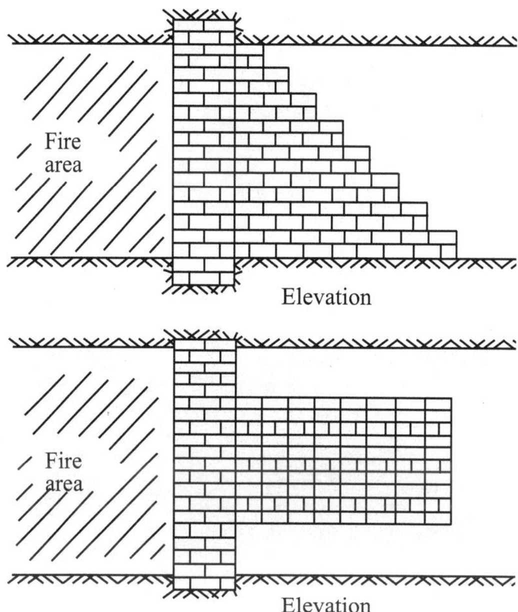

Figure 1.27 Buttressing of single-brick stopping.

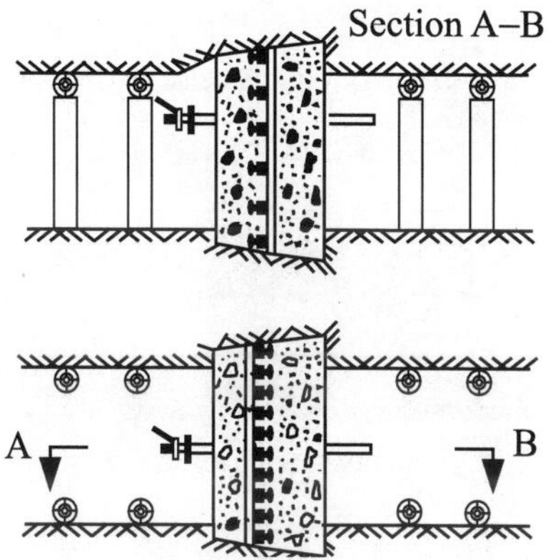

Figure 1.28 Reinforced concrete stopping.

Packwall stoppings

These are specially erected where they are subjected to excessive rock pressure. There are several types of packwall stoppings.

Rock-filled packwall stoppings (Fig. 1. 29)

A single pack of finely broken rock 3 to 5 m thick, well plastered and injected with slurry of stone dust, will seal a fire effectively. It may be faced with a brickwall on the outbye side.

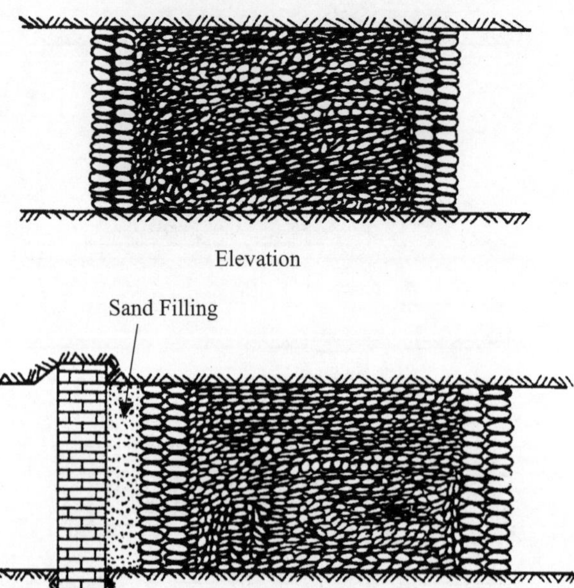

Figure 1.29 Rock-filled packwall stopping.

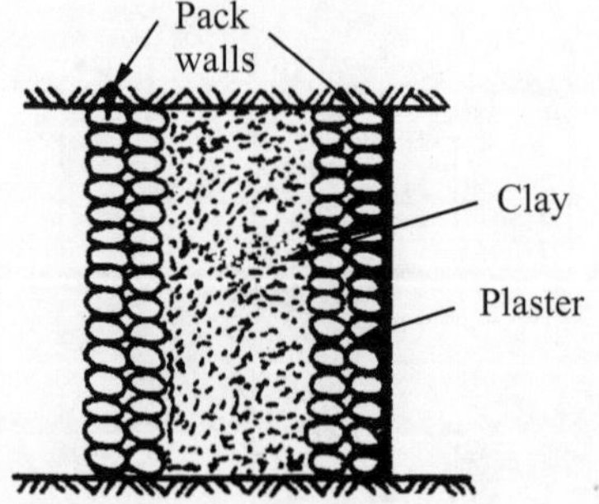

Figure 1.30 Rock-and-loam packwall stopping.

Rock-and-loam packwall stoppings
Two rock walls are erected with the space between them filled with loam (Fig. 1.30).

Post-and-loam packwall stoppings
This type of stopping has been successfully used in sealing several mine fires and worked-out sections in European mines. Its chief merit is that under excessive rock pressure it becomes tighter and will not crack or break. It may be constructed as a single or double stopping.

A single stopping (Fig. 1.31) is formed of alternate layers of plastic loam and short lengths of mine timber or posts. At first, a layer of loam is placed in the bottom hitch. A row of posts of fairly uniform size, 15 to 17 cm in diameter and

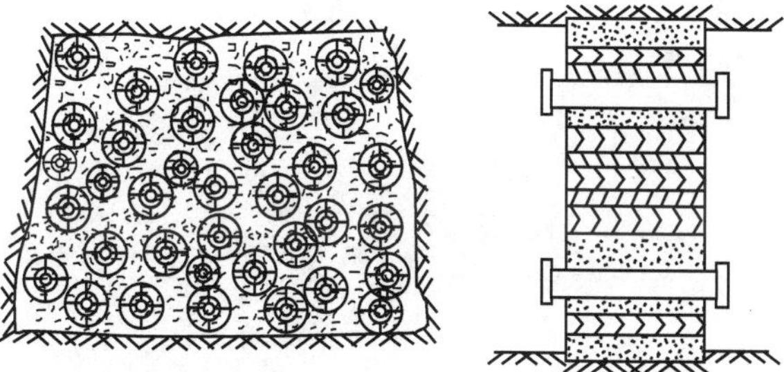

Figure 1.31 Post-and-loam single packwall stopping.

0.8 to 1.2 m in length, is then laid on it parallel to the axis of the roadway. A layer of loam is next placed on the posts and is well tamped between them. Another layer of posts is added. The operations of putting alternate layers of posts and loam are repeated till the stopping is completed.

A double stopping (Fig. 1.32) is erected by constructing two single stoppings 0.8 m apart, with the space between them filled with broken rock which should be injected with cement-stone dust slurry. Wooden wedges are driven in the stoppings to make up for their shrinkage. A combination of brick and post-and-loam stopping is shown in Fig. 1.33.

Special stoppings

Wire-mesh stoppings sprayed with gypsum slurry or permitted mine sealant have been used in mines abroad to serve as stoppings. The stopping consists of an adjustable channel steel frame bolted to the roof and spiked to the floor to which a steel wire mesh is tied, which is sprayed with the sealant to form an air-tight stopping. A hatch or door may be provided. The stopping is easy to erect and cheaper than concrete block or similar stoppings.

1.1.4.2.2.2 Sealing off with explosion hazard

When there is danger of a firegas- or firedamp-explosion during or after sealing-off operations, utmost care must be taken to see that an explosion does not take place during sealing, which might cause a dust explosion, and that, if it occurred after sealing, it is contained by explosion-proof stoppings. Explosion-proof and air-tight temporary stoppings should first be erected in the intake and return airways, followed after a certain time elapse by permanent stoppings. Sealing off a fire thus reduces to a race between depletion of oxygen and formation of a flammable mixture of combustible gases. Where inert gas injection in good time is possible, the formation of flammable mixtures may be eliminated during sealing.

The following precautionary measures should be adopted:

(1) The area to be sealed should be chosen so that a minimum number of stoppings is required by making the best use of barrier pillars.
(2) The stoppings should be sited as far from the fireseat as possible (300 m or more) in order that the work may be completed and men withdrawn before

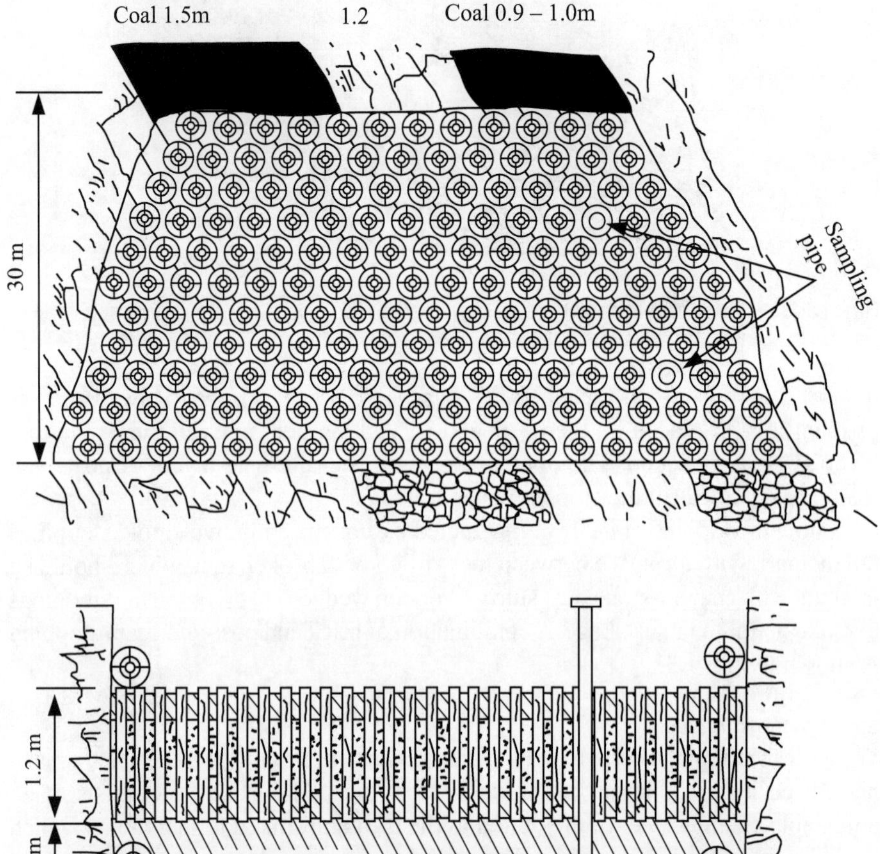

Coal 1.5m
1.2
Coal 0.9 – 1.0m
30 m
Sampling pipe
1.2 m
0.8 m
Clay filling
1.2 m
5.5 – 6.5 m

Figure 1.32 Post-and-loam double packwall stopping in gate road of a steep seam.

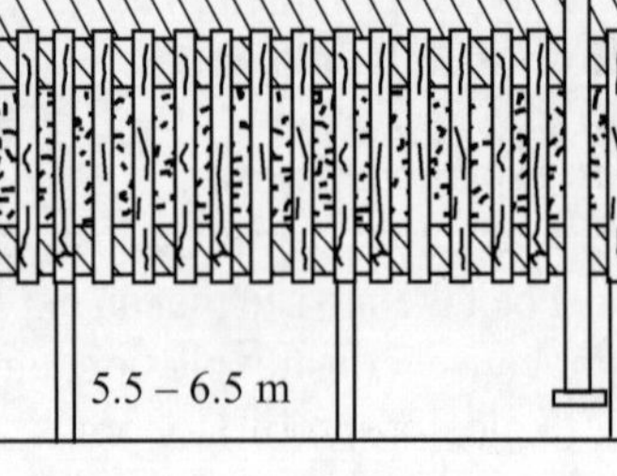

Figure 1.33 Combination brick-and-post-and-loam stopping.

a flammable gas mixture is formed in the larger volume of air enclosed. One should, however, remember that with a large sealed area, it becomes difficult to interpret the analyses of air samples taken from behind the stoppings as the problems of balancing the ventilation pressures at stoppings increase and it is more difficult to control the air leakages.

(3) The area to be sealed should be cleared of pipes, cables, and other metallic materials. Old batteries should not be left behind in the goaf as they are another potential ignition source.

(4) Samples from the fire area should be collected at shorter intervals of time and analyzed as quickly as possible in order that the stopping builders may be withdrawn, should the methane content near the fire become dangerously high. The result of the analyses should preferably be represented in the form of a graph so that the make of gas can be seen at a glance during sealing.

(5) Under no circumstances must the ventilation be interrupted when building stoppings. Any changes in ventilation especially restriction or reduction of air quantities should be done with extreme care. It should be avoided since inadequate ventilation causes firedamp to accumulate or other dangers to arise from migration of firedamp or firegases. To maintain sufficient ventilation through the fire area until the time for sealing off and also to enable rescue crew to pass through for purposes of exploration or recovery at some time, a ventilation tunnel or an equivalent is generally incorporated in each stopping. A steel pipe of at least 700 mm diameter fitted with a tight door or blank flange arranged near the floor of the stopping will be very satisfactory.

(6) In order that an explosion of firedamp or firegases during sealing is not propagated by coal dust towards the stoppings at which men are working, emergency stone-dust barriers of the German storeyed-type should be erected between the fireseat and the stopping in the early stages of the sealing operation. Where such barriers cannot be erected, the roadways inbye the stoppings should be stonedusted heavily to afford some degree of protection for the men employed in the erection of the stoppings.

(7) When the temporary stoppings on the intake and return sides are completely erected, the ventilation pipe left in them should be closed at the same time under all circumstances. Immediately after the closure of the pipes, all men should be withdrawn from the mine as promptly as possible for at least 12 hours (safe period is normally 24 hours) which is the critical period during which methane may reach its flammable range before the oxygen is reduced to 12 per cent or less. The main fan(s) and the fan-drift must be regularly checked using tube breathing apparatus; no naked lights should be used in the area of the fan evasee.

(8) The construction of the permanent stoppings, which is usually done under the supervision of a rescue team, should begin only after the 12-hour period has elapsed and after it has been found from the analysis of air samples from points at a minimum distance of 5 m behind the stoppings that no explosion hazard

exists. Minimum number of authorized persons must be allowed underground and a record made of all persons entering and leaving the mine.

(9) During the erection of the permanent stoppings, the temporary stoppings in the intake airways must be continuously watched for air leakage.

(10) The pressure at stoppings must be balanced after sealing.

(11) All events should be logged under the general heading 'Time, Event, Action Taken' and the records kept in case the sealed area is to be reopened at a later date.

(12) Telephonic communication between all stoppings, the fresh-air base, and the surface control room is desirable.

(13) Alternative plans for re-siting of stoppings should be prepared if found necessary.

1.1.4.2.2.2.1 Temporary stoppings

As temporary stoppings, sand-bag or stone dust-bag stoppings of 4 to 6 m thickness have been found to be effective.

Gypsum stoppings

Stoppings constructed of a quick-setting gypsum compound offer a quicker, easier, and safer means of sealing off fire areas than by the use of sand bags.

The German experience with gypsum stoppings erected in mines has been quite satisfactory. The proven method of erecting a stopping consists in pneumatically injecting dry gypsum powder by a compressed air-driven guniting machine between two tight shutterings and wetting it with water at the same time to form a slurry between the shutterings, which soon sets to a hard mass.

The thickness of a gypsum stopping as recommended by the Central Mine Rescue Station, Essen, F.R.G. is given as:

2 m	for roadways of heights up to 3 m;
2.5 m	for roadways of heights up to 3.5 m; and
Roadway height	for roadways of heights greater than 3.5 m.

Experience is lacking with stoppings in roadways larger than 12.5 m^2 cross-section.

For every m^3 of stopping volume, about 1.3 t gypsum and 0.8 to 0.9 m^3 water are required.

The site of the stopping should be carefully selected as with other types of stoppings. The shutterings (Fig. 1.34) are erected of horizontal boards nailed to wooden posts (two, three or more, depending on the roadway cross-section). The inbye shuttering edges and the sides and roof of the roadway are stuffed with silicate fibre wool and the shuttering is then nailed with silicate fibre mats to prevent the flow of slurry into the fire area. The front shuttering is similarly nailed from inside leaving an opening which can be used as an observation window during the injection of gypsum. The injection pipes, two horizontal and one inclined upwards, are inserted into the front shuttering. A sampling pipe passes through both the shutterings.

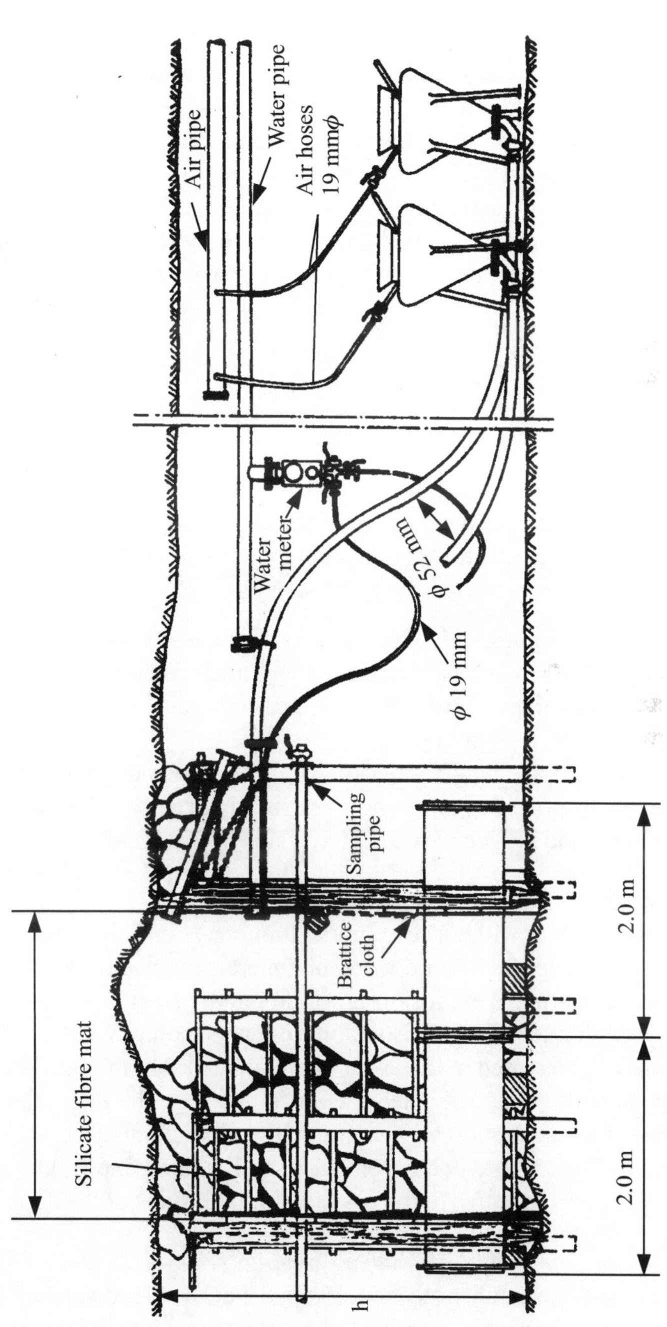

Figure 1.34 Erection of gypsum stopping

For quick sealing, two or more injection or placing units may be necessary, which may be installed at a convenient and safe place up to 300 m away from the site of the stopping. A single injection machine can blow on an average 2000 kg of gypsum per hour, so that two machines can blow 60,000 kg in eight hours with a total labour force of 8 to 10 men. About 16 to 20 manshifts are necessary for the erection of a stopping which may take 25 to 35 t of gypsum.

According to British practice, 75 mm × 75 mm wooden frames are erected across the roadway at about 1m intervals. The inbye frame is covered with fire-retardant slabs which are shaped to allow pipes to pass through the stopping. The following frame is covered in the same manner, working upwards to the roof as required, allowing filling of a section by pumping slurry between the two shutterings. After completion of the stopping, the surrounding strata are injected with gypsum (Hardstop). The thickness of the stopping is taken as equal to

$$\frac{\text{Perimeter of the roadway}}{2} + 0.3 \text{ (m)}$$

Compared with sand-bag stoppings, gypsum stoppings have the following advantages:

(1) Less material consumption;
(2) Can withstand about four times the explosion pressures;
(3) Saving in manshifts consumption by more than 50 per cent; and
(4) Greater safety in erection of the stoppings.

Gypsum stoppings also score over double-brick stoppings in savings in manshifts. The air-tightness achieved with them is comparable to that achieved with brick stoppings. Only certain precautions must be taken when erecting them especially in broken ground.

A water stopping may be created in both tail and main gates for rapid closure of a panel if creation of a low point is not strictly necessary for the normal working of the panel and sufficient water is available to the panel.

1.1.4.2.2.2.2 Permanent stoppings

For quick sealing without temporary stoppings, explosion-proof steel fire doors and wedge stoppings of hard wood or concrete may be used.

When constructed explosion-proof, fire doors erected in the intake and return airways of districts for their isolation from one another will be satisfactory. They need only to be closed in the event of an outbreak of fire. The doors should close in the same direction in which the air is flowing. The door frame is firmly set inclined at an inclination of 8° between the roof and floor with the door pressing against it. To facilitate door opening, a small hinged flap is provided for release of pressure and to equalize the pressure on both sides of the door.

Wooden- or concrete-block wedge stoppings (Figs. 1.35 and 1.36)

They consist of a number of wedge-shaped blocks of hardwood or concrete placed skin to skin in the conical opening left in the brickwork built into the roof, sides, and

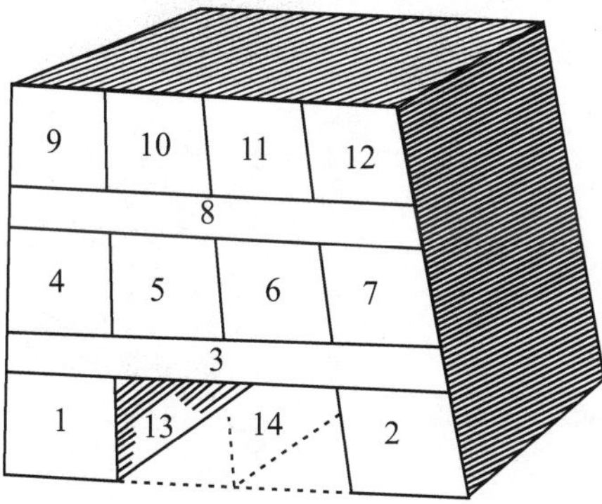

Figure 1.35 Wooden wedge stopping.

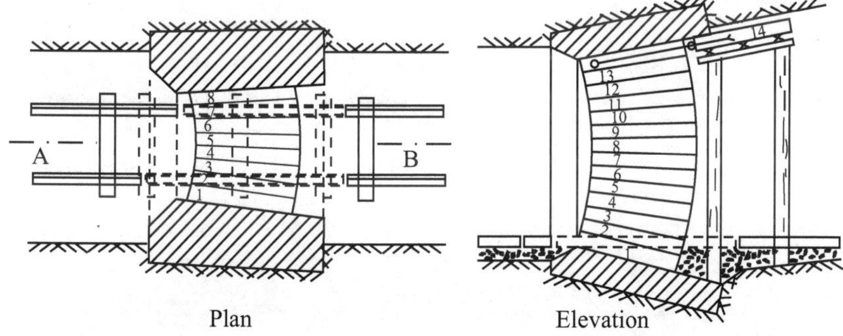

Figure 1.36 Concrete block wedge stopping

floor at the selected site. The wedges are serially numbered to facilitate their quick placement. The closing wedges in all the intake and return stoppings are inserted at the same time. In the event of an explosion the wedges tighten themselves and stop the explosion from propagation.

Gypsum stoppings

Gypsum stoppings which tend to lower from the roof unless regularly attended to, may serve as permanent stoppings. A two-brick thick wall hitched into the sides, roof, and floor is erected 2 m outbye the stopping and the space between injected with a mixture of stone dust, cement and water to ensure complete air-tightness (Fig. 1.37)

1.1.4.2.2.3 Fire-stopping fittings

In one or more of the fire-stoppings, the following fittings must be provided during their erection:

(1) A sampling pipe, 25 or 50 mm in diameter, to be as near the centre of the stopping as is convenient. It is sometimes fitted with a sampling line for collecting air samples from the sealed area passing through both temporary and permanent stoppings. The sampling line should be fitted with a valve. On

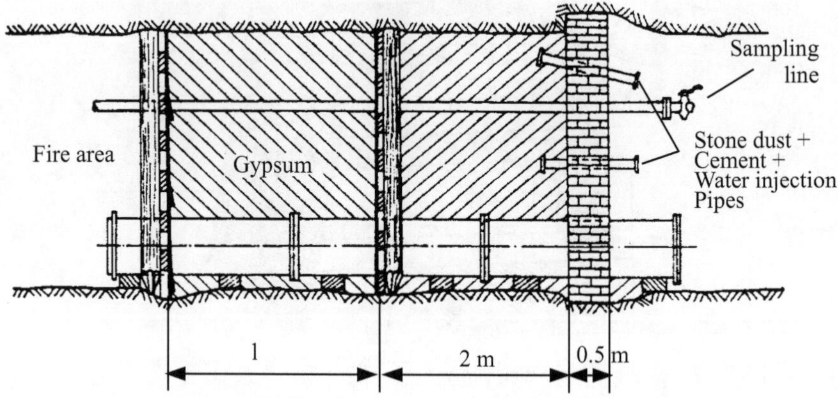

Figure 1.37 Gypsum stopping.

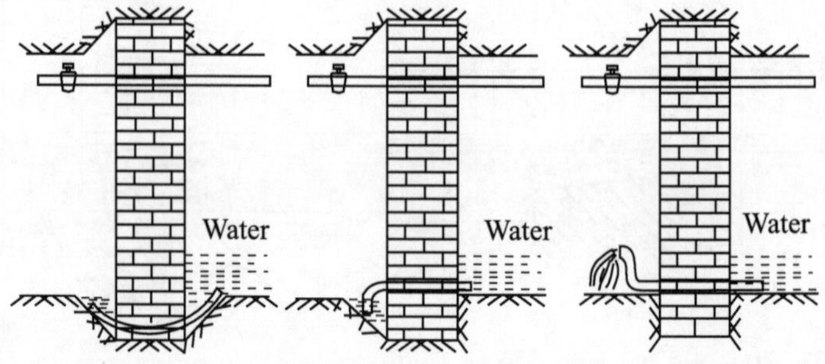

Figure 1.38 Water seals in stopping.

stoppings erected in rise or dip workings, three sampling pipes are advisable at the floor, centre, and top;

(2) A pipe with a valve for 'bleeding off' excess pressure of firegases and firedamp in a controlled manner. It should be at least 150 mm in diameter;
(3) A pipe with a valve and a manometer to take water gauge readings;
(4) A pipe for purposes of flooding or flushing the fire area with clay or sand or sealant material at a later date if required;
(5) A pipe for application of inert nitrogen or nitrogen foam; and
(6) A suitable gulley trap (water seal) to permit passage of mine water which may accumulate behind the stopping without leakage of air where the affected area is wet (Fig. 1.38). Water seals are usually self-sealing and work automatically.

1.1.4.2.2.4 Inspection of fire-stoppings

All fire-stoppings should be patrolled regularly for the following:

(1) Any cracks in or around the stopping that may have developed;
(2) Condition of the roadway support and the strata near the stopping;
(3) Proper closure of the valves;

(4) Temperature of water flowing out of the water seal when one is constructed; and
(5) Unhindered accessibility to the stopping.

The results of each inspection should be noted on a board hung near each stopping and recorded in a register kept for the purpose. Samples of air should also be collected through sample pipes of one or more suitably located stoppings to determine the status of the fire. Any unusual circumstances should be immediately reported to the mine manager.

In detecting air leakages at stoppings, one has to deal with very small air velocities which are difficult to determine.

When testing for air leakages, one or more of the following methods are frequently used:

(1) Feeling the stopping to find out if there are any hot or warm spots; hot or warm spots may not necessarily indicate the temperatures within the sealed area but they are definitely a pointer to a high temperature condition in the area;
(2) Detecting any hissing sound by putting an ear to the stopping;
(3) Observing air movements by creating small dust clouds; and
(4) Testing the atmosphere at the stopping with a canary and flame safety lamp or carbon monoxide indicator.

All of the above methods are uncertain. More convenient and efficient is the Smoke Tube Method. The smoke tube (Fig. 1.39) consists of a glass tube filled with silica gel impregnated with titanium tetrachloride ($TiCl_4$). By pumping air through it by means of a rubber aspirator bulb, the tetrachloride which vaporizes easily (boiling point 136.4°C) streams out of the tube and, on coming in contact with air, produces thick bluish-white clouds of titanium dioxide hydrate which have the same density as mine air and remain in still air for a long time. The movements of the clouds are visible at the lowest leakage air velocities. To check the air velocity, the travel of smoke must be timed over a premeasured distance. Tracer gas, sulphur hexafluoride (SF_6), krypton[85], can also be employed to check leakages into or from sealed area. An infrared laser camera is used for detection and location of SF_6 leaks. Auergesellschaft, Germany manufacture an electrically-operated smoke pump or generator that produce a dense white sulphur trioxide smoke 10 times that produced with a smoke tube using an aspirator bulb.

Figure 1.39 Smoke tube with aspirator bulb.

Recently, ultrasonic anemometry has been developed to measure very low air velocities.

1.1.4.2.2.5 Balancing of pressures at stoppings

This technique has been used successfully for fighting mine fires in the U.K. since the early 1950s. It is usually impossible to construct completely air-tight stoppings. When pressure on all sides of a sealed-off area is not the same due to the peculiar location of the area with respect to the ventilation system or pressure loss in airways, uncontrolled leakage of fresh air from the intake into the area and leakage of methane and noxious firegases out of the area may take place through leaky stoppings as well as through cracks and fissures in the strata around the stoppings. Even if the pressures on the stoppings are balanced by removing or resiting of doors, erection of further stoppings, air-crossings, regulators, pressure-balancing roadways or ducts, or fans (booster and auxiliary), leakages through them may take place when the pressure in the sealed-off area is less or greater than the pressure outside the stoppings. Under such conditions, it will be necessary to provide a balancing chamber at each leaky stopping to enable the pressure on the outbye face of the stopping to be controlled for a long period of time. After sealing off, it would be advantageous to conduct a pressure survey local to the stoppings, which will provide necessary information for balancing of pressures. The pressure required in a balancing chamber may be either positive or negative relative to the adjacent airway at any point of time.

A balancing chamber is formed immediately after the explosion hazard period has passed by, constructing an air-tight steel fire door in a wall at about 5 m outbye the stopping. The pressure of air in the chamber is controlled so that it is equal to the pressure inside the stopping. In practice, when the pressure is inward, the pressure in the chamber is controlled to be less by 1 to 2 mm, whilst when the pressure is outward, the pressure in the chamber is controlled to be higher by 1 to 2 mm. A compressed-air venturi ejector or air mover where compressed air supply is available at the site, or an electrically-driven reversible auxiliary axial-flow fan (Fig. 1.40) which will force air to or exhaust air from the chamber as circumstances demand, will be found to be a satisfactory means of controlling the chamber pressure. Long chambers make control easier and are to be preferred at stoppings in fractured ground liable to leakage. The technique requires a number of days to successfully extinguish a fire.

1.1.4.2.3 Sealing off the entire mine

Controlling fires in dry, dusty, and gassy bituminous coal mines is extremely hazardous. If, due to misfortune, a gas or dust explosion takes place during fire-fighting, the explosion may spread throughout the entire mine and even to the surface making it impossible to have a fresh-air base inside the mine from which to carry out rescue and recovery operations. In such a case, the entire mine will require to be sealed at the surface by closing the shaft top and the fan-drift of the main fan. A sampling pipe with a valve connection should be left in the shaft covering or fan-drift to enable air samples and pressure gauge readings to be taken.

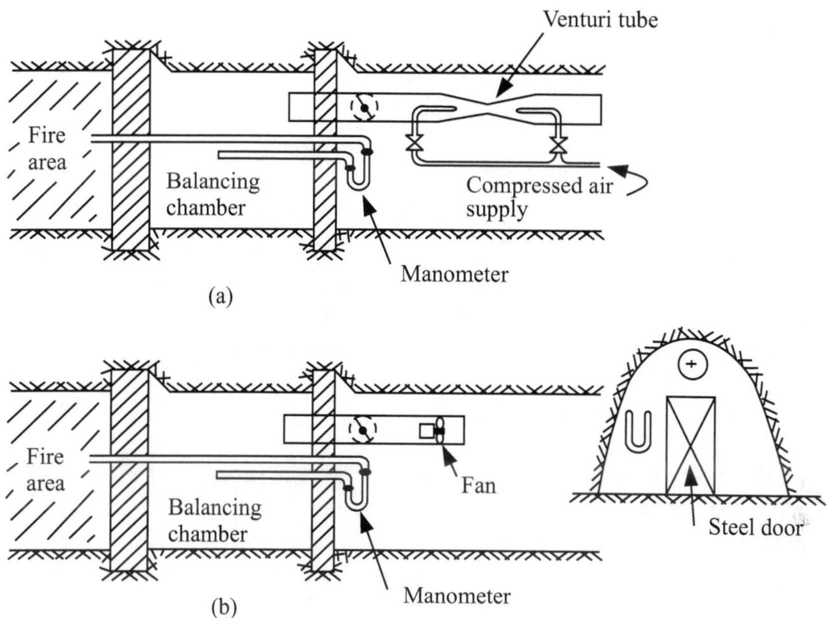

Figure 1.40 Balancing of pressure at a stopping by a pressure chamber: (a) using a compressed-air venturi injector; (b) using an auxiliary fan.

But it should be remembered that the samples will not usually give a correct picture of the conditions inside the mine as only light gases rise to the shaft top and the heavier ones do not come into the sample. Owing to the failure of the pumps in the pitbottom main sump, the lower levels may be flooded with water making the recovery operations very difficult.

1.1.4.2.4 Flooding the fire area or the entire mine

Flooding a fire area is the last resort after direct attack and sealing have failed. A coal mine is flooded when fires, after a powerful explosion, have assumed such proportions that all other methods of fire-fighting will fail or cannot be employed due to explosion hazard and the entire mine is to be saved from destruction.

To flood a fire area effectively, an adequate quantity of water must first be available and the fire area must be suitably located, such as dip-side workings, isolated from other workings with coal barriers or barrier pillars, so that water pumped or allowed to flow into it will flood it.

Flooding has the following disadvantages:

(1) Heavy damage to the mine workings and equipment;
(2) Difficulty of obtaining the required amount of water in a short period of time;
(3) Impossibility of ascertaining that the water is in contact with the entire roof and that the fire has been extinguished;

(4) Possibility of generating water gas by an insufficient amount of water;
(5) Heavy expenditure on dewatering;
(6) Danger of 'water blast' during de-watering;
(7) Impossibility of recovering resources in some instances. For recovery with flooding, one may have to erect several dams, which may be very expensive;
(8) Possibility of the fire being reinitiated or rekindled after de-watering in a few weeks due perhaps to an increase in the reactivity of coal and, hence, liability of coal to spontaneous combustion;
(9) When flooding the entire mine, existence of adequate barriers between it and the adjoining mines to withstand the head of water in the flooded mine; and
(10) Loss of entire mine production.

1.1.4.2.5 Hydraulic flushing of enclosed area with sand and other materials

The method can be recommended where the strata are so broken that neither sealing nor flooding will be effective. Generally, the fire is sealed off with stoppings in the usual manner and then the sealed area is flushed with a clay-water, sand-water, sand-crushed rock-water, or sand-clay-water-mixture through pipes left in the stoppings. In metal mines, mill tailings as a sludge may be used. Experience has shown that solids fill the voids completely, reduce and, in certain places, eliminate fire gases, cool the adjacent rocks, and offer support to the ground.

During flushing, care should be taken so that the slurry is not directed straight on to the fireseat but at a point near it so that water gas explosion from dissociation of water does not take place.

For controlling a fire in the goaf in hydraulic stowing mines, the fireseat should preferably be encircled with a girdle of sand barrier.

Hydraulic flushing using clay or sand through holes drilled from the surface is not very effective in extinguishing fires as it cannot be ensured that all the roadways and openings are covered. Also, a cone is formed at the borehole site and the fill shrinks on drying leaving large gaps.

1.1.4.2.6 Introducing inert gas into the fire area

Fighting mine fires with inert gases has been practised at different times since the 1950s in the USA, many countries of Europe, and in India. It has now come to be recognised as a well-proven technique for combating open and incipient mine fires. It is based on the principle that an inert gas reduces the oxygen content of mine air reaching the fireseat to such a level that the explosion hazard is eliminated and the intensity of the fire is reduced. The development of the fire is thus restricted, and may be extinguished altogether. The method can be applied on its own as a primary firefighting method or used in conjunction with the conventional fire-fighting methods to hasten extinguishment of a fire. Carbon dioxide, combustion gases, and nitrogen have been used as inert gases. Nitrogen is the most commonly used gas in the coal-mining industries of Europe and India. In Indian coal mines, it has been used for combating mine fires in Lodna, Sijua, Laikdih Deep, GDK9 Incline, Madujor, Damodar OCP, Ramagundam, and Chirimiri collieries.

The advantages of fighting fires with inert gases are:

(1) It offers maximum possible safety against risk of explosions and spread of fire if the inert gas could be introduced in good time;
(2) The inert gas penetrates easier into cracks and cavities than clay or sand;
(3) Owing to improved climatic conditions in the fire area, the fire-fighting brigades can operate for longer periods;
(4) The location of stoppings is of secondary importance in fighting a fire if the inert gas could be injected early. An inerted fire area is recovered in stages by advancing the intake stoppings with continuous flushing out of the gases from the fire area with the inert gas. When this is done, stoppings on the return side may be eliminated;
(5) The time interval between sealing and recovery of a sealed-off fire area is shorter due to faster cooling off of the area. It may be possible to effect a smooth transition between sealing and re-opening of a fire area;
(6) Recovery work is negligible and, hence, rapid;
(7) It is possible to work without the use of breathing apparatus;
(8) The rescue and recovery crew work under improved working conditions with reduced temperatures and relative humidity;
(9) It prevents outbreak of fire in workings during idle periods.

For inertization of mine fires, the following practices are adopted:

(1) Inertization by flushing the fireseat with inert gas maintaining normal ventilation in the working district/section (Local Inertization); and
(2) Inertization by flooding a sealed-off area with inert gas (Area or Zone Inertization).

With local inertization (Fig. 1.41), the incipient fireseat, usually in the goaf behind active faces, is directly flushed with the inert gas, nitrogen, with quantities

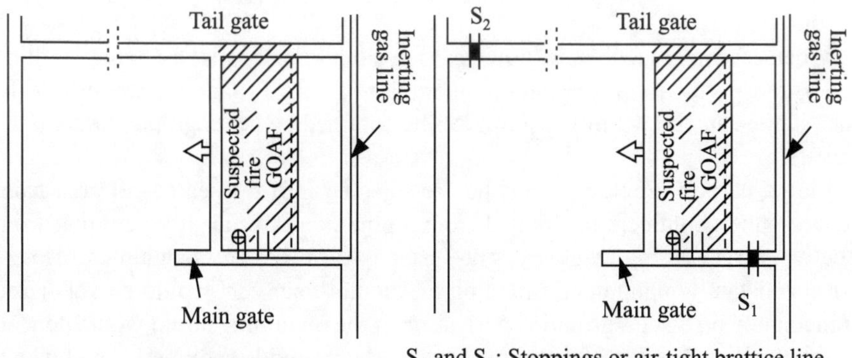

Figure 1.41 Methods of inertization of mine fires.

usually well below 100 m^3 /min. The stray air currents reaching the fire are almost completely replaced by the gas. The oxygen content at the fireseat must be reduced to between I and 5 per cent by volume. If a fire cannot be controlled with continuous injection of inert gas, one should examine whether the face/ district needs to be abandoned with salvage of equipment or take recourse to a long-term inertization until the face/district has been extracted. Precautionary local inertization can also be used for preventing or retarding spontaneous heating in goaves behind faces in thick to very thick seams worked by sub-level caving methods. This is done by decreasing the oxygen content to less than 15 per cent.

With area or zone inertization (Fig. 1.41), the inert gas is introduced into a fire area which has been sealed on all sides or at least on the intake side with the object of rendering flammable gas mixtures non-flammable, containing the development of the fire, and recovering the mine workings expeditiously. It is mainly used against open fires and has been employed in only a few individual cases of incipient fires to eliminate the danger of an explosion in the goaf. To fight open fires, the oxygen content of the air reaching the fireseat must be reduced to below 10 per cent by volume. The inert gas requirement is usually between 100 and 500 m^3 N_2/min.

Under favourable conditions, a fireseat in the goaf can be effectively fought by local inertization following area inertization, which will eliminate the risk of explosion. A saving in the construction of fire-stoppings may be achieved.

1.1.4.2.6.1 Inert gases for inertization

The inert gases which have been successfully used for inertization are carbon dioxide, combustion gases, and nitrogen.

Carbon dioxide

Since carbon dioxide is one-and-a-half times heavier than air, it is particularly suitable for application in steeply inclined mine workings including shafts where there is no appreciable air flow. It eliminates flammable gas mixtures and exerts a blanketing effect on fires. Carbon dioxide may be used in the form of gas, liquid, or solid (dry ice).

When used in gaseous state, liquid carbon dioxide is vaporized and the resulting gas is transported in tankers at a temperature of – 32°C and at a pressure of 18 bar. At present, about 4 m^3CO_2/min can be obtained by heating units fitted to the tankers.

Liquid carbon dioxide may either be injected into the sealed-off area from underground containers or drained from a pipe (water or air line) coming from a delivery truck or road tanker on the surface. It is necessary that a pressure of 7 bar is constantly maintained in the pipe. About 40 per cent would be vaporized immediately on discharge and vaporization of the remaining liquid would depend on the temperature. If the pressure drops, carbon dioxide snow is formed which may block the pipe. Owing to the occurrence of electrostatic charges, the end of the line must not end in flammable gas mixtures.

Dry ice is used in the form of small cakes. It suffers from the disadvantage that explosive volatilization takes place on contact with fire.

Carbon dioxide, however, did not find wide application in combating mine fires for the following reasons:

(1) It is not available in large quantities;
(2) The maximum prescribed limit (0.5 or 1.0 per cent by volume) in the air coming from a fire area is quickly reached and exceeded; .
(3) It is absorbed by the adjacent strata; and
(4) Reduction of CO_2 to CO at high temperatures at the seat of fire may introduce an additional hazard.

Combustion gases

Combustion gas produced in a combustion-type inert gas generator burning fuel oil as in Poland, or in a kerosene-fuelled jet engine, as in the ertswhile USSR, Poland and Czechoslovakia, may be used to provide an unlimited supply of inert gas. The generators are operated above ground and the inert gas is forced through a pipeline by a compressor, whereas the jet engines are located underground in an airway through which the entire intake air current to the fire must pass. The combustion gas consists of about 80 per cent N_2, 13 per cent CO_2, and the remaining residual oxygen, CO, SO_2, NO_x, and water vapour. In Eastern Europe, inert gas generators and turbines with capacities between 100 and 1500 ml/min have been used.

The disadvantages of the use of combustion gases for inertization of mine fires are:

(1) The gases have a high temperature requiring large quantities of water for cooling and outlay on equipment;
(2) The fairly high water vapour content has an adverse effect on climatic conditions in the fire area;
(3) Absence of cooling effect underground;
(4) The transportation and use of kerosene (flash point about 45°C) below ground in coal mines pose a threat to mine safety;
(5) Impossibility of correct interpretation of the condition of the fire by gas analysis and;
(6) Costly maintenance.

For successful application of combustion gases, it is necessary that the fire area is tightly sealed so that the gases do not stream out into active mine workings. One must constantly check on the oxygen content in the mine air. For long-term inertization, the economic feasibility of the use of combustion gases may be examined.

Nitrogen

Nitrogen is the most commonly used gas for inertization of major mine fires. Fighting mine fires with nitrogen has become a standard method in West European coal mines. Nitrogen may be used directly as a liquid against mine fires or in gaseous state by delivering it as liquid to the mine site through fixed pipelines or road tankers, vaporizing it in an evaporator and conveying it into the mine by means of a pipeline or flexible hose.

The advantages of nitrogen for inertization are:

(1) Delivery of liquid nitrogen to the site is simple;
(2) Cold (10°C to 15°C), dry, and pure gas is obtained;
(3) It is readily available in large quantities;
(4) It enables salvaging of face equipment after a longwall face reaches its planned boundary of extraction by precautionary inertization of the goaf, keeping the oxygen level below 12 per cent; and
(5) It is slightly cheaper than carbon dioxide and more costly than combustion gases.

For direct application of liquid nitrogen for fire control, the nitrogen is transported to the place of use in insulated containers and then atomized behind the fire-stopping using nitrogen-atomizing nozzles. The advantages claimed for this method are that the positive pressure resulting from vaporization prevents air leakages into the fire area and that the heat of vaporization is drawn from the fire gases and the adjacent strata, thereby exerting a cooling effect. In shallow mines, liquid nitrogen may be introduced into the fire area through a surface borehole to reduce the risk of explosion while building fire-stoppings.

Inertization with gaseous nitrogen obtained by vaporising liquid nitrogen at the mine site is the most commonly used method of combating mine fires.

Production of nitrogen

Liquid nitrogen in bulk is produced at major chemical works by the Linde air liquefaction process. Recent developments centre round production of small- to medium-size plants based on special techniques of nitrogen production.

The pressure swing adsorption plant operates on the principle that compressed ambient air separates into nitrogen and oxygen-rich gas when passed through carbon molecular sieves through whose internal pore system N_2 and O_2 diffuse at different rates. The plant has a capacity of up to 15 m^3 /min. Such plants can be used for long-term inertization or for precautionary inertization to prevent fires from breaking out.

Mobile plants with capacities of 20 m^3 /min are currently under development. If necessary, several plants can be operated in parallel.

Mobile plants operating on fractional distillation of liquid air employing the low-temperature process have been developed which will produce small volumes of nitrogen for long-term inertization. The air is compressed, cooled, and liquefied in a cold box. The liquefied air is then fractionated into nitrogen and oxygen of medium purity in a rectifying column. The individual units have a rated capacity of about 15 m^3/min N_2. Larger nitrogen flow rates can be obtained by operating in parallel in a modular arrangement.

Vaporization of liquid nitrogen

The liquid nitrogen delivered to the mine site at a very low temperature (–196°C) by road tankers (usually 38-t capacity) is transferred to stationary or transportable storage tanks which are double-walled, insulated, high-pressure containers. It is vaporized to the gaseous state by means of evaporators. The following types of evaporators are currently in use [16]

(1) Powered evaporators.
   (a) Oil-fired water-bath evaporators with external heating;
   (b) Propane-fired water-bath evaporators with internal heating; and
   (c) Electrically-heated evaporators;
(2) Ambient-air evaporators.

Water-bath evaporators operate on the principle that liquid nitrogen vaporizes as it passes through pipe coils in a heated water bath. The optimal temperature of a water bath is 20° to 30°C. About 600 kJ are required to vaporize 1 kg of liquid nitrogen and warm it up to +5°C. They have capacities of 65, 100, 125, and 300 m^3 N_2/min. They can be regulated to dispense nitrogen flow rates between 5 and 120 m^3 /min.

Air evaporators consist of nests of finned tubes of aluminium through which liquid nitrogen passes and vaporizes by drawing heat from the ambient air. After-heaters are used on the downstream side to warm up the gas 0° to 15°C. Electrical trim heaters with or without water baths are used for this purpose.

Transmission of nitrogen underground

When contemplating fighting mine fires with nitrogen, an 'inertization plan' must be prepared which covers not only active working faces/districts but also drivages using fast-heading machines. Besides setting out actions to be taken on the surface and underground, the inertization plan clearly specifies which of the existing pipe-ranges in shafts and pipelines in roadways can be utilized as inert gas lines in an emergency without affecting the fire-fighting operations. The position of the inert gas lines in the shaft section and their layout in the mine workings with the controlling valves should be shown on a drawing which forms part of the inertization plan. In case the existing lines cannot be made available for transmission of nitrogen, a sufficient length of fire-resistant, antistatic flexible hose must be kept in readiness. In mines where spontaneous combustion is a frequent cause of mine fires, it is prudent to install a shaft range specifically for inert gas as experience has shown that installation of hoses in the shaft under emergency conditions is an arduous and time-consuming operation. The pipelines or hose lines used for transmission of nitrogen from the surface to the point of application underground must be suitable for the required flow rate and permissible pressure drop. The shaft ranges and the underground gas lines are generally designed for a flow rate of 300 m^3/min although large quantities cannot always be supplied without the manufactures' cooperation. For a given situation, the minimum and maximum flow-rates should be determined. The diameter of the inert gas lines lies between 50 and 400 mm, the usual diameter being 150 to 200 mm. The pressure at the start of the inert gas lines is usually 5 to 10 bar. The friction coefficient for the gas lines can be calculated using the following formula [16]:

$$\lambda = \frac{1}{[2\lg(8.41D)]^2}$$

where D is the diameter of the pipeline in mm. In order to achieve the desired reduction in oxygen concentration, it is essential that a correct proportion be established between the inert gas flow-rate and the ventilating air flow-rate.

1.1.4.2.6.2 Monitoring the results of inertization

In order to monitor the results of inertization and to determine the success of fire-fighting, the composition of the gases in the fire area and the ventilating air currents immediately downstream of the fire area must be continuously monitored.

For this purpose, continuous remote environmental monitoring and control systems will prove to be most effective. This may be supplemented by collecting gas samples at regular intervals and analyzing them immediately. A sufficient number of portable gas-measuring/monitoring instruments such as detector tubes and O_2–, CH_4–, and CO– hand-measuring instruments should be made available to those engaged in fire-fighting and/ or recovery operations. Also, the volumetric flow-rate and pressure and temperature of the nitrogen gas must be monitored before its entry into the shaft range.

Experience with inertization of mine fires has shown that the success of the method depends on the speed with which inertization can be applied. A maximum of 12 hours for, all the preparatory jobs may be allowed. It must be borne in mind that the inertization method will not displace the conventional fire-fighting methods. A deep-seated fire will almost never be completely extinguished by introduction of nitrogen. Even with an open fire, direct fire-fighting operations must be undertaken while preparing for or during inertization.

1.1.4.2.6.3 Deployment of rescue workers in inert atmospheres

Working in inert atmospheres is at least as hazardous as working in high concentrations of firegases. Special precautions to be taken are:

(1) The rescue workers must work at some distance from the point of nitrogen discharge due to the deafening noise produced in the vicinity of the jet of nitrogen;
(2) A rescue brigade should carry at least two oxygen self-rescuers throughout their operation; and
(3) If the supply of nitrogen is interrupted, the men must be withdrawn immediately from the fire area.

1.1.4.2.7 Special methods of fire-fighting

Fire-fighting with high-expansion foam

High-expansion foam has been used especially for successfully combating roadway fires which cannot be successfully fought with hand fire-extinguishers or water due to smoke and heat. The quenching effect of the foam is due to the water it carries with it to the fire. The vapour formed by the evaporation of water in the

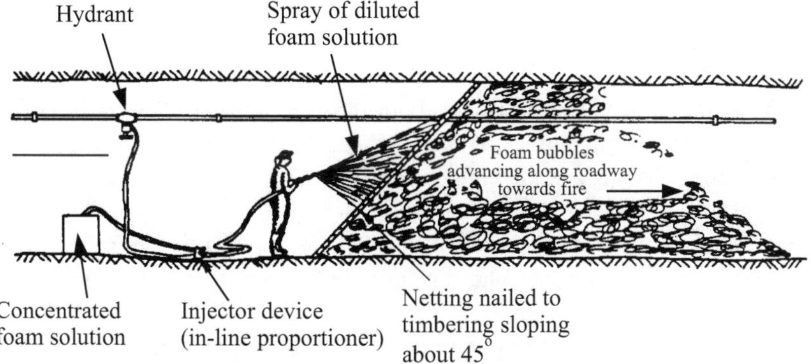

Figure 1.42 High-expansion foam plug (SMRE).

walls of the foam bubbles has a blanketing effect upon the fire besides its cooling action by virtue of its latent heat of vaporisation.

According to the method as originally developed by the then Safety in Mines Research Establishment, UK, the foam is formed by uniformly spraying a dilute aqueous solution of a foaming compound on to an inclined or vertical net stretched across the entire roadway cross-section and placed as near to the fire as possible on the intake side (Fig. 1.42). The ventilating current passing through the net which is continuously wetted, produces on the return side of the net bubbles which coalesce to form a mass of foam that quickly fills the roadway, creating a foam-plug that is moved towards the fire by the ventilating current. The volume occupied by the foam generated is 500 to 1000 times the volume of the sprayed solution. The foam, can climb over obstructions, turn sharp corners, and expand into sectional enlargements. The length of foam-plug that can be formed depends on the available ventilating pressure, nature of the roadway surface, and stability and other properties of the foam. The velocity of the foam front varies linearly with the air velocity which should be sufficient to yield a tight plug. The foam should be produced at such a rate which will ensure that, when it reaches the fire, it contains at least 0.3 kg H_2O per cubic metre of foam.

From the experience gained in the experimental underground roadway Buxton, UK, the US Bureau of Mines Experimental Coal Mine, Bruceton, and the Chamber of Mines South Africa, the following conclusions could be drawn regarding efficient application of the foam-plug method in fighting mine fires:

(1) The method should generally be used in roadways well outbye a coal face or open goaf since the foam plug will reduce the air-flow and may cause danger of firedamp accumulation.
(2) The method is not suitable for fighting fires in roadways dipping greater than 1 in 5 or rising greater than 1 in 10.
(3) Sufficient ventilation pressure must be available and the mean air velocity through the net must generally not be less than about 0.3 m/s nor exceed 2 m/s.

(4) The method is not effective on deep-seated fires which are rapidly advancing or buried under massive roof falls. Also, it cannot be used in dead-end places.
(5) The hydrant pressure should be about 7 bar(s)
(6) Ammonium lauryl sulphate is the best foaming compound which produces a stable foam having a water content of 0.2 to 0.3 kg or more per cubic metre of foam.
(7) The solution must contain at least 2 per cent (by volume) foaming compound. The rate of feeding the solution must lie between 0.002 and 0.001 of the volumetric rate of air supply.

To increase the scope of application of the high-expansion foam in fighting fires, the US Bureau of Mines perfected a practical foam generator that forces foam directly to the fire through a plastic tubing independent of mine ventilation for making the foam-plug. Mine Safety Appliances Co., the USA brought out transportable foam generators or foamakers into the market that will fit into the category of secondary fire-fighting equipment to fight localized mine fires not accessible to direct attack with conventional fire-fighting equipment and might have to be sealed off. The foam can be produced at such a rate that the time of travel between the foam generator and the farthest limit of a fire is three hours.

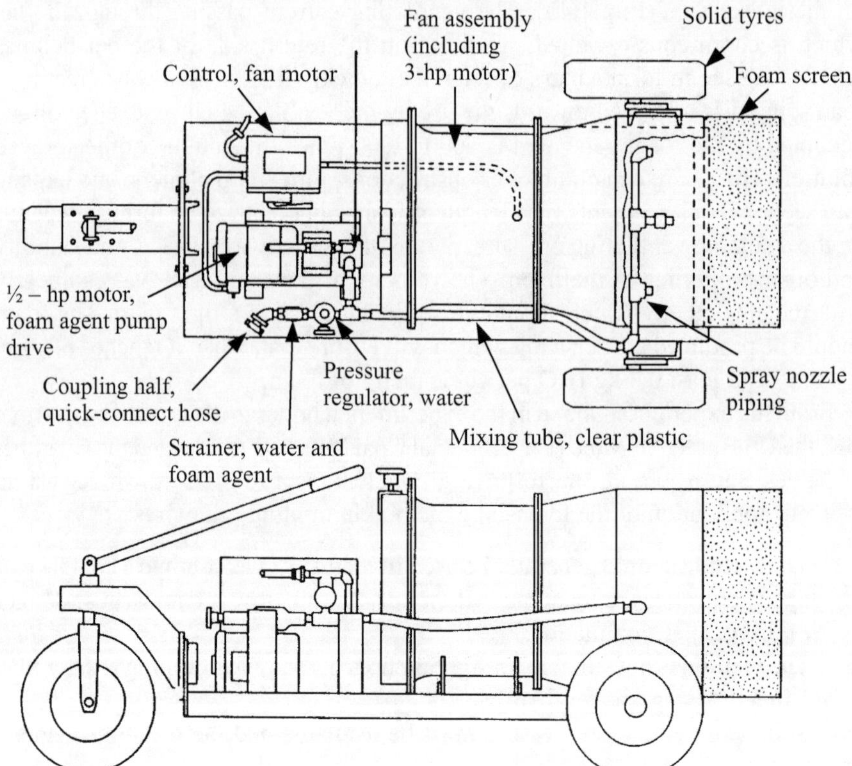

Figure 1.43 M.S.A. Mine Model Foamaker generator.

The MSA Mine Model Foamaker (Fig. 1.43) is available in two models with foam output capacities of about 85 m^3 (3 000 cfm) and about 113 m^3 (4000 cfm) as rubber-tyre or skid-mounted units. It consists of a 3.5-hp axial-vane fan which produces sufficient pressure to inflate and unwind a roll of tough polyethylene tubing when attached to it. The tubing will not pass the fire and the excess length will automatically melt to discharge the foam at the fire. The fan is provided with a louvre at its intake end to control the inlet air supply and, hence, the rate of foam production, while at its discharge end a screen of polyester fibre cloth or fibre-glass netting is fitted which is sprayed with a mixture of foam concentrate and water using full cone nozzles. The fan aerates the mixture into a frothy and bubbling foam which is then driven through the tubing. A flow of 136 litres per minute of water at an inlet pressure of 2 bar will be required. A foam proportioning pump adjusts the quantity of the foam concentrate, depending on the quantity of water used and the length of tubing required.

The advantages of transportable foam generators are:

(1) They can be quickly put into service within a minute of their installation;
(2) Being simple and rugged in construction, they can be easily operated by non-technical personnel;
(3) The full water content of the foam reaches the fire and is not drained off during transportation; and
(4) Two or more units can be set up around a fire area if it is necessary to apply foam from more than one direction.

MSA also developed Model 700 Foamaker as a permanently installed automatic fire-fighting system for combating fires at belt drives. Foam may also be used to put out an underground fire by introducing it through boreholes from the surface to the fire area.

High-pressure nitrogen foam developed in the Czech Republic has been successfully used for prevention and suppression of spontaneous heating of coal in goaves of longwall faces.

Fire-fighting with antipyrogene mixtures and solutions

In Czechoslovakia, incipient and open mine fires in roadways were successfully fought with antipyrogene mixtures and solutions [17]. For deep-seated fires due to spontaneous heating in roof coal of roadways, injection of sodium silicate-clay-water mixtures into the fireseat proved to be effective in extinguishing the fire (Fig. 1.44). For open fires in roadways, direct attack with two streams of sodium silicate and calcium chloride proved to be successful. The two solutions mix to form a white gelatinous layer on the fire. The solutions can also be used to spray roadway sides and roof so that the fire does not advance on the fresh-air side. Figure 1.45 shows a simple arrangement for producing fire streams of the two chemical solutions.

Fire-fighting with dry fly-ash injections

The US Bureau of Mines successfully experimented with remote sealing in abandoned mines using dry fly-ash or fly ash-benotonite-portland cement

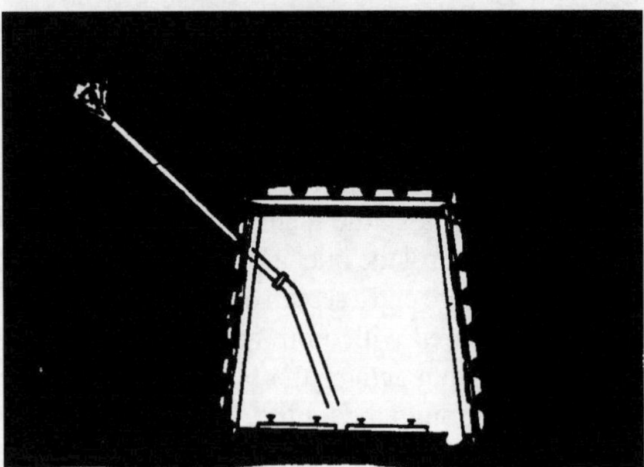

Figure 1.44 Fighting seam fire with antipyrogene injection.

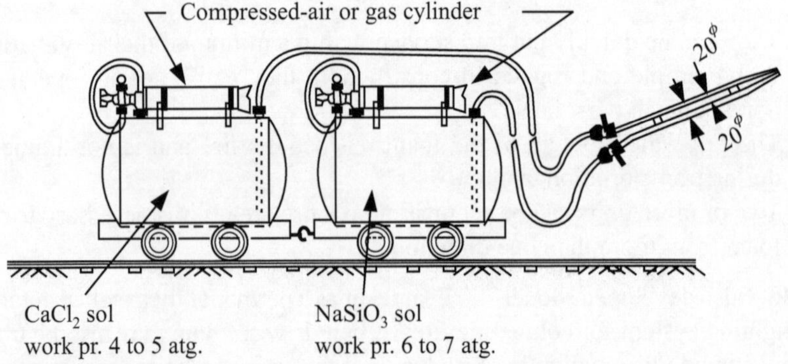

Figure 1.45 Arrangement of antipyrogene injection equipment.

mixture injections through surface boreholes. Fly ash is fluidized with an inert gas (nitrogen or inert gas from a combustion-type inert gas generator) and transported pneumatically or by compressed inert gas through the borehole to form incombustible barriers in mine workings enclosing the fire area that would restrict the fire's advance by cutting off its oxygen supply without exposing the miners to the hazard.

1.1.4.2.8 Ventilation control in fire-fighting

When fighting a mine fire, the mining engineer is too often confronted with the problem of effecting changes in the mine ventilation system so that the fire does not spread unnecessarily, the workmen are safely withdrawn, and other dangers do not arise.

There are four methods of ventilation control for control of fires:

(1) Reversal of mine ventilation;
(2) Short-circuiting;
(3) Isolation of fire; and

(4) Regulation of air quantities.

No general rule can be given as definite; knowledge of local and general conditions in each case will be necessary. The choice of one or more of the above methods depends on the location of the fire with respect to the ventilation system and the position of the workmen at the time the fire.

The reversal of mine ventilation following a mine fire is a controversial subject. The important factors to be considered before reversing the direction of air flow are:

(1) Stage of fire;
(2) Location of the fire with respect to the ventilation system;
(3) Presence of workers in mine workings;
(4) Type of fan; and
(5) Type of doors.

When a fire in a fiery and dusty mine assumes serious proportions and threatens to engulf the entire mine in a series of mine explosions, one should be prepared for all eventualities.

As a general rule, the main fan should not be reversed unless the fire is in the junction of the main intake splits, in the downcast shaft, or near the pitbottom of a downcast shaft. With fire in a timbered downcast shaft, reversal of ventilation due to heating of air may take place much to the advantage of workmen.

The type of axial-flow fan is important in that when the fan is reversed, it will operate at a lower efficiency so that its air output which should be of a necessary size, and pressure decrease which may result in the formation of flammable atmospheres inside the mine. For the fan to run in the reverse direction as long as required, it must have mechanical stability and an assured power supply. Fan performance curves must be available. Provision for reversal of mine ventilation should be made in all mines.

The ventilation doors should be equipped with latches so that they do not open on reversal of the direction of air-flow which must get to where it is required.

Short-circuiting the fire gases at a particular place by opening ventilation doors will lead the firegases directly to the return air current without having to go through other mine workings. One may also short-circuit the fresh-air current going to a fire so that the fire is starved of oxygen. Simultaneously with short-circuiting, any doors in the short-circuited area should be closed to prevent air movements in the area. The disadvantages of the short-circuiting method are that, in gassy mines, accumulation of firedamp takes place and that the load on the main fan increases which condition should, however, be checked by calculations.

Complete isolation of a fire is possible in mines which are divided into fire sections by means of fire doors and preparatory stoppings. The fire doors can also be used for reducing the quantity of air flowing through a fire area to control the spread of fire.

When a fire is in a main intake airway, one may slow down the main fan, adjust the damper in the fan-drift, redistribute air currents to obtain a reduced air-flow to the fire, or reverse the mine ventilation if the fire has assumed serious proportions threatening the lives of workmen working over a part or whole of the mine.

Failure or shutdown of the main fan scheduled to run for any reason, or its stoppage or reversal may bring about a situation in which fresh-air bases are impossible to establish and nothing is known of air directions. The major decision on stoppage or slowing down or reversal should be taken only after thorough consultations with all the senior mine officials involved.

It should be remembered that withdrawal or evacuation of men should be the foremost concern of the mine management before any one of the above methods of controlling ventilation is adopted and also that the method of ventilation chosen may be modified during firefighting if conditions so warrant.

Mathematical models and computer software have been developed for simulating the effect of fire on mine ventilating system.

1.1.4.2.9 Firefighting organization

As fire hazard is always present, every mine, no matter how small, should perfect and maintain its own firefighting and rescue organization to ensure maximum safety and escape strategy by:

(a) Training rescue crew and other personnel through a continuing education programme;
(b) Preparing a detailed plan of action (mine emergency response plan) in which all workmen, supervisory officials, rescue crew, and management know what they are required to do at the time of a mine fire or other emergency. The approved plan of action outlined in standing orders prepared by the mine management should include a specific firefighting and evacuation plan designed to acquaint miners on all shifts with procedures for:
    (i) evacuation of all miners not required for firefighting,
    (ii) rapid assembly and transportation of necessary men, fire-extinguishing equipment, and rescue apparatus to the place of fire, and
    (iii) operation of the fire-extinguishing equipment available in the mine;
(c) Providing necessary fire-fighting facilities at suitable places in the mine as well as providing for their care and maintenance;
(d) Providing a widespread telephone or other communications system with one or more direct connections to the surface, so that instruction and information can flow promptly between the person in-charge underground and the person in-charge on the surface
(e) Providing copies of firefighting plans or maps at suitable places underground and on the surface; and
(f) Laying down a procedure for conducting firefighting operations.

At least two mine workers in each working section on each production shift should be proficient in the use of fire-fighting facilities and know their location.

For an effective organization of fire-fighting, it may be advantageous to divide a mine into large zones in such a way that a fire anywhere in a particular zone will require a common set of immediate actions and a set of actions applicable to the particular zone. This will enable planning of actions in greater detail to combat the fire.

Training
All mine personnel must be trained to recognize and eliminate fire hazards, to evaluate and control fires, and to protect themselves and others in the event of a fire. Training of a few selected personnel in proper use of all available fire-fighting facilities is essential in organizing effective fire-fighting services at mines. The need for training with use of gas masks and breathing apparatus is obvious. Training will create a consciousness of fire and fire hazards among all mine personnel. A record of the training programmes must be maintained by the mine management.

Procedure after fire
At the appearance of any sign of fire (sweating, petrolic smell, tarry smell), the workman who notices it should inform the nearest supervisory official as soon as practicable. With the discovery of an open fire, he and any other persons in the vicinity of the fire should make a prompt effort to extinguish it with water, stone dust, or hand fire-extinguisher and inform the nearest supervisory official without delay. The official who is warned of the occurrence of a fire should immediately inform the manager of the mine or, in his absence, the principal official in-charge. If the fire cannot be easily and quickly extinguished or if the smoke from the fire is too dense to permit investigation, he should immediately remove all workmen in the section, in particular, on the return side, warn by telephone, or any other approved fire-warning alarm system, all workmen and supervisory officials working in other parts of the mine likely to be affected by firegases or a possible explosion, and inform the manager and ask for ratification of his action.

The evacuation of workmen from widely dispersed workplaces with little or no means of communication as in mines laid out on the horizontal system can demand considerable time – up to one-and-a-half hours or more. In large deep mines, the evacuation time may exceed the rated capacity of filter self-rescuers which is approximately 60 min operating time in an environment of 1 per cent CO. Any delay in warning miners to don their self-rescuers can, therefore, prove disastrous. Fire-warning alarm systems are varied. One must make a choice taking into account reliability, efficiency of operation, and cost.

In metal mines which have usually a network of compressed-air lines throughout the mines, the stench alarm system has been very successfully used for several years, which will take from 5 to 20 minutes to warn the miners, depending on the length of air lines and quantity of air used.

Ethyl mercaptan (C_2H_5SH) and eucalyptus are the commonest liquid stenches used as warning agents. Ethyl mercaptan has the very disagreeable odour of rotten cabbage, while eucalyptus has a characteristic odour which cannot be easily missed. The liquid stench is introduced into all compressed-air mains at the surface compressor plant (Fig. 1.46) and also sprayed into the downcast shaft. The disadvantages of the stench system are that workmen working in isolated

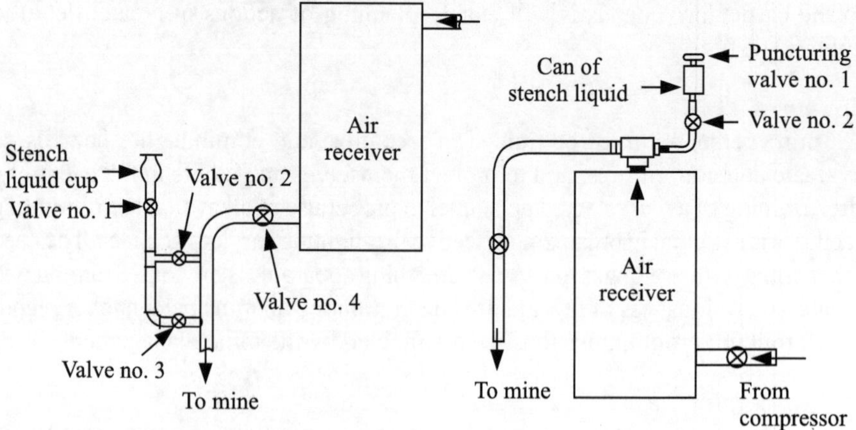

Figure 1.46 Stench injector devices.

places and using no compressed air might not be warned in time and that it can only warn workers to evacuate the mine without giving them any information on the type of danger.

Recent studies by the US Bureau of Mines [18] showed that ethyl mercaptan is toxic, causing debility in workers, and also reactive with iron oxide, resulting in fading of the odour during its travel over long distances in steel pipes. Tetrahydrothiophane (THT) is found to have ideal properties for mine stench warning. It is far less toxic than ethyl mercaptan, non-reactive with iron oxide, and its odour is recognisable in concentrations as low as 20 ppb but is not overwhelming at high concentrations.

The principal disadvantages of the stench system are the time required for the odour to reach the most remote workplaces and the tendency for some parts of a mine to be missed altogether due to low air velocities in them or backing-up of firegases. Telephones are effective only where workmen are close enough to hear the phone ring.

A device which automatically flashes a warning by short flashes followed by long flashes indicating the level where an emergency has been reported may be used for warning underground personnel, but the reliability of such a system would not be high.

The US Bureau of Mines developed a novel fire-warning alarm system [19] which enables instantaneous warning of all underground personnel. The warning alarm is sent by an ultra-low frequency electromagnetic signal from a transmitter, which penetrates through mine rock to small receivers worn on the person of the underground personnel (personal pagers) who thus receive the fire-warning signals. The transmitter can be located either on the surface or underground.

Leaky feeder digital radio communication system has been successfully developed superseding the page phone system to operate in deep mining conditions with difficult propagation condition for radio waves. The leaky feeder system consists of a flexible coaxial concentric radiating antenna cable (leaky feeder cable) which covers a complex system of mine workings, with radio signal providing two-way communications for ensuring a high level of reliability and safety for miners underground. To maintain the necessary frequency level, bidirectional line amplifiers are installed every 350–500 metres, fed from 12 V lines. Due to modular design, the system may achieve unlimited communication by connecting several base stations. The leaky feeder system, also called a distributed antenna system, withstands high/low temperatures, moisture, vibration and corrosion. It works independently, is simple to use, and it takes very little time to install and maintain. It provides a network of sirens and alarms for communication in emergency situations, including evacuation of affected miners.

Mine Site Technologies is a leading manufacturer of underground communication and tracking system.

As the system may be susceptible to damage from fires or explosions, technology is under development as an initiative of NIOSH to provide a two-way communications system that can directly communicate with miners after a mine accident or with others on the mine surface with only an underground transceiver and an antenna.

On being warned, the workmen should follow the evacuation plan and proceed to a refuge chamber, shaft or adjacent mines where connected. The escapeway must be clearly marked, preferably by red reflectors. Full-scale fire drills in which all miners participate should be held at regular intervals using non-toxic smoke bombs or smoke generators to familiarize them with the approved firefighting and evacuation plan besides throwing light on any deficiencies in the reporting system, evacuation, isolation of fire, etc. The escapeways should always be kept in a safe condition for travel and be reasonably free from falls, standing water, and other obstructions to the extent that men can escape quickly in an emergency. They should be examined at regular intervals. When the escapeways are shafts, they should be equipped with a hoist and cages. Where an escapeway is inclined at between 19° and 25°, it should be equipped with either a stairway (ladderway) or cleats, and when the inclination is more than 45°, only a ladderway should be installed. An escapeway plan should be hung at a suitable place in each working section. The withdrawal of workmen should be accomplished in an orderly manner so that every man may be accurately accounted for. Computers may be used to simulate evacuation of a mine in a variety of emergency situations without conducting fire-drills. It is possible to predict various mine evacuation times for the different evacuation strategies.

The manager or, in his absence, the principal official present at the surface, should immediately set the mine rescue alarm plan into action and set up emergency underground and surface organizations as outlined in Chapter 7.

Firefighting facilities

The efficiency of a mine fire-fighting organization depends on the availability of adequate and proper firefighting facilities at suitable places underground as well as on their constant maintenance so that they operate reliably at peak operating efficiency at all times. It is advisable for large mines to appoint a 'fire boss', or 'fire deputy' and a few assistants to him, who will be responsible for fire protection, training of firefighting personnel, and education of all workmen in safety.

Communication

Every mine should have adequate communication facilities between suitable points underground and the mine surface so that alarms can be sent in emergencies at all times. Telephones are the simplest most reliable and quickest means of communication in mines. They should be provided at the top and bottom of every shaft or main entry, at each shaft-landing, at loading stations, and on the intake and return sides of ventilating districts. One major problem with a telephone system is that the bell or siren might not be heard over the normal mining noises. In large mines with extensive mine workings, it may be advantageous to set up a telephone exchange underground which is connected to key points on the mine surface and to a surface telephone exchange. The fire alarm is conveyed through a preplanned chain of priority calls.

Plans

At every mine, there should be provided in the control and mine rescue room as well as at suitable places underground, a complete set of plans and sections of the mine and fire-fighting plans showing the mine ventilation, escape routes and means, water lines with diameters, hydrants and water pressure, location of fire stations and hose stations, fire trucks, fire doors, stone-dust-and water-barriers, preparatory fire-stoppings. Fireproof zones, telephones, compressed-air, pumping, and electrical systems and locations, SCSR caches, track haulage, etc., all in approved symbols.

Conducting fire-fighting operations

With fires which are not serious, the manager or, in his absence, the official in-charge should formulate a plan for safe conduct of the work in consultation with his experienced colleagues who are conversant with local conditions and are well-versed in the procedures following mine fires. The plan provides for the removal of endangered workmen if they have not been removed or warned earlier, pinpointing the location of the fire and the strategy of fire-fighting, selection of suitable sites and type of stoppings and their order of erection. Some exploration work by mine rescue or gas mask reconnaissance crew may be necessary to throw some light on the situation. The plan must be strictly followed with no essential deviation from it. The manager should direct the fire-fighting operations from a control room on the surface. If the manager is of the opinion that his presence underground is necessary at times, he should keep the control room, in his absence, under the charge of a responsible senior mine official.

Fire-fighting procedures must be kept under constant review and innovations and improvements made as and when required.

With large fires, emergency underground and surface organisations as outlined in Chapter 7 should be set up to fight them.

1.2 Surface Fires in Coalfields

The Jharia and Raniganj coalfields in India are characterized by many surface fires, some of which started in the 1920s or 1930s and continue to burn till today. In the Jharia Coalfield, there are at present 70 surface fires covering an area of 17 km^2 blocking about 48 million tonnes of coal. Rampant exploitation and unscientific mining over several decades by private mine owners were the principal causes of surface fires in Indian coalfields. Some efforts had been made by the coal companies to control the fires by trying to cut off oxygen supply both to the surface and underground fires by blanketing the surface with sand and by cutting trenches. These fires have caused huge losses of prime coking coal in the Jharia Coalfield and also caused huge losses of superior quality non-coking coal in the Raniganj Coalfield. They are also causing serious environmental pollution problems due to continuous liberation of heat, vapour, and smoke together with noxious gases and production of leachate from the refuse posing health and safety problems for the people of the coalfields besides preventing economic exploitation of underground seams as well as overall economic development in the coal-bearing regions. They have thus become a national problem and the social cost to put out the fires is enormous.

Areas of high temperature or hot spots may be identified by satellite imagery.

1.2.1 Causes of surface fires

Surface fires are caused due to ignition of (a) coal refuse banks, piles, or heaps comprising rejected mine dirt from physical coal cleaning, washery rejects, boiler ash, and other discarded materials containing considerable amount of organic matter as well as of coal faces in opencast mines, (b) coal stacks stockpiled at random, (c) outcrops of seams, (d) and quarry overburden dumps with high carbonaceous material including carbonaceous shale.

The possible causes of ignition are:

(1) Spontaneous combustion; this is the most common cause of ignition of refuse banks and coal stacks as well as of coal faces in opencast mines;
(2) Careless burning of trash and/or garbage from nearby dwellings;
(3) Fires due to burning of dried vegetation when not insulated from the refuse pile;
(4) Underground fires in shallow mines reaching the surface through cracks due to subsidence;
(5) Dumping of hot ashes;
(6) Intentional ignition to create clay, which may be used as road base materials; and
(7) Camp fires left burning; and illicit distillation of liquor.

1.2.2 Coal refuse fires

1.2.2.1 Preventions of coal refuse fires

It should be borne in mind that prevention of fires is cheaper than their extinguishment. The following measures may be adopted to reduce the fire risk:

(1) Selecting suitable coal refuse sites. A flat gently sloping site is satisfactory. A hollow or a valley is an excellent site. Steep hill slopes are usually not satisfactory and, when used, extra site preparation and disposal costs would be incurred. The foundation of the disposal area should be stable. All vegetation and undesirable materials should be removed from the land before refuse is disposed of upon it.
(2) Compacting reactive refuse materials using mobile equipment such as normal truck, dozer, scraper and front-end loader, to minimize flow of air through the pile. For maximum compaction of highly reactive materials, rollers can be employed followed by a sealing layer of inert material before a second layer is applied, in addition to an impervious seal at the edges. The thickness of the compacted layers should not exceed 60 cm.
(3) Prohibiting placement of flammable materials on the pile, for example, wood sawdust, sacking, waste oil, oily rags, and containers for oil, grease, paints, etc.
(4) Quenching boiler ashes before disposal on the pile
(5) Avoiding and restricting mixing of older refuse with fresh refuse. A fireproof barrier of clay or inert material should be constructed between old and new refuse piles.
(6) Sealing off main entries of abandoned shallow mines so that there is no chimney effect and the air does not flow through subsidence cracks to the refuse material.
(7) Refuse piles should not be constructed so as to impede drainage or impound water.
(8) Inspecting the pile regularly to detect fumes, the characteristic smell of gases, etc. from hot spots.

1.2.2.2 Fighting coal refuse fires

Various methods or techniques are available to fight refuse fires. The extinguishment of a burning refuse fire is a difficult and costly operation. The selection of a method or a combination of methods depends on the size and nature of the pile, progress of the fire, the availability of suitable extinguishing materials and equipment, and proximity of homes. Each fire represents an individual problem and one must tailor a technique selected to suit the given situation.

Experience has shown that the following methods can be used:

(i) Digging out;
(ii) Trenching;
(iii) Direct quenching with water;

(iv) Blanketing with inert material;
(v) Injection of a slurry of incombustible material and water; and
(vi) Use of water sprays.

Digging out
If a fire is in the initial stage, the burning material may be dug and loaded out by mechanical means, removed, and spread out to cool by exposure to air or be quenched with water. The area from which the burning material has been removed should be regraded, covered with an inert material and compacted again. The method has the disadvantage that when the pile is disturbed, fresh surfaces are exposed to the air, resulting in an increase in concentration of fumes.

Trenching
If a fire is in the very early stage, the burning area may be isolated from the remainder by cutting trenches or ditches to the bare soil underneath. The isolated hot material can then be quenched with water. The trench may be lined with clay to minimize entrance of air into the porous pile material. Trenching may fail if it is not wide enough and not completed quickly so that the jumping across of fire may be prevented.

Direct quenching with water
Where an abundant supply of water is available, it may be used by pumping it on to the fire and in the immediate vicinity. Where the fire is intense, water cooling may be required before and during the excavating operations.

Use of external jets of water may cause formation of deep fissures by the percolating water or by the water running on the surface of the pile in small rivulets. These fissures allow air to enter the pile and fuel the fire. This method poses a danger of explosion due to formation of water gas. An explosion may open up the pile to air and cause the fire to spread besides presenting a hazard to workmen.

Water applied internally into the pile through pipes inserted into it has limited success in extinguishing the fire as, after treatment, there is usually recurrence of fire on a larger scale, probably due to the creation of additional passages for air to enter by the water draining away.

Blanketing
It aims at cutting off air supply to the burning area by applying a blanket or covering seal of an incombustible material such as limestone dust, fly-ash, shale dust, earth, or clay. It is often effective if the blanket is sufficiently thick (greater than 3 m), completely covers the affected area (particularly the lower parts of the surrounding slopes) consolidated, and is maintained airtight. Sand alone does not form a good blanket unless covered with a clay layer. Constant inspection and maintenance are essential to ensure a continuous seal.

Use of water sprays
Continuous water spraying, especially in the early stages of a fire, is very effective in controlling the fire. Water will seep down into the burning pile without undue

surface disturbance cooling it. Once the fire is under control, spraying may be reduced to three to four hours each day. To prevent channelling, water sprays should be moved at intervals.

Slurry injection or grouting

Slurries of incombustible materials have been used successfully to control fires in refuse banks by injection through pipes inserted into the fire area [20]. Limestone dust, fly ash, shale, or clay may be used. Limestone dust is preferred because it liberates carbon dioxide upon heating, heating, together with the water in the slurry, will reduce the temperature so that heat is dissipated faster than it is produced. On account of its easy availability in many areas as a waste product, fly ash makes an excellent grouting material.

Where sufficiently weathered and disintegrated clay and shales are present in a pile, as determined by analysis of the refuse material, and plenty of water is available, grouting may not be necessary.

The disadvantages of using water sprays are:

(1) The steam formed has a high latent heat which is released on condensation, raising the temperature of the adjacent cooler refuse, producing a condition for the start of a further active heating.
(2) Stoppage of water spraying for a short period for any reason may offset the progress made during a number of days of regular treatment.
(3) The stability of the pile may be adversely affected due to the use of large quantities of water.

Precautions

Serious accidents may occur if proper safety precautions are not taken. When fighting a fire, the following precautions should be taken:

(1) A programme of gas testing by a gas detector. Action to be taken when and if gas is found and rescue of workmen decided upon.
(2) Suitable breathing apparatus should be available for all those immediately connected with the work in the danger area.
(3) Machine operators should be instructed on the action to be taken in the event of a machine breakdown in the danger area.
(4) A telephone or other means of communication should be provided.
(5) A first-aid worker should be in attendance.
(6) A hand-held IR-instrument should be provided for locating hot spots and temperature gradients in the pile. It will be extremely useful in developing a proper fire-fighting strategy.
(7) At the end of a day, all men should be accounted for.

1.2.3 Coal-stack fires

1.2.3.1 Prevention of coal-stack fire

Coal is stored on the ground for long-term storage in stacks exceeding 200 or 300 t, or in enclosed bins, bunkers, and silos for short-term storage. Owing to improper storage, all coals heat spontaneously due to oxidation ultimately reaching the temperature of ignition unless steps are taken to prevent it.

In general, there is little danger in storing coals that have been screened or sized to separate fines. A pile of uniform lumps such as cobbles, cubes, and nuts is honeycombed with air passages which will permit sufficient air to circulate freely in order to carry off whatever heat is generated. Piles consisting of all fines rarely cause trouble as the mass is so compact that air cannot circulate and provide the necessary oxygen for oxidation. Run-of-mine coal is difficult to store safely because of the presence of lumps and fines in the pile, which restrict air circulation and promote spontaneous heating. Compacting is recommended when stacking such coal. High humidity or damp conditions favour self-ignition of coal in storage.

A good basic rule to follow in storage of coal is to either ensure complete and continuous ventilation or seal the coal mass airtight. Insofar as storage is concerned, the important properties of coal which contribute to the rate of oxidation are (a) its rank, (b) content of natural moisture, (c) sulphur content, (d) temperature at which coal is stacked, and (e) tendency to slaking. Lower-rank coals have a greater tendency to heat spontaneously. Coals which are susceptible to spontaneous heating should always be stored separately from coals which are relatively safe.

The techniques of proper storage and handling developed in recent years have made storage or stockpiling of coal entirely safe. The current method of storage is the layering method with compaction.

The following guidelines may be observed when storing coal for long periods which will control or eliminate the spontaneous ignition hazard:

Height of stockpile

The height of a coal stack depends on the strength of the coal, liability of the coal to spontaneous combustion, and whether it is deposited in layers with compaction or not. Uncompacted piles should not normally be stacked to heights greater than 3 m; with compaction, the height can be raised to 10 m or more, provided proper supervision and scientific control are exercised.

Selection and preparation of site

The site of a coal stack must be carefully selected, taking into account the quantity of coal to be stored, cost of preparation of the site, methods of storage and reclamation, and drainage. It should be located away from any source of heat such as steam or hot water lines, furnaces, smoke stacks, or any refuse bank which has a history of heating.

The site should be located on solid ground, preferably on high ground, free of all brush, growth or trash, mounds, and ditches. Structures such as pylons, posts, poles and vertical columns of any kind should not be allowed to remain in the storage area. If it is possible, the pile should be located where it is naturally protected from prevailing winds by structures or landscape. In order to reduce the ventilating effect of wind, stacks of compactly stored coals should be arranged in an elongated shape with the ends facing the prevailing wind. A brick or concrete wall not less than 1 m high built around the site will reduce the entry of air at the skirt of the stack which is the most vulnerable place.

The site should be levelled off and compacted with a bulldozer. Ashes or cinders should not be used which might permit entrance of air under the pile. If necessary, a well-compacted foundation may be laid using crushed waste rock. A concrete base may be considered for permanent stacking.

If possible, different types of coal should be stacked separately.

Laying out stack

Flat-topped rectangular piles should be preferred over conical piles for ease of working with heavy mobile equipment, but it may be otherwise shaped to suit local conditions.

To start the pile, the site should covered with an initial layer of fine coal, 30 to 60 cm in thickness, immediately before stacking, and compacted with mobile rubber-tyred equipment to eliminate all air spaces. Crawler-type machines are less effective in compaction than the rubber-tyred types.

Each load should be tipped close to or overlapping the previous one so that the pile grows laterally but not vertically. The loads so tipped are bulldozed to give a layer 25 to 30 cm in thickness over the whole area. The top of the layer must be compacted as it is formed particularly when stacking bituminous coal so that mobile vehicles can run over it.

When the whole of the site has been covered in this way, a second layer is laid down in the same way and the procedure continued until the pile is completely built up to its planned height. The sides of the pile should have as gentle a slope as space limitations, permit. Ordinarily, the inclination should be 14° to 35°. The sides as well as the top of the pile should be carefully compacted. The top of the pile should be finished with a slight crown to help in shedding water.

As a final step, the whole pile should be capped or sealed in some manner with an airtight covering so that air does not flow into and out of the pile (Fig. 1.47). Coverings that have been tried are asphalt emulsions having 40 per cent water stored for longer periods of time, coal fines and lumps, and chemical coatings. It is now generally recommended to seal the whole pile with a 30 cm layer of fines covered with an additional 30 cm layer of well-screened lump coal to hold down the fines, which gives a satisfactory sealing. Sheets of heavy plastic may be drawn over the edges of the heap as well as around the base to prevent air from entering and to help seal the fire and prevent further oxidation.

Supervision

To check the temperature in the pile at regular intervals during the first three months of the life of the stacks, 25-mm capped steel pipes closed at the bottom may be driven on 3 to 6 m centres down to within 30 to 60 cm of the bottom of the pile. An armoured type of maximum reading thermometer may be used to measure the temperature at varying depths. Alternatively, a series of thermocouples may be inserted into the pipes. A practical method of detection that may be used consists

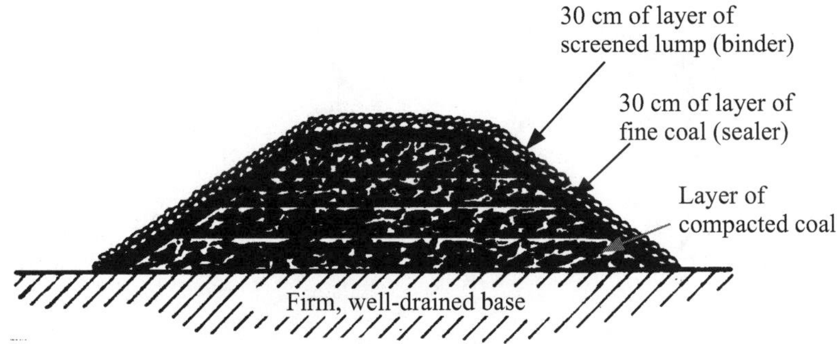

Figure 1.47 Airtight capping of a pile.

of introducing long steel rods in suspected hot places in the coal, leaving them for a few minutes, withdrawing them, and feeling their temperature.

To eliminate chimney effects created by vertical pipes, horizontal pipes may be driven to monitor the temperatures, which may require reclamation from top downwards.

When the coal temperatures are less than 35°C, temperature readings may be taken fortnightly but when the temperature exceeds 35°C, they may be taken weekly. When the temperature reaches 45°C, consultations should be held to chart out a future course of action to deal with the situation as spontaneous combustion is liable to occur as the critical temperature of about 70°C is reached.

Thermal infrared imaging technique may be used to identify higher than ambient temperatures in the pile.

1.2.3.2 Dealing with fires

The first physical indication is often given by a characteristic bake house smell. In the later stages, steam rising early in humid mornings from a small area of the pile and odour of burning coal may be noticed. A white, sometimes yellowish, greenish incrustation on pieces of coal may also indicate that heating is occurring.

When heating develops in a large pile, it may be impractical to spread out the coal to cool. When the location and extent of a fire have been determined, the coal in the heated zone may be dug out as promptly as possible and drenched with water as it is exposed.

Another method consists of driving pointed 25 to 50 mm pipes with the lower 1 m perforated with 10 mm holes (Water spear) down into the pile and supplying water to the pipes. Because of the possibility of an explosion and accidents, it is advisable that men are kept a safe distance away. The fire will be extinguished if the pile is thoroughly flooded with water to ensure that all parts of the pile are thoroughly wetted.

Continuous water spraying (Fig. 1.48) is very effective in controlling a fire in its early stages. Water will seep down into the pile without undue disturbance of its surface.

Dry ice may be used to put out coal-pile fires. This is based on the fact that if oxygen is prevented from reaching the coal, the fire will be extinguished. Dry ice

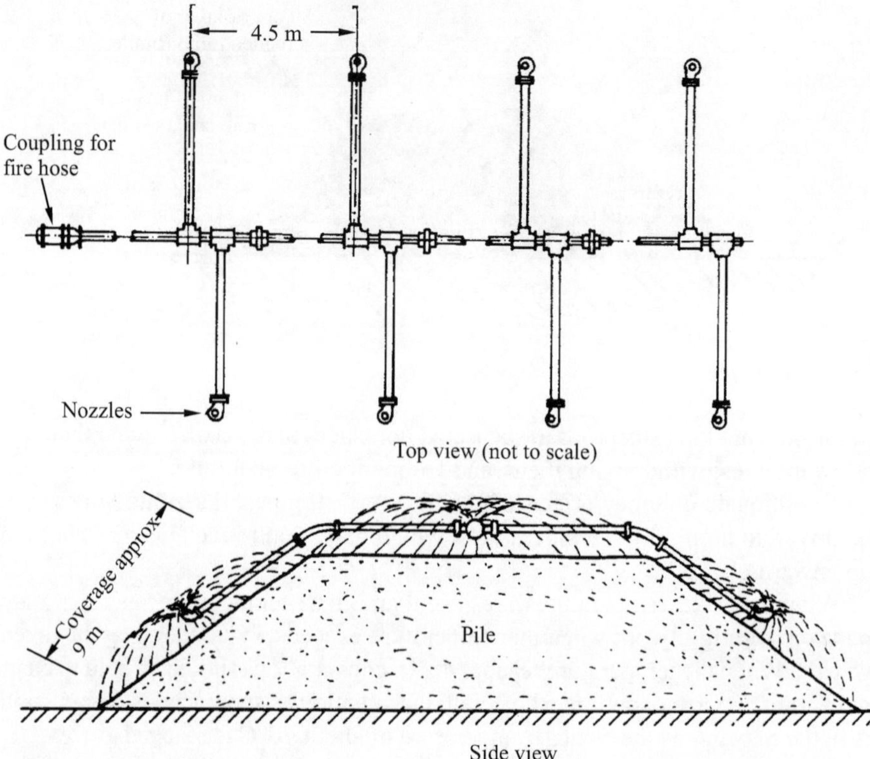

Figure 1.48 Water spraying a pile.

was used successfully in the USA in tackling stubborn fires in storage piles of 25,000 t [21]. Blocks of dry ice were buried 30 cm above the fire spot to effectively smother it. Fires deep inside a coal pile were tackled by using hollow pipes filled with broken pieces of dry ice and capped.

Chemical inhibitors may be used to retard spontaneous heating in coal piles. A solution or slurry of an inhibitor may be sprayed on to the top of each layer as it is laid down. A spray of lime and sodium silicate has been found to have a pronounced inhibiting effect on the oxidation and heating of coal [21].

1.2.4 Fires in coal storage silos

Fires may develop in ROM coal storage bunkers and silos which are usually of 15 to 30 m diameter and 20 to 60 m high located at mine sites or preparation plants under certain loading or storage conditions. They are caused mainly due to spontaneous combustion of coal, but the frequency of their incidence and hazard to life are insignificant. The silos which may be either open-top type with a roof covering to keep off rain water or closed-top type with vent and access holes around the roof area rely on natural air ventilation or forced air convection by means of exhaust fans where necessary. Fires in silos are best avoided by proper design so that there are no dead storage areas.

Owing to the disturbance caused to stored coal during the drawing-off operation, the most effective method of detecting coal silo fires is by the use of gaseous products-of-combustion detectors which measure CO and CO_2 concentrations with a high sensitivity.

Water is the most effective fire extinguishing agent for suppressing fires within a coal silo. A manually-operated water pipeline system with fixed water spray nozzles will suffice for this purpose.

1.2.5 Fires in opencast coal mines

Fires occur during mining of thick bituminous and non-coking coal seams liable to spontaneous heating and brown coal seams by the opencast mining method. The conditions favourable for occurrence of fires in hard coal mines are:

(1) presence of micro- and macro-cracks in massive coal benches providing greater access of atmospheric oxygen to coal surfaces;
(2) long exposure of coal benches to the atmosphere; and
(3) accumulation of loose coal at the toe of the benches.
(4) availability of pyrite bearing coal seams, reaction with ANFO explosive charges with weathering - oxidation products of pyrite.

The following measures may be adopted to prevent or minimise the risk of self-heating:

(1) Regular inspection of the exposed surfaces of coal benches to detect any signs of heating;
(2) Spraying the exposed coal surfaces with an inhibitor or antipyrogene to form a protective surface coating and infusing the inhibitor chemical to fill up the microcracks in the solid coal;
(3) Cleaning the toe of the coal benches of loose coal or spraying the loose coal with a fire-protective surface coating; and
(4) Laying water pipelines on the coal benches and the floor of the seam being worked if the problem of occurrence of spontaneous heating is serious.

Appendix I gives Regulations 116 to 119 of the Coal Mines Regulations, 1957, dealing with precautions against dangers from fires, dust, gas, and water to be observed in Indian coal mines.

1.3 Fires in Underground Sulphide Ore Mines

Many fires had occurred in the past in underground sulphide ore mines in the USA, Spain, Australia, and Canada due to spontaneous combustion of reactive sulphide ores. They constitute the principal underground metal mine fires. Iron sulphides generally have the greatest tendency to oxidize, particularly pyrrhotite. The US Bureau of Mines conducted a literature survey of this growing problem, giving the hazards associated with their mining, oxidation mechanism, and Prevention and control techniques [23].

As with coal, sulphides generate heat from spontaneous oxidation, and if the heat is not dissipated fast enough by the ventilating current, the temperature increase to above 100°C, producing intense heat sufficient to cause an outbreak of fire in combustible materials in contact with or in the immediate neighbourhood, producing significant quantities of toxic sulphur dioxide and carbon monoxide. Owing to the generation of a large amount of heat, extremely difficult environmental conditions may be created at the workplace and, when associated with crushed decaying timber, the fire may assume serious proportions which may be difficult to control.

The sulphide oxidation process is complex and depends largely on physical, chemical, and electrochemical factors which interdependently combine in the oxidation process. The important factors are the ore fineness, moisture content, water content of ore, porosity and permeability of the ore, temperature, depth of mine, ventilation, acidity of mine water, oxygen availability, minerological composition, sulphide type and sulphide content, and association with different sulphides and gangue minerals.

Fires due to spontaneous combustion in sulphide ore mines occur in mined-out stope containing highly fractured backfill with a large sulphide content with timber left in or against the backfill, in abandoned areas, and after caving during mining. Explosion of sulphide dust during or after blasting produces very high temperatures at which combustibles ignite.

The measures for prevention and control of sulphide ore mine fires are common with those for coal mine fires.

CHAPTER 2

Mine Explosions

Mine explosions are generally regarded as a serious and constant hazard in underground coal mining operations. They are caused by ignition of firedamp (firedamp explosions) or coal dust (coal-dust explosions) or both (mixed explosions). They are sudden combustion processes of great intensity, which are accompanied by release of large quantities of heat energy and in which the original gas or solid substance is converted into gaseous products.

In metal mines, explosions are usually rare occurrences. Explosions due to methane formed by the decomposition of vegetable matter have been reported in metal mines at different times. Explosions due to sulphide ore dust have been reported in the past from a few base metal mines mining ores containing a high proportion of iron pyrite. Explosions of blast-generated gases in long blastholes (30 m or more) which did not break through after blasting have been documented in Canadian and Australian mines. Sulphide-dust explosions have occurred in development blasting in a Canadian base metal mine belonging to Brunswick Mining & Smelting Corporation Ltd. Accidental explosions in sulphide ore mines using ANFO explosives have been ascribed to the reactions between ANFO explosive charges and pyrite oxidation products.

In India, between 1900 and 1980, 21 explosions occurred, the worst disaster being that in Dhori Colliery (1965) where 268 miners were killed.

Some explosions of methane and/or coal dust have been believed to have occurred due to lightning penetration into the goaves of underground coal mines.

2.1 Firedamp Explosions

Methane present in coal mines is a by-product of the coalification process during which the coal was formed from vegetable matter. It exists in the coal seam both in an adsorbed state, adhering to the internal micropore surface of the coal matrix, and in a compressed state in the fracture system of the seam. It is also present in the adjacent strata compressed in the fracture system of the rock. When the seam is mined, the equilibrium that existed in the coal seam and the surrounding strata under the confining pressure is disturbed and the gas is liberated from both the seam being mined and the adjacent strata, thereby posing a serious hazard unless sufficient air quantity is circulated through the mine to dilute its concentration in the general ventilation to less than the safe prescribed limit. The amount of methane stored within the coal increases with the coal rank, depth of cover over the seam, and the reservoir pressure. The volume of methane released as the coal is being mined forms the 'base emission' while the emission from other sources forms the 'secondary emission' .

Methane burns in air when ignited with a pale blue flame, but, when it is mixed with air, it can explode on ignition. The combustion and explosion take place according to the equation

$$CH_4 + 2(O_2 + 4N_2) = CO_2 + 2H_2O + 8N_2$$

One volume of methane requires two volumes of oxygen or 10 volumes of atmospheric air for its complete combustion. Theoretically, therefore, the optimum or stoichiometric mixture is formed at 9.5 per cent methane. Methane, however, forms flammable mixtures with air over a range of approximately 5 to 15 per cent.

If the methane content of a methane–air mixture is greater than 9.5 per cent, the oxygen present will not be sufficient for its complete combustion and if it is less than 9.5 per cent, oxygen or atmospheric air will be in excess.

A pure firedamp explosion does not extend over a wide area unless there has been emission or accumulation of large quantities of methane.

2.1.1 Limits of flammability, flammable limits, or explosive limits

The flammable limits of methane–air mixtures are the limits of concentration of methane in air between which a flame can be propagated throughout the mixtures. The boundary-line mixtures with minimum and maximum concentration of methane in air, which if ignited, will just propagate flame are known as the lower and upper flammable or explosive limits. Flammability limits of methane have been extensively studied. The lower and upper flammable limits (LFL and UFL) are approximately 5 (33 g/m^3) and 15 (100 g/m^3) respectively. Explosions at the flammable limits are rather weak and slow-burning, while at the stoichiometric concentration, they are most violently explosive. A mixture containing less than 5 per cent methane, although not flammable under normal conditions, may explode when at a high temperature or when compressed adiabatically due to blasting or a coal-dust explosion. Also, a mixture containing 15 to 100 per cent methane in which electric sparks can be generated without any explosion taking place is dangerous in a mine as it may pass through the flammable range on dilution with air in mine workings.

The limits of flammability are not fundamental characteristics of the gas but depend on experimental conditions. They are influenced by the presence of other combustible or inert gases, temperature, pressure, intensity of turbulence, diameter of the experimental tube, direction of flame propagation, oxygen concentration, intensity of ignition source, and presence of coal dust.

The lower flammable limit of methane is found to be independent of oxygen concentration above 20 per cent. It decreases linearly from 5 per cent to zero as

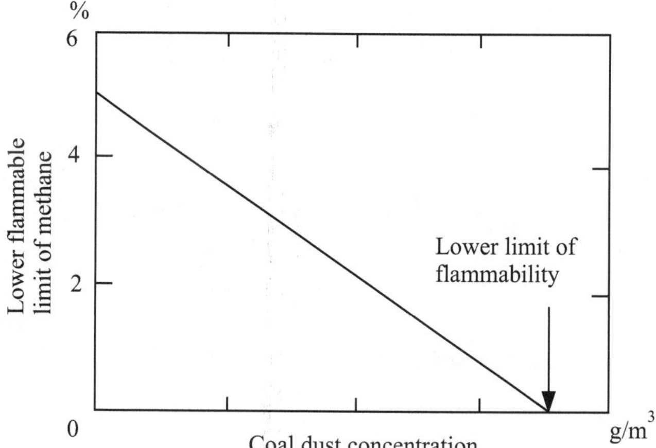

Figure 2.1 Variation of lower flammable limit of methane with coal dust concentration.

the air-borne coal dust concentration increases from zero to its lower limit of flammability (Fig. 2. 1).

The presence of other combustible gases like ethane, carbon monoxide, hydrogen, etc., which have, like methane, lower and upper flammable limits also reduces the lower limit which can be determined by using the Le Chatelier relation:

$$\frac{100}{L} = \frac{p_1}{l_1} + \frac{p_2}{l_2} + \frac{p_3}{l_3} + \cdots$$

where $p_1, p_2, p_3, \ldots$ are the percentages of the component gases in the mixture ($p_1 + p_2 + p_3 + \cdots = 100$ per cent) and l_1, l_2, $l_3 \ldots$ their percentage lower limits.

The presence of inert gases has a damping effect on the flammability of methane–air mixtures. Carbon dioxide is more effective than nitrogen.

2.1.2 Ignition point or ignition temperature

The ignition point of flammable firedamp–air mixtures is given as 650° to 750°C. The ignition point is the minimum temperature to which a portion of the mixture must be raised in order to initiate or cause a rapidly accelerating reaction in the whole of the accumulation with the accompaniment of a flame. It does not refer to the temperature of the igniting source which must obviously be at a higher temperature. It is not a definite temperature but depends upon the nature of the source of ignition whether flame, spark, etc and shape and size of the space where ignition occurs, methane content, temperature of the surroundings, pressure, oxygen concentration, presence of other gases, and turbulence. The ignition point of pure methane in oxygen is 550°C.

A characteristic property of firedamp is that when it comes into contact with an igniting source, the temperature of which is comparatively a little above its ignition point, a certain time must elapse before it is ignited. This period is known as the 'ignition lag' or induction time and it depends on the temperature, pressure, gas concentration and presence of other combustible gases. Thus, Naylor and Wheeler [24] found that with a 6.5 per cent methane–air mixture and a source of heat at a temperature of 700°C, the lag was 11 s and at 1175°C only 0.1 s. The ignition lag is explained as arising due to the reaction of methane with oxygen only after it has absorbed a definite quantity of heat (22.1 kcal/mol) [25].

2.1.3 Explosion characteristics

Flame temperature

The flame temperature of a flammable firedamp–air mixture is the temperature just at the moment of its explosion. It depends on the concentration of firedamp, uniformity of the mixture, turbulence, confinement, and heat losses. It is maximum at the stoichiometric concentration and is less at the lower and upper flammable limits. The temperature, however, does not remain constant but at once comes down to mine roadway temperature due to the explosion gases mixing with the rest of the cooler air and also coming into contact with cooler roadway surfaces. The adiabatic flame temperature for a stoichiometric methane–air mixture is 2200 K.

Explosion pressure

The explosion pressure depends on the flame temperature and confinement. The maximum explosion pressure of a methane–air mixture (760 mm Hg, 20°C) when ignited in a closed vessel is given as 7.2 bar(g) [26]. In mine workings, however, the explosion pressure may exceed this value. The shock wave (pressure wave) travelling ahead of the explosion flame will compress any firedamp accumulation encountered on its way to a pressure greater than 1 bar(g). Upon ignition of such an accumulation, the maximum explosion pressure of the resulting explosion will be much greater than 7 bar(g). This explains the observation generally made that severe damage from a firedamp explosion does not occur at the seat of the explosion but away from it.

Experiments on gas explosion phenomena in the US Bureau of Mines (USBM) Experimental Coal Mine [27] using natural gas (83 per cent CH_4, 16 per cent C_2H_6, and 1 per cent N_2) showed that the highest explosion pressure occurs in the gas zone and that the pressure decays exponentially with distance outbye the gas zone. Flammability data for quiescent methane–air mixtures in a 21-litre flammability test chamber using a strong electric spark as the ignition source obtained by the US Bureau of Mines [28] are shown in Fig. 2.2. The peak explosion pressure ratio is the peak explosion pressure divided by the initial pressure of the mixture.

Figure 2.3 gives the flammability diagram for stoichiometric methane–air mixtures with added inhibitor nitrogen gas and dusts in an 8-litre flammability test chamber, in which the order or relative effectiveness of the various inhibitors in

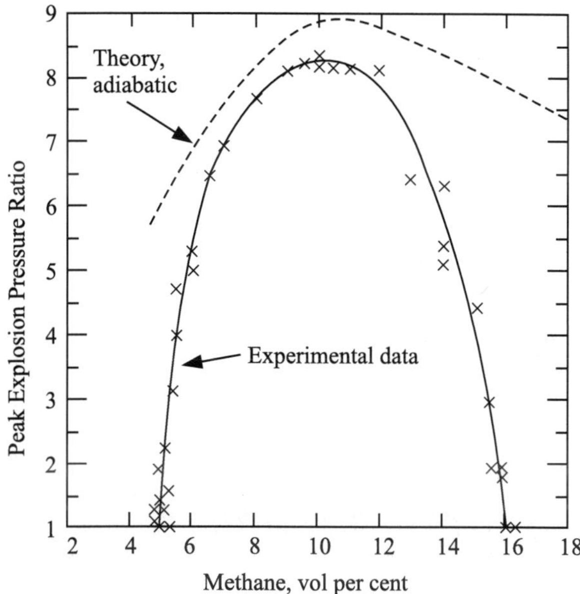

Figure 2.2 Explosion pressure for quiescent methane–air mixtures.

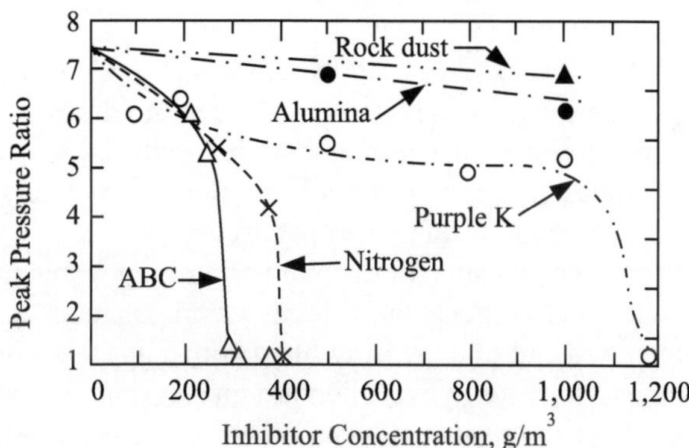

Figure 2.3 Effect of inhibitors on explosion pressure of stoichiometric methane–air mixture in a 8-litre test chamber.

extinguishing methane explosions is obtained as $NH_4H_2PO_4 > KHCO_3 > Al_2O_3 = CaCO_3$. Table 2.1 gives the inhibitor concentrations to inert a stoichiometric methane–air mixture [29].

Flame length

Experiments in the USBM Experimental Coal Mine [27] showed that the length of flame increases as the gas concentration in a gas zone increases from the lower limit of flammability to about 12 per cent, after which it decreases; the limited data indicate that the length of the flame is directly proportional to the volume of the zone and, for a given roadway cross-section, the total flame length is four-and-a-half times the length of the gas zone for 9.5 per cent mixtures and five times the length for 12 per cent mixtures.

Table 2.1 Inhibitor concentrations required to inert a stoichiometric methane–air mixture

Inhibitor	Inerting concentration	
	g/m³	wt.%
ABC ($NH_4H_2PO_4$)	290	81
Nitrogen gas (N_2)	400	86
Purple K($KHCO_3$)	1150	95
Alumina (Al_2O_3)	>1200	>95
Rock dust ($CaCO_3$)	>1200	>95

Velocity of propagation of flame or flame velocity

The velocity of propagation of a firedamp explosion flame is very small. It depends on the following factors:

(1) *Methane content of mine air* The velocity of flame propagation increases with increasing firedamp content from the lower flammable limit upwards. After reaching the maximum value at the optimum concentration, the velocity decreases.

(2) *Condition of the gas mixture, whether it is at rest or in motion* It has been found from experiments conducted in quiescent mixtures in tubes that the maximum velocity of propagation is not greater than 0.6 m/s [25]. On the other hand, when the gas mixture is in motion, the velocity may quickly increase to a few hundreds of metres per second.

(3) *Point of ignition* The location of the point of ignition within the body of the gas mixture markedly affects the velocity of propagation. If ignition takes place at the closed end of a roadway filled with a gas mixture, the speed of propagation and severity of explosion are greater than when ignition takes place at the outbye end of the roadway. When ignited at the outbye end, rapid burning rather than an explosion develops. It is for this reason that the 'fire boss' in the early days of mining could intentionally ignite gas as he entered a heading without igniting an explosion.

(4) *Length of gas zone* Experiments in gas zones in the USBM Experimental Coal Mine [27] showed that the velocity of flame propagation of a gas explosion increases from zero at the point of ignition to a maximum at a distance of about twice that of the original length of the gas body; the maximum flame velocity for the 7.5 m zone is about 99 m/s and that for the 15 m zone is 533 m/s.

(5) *Presence of obstacles in the path or change in area of roadway cross-section.* If a roadway in which an explosion has occurred has objects or obstacles which decrease its area of cross-section, the velocity of propagation of the explosion rises to a few hundreds of metres per second.

Direct blast and backlash

Firedamp explosions are characterized by two distinct operations: the direct blast and the indirect blast or backlash. In the direct blast, a pressure wave of great force and speed travels ahead of the explosion flame. The backlash is caused by the vacuum arising out of the cooling of the explosion gases and condensation of water vapour and is of less intensity than the direct blast but traverses the same path backwards. When the concentration of methane is greater than 9.5, two types of explosion flame occur, the primary and secondary flames. The primary flame propagates at a greater velocity and consumes the entire available oxygen. The secondary flame is produced later by the burning of the unburnt gas with the help of oxygen supplied by the blacklash. It propagates slowly in the direction opposite to that of the primary flame.

Explosion gases

The chemical composition of the products of a firedamp explosion depends greatly upon whether it is a pure firedamp explosion or a mixed explosion of firedamp and coal dust. With a pure gas explosion, carbon dioxide is always formed and carbon monoxide is frequently found. A certain amount of oxygen is also found in the explosion gases due to fresh air supplied by the backlash.

2.1.4 Estimation of hazard due to firedamp in mines

The hazard posed by firedamp to mine safety may be estimated by:

(1) determining the gas emission indices or rates in return air currents (m^3 CH_4/t and of r.o.m or saleable output) in coal mines;
(2) determining the concentration of methane at working faces; and
(3) the number, type and size of firedamp accumulations.

The gas emission index or emission rate is determined by using the formula

$$q_{CH4} = \frac{c \times 60 \times 24 \times Q_{air}}{100 \times O \times K} = \frac{c \times 14.4 \times Q_{air}}{O \times K}$$

where c = methane content in return air current (Vol. %)

Q_{air} = return air current quantity (m^3/min)

O = mined or saleable output (*t/d*)

K= a factor given by the ratio $\dfrac{\text{max.conc.of methane on any day in a week}}{\text{average concentration of methane in the week}}$

It varies between 1 and 2, depending on the degree of mechanization; for mechanized faces, K lies between 1.5 and 2.

On the basis of the gas emission index, coal mines in different countries have been classified into degrees/categories of gassiness. The national system of classification of mines for India, Poland and the USSR is given in Tables 2.2 to 2.4.

Table 2.2 Indian classification

Degree of gassiness	Gas emission index (m^3 CH_4 / t output)
I	< 1
II	1– 10
III	> 10

Table 2.3 Polish classification

Category of gassiness	Gas emission index (m^3 CH4/t output)
I	< 5
II	5–10
III	10–15
IV	> 15

Table 2.4 Russian classification

Category of gassiness	Gas emission index (m^3 CH_4/t output)
I	< 5
II	5–10
III	10–15
Outside the categories	> 15

For gassy non-coal mines, any one of the coal mine classification criteria is usually applied or no classification criteria exist.

A firedamp accumulation in a mine working is said to take place when the percentage of firedamp in the general body of the air current flowing in the mine working is more than that prescribed by the mining regulation (1.25 per cent in India, 1 per cent in Europe).

2.1.5 Causes of firedamp explosions

The greatest number of firedamp explosions occur in active mine workings in face areas and headings. The various causes of firedamp explosions in mines may be grouped under the following headings:

(a) Negligence of miners
(b) Use of damaged safety lamps and their improper handling
(c) Blasting
(d) Mine fires
(e) Friction
(f) Electric sparks
(g) Other special causes

Negligence of miners
Smoking, starting fires or opening of flame safety lamps on the part of miners had in the past resulted in firedamp ignitions. Explosions from such causes reflect discredit on all concerned.

Use of damaged safety lamps and their improper handling
A safety lamp is safe only when its various parts are clean, in good condition, all parts are properly assembled, and it is properly handled.

Blasting
Blasting in coal and roadhead rippings and drifts represented a dangerous source of ignition of firedamp in the past. With the development of new and safer explosives and improved shotfiring techniques during the past three decades and explosion protection on roadheading machines, the number of explosions due to this has decreased considerably.

Mine fires
Mine fires can easily bring about ignition of flammable firedamp–air mixtures in contact with them. When fighting a fire in a gassy mine, care should be taken to prevent firedamp content of mine air from rising to flammable proportions.

Friction
Frictional heating and frictional sparks can, under certain circumstances, ignite flammable firedamp–air mixtures. Frictional ignition in mines may take place due to: (a) friction between metal and metal, (b) friction between metal (especially steel) and rock, and (c) friction between rock and rock.

Frictional heatings are seldom the cause of ignition of flammable firedamp–air mixtures.

The degree of ignition hazard from metal-to-metal contact is determined by the properties of the more readily oxidizable metal. Extensive research carried out in the FRG and the UK on the possible ignition of flammable firedamp mixtures by incendive metal sparks has clearly shown that the ignition hazard from the incendive particles of iron is extremely less and that danger may be feared from aluminium and its alloys [30].

Friction between metal and rock poses the greatest ignition hazard in coal mines using cutting machines (cutters, continuous miners, power loaders). Several firedamp explosions in mines in recent years have been attributed to frictional sparking during cutting and drilling operations in seams containing hard siliceous bands or inclusion of iron pyrite nodules. Investigations showed that the nature of the rock, particularly the quartz content and its grain size, is far more important than the type of picks or bits used. It is now generally accepted that ignition of flammable firedamp–air mixtures by a pick cutting rock occurs at or near the rock surface after the pick has passed and is caused by the hot material left behind the pick, which is likely to be at temperatures exceeding 1200°C and that the type of rock most likely to cause ignitions will have a quartz content greater than 30% and a grain size greater than 10 μm [31].

Recent tests have shown that the hard metal or tungsten carbide insert of a bit can produce an ignition but that the steel shank produces an ignition far more easily.

Some early mine explosions in the UK and Canada were attributed to friction between rock and rock caused by the fall or caving in of sandstone roof rocks in goaves. Experiments conducted in the UK showed that the ignition of firedamp by the impact of rocks may take place by its direct contact with the hot patches on the contacting rock surfaces and that siliceous or quartz-bearing sandstones can produce ignitions.

Explosions of blast-generated gases in long boreholes (30 m or more) in base metal mines in Canada and Australia have been attributed to rock falling into the holes producing frictional sparks.

Despite extensive research, the exact mechanism of the ignition process is not well understood. The frictional ignition hazard depends on the nature of the contacting materials, the composition of the flammable gas mixture, the rate of energy release, and the type of frictional contact of the materials.

Electric sparks

The electrification of coal mines has introduced into the mines an ever-present source of ignition – electric sparks igniting not only combustible materials but also flammable firedamp–air mixtures. Sparks may be produced from switchgear, damaged cables, signalling apparatus, and faulty electrical equipment. Although electric sparks usually have a much higher temperature than ordinary flames, it may happen that a spark has a very short life and its electrical energy is not sufficient to cause ignition of the mixture in that time. The minimum energy of a spark causing ignition of a flammable firedamp mixture varies with methane concentration, humidity, oxygen content of the atmosphere, temperature, pressure and turbulence.

The variation of the minimum ignition energy with different methane–air mixtures is shown [32] in Fig. 2.4, from which it is seen that the most flammable mixture for ignition by an electric spark occurs at 8.3 per cent methane, irrespective of the type of spark (low-voltage inductive or high-voltage capacitive) and that the minimum ignition energy is as low as 0.28 mJ (mWs)

Other special causes

Some of the mine explosions in recent years have been ascribed to ignition of firedamp– or dust–air mixtures by sparks of static or frictional electricity having adequate energy which will be some fraction of the total stored energy. In gassy coal mines, electrostatic charges in excess of 300 V must be viewed with caution.

Ordinary belts passing over pulleys can accumulate static charges sufficient to produce sparks capable of igniting flammable firedamp or coal-dust–air mixtures. Dust-laden mine air passing through ducting can electrify the ducting by friction.

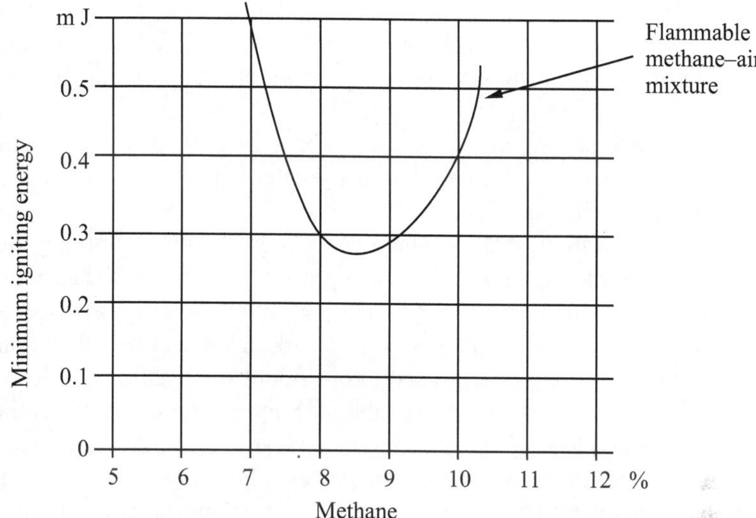

Figure 2.4 Variation of minimum igniting energy with varying methane concentration for ignition with high-voltage capacitive spark.

Warm dry atmospheres are favourable to the development of static charges by friction.

Methane blowers, when they catch fire, can become a cause of mine explosions.

2.1.6 Prevention of firedamp explosions

No practical measures exist for arresting firedamp explosions in coal mines. The only thing that can be done is to step up protective measures.

The various measures against the firedamp explosion hazard in mines can be divided into the following three groups:

2.1.6.1 Measures against accumulation of dangerous firedamp mixtures in mine workings from the beginning

The most effective method of preventing firedamp explosions in mines is by providing adequate ventilation which will dilute the firedamp, besides other harmful gases, to well below limits that may be prescribed for different mine workings and carry it away to the surface. Frequent sampling of mine air for methane at several points in the mine is, therefore, an important measure for prevention of firedamp explosions.

The following important points should be borne in mind:

(i) The mine should be mechanically ventilated by the exhaust ventilation method. A reserve or standby main fan having an independent drive and power circuit when electric motors are used should be provided especially in mines with a methane emission greater than 5 m^3 per tonne of daily output.

Every main fan shall be so installed and positioned that it is not damaged by a possible explosion as far as possible. It should be fitted with an automatic alarm or signal device to alert persons on duty, should it slow down or stop.

(ii) The mine equivalent orifice should be as large as possible (> 2 m^2)

(iii) The ventilation of mine workings greater than 3 m in length should not be done by diffusion alone.

(iv) The ventilation of development headings should be done by utilizing the mine ventilating pressure as far as practicable. Air which has passed through any abandoned area which is inaccessible or unsafe for inspection should not be used to ventilate any active workings in a mine. If auxiliary fans are required to be properly used, they should be installed and located so that air is delivered within 5 m of the face and recirculation of ventilating air is eliminated to keep the working face clear of flammable and noxious gases, dust, and explosive fumes. In places where auxiliary fans are used, the ventilation during weekends and idle shifts should be by means of the primary air current conducted into the place in a manner to prevent accumulation of firedamp.

(v) Ventilation doors should be correctly located and kept closed except when men, equipment and trains are passing through them. They should always be in good repair and be self-closing.

(vi) The mine ventilation system should be planned so that simple, effective, and reliable ventilation of all workings is assured. Where multiple main fans are used, the ventilation system should be so arranged that no adverse air reversal will occur in the event of failure or stoppage of any fan or fans. Predictions of firedamp emission for different sites in a coalfield will greatly assist in planning safe ventilation systems for mines.

(vii) Seams should be extracted, as a rule, from top downwards to decrease the methane levels in the lower seams.

(viii) The method of extraction should be selected so that it guarantees an easy and safe ventilation of the faces by air dilution with adequate velocities at the face and at the waste edge. Face air velocities of up to 4 m/s or more are being used today on modern longwall faces in very gassy seams to mine coal safely.

In high-capacity longwall faces with strong methane emissions and high ventilating air requirements, faces laid with W-ventilation system will enable larger air quantities to flow through them besides providing a middle gate for drilling additional methane drainage holes.

(ix) A particularly high standard of unit ventilation by separate ventilation splits should be maintained in each mechanized mining section and in districts/panels liable to gas outbursts.

(x) In bord and pillar and longwall retreating panels in very gassy seams worked with caving, the firedamp content in the goaves behind the active faces must be controlled by in-mine local or central drainage of goaves or drainage through surface ventilation boreholes. Bleeder systems with bleeder entries and bleeder entry connections as in American mining practice can be successfully employed to move firedamp–air mixtures continuously from the caved areas behind retreating longwall faces away to the return airways, and to minimize the hazard of expansion of goaf gases due to changes in atmospheric pressure (Fig. 2.5) and their release into faces and gate roads as unusual emissions during the rapid closure of the goaf, just behind the face supports or not far away from them, when caving takes place periodically.

(xi) Mining with backfilling (Fig. 2.6) or solid stowing of the waste/goaf, especially hydraulic filling, prevents formation of methane reservoirs in goaves.

(xii) Horizontal methane drainage holes drilled into a seam in advance of a panel must be sealed before they are intercepted during extraction of the panel to prevent methane from being discharged forming flammable methane mixtures.

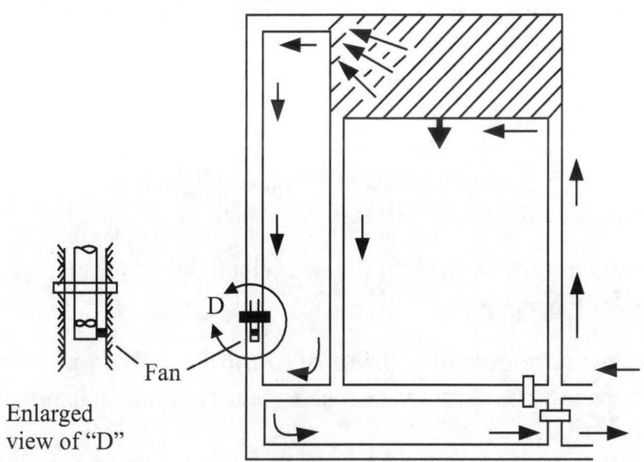

Fig.2.5 Bleeder system of ventilation of a retreating longwall face.

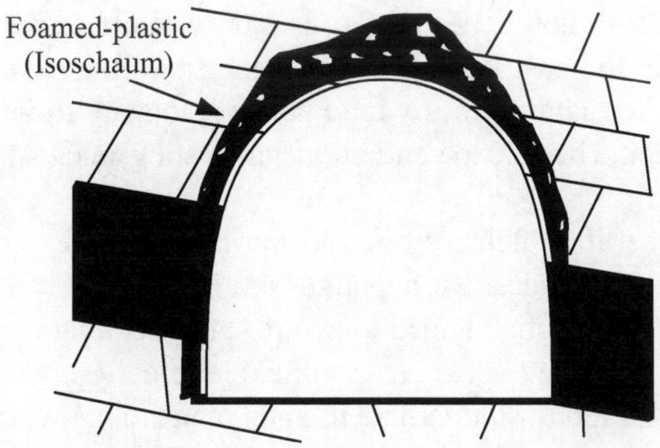

Fig. 2.6 Roof voids/cavities filled with foamed plastic.

(xiii) Air currents and methane emission should be checked by systematic measurement of air quantities and their methane concentration. Special examinations for firedamp layering should be made during periods of falling barometric pressure in ascensionally-ventilated roadways adjacent to old workings, within the areas of moving ground behind faces, and high points at which gas will tend to accumulate and layer. If, at any time, the air at any working place contains a methane accumulation, changes or adjustments in ventilation should be made at once so that such air contains less than the prescribed value. While making such changes or adjustments, power to electric equipment located in such places should be cut off. All personnel may have to be withdrawn from the area, depending on the concentration of methane.

For judging the possibility of formation of methane layering, the Middendorf formula [33] may be used to calculate the 'layering index':

$$S_{\text{Index}} = \sqrt[3]{\frac{24v^2}{c\,\sqrt{F}}}$$

where v is the mean velocity (m/s);

c is the mean methane content of air current (% CH_4);

F is the area of the cross-section of the airway at the measuring station (m^2).

If $S_{\text{Index}} < 2$, there is probable danger of methane layering

$S_{\text{index}} > 2$, there is no danger of methane layering.

A correction factor must be used for the rising inclination and change in the cross-sectional area of the airway.

2.1.6.2 *Measures against ignition of flammable firedamp mixtures*

The various preventive measures to be taken against ignition of flammable firedamp mixtures in mines are:

(i) All persons should be prohibited from carrying smoking articles (pipes, cigars, cigarettes, tobacco other than chewing tobacco or snuff), matches or other spark- or flame-making devices into the workings. All men entering the mine should be searched for contraband.

(ii) All coal mines should be treated as safety-lamp mines as a number of explosions in the past had occurred in the so-called naked-light mines. In short-life naked-lamp mines where naked lights are to be retained, special attentions should be paid to ventilation, gas-testing, and to precautions against coal dust.

(iii) (a) Only certified flame-proof and intrinsically-safe apparatus should be used in coal mines. The apparatus should be properly installed, protected, operated, and maintained to assure safe operating conditions.

(b) If, in a district or part of a mine, electrically-operated equipment is not required for immediate use and men are not working there, power should be cut off in that district or part of the mine. Tests for methane should be made immediately before the equipment is energized.

(c) Trailing cables which are vulnerable to damage should be suspended from hangers, specially provided for the purpose, and, if they are present in the face area, should be suitably protected against damage from any cause.

(d) To prevent ignition from electrostatic charges, all ventilation ductings should be earthed and only antistatic polythene sheeting, hoses, and belts used.

(e) A reliable methane monitor or cut-out that will automatically cut off power supply to the electrical equipment when the methane concentration reaches the prescribed maximum percentage may be installed in endangered mine workings.

(f) A methane monitor should be installed, when available, on any electric face-cutting equipment, continuous miner, longwall face equipment, and loading equipment to automatically de-energize equipment or give a warning automatically when the concentration of methane reaches the maximum prescribed limit. The methane monitors shall be properly maintained to keep them operative and checked at regular intervals for operating accuracy.

(g) When a main fan is stopped for any reason, electrical power should be immediately cut off in return airways. After the fan has been restarted, the power shall not be switched on unless normal ventilation and safe conditions have been restored.

(h) In places where auxiliary fans are used, the auxiliary fans should not be operated during stoppage of normal mine ventilation. Accumulations of methane should be removed after restoration of normal mine ventilation before the fans are operated. In a place ventilated with an auxiliary fan, if the auxiliary fan is stopped or fails, electrical equipment operating in the place should be stopped and the power disconnected at the power source until the ventilation is restored. The auxiliary fan should be maintained so that the impeller does not strike the casing.

(i) Changes in ventilation affecting the main air current or any split thereof should be made only when the mine is idle. The power supply should be cut off from the affected area before changes are made.

(iv) Production of excessive frictional heat with conveyors, brakes, and bearings should be avoided by good installation and proper maintenance.

The production of frictional sparks, especially by metal-to-rock contact as with face-cutting, drilling, continuous mining, and longwall powerloading equipment, should be avoided as far as possible. Pyritic intrusions in coal seams have a significant frictional ignition potential due to sulphur flames produced by cutting bits striking pyrite.

Besides producing frictional sparks, cutting bits of mining machines, when they are worn or broken, are especially hazardous if they scrape against instead of cutting into the material.

The precautionary measures against frictional ignitions during cutting of seams by jib coalcutters consist in selecting an appropriate cutting horizon and lower pick speeds, wet-cutting using external water sprays directed at the ingoing and outgoing pick or using 'whale jibs' in which the water is piped to a number of points around the apex of the jib, providing a water mist in the cut, introducing an inert gas such as carbon dioxide or nitrogen into the cut, or ventilating the cut. Adequate ventilation of the cut using a water spray device provides the most effective known means of preventing frictional ignitions.

With power-loading on longwall faces using shearer loaders, the frictional ignition hazard varies greatly, depending on the type of shearer loader used (conventional fixed drum shearer loader, ranging drum shearer loader, floor or conveyor-mounted trepanner), whether cutting with or against the ventilation, presence of hard dirt bands or quartzitic pyrite nodules in the seam or floor, standard of ventilation, cutting speed, type of pick, and sharpness of cutting picks. Research has shown that point-attack picks cause ignitions much more easily than radial- or forward-attack picks and the risk of ignition diminishes significantly below pick linear cutting speed of 1.5 m/s. Experience in British mines working thin seams has shown that with good standards of ventilation, the frictional ignitions can be confined to the neighbourhood of the power leader, that the incidence of ignition in thin seams resulting from picks striking the floor is much greater than from picks striking the roof due to the cutting zone at the floor being most difficult to ventilate, and that the risk of ignition is least with L-shaped outboard arm ranging drum shearer loaders and maximum with conveyor-mounted trepanners [15].

The risk of frictional ignitions by ripper-type continuous miners can be prevented or minimized by modified bit design and using carefully-engineered back sprays on the ripper drum with adequate spray pressure at the nozzle applied directly at the coalcutting bits.

Owing to the dominant role played by friction as an ignition source, one may divide the mine into abnormally high-suspect zones or areas of frictional ignitions, in which an intensive programme to eliminate frictional ignitions may be undertaken.

(v) Use of materials constructed of light alloys should be prohibited to eliminate incendive sparking.

(vi) Spontaneous heating of coal should be controlled by proper planning of mine development as well as coal extraction, good ventilation system, and inspection. Mine fires should be detected in their early stages.

(vii) Blasting with explosives should be restricted to a minimum. Immediately before firing a shot or a group of multiple shots and after blasting is completed, examination for methane should be made. Mechanical winning and heading machines and blasting devices such as Hydrox, Cardox, and Airbreaker shells may be used as alternatives to ordinary explosives for breaking down coal. Pulsed-infusion shotfiring in combination with deep-hole water infusion

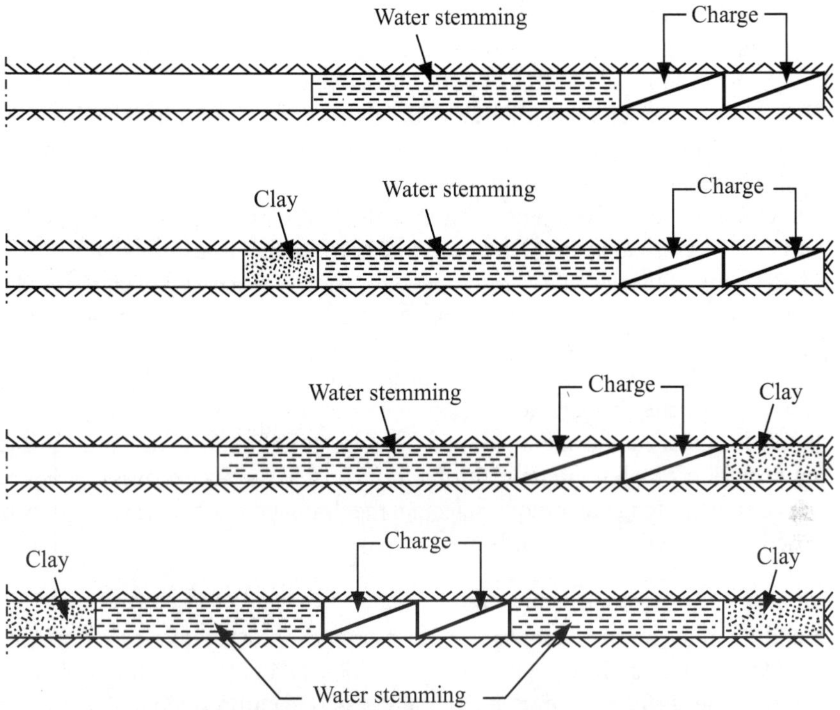

Figure 2.7 Methods of charging a shothole with water stemming.

may also be employed for getting coal without machine-cutting. Methods of charging a shothole with water stemming are shown in Fig. 2.7.

(viii) Welding, flame-cutting, grinding, and soldering operations must be done only after taking extreme precautions. Examinations for methane should be made immediately before and periodically, during such work.

(ix) All mobile diesel-powered equipment must be inspected and maintained in the approved condition in accordance with the instructions furnished by the manufacturer. Particular attention should be paid to the flame arresters in the intake and exhaust systems, the exhaust cooling system, and the surface temperature, of the engine and components of the exhaust system.

2.1.6.3 Control of firedamp emission

The need to extract seams having greater methane content at greater depths, the use of intensively-worked high-production extraction methods, such as longwall mining, and the need to mine more gassy seams have all led to methane problems in mines even when the emission rates are not excessively high. In mines where it is not possible to control the methane concentration by general ventilation, which may be extremely expensive, drainage techniques must be adopted to enhance mine safety by extracting as much methane as possible from the strata before it mixes with the air in the coal faces and roadways, and obtain increased production rates. No single technique can be universally applied since the rate of methane emission in a seam depends on the rank of coal, pressure of gas, permeability of the seam, type and nature of the strata overlying and underlying the seam, presence of other seams and the sequence of their extraction, severity of faulting and folding, relaxation of the strata resulting from coal extraction, and the extraction methods. Investigations should be carried out to predict the anticipated emission rates and movement of methane from seams in the roof and floor through geologic studies, studies on the physical properties of the coal seam being mined now and of those likely to be mined in the future, and collection and analysis of gas emission data from new and existing coal mines so that an effective system for methane control and ventilation may be designed.

2.1.6.3.1 *Methane drainage techniques*

Methane drainage can be accomplished by a variety of underground and surface techniques for control of methane during mining or in advance of mining. For the success of any drainage technique selected, the drainage system must be properly designed and effectively controlled.

2.1.6.3.1.1 *Underground techniques*

The major underground techniques for methane drainage use cross-measure boreholes, superjacent headings, gob gas cavities, and horizontal boreholes.

On the mine surface, the drained methane gas is usually conducted away to be burnt in a boiler house for power generation.

Cross-measure boreholes

This is by far the most common method of methane control on European longwall faces. Cross-measures boreholes are drilled from the gate roads of advancing longwall faces into the adjacent strata above and/or below the seam being worked over the waste area and close to the working face (Fig. 2.8) usually using special underground rotary drills (Fig. 2.9). Methane is drained by applying suction pressure to the hole, and the methane–air mixture is drawn into a pipeline which may extend to the surface. The diameter of the boreholes varies between 65 and 120 mm. The spacing of the boreholes is important as too wide a spacing will allow a significant proportion of gas to escape into the mine workings, while too close a spacing will involve unnecessary and expensive drilling. The usual distance between the holes is 10 to 30 m when the zones of influence of the individual holes just meet. The optimum spacing is determined by a certain amount of trial-and-error drilling. A properly designed borehole pattern, can capture 50 to 80 per cent of the total methane emission. The boreholes are drilled at angles varying from 30° to 60° to the bedding plane. The length of holes may vary between 25 and 40 m, exceptionally reaching 150 m. Holes drilled at right-angles to the line of the gate roads have been found from experience to be more successful than holes angled towards the face.

The efficiency of the borehole-to-strata seal (standpipe seal) is of vital importance since it not only affects the purity of the gas but also the zone of influence of the boreholes and the effectiveness of the drainage system.

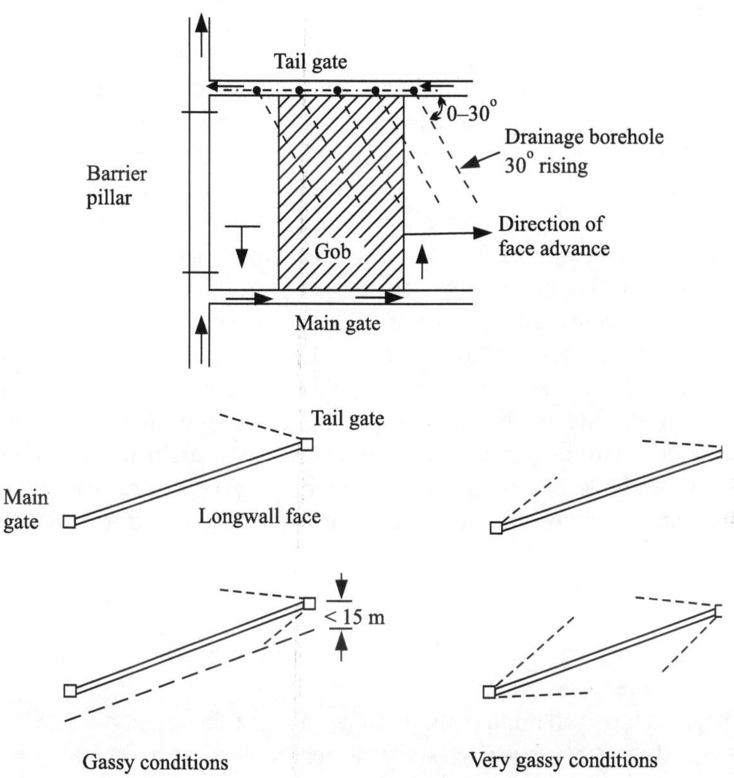

Figure 2.8 Methane drainage through cross-measure boreholes.

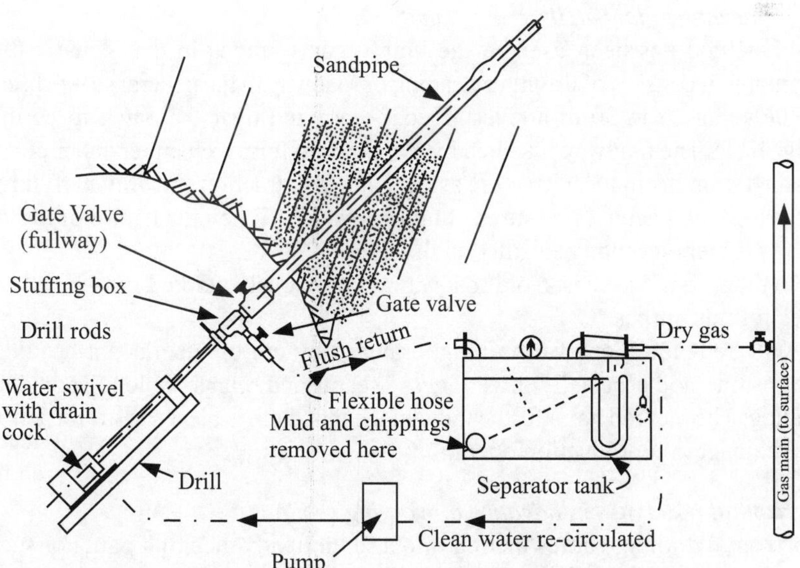

Figure 2.9 Drilling set-up for methane drainage boreholes (Edeco Mini-Hydrack).

The drainage of gas is normally carried out through boreholes from the return gate or the tail gate but drainage from the main gate is also sometimes practised when gassy and very gassy seams occur in the floor of and close to the seam being worked to prevent methane from entering the air stream in the vicinity of electrical apparatus. Drainage of floor strata will permit extraction of a lower seam by retreating longwall. As a rule, boreholes at a distance of 10 to 20 m behind the face begin to yield gas, the yield reaching a maximum from a borehole at a distance of about 40 to 75 m from the face. The yield of gas from a borehole stops at a distance of 100 m behind the face.

Drainage boreholes drilled in the floor of a seam are not as productive as those in the roof due to decreased relaxation and fracture of the floor strata, the relatively short life, and the adverse effect of water of the strata on gas drainage on account of inflow of water into the holes. A larger number of holes in different directions and inclinations will be required. However, drilling of drainage boreholes in the floor is frequently necessary to drain off excessive gas pressures caused by strata movement and to control floor outbursts. The holes are spaced at wider intervals, 40 to 80 m apart and are drilled downwards sub-horizontal to 60° under the waste area.

If an overlying seam causes excessively high methane levels in a mine, the overlying seam can be drained of gas by means of boreholes drilled from the return gate in the lower seam.

With retreat longwall mining, the drainage of strata above and/or below the seam being worked cannot be practised since the boreholes cease to function because of area collapse as the face advances past them. With two tail gates (double entry), however, methane entering the mine opening can be controlled (Fig. 2. 10).

Superjacent headings (Hirschbach method)

This method has been used in the highly gassy mines in the Saar Coalfield, Germany. It consists of driving a heading or roadway in the general strike direction in the strata 20 to 30 m above the coal seam and over the panel to be mined (Fig. 2.11). The roadway is sealed by stoppings to form a chamber and methane is drained from the induced fracture system due to extraction and drawn off through the seal using vacuum pressures of up to 3 m WG. When the nature of the strata allows, boreholes may be drilled in the floor.

In order to reduce costs, old roadways in previously worked-out seams can be used for this purpose.

With retreating longwall mining, drainage by use of superjacent headings is the best method especially in very gassy seams and seams liable to spontaneous heating. The method has a further advantage that there is clear separation between the drainage and production operations.

Horizontal boreholes in advance of working sections

Horizontal drainage holes drilled into a seam in advance of a panel or section (Fig. 2.12) can effectively lower methane emission levels at the working faces by diverting some of the methane in the coal to the holes. The rate at

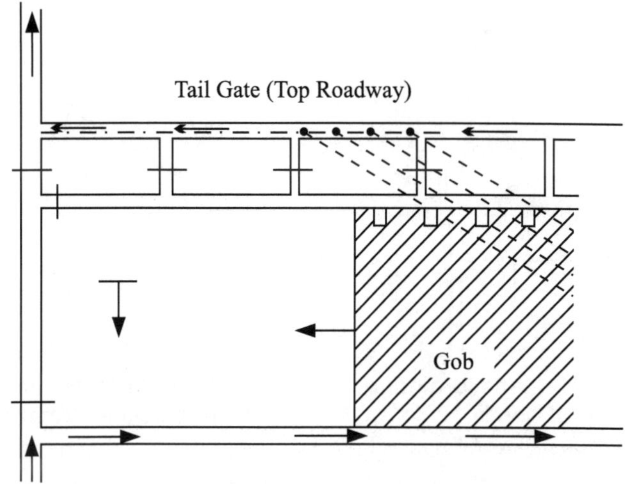

Figure 2.10 Methane drainage with double entry retreating longwall.

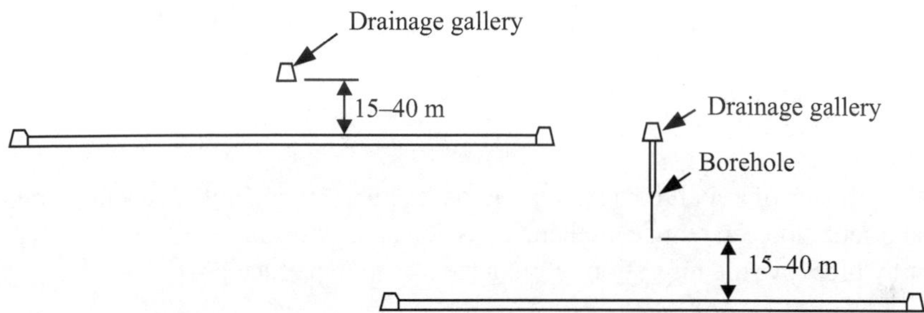

Figure 2.11 Methane drainage through superjacent headings (Hirschbach method).

which the gas can be removed from the section depends on the length of the drainage holes and applied section. Generally, the length of the drainage holes should be at least equal to the width of the section. After the section is advanced halfway along the drainage holes, the hole drilling phase is repeated. This technique is well suited for adoption in deep mines and mines with an inaccessible topography. The drilling programme can be incorporated into the mine development plan.

Horizontal drainage holes may also be drilled on both sides of single coal or stone headings in highly gassy seams during their fast drivage by the use of machines to reduce gas emission into them.

Horizontal boreholes from shafts

The US Bureau of Mines successfully demonstrated that large quantities of methane can be drained through long horizontal boreholes drilled on a radial pattern into a virgin coal seam from the bottom of an air shaft (Fig. 2.13) long before the shaft is needed for ventilation. The advance drainage decreases the gas pressure within the seam over a large area around the shaft and reduces the

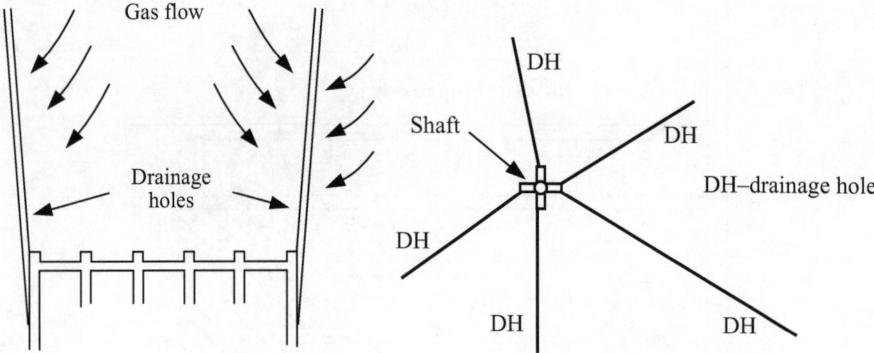

Figure 2.12 Methane drainage through horizontal boreholes in an advancing section.

Figure 2.13 Methane drainage through horizontal boreholes from shaft.

methane load in the ventilating air. The successful application of this technique of de-gassification, however, depends on the *in situ* permeability of the coal seam and the hole direction relative to the cleat. This technique has been successfully applied in some mines in the USA.

Water infusion

Water infusion of a coal seam having a good fracture permeability and a favourable cleat orientation can reduce methane emission at the working face by 80 to 90 per cent by blocking the migration of methane towards the face [34].

Goaf/gob drainage

In very gassy mines, large quantities of methane may flow into the gob from the fractured strata above the coal seam. The large volume of the accumulated gas frequently poses severe ventilation problems. The gob may be drained by gas- or pack-cavities.

Gas cavities or corridors are left in the gob either parallel to the gate roads with open caving of the gob (Fig. 2.14) or parallel to the face in the gob stowed pneumatically (Fig. 2.15). Methane is drained under a low suction from the cavities through pipes connected to the drainage pipeline. In the conventional method, the cavities are constructed of timber lagging and steel wire mesh. This method had been employed as a secondary drainage method in some mines in Germany and France to drain gas which could not be captured by cross-measure boreholes or superjacent headings.

2.1.6.3.1.2 Surface techniques

The surface techniques for methane drainage involve draining the methane from a virgin seam prior to mining as well as drainage of gob areas by means of boreholes drilled from the surface up to a mining depth of 500–600 m. They have several advantages such as gob drainage is independent of coal extraction, there is no

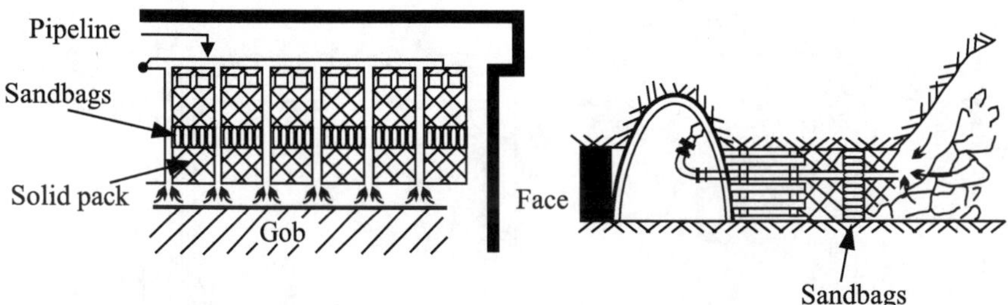

Figure 2.14 Methane drainage through gas cavities with caving of goaf.

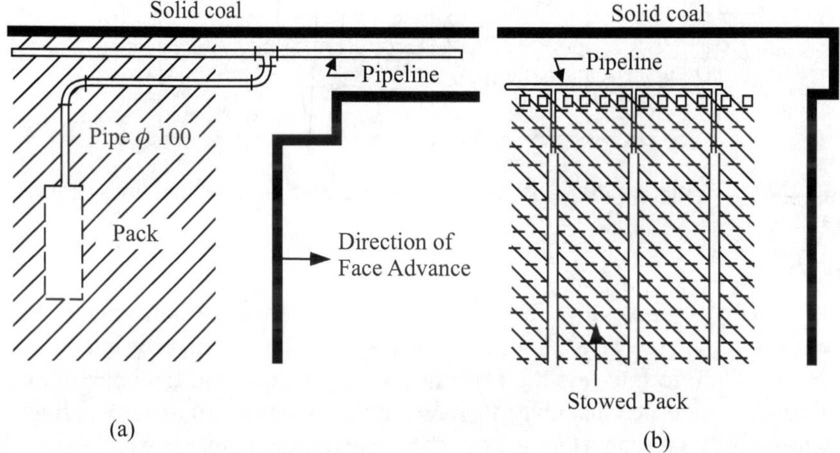

Figure 2.15 Methane drainage through pack-cavities.

necessity of laying a pipeline underground, the amount of drilling required is decreased and the efficiency is high.

Vertical boreholes into virgin coal seam (Fig. 2.16)

In this method, vertical boreholes (less than 250 mm diameter) are drilled into the virgin coal seam. The holes are cased and water in the seam pumped off when methane flows out of the coal. The effectiveness of the gas flow into the borehole depends on the seam permeability and the pressure of the gas. The initial production is normally at low rates. However, by hydraulic stimulation of the coal seam, the naturally occurring fractures in the coal seam are enlarged and extended beyond the borehole by hydraulic pressure and injection of gelled sandbearing water through perforations in the casing. When the water is pumped out, the sand props open the fractures and thus increase the permeability. After stimulation, the drainage is increased several fold. The chief advantage of this technique is that the drainage can be carried out long before mining takes place, but its main disadvantages are that it may cause roof problems during mining due to roof damage, the cost per borehole can be high in difficult terrain, and large quantities of water are required before drainage can start.

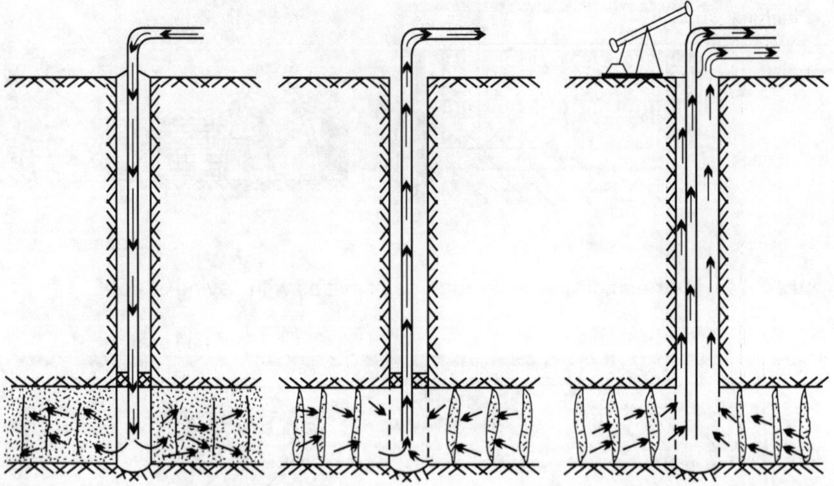

Figure 2.16 Methane drainage through surface vertical boreholes into virgin coal seam.

Slant boreholes into virgin coal seam

This method combines the features of horizontal drainage holes and vertical boreholes from the surface. Slant holes are drilled from the surface by intentionally deflecting them to intersect the seam at a suitable angle and to continue in the coal parallel to the bedding plane thereby maximizing the natural vertical fracture system of the coal seam (Fig. 2.17). Also, one vertical borehole can be used for several slant holes. At present, this technique needs further development before it can become effective and economical. The technique poses problems of bit control and borehole surveying as well as of de-watering.

Vertical boreholes into gob areas (Fig. 2.18)

Gob drainage with vertical boreholes has met with varying degrees of success in the USA and the erstwhile USSR coal mines. The holes are drilled ahead of

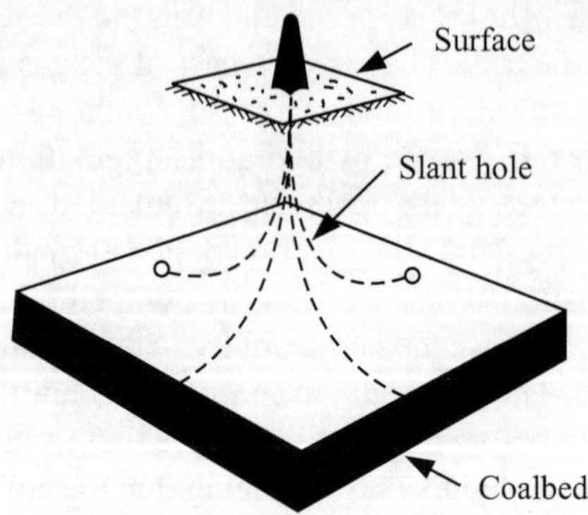

Figure 2.17 Methane drainage through surface slant boreholes info virgin coal seam.

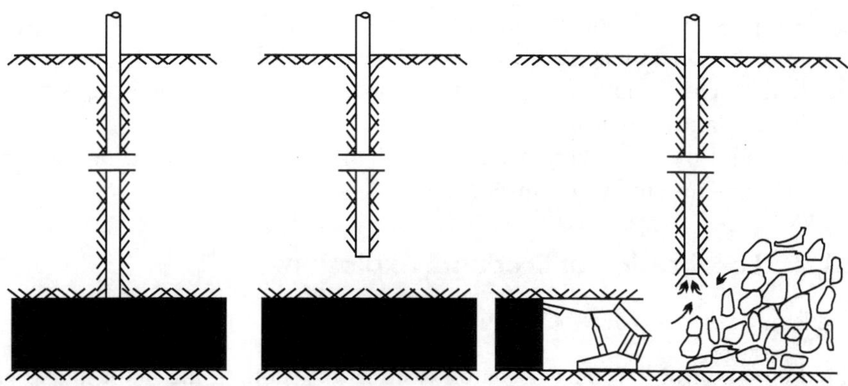

Figure 2.18 Methane recovery through surface vertical boreholes into goaf area.

mining to intersect the seam or terminate in the immediate roof above the seam. When the mining face passes the hole, methane is released into the gob from the fractured strata and flows to the hole to be drawn to the surface. The bottom 30 to 80 m of the cased hole is slotted or perforated to allow the hole to stay open when the roof caves. Experience has shown that large quantities of methane can be removed this way and that methane emission underground is reduced by more than 50 per cent. The method can be economical in shallow mines.

2.1.6.3.2 Control of gas outbursts

In seams liable to gas outbursts, special precautions should be observed in their working . Pre-draining the methane at a controlled rate by advance boreholes, drilling large-diameter de-gassing and de-stressing boreholes in the seam, high-pressure infusion of coal with water or $CaCl_2$ solution (30 per cent), extraction of protective seams, above or below the suspect seam, and de-stress blasting by remote shotfiring (shock or volley firing) are the most important measures against gas outbursts.

2.1.6.3.3 Inspections and reports

In coal mines, inspections should be carried out during every shift in every part of the district which is required to be ventilated to test for:

(a) The presence of methane in the general body of the air in the working places and in mine airways and for oxygen-deficiency, besides examining the state of ventilation, state of the roof and sides, and general safety.

(b) The accumulation of gas at the ends of longwall faces, face rippings, goaf edges, the faces of advanced headings, blind ends, faults, fissures, dykes, and cavities or high places in the roof hanging. To test for methane, an approved methane detector should be used and a permissible flame safety lamp may be used as a supplementary testing device. An early worker warning system may be used in hazardous locations or areas.

(c) The presence of methane before an intentional roof fall in pillar workings; if, in such an examination, the methane level is found to exceed the prescribed limit, such roof falls should not be allowed to take place unless adjustments in ventilation are made.
(d) A record of all measurements should be kept and maintained in the mine office on the surface for inspection.

2.1.7 Localization of firedamp explosions

Firedamp explosions may be localized in the following ways:

(1) Formation of several ventilation districts by splitting the main intake air current so that each district has separate intake and return airways; air-crossings should be avoided as far as practicable or should be constructed of robust construction;
(2) Erecting explosion-proof blasting dams in long development headings in gassy mines (Fig. 2.19);
(3) Adopting measures against initiation of coal-dust explosions and their propagation; and
(4) Maintaining an efficient rescue and recovery organization.

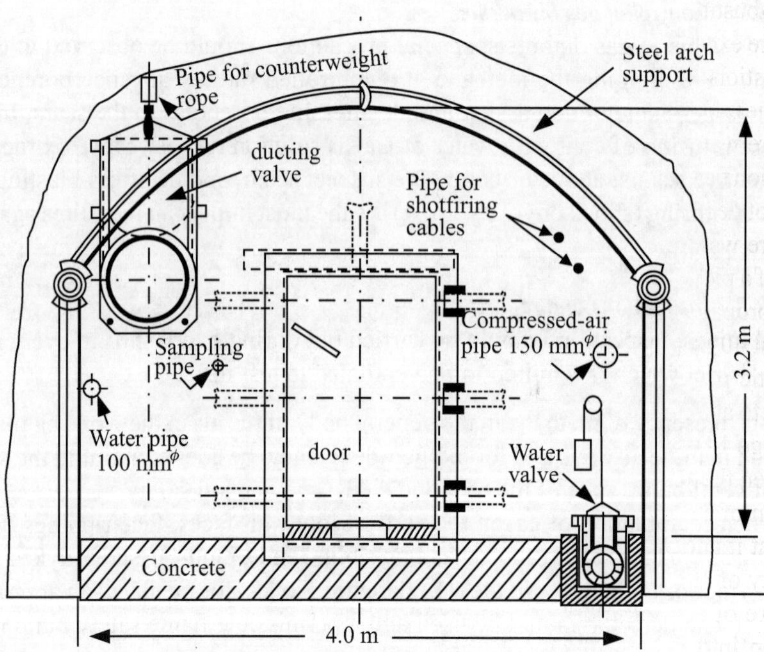

Figure 2.19 Blasting dam/stopping.

2.2 Coal-dust Explosions

A coal-dust or any industrial dust explosion is a sudden combustion process of great intensity characterized by mechanical destructive effects through pressure and heat. For an ignition to take place, the combustible dust must be present in the form of a thick cloud having a definite mixing ratio with oxygen, and a source of ignition of sufficient intensity in the form of flame must be present to initiate a combustion wave.

2.2.1 Development of coal-dust explosions

The exact ignition mechanisms of flammable dust–air mixtures are not clear. The view commonly held at present is that surface oxidation of coal-dust particles, partial de-volatilization of solid coal particles, ignition of the volatiles–air mixture in the space between particles, and combustion of solid particles are conjointly responsible for the development of a coal-dust explosion. Experience has shown that a coal-dust explosion often develops in stages. The first stage of ignition is often a puff which is a sudden combustion of a part or the whole of the airborne dust marked by a very high temperature but without any dynamic effects. If the whole of the dust is consumed, the combustion of the dust–air mixture ends with the puff. On the other hand, if a part of the dust is consumed, the puff may eventually lead to an intense main explosion. During the transition from the puff to the explosion, there takes place an increase in pressure in the burning layers due to the transfer of the heat of combustion to the surrounding unburnt layers, mainly by radiation. When the pressure exceeds a certain value, a full-fledged explosion is developed in which the combustion takes place at such a rapid rate (velocity of propagation) that the whole of the heat liberated is transferred without loss to the surrounding unburnt layers. A pressure wave is developed which passes through the unburnt layers ahead of the explosion flame. Once the pressure wave is formed, the propagation of the explosion does not depend any more upon the presence of a flammable dust–air mixture. The pressure wave will itself stir up the deposited dust, creating necessary fuel in the form of a pioneering cloud for the following flame. Thus, the dispersion of dust and flame propagation processes are intercoupled. In general, in the run-up zone which is about 40 to 60 m or more, the flame velocity increases from 0 to about 100 m/s, the static pressure amounts to about 0.5 bar, and the dynamic pressure increases from 0 to about 10 kN/m^2. In a fully-developed explosion, the static pressure lies in the range 1–3 bar and the dynamic pressure between 10 and 50 kN/m^2.

When the rate of propagation of an explosion assumes the greatest values, the ignition of a dust–air mixture takes place at the instant of arrival of the pressure wave at it and the explosion assumes the character of a detonation with a flame velocity of 1000 m/s or more, static pressure between 5 and 10 bar and dynamic pressure of about 100 kN/m^2 [35]. In practice, however, dust explosions do not develop into detonations, being governed by the amount of fine dust and the characteristics of the dust–air mixtures.

2.2.2 Flammability or explosive limits

The flammability or explosiveness of a dust is defined as its ability, when in the form of a cloud, to spread or propagate ignition to all points where dust–air mixtures of corresponding concentration are present.

Like methane–air mixtures, a heterogeneous coal dust–air mixture has lower and upper limits of flammability or explosive limits, but the range of flammability is very wide, much wider than in the case of firedamp mixtures.

The lower or lean flammability limit is not an absolute quantity. It depends on the particle size and the chemical composition of the dust, nature and intensity of the igniting source, time of contact with the source, turbulence of the dust cloud, uniformity of dust dispersion, purity of the sample, and the composition of the atmosphere, specially the methane and oxygen contents. USBM researches on Pittsburgh and Pocohontas Seams coal dusts [36] showed that the lower limit is independent of the particle size for all sizes below some threshold or characteristic value above which the limit increases significantly with increase in particle size until a critical size is reached above which the dust cloud is non-explosive at any concentration or entirely non-ignitible at any reasonable temperature (Fig. 2.20). Bituminous coals have a lower limit of flammability which is variously reported to vary widely between 30 and 300 g/Nm^3 [37].

The upper limit of flammability or upper explosive limit is indefinite and has not been determined because of experimental difficulties of maintaining dust clouds of high concentrations. The upper limit is of little practical utility as it is unlikely ever to be reached under mining conditions.

As with methane–air mixtures, explosions of limit dust–air mixtures are weak. Curves obtained by plotting explosion pressures and rates of pressure rise against concentration show that the explosion pressure and rates of pressure rise are at a minimum at the lower limit of concentration and then gradually increase until an

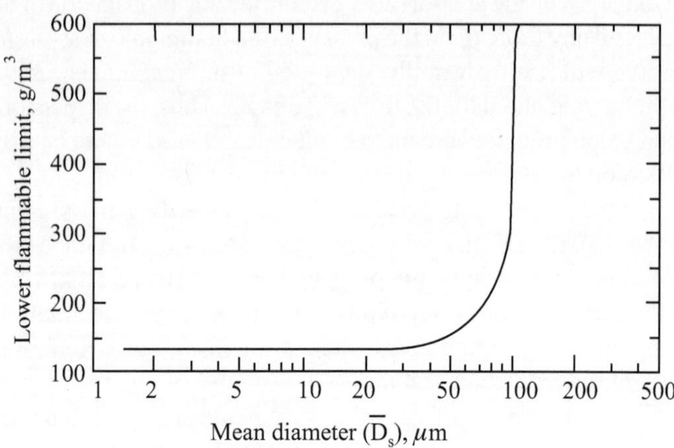

Figure 2.20 Lower flammable limit as a function of particle size for Pittsburg coal dust using 8-litre test chamber at 25°C (USBM).

optimum concentration is reached, after which they slowly decrease with further increase in concentration. The most violent explosions are produced when the concentration is about 10 times the lower limit (400 to 500 g/Nm^3) although for complete combustion only 113 g/Nm^3 (pure carbon) would be sufficient. With dust concentrations greater than the optimum, absorption of heat by the unburnt dust is apparently the reason for less than maximum explosion pressures.

2.2.3 Ignition of Coal Dust–Air Mixtures

Ignition of dust–air mixtures is not so rapidly brought about as with gas–air mixtures. In general, a rather larger source of heat is required. The ignition temperature of a coal-dust cloud depends on the rank of the coal, nature and intensity of ignition source, particle size, moisture and ash contents, and oxygen concentration. It is usually determined in the laboratory as the lowest furnace temperature at which a given size of dust ignites when dispersed into the furnace of a standard test apparatus (1.2-litre Hartmann furnace in the U.S.A) as a uniform cloud. The temperature so measured is also referred to as the minimum thermal auto-ignition temperature (AIT) as the explosion of a dust cloud is caused by its intrinsic reactivity at an elevated temperature. The ignition temperature decreases as the rank of the coal decreases from the anthracites to sub-bituminous coals. It varies between 900°C and 600°C for relatively low-ash coals. Moisture in dust particles and in the surrounding atmosphere raises the ignition temperature of the dust because of the heat absorbed for heating and vaporization of the moisture. With decreasing oxygen concentration, the ignition temperature increases. Figure 2.21 shows the minimum auto-ignition temperature as a function of particle size for Pittsburg and Pocohontas coal dust obtained using the 1.2-litre Hartmann furnace [36].

The electrical ignitibility of a coal dust is determined by using an electric spark source for ignition of dust clouds. The minimum spark ignition energy of a dust

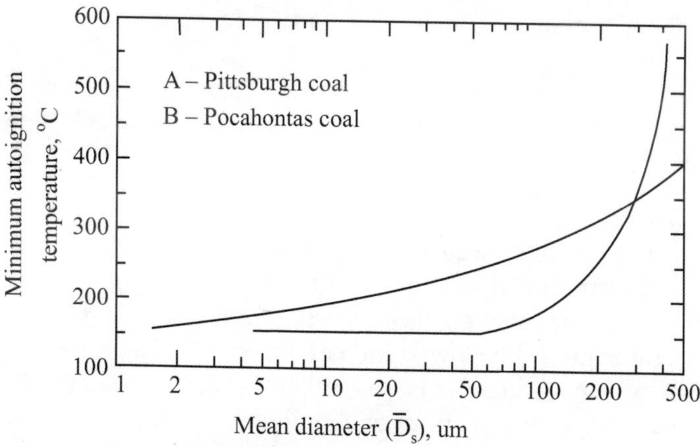

Figure 2.21 Minimum auto-ignition temperature of Pittsburg and Pocahonta coal dusts as a function of particle size using 1.2–1 Hartmann furnace (USBN).

cloud decreases with increasing temperature of the dust cloud. The minimum spark energy for electrical ignition of dust clouds of different coals lies between 40 and 120 mJ.

The very large amount of coal-dust explosion test data obtained by the US Bureau of Mines [37] show that the ignitibility characteristics of a dust must be separated from the propagation characteristics.

2.2.4 Factors affecting development of coal-dust explosions

The flammability or explosibility of coal dust–air mixtures has been the subject of many investigations carried out in laboratories, surface experimental galleries, and experimental coal mines in many coal mining countries of the world. The work in experimental coal mines centred around the origin, propagation, and control of coal-dust explosions.

The following physical and chemical factors exercise an important influence on the flammability of coal dust–air mixtures and propagation and control of coal-dust explosions in mines.

Particle size

Thermal ignitibility studies on coals of different volatile contents have shown that coal-dust particles up to 750 to 1000 μm [36] take part in explosion, depending on the rank of the coal, nature and intensity of the ignition source, and oxygen concentration and that fine particles control the ignition, violence, and speed of flame propagation. Dangerous are the particles which lie between 10 and 100 μm size. The loss of flammability of dust below the 10 μm size is explained as due to chemical decomposition of dust at that degree of fineness, a tendency to agglomerate, and rapid oxidation on initial exposure to air, thereby becoming less easily ignitible. At larger particle sizes, the rate of de-volatilization decreases rapidly due to the relatively short pre-heating time available. This tends to limit the overall rate of flame propagation through the mixture and the mass concentration of dust required to produce a limit concentration of combustible volatiles increases markedly [36].

Decrease in particle size also increases the capacitance of dust clouds with possible development of electrostatic discharges of sufficient intensity under suitable conditions, which may ignite a dust cloud.

Dustiness of mine workings

It is customary to express the quantity of deposited dust in g/m^3 of mine excavation and the concentration of airborne dust in g/Nm^3 of air, though, without knowledge of the particle size distribution, these expressions are meaningless.

The determination of the lowest limit of the deposited dust in a mine working at which an explosion can occur is very difficult as the whole of the dust need not necessarily be suspended in air for an ignition to take place. From experiments conducted in experimental mines [25], it had been found that a mine working is dangerously dusty if it contains 100 to 120 g/m^3 and that the most violent explosions occur at 300 to 400 g/m^3.

The minimum density of a dust cloud, which will propagate an explosion, depends on the nature of the source of ignition, fineness of the dust, rank of the coal, and other parameters. The dust cloud must be dense immediately surrounding the ignition source so that one cannot see through it. As the dust concentration in mine air currents is not sufficient to propagate an explosion, the explosion must stir up the deposited dust along its path to create a cloud for its propagation.

Figure 2.22 shows a typical thermal ignitibility curve for a coal dust showing the relation between the ignition temperature and the coal-dust concentration. It represents the boundary between ignitable and non-ignitible mass concentrations at a given thermal ignition temperature. It will be seen that the minimum value of the ignition temperature is approached asymptotically at the higher dust concentrations.

Volatile matter content

The flammability of a coal dust depends greatly on its combustible volatile matter; it increases with increasing volatile content. The volatile matter is usually calculated on a dry, ash-free basis using the formula.

$$\% \text{ VM} = \frac{\% \text{ VM (from analysis)} \times 100}{100 - \% \text{ ash} - \% \text{ moisture}}$$

As the right-hand side of the above formula may be written as

$$\frac{\% \text{ VM}}{\%\text{VM} + \% \text{ FC}}$$

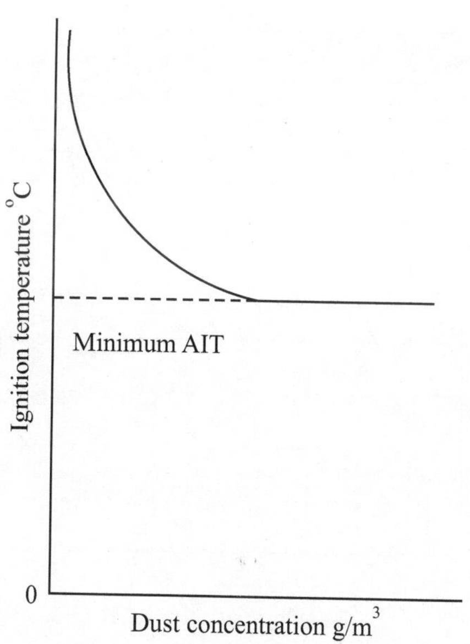

Figure 2.22 A typical thermal ignitibility curve for a bituminous coal dust in air.

the percentage of volatile matter on a dry, ash-free basis is sometimes called the volatile-combustible ratio or simply the volatile ratio of coal.

Several investigations in laboratories, surface experimental galleries, and experimental coal mines on the flammability of coal dusts had shown that coal dusts with VM < 10 per cent are non-flammable, those with VM = 10 to 14 per cent are less flammable, whilst those with VM > 14 per cent are highly flammable. The increase in flammability, however, is different for different coals. For low-volatile coals, the flammability measured by the amount of incombustible required to prevent explosion flame propagation, increases almost linearly with increasing volatile ratio. But above about 25 per cent, the volatile ratio in the range of medium-and high-volatile bituminous coals, the flammability rises only slightly with increasing volatile ratio. From statistics of coal-dust explosions in the coal mines of Germany and the UK, it was noticed that explosions did not take place with coal dust containing less than 20 per cent volatile matter (DAF).

Figure 2.23 shows the effect of volatile matter (DAF basis) on the flammability of American Coals [38].

Percentage of ash

An increase in ash content or presence of inert foreign material reduces the ignitibility or flammability of coal dust because of heat absorption. Stone-dusting in coal mines is a practical application of the use of inert dust to prevent an explosion from taking place.

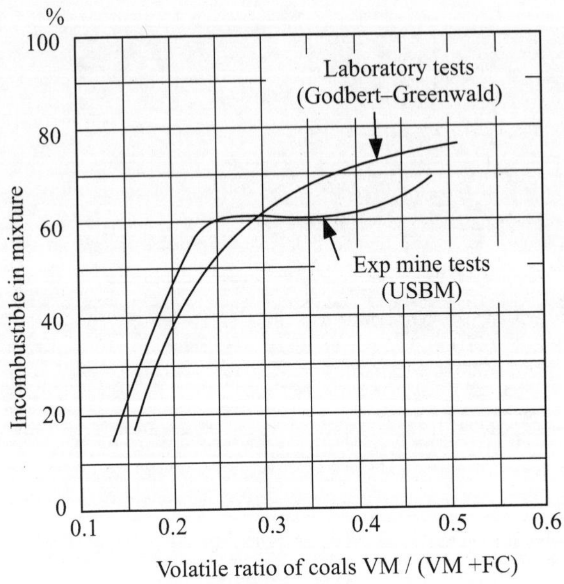

Figure 2.23 Variation of flammability with volatile ratio of American Coals.

Percentage of moisture
Moisture in dust particles raises the ignition temperature of the dust. It exerts a cooling effect because heat is absorbed during its heating and vaporization, thereby reducing the energy available for ignition of the dust cloud. It also tends to wet and agglomerate the fine particles of dust, reducing their dispersability. Coal dust loses its dispersability with a moisture content of 25 to 30 per cent. It loses explosibility at 50% moisture content. The effect of moisture on flammability is unimportant below about 10 per cent.

The drying out of the deep mine workings due to air currents increases the hazard due to coal dust in winter more than in summer months.

Oxygen concentration
Variations in oxygen concentration affect the ease of ignition of dust clouds and the explosion pressures. With decreasing oxygen concentration, the ignition energy required increases, ignition temperature increases, and maximum explosion pressure decreases.

Nature and intensity of ignition source
The nature and intensity of the ignition source (temperature, size of spark or flame, etc.) exert a great influence on the flammability of the mine dust under mining conditions as they determine the dust-raising capacity and turbulence induced within the cloud. Explosions initiated by strong sources develop faster and cause more damage than explosions initiated by weak sources. The igniting sources more often than not are the flame of an exploding firedamp, flame accompanying the detonation of an explosive, or an electric spark caused by a damaged electric cable.

Percentage of firedamp in mine air
The presence of firedamp in air in percentages less than its own lower limit reduces the lower explosive limit of coal dust by replacing the coal on a weight thermal basis. One per cent CH_4 (by volume) in $1 m^3$ of air is equivalent to about 12 g of coal dust. The flammability of coal dust increases almost directly in proportion to the percentage of firedamp (Fig. 2.24) [39].

Turbulence
As the combustion of dust takes place at the surface of the dust particles, the rate of reaction, therefore, depends on how intimately the dust and oxygen are mixed. Turbulent mixing of dust and air will result in more violent explosions than those caused by ignition in relatively quiescent mixtures.

Surrounding conditions
The size, shape, constrictions, obstructions, branching, length, and nature and condition of the surfaces of mine workings exert an important influence on the development of coal-dust explosions as they increase or decrease the progress of a flame by holding or releasing the pressure.

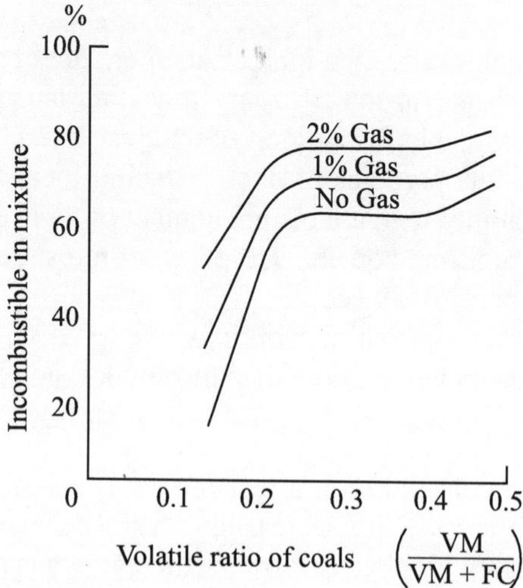

Fig. 2.24 Effect of firedamp on flammability of coal-dust clouds.

2.2.5 Explosion characteristics of coal dust

Flame or explosion temperature

The maximum flame temperatures occur at stoichiometric concentrations. The theoretical calculated flame temperature for stoichiometric mixtures is about 2500°K (at constant volume). In practice, the temperatures obtained lie between 800° and 1000°C [40]

Maximum explosion pressure

Maximum explosion pressures up to 7 bar have been obtained experimentally for dusts of different coals. They depend on the rank of the coal, particle size, concentration, and turbulence.

The rate of pressure rise is the ratio of the increase in explosion pressure to the time interval of that increase during which energy is released. The maximum rate of pressure rise is obtained at the steepest slope of the pressure–time curve. The destructiveness of a dust explosion depends primarily upon the rate of pressure rise. The rates of pressure rise are, however, less than with gas explosions. In practice, a dust cloud is rarely ignited under optimum concentration conditions for development of maximum explosion pressures.

Another expression, the 'peak explosion pressure ratio' is sometimes used. It is defined as the ratio of maximum explosion pressure to the initial pressure at ignition with a small correction for the pressure rise caused by the ignition source by itself.

$$\text{Peak pressure ratio} = \frac{P_{max} - \Delta P(\text{ignitor})}{P_{initial}}$$

where P_{max} is the maximum explosion pressure (absolute) during an experiment, ΔP (ignitor) is the pressure rise due to the ignitor ignition source by itself and $P_{initial}$ is the pressure prior to ignition (~I atm absolute).

Rate of propagation of explosion flame or flame velocity

Velocities of propagation of explosion flame up to 2000 m/s or more (usually 200 to 300 m/s) are encountered in mines. In a roadway of constant cross-section which is more or less uniformly dusty, the velocity of flame propagation and explosion pressure increase with the distance from the seat of the explosion. The velocity is greatly affected by sudden variations in cross-section of the mine workings through which the explosion passes, the amount of dispersed stone dust, and the pressure release into adjacent areas.

The average burning velocity of a coal dust–air mixture is given by the ratio

$$\frac{\text{Average flame speed}}{\text{Expansion ratio}} = \frac{\text{Max.travel distance}}{\text{Time to peak pressure}} \times \frac{1}{\text{Expansion ratio}}$$

The expansion ratio is the density of the unburnt mixture divided by the density of the burnt gas combustion products. The finer dusts are characterized by maximum burning velocities in the range of 30 to 35 cm/s, while the very coarse dusts are characterized by maximum velocities as low as 10 cm/s [37].

Indices for rating the relative explosibility hazard of coal dusts

The severity and destructiveness of an explosion from a coal dust are related to its ease of ignition, maximum explosion pressure, maximum rate of pressure rise, and confinement. The relative explosibility hazard of coal dusts is determined by comparison of their flammability data between themselves or with those obtained for a standard size dust of a coal seam chosen as a standard. The following terms, indices, and coefficients are used:

Ignition sensitivity

It is a function of the ignition temperature and minimum ignition energy [41].

Ignition sensitivity

$$\frac{\text{Ign. Temp.} \times \text{Min.Ing.Energy} \times \text{Min.Conc. Standard Coal Dust}}{(\text{Ign.Temp.} \times \text{Min.Ign. Engergy} \times \text{Min.Conc.})\text{ Sample dust}}$$

Ignition severity

It is a function of the maximum explosion pressure and the maximum rate of pressure rise.

Ignition severity =

$$\frac{\text{(Max.Explo.Press} \times \text{Max.Rate of Press.Rise) Sample dust}}{\text{(Max.Explo.Press} \times \text{Max.Rate of Press.Rise) Standard coal dust}}$$

Explosibility Index = Ignition Sensitivity × Explosion Severity

Depending on the explosibility index, the coal-dust explosions may be classified as follows [41]:

Type of explosion	Explosibility index
Weak	< 0.1
Moderate	0.1–1.0
Strong	1.0–10
Severe	> 10

Index ratings based on the above have, however, fallen out of favour.

In Germany, a coefficient of explosibility is calculated from data obtained on coal-dust explosion in large closed test vessels as

$$k_{ex} = \sqrt{(\text{Max.rate of pressure rise} \times \text{avg. rate of press.rise})} \text{ bar/s}$$

The explosibility factor or simply the explosibility of a coal-dust deposit is given by

$$Z = \frac{S}{100 - S}$$

where S is the amount of total inert matter (per cent) that must be present in a unit mass of coal dust to prevent flame propagation through the mixture as determined by test.

Explosion gases

As the oxygen of the mine air is nearly always not enough for complete combustion of all the dust present in mine workings through which the explosion flame passes, carbon monoxide is always found in the explosion gases in concentrations up to as high as 14 per cent. The toll of lives taken by a coal-dust explosion is not merely due to the effects of the explosion flame or force but mainly due to the breathing of the poisonous carbon monoxide gas.

Formation of coke crust and soot deposits

In a coal-dust explosion, its pressure wave and flame radiate intense heat which can melt metals and convert organic matter into coke and ash. Owing to insufficient oxygen, only a part of the coal dust is completely burnt into ash whilst the remaining dust gets coked and deposited as characteristic crust or globules on roadway supports and on the sides and roof of the roadways through which the explosion passes. The presence of visible traces of coke crust after an explosion depends on the caking properties of the coal. Bituminous coals yield larger coke crusts than non-coking coals which yield granular crusts.

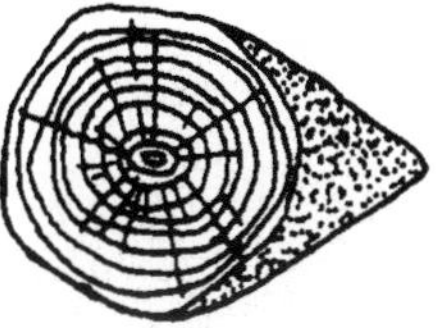

Figure 2.25 Coke crust on bars and props.

Experience with large explosions in mines has often shown that the coke crust is invariably formed on the reverse or sheltered side of the roadway supports or projections (Fig. 2.25) and that it is found on the 'windward' side of the supports or projections near the seat of the explosion. In small explosions with velocities, on the other hand, the coke crust is formed on all sides of the supports. Experiments in the US Bureau of Mines Experimental Coal Mine [42] showed that an explosion flame can traverse an area without producing coke and that as the explosion flame velocity increases, the amount of coke produced decreases.

Soot is deposited in and beyond the area traversed by the explosion flame. Soot deposits are generally thicker in the explosion area. Soot may be deposited as a continuous layer on horizontal surfaces or form a lacy network or stringers at the roof and on vertical surfaces.

2.2.6 Comparison of coal dust and firedamp

Coal dust and firedamp have many common properties besides their characteristic features:

(1) Both have lower and upper limits of flammability. Explosions of limit mixtures are weak.
(2) The ignition temperature of firedamp is 650° to 750°C while that of dry airborne dust is 600° to 900°C.
(3) The heats of combustion and explosion temperatures are nearly the same.
(4) The flammability of firedamp is generally the same throughout the mine. On the other hand, the ignition and flammability of dust in mine workings vary greatly, depending on fineness, volatile matter, ash, moisture, etc.
(5) The propagation of firedamp explosions takes place due to conduction of heat. With coal-dust explosions, on the other hand, radiation of intense heat by the pressure wave as well as the explosion flame plays an important part in their propagation.
(6) The maximum pressures developed in some dust explosions are higher than in firedamp explosions. The rates of pressure rise are, however, generally lower than those obtained in firedamp explosions.
(7) Coal-dust explosions are frequently more disastrous in their effects than firedamp explosions because of their longer duration.
(8) With firedamp explosions, carbon monoxide is frequently found. With coal-dust explosions, on the other hand, carbon monoxide is always found.

(9) The ignition of a coal-dust explosion even with the strongest igniting source requires at least 100 ms, while with a firedamp explosion only 1 to 2 ms is required [43].

(10) The velocity of propagation of coal-dust explosions is generally higher than that of firedamp explosions.

2.2.7 Dust explosion test apparatus

Various types of apparatus for studying the flammability behaviour of coal dust– air mixtures have been described in the literature on coal-dust explosions. The different types of test chambers used and varying procedures adopted make it difficult to compare results obtained by them. Over the years, larger and more spherical test chambers have been developed with uniform dust dispersion and adequate strength of the ignition source for hard-to-ignite dusts and dust-inhibitor mixtures which would give dust explosion data that correlate well with large-scale tests and experimental mine results. In these test chambers, it is possible to measure the lower and upper limits of flammability, explosion pressures and rates of pressure rise, explosion temperatures, minimum ignition energies, minimum oxygen concentrations for flammability, and amounts of inhibitors necessary to prevent explosions.

Figure 2.26 gives a diagrammatic arrangement of the Godbert–Greenwald apparatus formerly used to evaluate the thermal ignitibility of dust clouds. It consists essentially of an electrically-heated vertical cylindrical tube (Alundum 3.9 cm × 23 cm) furnace through which a weighed amount of coal dust is projected downwards as a uniform cloud by a controlled blast of air directed at the dust

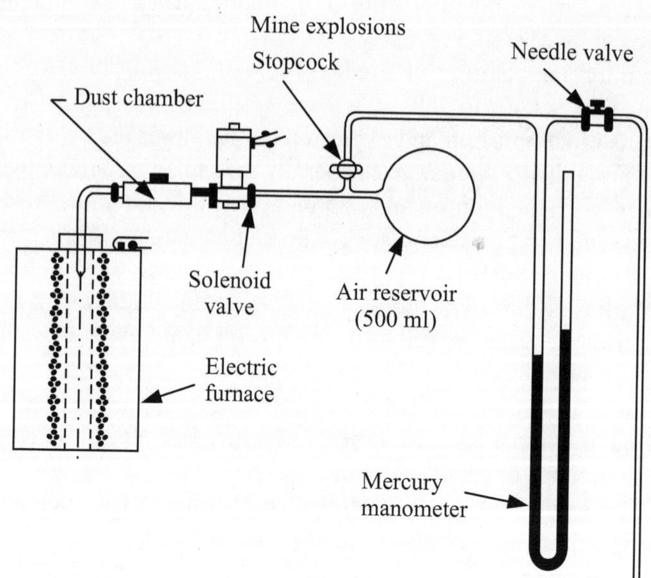

Figure 2.26 Godbert–Greenwald apparatus.

sample placed in a small chamber at the top of the tube. The lowest temperature of the furnace at which flame issues out of the open bottom end of the tube gives the thermal ignition point.

The Godbert–Greenwald furnace suffers from the drawbacks that the dust cloud is not completely confined within the furnace and its concentration is not accurately known, short exposure time of the dust cloud in the high-temperature region, and uncertainty as to the vertical temperature uniformity.

An improved version of the above furnace is the 1.2-litre cylindrical Hartmann ceramic furnace or the bomb developed in the 1930s which became a standard dust explosibility apparatus in the USA and which generated the largest amount of dust explosion data. This apparatus, however, has serious deficiencies such as non-uniform dust dispersion, inadequacy of the ignition source for many dusts, and lack of agreement with large-scale tests. An 8-litre flammability chamber was developed by the US Bureau of Mines for coal-dust and gas explosion studies. Figure 2.27 gives a schematic diagram of the chamber and the air-dispersion tank. The instrumentation includes a pressure transducer, an oxygen sensor, and an optical dust probe. The pressure transducer measures partial pressures when mixing gases and also explosion pressures after ignition. The oxygen analyzer uses a polarographic method to measure the partial pressure of oxygen. The optical dust probe is used to study the dust dispersion by measuring the attenuation of near-infrared light at a wavelength of 0.95 μm. The standard ignitor is an array of four electrically activated pyrotechnic matches which deposit their energy (140 J) in about 0.05 s. The conical dispersion cup significantly improves the effectiveness and reproducibility of the dust dispersion.

The normal procedure is to spread a measured mass of dust uniformly around the disperser cone, partially evacuate the chamber to about 0.2 to 0.3 atm, disperse the dust by an air impulse injected by the air-dispersion tank (pressurized to 5 atm), raising the chamber pressure to 1.0 atm, and energise the ignition source, allowing 0.1 s after the duration of the air impulse (0.2 s).

The 8-litre chamber produced much valuable data on the flammability of coals and other dusts. Owing to the limitation of the maximum ignition energy that could be used and use of test chambers up to 1 m^3 in European countries, the Bureau of Mines developed a 20-litre explosibility test chamber (Fig. 2.28) which can be used for explosibility testing of dusts, gases, and their mixtures using stronger ignition sources at lower and higher initial pressures. The data obtained have shown good agreement with data obtained from full-scale tests in an experimental mine [28].

At the Bergbau-Versuchssrecke (Mining Experimental Gallery), Dortmund Derne, Germany, test chambers of 1.2-litre to 30 m^3 capacity are available for coal-dust explosibility studies. For routine testing, 1m^3 and 40-litre capacity test chambers are used. Figure 2.29 shows the 40-litre test chamber [44]. The dust to be tested is kept at a pressure of 9 bar(g) in a dust chamber outside the test vessel. It is dispersed after the opening of the solenoid valve and, after a delay of 170 ms, a chemical ignitor (5 kJ) ignites the dust cloud. The explosion pressure variation

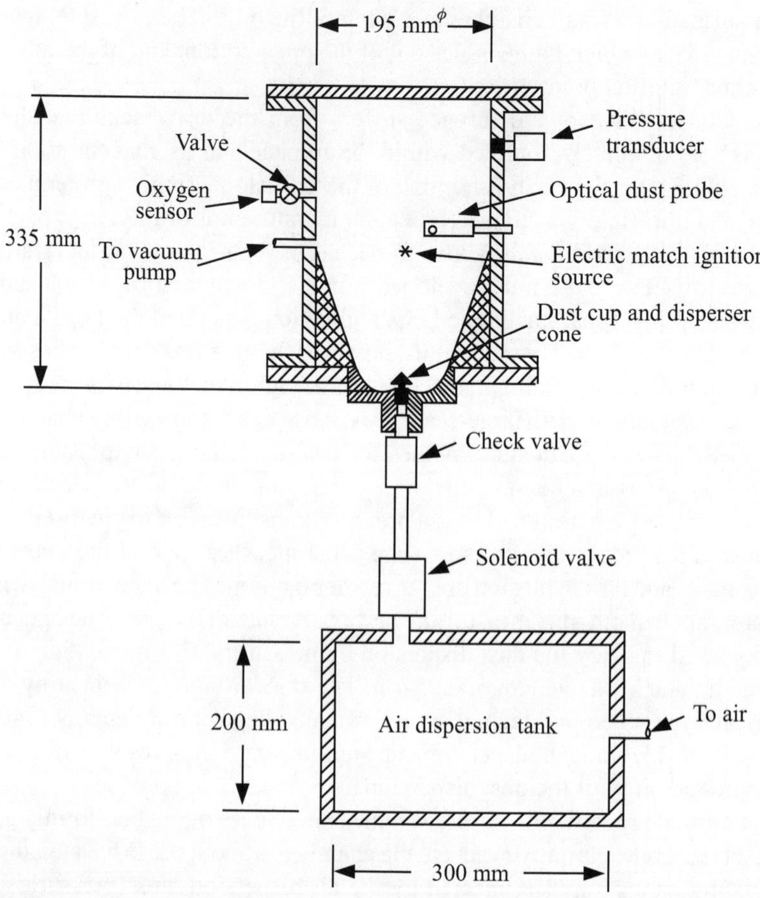

Figure 2.27 USBM 8-litre flammability chamber.

with time is recorded from which a coefficient of explosibility is calculated (Fig. 2.30).

2.2.8 Causes of coal-dust explosions in mines

In practice, the causes that bring about ignition of flammable dust–air mixtures are very similar to those operating in the ignition of flammable methane–air mixtures, but the explosion hazard, in general, is rather greater as coal dust is a normal accompaniment of the coal winning process and can be easily raised into the mine air as a dust cloud, particularly in winter when danger of dust explosions is likely to be more when the mine air is drier. For a coal-dust explosion to take place in mines, two conditions must be fulfilled. The dust must be present as a dense cloud and a source of ignition in the form of a flame must be present.

The various causes of direct ignition of a dust cloud can be classified as

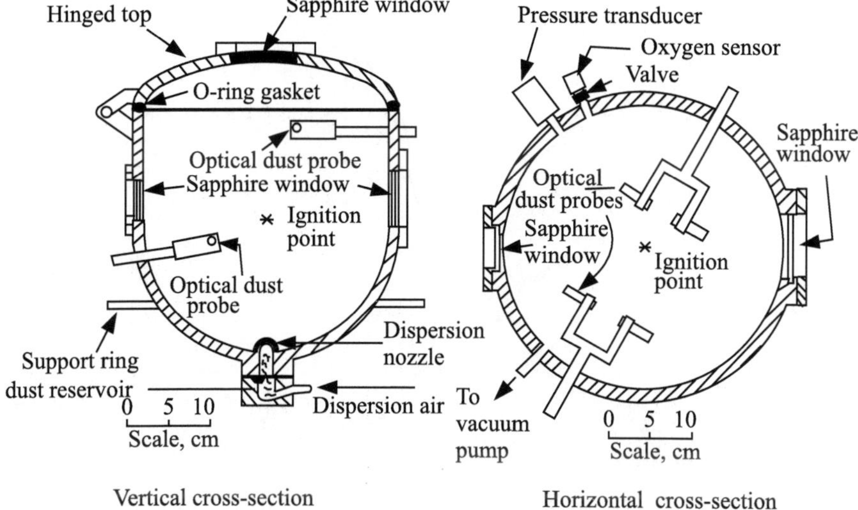

Figure 2.28 U.S.B.M.20-*l* Explosibility test chamber.

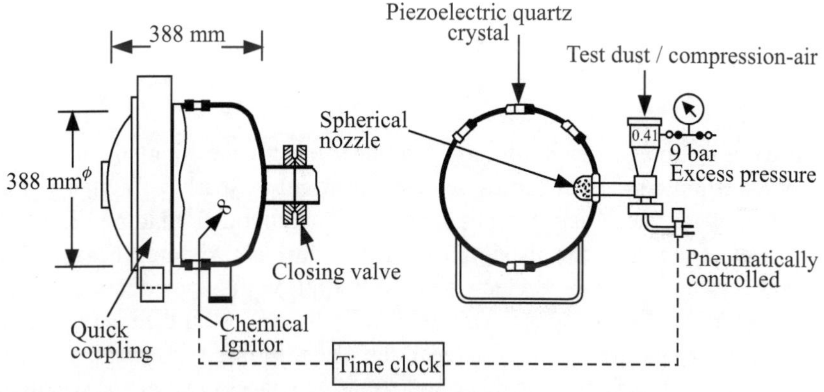

Figure 2.29 German 40–*l* explosibility test chamber.

(a) naked flames
(b) friction
(c) electric sparks
(d) firedamp explosions

Naked flames

A naked flame is the easiest means of igniting a dust cloud as the source of heat is of considerable size and a larger part of the dust cloud can be heated.

Friction

Hot surfaces as a result of mechanical friction, such as overheated bearings, may ignite surrounding explosive dusty atmospheres.

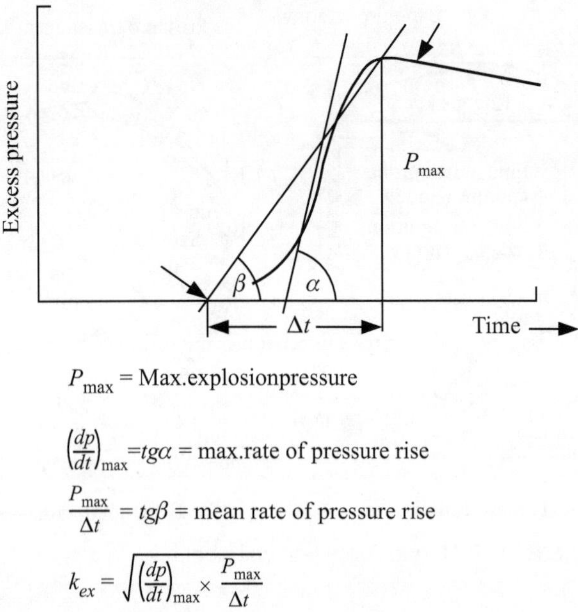

Figure 2.30 Calculation of coefficient of explosibility.

Electric sparks

Electric sparks from short-circuiting and arcing at electrical equipment or overhead trolley wires may ignite an explosive dust–air mixture. Sparks of higher voltage and amperage are necessary than in the case of flammable firedamp mixtures.

Static electric sparks can also ignite explosive dust–air mixtures. Fine particles of dust may readily become electrified by friction with air or ducting through which they pass. As the electric charge on a body resides on the surface, a dust cloud has a very large capacity. Under suitable conditions, a discharge or sudden recombination of separated positive and negative charges can occur which can then act as a source of ignition. With increasing humidity, however, the electric potential falls.

Firedamp explosions

A firedamp explosion is the commonest source of initiation of a coal-dust explosion. Besides posing the danger of such direct ignition, a firedamp explosion may raise the deposited dust from the mine floor, sides, or roof into mine air very quickly before its flame has ceased and then propagate as a coal-dust explosion. A very small gas explosion initiated by accidental ignition of a small quantity of flammable firedamp mixture (approximately 0.4 m^3 volume may thus bring about a much bigger coal-dust explosion. This danger is particularly great in long headings than on long coal faces due to the low air velocities and a lack of adequate pressure relief except in one direction towards the entrance of the heading. An explosion in pure coal dust may not develop when layered gas is ignited or when the gas is ignited at the outbye end. It is significant that most firedamp explosions do not develop into coal-dust explosions due to their failure to raise a sufficiently dense dust cloud.

2.2.9 Prevention and suppression of coal-dust explosions

It is well-known that it is much easier to prevent a coal-dust explosion being initiated than to suppress one.

The measures for prevention and suppression of coal-dust explosions can be divided into the following three groups:

2.2.9.1 Measures which prevent or reduce formation and dissemination of coal dust underground

The elimination of coal dust in mines would be the logical means of eliminating coal-dust explosion hazard, but unfortunately, this is virtually, impossible. Much can, however, be done to reduce the formation, distribution and accumulation of coal dust in mine workings.

The following important measures should be adopted:

(i) On longwall faces, water infusion of the coal face to reduce respirable dust at low or high water pressures where the seam and adjacent strata allow. The different methods of infusion of coal *in situ* before it is mined as practised in European mines are shown in Fig. 2.31. Infusion is generally practised on faces in seams which are ploughable. As it is difficult to infuse fast-moving mechanized faces with non-cyclical mining, the method of long (deep)-hole low-pressure infusion by means of holes drilled into the seam parallel to the face in advance of the coal face from the advanced gate roads will be the most satisfactory method. Long-hole high-pressure infusion may also be applied as a larger area of coal can be infused. The effectiveness of coal face infusion depends on the amount of water injected and its uniform distribution in coal. The amount of water required lies between 8 and 10 litres per solid cubic metre of coal. Insertion of a solid calcium chloride cartridge into the infusion hole prior to infusion has been shown to decrease the total dust make considerably (up to 50 per cent) [45]. Water mixed with surfactants improves dust suppression compared to plain water. The disadvantages of wetting of coal seams before its extraction are consumption of considerable amounts of water and energy and the possibility of wetting a whole section of the seam.

(ii) Wet winning of coal using wet pneumatic picks where used.

(iii) With machine-cutting by means of coal cutters, using sharp picks of a suitable type, selecting optimal cutting and travelling speeds of the machine, using gummer and wet-cutting; with continuous miners by using scrubbers on them.

(iv) When blasting in coal, use of stemming cartridges or ampoules of calcium chloride powder containing 82 to 85 per cent $CaCl_2$ and 15 to 18 per cent

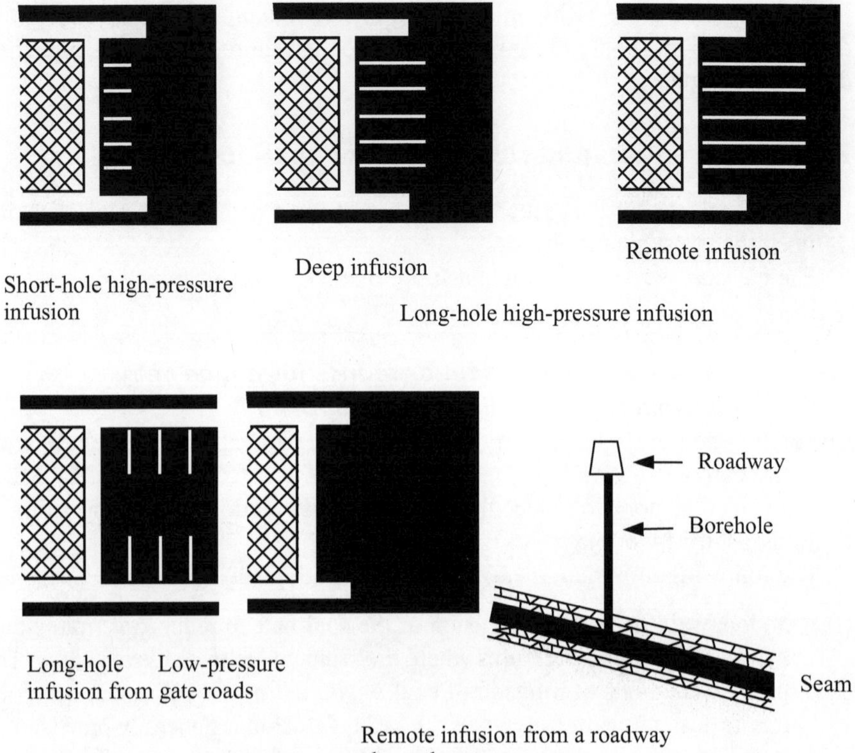

Figure 2.31 Methods of water infusion of longwall faces.

water of crystallization reduces considerably the dust produced by shotfiring due to the formation of a large number of droplets as a result of distribution of hygroscopic salt particles in the fume cloud containing a considerable amount of water vapour, which bind the dust.

(v) With power loading using the conventional shearer loaders, by not using too many cutting bits which should be sharp and of a suitable type and bit lacing, selecting a suitable drum design with vane angle greater than 12°, operating at optimal rotational speed of the drum by using a two-speed gearbox, and at optimal travelling speed of the machine, with proper direction of drum rotation, preferably roof to floor; introducing water to the bit clearance line through the hollow drumshaft by having sprays in the shell or barrel (barrel release) or mounted on the vanes (vane release); flushing the cutting edges of the bits with sprays located either in or close to the bit boxes (behind-the-bit flushing, Fig. 2.32) and using external water sprays on the body of the shearer on the face side to deliver water to strategic areas. Internal water sprays with a water pressure greater than 15 bar have been found to be more effective than external water sprays. In hot and deep mines, or in seams with soft floor, the internal water feed may be phased so that water comes out through the nozzle outlets near the

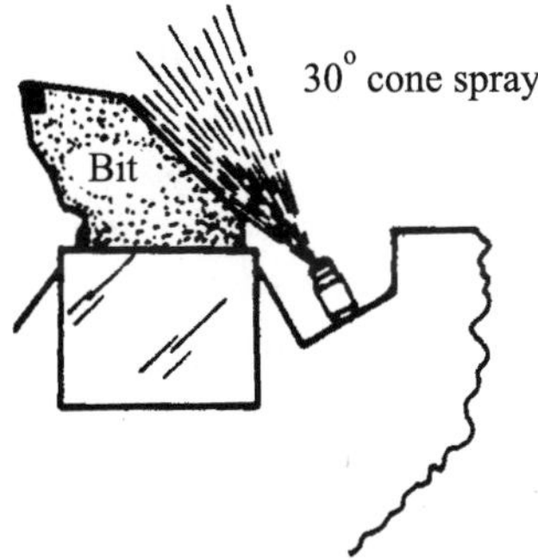

Figure 2.32 Behind-the-bit spray system.

bits only when they are actually cutting, since spraying the dust already generated is not effective enough.

(vi) Thoroughly wetting the coal pile before it is manually or mechanically loaded. Using such types of conveyors with which the dust production is minimum.

(vii) With belt conveyors;

(a) covering them along their length with a hood (Fig. 2.33);

(b) complete shrouding or boxing of the conveyor for a certain distance before the entry and after the exit when passing through air-locks with some form of seal (suspended conveyor belting) to allow passage of materials;

(c) having properly designed and installed chutes and skirt boards at transfer and loading points. It is most advantageous to hood or enclose the transfer points; and

(d) water spraying transfer and loading points.

(viii)Using large-capacity mine cars.

(ix) Water spraying full and empty trains during their transit.

(x) With rope haulages, raising the haulage ropes by correct siting of the rollers to prevent contact with the floor containing dust.

(xi) Preventing spillage and degradation of coal during transport on haulage roads by:

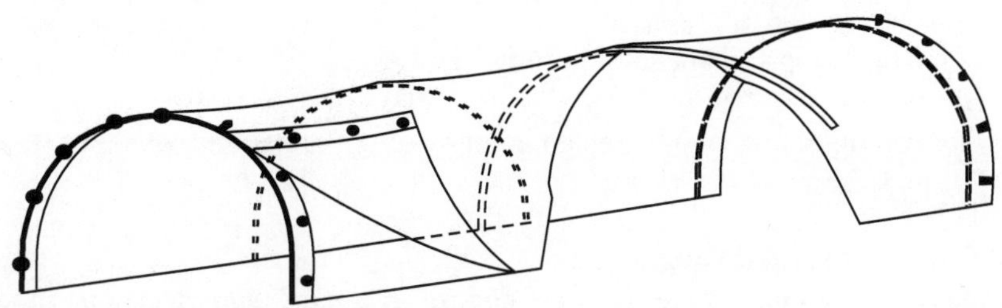

Figure 2.33 Covering hood for belt conveyors.

(a) using undamaged, well-maintained dust-tight cars;
(b) avoiding overloading of cars so that there is no spillage in transit;
(c) using retarders and creepers to avoid violent collisions;
(d) maintaining the haulage track in good condition; and
(e) on coal conveyor roadways, reducing spillage by selecting proper belt width and speed for operating the conveyor at 75% of its full rated capacity, by good alignment and transverse levelling providing adequate bunker capacity at loading points, centralizing the flow of coal, and keeping the number of belt joints to the minimum and also sealing them.

(xii) Restricting velocities of air currents in mine airways to less than 3 m/s if possible.

(xiii) Adopting homotropal ventilation where the ventilating air travels in the same direction as the coal to reduce dust pick-up.

(xiv) Preventing dust accumulation in mine workings by:
(a) dry suction at loading and unloading points at which large quantities of dust are produced which cannot be suppressed in the ordinary way, and removing dust by means of collectors which may be of the fabric, dry cyclone, or wet impingement type;
b) incorporating a dust collector in the auxiliary ventilation system in development drivages and headings;
c) cleaning systematically and regularly main haulage roads and main return airways of deposited dust (three to four times a year) using transportable roadway suction apparatus;
(d) cleaning regularly and systematically at and near transfer and loading points;
(e) installing skip-hoisting in upcast shafts; and
(f) locating dry coal preparation plants far away from downcast shafts (not less than 80 m).

(xv) Selecting a method of coal winning with which dust production is the least. Winning by coal ploughs produces much less dust than by shearer loaders.

(xvi) Controlled caving of roof coal in very thick seams mined by the sub-level caving method using close-fitting shields.

(xvii) Consolidating the floor dust to prevent it from being raised.

In open cast coal mines, important dust sources include:
(1) Mine haul roads
(2) Removal of top soil ahead of mining
(3) Blasting of coal
(4) Stockpiling of coal and its reclamation by use of reclaiming equipment
(5) Tailings dams

2.2.9.1.1 Dust modelling

At the mine planning stage, for dust control in mines, predictive dust models using computers have been developed for major contributions from both point and non-point sources taking into account the given meteorological data over the area to predict dust impact. Appropriate dust control options are provided. Owing to inaccurate estimate of the various variable factors, the control options should be tested before their acceptance.

2.2.9.2 *Measures against ignition of dust accumulations*

These measures comprise:

(i) Measures against ignition of flammable firedamp mixtures;
(ii) Neutralization or consolidation of dust at working coal faces within a radius of 10 to 20 m before shotfiring by means of water or inert dust; and
(iii) Neutralization of dust in roadways by means of water, inert stone dust, and hygroscopic salts.

2.2.9.3 *Measures against explosion propagation*

Dustless zones in mine workings might at first seem to be a logical means of arresting a coal-dust explosion. But experience has shown that strong explosions can easily propagate through several hundred metres of nearly dust-free zones due to burning dust being transported in the moving air column.

The protective measures which have been found in practice to have varying degrees of effectiveness in arresting explosion propagation in the coal mines so that an explosion is confined to the part of the workings in which it might occur are:,

(a) Generalized wetting of coal dust
(b) Generalized stonedusting (rockdusting)
(c) Stonedust (rockdust) barriers
(d) Explosion stoppings
(e) Salt zones
(f) Water barriers
(g) Triggered barriers

2.2.9.3.1 *Generalized wetting of coal dust*

Wetting of coal dust as an effective means of arresting propagation of coal-dust explosions in dry mine workings was known ever since the explosion hazard of coal dust was recognized. For water to be effective, it must be present in sufficient quantity and be mixed intimately with coal dust. The percentage of admixed water (by weight) required to prevent propagation of a coal-dust explosion depends on the fineness of dust, strength of the ignition source, volatile content of coal, and the amount of stone dust present. It should not be less than 50 per cent. In practice, coal dust is wetted over a length of roadway at least 8 m near a working face by washing down excessive deposits of it on the side and roof surfaces to the floor by means of hoses thereby converting the dust into mud. The frequency of water washing depends upon the dryness of dust and frequency of blasting. Water spraying using water-spray nozzles installed not more than 10 to 20 m from working faces have been regarded as effective means of combating initiation of coal dust and firedamp explosions by blasting. To increase the wettability of coal dust which neither adsorbs nor absorbs water readily, a wetting agent may be added to the water.

The disadvantages of water as an inert for neutralizing the coal-dust explosion hazard are:

(a) Wetting must be done continuously by streams of water which must be available in sufficient quantity;
(b) Relative humidity of mine atmosphere is increased;
(c) Heaving of floor, if soft, occurs; and
(d) Cost of the plant is high as the entire mine workings must be equipped with water mains.

The use of water is justified if the relative humidity in mine workings exceeds 90 to 95 per cent. One should remember that spraying water in a mine roadway will not free it permanently from the danger of explosion.

2.2.9.3.2 *Generalized stonedusting*

The British engineer W. Garforth first observed in the year 1891 that an explosion did not propagate to a part of a mine which was well stonedusted. With this began stonedusting in Britain with it being officially adopted in 1920. It was after the greatest explosion of all times that occurred in the year 1907 in the Courieres mine in France that French scientists and engineers, notably M.J. Taffanel and a German engineer, Beyling, engaged themselves, with stonedusting. Stonedusting was officially adopted in France in 1911 and in Germany in 1926. Today, generalized stonedusting is done in mines of almost all coal-mining countries of the world.

Generalized stonedusting consists in applying stone dust on the sides, roof and floor of all mine workings except those within 10 m or less of all working faces so that it overlays the deposited coal dust and thus prevents the latter from taking part in an explosion. If a mine or any part of it is naturally 'too wet' (condition wherein water exudes if a ball of dust is squeezed in the hands) or too high in incombustible content to propagate an explosion, stonedusting is not required in that mine or part thereof.

The value of stone dust application is due to the following facts:

(a) When coal dust is mixed with enough inert or incombustible dust, it will not explode or assist in propagation of an explosion. An addition of about 40 per cent stone dust causes a 50 to 90 per cent reduction in flame velocity.
(b) When incombustible dust is raised into an explosion flame in a sufficiently dense cloud, it gets heated up taking away heat from the flame. Greater the amount of stone dust in the flame, greater is the cooling effect. In the case of coal-dust explosions, the incombustible dust also serves to shield or blanket the coal-dust particles from the heat of radiation so that they do not take part in combustion any more and also hinder diffusion of oxygen and gases into and from the burning coal particles.

As coal dust is constantly produced as a result of mining operations and gets deposited by ventilating currents in mine workings, one application of stone dust will not suffice to keep the mine workings immune from explosions. Stonedusting must be applied at regular intervals of time after it has been first applied as this gives some assurance that adequate mixing of coal dust and stone dust is taking place and the areas can be safely travelled.

On the basis of tests carried out in surface experimental galleries, different countries have prescribed different minimum percentages of incombustible content in the combined coal dust, stone dust and other dusts on the floor, roof, and sides of mine roadways at all times. Moisture contained in the mine dust is considered as a part of the incombustible content of the dust. The minimum incombustible content by mass required of mine dust is 70 per cent in India, 80 per cent in Germany, and 65 per cent in the USA. It depends on the character of coal, specially its volatile content on ash-free dry basis, the fineness of the dust produced, and the percentage of methane present in the mine atmosphere. Where methane is present in any ventilation current, the minimum incombustible content, S per cent must be raised by ($100 - S$ per cent/5) for each 1 per cent increase of methane in the general body of the air over a period of time.

For a given coal, the quantity of stone dust to be applied in mine workings can be calculated from the relation

$$\frac{0.01a + x}{1 + x} = \frac{b}{100} \qquad \text{or} \qquad x = \frac{b - a}{100 - b}$$

where x is the quantity of stone dust required (kg stone dust/kg mine dust);

a is the percentage of incombustible matter already present in the mine dust;

b is the prescribed minimum percentage of incombustible content.

About 3 to 7 kg stone dust per tonne of coal output may be required.

In base metal mines, the use of stone dust is not recommended due to the large amounts which would be required and the difficulties due to caking.

2.2.9.3.2.1 Characteristics of suitable stone dust

All stone dusts used for stonedusting and other purposes in mines must fulfil certain requirements in respect of fineness, dispersability, combustible matter, and effect on health. Different countries have prescribed different specifications for a suitable stone dust (Table 2.5).

A suitable stone dust should not be hygroscopic so that it does not cake when not directly wetted by water from the strata. It should be readily dispersible into the air when blown by the mouth or by a suitable appliance, and be soluble in the fluids of the lungs. It should also be as light in colour as possible, preferably white, so that it makes it easier to detect deposition of a thin surface layer of coal dust where coal dust is building up.

Table 2.5 Specifications of stone dust in some countries

	Germany	**USA**	**UK**	**India**
Fineness	100% through sieve of 144 mesh/cm^2 and at least 50% through sieve of 6400 mesh/cm^2, by mass	100% through 20-mesh per linear inch sieve and at least 80% through 200-mesh sieve, by mass	100% through BS 60-mesh sieve and at least 75% through 240 mesh sieve, by mass	100% through 60-mesh and at least 50% and not more than 75% through 240-mesh sieve, by mass
Combustible matter	<3%	<5%	Not specified	Not specified
Total free and combined	< 10% by mass in fraction< 20μ			
Silica content	5% in the respirable fraction < 5μ	<4%	Not specified	Free silica < 5%

The standard stone dust is prepared in special mills out of shale, dolomite, gypsum, or limestone. Gypsum dust is the most effective of all. Owing to its cheapness, easy availability, white colour, low silica content, and little tendency to cake. Limestone dust is, however, the most commonly used in mines throughout the world.

Relative effectiveness of various inhibitor dusts in inerting coal dust accumulations as supplements or substitutes for stone dust especially in very gassy coal mines as determined by the US Bureau of Mines in an 8-litre chamber and in full-scale tests in the Experimental Mine is given in Table 2.6 [18]. It will be seen that $NH_4H_2PO_4$, ABC are remarkably the most effective of the dusts studied. But the cost effectiveness and effect on health remains to be studied.

Table 2.6 Relative efficacy of inhibitors in inerting coal dust accumulations

	% Inert content required in	
Inhibitor dust	Experimental mine	8-litre Chamber
NH_4 H_2PO_4, ABC	25–30	28–12
NaCl, BCD	40–45	50–55
KCI, Super K	40–45	55–60
$CaCO_3$, stone dust	70–72	65–70
$KHCO_3$, Purple K	70–75	77–82

2.2.9.3.2.2 *Stone dust application*

As deposition of coal dust takes place continuously, stonedusting should be done in the right place in such a manner and at such intervals of time as will ensure that the mine dust on the floor, roof, and sides throughout will always consist of a mixture containing not less than the prescribed minimum percentage of incombustible matter. Excessive or blanket stonedusting of the floor of mine workings can never compensate for deficiency of stone dust on the sides and roof.

Before applying stone dust for the first time, all accumulations of coal dust, float coal dust, loose coal and other combustible materials should be loaded out, as far as practicable. This reduces the required amount of stone dust and facilitates mixing of the stone dust with the coal dust. Stonedusting should begin in active sections of the mine where explosions would be most likely to originate (within 10 m of active coal faces) and advance from the faces outwards to the mine's main entrance as the faces advance. Before workings are abandoned, the floor, roof, and sides must be dusted.

Stone dust can be applied by hand or by mechanical means using stone- dusting machines.

Hand-dusting by broadcasting with hand scoops is cumbersome, has low capacity, does not ensure even distribution of stone dust over the roof and sides and, in consequence, is not suitable for large or mechanized mines. A man can stonedust 15 to 20 m of a roadway, 9 to 11 m^2 in cross-section, per shift [25]. In machine-dusted mines, hand-dusting is confined to within two cuts of a face.

Mechanized dusting or mechanical spreading of dust is ideal for large and mechanized mines as it is the most economical, efficient, and rapid method. Stonedusting machines, also called stone dust distributors, blow fluidized dust onto mine surfaces through tubing or hose which may be up to 200 m long. They have high capacities so that a considerable amount of dust can be applied in a very short time when an opportunity offers. Both low-pressure and high-pressure machines are available in the market. The low-pressure machines are portable machines which can be moved from one face to another for face-area stonedusting as soon as a face is loaded out. The high-pressure machines have dust capacities up to one tonne per minute and are used for applying dust in intake haulage roadways and return airways as well as in face areas. The well-known machines are those manufactured by the Mine Safety Appliances Co., Pittsburg, USA and the American Mine Door Co., Ohio, USA. They are powered by 5 to 20 hp electric motors and are available as tow-behind, skid-, track- or rubber tyre-mounted units (Fig. 2.34). Their minimum heights are 400 mm on skids, 558 mm on rubber tyres, and 635 mm above rail on wheels. The skid-mounted machines may be mounted on shuttle cars, belts, or mine cars. The tyre- and track-mounted units may be of portable, mobile, or towed type. Experience has shown that the tyre-mounted unit towed by a battery-operated tractor provides the maximum flexibility, manoeuvrability, and range. In mine workings containing compressed-air lines, compressed-air operated tank-type dusting machines may also be employed.

Mechanical dusting should be carried out only when the workplaces to which the dust is carried by ventilating currents are free of workmen. It must be carried out between shifts, on idle shifts or weekends, by gangs specially trained for the purpose.

Auxiliary exhaust fans when used to improve ventilation can also be utilized for stonedusting by introducing dust at the fan discharge.

Figure 2.34 M.S.A. Type SC Rockdust distributor.

In mines with extensive mine workings where the handling and distribution of stone dust would consume considerable number of manshifts, the so-called 'bulk stonedusting system' may be adopted with which the total capital invested can be realized within a short time. In the bulk stonedusting system as practised in the US mining industry, the stone dust is transferred from a surface storage bin into large-capacity bulk supply cars underground through a lined borehole (Fig. 2.35) by means of an aerator feeder. The bulk cars are transported to different sections of the mine where the stone dust is transferred to stonedusting machines by screw-type conveyors. In a shift, two stonedusting men can handle about 20t bulk stone dust including the filling of the bulk car at the borehole, transporting it to the section, filling the hopper of the dusting machine and stonedusting.

MSA developed a pressure tank automated stonedusting system (Fig. 2.36). It is a pneumatic conveying system composed of modular units which can be grouped to suit mine layout. A storage bin located on the surface supplies stone dust to a main supply pressure tank underground, which supplies dust to inbye pressure tanks spaced about 1000 m apart, being connected by light-weight pipelines. Each tank has a compressor to build up pressure automatically and to fluidize the stone

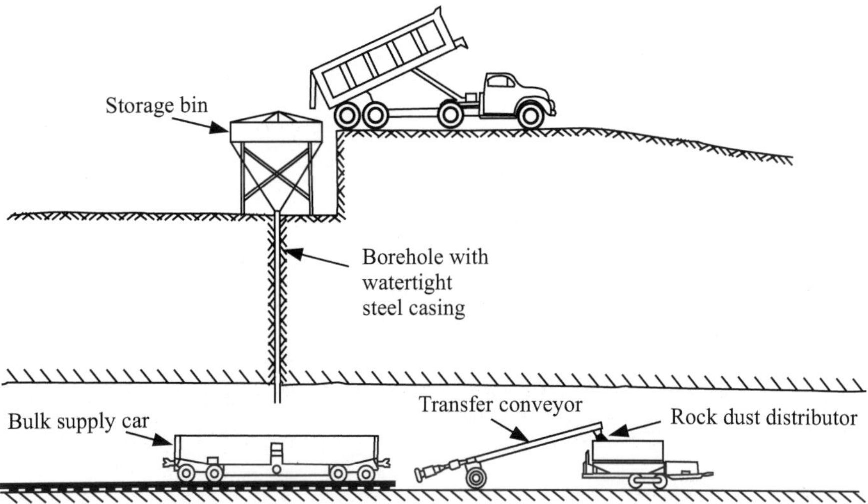

Fig. 2.35 M.S.A Bulk Rockdusting System.

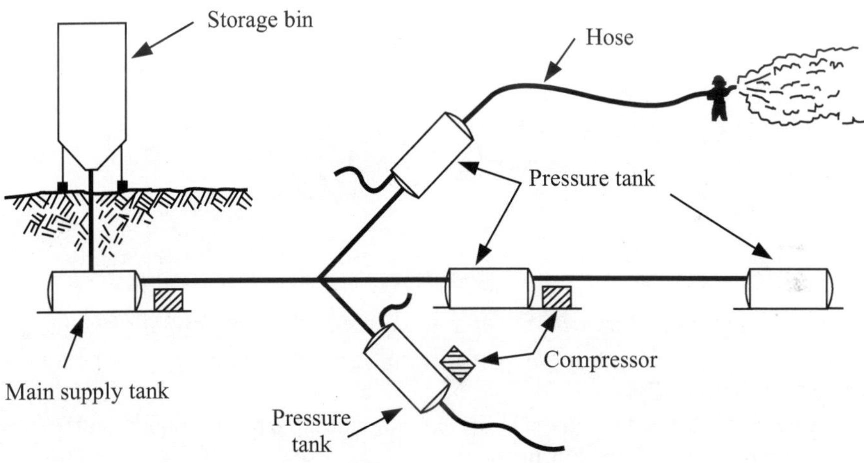

Figure 2.36 M.S.A. Pressure tank automated rockdusting system.

dust. Figure 2.37 shows the construction of a pressure tank fitted with a modulating valve which is essentially an air-stone dust mixing valve, maintaining a constant line pressure and maximum flow of stone dust.

The cost of stonedusting depends on the cost of labour, the method of stonedusting adopted, and the system of mining by longwall or bord and pillar.

To increase the adherence of the stone dust on the sides and roof of roadways which are dry and smooth or where stonedusting is to be done during a working shift without creating intolerable dust clouds downwind, wet stonedusting method was developed in the USA. Wet stonedusting consists of spraying a premixed stone dust slurry by means of a guniting machine through a guniting nozzle or

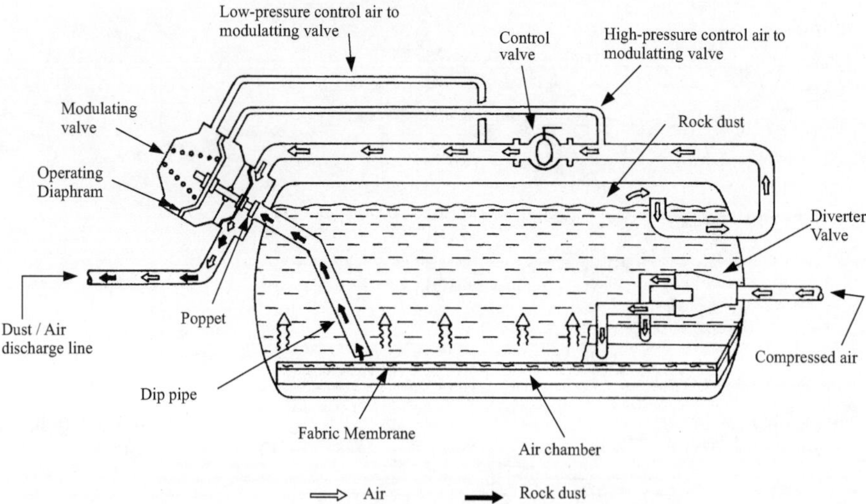

Figure 2.37 Construction of a pressure tank fitted with a modulating valve.

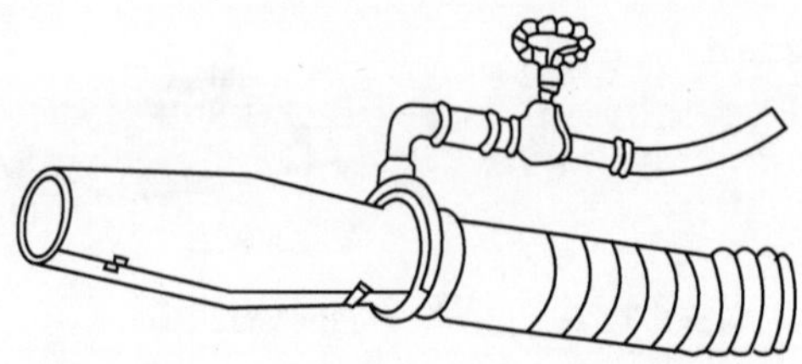

Figure 2.38 Wet nozzle.

by mixing dry stone dust with water at the nozzle of a commercial stonedusting machine (Fig. 2.38). It is limited to side and roof surfaces, the floor being dry stonedusted manually.

Experiments carried out in the U.S. Experimental Coal Mine on the effectiveness of wet stonedusting in arresting propagation of explosion had shown [46, 47] that:

(a) a mixture of 20 to 30 litres of water with about 45 kg dust gives good results from the standpoint of adherence;
(b) wet stone dust should be applied at a rate of not less than 0.92 kg dust per square metre of surface area to yield a good covering of the side-roof surfaces;
(c) the rate of drying of the stone dust varies with the air velocity and relative humidity; with normal air currents and relative humidities below 80 per cent, the stone dust dries completely in one to three days and at humidities of 80 to 90 per cent, it dries in about a week; and
(d) wet stonedusting is less effective than dry stonedusting in arresting the propagation of an explosion.

2.2.9.3.2.3 Testing of stone dust before use in mines

Stone dust must be tested at the mine laboratory for fineness, purity, and dispersability.

Testing for fineness

From the consignment arriving at the mine, a gross sample of approximately 2 kg is taken and reduced to 250 g by coning and quartering or by means of a sample divider. The representative sample is taken in an air-tight container to the mine laboratory where it is spread on a tray and allowed to dry for 24 hours. 100 g of the air-dried sample is then sieved using prescribed sieves and the amount of dust remaining on the sieves and in the receiver weighed to find the percentage fraction.

Testing for dispersability

The dispersability of a dust may be defined as the ease with which a mass of dust at rest can be raised and dispersed into the air when blown upon.

The simple test which satisfies mining regulations consists in spreading the dust on the palm and seeing if a portion of it can be blown off by the mouth or using a suitable appliance.

For impregnated or water-proofed dusts which remain freely dispersible under wet mine conditions, the above test will yield erroneous results as they are usually finer than untreated dusts and have stronger cohesive forces between particles so that when blown by the mouth they do not readily disperse but leave a portion on the palm. To test the dispersability of untreated and treated dusts, a method had, been developed in the Saar Coalfied [48], Germany in which an accurately weighed stone-dust sample placed in a clean dry glass basin or bowl is blown out for a definite period by means of air flowing out of a capillary nozzle which is constantly moved without touching the glass basin. The stone dust is deemed to be dispersible if the percentage of the dispersible fraction exceeds a definite value.

2.2.9.3.2.4 Mine dust sampling

The only certain means of controlling the adequacy of stonedusting is by taking samples of the mine dust from appropriate locations at regular intervals depending on the intensity of coal-dust production in the mine and testing them for their incombustible contents. Sampling procedures are laid down in mining regulations. A mine is divided into zones or sampling lengths which should be distinctly demarcated, and a representative sample is taken from each zone at such intervals of time as may be prescribed. The length of a zone should not be less than 50 m. The length, number and location of such zones should be clearly shown on a plan called the sampling plan. The mine workings and places in them from which it is not necessary to collect samples are the main shafts, production faces, development headings for opening up of longwall faces, loading and transfer points, and workings and places which are naturally wet or treated with dust-binding salts. The results of the analysis or tests should be recorded in a special book (dust register) kept at the mine for the purpose, which shall also show the place (location in the zones), the date of last stonedusting at the sampling place, and time of sampling. In general, there should always be liaison between the stonedusting and sampling operations to avoid the possibility of sampling immediately after stonedusting, which would give a false sense of security. The first sample should be collected about one week after stonedusting for the first time. Further samples should be collected about one week before stonedusting.

It must be clearly understood that while sampling can indicate that a length of roadway is in a dangerous condition if the samples are below standard, it cannot give an assurance that samples with incombustible contents above the prescribed value reflect safe conditions. This is because the presence of coal-rich patches or coal-rich surface layers would not be revealed by the present sampling techniques which are designed to give only the average composition of the dust at the time of sampling. Also, the samples cannot reflect changing conditions within the sampling cycle. Thus routine samples cannot give a completely reliable picture of the coal-dust explosion hazard in a mine roadway.

Equipment and method of sampling

The mine dust sampling equipment commonly used consists of:

(1) A sampling scoop or dust pan having a width of 100 or 150 mm to collect the sample;
(2) A brush, 50 mm wide;
(3) A standard sieve(s) of prescribed mesh (BSS 60-mesh in the UK, 20-mesh in the USA, 60-mesh for dry sample and 18-mesh for wet sample in India);
(4) One or two pieces of oil-cloth or rubberized cloth, about 60 cm × 60 cm, on which to mix the representative sample and to quarter it until there is just sufficient to sieve;
(5) Sample containers, 250 or 500 ml, or envelopes and labels that can be pasted on them to carry the samples from the mine to the laboratory;
(6) A pencil and a book; and
(7) A carrying canvas sack or sectionalized carrier box to carry 30 to 36 samples.

The collection of a representative sample from a zone is usually by the method of strip sampling by which the mine dust is collected from a succession of transverse strips as nearly as may be of equal width (100 or 150 mm) taken at such number of places or such distance from one another over such length of zone as may be prescribed by regulations. When collecting a sample, the sampler should walk against the ventilating current.

At any sampling section, two kinds of samples are collected: the floor sample and the side-roof sample. The floor sample comprises dust collected to a maximum depth of 25 mm on the floor from side to side provided that loose material is found to that depth, while the side-roof sample comprises dust collected to a depth of 5 or 6 mm as near as may be on the roof and sides. The surfaces of fixed structures are considered to be part of the roof and sides.

The floor and side-roof samples may be combined into a single sample and a single representative sample (250 to 500 g) obtained after mixing, quartering, drying in the air if necessary, and passing a portion through the prescribed sieve (peripheral or band sampling) or separate representative samples obtained from each of them. Intensive sampling studies conducted by the US Bureau of Mines [49] had revealed that band sampling can be substituted for the more time-consuming and tedious floor and side-roof sampling without any sacrifice of safety. But one serious disadvantage of band sampling is that in mines excess stone dust will be spread on the floor with little or no stone dust on the roof and sides and vice versa. Collection of separate floor and side-roof samples is, therefore, the more reliable method of ascertaining the adequacy of stonedusting.

The incombustible matter of the total dust at a sampling place is given by

$$I_s = \frac{I_{sr}W_{sr} + I_f W_f}{W_{sr} + W_f}$$

where I_{sr} is the combustible content of the side-roof
I_f is the combustible content of the floor sample, per cent
W_{sr} is the mass of the side-roof sample, kg per linear metre
W_f is the mass of the floor sample, kg per linear metre.

A sample representative of a length of roadway may also be collected by a method of 'spot sampling' by which the dust for a particular sample is collected from one point for each metre length of the roadway.

Analysis of mine dust samples

The representative mine dust samples are analyzed for the incombustible matter content by approved methods of analysis. Chemical analysis in the laboratory is by far the most reliable of all the methods. Less accurate but simpler and more rapid are the colorimeter and volumeter methods of estimation with which the time and labour required for collecting and analyzing mine dust samples area considerably reduced. Portable coal dust/rock dust analysers for on-the-spot evaluation of the adequacy of stonedusting have been developed in the USA which will indicate the incombustible content of mine dusts over a range of 50 to 100 per cent incombustible within ± 2 or 3 per cent of the chemically determined incombustible content for 80 per cent of the standard samples with prescribed specifications.

Chemical analysis

For routine dust analysis, chemical analysis consists of determination of the moisture and ash contents.

Moisture content

A weighed quantity (1 g) of the representative sample is dried at a temperature between 105° and 110°C. The loss of mass represents the moisture.

$$\%\text{Moisture in sample} = \frac{\text{Mass loss of moisture}}{\text{Mass of dust sample}} \times 100$$

Ash (incinerated residue) content

In the high temperature incineration method, the residue remaining after moisture determination is heated to a temperature of 925° ± 25°C in a muffle furnace for one or two hours until it no longer loses mass and the mass of the incinerated residue determined.

$$\%\text{ Ash} = \frac{\text{Mass of residue}}{\text{Mass of original sample}} \times 100$$

The sum of the masses of the moisture and incinerated residue is reckoned as the incombustible matter and is expressed as a percentage of the total mass of the dust

In the case of dust samples containing carbonates, as happens when limestone dust is used for stonedusting, the mass of carbon dioxide liberated during incineration should be reckoned as incombustible matter. The carbon dioxide content of the sample can be determined by treating a weighed portion of the sample with dilute (10 per cent) hydrochloric acid and finding the loss in mass or measuring the volume of carbon dioxide given off and calculating its mass.

$$\%\text{ CO}_2 = \frac{\text{Mass loss of CO}_2}{\text{Mass of original sample}} \times 100$$

If it is necessary for a sample to be air-dried before being sieved through a prescribed sieve, a correction must be applied to the incombustible matter determined for the loss of moisture during drying.

In the low-temperature incineration method, the dust sample is incinerated at a temperature of not less than 500°C and not more than 530°C until its mass is constant. This temperature is sufficient to complete the combustion of the organic matter but not high enough to decompose the carbonates.

Colorimetric methods

There are two practical rapid methods:

(1) Usual colour comparison method; and
(2) Colour measurement method using a reflectometer (instrument sorting).

In the visual colour comparison method, the colour of a representative sample is compared in the mine with that of standard dust mixtures prepared from actual mine dust samples and known to contain definite percentages of incombustible matter. To eliminate underground all samples that contain 80 per cent or more incombustible matter which would mean a considerable saving in effort, only a single standard dust mixture containing 80 per cent incombustible need be used.

In the colour measurement method by reflectometer, the light-reflective properties of the surface of mine dust samples are measured by means of photoelectric cells. The reflectometer must first be calibrated for different mines and seams by conducting tests on standard dust mixtures for each mine and seam and plotting the relation between the inert content of the dusts as obtained by chemical analysis and reflectometer readings. From the calibration curves, the percentage of inert content in an actual mine dust sample corresponding to the reflectometer reading obtained can be read off. The reflectometer can be used to sort dusts having an inert content between 50 and 80 per cent.

An obvious disadvantage of the colorimetric method is that the colour of mine dust samples is affected by various contaminants, particle size of coal dust, rank of coal, particle size of stone dust, moisture content, degree of mixing of coal and stone dust, lighting conditions, etc.

Volumeter method

This method is suitable for all dusts except those containing gypsum. It consists in measuring the specific volume of a weighed quantity of representative mine dust sample by the so-called volumeter. The specific volume of a mine dust sample is given by the sum of the specific volumes of its constituents, namely, the coal dust, stone dust, and other dusts. If the specific volumes of standard dust mixtures prepared from actual mine dust samples containing known percentages of incombustible matter can be determined and a graph drawn therefrom, then the percentage of incombustible matter corresponding to the measured specific volume of a dust sample collected can be read off.

The volumeter consists of a 50-ml flat-bottomed glass flask with a ground glass neck into which fits an open measuring stem, about 20 cm long and 1.3 cm in diameter, graduated from zero at the top to 100 at the bottom (Fig. 2.39). The volume of the flask plus stem is 59.6 up to the 100 graduation mark and 60.2 up to the zero graduation mark.

To use the apparatus, 25 ml of methylated spirit is first run into the flask and 25 g of the dust sample to be tested is then poured into it. After inserting the measuring stem into the vaselined neck of the flask, the flask is vigorously shaken by hand for two minutes to remove all air bubbles. The other 25 ml of the spirit is then poured through the open end of the measuring stem and the reading of the level of the liquid in the stem noted. By reference to the calibration graphs obtained for standard dust mixtures for different seams, the incombustible matter in a dust sample in any seam can be found out from the reading on the graduated stem.

To safeguard against any discrepancy when using the volumeter method, one in every 50 samples should be check-tested by chemical analysis. The accuracy that can be obtained with this method is ± 4 per cent [50].

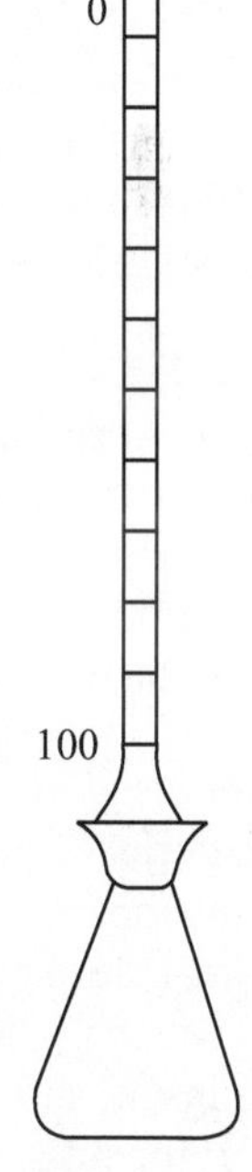

Figure 2.39
Volumeter.

Combination of the colorimeter and volumeter methods
When an increased throughput of samples is to be achieved, a combination of colorimetric sorting and volumeter testing may be used. The samples are first sorted by the colorimetric method and those that are darker in colour than the standard dust are analysed by the volumeter method.

2.2.9.3.2.5 *Efficacy of stonedusting*

Extensive investigations carried out in the Tremonia Experimental Mine, Germany to test the efficacy of stonedusting in suppressing coal-dust explosions [51] revealed that the legislative requirement of mine dust gives no guarantee that an explosion will not propagate through a stonedusted roadway. The experiments clearly brought to light the following important facts:

(1) Stone dust does not form an intimate mixture with coal dust as was originally assumed;
(2) Stone dust when overlain by a layer of coal dust does not prevent explosion propagation; and
(3) Stone dust is effective only when it overlays coal dust in a quantity which is four to six times the weight of coal dust.

From the foregoing, it is evident that stonedusting as a practical measure does not offer adequate protection against propagation of coal-dust explosions unless the coal dust and stone dust are thoroughly mixed and the stone dust overlays the coal dust in a large quantity which may not be achieved in wet roadways, haulage roadways with belt conveyors or parked mine cars at transfer points, longwall faces, head- and tail-gate areas, return airways, and isolated sections. It can only be considered as an additional or secondary measure of safety. Stonedusting can be effective only in mine workings where coal dust deposition is less.

2.2.9.3.3 Stone-dust barriers

Stone-dust barriers as a means of suppression of coal-dust explosions were first proposed by M.J. Taffanel and are today extensively used in Indian and many overseas mines. A stone-dust barrier is a device which uses the dynamic pressure of an explosion to release and disperse a mass of stone dust in the form of a thick cloud into the path of an oncoming explosion flame, thereby smothering the flame.

Barrier design
Experience has shown that of the various designs of barriers evolved and tested in Germany, Poland, and the USA, the shelf barrier, consisting of a number of dust-laden shelves independently supported transverse to and along the roadway in which it (the barrier) is installed, is the most practical design, being less difficult to install and maintain. It occupies a length of 25 to 40 m of the roadway.

Stone-dust barriers are installed in strategic areas of the mine such as roadways leading from shafts or their pitbottoms, in all level and inclined roadways including gate roads and development headings, and near roadway junctions.

Two designs of shelves are commonly used in mines, the German (Improved Dortmund-type) Shelf and the Polish Shelf. The German Shelf (Fig. 2.40) consists of several loose planks, maximum 60 cm long and 10 to 15 cm wide, which are abutted along their length with the ends supported by cross pieces which rest upon two long transverse bars with their ends resting loosely on rigid shelf supports. The Polish Shelf (Fig. 2.41) is composed of several short planks, 10 to 15 cm wide and 35 to 50 cm long, laid alongside one another in the direction of the roadway.

There are two types of German or Polish Shelf, the Light Shelf and the Heavy Shelf. In German mines, both the German and Polish Shelves are officially approved for use, while in the U.K. and India, only the Polish Shelf is the officially approved one. The specifications of the light (Type 1) and heavy (Type 2) German shelves as officially approved for use in German mines in roadways up to 4 m high are given below:

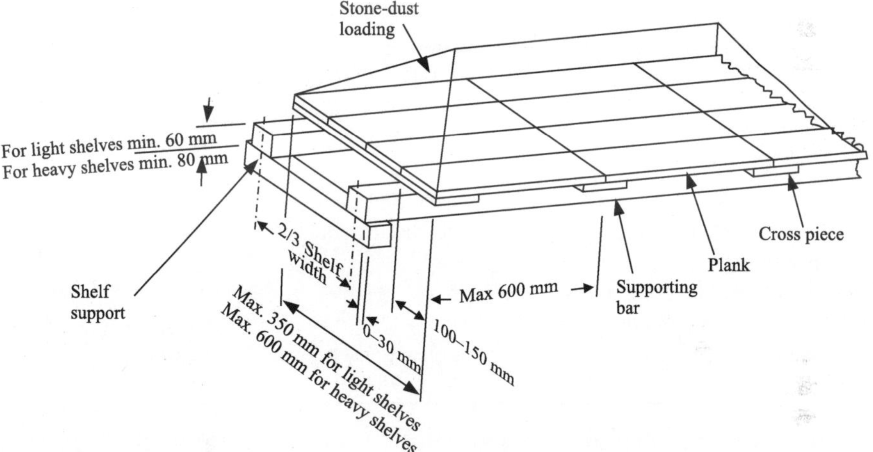

Figure 2.40 German Shelf

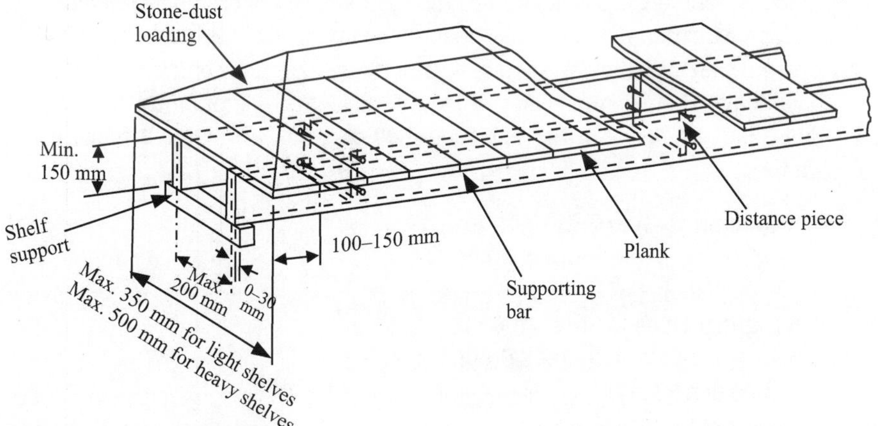

Figure 2.41 Polish shelf

	Light Shelves	Heavy
Width of shelves	max. 35 cm	60 cm
Width of planks	10–15 cm	10–15 cm
Length of planks	max. 60 cm	60 cm
Height of supporting bars	at least 6 cm	8 cm
Distance between supporting bars (centre to centre)	2/3 of shelf width	
Mass of shelves/deflection in length of shelf	max. 15 kg/m	20 kg/m
Deflection of supporting bars	Max. 2 per cent span width	
Dust loading on shelf	at least 50 kg max. 100 kg	150 kg 300 kg

The specifications of the light and heavy Polish shelves as officially approved for use in German mines in roadways up to 4 m high are given below:

	Light Shelves	Heavy
Width of shelves	max. 35 cm	50 cm
Width of planks	10–15 cm	10–15 cm
Length of planks	max. 35 cm	50 cm
Height of supporting bars	at least 15 cm	15 cm
Distance between supporting bars (centre to centre)	max. 20 cm	20 cm
Mass of shelves/m length of shelf	max. 15 kg/m	15 kg/m
Dust loading/length of shelf	at least 30 kg/m max. 35 kg	60 kg/m 70 kg/m

The following rules govern the erection of stone-dust barriers of both types in German mines:

(1) A stone-dust barrier must carry not less than 400 kg stone dust per square metre of average cross-section of the roadway in which it is installed.

(2) At least a quarter of the total dust loading of any one barrier must be distributed on light shelves which must flank the heavy shelves of the barrier at either end. The heavy shelves must carry at least a quarter of the total dust loading.

(3) The distance between the adjacent shelves of a barrier must be as given under:

German shelves	min. 1.50 m max. 5.00 m
Polish shelves	
Light shelves	min. 1.00 m max. 2.00 m
Between heavy shelves or between a heavy	

and a light shelf min. 1.25 m
max. 2.50 m

(4) The bottom of the shelves should be at a height greater than half the roadway height but not exceed 2.60 m. The clearance between the ends of the shelves and the sides of the roadway should be at least 5 cm.
(5) The brackets supporting the entire shelf must be rigidly fixed to the ground or roadway support. The shelf should never be suspended from chains or wire ropes which tend to swing.
(6) The shelf supports at the brackets must be horizontal and have a smooth bearing surface; they should not project beyond the shelf supports by more than 3 cm.
(7) The supporting bars must be rectangular in section.
(8) The gaps between the planks must be covered with thin scantlings or strips having a maximum width equal to the width of the planks.
(9) The clear space (vertical distance) between the top of the dust loading and the inner edge of the roof bar or crown segment of the steel arched support, as the case may be, must be at least 15 cm.
(10) The dust loading must be approximately symmetrical with respect to the centre of the roadway and must occupy at least two-thirds of the maximum width of the roadway.
(11) The dust loading on the shelves must not be covered.
(12) In the vicinity of a barrier, ventilation ducting, overhung belt conveyors, pipes, and other obstructions which seriously affect the effectiveness of a barrier must not be present.
(13) The barriers should not be installed at roadway junctions, at curves, or in widened portions. They can, however, be installed near roadway junctions.
(14) The distance between barriers should not exceed 200 m in gate roadways of longwall faces and 400 m main roadways.

In the UK, the stone-dust barriers are of three types: the light, intermediate, and heavy barriers. Two types of Polish Shelves are used. The light shelf the width of which should not exceed 35 cm, has a dust loading not more than 29.8 kg/m shelf length, while the heavy shelf, the width of which should not be less than 35 cm and not more than 50 cm, is loaded with not more than 59.6 kg/m. The light barrier carries a total dust loading of at least 107.4 kg per square metre of average roadway cross-section and comprises all shelves of the light type. The intermediate barrier carries a dust loading of 195.3 kg per square metre roadway cross-section and comprises not more than one-third of the shelves of the heavy type. The heavy barrier carries a dust loading of at least 390.6 kg per square metre of average roadway cross-section comprising not less than one-third of the shelves of the light type.

The distance between the adjacent shelves are:

Light shelves min. 0.91 in
max. 2.10 in

Between heavy shelves or between a heavy and a light shelf	min. 1.22 m max. 2.59 in

In India, the stone-dust barriers were officially adopted in the year 1963. Their design is similar to that of the UK one.

Barriers for special purposes
They are erected for special purposes such as for protection of men engaged in sealing off fire areas in mines. They are quick-acting and can be quickly erected. They carry 100 kg stone dust per square metre of roadway cross-section.

German 'Quick Barrier'
There are two types of quick barriers: the frame barrier and the so-called improvised barrier' (German Behelfs-Schnellspere).

The frame barrier (Figure 2.42) consists of several light shelves arranged in a light frame, 2. 10 m high and 1 m wide. The shelves are of plywood, 16 cm wide with a 5-cm deep layer of stone dust on each so that a gap of 5 cm between successive shelves is left for the ventilating current to pass through. The staggered placement of the frames allows room for men to travel through the barrier. The frames are either suspended from the roof or wedged tightly between the roof and floor. Figure 2.42 also shows the arrangement of the frames in narrow and wide roadways [52]. lt takes about 40 minutes for four experienced men to erect these barriers.

The improvised barrier (Fig. 2.43) consists of several dust-laden shelves arranged one above the other on shelf supports nailed to the side props of timber sets and centre props erected specifically for the purpose on one or both sides of them, depending on whether a staggered passage way is to be left or not. The shelves are longer and wider (width 30 cm) than those of the frame barrier.

It is recommended that quick barriers be installed, as far as practicable, 30 to 40 m from the fireseat and 100 m outbye the temporary stopping.

2.2.9.3.3.4 *Efficacy of stone-dust barriers*

All stone-dust barriers depend for their effective operation on the formation of a thick cloud of stone dust by the pressure wave of a coal-dust or firedamp explosion before being passed by the flame of the explosion. Studies and experience with explosions in experimental and operating coal mines had shown that the force of an explosion and the time interval between dust discharge and flame arrival at the barrier, which depend upon the design and location of the barrier, the presence of flammable firedamp–air mixture, and the intensity of the explosions, determine the efficacy of a stone-dust barrier. A weak explosion may not throw the shelves off their supports. If the time interval between dust release and flame arrival is too long, a greater part of the dust falls to the floor but if it is too short, the dust does not get adequately dispersed. Investigations have shown that a time interval of 0. 1 to 0.2 s [40] is sufficient enough to create a flame-quenching cloud.

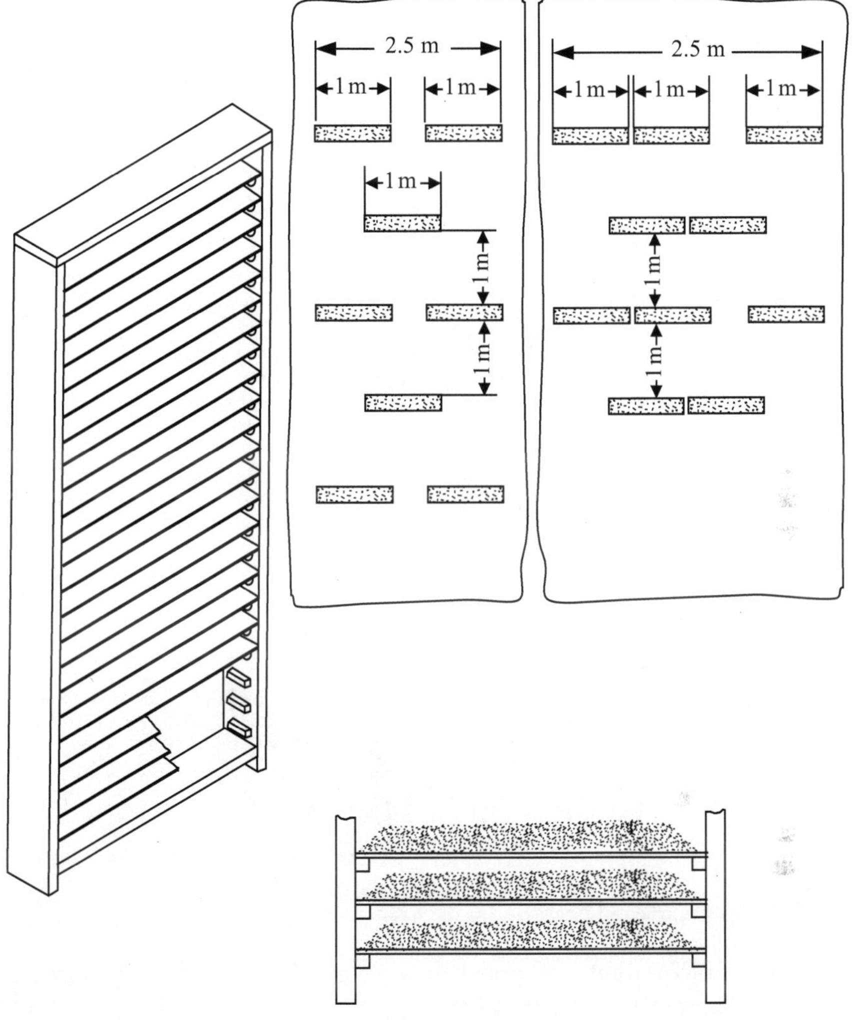

Figure 2.42 Frame barrier.

In practice, stone-dust barriers may fail under any one of the following circumstances:

(1) When the barrier itself lies in a flammable firedamp–air mixture or firedamp occurs as a roof layer;
(2) When flame velocities are high (exceeding about 500 m/s), as when a dust explosion is initiated by a powerful firedamp explosion or is assisted by firedamp during its propagation;
(3) When the barrier is located less than 40 to 60 m or far from a face or other potential point of ignition, so that the dynamic pressure is less than the minimum required, which normally lies between 3 and 5 kN/m^2 ; and

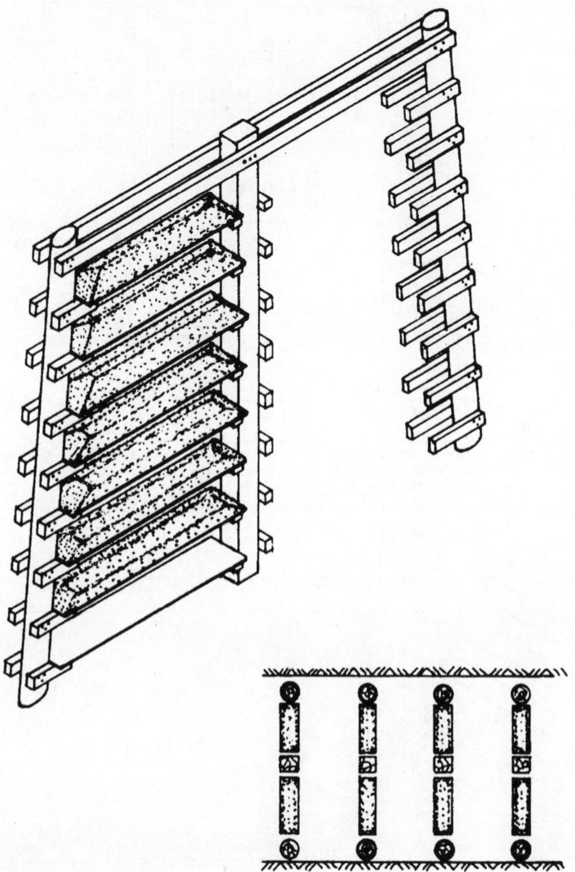

Figure 2.43 Improvised barrier.

(4) When an explosion is initiated by a weak ignition source and sufficient dynamic pressure is not built up.

The type, siting, design, installation, and maintenance of stone-dust barriers to be provided in longwall and bord and pillar workings in gassy seams of Indian coal mines in accordance with the sub-regulation (2) of Regulation 123C of the Coal Mines Regulations, 1957 (Appendix 1) are specified in the DGMS Circular No. 6 (Legis) 75.

2.2.9.3.4 Explosion-proof stoppings

Unlike stone-dust barriers, explosion-proof stoppings localize firedamp or coal-dust explosions by isolating completely the area from the rest of the mine. An explosion-proof stopping must, therefore, withstand, without being damaged, the full explosion pressure and also bring about extinction of the explosion flame by starving it of oxygen. It is mainly used for localizing explosions in parts of a mine in which there is less likelihood of widespread propagation of an explosion such as development workings in coal and stone. In practice, explosion-proof stoppings are frequently erected in sealing off fire areas where there is danger of explosion due to firedamp or fire gases.

The stoppings may be constructed of brickwork, concrete, or timber. Wedge stoppings of brick, concrete blocks and wood have been successfully used. Frequently, heavy single-wing steel doors about 20 mm thick erected in a solid stopping are used. They have the advantage that they can be closed quickly. They can also be used as 'blasting dams' in mine development work in gassy mines.

2.2.9.3.5 Salt zones

Owing to the limited efficacy of generalized stonedusting in preventing propagation of coal-dust explosions, experiments with salt zones were conducted in Germany to find a much more effective substitute. Three fundamentally different processes were developed, namely, the Salt Crust Process, the Calcium Chloride or Magnesium Chloride Paste Process, and, the Calcium Chloride Powder Process, all of which have proved to be very effective in rendering coal dust indispersible so that it does not take part in the explosion. Calcium chloride is widely used in Germany and a few other countries in Europe in paste or powder form for dust binding in mine roadways, particularly in gate roads.

Salt crust process

This process was first tried out at Beekerwerth Colliery in the Ruhr Coalfied. It consists of coating the sides, roof, and floor of a length of a roadway with a plastic mixture of rock salt (fine and coarse) containing about 96 per cent NaCl and water by means of guniting equipment and wetting with sprays of water as dry salt crust is formed and a large quantity of coal dust is deposited on the crust. Under the influence of the ventilating current, the water evaporates and the salt crystallizes through the coal dust, forming with it a hard black crust. A great disadvantage of this process, however, is that it cannot be used where the relative humidity exceeds 80 per cent as no recrystallization takes place. In very dry conditions with relative humidity below 55 per cent, water evaporates so rapidly that frequent re-wetting becomes necessary, which makes the method uneconomical.

Calcium chloride/Magnesium chloride paste process

This process depends for its action not upon the formation of a crust by alternate processes of solution and crystallization but upon continued wetting of the coal dust by the hygroscopic action of calcium chloride or magnesium chloride paste which causes the dust particles to adhere or bind by extracting moisture from the atmosphere. The hygroscopicity of the calcium chloride or magnesium chloride alone will not suffice to wet the dust unless a wetting agent (1 to 1.5 per cent) is added to it. To improve adherence to rock surfaces, a gelatinous compound, magnesium hydroxide (2 to 3 per cent), is added to the calcium chloride or magnesium chloride solution which then assumes a pudding-like appearance. The percentage of calcium chloride or magnesium chloride depends on the prevailing climatic conditions. It must be such that the paste maintains its pudding-like state for as long a time a practicable. At higher temperatures and relative humidities, the required concentration of the solution will be less than at lower temperatures and relative humidities. Figure 2.44 shows the variation of $CaCl_2$ concentration with the relative humidity at 30°C [17]. The optimum concentration is best determined by trials. The quantity and kind of wetting agent depend on the quantity of coal dust to be neutralized by the paste in a given time. It should be non-ionizing and also be cheaply available. Polyglycol ethers are the best wetting agents. One kg paste binds about 5 kg dust and, when applying for the first time, a 5 kg paste per square metre surface area is required [53] so that, with a roadway perimeter of 10 m (excluding floor), 50 kg paste per metre length of roadway will be required.

A calcium chloride paste zone in a roadway is prepared by spraying the side-roof surfaces over a length of at least 80 m of the roadway with the paste and spreading flaked calcium chloride, a mixture of monohydrate and dihydrate of calcium chloride containing a wetting agent, evenly over the floor. The paste, if properly applied, remains effective for a period of a few weeks to six months, depending on the amount of dust deposition, after which it should be sprayed fresh.

Experiments conducted at the German Experimental Mine under the severest experimental conditions have shown that the flame of a firedamp or coal-dust explosion striking into the paste zone is extinguished within the first few metres of the zone [54].

The dust-binding capacity of calcium chloride paste which is given by the mass of coal dust neutralized per unit mass of the paste depends on the size of coal dust, the rank of the coal, the amount of dust deposition per day, the kind and concentration of the wetting agent, the 2 amount of support material, and the thickness of the paste layer [55].

Like a stone-dust barrier, a calcium chloride- or magnesium chloride-paste zone will fail to suppress an explosion if it is filled with a flammable firedamp mixture or has a layer of firedamp at the roof.

On the European continent, greater reliance is placed on calcium chloride paste-zones than on generalized stonedusting or stone-dust barriers. Calcium chloride has a slight corrosive effect on rails, ropes, etc., which should be kept out of contact with the salt.

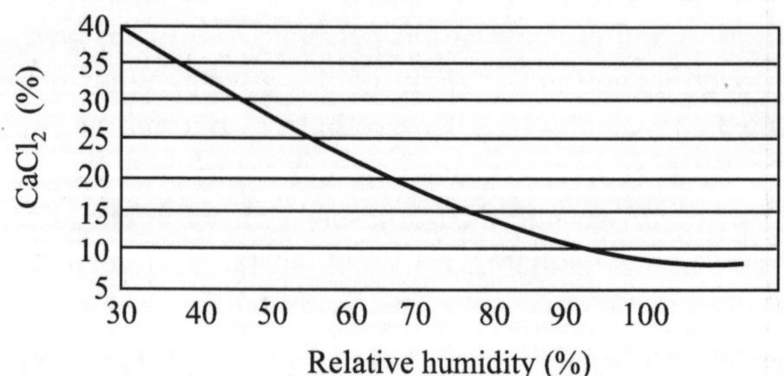

Figure 2.44 Variation of $CaCl_2$ concentration with relative humidity at 30°C.

Calcium chloride powder process

The calcium chloride/magnesium chloride paste process suffers from a serious disadvantage that the paste, containing 20 to 30 per cent hygroscopic salt, must be transported in special containers to the place of use or pumped using high -pressure pumps where it is not possible to transport the containers. To overcome this difficulty, Chemische Fabrik Kalk GmbH, Germany developed in 1965 the Montan Powder Process, in which a fine-grained high-percentage calcium chloride powder (80 to 85 per cent monohydrate $CaCl_2$, H_2O) containing a wetting agent (3 per cent) is used in place of the paste. Sodium chloride is added to serve as support material to promote adherence to clean surfaces and to extend the interval between applications. On account of its large surface area, the powder adheres to the roof and vertical surfaces. It takes up water vapour from the ventilating air becoming a solution and forms a paste with the deposited dust. The wetting agent acts through the paste. One kg powder takes up 1.3 litres of water at 50 per cent humidity, 2 litres of water at 70 per cent humidity, and 4.6 litres of water at 90 per cent humidity. Depending on the relative humidity of the ventilating air, 1 kg powder binds 4 to 7 kg mine dust for humidities between 50 and 90 per cent.

The powder is applied by machines which blow fluidized powder onto roadway surfaces through antistatic tubing. Two men can apply powder over 60 to 300 m of a roadway in a shift. Hands, arms, faces, and other uncovered parts of the body must be protected using protective creams. Electrical installations may be protected by a plastic film.

The normal frequency of application depends on the amount of coal dust deposited, that is, the output, and lies in general between one and six weeks. At the pithead, 1 t of powder (80 per cent $CaCl_2$) costs four to five times the cost of 1 t paste (20 to 30 per cent $CaCl_2$).

The advantages of the powder process over the paste process are that the storage and transportation of powder in plastic sacks are simpler; roadway roof, sides, and floor can be treated in one operation; it is less corrosive and can be used under all humid conditions generally prevalent in mines. A disadvantage of the powder is its high dispersability, which causes it to be carried over long distances. For this reason, the intake airways must be dusted when there are no men on the face. The addition of sodium chloride as support material makes it dispersible with difficulty.

2..2.9.3.6 Water barriers

Since the early 1960s, interest has revived in the use of passive water barriers, also called water-trough barriers, as an alternative to stone-dust barriers for suppression of coal-dust explosions in mines. Water has the following advantages over stone dust:

(a) its heat capacity is about five times that of dust;
(b) its efficacy is not affected by underground climatic conditions; and
(c) it is available in all mine roadways.

A water barrier consists of a number of water-filled troughs or containers of suitable material supported on horizontal shelves in the vicinity of the mine roof as in the case of a stone-dust barrier. The containers shatter or burst under the action of the pressure wave or shock wave ahead of the propagating flame of an explosion releasing and dispersing water in all directions in the path of the explosion flame. In some countries, water barriers have become the principal means of protection against coal-dust explosions.

Water barriers offer advantages over stone-dust barriers in cheapness and ease of installation and maintenance. Extensive tests on the performance of water barriers carried out in the Tremonia Experimental Mine, Germany showed that in quenching explosion flames, water barriers are roughly equivalent to stone-dust barriers and that 200 litres of water per square metre of roadway cross-section would be necessary for the same effect as 400 kg stone dust per square metre on Dortmund shelves [56]. Besides the magnitude of the dynamic pressure, the shattering of the water troughs is influenced by the trough material used, trough shape, method of installation, and trough lids or covering. Wood and sheet steel are not suitable materials. Troughs made of certain varieties of hard PVC or foamed polystyrol (Styropor) have been found to be most suitable materials as they are easily shattered at low wind pressures, giving good water distribution. The troughs must be designed so that they maintain their shape with little sacrifice of their fragility. Only troughs with approval certificates should be used. The method of installation of the troughs in a roadway cross-section exercises a great influence on the shattering of the troughs. Troughs placed with their longer axis at right-angles to the roadway axis offer greater frontal area to the dynamic pressure than when they are placed parallel to the axis of the roadway.

Contrary to expectations, troughs supported in the roadway cross-section with their edges resting on the transverse supporting frame have been found to shatter more easily than troughs supported on transverse bars. This is because the former are subjected to the full dynamic pressure and cannot be displaced as happens with the latter. Also, the use of loose lids to prevent evaporation of water does not in any way affect the distribution of water in the direction of the roof as the lid lifts itself off the trough.

Water barriers are at present-widely used in German coal mines. Their design and installation procedures are laid down in the regulations. Depending on the method of support, two types of water barriers have been approved for use in mine roadways less than 4 m in height or less than the maximum width at the site of installation – Type I and Type 2. In Type 1 barriers, the troughs are supported with their total upper lip surface resting on transverse supporting frames while in Type 2 barriers, the troughs are placed over transverse bars. Figure 2.45 illustrates the prescribed method of installation of water troughs carried by a shelf in a roadway cross-section as well as the two types of approved trough construction.

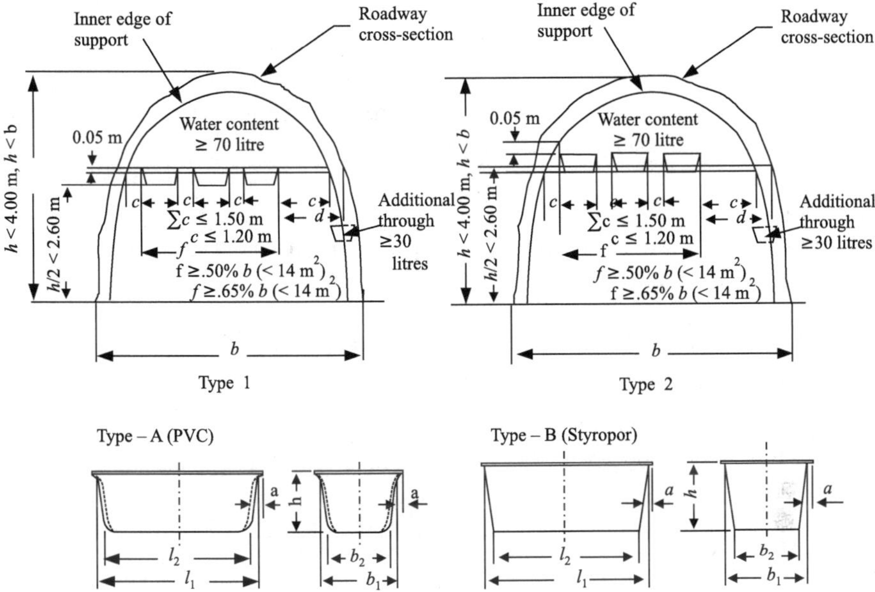

Figure 2.45 German water (trough) barrier (schematic)
l_1 = 760; l_2=720; a = 25; b_1=500; b_2=450; h=270; Vol=831.

The following rules govern the erection of water barriers in German mines:

(i) The water barriers must at all times contain a total quantity of at least 200 litres of water per square metre roadway cross-section or at least 5 litres per m^3 roadway volume and must be at least 20 m long.

(ii) The distance between two shelves must be at least 1.2 m.

(iii) The space between lips of adjacent troughs carried by a shelf must not be greater than 1.20 m and the total space between troughs in a row of troughs must not exceed 1.50 m. A row of troughs is identified as a number of troughs supported across the roadways from side to side.

(iv) The distance between the outer troughs of a row and roadways side or rib must not exceed 1 m. Where this distance exceeds 1 m, an additional trough containing at least 30 litres of water must be installed at the rib.

(v) The troughs must cover, at the site of installation, at least 50 per cent maximum roadway width for roadway cross-sections up to 14 m^2 , and 65 per cent maximum roadway width for roadway cross-sections exceeding up to 14 m^2 and 65 per cent maximum roadway width for railway cross-sections exceeding 14 m^2.

(vi) The bottom of the troughs must be at a height of at least half the height of he roadway but not exceed 2.60 m.

(vii) When the top lip or edge of the troughs is higher than 1.70 m above the roadway floor, the trough walls must be designed so that the water level can be recognized against marked graduations or a float provided in each trough.

(viii) With Type 2 barriers, the vertical space between the top edge of the trough and the inner edge of the roof support must be at least 10 cm.

(ix) The troughs must carry at least 70 litres of water.

(x) At all places where barriers are installed, water from a water pipe must be available. Water hoses must be provided.

(xi) Water barriers must be located at least 100 m away from stone-dust barriers.

(xii) The distance between barriers must not be greater than 200 m in gate roadways and 400 m in main roadways,

Figure 2.46 shows a water barrier in the main gate of a mechanized longwall face.

Figure 2.47 shows the modified German trough recommended by the U.S. Bureau of Mines for use in water barrier installations on belt conveyor roads [57]. In this design, the side lip supports are removed and the front and rear lips of the

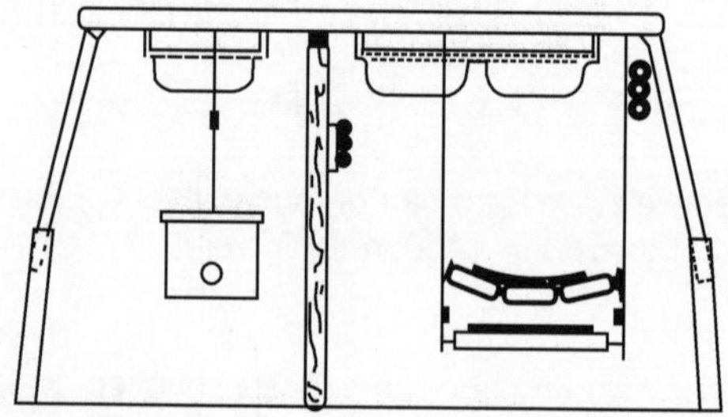

Figure 2.46 Water troughs in the cross-section of the gate road of an advancing longwall face.

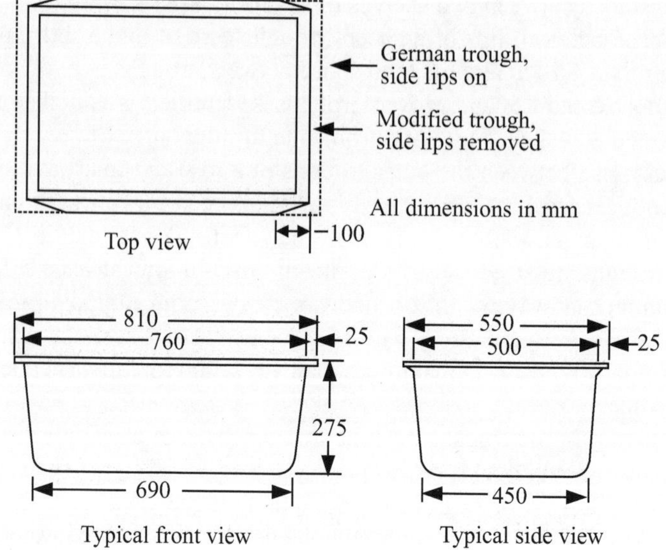

Figure 2.47 Modified German/Trough.

modified trough rest on the framework so that, in the event of an explosion, the trough falls pivoting about its rear lip. Such a design is expected to be effective in suppressing weak coal-dust explosions.

Investigations carried out in the Experimental Mines in Germany and in the USA has shown that water barriers in which large quantities of water are concentrated in troughs mounted on shelves close together forming a short barrier system length are reliably effective in suppressing moderate to strong coal-dust explosions with static pressures lying in the range 1 to 3 bar, wind pressures between 40 and 50 kN/m^2 , and flame velocities 76 to over 300 m/s. They have also shown that such barriers can be ineffective:

(1) When an explosion is initiated close to (less than 40 m) or far from the barrier or initiated by a weak ignition source, resulting in a weak or slow-moving explosion with flame speed less than 76 m/s [58], or

(2) when an explosion is very strong or violent, detonation-like, so that the time lapse between the arrivals of the pressure wave front and flame at the barrier become too short (less than 0. 1 s) to disperse water into the roadway cross-section or

(3) when an explosion spreads into an adjacent roadway through interconnecting crosscuts.

To overcome the above limitations of concentrated water barriers, 'distributed water barriers' were developed in Germany in which rows of water-filled troughs on shelves are 'distributed' as much as 10 to 30 m apart along the roadway so that the total barrier system is several hundred metres long. This increases the probability that a few shelves will be at some optimum distance from the explosion origin to suppress the explosion flame. The distributed barriers were found to be effective in suppressing slow-moving to powerful explosions with static pressure of up to about 6 bar, dynamic pressures of up to 1.6 bar, and flame velocities between 30 and 500 m/s.

With distributed barriers, the quantity of extinguishing water is expressed in litre or kg per cubic metre of roadway volume. The quantity of water required, as found from trials in experimental mines, lies between 0.5 and 1 litre per m^3 and the number of troughs or containers required is no more than with the concentrated barriers.

The US Bureau of Mines developed three types of water barriers especially for use against slow-moving explosions. One barrier is a modification of the conventional German barrier which responds to dynamic pressures whereas the second and third types respond to rise in static pressures developed ahead of the explosion for their operation. All the three types were found to be effective against weak dust explosions.

2.2.9.3.7 *Triggered barriers*

Stone-dust and water barriers suffer from the disadvantages that they depend for their action on the dynamic pressure generated by the explosion. To make their operation independent of pressure, work on the so-called 'triggered barriers' was started in some of the European countries around 1966. A triggered barrier consists of a sensor or detector, a disperser, and an extinguishing agent. The sensor, located upstream of the disperser, detects a developing explosion and sends a signal to the disperser which disperses the extinguishing agent into the path of the explosion flame. Triggered barrier systems and several extinguishing agents were investigated in large-diameter galleries and experimental mines against firedamp and coal-dust explosions propagation. Firedamp explosions were successfully suppressed in large-diameter pipes by use of dry extinguishing powders as well as water.

A suitable sensor must be sufficiently sensitive to react to temperature changes or to radiation from the flame of any size of explosion. On the other hand, it must be selective, so that it would not react to extraneous effects and influences such as those due to mechanical shocks, cable faults, air-blast shocks produced from normal blasting work, mine lighting, and heat from flame lamps or other sources. Its performance should not be impaired by dust, oil, or water. The photo-electric (infrared and ultraviolet) and thermocouple sensors have their own advantages and disadvantages. By suitable design, some of the disadvantages can, however, be overcome. UV-sensors have been found to be unreliable in operation with coal-dust explosions in which an unburnt cloud of coal dust between the flame and the sensor may attenuate the UV-radiation to an insignificant level.

There are two types of extinguishant dispersion systems. In one system, the extinguishing water contained in a trough or the extinguishing powder held in a polythene bag or polythene-covered container is dispersed by a detonating cord. In the second system, the extinguishing agent which may be water or powder, is contained in the disperser under a stored force (pressurized nitrogen gas or Halon 1301) and is dispersed when a detonator bursts the sealing disc or diaphragm of a quick-release valve of an inverted high-pressure steel cylinder containing the suppressant water or powder and nitrogen at a pressure of 30, 60, or 120 bar(g).

It is essential that the extinguishant is discharged at a high rate and that the time interval between the onset of discharge and flame arrival does not exceed the time necessary for full discharge.

The relative effectiveness of the extinguishing agents tried has been found to be as follows [59]:

$$KHCO_3 < \text{Water} < \text{Water mixed with Halon 1301 } (CF_3Br) < \text{Halon } (CF_3Br)$$

Water is two to three times as effective as potassium bicarbonate, whereas the hybrids and Halon alone are only marginally superior to water. Triggered barriers have the following advantages over the conventional barriers:

(1) They are applicable in all regions of a mine;
(2) They find particular application in thin seams where there is insufficient headroom for passive barriers;

(3) They can be used to suppress firedamp explosions;
(4) Much less extinguishant will be required; and
(5) Minimum barrier maintenance.

Triggered barriers, however, have not found general application in mines.

Recently, a new type of bagged stone-dust barrier system was developed in South African and is currently in use in African and Australian coal mines. The stone dust, instead of being spread on wooden shelves as in conventional barriers, is contained in bags suspended from the roof of the roadway. It is claimed that the system is as effective as stone-dust or water trough barriers, with the added advantages of easier installation and simpler maintenance.

Roadheaders for mine development in European mines are being equipped with active triggered barriers in which methane ignited near the cutter head triggers release of a fire extinguishing agent.

2.3 Investigation of Mine Explosions

When investigating the possible cause of origin and course of a coal mine explosion, all the principal underground evidence available immediately after the explosion should be carefully collected. Some of the evidence obtained may be conflicting in nature due to the effect of backlash. The knowledge of the conditions obtained before the explosion, the nature of operations being carried out about the time of the explosion, and the gassiness of the mine may offer vital clues.

The evidence that may be available and collected immediately after an explosion before any changes occur, consists of the following:

(1) Displacement of loaded mine cars, strong steel supports, machinery or other heavy objects, and bending of steel beams, which may serve as the best guide for ascertaining the direction in which the explosion force has travelled through the mine workings;
(2) Charring or burning of materials sensitive to flame such as paper, fibres of torn timber, and pieces of clothing which may give on minute examination in the laboratory valuable information on the passage of the explosion flame;
(3) Formation of traces of coke crust or globules on roadway supports or projections as well as on sides and roof, which not only indicate with definiteness the passage of a coal-dust explosion flame but may also throw light on the intensity of the explosion;
(4) Formation of soot deposit occurring as a layer on horizontal surfaces or as a lacy network or stringers at the roof, which would indicate the passage of the coal-dust explosion flame;
(5) Nature of death or injury of the victims, whether by burning, violence, suffocation, or poisoning by afterdamp, which it may give clues to the type of explosion that may have occurred;
(6) Position of dead bodies as obtained from the records of the rescue brigades engaged in rescue and recovery operations following the explosion as well as of equipment in relation to what might have been expected in normal

operation, which may give valuable information on the operations being carried out and on any unusual happening about that time;

(7) Defective electrical apparatus and machinery or defective or damaged safety lamps, which may pinpoint the cause of the origin of the explosion. After careful examination underground, these should be removed to the surface for a detailed examination;

(8) Discovery of contraband, such as matches or other flame-making devices, which may indicate negligence of miners as a possible cause of ignition;

(9) Signs of blown-out shot which would locate the seat of the explosion;

(10) Evidence of survivors and rescue men as well as of workers and officials in other shifts obtained as soon as possible after the explosion and kept as accurate records which may throw useful light on the conditions obtained prior to the explosion as well as at the time of the explosion;

(11) Analyses of air samples collected and analyzed immediately after the explosion, which may give a clue to the type of explosion that might have occurred; and

(12) Immediate past history of the mine and the affected part or parts thereof especially the ventilation difficulties, operation of ventilating appliances, and the seriousness of dust hazard from official reports and records, which may give a general appreciation of the explosion hazard existing in the mine.

The early stages of the investigation are generally hampered by the urgent needs of rescue, exploration, and recovery work. It is important that vital evidence is preserved for detailed investigations which should follow as early as possible.

All the evidence and data collected must be marked on a large-scale plan of the working. By careful analysis of the evidence, the most likely sequence of events and the most probable causes of the origin and seat and spread of the explosion may be inferred.

In investigations of complex accidents, a number of hazard analysis and accident investigation techniques have been developed involving the application of scientific and management principles such as the Scientific Method (Research Technique) Change Analysis, Gross Hazard Analysis, Failure Mode and Effect Analysis, and Fault Tree Analysis, any one of which may be used in making decisions.

Investigations into the causes and circumstances of a mine explosion are usually carried out by a Court of Enquiry set up by the State comprising, as its members, impartial persons who-have had a wide experience of varied mining conditions and who are specialists in their field. The final report of the Court of Enquiry reveals in all probability the basic causes leading to the disaster and the roles of the mine management and mine workers.

2.4 Sulphide Ore-Dust Explosions

Sulphide ore-dust explosions have occurred in Canadian base metal mines mining metal sulphide ores containing pyrite and pyrrhotite during the blasting operations in development headings and in production workings of cut-and-fill and blasthole stopes. The sulphide ore dust generated provided both the fuel and oxygen while blasting provided the ignition source.

Pyrite is consumed according to one of the following reactions to form haematite (Fe_2O_3), magnetite (Fe_3O_4), and the toxic sulphur dioxide (SO_2):

$$3\ FeS_2 + 8O_2 \longrightarrow Fe_3O_4 + 6O_2 + \text{heat}$$

$$4\ FeS_2 + 11O_2 \longrightarrow 2Fe_2O_3 + 8SO_2 + \text{heat}$$

The haematite is deposited as a red dust in the blast area, while the to toxic sulphur dioxide contaminates the underground workings necessitating its dilution and/or removal by the mine ventilation system.

Like coal-dust explosions, the primary or main explosion may produce a shock wave which may be strong enough to disperse the dust deposited on the walls of the opening to be ignited by the following flame front moving through the dust cloud, thereby propagating the explosion over distances as long as the flammable dust–air mixtures feed the combustion process; the extent of propagation is, however, usually shorter [60].

Systematic investigations on the theoretical and practical aspects of sulphide-ore dust explosions began in the early 1990s in Canada. They have thrown some light on the ignition of sulphide ore-dust clouds by explosives and the practical measures that may be adopted to minimize the explosion hazard in mines during blasting.

The various precautionary measures and their combination that may be adopted to combat the explosion hazard in mines are:

(1) Selecting the proper type of explosives with low incendivity, i.e., with low explosion temperatures which will not adversely affect fragmentation;
(2) Selecting a drillhole pattern which will prevent rifling of the explosive energy from the drillhole [61];
(3) Accurate drilling of the holes for successful application of incendive explosives;
(4) Careful loading of the explosive charge in holes to maintain high compaction ratios at an effective level;
(5) Tamping inert stemming cartridges in the unloaded collar of each hole;
(6) Washing down the walls and backs in the development headings before blasting; and
(7) Creating water mist curtains at the face during a blast.

CHAPTER 3

Mine Gases

Normal ambient air is a mixture of gases containing 78.10 per cent nitrogen, 20.93 per cent oxygen, 0.03 per cent carbon dioxide, 0.94 per cent argon, and traces of hydrogen, helium and other rare gases together with a variable amount of water vapour (0.1 to 3 per cent, according to the relative humidity). 'Atmosphere' is another word for air.

Pure gases seldom exist in the workplace. Generally, as air is circulated through a mine, its composition only changes a little. It loses some of its oxygen due to worker's breathing and oxidation processes in the mine. It picks up other contaminant gases often produced in mines under normal conditions, namely carbon dioxide, carbon monoxide, oxides of nitrogen, sulphur dioxide, hydrogen sulphide, and aldehydes. When the mine gives off methane, large or small amounts of it may also be liberated into the mine air. In metal mines, hydrocyanic acid may be found in the vicinity of sand-filled areas, being formed by the action of acid water on the cyanide content of sand pulp. In mines where cooling plants are used, Freon 11 and Freon 12 may also be found in mine air. With adequate ventilation, all these gases are diluted and rendered harmless and carried away so that the oxygen content in mine air stands at about 20 per cent, with the noxious gases present only in traces not exceeding the prescribed threshold limit values.

Under abnormal conditions, such as during mine fires and after explosions, the composition of the mine air may, however, undergo significant changes. Dangerous quantities of asphyxiating or poisonous gases and atmosphere devoid of oxygen may be encountered in mine workings in which only rescue men equipped with respiratory protective equipment can work. Knowledge of the different gases, in particular their physical properties and toxicity and methods of their detection or estimation other than by the gas-volumetric method is, therefore, essential for every rescue man. It will also be necessary to know the allowable exposure levels for the mine gases below which the health of a worker is not affected.

3.1 Threshold Limit Value (TLV)

The threshold limit value of a toxic gas, fume or vapour is the minimum airborne concentration of the gas, fume, or vapour below which no adverse health effect or poisoning will occur from exposure for a working lifetime and above which injury will result from repeated exposure day after day in workplace air. Determination of the threshold limit values is often a difficult problem. Every year the American Conference of Governmental Industrial Hygienists review and specify threshold limit values for a very large number of industrial materials, which are generally adopted as reference values throughout the world. Data available from extensive assessment studies should be taken into account in determining the proper values.

There are three types or categories of threshold limit values:

Threshold limit value – time-weighted average limit (TLV – TWA).

Threshold limit value – short-term exposure limit (TLV – STEL).

Threshold limit value – ceiling (TLV – C).

Time-weighted average (TLV – TWA)
It refers to the average concentration to which a worker is exposed over the course of a work week. It is calculated on the basis of a 40-hour work week and is expressed in either parts of gas, fume, or vapour per million parts of contaminated air by volume (ppm.) or in approximate milligrams of substance per cubic metre of air (mg/m^3). 0.1 vol per cent = 0.00 1 = 1000 ppm. Time-weighted averages allow for excursions above the TLV for short periods without injury to health (up to a specified maximum), provided they are compensated by equivalent excursions below the limit during the work day. The excursion depends on various factors such as the nature of hazard, whether it has cumulative effects, whether exposure to very high concentrations even for short periods can cause acute poisoning, the frequency with which the TLV is exceeded, and the duration of the excessive concentration.

Short-term exposure limits (TLV – STEL)
These are maximum concentrations to which a worker can be exposed for a period of up to 15 minutes at any one time without suffering from intolerable irritation, materially reduced work efficiency, etc., provided that the exposure does not occur more than four times a day with at least 60 minutes between exposure periods.

Ceiling concentrations (TLV – C)
These are maximum allowable concentrations (MACs) that should not be exceeded even instantaneously.

It should be stressed that TLVs are intended only as a guide and should be used as not fine dividing lines between safe and dangerous concentrations. Exposure within allowable levels can be achieved by means of well-designed control measures which will minimise, the gas or fume in the workplace air and good work practices which will ensure safe working conditions.

For measurement of concentration of gases encountered in mine atmospheres, a number of single and multi-gas detectors and monitors with state-of-the-art gas detection instrumentation are available in the market, which can continuously detect and display the gas concentration of a single gas of concern or all gases simultaneously.

Gas concentration is commonly measured in percentage (%) by volume and parts per million (ppm). They are easily converted to one another by using the basic relation.

$$\% \times 10000 = \text{ppm}$$

Contamination limits are only quoted in milligrams per cubicmetre (mg/m³). The following relation is used to convert concentrations from ppm at 20°C to mg/m³.

$$\text{mg/m}^3 = (\text{ppm} \times M) \div 24.4$$

where M is the molecular weight of the gas and 24.04 is a gas constant.

In the following, the causes, sources, effects, detection and estimation of mine gases will be described.

3.2 Oxygen (O_2)

Oxygen is a colourless, tasteless, and odourless gas which is 1. 1 times heavier than air. Its density is 1.428 kg/Nm³. It is slightly soluble in water, 100 volumes of water dissolving at 20°C, 3 volumes of the gas. The critical temperature is –119°C and the critical pressure 50 atm. Liquid oxygen has a light to steel blue colour; it has a specific gravity of 1.12 (water = 1) and boils at –183°C at a pressure of 760 Torr.

Oxygen is essential to human, animal, and vegetable life. The average person will consume approximately 740 litres of oxygen (1 kg of oxygen) per 24 hours. By breathing, oxygen is absorbed by the blood and carried to the cells of the body. It is an extremely reactive element which combines with many elements (oxidation) with evolution of heat. Depending on the rate of oxidation, one distinguishes between the terms slow oxidation, combustion, explosion, and detonation.

In mines, the oxygen content in mine air decreases due to breathing by men, burning of flame safety lamps, absorption by acidic mine water, and gradual oxidation of organic and inorganic substances such as mine timber, coal, and pyrites. The oxygen content, however, decreases considerably immediately after a mine fire or explosion or due to appearance of other gases in higher concentrations. In most cases, the reduction in oxygen is attended with an increase in carbon dioxide content.

The biological effect of oxygen depletion is similar to asphyxiation. Oxygen depletion producing a hazardous condition occurs when it is consumed by oxidation from the surrounding air without fresh air replacing the consumed oxygen or by displacement from another gas.

A fall in oxygen from its usual level of 21 per cent in air to 18 per cent does not represent any danger to human life, although it is advised not to enter a work place with less than 18 per cent oxygen. When it falls from 18 to 15 per cent, the breathing becomes laboured and muscular skill is diminished (anoxia); when it falls from 14 to 10 per cent, a man is still conscious but has faulty judgement (not obvious to himself) and he becomes fatigued very quickly, with a further fall from 10 to 6 per cent, he collapses due to inadequate supply of oxygen to the brain but can be revived by fresh air or oxygen. Increased oxygen demands during periods of hard work may result in oxygen-deficiency symptoms at much higher percentages. Oxygen deficiency in circulating air of self-contained breathing apparatus caused by the wearer of the apparatus forgetting to turn on the oxygen cylinder valve leads to similar effects. The threshold limit value of oxygen is given as 19.5 ppm.

The adequacy of oxygen in mine air may be ascertained by means of a flame safety lamp, the flame of which becomes dim and small and finally goes out when the oxygen content falls to about 16 per cent, whether carbon dioxide be present or not. Small amounts of methane tend to decrease this value somewhat; for example, when the atmosphere contains 1 per cent methane, extinction occurs with about 15 per cent oxygen. An acetylene lamp does not give a warning of the presence of an irrespirable atmosphere as it burns in oxygen concentrations up to 12 per cent and is extinguished at 10 per cent.

The inhalation of pure oxygen under normal conditions for a limited period up to 6 hours has no harmful effects. With self-contained breathing apparatus, the oxygen content in the circulating air lies between 40 and 60 per cent. In abnormally high concentrations, irritation of the lungs may develop. Pure oxygen at 1 atm has the same effect on the body as air compressed to about 5 atm pressure. Pure oxygen at elevated pressures and air at pressures above 5 atm may adversely affect the body. For this reason, special precautions must be taken when working in tunnels under higher-than-normal oxygen pressures.

3.2.1 Detection and estimation

The ambient air oxygen concentration can be measured by use of an oxygen indicator, analyzer, meter, or detector notably manufactured by MSA/Auer, Dräger, Riken, Oldham, Sieger, and others based either on the electrochemical reduction of oxygen in a galvanic cell or on the paramagnetic property of oxygen.

The oxygen indicators, meters or personal monitors are hand-held instruments based on the principle of electrochemical reduction of oxygen. They sample the atmosphere for oxygen deficiency or oxygen surplus by diffusion and measure concentrations of oxygen over a range of 0 to 25 per cent with an accuracy of ± 0.2 per cent O_2.

These instruments use an electrochemical cell, also known as a fuel cell, as an oxygen sensor. The cell contains two dissimilar electrodes, a gold cathode and a lead anode, in a basic electrolyte (Fig. 3.1). The entire cell is encapsulated in inert plastic which is sealed off. A thin teflon membrane protects the sensing electrode and allows oxygen to diffuse into the cell where it is dissolved in the electrolyte. The oxygen reacts at the gold cathode, giving it a positive charge. The anode is negatively charged through the formation of lead oxide and water so that a low electric current proportional to the oxygen concentration can flow between the cathode and anode. This current is used as a measuring signal which is amplified

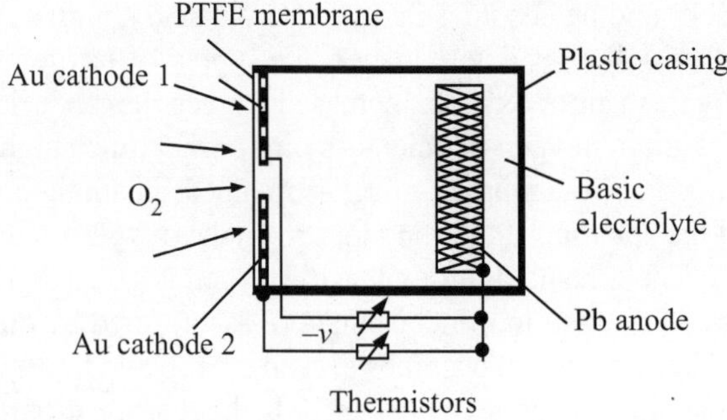

Figure 3.1 Fuel cell

through a solid-state electronic circuit and transmitted to the indicator and the alarm unit if the oxygen level falls below the set value.

The main advantages of the electrochemical sensing cell are its remarkable stability and rapid response over a long period and negligible influence of pressure or humidity variations. The microprocessor controls the measurement and processes the temperature-compensated signal to display a non-ambiguous value.

The main disadvantage of the cell, however, is that the gradual conversion of the lead anode to lead oxide limits its life. The sensor capsule must then be replaced. The life span of the cell at room temperature and sea-level pressure is given as one year.

Since the response is linear, the instrument can be single-point calibrated using known oxygen concentrations.

The instrument is equipped with a rechargeable NiCd battery pack or a 9-V dry cell. The housing is made of antistatic plastic material. Fig. 3.2 shows MSA/ Auer, Draeger, Riken Keiki, and Sabre oxygen personal monitors.

3.3 Nitrogen (N_2)

Nitrogen is a colourless, tasteless, and odourless gas. It is slightly lighter than normal air, its specific gravity being 0.967. It has a density of 1.254 kg/Nm^3. Its critical temperature is –146°C and the critical pressure 35 atm. Liquid nitrogen boils at –196°C. The gas is slightly soluble in water, 100 volumes of water dissolving at 15°C, 1.8 volumes of nitrogen. It is chemically inert; it is not combustible and, hence, also not a supporter of combustion.

As part of the air, nitrogen is found throughout the mine. It may stream out of pores of coal seams and adjacent strata. It occurs in gas outbursts in potash and copper slate mines.

Nitrogen undergoes no alteration in the process of breathing , has no metabolic function and is not poisonous but suffocates due to lack of oxygen when present in an amount greatly in excess of that normally found in air. In the absence of oxygen, it becomes a lethal asphyxiant. Under very high pressures, mental confusion, incoordination, etc., sometimes result due probably to the anaesthetic action of the nitrogen present in abnormally high concentrations.

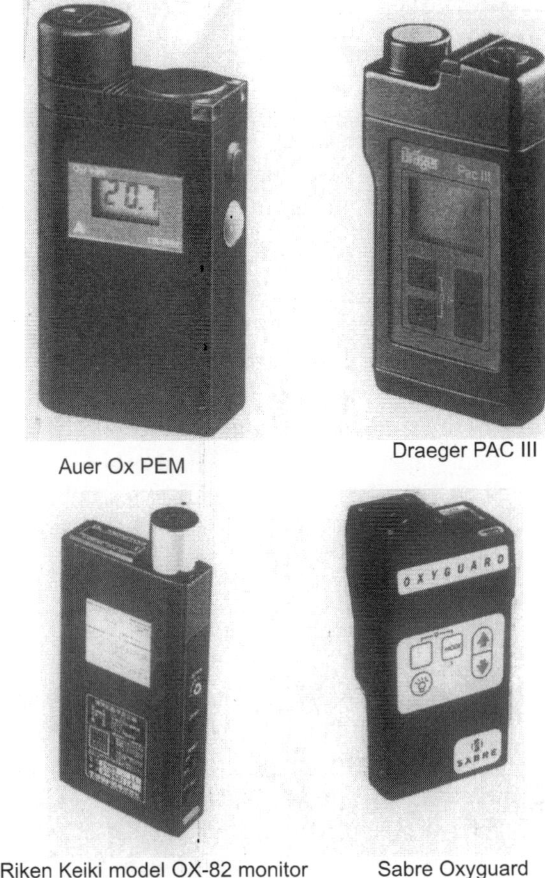

Figure 3.2 Personal oxygen monitors

3.4 Carbon Dioxide (CO_2)

Carbon dioxide, commonly called black damp, is a colourless, odourless gas having a slight acid taste. It is about one-and-a-half times heavier than air and, in consequence, is found in low-lying places in mines. It is extremely soluble in water, 100 volumes of water dissolving at 15°C, 100 volumes of the gas forming a weak acid. The critical temperature is –31.9°C. Carbon dioxide is not combustible and does not support combustion nor sustain life.

It is produced in mines from the following causes:

(1) Breathing of men (average 50 litres per hour per worker); produced in the human body and exhaled in the respiratory process.

(2) Burning of flames (0. 15 to 5 litres per minute per lamp);

(3) Decay of mine timber;

(4) Slow oxidation of coal in coal mines;

(5) Exudation in pure state or associated with methane from the coal seams and adjacent strata;
(6) Gas outbursts in coal and potash mines;
(7) Blasting;
(8) Use of internal combustion engines, such as diesel locomotives; and
(9) Mine fires and explosions in afterdamp.

In the potash mines of the Werra-Basin, Germany, about 40 to 50 gas and potash-outbursts occur in a year with an average intensity of 1800 t per outburst [62]. The carbon dioxide content of mine air increases continuously as the air passes through the mine workings. Its average value depends on the intensity of ventilation. In adequately-ventilated mines, the CO_2-content of mine air is generally kept below 0.5 per cent, irrespective of whether the mine is a coal or metalliferous mine. Higher concentrations of carbon dioxide may also occur in the circulating air of a self-contained breathing apparatus if, by mistake, a used-up regenerating canister has been used. The exhalation of carbon dioxide by escaping workers in refuge stations can create hazards.

Carbon dioxide in small concentrations of up to 3 per cent has the peculiar, function of regulating the breathing apparatus of man. Investigations show that the rate of breathing and the quantity of air inhaled per breath depend on the CO_2-content in the alveoli.

Carbon dioxide is not poisonous in the real sense but is asphyxiating. It is difficult to fix safe, harmful, and dangerous limits of carbon dioxide in mine air as the resistance of different individuals to the effects of carbon dioxide inhalation varies greatly. At even 0.5 per cent or 5000 ppm, breathing becomes a little deeper and faster; at 2 per cent, the rate and depth of breathing increase by 50 per cent; at 4 per cent, breathing becomes much faster (about three times), and, with physical exertion over several hours, headache, palpitation of the heart, and weakness result; at 8 to 10 per cent, after half to one hour of work, suffocation and unconsciousness occur; in the vicinity of 20 per cent, death occurs after 20 to 30 minutes of breathing unless the victim is removed to a source of fresh air. The above-mentioned symptoms are observed when the oxygen content of air decreases with increasing carbon dioxide content. When, however, the oxygen content is greater than 20 per cent, the toxic effects of carbon dioxide will be less pronounced. The threshold limit value of carbon dioxide is given as 5000 ppm.

Figure 3.3 shows the increase in pulmonary ventilation with increase in the carbon dioxide concentration in air [63].

3.4.1 Detection and estimation

The detection and estimation of carbon dioxide in mine air may be done by means of a flame safety lamp or hand-measuring instruments utilizing detector tubes.

Carbon dioxide exerts an extinguishing effect on the flame of a flame safety lamp. It is, however, difficult to determine exactly the concentration at which

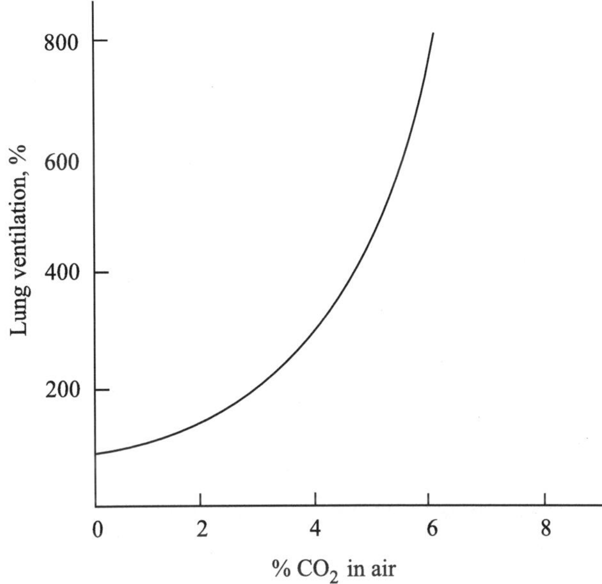

Figure 3.3 Increase in lung ventilation with increase in CO_2 concentration.

the flame becomes dim or starts extinguishing as these depend not only on the concentration of carbon dioxide but also on the oxygen content of mine air and other factors. In still air, the flame extinguishes at a lower concentration than in moving air. Also, the burning of the flame depends on the flame temperature. In still air, the flame of a safety lamp is extinguished at a CO_2 concentration of 3 to 4 per cent. A flammable methane air mixture is incapable of supporting flame propagation when the carbon dioxide concentration is 25 per cent.

Hand-held detectors using colorimetric indicating detectors using detector tubes provide a rapid economical method for manual sampling of more than 100 different toxic gases, fumes, and vapours in the threshold limit ranges. A detector consists of a dosing pump of bellows-, rubber aspirator bulb-, or piston-type and a package of detector tubes which are glass tubes with fused break-off tips filled with an indicating chemical substance which changes colour in the presence of the gas being tested. When an accurate sample of ambient air is drawn through a detector tube, a colour change results over a length which is proportional to the gas concentration which is read off on the concentration scale printed on the tube for direct reading or the length of colour stain compared with an accompanying scale. The tubes are calibrated for a single gas and calibration curves drawn. Figure 3.4 shows a typical calibration curve that will be obtained for a detector tube on the basis of measurements with a given number of aspirations [64]. It will be seen that the gradient is at first very steep, followed by a rounding off and an almost linear course.

The specificity of the indicating chemical is so high that reaction only takes place when the gas component to be measured is unaffected by other gases which

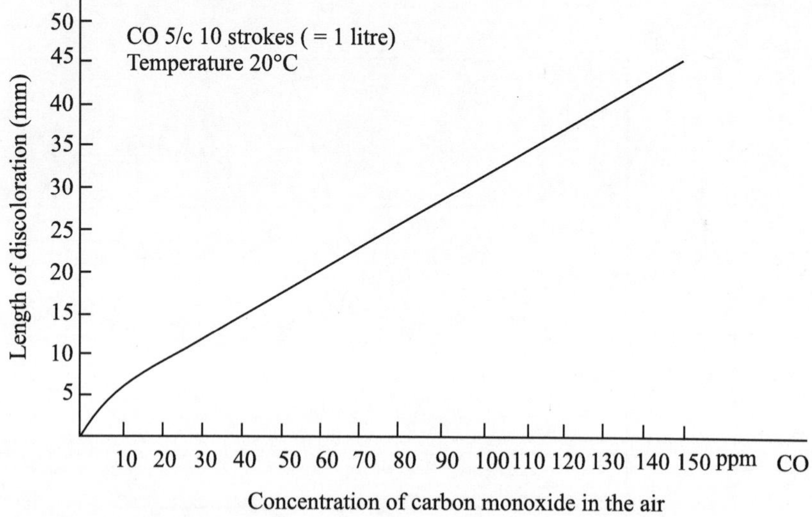

Figure 3.4 Calibration curve for the Dräger carbon monoxide 5/c tube

may be present at the same time. Where the chemical can react with other gases and vapours to give a colour change, the interfering components are removed by a pre-cleansing layer or guard chemical in the detector tube. The shelf life of the detector tubes is taken as two years.

The well-known manufacturers of detectors used in mines in the world include Mine Safety Appliance Co., (USA), Auergesells chaft GmbH (Germany), and Draegerwerk AG (Germany).

The MSA Universal Tester (Fig. 3.5(a)) has a variable-volume piston-type pump. The operator draws the handle of the pump to the preset position which controls the volume of the sample to be drawn at four levels, 25, 50, 75, or 100 ml. Sampling lines of various lengths can be used with the pump to test for the presence of toxic atmospheres in hard-to-reach areas. The MSA also manufacture detectors/testers using aspirator bulbs. The Auer Gas Tester (Fig. 3.5(b)) has an aspirator bulb to draw a sample of ambient air through the detector tube.

Manufacturers of mine and industrial safety products have brought out in the market continuously operating and electronically-controlled detector tube pumps. Figure 3.5(d) shows MSA/Auer Toximeter II which has a stroke volume (electronic stroke 100 + 5 ml) which is regulated by a temperature-compensated differential pressure sensor. The detector tube is inserted on the inlet side.

The Dräger Multigas Detector (Fig. 3.5(c)) has a hand-operated bellows pump which supplies 100 ml at each stroke. The pump head has an aperture into which the detector tube to be used is inserted. The bellows, made from neoprene, has a valve which closes when the air sample is drawn in and opens on squeezing the bellows. To draw a sample, the bellows are first

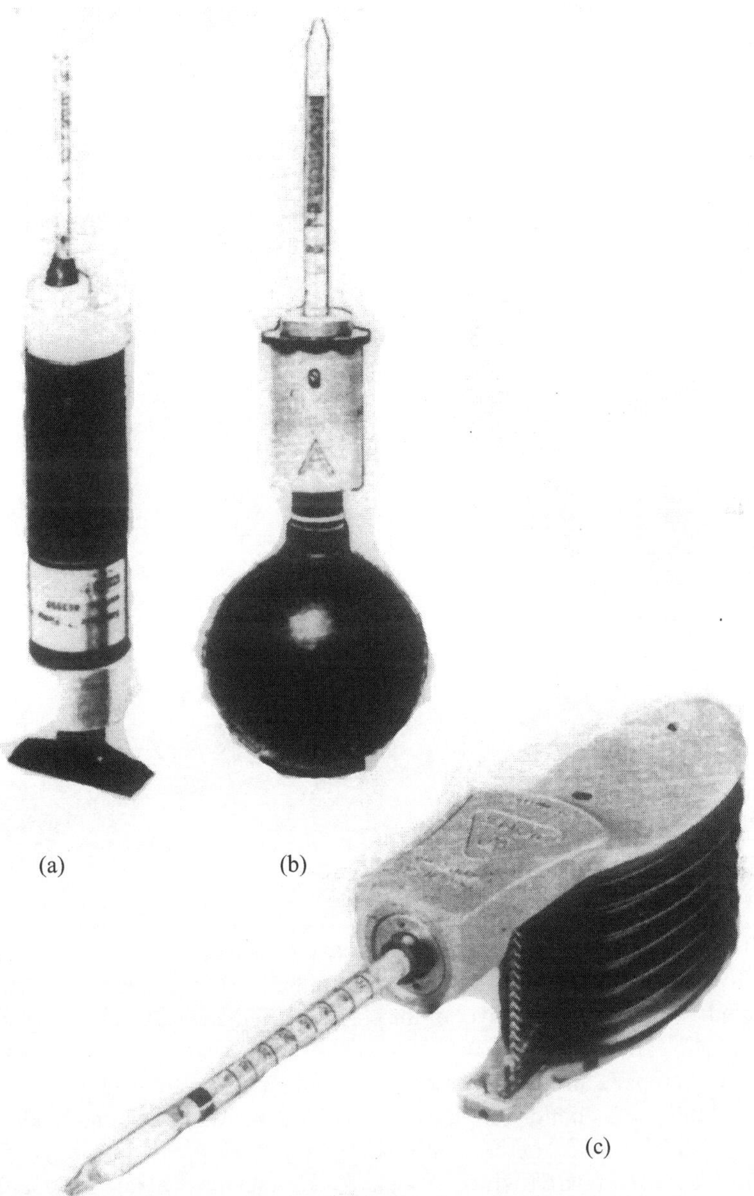

(a) (b) (c)

Figure 3.5 Multi-gas detectors using detector tubes; (a) MSA; (b) Auer; (c) Dräger.

compressed and then released, the end of the suction process being reached when the limit chain is taut. The opening time during which the sample is drawn depends on the resistance of the detector tube. It may vary from 3 to 40 s. The range of the opening time is indicated in the instructions for use of the detector tubes.

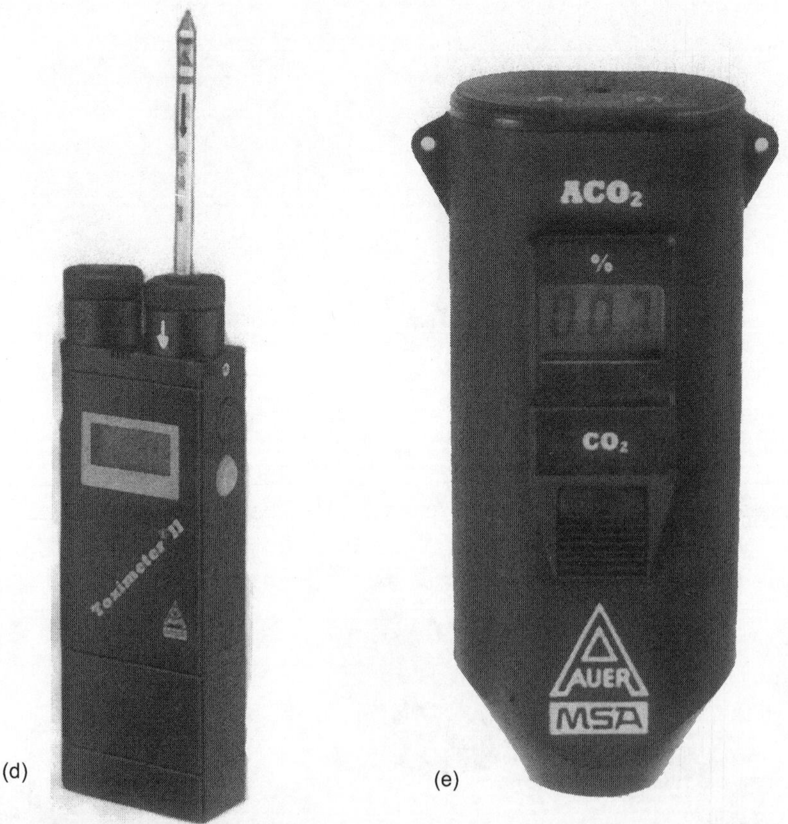

(d) (e)

Figure 3.5 contd. (d) Auer toximeter II; (e) Auer ACO_2 indicator.

The Dräger carbon dioxide detector tube has two measuring ranges of 0.1 to 1.2 vol . %~ (five strokes) and 0.5 to 6 vol. %~ (one stroke). The tube contains a pre-cleansing layer and a white indicating layer of the chemical, hydrazine, which changes colour to bluish-violet due to reaction with carbon dioxide. The presence of other gases and moisture in ambient air does not affect the reading of the instrument.

The Auer ACO_2 hand-held indicator (Fig. 3.5(e)) uses an electrochemical sensor operating over the concentration range 0.03–100 vol. %~. It samples the atmosphere by diffusion. An easily replaceable electrolyte chamber provides the sensor a life expectancy of up to 12–24 months, depending on its operation. The recommended replacement of electrolyte is every three months. The instrument is controlled by a microprocessor and powered by four standard 1.5 V batteries. All functions can be selected with a single pushbutton. The instrument has two adjustable alarm thresholds, factory-set, at 0.5 vol. % CO_2(TLV) and a main alarm at 1.0 vol.%. It is housed in dust- and waterproof antistatic material and weighs approximately 310 g with batteries.

3.5 Carbon Monoxide (CO)

Carbon monoxide, commonly called white damp, is a colourless, tasteless, odourless, and non-irritating gas. It is slightly lighter than air, with which it mixes easily; its density is 1.250 kg/N m^3. Its critical temperature is –140°C and critical pressure 34.6 atm. It is not very soluble in water, 100 volumes of water dissolving 2.3 volumes of carbon monoxide at 20°C. It is not a supporter of combustion but burns in air at about 700°C with a light-blue flame to carbon dioxide. When mixed with air in certain proportions, it explodes, the flammable range being 12.5 to 75 vol. % CO. Such mixtures may be formed following a mine fire or an explosion. Carbon monoxide is not absorbed by charcoal or alkalies which compose the absorbents of most gas masks. It can be oxidized by special catalysts such as hopcalite to carbon dioxide.

Carbon monoxide is formed in mines as a result of uncontrolled combustion of substances such as timber and coal. The principal causes of its formation are mine fires and coal-dust explosions. Small quantities of carbon monoxide may also be produced from slow oxidation of timber and coal at mine temperatures, blasting, and use of diesel equipment. With mine fires, it is found near the seat of fire in the return air current coming from the fire and in sealed-off areas until the extinguishment of the fire.

After explosions, it is found throughout the mine. It does not seek high or low parts of the mine.

3.5.1 Physiological effects

Carbon monoxide is by far the most dangerous gas encountered in coal and metal mines. It is a deadly poison. Its poisonous character is due to its great affinity for the vital haemoglobin (oxygen-carrier) of the blood. The affinity is 200 to 300 times that of oxygen, forming a more stable compound than oxyhaemoglobin ($Hb.O_2$) called carboxyhaemoglobin (Hb. CO, bright pink compound). Once the haemoglobin combines with carbon monoxide, it cannot combine with oxygen, thereby reducing the oxygen-carrying capacity of the blood which deprives the brain and body tissues of the oxygen they require for normal functioning. The rate at which carbon monoxide combines with the haemoglobin depends on the exposure time, the CO-concentration, and the activity being performed. An individual's response will vary depending on his age and general physical condition. Carbon monoxide is non-toxic to insects and other lower forms of life which have no red blood cells.

The reaction between O_2, CO, and haemoglobin is reversible and may be represented as

$$HbO_2 + CO \rightleftharpoons HbCO + O_2$$

The equilibrium constant

$$K = \frac{[O_2].[HbCO]}{[CO].[HbO_2]}$$

The equation can be rearranged as

$$\frac{[HbCO]}{[HbO_2]} = K\frac{[CO]}{[O_2]}$$

$$\frac{[HbCO]}{[HbCO]+[HbO_2]} = \frac{K[CO]}{[O_2]+K[CO]}$$

By multiplying both sides of the equation with 100, the left-hand side gives the percentage HbCO-saturation of the total Hb

$$\%HbCO = \frac{100\,.\,K[CO]}{[O_2]+K[CO]}$$

Using Vol.–% in place of molar concentration and taking the oxygen concentration in the alveolar air as constant and equal to 15 per cent, the above relation becomes

$$\%HbCO = \frac{100\,.\,K\%\,CO}{15+K\,\%CO} = \frac{100\%\,CO}{(15/K)+\%CO}$$

Taking $K = 300$, we get

$$\%HbCO = \frac{100\,.\,K\%\,CO}{0.05+\%CO}$$

By using this relation, one can easily determine the percentage saturation of the human blood with CO for any given concentration of carbon monoxide in air.

Carbon monoxide in commonly referred to as the silent killer. It often affects the victims in such a manner that they fail to recognize the danger until it is too late. When the percentage blood saturation exceeds 60, there is a great possibility of immediate death. Figure 3.6 gives a chart, 'Physiological effects of carbon monoxide on human beings,' prepared by the Staubinstitut für Staublungenforschung and Gewerbehygiene, Germany [65]. It shows the relationships between the CO-concentration (range 0.005 to 0.1 per cent CO), time of exposure, and percentage saturation of blood as well as the after-effects or symptoms of poisoning observed on a normal healthy human being. It is clear from the chart that even very small concentrations of the gas are harmful. From the chart, Table 3.1 is prepared to serve as a guide when working in mine atmospheres containing carbon monoxide. The threshold limit value is 50 ppm. A 70–80% blood saturation by CO will cause death.

Table 3.1 Physiological effects of mine air CO concentrations

CO concentration vol-%	Time of exposure	Symptoms	Work in such atmospheres
≤ 0.005	After a few hours	No perceptible symptoms or only weak symptoms	Unrestricted without respiratory protective equipment
0.010	After 6 hours	Slight headache and short breath during physical exertion	Not longer than 6 hours without respiratory protective equipment
0.020	After 2 hours	Headache, suffocation, faintness, dizziness	By rescue men without respiratory protective equipment not longer than 2 hours
0.030	After 1.5 hours	Headache, suffocation, faintness, dizziness	When CO-concentration exceeds 0.02 per cent, respiratory protective equipment to be used
0.060	Less than 1 hour	Headache, suffocation, faintness, dizziness	
	Slightly less than 2 hours	Unconsciousness	
0.10	After 1.5 hours	Unconsciousness	
	After 4 hours	Possible death	

3.5.2 Detection and estimation

For detection and estimation of carbon monoxide in mine atmospheres, the following methods are used:

(1) Canary birds
(2) Colorimetric indicating detectors
(3) Electronic measuring (indicating and monitoring) instruments

Canaries provide a simple method for detection of carbon monoxide in mine atmospheres. On account of their much faster breathing rates (about 20 times) due to high basal metabolic rate canaries are affected more quickly by the gas than a human being and thus give a warning signal for man to retreat to fresh air.

Birds are taken in small cages (two or three per cage) to places where carbon monoxide may be expected and their behaviour observed. When, at a place, a bird shows signs of distress (unsteady on its perch), the place should not be entered and any mine workings likely to be affected by the poisonous gas should be vacated forthwith.

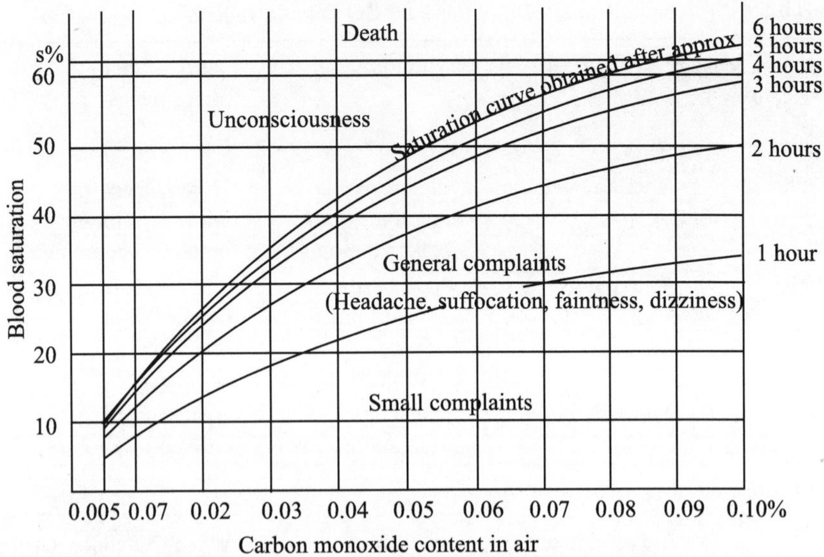

Figure 3.6 Physiological effects of carbon monoxide on human beings.

Investigations carried out both in laboratories and underground on the behaviour resistance, and symptoms of poisoning of warm-blooded canaries and mice had shown [25] that

(a) at low concentrations of carbon monoxide less than 0.1 per cent, men, especially those doing physical exertion, are affected earlier than mice and canaries;

(b) at CO-concentrations greater than 0.18 per cent, the canaries are three times more sensitive than mice and 6 to 10 times more sensitive than men at rest.

(c) there are individual differences in birds and mice in respect to their sensitivity as amongst men; and

(d) canaries are likely to be acclimatized to very small percentages of carbon monoxide.

For these reasons, canaries as living detectors have been entirely replaced by colorimetric indicating detectors and electronic gas measuring instruments.

The colorimetric stain tube methods developed work on the same principle. In each case, the manufacturer develops a detector tube that changes colour along the length of the tube in proportion to the concentration of the gas in the air. A known quantity of air, usually in multiples of 100 ml is drawn through the tube after the two glass ends have been broken and the tube is properly inserted into the pump. Most pumps are designed to draw 100 ml per stroke.

The MSA Universal Tester/Detector, Auer Gas Tester, and Dräger Multigas Detector using length-of-stain detector tubes, provide a rapid method of on-the-spot measurement of the concentration of carbon monoxide in the range 10 to 1000 ppm or 0 to 3000 ppm depending on the amount of air sampled.

The M.S.A. detector tube contains yellow silica gel impregnated with palladium sulphate and ammonium molybdate. When an ambient air sample containing carbon monoxide is drawn through the tube, the yellow silica gel turns to a shade of green, the intensity of which depends on the CO-concentration in the sample. The discoloration in the tube is compared with a colour comparison standard scale or tube to obtain the toxicant concentration.

The Dräger tube contains a white indicating layer of iodine pentoxide, selenium dioxide, and fuming sulphuric acid which turns brownish-green in the presence of carbon monoxide.

$$5CO + I_2O_5 \xrightarrow[\text{(brownish-green colour)}]{SeO_2 + H_2SO_4} I_2 + 5CO_2$$

As water vapour, gasoline vapour, hydrogen sulphide, nitrogen dioxide, ethylene, and acetylene ordinarily encountered in mines with carbon monoxide interfere with the CO reading, they are removed by a pre-cleansing layer of a guard chemical, a chromium compound contained within each tube. With high concentrations of hydrocarbon gases, the capacity of the pre-cleansing layer may not be sufficient. A pre-tube containing activated charcoal is inserted into the detector tube.

Dräger tubes for detection of carbon monoxide in dual-reading and single reading types have the ranges

Dual-range types

CO 5/c	5 to 150 ppm with 10 strokes and 100 to 700 ppm with two strokes
CO 10/b	10 to 300 ppm with 10 strokes and 100 to 3000 ppm with one stroke

Single-range types

CO	0.3%/a	0.3 to 4 vol.% with one stroke
CO	0.5%/a	0.5 to 7 vol. % one stroke

Auer developed the Toximeter II for use in conjunction with Auer detector tubes, which uses a battery-operated pump electronically controlled to draw a sample of air through the detector tube at a rate of 100 ml per basic time unit of 25 s. The basic time unit can be automatically multiplied by means of an electronic multiplier. The number of measurements that can be made per battery charge varies between 100 and 800, depending on the time of measurement. The chief advantages of the Toximeter compared with the manually-operated detectors are time saving through automatic operation, for both intermittent measurement and continuous air monitoring, and greater reliability. It can be used for collecting samples in or drawing samples from sampling tubes or sample containers and as a pump of a smoke generator to generate smoke with smoke tubes or smoke cartridges.

The Dräger Quantimeter is an automatic model of the Dräger Multigas Detector based on bellows pump. A fixed volume of 100 ml is drawn through the detector tube per stroke. The number of strokes is selected before measurement and, operation takes place automatically. More than 500 pump strokes can be obtained per battery charge. It weighs 5 kgf.

Carbon monoxide indicators, meters, monitors

For frequent measurement of carbon monoxide, a portable electronic measuring instrument is more accurate and economical than a detector with detector tubes. It is a self-contained battery-powered instrument capable of measuring CO in air in a range of 0 to 100 or 0 to 500 ppm by volume.

The MSA / AUER carbon monoxide indicator 'MiniCO'(Fig. 3.7)

The MiniCO indicator is a hand-held battery-powered instrument with a measuring range of 0 to 100 ppm CO in air (Model I) or 0 to 500 ppm CO (Model II) and minimum detectable concentration of 2 ppm.

The sensor is an electrochemical polarographic cell containing sulphuric acid as electrolyte. The cell which is a sealed unit is self-sustaining without any consumable electrode. The sample is introduced to the sensor by diffusion through a gas-permeable tetrafluoroethylene membrane. The cell electro-oxidizes CO to CO_2 in proportion to the partial pressure of CO in the sample chamber. The resulting electrochemical signal is amplified and temperature-compensated to drive the meter. The potentiostat holds the working electrode at a constant potential with respect to the reference electrode.

Figure 3.7 MSA/Auer carbon monoxide indicator 'MiniCO'

For checking the response of the instrument, zero and span calibration checks are performed by means of a calibration check kit. The checks should not be performed for at least two hours after installing a new sensor cell or batteries. Changes in atmospheric pressure will cause changes in calibration. The reading decreases as the altitude increases and increases as the altitude decreases.

To measure the CO-concentration, the sensor plug is removed to let the air enter the cell. The sample switch is pressed and held for 45 seconds and the reading taken with the switch pressed. The battery check indicator light must remain lit throughout the sampling period.

The sensor cell should give a service life of a minimum of six months. The battery power supply should last up to 12 months under normal use or 400 hours of continuous operation. Figure 3.8 gives a simplified block diagram of the MiniCO carbon monoxide indicator.

For continuous monitoring of the ambient air for CO-concentration, hand-held personal monitors have been developed by Auer (TOX-PEM CO), Draeger (Comopac), Ricken Keiki (Model CO-82), Sabre (Model PM 200), and others which are small and lightweight in design and can be carried in the breast pocket or worn around the neck.

The portable monitoring instruments using fuel cells, also called indicators, provide direct readings as well as audible and visual alarms if preset at 50 ppm concentration or at any other desired level. They are used for on-the-spot measurement of carbon monoxide in air for fixed-point continuous monitoring in any location in a range of 0 to 100 or 0 to 500 ppm. The rechargeable 2.4 V Ni-Cd battery pack sealed in a plastic case provides 8 to 10 hours of sampling in a fully charged condition. A small pump draws an air sample into the inlet through a flowmeter and a factory-set flow control valve. A portion of the sample is routed through an interferant filter to minimize their effects and into the sensor sample chamber. The sample then exhausts through a port in the sample chamber.

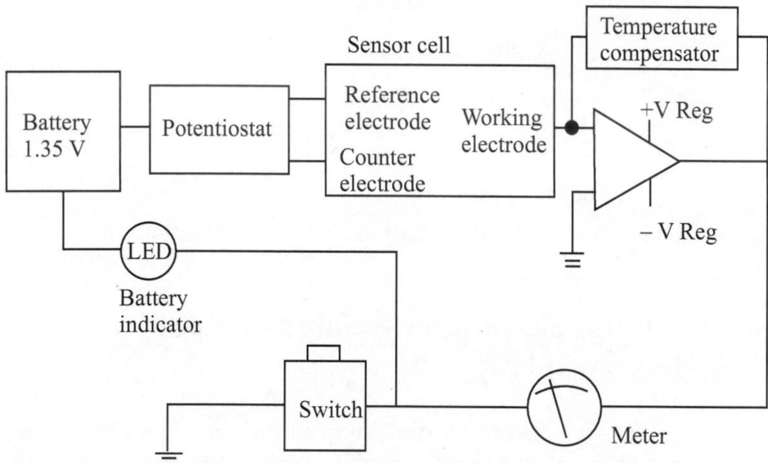

Figure 3.8 Simplified block diagram of MiniCO carbon monoxide indicator.

The following table lists the interferants and their concentrations equivalent to 1 ppm carbon monoxide or less:

Methane (CH_4)	10,000 ppm
Ammonia (NH_3)	1,000 ppm
Sulphur dioxide (SO_2)	500 ppm
Hydrogen (H_2)	60 ppm
Hydrogen sulphide (H_2S)	30 ppm
Nitrogen dioxide (NO_2)	12 ppm
Propane (C_3H_8)	5 ppm
Nitric oxide (NO)	3 ppm
Ethylene (C_2H_4)	2 ppm
Acetylene (C_2H_2)	1 ppm

In dusty environments, an external dust filter would be necessary. Use of a sample humidifier is recommended when sampling for more than one hour per day and/or the relative humidity is less than 50 per cent.

A variety of sampling lines and probe rods are available for testing atmospheres in remote locations. The instruments are equipped with a carrying handle and a shoulder – waist harness.

Figure 3.9 shows the block diagram of portable carbon monoxide indicators.

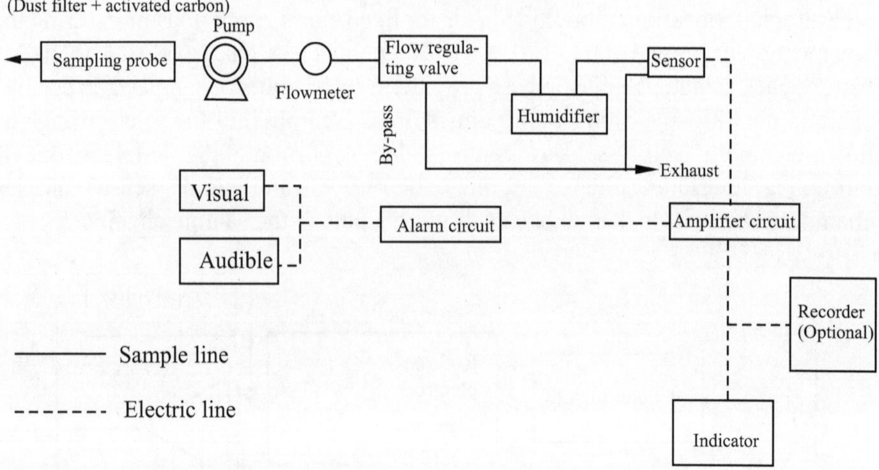

Figure 3.9 Block diagram of portable carbon monoxide indicator.

3.6 Hydrogen Sulphide or Sulphuretted Hydrogen (H_2S)

Hydrogen sulphide, referred to as stinkdamp in the early days of mining, is a colourless gas having a sickly sweet taste and a disagreeable odour of rotten eggs. It has a density of 1.5 kg/Nm^3.

It is 1.2 times heavier than air. It is easily soluble in water, 1 volume of water dissolving about 3 volumes of H_2S. It is combustible and forms flammable mixtures when mixed with air, the flammable range being 4.3 to 45 volume per cent H_2S.

Hydrogen sulphide is produced in mines from the following causes:

(1) Spontaneous heating of coal containing sulphur;
(2) Decay of organic matter, especially timber;
(3) Action of acidic mine waters on sulphides;
(4) Emission from fissures and joints, especially in potash mines;
(5) Emission from water of mineral springs when intersected;
(6) Emission in association with firedamp;
(7) Bacterial action on sulphides and sulphates in water; and
(8) Dust explosions in sulphide ore mines.

Hydrogen sulphide is a highly poisonous gas. It is more poisonous than carbon monoxide, but it gives an immediate warning. The exact low limit below which it ceases to act as a poison has not been determined. The threshold limit value is given as 10 ppm (15 mg/m^3) . The effects of exposure to various concentrations of hydrogen sulphide in air are [66]:

0.005 to 0.01 vol. %H_2S	Mild conjunctivitis and respiratory tract irritation after one-hour exposure
0.02 to 0.03	Marked conjunctivitis and respiratory tract irritation after one-hour exposure
0.05 to 0.07	Dangerous after half/to one hour exposure
0.07 to 0.20	Rapid unconsciousness, cessation of respiration and death in a few minutes at the higher concentrations

3.6.1 Detection and estimation

Hydrogen sulphide can be detected by its smell of rotten eggs even at concentrations as low as 0.0001 per cent (1 ppm). This distinctive odour, however, is noticed only in concentrations less than 0.2 per cent as at higher concentrations or following continued exposure to concentrations as low as 0. 0 1 per cent, the gas paralyzes the sense of smell and the sensory response is not proportional to the concentration of the gas.

Hydrogen sulphide can be detected by using colorimetric indicating detectors. The MSA detector consists essentially of palladium chloride in an acetone–water solution, sealed in a small glass tube which is surrounded with absorbent cotton. The presence of hydrogen sulphide is indicated by a colour change to dark in the cotton when the tube is crushed between the thumb and forefinger; the discoloration is compared with the scale on a standard colour chart supplied.

Length-of-stain hydrogen sulphide detectors using detector tubes are also available from Dräger, MSA, Auer, and others. The detector tube of the MSA

Hydrogen Sulphide Detector (Fig. 3.10) contains white granules of activated aluminium oxide coated with silver cyanide which turn greyish-black on coming into contact with the hydrogen sulphide in the air sample drawn through the tube. From the length of travel of discoloration through the granules, the percentage of hydrogen sulphide in the air sample is directly read off the calibrated graduated scale. The instrument has a measuring range of 0 to 800 ppm.

The Dräger detector tube has a white indicating layer of a lead compound which changes colour to pale brown in the presence of hydrogen sulphide.

$$H_2S + Pb^{2+} \longrightarrow PbS + 2H^+$$

Lead compound — Pale brown lead sulphide

The ranges of measurement are 1 to 20 ppm and 10 to 200 ppm. The detectors are sensitive to more than one contaminant and so the results must be interpreted with care. For example, in the presence of SO_2, the H_2S indication is somewhat high; a mixture of 5 ppm H_2S and 40 ppm SO_2 gives an indication of about 8 ppm H_2S while SO_2 alone does not discolour the indicating layer [63].

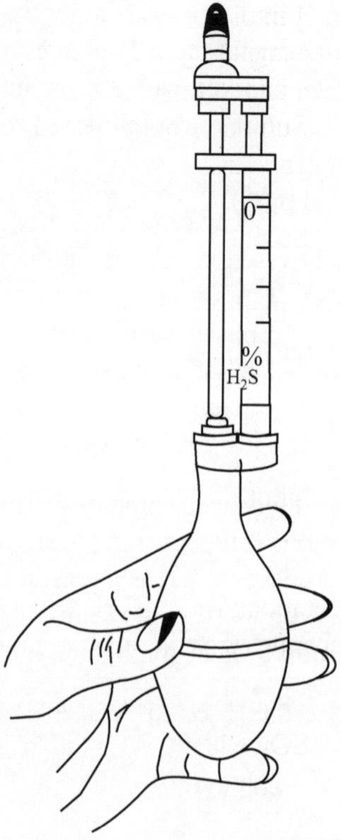

Figure 3.10 MSA hydrogen sulphide detector.

Portable hydrogen sulphide indicators

Like portable carbon monoxide indicators/monitors, these are self-contained battery-powered solid-state instruments using an electrochemical polarographic cell for their operation. They provide direct readings as well as audible and visual alarms if concentrations exceed preset limits on the low and high ranges. The measuring ranges are 0 to 20 and 0 to 100 ppm H_2S in air with a minimum detectable concentration of 0.5 ppm. A small pump draws a sample of air which is analyzed for hydrogen sulphide. The instrument can be carried using the handle or slung over the shoulder using the strap. Such indicators are manufactured by leading manufacturers of rescue and gas detection equipment.

3.7 Sulphur Dioxide (SO_2)

Sulphur dioxide, the primary oxide of sulphur, is a colourless, suffocating, and irritating gas with a strong pungent sulphurous smell. It is 2.21 times heavier than air and it tends to settle into low-lying areas.

Sulphur dioxide is produced with other gases in mines mining sulphide ore from blasting, mine fire and explosions, and as a product of complete combustion of fuel in diesel engines. As the production of sulphur dioxide in the exhaust gases is related directly to the amount of sulphur in the fuel, one must purchase diesel fuel keeping this in mind.

Sulphur dioxide is a very poisonous gas. It is extremely irritating to the eyes and respiratory passages which it attacks even at a concentration of 0.002 per cent (20 ppm). The threshold limit value is given as 5 ppm (13 mg/m^3).

Sulphur dioxide damages plants which are more sensitive than human beings, causing the loss of chlorophyll (chlorosis) and tissues of leaf cells (plasmolysis). The damaging effect depends on the concentration, presence of particulants and length of exposure.

3.7.1 Detection and estimation

Sulphur dioxide can be detected by using colorimetric indicating detectors and detector tubes.

The Dräger detector tube (1/a) has a white pre-cleansing layer of a copper compound to retain hydrogen sulphide, a blue indicating layer iodine/starch which changes to white in the presence of sulphur dioxide.

$$SO_2 + \underset{\text{Iodine}}{I_2} + 2H_2O \xrightarrow{\text{starch}} H_2SO_4 + 2HI$$

The measuring range is 1 to 25 ppm. SO_2.

Oxides of nitrogen (NO, NO_2) cause minor errors indicating lower values of hydrogen sulphide concentration. For this reason, sulphur dioxide in the exhaust from a diesel engine cannot be measured by means of detector tubes.

3.8 Nitrous Fumes (Oxides of Nitrogen) (NO_x)

These consist of a mixture of different toxic oxides of nitrogen as NO, NO_2, N_2O_3 and N_2O_4 having a biting and choking smell. They are yellow to reddish-brown, in colour and have a smell of blasting powder fumes. They are easily dissolved by the moisture in mine air and contribute to smog or haze.

Nitrous fumes are formed during blasting by high explosives such as gelatine dynamite due to incomplete detonation. They tend to settle in the freshly blasted and dry muck pile, being about one-and-a-half times heavier than air. They are released when the muck pile is disturbed, posing a hazard to the loader-operator, or anyone else in the vicinity.

Nitrous fumes are also produced during the combustion process inside the cylinders of a diesel engine. The amount formed depends on the maximum temperature reached in the cylinders during the combustion cycle, the amount of oxygen available for completion of the chemical reaction, and engine maintenance. The principal oxide of nitrogen formed is nitric oxide which however, being unstable, rapidly oxidizes to nitrogen dioxide in the presence of oxygen, both in the exhaust pipe and in the mine air.

Nitrous fumes are highly poisonous. They are 7 to 10 times more toxic than carbon monoxide; nitrogen dioxide is 5 times more toxic than nitric oxide. The toxic effect is often delayed. Persons exposed to high concentrations may not exhibit ill-effects for several days or weeks and fatalities may occur suddenly. When noticed, the mouth and nose should be covered with a damp handkerchief. Lives of intensive care patients can sometimes be saved by inhalation of NO gas.

The nitrogen dioxide combines with the haemoglobin of the blood about 300,000 times more readily than oxygen to form an extremely stable compound, thereby quickly reducing the oxygen-carrying capacity of the blood. The threshold limit value is given as 5 ppm nitrogen dioxide.

Even at low concentrations (10 to 20 ppm), nitrogen dioxide exerts corrosive effect on lung tissues. It penetrates air passages all the way down to the alveoli, where respiratory exchange takes place. As nitrogen dioxide is fairly soluble in water, forming nitric acid, the moist air passages of the nose, throat, and lungs are irritated immediately. The nitric acid attacks the thin-walled blood vessels of the alveoli causing them to be permeable to the plasma of the blood. A concentration of 200 to 700 ppm is rapidly fatal after a short exposure. When it is suspected that a person is exposed to poisoning, no artificial respiration should be attempted, but instead his body should be kept warm and oxygen administered. A cigarette will taste sickly sweet when smoked by him.

Once formed, nitrous fumes are not affected by water scrubbers. Catalytic mufflers do not reduce them by any appreciable amount.

The most effective means of dealing with nitrous fumes are by providing rapid dilution of the exhaust gases with large quantities of air, providing adequate ventilation, and purchase of diesel equipment with pre-combustion (indirect injection) engines which produce cleaner exhaust.

The harmful NO_x can be removed from diesel engine exhaust gases by using a three-way catalyst containing platinum, palladium, and rhodium in the catalytic converter used, in which platinum and palladium oxidize the harmful CO and unburnt hydrocarbons to harmless CO_2 and water while rhodium reduces the harmful NO_x to harmless nitrogen.

3.8.1 Detection and estimation

Nitrous fumes can be detected by colour-stain detector tubes in concentrations of up to 100 ppm. The Dräger detector tubes measure nitrous fumes ($NO + NO_2$) in the ranges 0.5 to 10, 2 to 50, and 5 to 100 ppm. The detector tube contains a reddish-brown oxidation layer containing a chromium compound and a yellow indicating layer of N-diphenyl benzidine which changes colour to dark bluish-grey in the presence of the fumes. The oxidation layer oxidizes NO to NO_2.

Personal nitrogen oxide samplers and hand-held direct-reading NO_2 detectors are now available in the market.

3.9 Hydrogen (H_2)

Hydrogen is an odourless, colourless, and tasteless gas. It is the lightest gas known. It has a density of 0.089 kg/Nm^3. It is slightly soluble in water. It does not support combustion but is combustible. It is flammable when mixed with air, the flammable limits being 4 and 75 per cent by volume. Like methane, it does not burn in the flame safety lamp. It is, however, more easily ignitible than methane.

Hydrogen rarely occurs in mines. It may be emitted from fissures in association with methane. It is sometimes found in firegases, especially during devolatilization of coal and in explosion gases. It is liberated during charging of electric storage batteries in underground charging stations. It may be liberated with CO when fighting a deep-seated large open fire of coal with a jet of water directed onto its centre. It may also be produced by the chemical action of strong acid waters on iron.

Hydrogen is not poisonous. The detection of hydrogen in firegases is done mainly by gas analysis.

3.10 Methane (CH_4)

Methane, also called marsh gas and commonly known by the name of firedamp in mines, is a colourless, odourless, and tasteless gas. It has a density of 0.7168 kg/Nm^3 and is 0.554 times as heavy as air so that it tends to rise to the roof of a mine working. It is soluble with difficulty in water, 100 volumes of water dissolving at 20°C 3.3 volumes of CH_4. It is combustible and, when mixed with air in certain proportions, it explodes, the flammable limits being 5 and 15 per cent. Although non-toxic by nature, methane reduces the oxygen concentration in mine atmosphere by dilution and thus acts as an asphyxiant. At 20 per cent, the gas burns around the flame of a flame safety lamp and at 9.5 per cent the flame is extinguished.

The presence of methane in a mine causes such a mine to be called a 'fiery', mine. Methane chiefly occurs in all virgin coal seams (including anthracite) and associated strata as free and adsorbed gas. It was formed as a by-product during the so called coalification process of vegetable matter when the seams were formed. Bituminous coals contain larger amounts of the gas than other coals. Methane enters mine workings out of coal seams and their adjacent strata as well as out of coal being mined (coal mine methane, CMM). It may also be found in the region of faults, dykes, slips, or rolls in roof cavities, above falls, high places and abandoned workings. It is given off in the form of (i) regular, slow and continuous emissions, (ii) blowers, and (iii) gas outbursts as primary occurrence. Methane emission rates are often unpredictable because of the varying interactions between geology, mining, ventilation and methane control measures/systems adopted owing to site-specific conditions and mining practices. The methane emission from a prospective coal mine can be forecast using coal cores taken during exploration drilling and measuring gas seeping from the core. Methane has also been reported to have occurred in salt, potash, sulphur, lead-zinc, silver, gold, tin and diamond mines but is much less common.

Methane is also found in the surface atmosphere in coalfields, being released during mining of coal seams and liberated into the atmosphere through the mine ventilation system and by the mine methane drainage systems adopted as a safety measure with transport of methane to the surface, where it is vented instead of utilizing it as a fuel for steam generation (ventilation air methane, VAM).

In technical literature of the early 1990s, occurrence of firedamp has been reported in mines worked for diamonds, gold, lead, silver, salt, tin, potash and quicksilver.

3.10.1 Detection and estimation

Besides the flame safety lamp which has the highest possible accuracy of 0.5 per cent and has been in use in coal mines for more than a century, there are, commercially available today various, types of approved or permissible hand-held instruments known as methanometers which are designed for rapid detection and/or estimation of methane in air with an accuracy which is about 10 times that obtained with the flame safety lamp which has come to be regarded today as a piece of backup equipment. Methanometers are self-contained battery-powered instruments and were first introduced in mines in 1954.

The operating principles of the methanometers commonly used in mines are:

(1) Catalytic combustion of methane present in a sample of atmosphere on the surface of a catalytically-activated pelletized filament or 'pellistor' which forms part of a balanced electrical bridge circuit. The combustion of the gas increases the temperature of the pellistor due to liberation of heat, 212 kcal/kg, causing a proportional change in its electrical resistance. The change in the resistance creates an imbalance in the balanced electrical Wheatstone bridge circuit, which is measured either on a meter with a calibrated scale or electronically translated into a reading as the percentage of methane with a digital display.

(2) Change in electrical resistance of a heated wire filament (100°C) through loss of heat due to the thermal conduction property of methane. Since the

Table 3.2 Relative heat conductivity of some gases

Air	1.00
Oxygen	1.01
Nitrogen	0.99
Hydrogen	7.13
Carbon dioxide	0.58
Carbon monoxide	0.96
Methane	1.23
Ethane	0.74
Propane	0.62

heated filament (active sensor) forms part of the Wheatstone bridge circuit, the change creates an imbalance in the circuit, which results in a deflection of a meter pointer in proportion to the methane concentration. The ability of a gas to conduct heat (the coefficient of thermal conductivity) is a specific physical property of the gas. Table 3.2 gives the relative heat conductivity of some gases taking the heat conductivity of air as 1[67].

The heat conductivity of a mixture of gases in a sample can be roughly determined by using the relation:

$$\lambda_{mixt} = \sum_{i=1}^{n} \lambda_i \cdot r_i$$

where λ_{mixt} is the heat conductivity of the gas mixture,

λ_i is the heat conductivity of the component gas i

r_i is the volume fraction of the component gas i.

Accurate readings of methane concentration can only be obtained with binary gas mixtures. It is necessary that the heat conductivity of the methane component in the binary mixture differs sufficiently from the heat conductivity of the accompanying gas. Gas mixtures consisting of more than two component gases can be considered as binary if the heat conductivities of the constituent gases are nearly such as those of CO, N_2, and O_2.

(3) Combination of catalytic combustion and heat conductivity principles.
(4) Differences in refractive indices of normal air and methane – air mixtures.

In comparison with the earlier models, the recent models of electric methane detectors, using a variety of sensors, are characterized by the following features:

(a) Small, compact, light in weight, modular design, and dust-proof;
(b) Microprocessor control permitting high measuring accuracy;
(c) An automatic sampling pump;
(d) Improved detector filament having a long life;
(e) Simplicity of operation by means of push button(s);
(f) Digital readout;
(g) Recharging of battery without having to open the instrument case, with automatic switch-off; long battery life;
(h) Robust construction with maximum shock and vibration resistance and easily accessible interior;
(i) Telescopic sampling probes for sampling in inaccessible places;
(j) Autocalibration,
(k) Continuous operation when required; able to store large numbers of gas readings (about 200)
(1) An adjustable alarm (audible and visual)
(m) Meter illumination in dark places;

(n) Wide temperature range;
(o) Sensor immune to noise;
(p) Provision of a data logger and software; and
(q) Also designed as multi-gas measuring instrument using sensors.

Most of the above features are common to other gas indicators. Before being approved for use in mines, methanometers are subjected to approval tests as may be laid down by mining law.

Methanometers, catalytic combustion-type

For spot measurement

These are hand-held instruments for routine use housed in an impact-resistant antistatic plastic case or stainless steel case powered by a rechargeable 2.4-V nickel–cadmium battery. A sample of atmosphere is drawn by diffusion and a natural draft created by heat on to a pair of heated pelletized filaments in the sensing head. One filament is catalytically treated while the other is not (inactive or compensator filament). These form half of a balanced Wheatstone electrical bridge circuit. The gas-detecting filament ('pellistor' or 'pelement') consists of a very small catalyzed ceramic bead supported on a coiled platinum filament of about 0.05 mm diameter. It operates at a temperature of about 450°C, needs little power, has practically no zero drift, and has a long life. The inactive filament, being exposed to the sample, helps to maintain circuit balance under changing conditions of flow, temperature, humidity, and carbon dioxide content.

When a mixture of methane gas and air comes into contact with the catalytic elements, rapid combustion of the gas takes place, raising the temperature and resistance of the leg of the bridge and throwing the bridge out of electrical balance. The imbalance is measured on the digital display.

A single charge of the battery provides approximately 200 readings. The instruments have a measuring range of 0 to 5 per cent and an accuracy of ± 0.1 per cent CH_4.

The instruments are also designed to give a continuous display of gas concentration.

Figure 3.11 gives schematic diagrams of methane detectors/ methanometers based on the principles of catalytic combustion, heat conductivity, and catalytic combustion – heat conductivity.

For continuous measurement

Methanometers for continuous determination of methane levels at strategic locations near the face and on equipment in mine workings are called methane monitors or automatic methanometers. They provide visual and audible alarms and, in some instruments, a continuous record of the methane concentration. When provided with an external relay unit, they can be used to automatically switch off electrical machinery as required. They are operated continuously from mine power mains or from a rechargeable nickel–cadmium battery (12 V, 7 Ah)

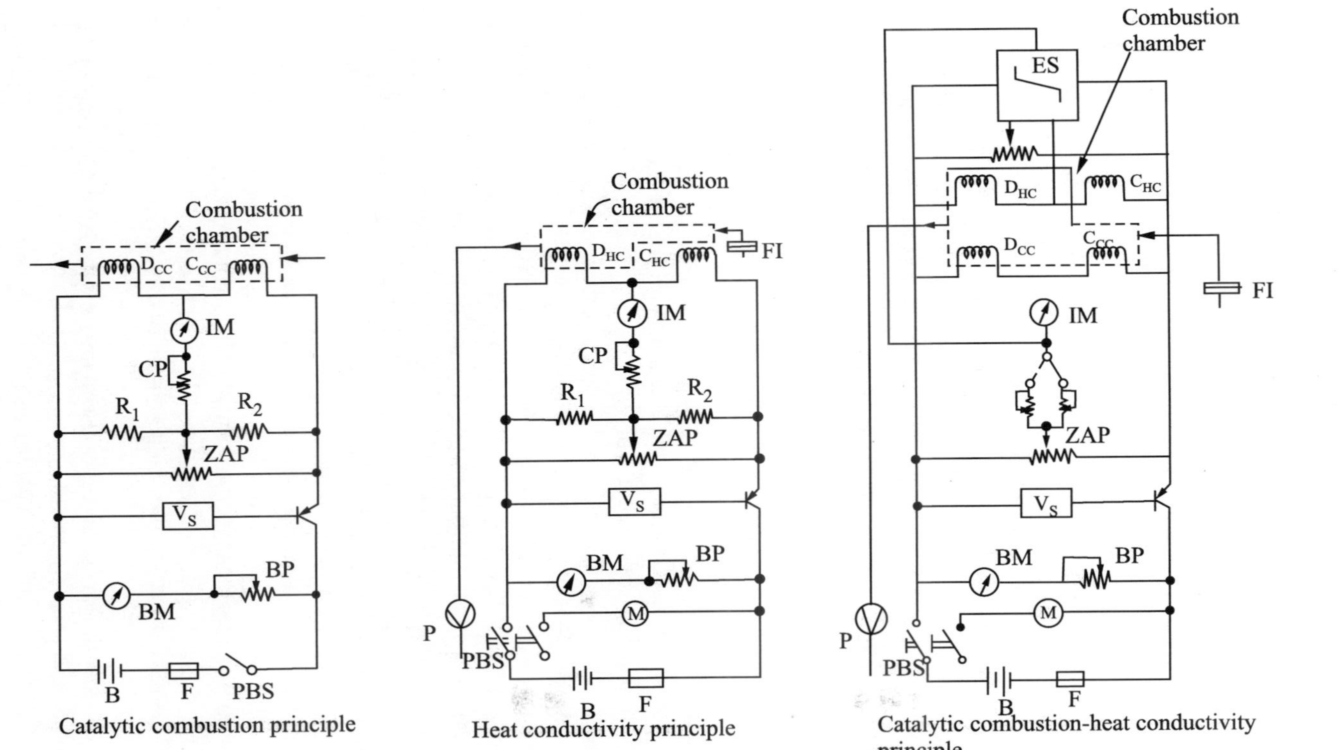

Figure 3.11 Schematic circuits and flow diagrams of methanometers of catalytic combustion, heat conductivity, and catalytic combustion–heat conductivity: types. D_{CC}, D_{HC}: detector filament; C_{CC}, C_{HC} : compensator filament; IM : indicating meter; CP: calibration potentiometer; R_1, R_2: bridge fixed resistors; ZAP: zero adjust potentiometer; VS: voltage stabiliser; BM: battery meter: BP: battery check potentiometer; B:Ni-Cd battery; F: fuse; PBS: push button ON/OFF switch; P: pump; M: motor; F: filter; ES: electronic switch.

which can power for 10 to 12 hours. The battery which is trickle-charged, will allow operation during weekend shutdowns or automatically on interruption to the power supply for any reason.

A methane monitor is usually of modular construction, which gives it flexibility in application. It is made up of a control module, a battery module and a recorder module, each housed in a robust case and connected by a flexible cable to a detector head or sensor housing which includes a sintered stainless steel flashback arrestor and filter unit, etc. to prevent flame propagation to the outside.

For continuously monitoring the concentration of methane in methane drainage systems either on the surface or underground, high-concentration methane monitors are commercially available.

A continuous methane monitoring system provides 24-hour surveillance of methane gas concentration in outbye ventilation splits inside the mine. Such a system consists of a group of methane sensors, power supplies, connecting cables, communication units, and recorders. The analogue output can also be transmitted to the surface via an approved telemetry system.

Modern handheld electronic methanometers are capable of operating for over twelve hours on battery charge and able to store large number of gas readings in on board data logging chips which can be retrieved later on the surface for display on PC's.

Methanometers, heat conductivity type

The thermal conductivity detector is used to measure high concentrations of methane in air in the range of 5 to 100 vol per cent. It has a built-in motor driven pump to draw a sample of atmosphere through a test chamber containing two thermal conductivity sensors consisting of thermally and electrically identical heated platinum wires. One sensor, the reference sensor, is hermetically sealed in a compensating chamber filled with air (as reference gas) while the other sensor is in a measuring chamber into which the air sample diffuses through a mesh. Flashback arrestors of sintered metal are located on the inlet and outlet of the measuring chamber. Moisture and carbon dioxide in the sample are removed by an absorption tube containing silica gel and soda-lime; dust and dirt are removed by an easily replaceable mechanical filter.

The detector and compensator sensors form part of a balanced electrical bridge circuit. When a mixture of methane in air is drawn through the instrument, it comes into contact with the detector sensor, the latter will cool due to heat loss at a rate depending on the concentration of methane. Thus the voltage across the sensor will decrease, thereby upsetting the bridge circuit and resulting in deflection of the meter pointer.

A well-known instrument approved for use in mines is the Auer Methano-meter M_5 10B, which is calibrated for a methane range of 5 to 100 vol per cent CH_4 with an accuracy of indication of ±0.2 vol. per cent CH_4. A single charge of battery provides approximately 900 readings. The pump capacity is at least 250 ml/min and it produces a maximum underpressure of 50 mbar. For sample containing carbon dioxide, it is necessary to insert an absorbent cartridge. A combination of the catalytic combustion principle for the low 0 to 2 per cent methane measuring range and the heat conductivity principle for the higher range of 1.6 to 5 per cent methane is incorporated in the Auer Methanometer M702 (Fig. 3.12). The combination of both principles provides unambiguous indication of all methane concentrations.

Heat conductivity-type methanometers are generally only used where great sensitivity is not required.

Interferometer

It is an optical detector which utilizes the optical properties of methane – air mixtures and compares the velocity of a beam of light through fresh air with that through a sample drawn into a measuring cell. The velocity of light is dependent on its wavelength and frequency. It has its greatest value in vacuum of 29979 × 10^8 m/s. When passing through a medium, its velocity becomes smaller. The ratio of the velocity of light in vacuum to that in the medium is the refraction number or refractive index.

Figure 3.12 Auer methanometer model M 702

When two sets of waves derived from the same light source travel outward, through a medium, they interfere with each other, producing what is called an interference pattern which is viewed as striped fringes through a telescope. When, however, they travel through two media having different refractive indices, a phase shift occurs and the fringes shift from their original position, depending on the difference between the refractive indices of the media.

Figure 3.13 gives the schematic diagram of an interferometer.

A beam of light supplied by a lamp bulb and made parallel by passing through a condenser lens splits into two coherent beams after striking a thick parallel-plane glass plate the inner or back surface of which is silvered. One of these beams is made to pass twice through a measuring gas chamber into which a gas sample can be introduced. The other is made to pass through two outer chambers (reference chambers) containing dry fresh air free of CO_2. The two beams unite later in a movable reflecting prism where they are reflected to pass through the objective

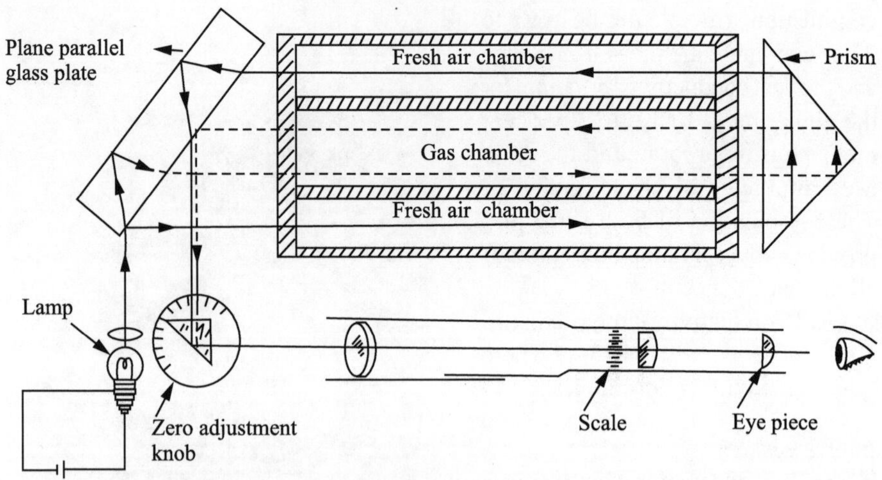

Figure 3.13 Schematic diagram of interferometer.

of a small telescope focused on an illuminated reading scale. They interfere with each other due to an optical path difference between them.

Let $l/2$	be the length of the chambers;
v	be the free space velocity of light;
λ	be the wave length of the monochromatic light used;
n_a	be the refractive index of air; and
n_m	be the refractive index of a mixture of gas and air.

The velocity of light in the chamber filled with air = v/n_a.
The velocity of light in the chamber filled with the mixture of gas and air = (v/n_m).

The optical path difference between the two light beams due to the difference in travel times through the chambers.

$$= \left(\frac{2 \times l/2}{v / n_m} - \frac{2 \times l/2}{v / n_a}\right) v = (n_m - n_a)l$$

If z is the number of fringes shifted, $(n_m - n_a)l = z\lambda$.

The amount of fringe shift is, therefore, proportional to $(n_m - n_a)$, which means that the larger the value of n_m, the more sensitive is the instrument.

If the concentration of the gas in air is x vol. per cent, the refractive index of the mixture of gas and air is given by

$$n_m = \left(1 - \frac{x}{100}\right) n_a + \frac{x}{100} n_g$$

where n_g is the refractive index of the gas.

$$x = \frac{100(n_m - n_a)}{n_g - n_a}$$

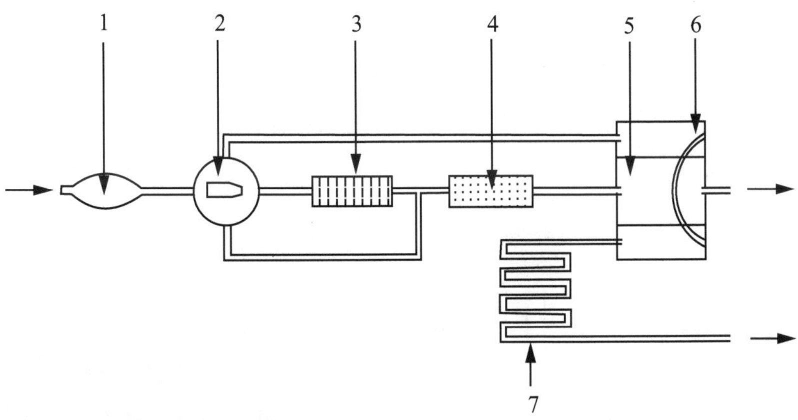

Figure 3.14 Schematic diagram of the sample flow through interferometer. 1: aspirator bulb; 2–4: way tap; 3: soda-lime filling; 4: silica gel; 5: measuring chamber; 6: reference chamber; 7: pressure-compensating tube.

The refractive index of any gas is affected by pressure and temperature variations, and the difference in refractive indices, therefore, depends upon pressure, P Torr, and temperature, T, K of the measuring gas and air in the chambers. If the instrument is adjusted at a pressure P_i and temperature T_i, the measured values of methane concentration must be multiplied by a correction factor $(T/T_i \,.\, P_i/P)$.

In general, the correction is negligible. The pressure difference between the measuring and reference chambers is eliminated by means of a 2 or 3 m long capillary tube at the exit of the reference chamber (Fig. 3.14)

The interferants which affect the readings are water vapour, carbon monoxide, and carbon dioxide. Water vapour and carbon monoxide from the air sample are removed by silica gel and soda-lime, respectively. Carbon monoxide, normally present in very small quantities, and oxygen deficiency cause positive errors, while hydrogen causes negative errors.

To take readings, the gas chamber is cleansed with fresh air by allowing it to flow through it by squeezing the aspirator bulb about five times. The press button switch is then operated to illuminate the ocular scale. Interference fringes will be observed through the eyepiece. The fringes consist of two black lines or stripes with coloured ones on either side of them. Of the two black lines, the one on the right is selected as the, 'index stripe'. The zero adjusting knob is next rotated until this black stripe shifts and coincides with the zero line of the ocular scale. This operation is called zero-setting of the instrument and the instrument is now ready for use (Fig. 3.15). Next, the aspirator bulb is squeezed at least five times to draw the air to be sampled into the gas chamber. After pressing the switch, the new position of the index stripe on the ocular scale directly gives the percentage of methane in the air sampled.

The measuring ranges are 0 to 6 per cent; 0 to 10 per cent; and 0 to 100 per cent and the time for a measurement is 15 to 20 seconds. Well-known manufacturers of interferometers are Carl Zeiss (Germany) and Riken Keiki Fine Instrument

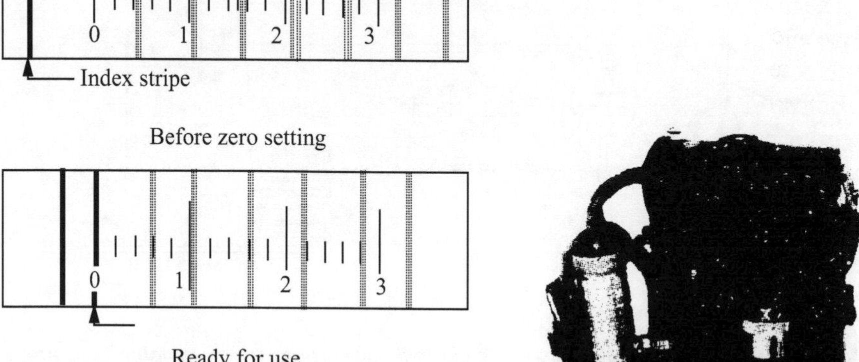

Figure 3.15 Zero-setting and taking gas reading.

Figure 3.16 Riken interferometer model 17.

Co. (Japan). Figure 3.16 shows the Riken Interferometer Model 17, which has dimensions 38 × 90 × 190 mm, weighing approximately 1.5 kg and using a 1.5-V dry battery.

Care and use of methanometers

There is a wide choice in methanometers and most methanometers designed today require relatively less maintenance and are easy to repair and use. Although designed sufficiently rugged for mining use, being precision instruments, all electronic gas detectors must carefully and regularly maintained and handled with reasonable care and intelligence at all times so that mine safety is not jeopardized.

The routine inspections, maintenance and testing of hand-held methanometers are usually carried out in the lamp-room by competent persons, who must check the following with fully-charged battery before the start of every shift:

(a) the external condition of the instrument;
(b) the proper assembly of the instrument case and the indicating meter window for any damage;
(c) battery voltage; and
(d) zero and calibration checks.

Detailed steps for checking the instrument are outlined in the instruction manual supplied with the instruments. In case the instrument requires recalibration or repair, it should be returned to the factory for service. A service manual is supplied for those customers who wish to carry out their own repairs.

The instruments are stored in lockers in which the users deposit the instruments at the end of the shift and from which they pick them up at the beginning of the shift.

Before going down the mine, the user must check the instrument reading by means of calibration check gas (methane 1.8, 2, or 2.5 per cent) from a calibration check kit provided in the lamp room.

The filters must be inspected and replaced as and when required. When a routine check indicates the need, the battery must be replaced.

Before making measurements underground, one should see that the instrument attains the surrounding temperature. The incidence of warm moist air entering a cooler instrument must be avoided. It is recommended that the instrument be checked by the user at regular intervals during the shift.

3.11 Radon

Radon is a noble gas produced by the decay or disintegration of radium-226 (^{226}Ra), which is one of the decay products of one of the three alpha-emitting principal isotopes or nuclides of natural uranium, U-238, for which uranium ore is mined. It is a colourless, tasteless, odourless, non-flammable, and radioactive gas having a density of approximately 9.73 kg/m^3 at 0° C and 100 kPa. It is chemically inert and non-toxic. Radon-222 (^{222}Rn) is the longest-lived isotope, with a half-life of

Table 3.3 Decay series of randon to lead

Name	Atomic No.	Mass No.	Range in air (cm)	Half-life	Principal radiation
Radium-226 (^{226}Ra)	88	226	3.39	1600 years	Alpha
↓					
Radon-222 (^{222}Rn)	86	222	4.12	3.82 days	Alpha
↓					
RaA (^{218}Po)	84	218	4.72	3.05 minutes	Alpha
↓					
RaB (^{214}Pb)	82	214	...	26.8 minutes	Beta, gamma
↓					
RaC (^{214}Bi)	83	214	...	19.7 minutes	Beta, gamma
↓					
RaC (^{214}Po)	84	214	6.97	1.64 μs	Alpha
↓					
Other long-lived daughters					
↓					
Stable lead (^{206}Pb)	82	206	...	Infinite	

3.82 days. All the radon isotopes undergo a radioactive decay chain, producing their short-lived decay products or radon progeny until equilibrium is reached, when stable lead (^{206}Pb) is formed (Table 3.3). During the decay process, often alpha particles, beta particles, and gamma rays are emitted. Thus, airborne radiation is a mixture of radon and its daughters. On account of the short half-lives of radon daughter products, their concentrations rapidly increase when a source of radon is present but rapidly decay when they are separated from the radon source, resulting in a significant variation with location and time as the ventilating air flows through the mine workings. Thus, the operation of any uranium mine cannot be conducted without extensive impact on the environment throughout the life of the mine.

The penetrating power of the three kinds of emission is inversely proportional to their ionizing power. Alpha particles are positively charged, are powerful oxidizing agents, and can travel 3.8 to 7.6 cm in air. They do not penetrate the outer layers of the skin and can be stopped by heavy clothing. Beta particles are much smaller than alpha particles, are negatively charged, and are 100 times more penetrating but about as damaging as gamma rays. Gamma radiation is an electromagnetic radiation, has no electric charge, and is 10,000 times more penetrating than alpha radiation, less damaging though it can be shielded by lead, concrete, etc. The whole body of the employee is prone to gamma radiation exposure, but in most uranium mines, the employee exposure is not excessive. Alpha radiation has a far greater potential to damage living tissues than the other kinds of radiation and is the main source of internal exposure in mines from inhalation, ingestion, and absorption of radioactive dust and radon daughter products. It is responsible for elevated levels of lung cancer in uranium miners. Beta and gamma radiations are sources of external radiation exposure. The relative contributions to the total absorbed dose of radiation depends on the method of mining, the ventilation system designed, and the dust suppression methods used.

Radon is found in trace quantities throughout the world in almost any kind of soil and rock in the earth's crust. Granite rocks contain more uranium, thorium, and potassium than any other kind of rock. Radon originates from man-made sources like nuclear power production and uranium mining. The United Nations Scientific Committee on the effects of Atomic Radiation (1988) has estimated that exposure to natural sources contributes more than 98% of the radiation dose to the population (excluding medical exposure). The global average human exposure from natural sources is 2.4 mSv/year (millisieverts per year), the variation depending on several factors such as height above sea level, the amount and type of radionuclides present in the soil, and the amount taken into the body through air, food, and drinking water.

Radon occurring in small concentrations in most hard rock mines may not pose any significant occupational hazard. Coal seams are also known to contain traces of radium which can produce radon in underground mines. A coal seam was mined for several years in the Dresden-Freital area in the former East Germany (Deutsche Democratische Republic) after the Second World War for the recovery of contained uranium [68]. In uranium mines, for obvious reasons, the radiation levels are generally quite high, being directly proportional to the grade of the uranium in the vicinity. The radon and thoron gases in the ore matrix diffuse out into the mine atmosphere through cracks and fissures or by way of mine water which dissolves radon and releases it into the mine air. The emanation is enhanced if the host rock has a weak or porous structure. Shortly after their release into mine air, radon and thoron gases undergo radioactive decay, producing their hazardous decay products.

The long-term radiation-induced lung cancer hazard of the uranium mine environment was first recognized in the late 1930s by a study of pitchblende miners of the Erzgebirge (Ore Mountains) in Germany and Czechoslovakia. Pitchblende is a mineral resource of radium as well as uranium. After about 15 years of pitchblende mining, the miners began to die of lung cancer and other diseases.

When radon gas is inhaled, because of its relatively long half-life, it tends to be exhaled, contributing little to the radiation dose. However, some of the radon dissolves in the body fluids and gets into the blood stream, where it and its daughter products irradiate various tissues and organs in the human body, which have different sensitivities to radiation. The short-lived respirable particulate daughter products in mine air attach themselves to respirable dust and penetrate deep into the lungs without lung clearance in the upper respiratory tract, causing cancer of the lung tissues and other organs. The radioactive respirable dust can be captured as ordinary respirable dust. The radiation hazards with uranium mining are in addition to the conventional non-radium related hazards normally associated with hard rock mining.

The radiation effects on human beings are of two types: somatic and genetic. The somatic effects are those which appear in the person who is actually exposed himself, while the genetic effects appear in subsequent generations after a latent period of 10 to 50 years due to their snow-balling.

The practical unit of exposure to radon daughters generally adopted is the working level (WL), which is defined as that concentration of daughter products in one litre of air which, on ultimate decay liberates a total energy equal to the emission of 1.3×10^5 MeV (mega electron volts) of alpha energy. In SI units, the WL corresponds to 2.1×10^5 J/m^3.

As air passes through the mine workings, the working level of the air increases.

In mining environments, a special unit, the working level month (WLM) is used to measure workers' exposure resulting from inhalation of air containing 1 WL of radon progeny for one working month. Exposure to 1 WL for 170 hours gives a dose of 1 WLM.

The International Commission on Radiological Protection recommends that all exposures (doses) be kept as low as is reasonably achievable (ALARA principle) which will ensure that mine operators do more than just meet the regulatory standards.

Studies of uranium miners in the U.S.A. and former Czechoslovakia showed that the miner is more likely to get lung cancer when his total exposure exceeds 120

WLM in a year [69]. Assuming that miners work 30 years, a maximum permissible annual dose of 4 WLM in any calendar year is generally recognized as a healthy standard in most countries of the world below which the health effect of radon is insignificant or does not occur; it has been shown by extensive scientific studies and technical investigations that at such an exposure level the human body can compensate for some of the damage caused by it, although there is no radiation exposure level which can be taken as absolutely safe. The threshold dose of 4 WLM is also referred to as the 'reference level of dose'.

The SI unit of radioactivity is the becquerel (Bq), where 1 Bq=1 disintegration per second.

Radiation dose terms frequently used are [70] :

The *absorbed dose* which refers to the amount of energy that is deposited in all tissues or organs per unit mass by the radiation. The SI unit for the absorbed dose is the gray (Gy). 1 gray = 1J/kg.

The *equivalent dose* which is the product of the absorbed dose and a factor related to the particular type of radiation.

The *effective dose* of radiation received by a person which is given by the sum of the equivalent doses received by all tissues or organs in the human body weighted by 'tissue weighting factors' which will reflect the different sensitivities to radiation of different organs and tissues in the human body. The SI unit for the equivalent and effective doses is the sievert (Sv). 1Sv = 1 J/kg.

The *committed effective dose* is a measure of the total effective dose received over the lifetime following an intake of a radionuclide (internal exposure).

The term *dose* may be used as a general term to denote either the absorbed dose (Gy) or the effective dose (Sv), depending on the situation.

The International Commission on Radiological Protection (ICR) recommended in 1991 standards for occupational and public dose limits on radiation protection. The standard for occupational effective dose limit is 20 mSv/year averaged over a period of five consecutive years with a maximum of 50 mSv in any one year, while the standard for the public dose limit is 1 mSv/year above the natural radiation background level, allowing a higher dose in any one year.

The ICRP recommendations have been accepted internationally by the International Atomic Energy Agency (IAEA), the World Health Organization (WHO), and the International Labour Organization (ILO) and are followed all over the world. In India, the Atomic Energy Regulatory Board (AERB) is the national competent regulatory authority which has accepted the ICRP standards and is primarily responsible for radiation protection and monitoring in uranium mining, milling and ancillary operations and nuclear power stations.

The relationship between the dose in WLM and the actual dose in sieverts to the target tissues in the lung is extremely complex, being dependent on many factors. The ICRP 66 (1994) suggests a conversion factor of 1 WLM = 5 mSv for occupational exposures, while some other studies recommend 10 mSv/WLM.

For monitoring radiation protection for ensuring compliance with regulation requirements, two types of monitoring programmes must be undertaken: a survey programme in which measurements at specified locations in a given area are carried out (grab sampling or continuous sampling) and direct assessment of an individual worker's exposure by personal dosimeters worn during work. For measuring radon in the air, scintillation cells in conjunction with photomultipliers and electronic counters are generally used. External cumulative gamma radiation is measured by thermoluminescence dosimeters.

High levels of radon and its daughter products in high-grade uranium mining environment can be controlled and countered by the following measures:

(1) Proper mine layout;
(2) Designing an effective ventilation system which will
  (i) provide an adequate quantity of fresh air or mine air containing as low a concentration of radon as possible to the working sections,
  (ii) provide high air velocities to keep the air residence time to a minimum, and
  (iii) avoid local recirculation of air;
(3) Selecting a suitable mining method so that the miners have little direct contact with the ore as far as practicable by remote-controlled operations and good material handling techniques to reduce exposure to radiation sources;
(4) Sealing off worked-out sections effectively;
(5) Using respiratory protective equipment in selected high-risk areas;
(6) Applying sealant coatings like shotcrete on exposed rock surfaces to act as a shield against exposure of mining crews to gamma rays;
(7) Adopting toxic uranium dust suppression measures;
(8) Worker education and training;
(9) Posting warning signs by the mine management in areas with high ionizing radiation; and
(10) Periodical medical check-ups which will provide information on the general health of the workers and, coupled with worker education, can reduce the incidence of lung cancer.

Other sources of radon on the mine surface as a consequence of mining uranium ore are ore stockpiles, mine waste rock piles, ore transportation, mine water disposal ponds, mill tailings ponds, crushing areas in the mill, and yellow cake packaging areas. Techniques have been developed to control the radioactive emanations from solid and liquid wastes produced to minimize any damage which may be caused to the environment.

Although one might expect radon daughters to travel over long distances on the earth's surface, in practice experience has shown that the radiation levels are very low due to the combination of rapidly increasing area with distance and vertical mixing with air due to air turbulence.

Although the general observation usually made is that lung cancer deaths are higher than in the general population, it got disproved by French uranium miners who after working over a period of many years did not suffer from lung cancer any more than the general population in France [69]. This was made possible by enforcement of stringent control measures for protection of the environment which more than just met the regulatory standards.

With few exceptions, uranium is mined in uranium ore mining countries with concentrations of 0.1–0.5% U_3O_8 in the uranium ore. According to IAEA Safety Guides Safety Series No. 95, 1989, notification and licensing may not be required for handling solid natural radioactive materials containing less than 0.05 wt% of the elements uranium or thorium. This means that very low grades do not pose serious environmental hazards from radiation in their mining and processing if proven control measures are adopted.

3.12 Gas Mixtures and Smoke

Many of the gases discussed earlier are generally found as mixtures in mine environment. These mixtures have been given rather graphic names as given below.

Firedamp It is actually methane and possibly trace amounts of other gases.
Blackdamp It refers in general to a mixture of carbon dioxide and nitrogen in an oxygen-deficient atmosphere.
Afterdamp It is the name given to the residual gaseous products and smoke after a major fire or explosion. It includes carbon monoxide, carbon dioxide, nitrogen, oxygen, hydrogen, and hydrocarbons. Its effects are generally those of carbon monoxide. One finds a creosote smell in the air.
Rock gas It is primarily nitrogen and carbon dioxide, creating an oxygen-deficient atmosphere. It normally enters the mine from adjacent rock strata at ordinary pressures.
Smoke It is made up of very small particles (soot and tars) suspended in the air. It may irritate the nostrils and throat when inhaled. It is not normally considered to be asphyxiating in character, although it may be mixed with gases such as carbon monoxide and other vapours in proportions too dangerous to inhale.

3.13 Gas Analyzers

These are extremely accurate instruments used for analysis of air samples containing a mixture of gases in the laboratory or for continuous ambient air monitoring in mines.

Infrared analyzers
The Luft-type infrared analyzer provides an accurate and continuous analysis of a single selected gas in a mixture of gases or vapours in real time. It operates on the non-dispersive (NDIR) principle based on the absorption of infrared radiation by heteroatomic molecular gases. Figure 3.17 shows the absorption of infrared radiation for gases CO, CO_2, and CH_4, which are of great interest in mining. It will be seen that high percentages of infrared radiation are absorbed over a

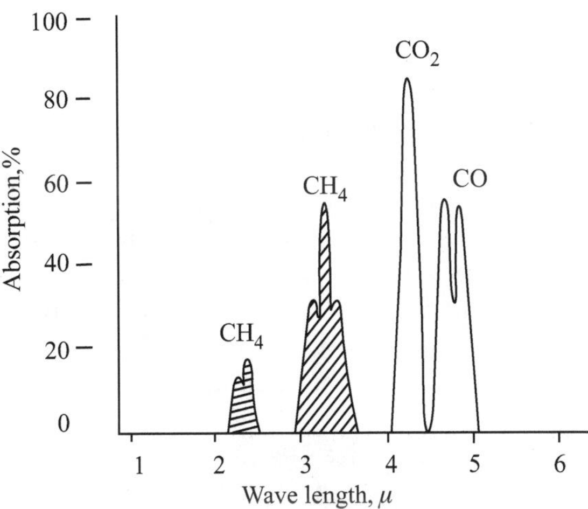

Figure 3.17 Absorption of infrared radiation by some gases.

band of wavelengths in the spectrum depending on the molecular structure and concentration of the component gas and that radiation at other wavelengths is virtually unaffected by it. The position of this band identifies the gas and the percentage of energy absorption is a measure of the gas concentration. This principle does not apply for elemental diatomic gases such as H_2, O_2, N_2, and the rare gases which are not infrared active, but it is applicable to almost all others. When measuring the concentration of a selected gas, the infrared wavelengths used include those of the absorption band of the gas to be measured.

The absorption of infrared radiation follows the exponential Lambert Beer law:

$$I = I_0 \cdot e^{-kcd}$$

where I is the transmitted intensity;
I_0 is the incident intensity;
k is a dimensionless extinction coefficient;
d is the length of path;
c is the gas concentration.

As the extinction coefficient for a given gas is a constant quantity, the transmitted radiation after absorption is a function of c and d. The length of the path in gas must, therefore, be selected depending on the expected gas concentrations to be measured. The higher the concentration, the shorter is the length of path.

Figure 3.18 gives a schematic diagram of an infrared analyzer. The instrument comprises an infrared source, a rotating interrupter or chopper vane, two side-by-side vertical cells or tubes, two receiving cells, a detector or diaphragm cell communicating with the receiving cells, an amplifier, a rectifier, and a recorder. Twin beams of infrared radiation from the source pass through the tubes. A single source is used in order to eliminate errors that would be caused by the differential ageing of two separate sources. The rotating chopper is placed between the source and the tubes to alternately block the radiation to the two tubes. This modulation of the beam is necessary for the operation of the measurement system.

The two tubes are a sample or analysis tube through which the sample gas is passed and a comparison or reference tube which is sealed and contains air or some other non-infrared absorbing reference gas. The tubes are made of brass with gold-plated bores or of aluminium with stainless steel insert, internally gold-plated. They are also available in stainless steel, nickel, and monel metal. The internal surfaces are highly polished to give the best optical and chemical conditions for analysis. The ends of the tubes are sealed with windows of material (sapphire, quartz, calcium fluoride, barium fluoride, etc.) transparent to the radiation wavelengths used.

The two receiving cells are an analysis receiving cell and a reference receiving cell which are placed beneath the two vertical tubes so that two beams of unequal energies passing out of the tubes during a measurement enter their respective receiving cells. They are filled with equal volumes of the pure sample of the gas to be measured so that the gas exerts an equal pressure on the diaphragm.

During a measurement, the amount of energy received by the analysis receiving cell remaining after absorption in the sample tube generates heat in the cell, which is related to the concentration of the gas to be measured in the mixture. The other reference receiving cell receives the energy without any absorption in the reference tube. As the volume of the gas on either side of the diaphragm is constant, different amounts of heat are generated in the cells due to unequal radiant energies resulting in unequal pressure rises and the change in position of the diaphragm causing a variation of capacitance. The periodic interruption of radiation

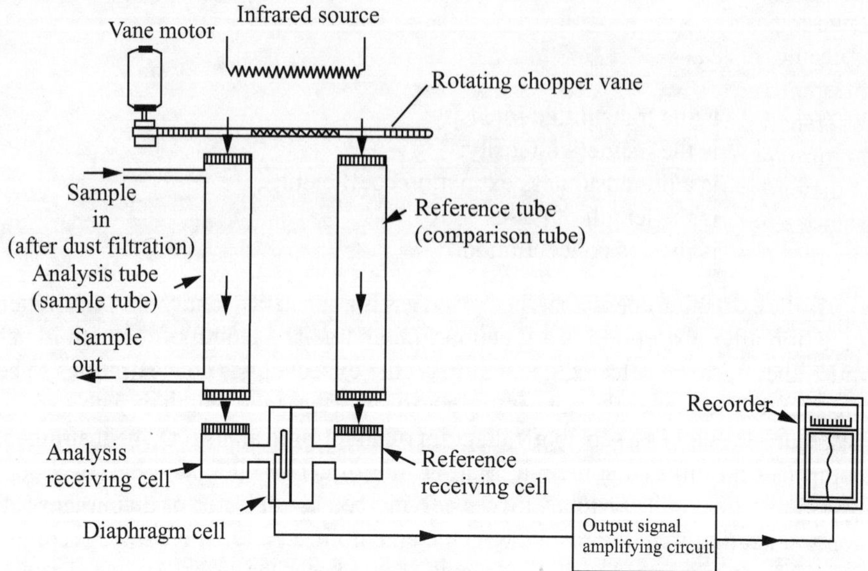

Figure 3.18 Schematic diagram of infrared analyser.

by the chopper, however, causes a corresponding reciprocating movement of the diaphragm at the frequency of the beam interruption. The change in capacitance provides an electrical output signal which is amplified, rectified and recorded on a chart recorder.

The zero-drift of the instrument is less than 1 per cent of full scale in 24 hours. The instrument can be operated at ambient temperatures up to +50°C.

The readings are affected by the presence of ethane, propane and butane gases, and dust. They are, however, practically not affected by CH_4 and CO_2 as they usually occur in mine air. The error caused by 5 per cent CO_2 or 5 per cent CH_4 is less than 10 ppm. The errors due to pressure and temperature variations are very small.

The instrument can be supplied with any desired measuring range or ranges. For control of methane-content of mine air, a range of 0 to 3 per cent CH_4 is selected. For control of CO-content in air currents produced due to spontaneous combustion or open fires, a range of 0 to 300 ppm is usually selected. All analyzers are fitted with solid-state electronics.

Gas chromatograph

Gas chromatography is a widely used high-precision analytical technique which uses a diverse group of methods to separate closely related components of complex mixtures of chemicals in a sample for the purpose of identification and quantification of the individual components constituting the sample mixture. A chromatograph is thus a chemical analysis instrument. It uses a coiled tubular column through which a sample to be analyzed is transported by an inert carrier gas called the mobile phase. This motion is inhibited by the adsorption of the molecules of each component either onto the coated column walls or onto the packing material in the column called the stationary phase. Depending on the degree of affinity of the molecules to the stationary phase, the molecules of the various components have different rates of progression along the column and reach the end of the column at different times thereby resulting in the separation of the various components of the mixture into discrete bands that can be analyzed qualitatively and quantitatively as they are swept by the carrier gas to a detector. A record of the effluent elute from the column after injection plotted against time is called a chromatogram. Figure 3.19 shows examples of good and bad separation of two components and Fig. 3.20 shows a typical chromatogram of a single compound. Chromatography can be divided into two categories: gas -liquid chromatography and gas-solid chromatography gas-liquid chromatography is mostly used for environmental analysis of liquid and gaseous mixtures. It is a standard method used for analysis of samples of mine atmosphere in the laboratory. The main components, nitrogen, oxygen, carbon dioxide and methane can be determined in as little time as 3 minutes while a complete analysis may take 10 minutes.

A chromatographic system consists of (1) a carrier gas supply, (2) a microsyringe for sample introduction, (3) the injection port, (4) the column and oven, (5) the detector, (6) an integrating recorder, and (7) accessories.

The most widely used carrier gases are helium, argon, nitrogen, and hydrogen of ultra high purity. Of these helium is the most recommended gas as it is inert, can be operated at high flow-rates and is the most convenient for a number of detectors. Because of its non-availability, hydrogen is the preferred gas if it is not a component to be measured in the sample. The flow-rate of the carrier gas must be adjusted to provide optimum column efficiency which can be ascertained by observing the peaks plotted on the strip chart of the recorder. As a general rule, low flow-rates and low temperatures will result in broad peaks which yield unsatisfactory quantitative data. Larger flow-rates will yield narrow width of peaks thus providing better resolution of adjacent peaks. As a starting point for packed columns, a flow-rate of 60 ml per minute is recommended.

Two designs of columns are used in gas chromatographs: packed columns and capillary columns.

Packed columns are typically a glass or stainless steel coil containing finely divided inert solid support material (e.g., diatomaceous earth) coated with a liquid or solid stationary phase. The nature of the coating material will be determined by the sample to be analyzed. Reliable information on their selection is available from the manufacturer. Packed columns have inner diameter of 2 to 5 mm and a length of 1.5 to 10 m.

Capillary columns are tubular columns having a very small internal diameter. Most columns are made of thin fused silica with a polymer outer coating and an inner coating of an active organic compound as stationary phase material. The internal diameters are typically between 0.25 and 0.32 mm with a total length of 10 to 100 m as a coiled configuration to fit in the instrument oven. High-resolution columns have

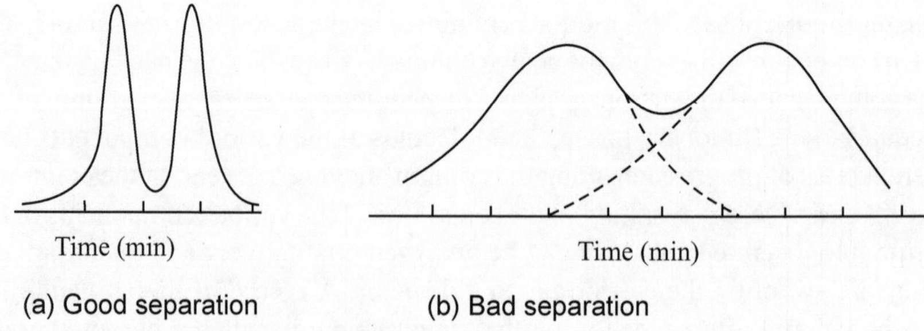

Figure 3.19 The separation of two components.

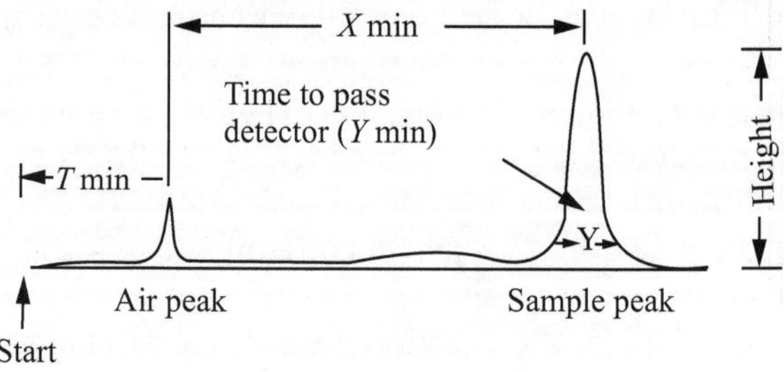

Figure 3.20 Schematic diagram of a gas chromatograph

diameters of 0.15 to 0.20 mm. Capillary columns provide a much higher separation efficiency than packed columns but can handle only a small quantity of sample (1–2 microlitre). Up to five separating columns may be accommodated and connected to the carrier gas stream by means of special column-switching valves.

The most common stationary phases used in gas chromatic columns are polysiloxanes, which contain certain substituent groups to change the phase polarity. The instrument manufacturers provide information on proper selection of a stationary phase so that it does not bleed out of the coated column due to excessive oven temperature fouling the detector. As molecular adsorption and rate of progression along the column depend on the temperature, the column temperature must be carefully controlled for precise work. The greatest level of separation occurs at reduced temperatures but this may result in very long duration times to reach the detector.

A variety of detectors for gas chromatography are available from the manufacturers. In general, each detector utilizes a unique characteristic of a molecule to generate a measurable electrical signal. The choice of a detector depends on the sensitivity to organic and inorganic compounds, selective detection ability and linearity. The various detectors that have been developed are the Flame Ionization Detector (FID), Thermal Conductivity Detector (TCD), Electron Capture Detector (ECD), Flame Photometric Detector (FPD) and Nitrogen Phosphorus Detector (NPD). The flame ionization and thermal conductivity detectors are the two most commonly used types on commercial gas chromatographs.

A FID uses a hydrogen/air flame and a collector plate. The effluent from the GC column passes through the flame which ionizes hydrocarbon and other molecules producing ions. The ions are attracted to the collector electrode producing electrons and the resulting electron current signal is amplified.

The FID is extremely sensitive to all organic compounds including hydrocarbons with a large dynamic range but is not sensitive to many inorganic compounds. Its only disadvantage is that it destroys the sample. It is not sensitive to CO, CO_2, H_2O, N_2 or O_2 which are normal flame products. Using Porapak-N as column material, the FID is used for measurement of CH_4, C_2H_6, C_2H_4 in mine atmospheres.

A TCD monitor changes in the thermal conductivity of the effluent. It can detect any sample molecules (organic or inorganic) that have thermal conductivity different from that of the carrier gas. It uses an electrically heated wire or thermistor as the sensing element whose temperature depends on the thermal conductivity of the effluent flowing around it. Changes in thermal conductivity causes a temperature rise in the element which is sensed as a change in resistance. The TCD consists of four tungsten–rhenium filaments in Wheatstone bridge configuration.

The TCD is commonly used for analysis of O_2, N_2, CO, CO_2, H_2S, NO, NO_2 etc in mine atmospheres using molecular sieve –5A as column material. The detector has a detectability of 1.9×10^{-9} g/ml. The GCs are generally designed to operate over an operating range of 20°–130°C which is suitable for most applications and the temperature may be thermostatically controlled. A high temperature TCD is also available which can be operated up to 400°C.

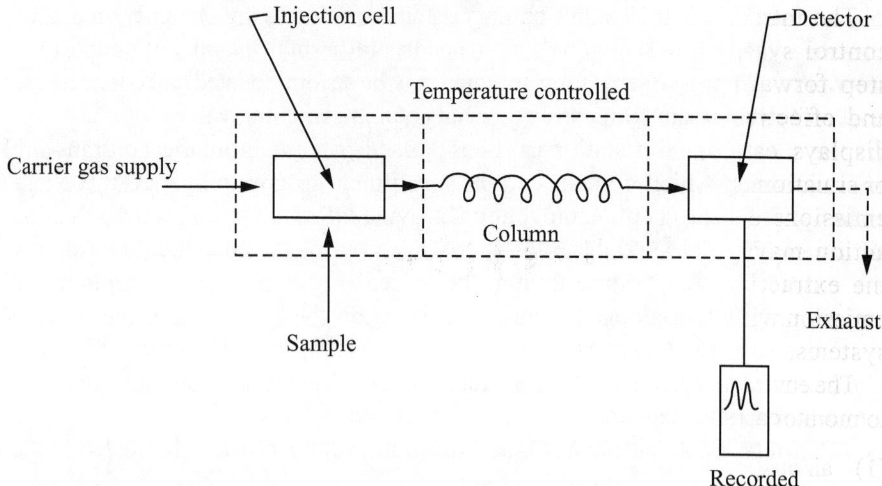

Figure 3.21

There are three ovens one for each of the injector, columns and detector (Fig. 3.21). The injector oven is designed for a temperature range 50°– 450°C settable in 1°C steps. The detector oven is designed and operated so that the detectors are kept at a higher temperature than the injectors and columns during heat-up and cool-down periods to minimize the risk of detector contamination. The column oven allows for fast heat-up and rapid cool-down resulting in faster analysis with minimum loss of operating time. If the temperature of any one of the three ovens rises more than 10°C above the set value, the instrument is automatically switched off thereby protecting the injectors, columns and detectors.

Modern gas chromatographs are microprocessor-controlled for isothermal as well as temperature-programmed operation and are of modular design to enable system configuration to be expanded as the analytical requirements increase. They have unique features of multi-function digital display of set parameters and actual values and diagnostics, built-in signature analysis, data protection, start-up and cool-down sequence, oven temperature protection, a computing integrator to determine the peak area and peak height, retention time, and provide a record of the chromatogram and final results.

Field gas chromatographs are also available in the market which are capable of the same analyses as fixed laboratory instruments

When using a gas chromatograph for analysis of mine atmosphere, the sample should be first passed through the TCD and then through the FID.

3.14 Mine Environmental Monitoring and Control

The effectiveness of engineering control measures for compliance with mining regulations can be ensured only if mine gas concentrations in mine workings are accurately monitored.

The introduction of continuous remote environmental monitoring and control system in mines, particularly in modern coal mines, is a great step forward in achieving increased mine safety, higher productivity, and effective utilisation of manpower. It provides, through alarms and displays, early warnings of impending abnormal and dangerous conditions or situations in mine workings such as spontaneous combustion and sudden emissions or layering of firedamp so that timely appropriate corrective action may be taken. Knowledge of average methane emission during the extraction of a seam as well as of the maximum actual-to-average emission will enable better design of mine ventilation and methane drainage systems.

The environmental monitoring and control system provides measuring facilities to monitor and control

(1) air quality (principal mine gases – methane, carbon monoxide, carbon dioxide, oxygen, nitrogen, and in certain very specific cases, hydrogen sulphide and sulphur dioxide — temperature and humidity);
(2) air flow rate, air velocity;
(3) differential pressure, static pressure;
(4) coal dust, submicrometre particulates;
(5) noise; and
(6) fans (auxiliary, booster, main) operation.

In modern mines, environmental monitoring forms an integral part of a comprehensive monitoring system which will provide comprehensive management information and control and includes monitoring and control of other underground or surface plants or systems such as:

coal face equipment;
coal clearance equipment;
electrical distribution;
pumps;
machine health;
management information; and
general purpose.

Transducers/sensors and any other measuring instruments that supply a continuous signal are used to measure the variable parameters and the outputs are transmitted via a data transmission system to a 'central control station' or 'mine control centre' on the mine surface.

3.14.1 Environmental monitoring systems

Depending on the number of underground sample points and the number of gases to be measured, one or more of the following basic systems of atmospheric monitoring may be used (Fig. 3.22):

(1) Where only a relatively small number of underground monitoring points are involved, sensors or self-contained analyzers are used and the output analogue signals, after amplification, are transmitted by a direct multi-core cable through an isolating zener safety barrier to a surface-mounted central monitoring station with data recording and audible or visual alarms systems. The system is simple and relatively inexpensive to install.

(2) The 'tube-bundle system' with individual nylon/polyethylene sampling tubes going to the sample points to aspirate gas samples for analysis by a microprocessor-based analyzer (or analyzers) at a central station on the surface, which measures or derives the various parameters. The parameters that can be handled by the system are methane, oxygen, nitrogen, carbon dioxide, carbon monoxide, Graham ratio, and oxygen deficiency.

The tube-bundle system is used where response times are not critical and high-accuracy instruments are desired in order to detect small changes in gas concentrations. As the instrument(s), pumps, and valves are located outside the mine, they are independent of the underground mine power and are easily accessible for maintenance repair and calibration. However, this system suffers from several limitations which generally does not make it useful for multi-purpose environmental monitoring. The system cannot be used for measuring physical parameters and certain absorptive gases, provides intermittent monitoring at one point where one analyzer is used for many tubes, and necessitates checking of the integrity of the sample tubes from time to time. Its primary use has been for detection of spontaneous combustion and other mine fires.

(3) Where a large number of points are to be monitored, a fast response is required and distances are large, appropriate sensors/transducers are used and the analogue outputs are encoded and transmitted via an approved data transmission system to a central control station (mine control centre) on the mine surface, consisting of one or more computers which check and process the data to determine and display the status of conditions in the mine. This system is called telemetry system.

The main advantages of the computerized mine environmental monitoring system (either tube-bundle or telemetry or a combination of them) lies in the continuous nature of the data received from the system and easy storage and retrieval of the data at a central location.

When selecting a permanent environmental monitoring system/equipment, the following points must be borne in mind:

(l) Cost of initial installation;
(2) Accuracy of equipment;
(3) Interference by other gases or electrical noise;
(4) In-built safety features – intrinsic safety;
(5) Ability to operate even when mine power is cut off for any reason;
(6) Ease of maintenance, availability of supplier technical back-up;
(7) Simplicity and sturdiness of construction, flame-proofness and vandal-proofness;

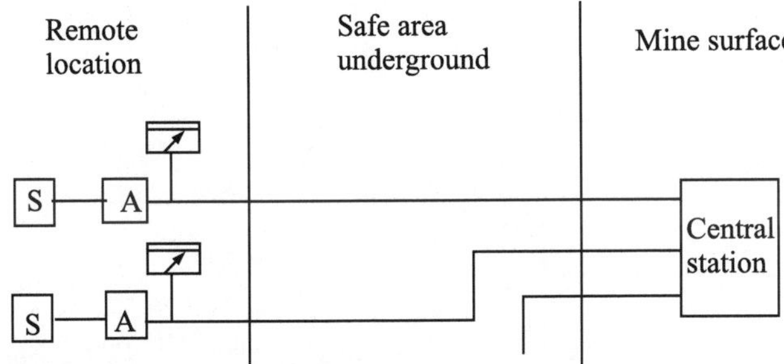

(i) System with sensors, amplifiers, local read-out (optional) at remote location in a hazardous area. Display, alarms at safe location underground or surface.

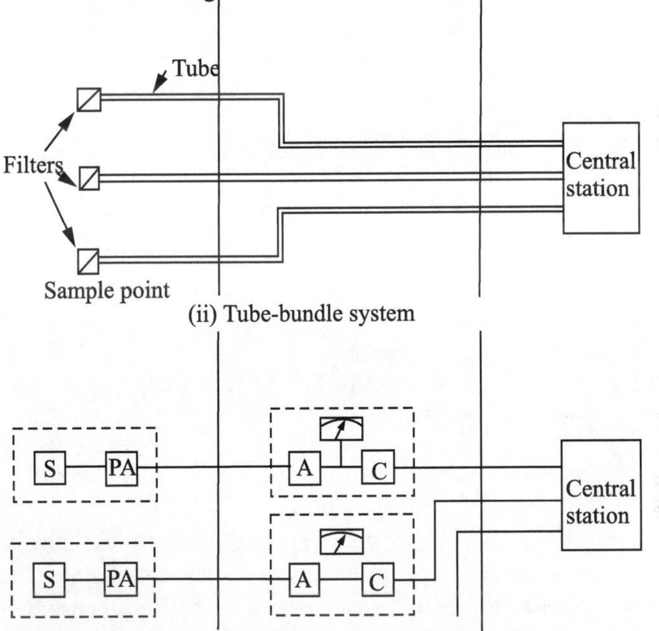

(ii) Tube-bundle system

(iii.a) System with sensors at sample points. Amplifiers, coders, local read-outs (optional) etc., at a safe location underground.

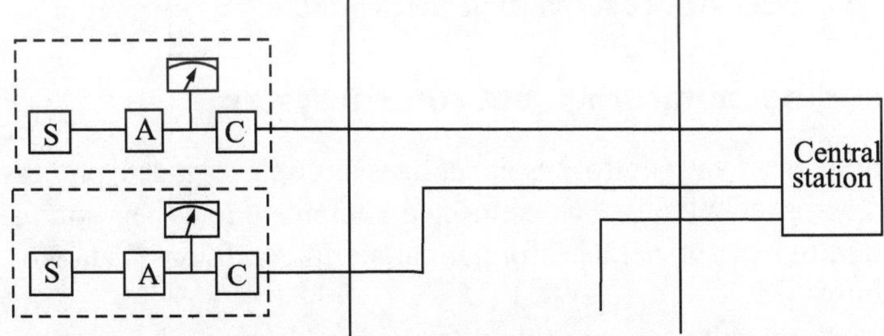

(iii.b) System with sensors, amplifiers, coders (FM), local read-out (optional) at remote locations in a hazardous area.

Figure 3.22 Systems of environmental monitoring.

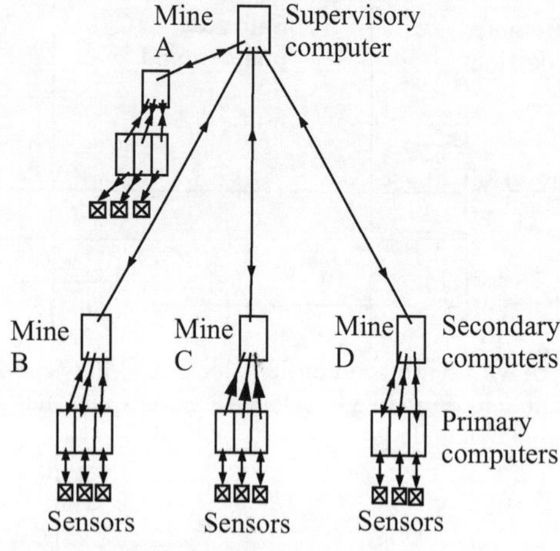

Figure 3.23 Supervisory management system.

(8) Speed of response;
(9) Accessibility for alarm-setting by underground personnel;
(10) High degree of reliability to provide necessary protection for which they are made;
(11) Real-time picture; and
(12) A sense of responsibility on the part of the mine management and technology gap at the mine.

Studies have shown that all costs incurred can be recovered in 6 to 12 months, depending on the size of the installation.

Mine control systems of two or more neighbouring mines may be connected to a central overall supervisory control system at one of the mines (Fig. 3.23) where information of a general or total system nature may be processed and stared, and reports issued, and where all normal primary information displays relating to mines may be called up. All interrogation and display facilities will, however, remain at the mine site which will be responsible for distributing its own reports.

3.14.2 Mine monitoring and control system

A mine monitoring and control system utilizes multiplexing, data processing, and microprocessor techniques. The connected computers and their software allow presentation of environmental information, alarm conditions, data storage, and calculations.

A mine monitoring and control system (Fig. 3.24) may be considered to be made up of the following basic parts:

(1) A central station or master station located at the mine surface in a control room or a mine control centre comprising a central processor or telemetry unit

that controls the operation of the transmission system and collects, analyzes, and handles monitoring data received from it;

(2) Computer software that performs the analysis of data and provides a variety of displays;

(3) A transmission system;

(4) Outstations or remote controllers that convert the transducer signals into data transmission signals; and

(5) Transducers/sensors.

3.14.2.1 Central station

The central station, also called the 'master station', forms the heart of the whole system. It comprises a telemetry unit and a control computer with control console and keyboard, one or two VDUS, and a printer.

The design of the telemetry unit varies from manufacturer to manufacturer, depending on the system used. Basically, it consists of a microprocessor-based scanner connected to the computer through an interface, to interrogate or scan, on instruction, the various outstations within a range of 10 km and decode the monitoring information for the computer to store, analyze and process. The computer commands entered through the keyboard are converted into signals by the computer interface for transmission to a particular outstation.

The other features of the telemetry unit are:

(1) Automatic control of outgoing telemetering lines, signalling by audio or visual alarm any defects occurring;

(2) A manual control for checking the correct functioning of the whole system;

(3) Graphic recording of information;

(4) Triggering alarms in the event of an overflow of the pre-adjusted thresholds;

(5) Control of specific equipment;

(6) A telephone link with each measuring point; and

(7) A device (Zener barrier) to supply intrinsically safe voltages and currents for powering the remote transducers.

A telemetry unit can be connected up to eight outstations. Its capacity can be extended by having several units.

Computers

Two computers are used in the control room/mine control centre. The primary computer (in computer rack), also called the control computer, operator's computer, or 'real-time' computer, will provide an accurate and reliable 'real-time' picture of what is happening on a minute-to-minute basis, and the secondary computer, also called the 'deferred-time' computer has a large memory and stores the basic data on system status for analysis and retrieval over a span of weeks and months (Fig. 3.25).

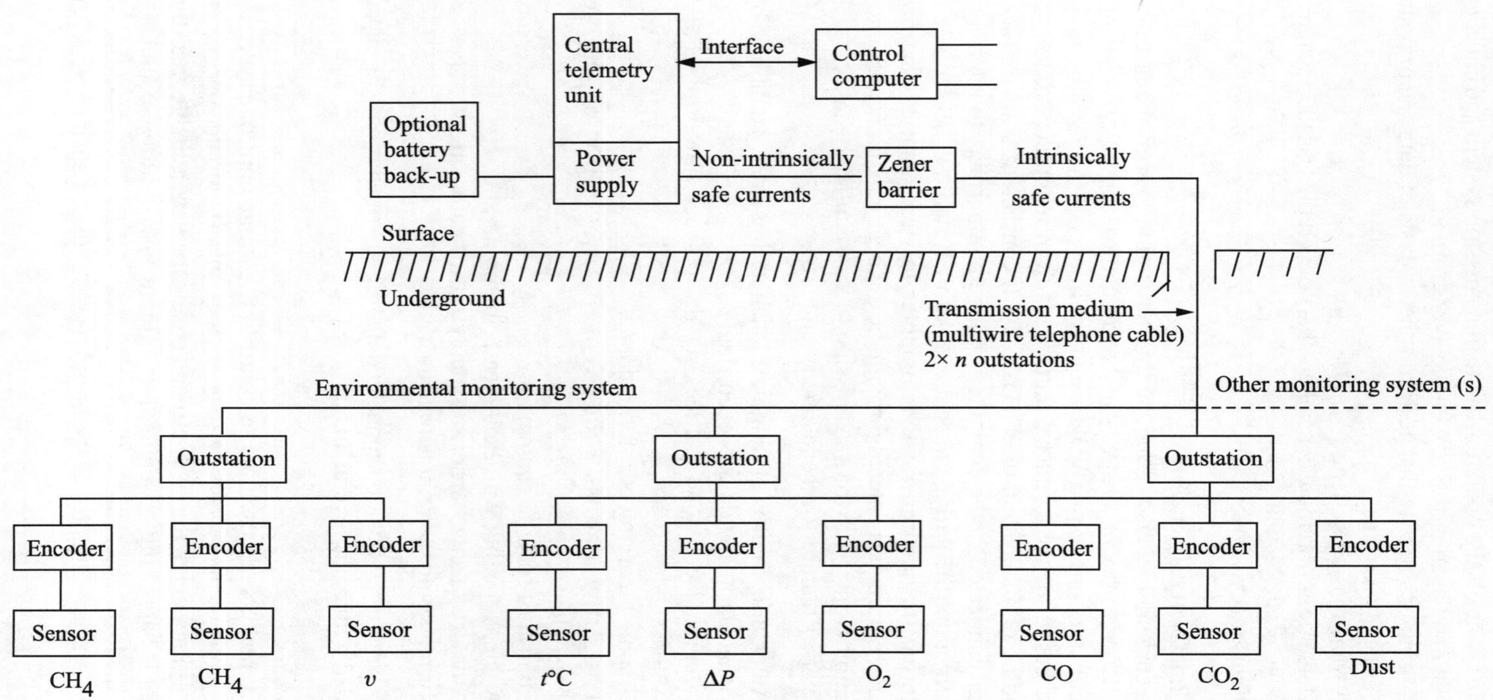

Figure 3.24 Mine monitoring and control system.

Both microcomputers and minicomputers are used in environmental monitoring and other applications. The dividing line between them is thin, although, generally speaking, minicomputers are more powerful, have more storage capacity, and are costlier than microcomputers.

In many cases, a standby computer is provided which can be switched into service in the event of failure of the primary computer.

The computer operator communicates with the operating system through the function keyboard and the computer writes messages for the operator on display screens. Alpha-numeric keys are used to input data to or generate commands from the computer. All other keys are divided into several blocks or sections, each of which performs a particular function.

British Coal (formerly the National Coal Board) developed a Standard Computer system for Mine Operations (MINOS) which can be described as a set of computer equipment, a basic computer programme called an 'operating system', and a set of application programmes which may be independent of the data transmission system to monitor and control a specific plant. The principal features of the MINOS system are:

(1) Use of standardized primary and secondary computers as well as software;
(2) Same keyboard;
(3) Similar displays on the VDUs irrespective of the manufacturer; and

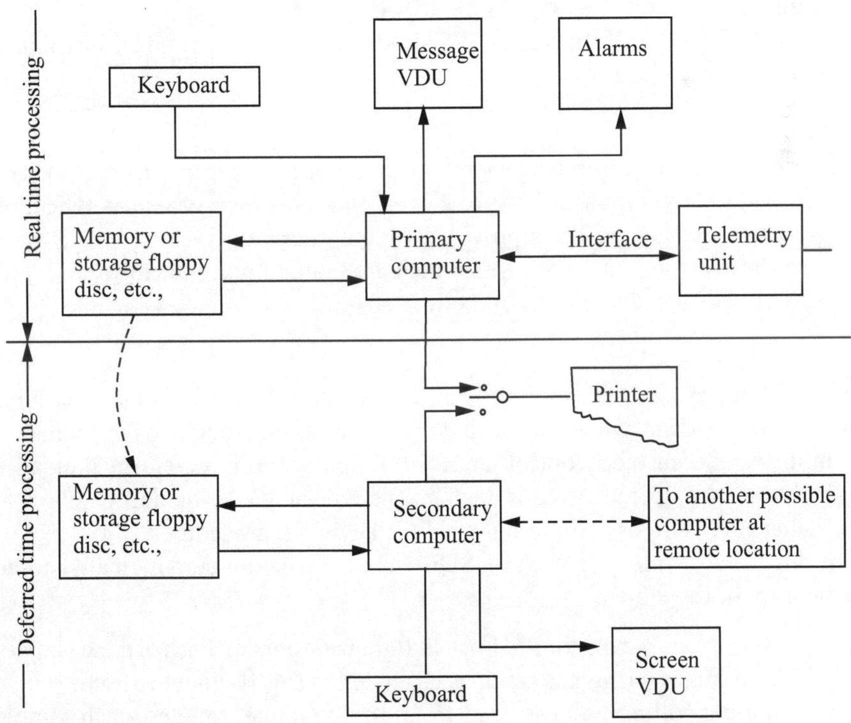

Figure 3.25 Data processing.

(4) Built-in flexibility which permits operation of the system to suit local circumstances.

The MINOS became a standard monitoring and control system for British collieries.

Recent advances in technology such as microcomputers and touch-pad keyboards have been included in the concept Micro-Minos system which has been successfully used to control and monitor other underground and/or surface plants or systems by using spare capacity in the existing outstations and/or incorporating further outstations.

When the computer capacity becomes a major constraint and several applications cannot be integrated in the single control computer, several microprocessors may be used, each carrying out a single function so that computing power is distributed. Such a distributed system offers a greater modularity in expanding the system and system reliability. A processing station could be located adjacent to a group of transducers. The local station would be able to process the data and provide visual displays or alarms. It would send these data to the central station only when requested.

A number of monitoring and control systems are manufactured in the USA, UK, France, Germany and other countries by companies such as Hawker Siddley Dynamics Engineering Ltd., John Davis & Sons (Derby) Ltd., Westinghouse Systems Ltd., Transmitton Ltd., Oldham France SA, Siemens and Huwood Controls Div. of Babcock Bristol Ltd., MSA.

Figures 3.26 and 3.27 show basic WESDAC Minos elements and the distributed computer system structure.

Software

The software, that is, computer programme or instructions, is tailor-made to each particular system. It forms the basis of the real-time operating system. Application programmes use the facilities provided by the operating system. There are a few well-proven software packages which are operating satisfactorily in many industrially-advanced countries of the world.

Data handling

The basic approach to monitoring is exception reporting, that is, all departures from set norms as and when they occur are processed and brought to the operator's attention at the surface control station through warning or alarm messages displayed on the operator's console. The operator may also request displays of the status of an item or plant through simple keyboard procedures.

In the Micro-Minos system of HSDE Ltd., the data are automatically stored in the form of three files:

(1) An 8-hour rolling trend formed from 48 10-minute samples. Each of these samples is the average of 1-minute readings taken during that 10-minute period.
(2) A 32-hour rolling trend formed from 48 40-minute samples, each sample being the average of readings received within the 40-minute period.

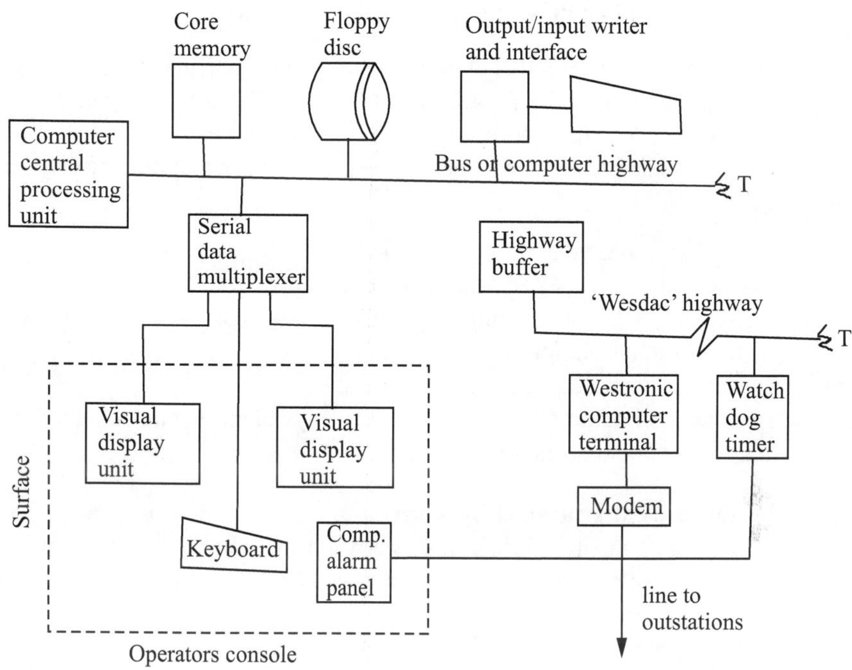

Figure 3.26 Basic Wesdac Minos elements

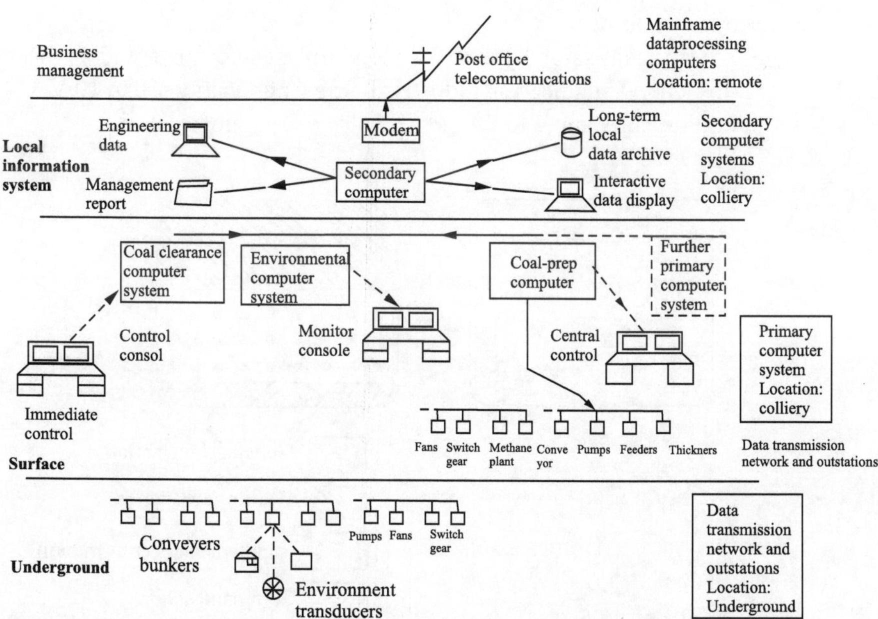

Figure 3.27 Wesdac-Minos computer system structure (distributed system).

(3) A 7-day rolling trend formed from 48 4-hour samples.

These files are used for trend analysis and summary reporting and are passed to a secondary computer for subsequent processing. Reports are presented on VDU-displays or in printed form.

When two VDUs are used, the screen space provides for four display areas as shown in Fig. 3.28.

Area 1: A full screen used for an overall display of environmental conditions underground, trends and interactive operations.

Area 2: Used solely for plain language, exception reports, and alarm messages for operator's attention.

Area 3: Used for detailed plant status information.

Area 4: It is the command echo area which displays plant commands given by the operator using the function keyboard.

3.14.2.2 Data Transmission System

Data and commands must be transmitted between the computer at the surface central station and the underground outstations as well as between the outstations and transducers at remote locations.

The transmission systems used are:

(1) Analogue transmission systems;
(2) Digital transmission systems
(3) Frequency-based communication systems

Transducer outputs are electrical signals which may be analogue – current voltage – or binary numbers.

The analogue transmission system is the simplest and most widely used technique in the general engineering industry. In mine applications, 0 to 10 V, 0.4 to 2 V DC and 0 to 1 mA and 4 to 20 mA signals are commonly used.

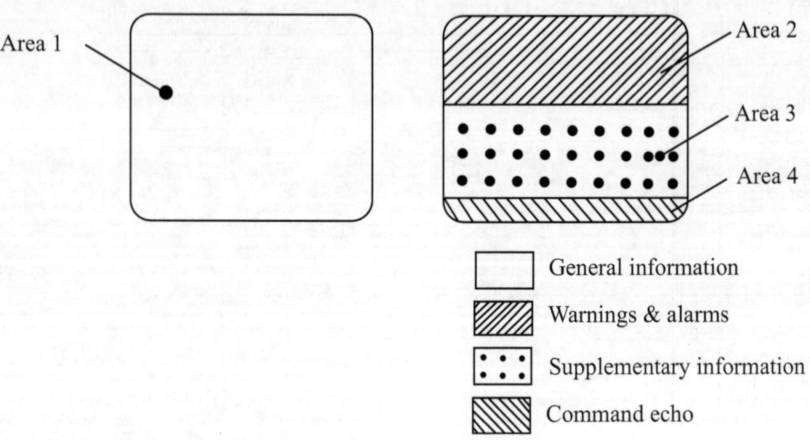

Figure 3.28 VDU screen allocations.

Owing to some inherent disadvantages in transmission of analogue voltage or current signals, digital and frequency-modulated signals are widely used in mines employing analogue voltage signals.

Digital signals are in the form of ON/OFF signals generated by the transducers as a series of electrical pulses (binary 1) and spaces (binary 0). The major advantages of digital transmission are that the accuracy and integrity of the binary signals are preserved from the transducers to the central station and that the digital circuitry is very inexpensive compared with the analogue circuitry of the conventional system. The disadvantage, however, is that sophisticated circuitry must be built into the transducer unit design.

Frequency-modulated signals with constant amplitudes are produced from the analogue voltage signals by the use of encoders (oscillators) within the outstation. They are, in fact, a form of analogue signals since the transmitted frequency is proportional to the variable parameter being measured. Typical frequencies in use are the 6 to 12 Hz and 6 to 12 kHz ranges. The higher frequency signals near the voice range are suitable for long distances. As frequency signals are AC, they are intrinsically safe and require much less power to transmit compared to analogue signals.

Multiplexing

Multiplexing can be applied to analogue, digital, or frequency signals. It allows several remote transducers to transmit information channels over the same single transmission facility without interfering with each other.

Analogue time-division multiplexing (TDM)

TDM allows transmission of several information channels over the same transmission facility on time-sharing basis. In mines, several cables may be run to one or more central points where a multiplexer unit is located. The use of such a system reduces the amount of cable required and cuts down the installation cost considerably.

Figure 3.29 shows a typical TDM system to multiplex five signals. A rotating switch, called a commutator or local selector, connects each information channel in a rotational sequence many times a second and the sample pulses are transmitted one after the other over the communication or transmission channel, dwelling on each contact only for the duration of one pulse. At the receiver end, another switch rotating in synchronism with the sensing commutator decommutates the pulses and connects them to corresponding addresses on the telemetry unit to reconstruct the original channel signals.

Digital time-division multiplexing

Figure 3.30 shows a typical digital time-division multiplexing system.

The digital signals are fed to the input gates which act like switches. Analogue signals are converted to their digital equivalents by an analogue-to-digital converter (ADC). The parallel-to-serial converter (P/S converter) acts as the commutator or the switching device and the serial data (output of the

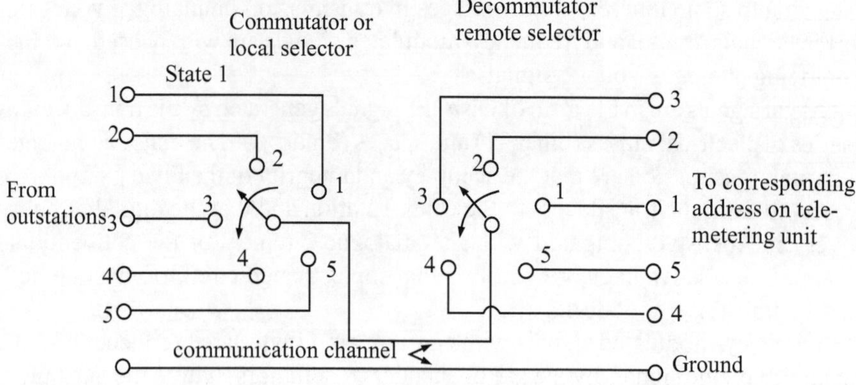

Figure 3.29 Analogue time-division multiplexing system (TDM).

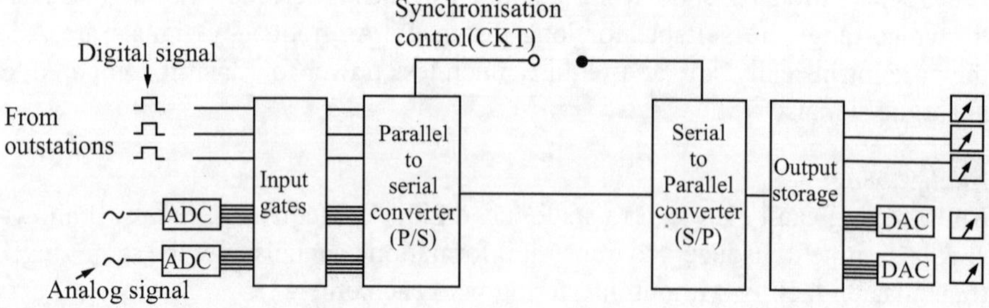

Figure 3.30 Digital time-division multiplexing system.

P/S converter) are then transmitted one after the other over the transmission facility to the line drivers. At the receiving end, a serial-to-parallel converter (S/P converter) converts them into parallel format, reconstructing the original analogue signals.

Frequency-division multiplexing (FDM)

A FDM system consists of a number of oscillators or transmitters of different frequencies, one for each information channel. The frequency of each transmitter is carefully chosen so that there is a minimum of interaction between the channels. The transmitters operate simultaneously and continuously. At the other end of the transmission channel, there are an equal number of filters matched to each oscillator. Each filter is designed to pass the frequency from a particular transmitter and reject all other frequencies. The technique is illustrated in Fig. 3.31. The advantages of FDM are its simplicity and insensitiveness to electrical disturbances. The disadvantages, however, are that the system is expensive, the number of channels which may be used is restricted (maximum 40), the accuracy of the transmitted data is restricted, the second and the third harmonics can cause false detection and, hence it is unreliable compared with the digital system.

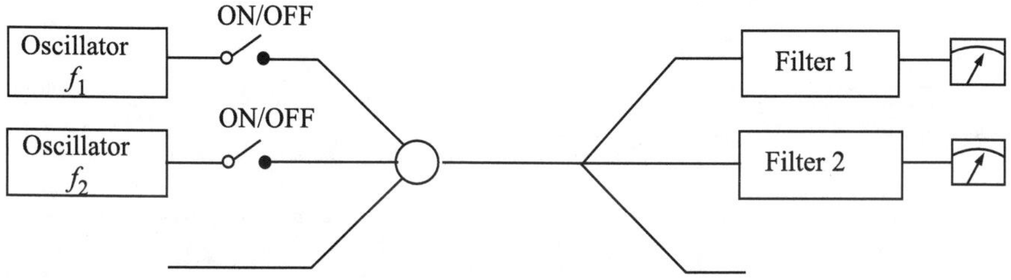

Figure 3.31 Frequency-division multiplexing system.

3.14.2.3 Transmission line (Telemetering cable network)

Monitoring and control signals are continuously transmitted two ways between transducer outstations and the central station over a cable network. The volume of and the speed at which the information may be required to be transmitted will determine the choice of the transmission channel. With FDM, the limiting factor is the highest value of the carrier frequency which may be propagated. The following types of transmission lines are commonly used:

(i) A twisted pair of wires or telephone cable (5 kHz);
(ii) A multi-core cable with twisted pairs (10 kHz); and
(iii) A high-frequency co-axial cable (10 MHz).

The standard twisted-pair mine telephone table (70 ohm/km) is most commonly used in mines. Multi-core and co-axial cables are expensive and require skilled maintenance. The cables must be intrinsically safe.

3.14.2.4 Outstations

Outstations perform data acquisition, analysis, and transmission functions. They also receive commands from the central station and execute them by switching on/off motors or actuators. They are connected in series, but a number of outstations (normally up to 16) are arranged together in a ring. In each ring, a cable runs down from the central station to one outstation. Other cables run from each outstation to another. There are six cores for each ring. These are the data down, data up, shift, transfer, identity and common cores. Each outstation can monitor up to 40 digital signals and up to eight analogue signals. The outstations are capable of being operated locally in the event of a failure of the telemetry link to the surface.

Each outstation has its own identity known as *address code* and by this means the precise source of an information bit can be recognized. A section of the telemetry unit is dedicated to that address and, when an outstation is poled, the state of each data bit is transmitted and filed in an appropriate address of the computer or control console, which can then be directly displayed. The outstation design contains local display of status.

3.14.2.5 Transducers

Transducers (also called sensors, monitors, detectors) are used to measure the variable parameters and are sited as near as possible to the sampling points. They

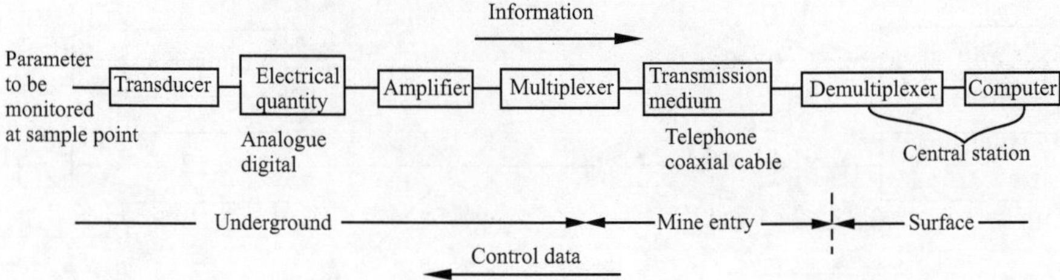

Figure 3.32 Transducer system.

produce information in the form of an electrical signal either as an analogue voltage in the range 0.4 to 2 V or a set of voltage-free microswitch or relay contacts at one or more preset alarm levels.

A transducer consists of a sensing element which may or may not be designed integral with an electronic circuit which will convert the signal received from it into an electric analogue voltage for further processing for transmission. The power supply is usually a battery. Most transducers use liquid crystal display (LCD) for local indication and calibration or a light emitting diode (LED). Figure 3.32 shows the transducer system. When selecting a transducer, the cost, accuracy, life, selectivity, response time, reliability, maintainability, and power requirement must be taken into account.

The transducer types used in environmental monitoring and the principles of their operations are listed in Table 3.4.

Table 3.4 Transducer types

Type		Operating range
Infrared gas sensor		
CO_2	Carbon dioxide	0–2% vol
CH_4	Methane	0–100% LEL
Electrochemical gas sensors		
CO	Carbon monoxide	0–50 ppm
H_2S	Hydrogen sulphide	0–500 ppm
SO_2	Sulphur dioxide	0–100 ppm
NO_2	Nitrogen dioxide	0–20 ppm
0_2	Oxygen	0–25%
H_2	Hydrogen	0–1000 ppm
Catalytic combustion sensor		
Flammable gases		0–5% V 0–100% LEL
Environmental sensors		
Ambient air temperature sensor		–10–+50°C
Air velocity/flow sensor		0.5–30 m/s
Pressure sensor		0–600 bargauge

Gas sensors are the heart of personal and fixed gas detectors protecting life and property in inhospitable environments in mining and other dangerous industries. They must be stable in operation, for which they are tested under extreme conditions so that they function reliably throughout their design life. They are supplied by approved sensor suppliers for the majority of instruments manufacturers that serve the markets.

CHAPTER 4

Outbursts of Coal and Gas

An outburst is a phenomenon characterized by sudden displacement or ejection into mine workings of either large volumes of fragmented rock with or without gas or large volumes of gas alone. The phenomenon is generally attributed to high gas pressures and/or overstressing due to accumulated stresses in rocks, although its mechanism is still not fully understood.

Outbursts occur in coal, salt, potash and metal mines. The gas emissions are generally firedamp, carbon dioxide, nitrogen, and hydrogen. In coal mines, the gas may be firedamp or carbon dioxide or their mixtures. Outbursts of carbon dioxide tend to be more severe than firedamp outbursts.

The potential hazards associated with outbursts are:

(1) Immediate risk from burial and subsequent asphyxiation of mine personnel by dust and/or gas in the vicinity of an outburst when it occurs with little or no warning;
(2) Death of mine personnel due to violent expulsions of rock and gas or moved equipment and supports in the outburst zone;
(3) Damage to equipment and mine workings;
(4) Formation of combustible or flammable gas mixtures in coal mines with risk of fire and explosion from damaged equipment; and
(5) Loss of production from the affected district, or loss of a mining horizon, or loss of a whole mine from frequent outbursting.

Outbursts are known to be confined to a few mining fields in the world, the well-known, of which are: the coalfields of Cevennen (France), Campine (Belgium), Ruhr (Germany), Wales, Derbyshire, Lancashire, North Staffordshire, Nottinghamshire, and Durham (UK), Silesia (Poland), Donez and Kuznets (Russia), Ostrava (Czechoslovakia), Lias and Pecs (Hungary), Ishikari and Hokkaido (Japan), Sydney and Bowen Basins (Australia), British Columbia (Canada), and Raniganj (India) Potash mining fields of Central Germany, Louisiana salt mining field (the USA) and gold mining fields of Kolar (India) and Witwatersrand (South Africa), About 100,000 gas outbursts have been reported from all over the world [71].

In coal mining, a distinction is sometimes made between gas outbursts and bumps. In a gas outburst, it is the gas which ejects out the coal-rock whilst in a bump, the gas may be released after sudden and violent failure of coal pillars under stress. In bumps, the stored elastic energy of rock and coal is released and the coal does not disintegrate so much into fine coal as with gas outbursts. The gas energy release depends on the quantity and pressure of gas stored in the coal and the quickness of the desorption ability. In large outbursts, both gas outbursts and bumps, may, however, occur at the same time due to joint action of rock and gas pressures. Several hundred tonnes of usually fine coal may be ejected in a fraction of a second and several hundred thousand cubic metres of gas may be evolved in large outbursts. The pressure of the enormous quantity of the instantaneously released gas may be sufficient to push back the ventilating intake air current several hundred metres and destroy the ventilation system. The gas emission generally stops rapidly but sometimes it may continue for a long period. Whereas CH_4 in the strata is a product of the coal-forming process, CO_2, with carbon dioxide outbursts, is introduced into the seams through igneous intrusions which cause partial devolatilisation of coal adjoining the intrusion with local increase in rank. Owing to the higher absorption capacity of coal for CO_2 than for CH_4, CO_2-outbursts are characterized by greater violence and seams containing CO_2 show the greatest proneness to outbursts.

Unlike bumps which often occur away from active faces, gas outbursts occur only at fresh faces of headings in coal, in virgin areas, in cross-measure drifts/cross-cuts, and at or in proximity to longwall faces. The majority of outbursts take place in the downward direction under the influence of gravity, but in some cases, they occur in an upward direction from the floor close to the working face (floor outbursts).

Hargraves [72] reviewed the literature published till 1982 on the subject of instantaneous outbursts of coal and gas.

4.1 Causes of Outbursts of Coal and Gas

Based on experiences with actual outbursts published in the mining literature, outbursts of rock/coal and/or gas may occur under the following conditions:

(1) When working gassy seams containing gas under high pressure. There is no minimum standard for the degree of gassiness at which a seam becomes outburst prone.

(2) When working seams which are relatively soft and friable or contain soft bands or layers in local sites as a result of traversing of the coal by innumerable cleavage planes. Such coals have a structure which, in the unconfined state, is incapable of withstanding stresses of any magnitude.

(3) When the adjacent roof and floor with outburst-prone coal are strong and the coal seam parts readily from them.

(4) Where the adjacent roof and floor are weak and the coal is soft.

(5) Where the extraction of a seam in flat measures is not complete and safety barrier pillars and other pillars or strips of seam are left unmined for whatsoever reason, and are mined at a later date often between goaves.

(6) Intersection of zones of intense abutment pressures of adjacent longwall faces in the same seam mined at different times leading to intensified stress in the front abutment zone (Fig. 4. 1).

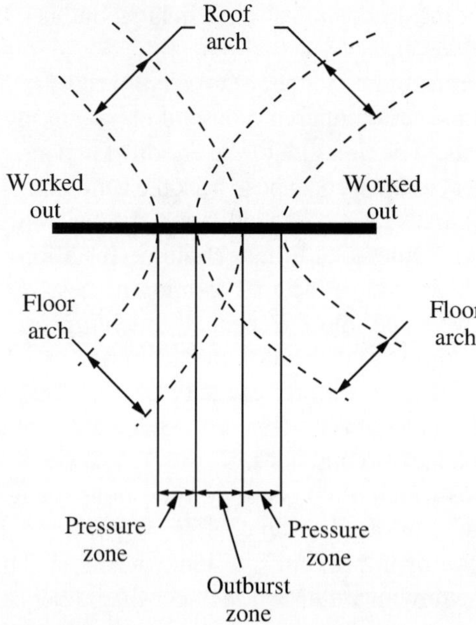

Figure 4.1 Intersection of abutment pressure zones of adjacent longwall faces.

(7) When driving a development coal heading in the front abutment pressure zone of a parallel longwall face approaching its boundary limit (Fig. 4.2).
(8) When a cross-measure drift/cross-cut intersects a seam.
(9) When driving a rise heading in a steeply-inclined seam.
(10) When extracting seams having outburst-prone coal with a sandstone roof.

An outburst in the face may occur when its front abutment pressure intersects the existing pressure zone of a worked-out face in an overlying

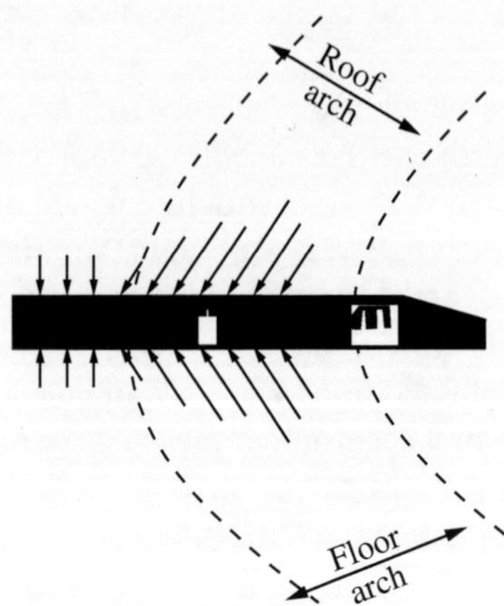

Figure 4.2 Development coal heading in the abutment pressure zone of a longwall face approaching its boundary limit.

seam. In semi-steep and steep measures, the coal tends to dislodge or run out aided by gravity (Fig. 4.3).

(11) Presence of a strong band or bands followed by a permeable and/or porous stratum and a coal seam or carbonaceous bed in the floor of the seam being worked, which is liable to floor outbursts [73].

(12) As the load stresses increase with depth due to superincumbent and lateral confinement and as the gassiness of the strata also increases with depth, outburst proneness increases with depth although it has not been categorically established in some coalfields. The shallowest outburst occurred at Collensville Colliery in Australia at 180 m depth. There is, however, no direct relationship between depth and proneness although the possibility of the incidence of violent outbursts is higher at greater depths, exceeding about 1200 m.

(13) Areas subject to severe tectonic forces due to faults, dykes, sills, and rolls, thickening and thinning of seams are more prone to outbursts. In such an area, outbursts in development headings are more frequent than in production faces, but the severity of outbursts in the latter is greater than in the former. Outbursts commonly occur on and adjoining faults and dykes.

(14) Exposure of roof over a large area in depillaring sections without caving taking place. Sudden fracture of the overhanging roof causes crushing of the coal stooks/ribs and a sudden outburst. Similarly, on longwall faces, if caving is inadequate, the strata overhang behind the face supports creating excessive stresses at the face due to cantilever action. The abutment zone does not advance with mining, which may result in a burst.

(15) At points of converging pillar lines in bord and pillar workings.

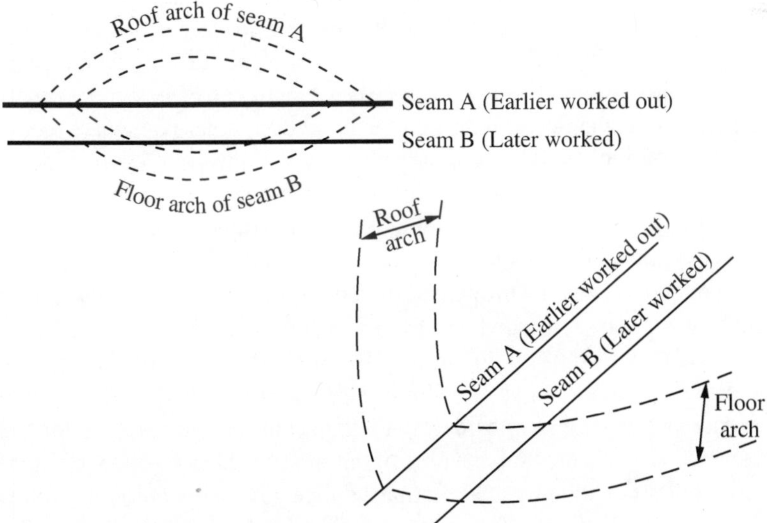

Figure 4.3 Intersection of floor pressure arch of a longwall face in an overlying seam with an underlying seam.

(16) When working thick seams which cannot be mined to full thickness in one pass and are developed in the floor, leaving roof coal.
(17) When working seams of high-rank coals which are generally more prone to outbursts than lower-rank coals. The coals usually affected are those of relatively high-rank bituminous and anthracite.
(18) When practising destress blasting, also called 'shock blasting' or inducer shotfiring, which may precipitate on outburst immediately following blasting or after a delay of several hours.
(19) High rates of face advance which will increase the gassiness of face coal and increase proneness.
(20) When mining under a hilly terrain with crests and valleys.

4.2 Prevention of Outbursts of Coal and Gas

When working seams subject to instantaneous outbursts of coal and gas, the potential outburst zone must be identified in advance and shown on mine plans. Suitable methods of development and extraction in these areas must be devised so that the danger or severity of the outburst is minimised.

The following precautionary measures may be adopted in development drivages in coal and on production faces in seams subject to outbursts:

4.2.1 In Development drivages in coal

(1) In inclined seams, headings in coal should be driven, as far as practicable, in the dip direction. They should be wide and driven slowly at a uniform rate to give greater time for gas release and stress relaxation. In case a rise heading has to be driven in a seam between two levels, a large diameter pilot hole should be bored connecting the levels and the heading driven along the hole [74]. Blasting for drivage should be used only when absolutely necessary and an alternative method of face advance is not available. The length of shotholes, the explosive charge per hole, and the number of holes per square metre must be optimized to avoid unnecessary shattering of the seam beyond the pull.
(2) Adopting shock blasting or inducer shotfiring over the entire face of the heading to advance the abutment zone away from the active working face. This method was first used in France in 1892 and came to be widely practised in many countries of Europe and the erstwhile USSR. The back ends of the shotholes are overcharged and fired in a round of more than six shots from a safe distance at the end of shift. This method reduces the elastic modulus and strength of the burst-prone high-stress zones or areas, causing the stress to decrease as well as transfer it to the adjacent rock so that they fail without violence. By this method, the time of outburst can be controlled, but it induces more outbursts than by any alternative face advance method. Development drivage in inclined seams through cross-cuts without advance boreholes and inducer shotfiring is fraught with danger of outbursts.

To reduce the incidence of outburst in a highly stressed area, the method has been modified by advance boring of one or more large-diameter holes (150 to 300 mm) which serve to degass and destress the coal face before the face is advanced.

Special precautions to be observed with inducer shotfiring;

(i) The number of shotholes in a round and charge per hole should be adequate.
(ii) Temporary and permanent supports should be set as soon as possible after firing and as close as possible to the heading face.
(iii) Electric power should be switched off prior to firing.
(iv) No person should be on the return side of the place and the persons engaged in firing shots should be at least 200 m from that place.
(v) There should be a ready means of communication between the firing station and the surface.
(vi) To reduce the damage from an ensuing outburst, a barricade may be erected at a short distance from the face to be shot to provide a strong obstruction over a major cross-section of the headings to the passage of coal and gas. Such barricades have been successfully used in France, Hungary and erstwhile USSR.
(vii) The firing of shots may be carried out from the mine surface or from special underground blast chambers.

(3) Heading drivage by a continuous miner should be done with advance boring of a large-diameter hole. The continuous miner should sump into the face at the roof and take a web of coal of the face so that very high drivage rates are not obtained. The miner should be operated by remote control.
(4) Advance predrainage of a seam to reduce the gas content below that for proneness by drilling lateral horizontal drainage holes in advance of a panel or by drilling boreholes from the surface into the virgin seam prior to development.
(5) Avoiding development in the abutment zone of adjoining faces in the same seam or neighbouring seams.
(6) Forming large size square pillars (up to 50 m) or long rectangular pillars in seams worked by the bord and pillar method. The width-to-height ratios for coal pillars in a given seam most conducive for coal and gas outbursts must be investigated.
(7) High pressure water infusion of coal through drillholes in the headings.

4.2.2 On production faces

(1) Longwall mining is preferable to bord and pillar mining due to minimum development work without pillar corners.
(2) Longwall advancing is preferable to longwall retreating.
(3) The longwall face should not make acute angles at the face ends.
(4) The longwall face should be laid, as far as possible, at right-angles to the boundary limit of worked-out faces in the same seam [75].

(5) A single-face advance is preferable to a two-face advance in two opposite directions, with the face making an angle of 10° to 15° with the direction of the main cleat of coal.
(6) In inclined seams, advancing the face in the dip direction is safest.
(7) With longwall advancing, the gate roads should either be very short or extend beyond the highly stressed front abutment zone.
(8) Caving or hydraulic filling/stowing should be practised, particularly in deep mines, as a method of ground control.
(9) Working a 'protective seam' underlying or overlying the suspect or protected seam with concentrated stress before mining the latter. The area affected by the vertical strata destressing lies between 50 and 100 m in both directions. If the protective and protected seams are worked at the same time, then the workings in the protective seam must be much ahead of those in the protected seam, by a distance which is determined by the vertical distance between the seams and the caving angle of the overlying strata. In very thick seams, the topmost slice, if extracted without leaving unmined pillars, could form the protective seam.
(10) Limiting the daily rate of face of advance on mechanized longwall faces. Should the rate of advance required be less than the economic one, mining of coal by inducer shotfiring may be considered.
(I1) Using advance water infusion of longwall faces to drive the gas away from highly stressed areas to drain out from the face. Depending on seam fracture permeability and cleat orientation, water infusion may, however, block migration of methane towards the face. It is practised in some countries abroad.
(12) Leaving larger safety barriers or barrier pillars.
(13) Providing each production face with independent intake and return airways.
(13) Laying down a special code of precautions which must be strictly followed.
(14) Inducer shotfiring may be applied as a last measure when natural destressing cannot be induced by a suitable face design and mining sequence.
(15) When planning for development of a mine, the sequence of extraction of different sections of the mine must be planned so that extraction of one does not cause overloading pressure on the others.
(16) Adopting coal extraction by monitor jets where geological factors allow. The formation of large cavities results in destressing of the seam.
(17) Providing life support systems for supply of respirable air in the event of an outburst.

4.2.3 Prediction of outbursts of coal and gas

It is nearly impossible to predict outbursts with any degree of accuracy. Some of the experiences made with actual outbursts in many countries have been contradictory.

Their magnitude is evaluated according to the amount of coal burst into the mine workings in tonnes. The various monitoring methods which have been used for early evaluation of the potential risk to miners are:

(1) Underground observations
(2) Gas measurements
(3) Measurements on coal
(4) Microseismic measurement

4.2.3.1 Underground observations

Underground observations consist of observation of local audible and visible premonitory signs and use of simple instruments and methods. The warning signs, usually given out in outburst zones several days or hours before their occurrence, include a change in the seam thickness, cracking noise from the coal mass, high gas emission due to periodic weighting when seams are overlain with hard sandstone or conglomerate, higher resistance to drilling in coal, closure of shotholes during their charging, weighting of supports and occurrence of microfractures and breaks in the roof and floor due to increased rock pressure, reduction in joint spacing, occurrence of roof polishing, and exudation of water. The immediate signs preceding an outburst are: bumps, sounds resembling booms or thunder, and falling of small pieces off the coal face.

4.2.3.2 Gas measurements

In the early days of prediction of outbursts, the concentration of evolved gases in the ventilating air as a result of their emission in the working place was used as an indicator of an outburst situation. In later years, a few empirical indices/values were developed under controlled field conditions for determining the degree of proneness.

Emission value or emission index

It is the emission rate of seam gas (CH_4/CO_2) at the working place per tonne of broken coal. The danger due to an outburst generally increases with increasing emission value. It is the simplest day-to-day predictive method.

Gassiness in a standard drainage hole in coal

The gassiness in a standard diameter hole drilled into the advancing face is measured. This is more suitable on inducer shotfiring faces than on continuous miner faces.

Gassiness index

This is determined as the initial gas emission or desorption from drillcuttings of standard particle size range obtained by drilling a standard diameter hole into the face. This method is used in some coal mines abroad.

Seam gas pressure

Virgin gas pressures above a definite value in seams subject to high rock pressures or in highly stressed sections of seams may be used as an index for determining the burst-proneness of seams.

4.2.3.3 Measurements on coal

Drillcuttings swell factor, given by the ratio

$$\frac{\text{Volume of drillcuttings}}{\text{Volume of hole drilled}}$$

is commonly used as a predictive index. It is important that the drill bit is sharp, the cuttings are collected in the high-pressure zone, and a standardized hole diameter is used. The volume of drillcuttings per metre length of drillhole is also used as a predictive index when it exceeds a certain value determined by experience with burst-prone areas.

Softening of coal due to increased fissuration takes place when approaching an outburst zone. This is revealed by a study of the microstructure of coal under an electron microscope.

4.2.3.4 Microseismic measurements

Microseismic measurements are finding increasing application in both coal and non-coal mines for locating and monitoring burst-prone areas several days in advance of failure.

Naturally-occurring rock noises result from small-scale structural adjustments actively taking place within the mine rock in those parts or zones of a mine in which rock stresses are continually changing due to the effect of mining and/or changing support conditions. The seismic energy transmitted through the rock is detected, recorded, and analysed by standard noise rate analysis techniques to determine the degree of structural stability of individual areas of the mine with unusual stress conditions as well as to estimate when failure is likely to occur.

Basic seismic equipment consists of a geophone(s) of velocity gauge-type or accelerometer-type to detect the seismic energy vibration and convert that vibration into an electrical signal, an application system, and monitoring and/or recording equipment.

4.2.3.5 Other measurements

Other measurements which have been developed are measurements of electrical resistivity of the roof and floor strata, deformation and stress measurements in strata using photoelastic techniques, and measurements for determination of *in situ* stress concentration changes by continuous recording of borehole deformation. Despite the advances made in rock mechanics, the mechanism of outbursts is not fully understood and the threat from them could not be fully controlled. The research that has been conducted so far generally aimed at a general understanding of the phenomenon and development of methods of a more empirical nature for detection, prevention, and control of outbursts in a given mining area.

In any comprehensive programme of research on outbursts of coal and gas, the following items of study/investigation in the laboratory, planning office, and field must receive attention:

(1) Gas-coal; confining rock permeability;
(2) Gas-coal adsorption and fast desorption characteristics;
(3) Seam gas compositions;
(4) Seam gas pressures;
(5) Face gassiness indices;
(6) Seam gas advance drainage techniques from underground and from the surface;
(7) Direction of coal cleating;
(8) Seam water content;
(9) Coal microstructure before and after outburst;
(10) Stress in virgin coal/rock; stress change movements in coal;
(11) Strength of coal/rock just before and after outburst;
(12) Elastic moduli of coal/rock;
(13) Geological-tectonic structure of the area being mined;
(14) Width of pressure arch, zone of intense pressure in the front abutment zone, and zone of relaxation;
(15) Where, how, and when of destressing; development of suitable destressing techniques by trial-and-error procedures;
(16) Mining geometry and mining sequence; and
(17) Microseismic and seismic monitoring for location and delineation of highstress areas; location of faults and some irregularities.

As mines become deeper and the outburst hazard seemingly becomes greater, microseismic monitoring will be increasingly used as a production tool by improving the geotechnical knowledge of the underground mines with a view to improve their design.

The number of occurrences of coal and gas outbursts has significantly reduced over the years due to various measures adopted but the danger cannot be eliminated altogether.

CHARTER 5

Sampling of Mine Atmospheres and Interpretation of their Analyses

Knowledge of the changing composition of mine atmosphere in a suspected or already affected area is essential for drawing any inferences on the development and/or extinction of mine fires and the explosion hazard therefrom. As mine atmosphere contains several gases, portable gas detectors cannot be used to advantage as they have definite limitations in their range of detection and are primarily designed for detection of one gas only. In chemical analysis of samples, however, the accuracy of analysis can easily be checked by duplicate samples and the gases may be determined regardless of their concentration.

In determining the composition of mine atmosphere by sampling, one should always remember that no analysis can be better than the sample. Non-representative samples and improper sampling procedures will yield erroneous results which may lead to incorrect interpretations and, in consequence, to unsafe or irrelevant recommendations or conclusions.

5.1 Sampling of Mine Atmospheres

5.1.1 Types of samples

The samples may be obtained by instantaneous sampling ('grab' or 'spot samples) or continuous sampling ('continuous' samples) methods.

Grab samples are taken over short periods of time of a few seconds to a minute or two and represent the mine atmosphere at a particular place and instant. They constitute the majority of samples taken in mines. A grab sample may be taken from one point (point sample) or over several points in the cross-section of a sampling place (cross-section sample).

Continuous samples are collected over longer periods of time and give the average composition. It is seldom necessary to take continuous samples as a number of grab samples taken at pre-determined intervals dictated by the urgency of information will provide more information than one continuous sample. The introduction of computerized continuous mine environmental monitoring and control systems in mines, however, offers many advantages since they can provide round-the-clock information on air quality and quantity at sampling points and can give early warnings of developing abnormal situations.

5.1.2 Sampling in accessible places

When detecting spontaneous combustion in a suspected area, samples may be collected in the return airway of the area or in the supposed course of gases coming from the area before the gases get diluted. When sampling in a return airway, the sampling point or place should be selected not nearer than 20 m of the last probable point of contamination of the moving air by the gases coming from the area. This is to ensure that the gases are thoroughly mixed with the air current so that the mixture has a uniform composition. A sample taken from mid-height of the place selected will give the average composition of the air.

In nearly-stagnant or slowly-moving air that has had no opportunity to mix, stratification of gases may occur and the composition, in consequence, may vary widely in vertical cross-section. To obtain a representative sample, several grab samples should be taken from various points in the cross-section. The sampling points should be fixed at three heights at specific distances below the roof, near the mid-height, and above the floor and the results averaged.

During sealing-off operations, the samples should be collected from the cross-section still left open. If the gases, especially at the roof, are hot, hand gloves must be worn.

When re-opening a sealed-off area, the samples may be taken in the opening or in the ventilation steel pipe of the return fire-stopping.

5.1.3 Sampling from sealed-off areas

The choice of place or places of sampling and the mode of collection of samples from a sealed-off area depend upon the number of seals or stoppings erected for its sealing off. With one or two stoppings, there is little choice in the selection of the sampling places. However, if there are several stoppings, the sampling places at any given time must be carefully selected taking into consideration the place of sampling or stopping with respect to fire and probable course of firegases, changes in barometric or fan pressure, occurrence of falls or previously constructed temporary stoppings, and position of the sampling pipe in stoppings. Samples from sealed-off areas should be taken only when the barometric pressure is relatively constant or falling.

When samples are to be taken through surface boreholes, either the boreholes must be cased or sampling lines inserted into them for the purpose of drawing samples through them to eliminate dilution or contamination of the samples. The samples should be marked whether the borehole was 'blowing', 'sucking' or relatively 'still'.

5.1.4 Construction of a sampling pipe or line at a stopping

When a stopping is constructed, unless conditions are unusual, a 25 or 50 mm diameter steel pipe should be built into it near the centre extending as far behind the stopping (greater than 20 m) as is convenient to reach but not too close to the

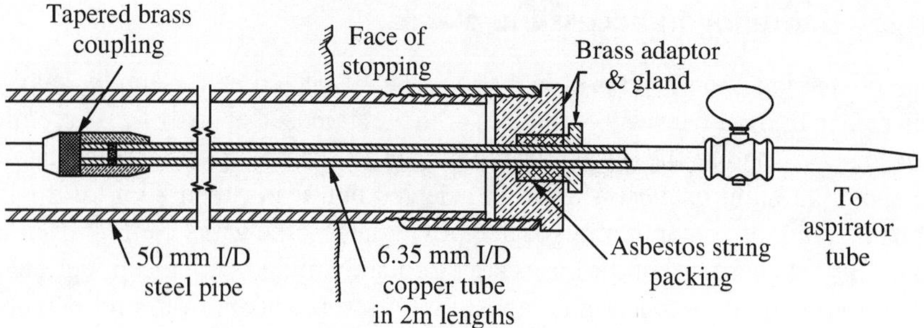

Figure 5.1 Copper sampling line

fire, which may show too low or too high a concentration of fire products. Samples are drawn either through the pipe or through a 6-mm inside diameter seamless copper sampling line or tube inserted and properly fitted into the pipe so that the whole assembly is airtight (Fig. 5. 1). Plastic probes may also be passed through the pipe to take samples.

Where sealed areas have gradients more than 6 per cent causing stratification of air, three sampling pipes should be built into the stoppings to collect samples near the roof, near the centre, and near the floor and then average their analyses.

5.1.5 Sampling equipment

Samples are collected in sample containers by replacing their original content with the atmosphere to be sampled. A sample should not suffer any contamination or change of composition during its collection as well as during its preservation between the time of sampling and the time of analysis.

Depending on the method of filling, sample containers are divided into vacuum-type containers and gas- or liquid-displacement containers.

The vacuum-type container (Fig. 5.2(a)) is an evacuated glass bulb, the neck of which has been sealed by heating and drawing to a tip during the final stage of evacuation. When collecting a sample at a point, the neck is broken at a breaking scratch mark provided on it when the surrounding atmosphere enters and fills the container at the prevailing pressure. The container is then sealed by means of a wax-filled cartridge or rubber cap. The usual capacity of the container is 250 to 300 ml.

The vacuum-type container may be used to sample in accessible places or from inaccessible places. Its great advantage is that it preserves the sample without any leakage or contamination until the sample is analyzed.

Gas- or liquid-displacement containers include ordinary glass bottles, polymer plastic bag, copper- , plastic- or glass-sampling containers or sampling tubes, and brass sampling capsules (Figs. 5.2(b)–(f)). Glass bottles and glass sampling containers can be filled by the gas- or liquid-displacement method while rubber bladders and brass sampling capsules are filled by the gas-displacement method only.

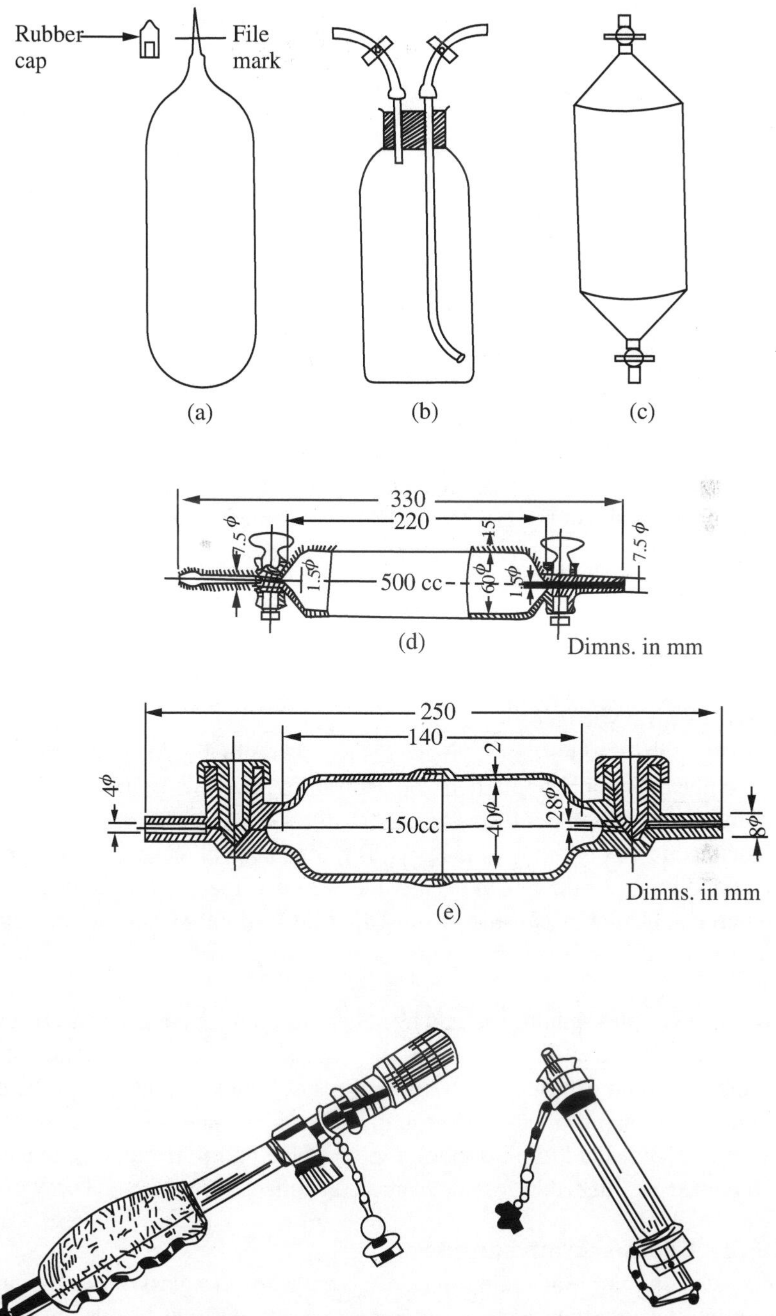

Figure 5.2 Sample containers (a) Vacuum container; (b) glass bottle; (c) copper container; (d) glass sampling tube; (e) plastic sampling tube; (f) brass capsule.

The gas sampling containers, with an airtight stopcock at each end, are made in capacities of 150, 250, and 500 ml. When used for sampling by water displacement, one of the short pieces of glass tubing joined at each end of the container has a capillary bore through it. The diameter of the capillary bore is chosen so that a 500 ml container drains out in about 40 seconds [76]. The containers are filled at the surface laboratory with acidified water coloured with methyl orange and taken underground in a suitably designed case. Mine water should never be used as bacteria in it can oxidize methane and carbon monoxide that may be present in the sample to carbon dioxide, giving erroneous results after chemical analysis.

The polymer plastic bags (PVC, teflon etc.) are protected by a fabric on the outside. They are inexpensive, light in weight, and accommodate a large volume of a sample suitable for analysis by fixed analyzers. An aspirator bulb or a football pump may be used for filling them with the sample.

The brass sampling capsules have the advantages that they are unbreakable, have no stop-cocks; are easily carried, and a large volume of a sample can be compressed into it by the brass hand pump. They are generally used when samples are to be collected for gas chromatographic analysis, for mailing to another place, or for retention for long periods. The cylinder has a capacity of 50 ml.

5.1.6 Collection of samples

5.1.6.1 Point samples

For taking grab or point samples in accessible places by liquid displacement using glass or plastic sample containers, no aspirating device is required as the water has only to be drained out of the container to collect samples.

When using a polymer plastic bag, it is folded and rolled to expel the previous sample and then pre-flushed at least twice before a final sample is taken.

When using a brass capsule, it must first be flushed with air at the sampling place by 10 strokes of the piston pump and the sample collected after 20 complete strokes.

Where a sample container cannot be held at a sampling point, a sampling probe, 6 mm inside diameter, may be used. With glass or plastic containers, the probe is connected to an aspirator bulb through a 120°-cock so that the probe can be flushed before a sample is drawn through it (Fig. 5.3). When using a brass capsule, the probe is connected to the suction nipple of the pump. Both the probe and the capsule must be flushed before the sample is collected in the usual way.

5.1.6.2 Cross-section samples

A cross-section sample at a sampling place is collected in a glass or plastic container by moving the inlet end of the container held vertically at a constant rate until the whole section is evenly covered (Fig. 5.4(a)). If the cross-section is large so that portions of the cross-section are beyond the reach of the sampler, the sample container can be tied to a stick and the cross-section traversed. When using a brass sample capsule, the cylinder is first flushed in the centre of the cross-section by

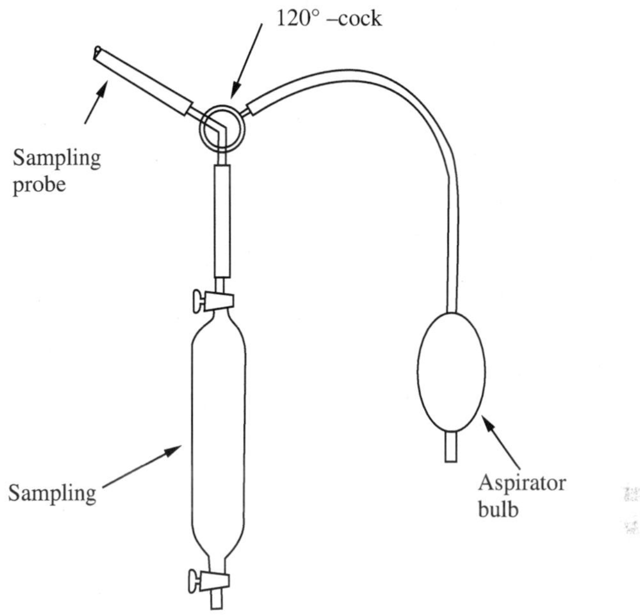

Figure 5.3 Arrangement for collecting a point sample with sampling probe.

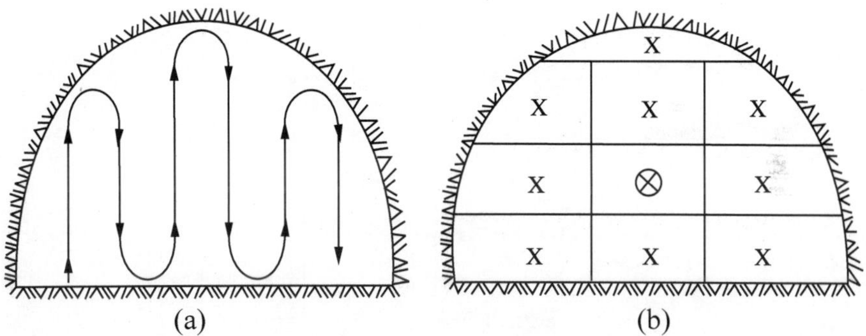

Figure 5.4 Cross-section sampling: (a) by traversing the cross-section; (b) by taking point samples in the cross-section.

10 strokes of a piston and the sample collected at 10 points using two strokes at each point (Fig. 5.4(b)).

5.1.6.3 Samples through sampling pipes of sealed-off areas

When a sampling pipe is blowing out, sample containers may be directly filled by gas displacement without the aid of an aspirating device. It is necessary for such direct sampling that the gas blows out of the sampling line over a longer duration with sufficient intensity. Before taking a sample, the sampling pipe must be purged of the gases already contained in it for a period of at least 5 minutes and then connected to the sample container by a short length of rubber tubing. The purging of the sampling pipeline may, however. create a dangerous atmosphere for the sampler. If the sampler is not equipped with a respiratory protective apparatus, he should carry a carbon monoxide detector and an oxygen-measuring instrument or a flame safety lamp with him.

When a sampling pipe is drawing in or when there is no pressure in it, a footpump, a Fletchers bellows, or a compressed-air ejector, where a compressed-air line is available, may be used to purge the sampling pipe of gases and to draw the sample into a glass or plastic sample container (Fig. 5.5). For collecting sample in a brass capsule, the suction nipple of the pump is connected by a short piece of tubing to the cock as in the arrangement shown in Fig. 5.6.

Sampling the atmosphere behind a stopping may have to be carried on for a period of a few months or longer.

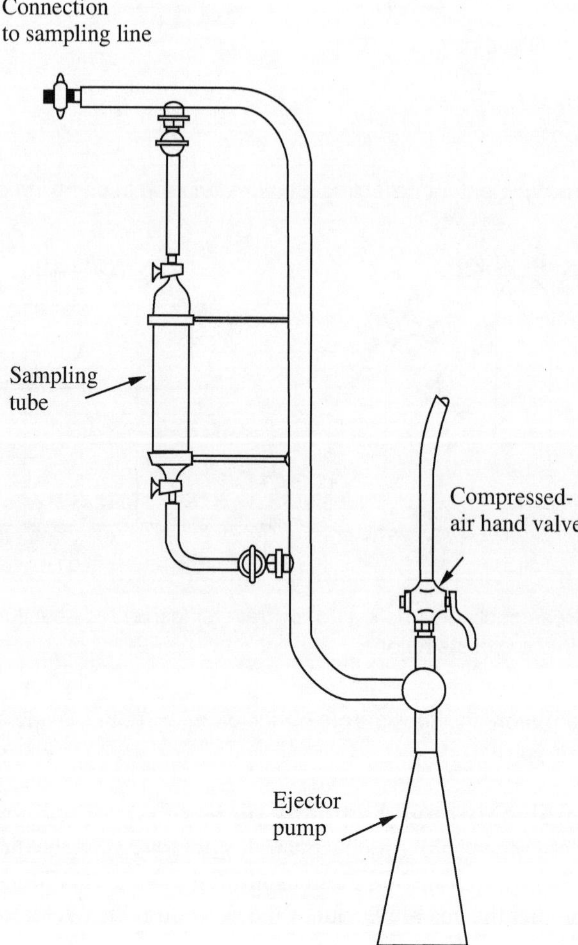

Figure 5.5 Arrangement for collecting sample in a glass or plastic sampling tube from a sealed off area.

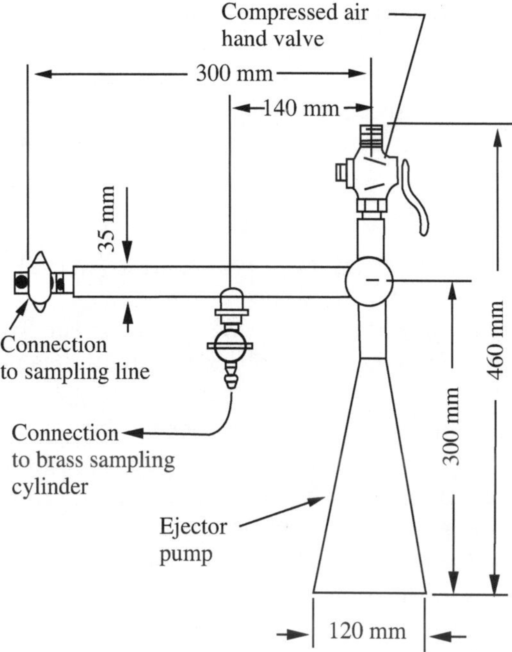

Figure 5.6 Arrangement for collecting sample in a brass cylinder from a sealed-off area.

5.2 Allied Measurements

Pressure across stoppings

When samples are collected from behind a stopping, the pressure across the stopping must be measured and recorded by the sampler. The pressure across a stopping may be positive ('blowing out'), negative ('drawing in') or neutral (pressure same on both sides). As the pressure difference is usually very small, an inclined tube manometer should be used. One side of the manometer should be connected to the sampling line while the other side is connected to a short length of rubber tubing which should be held in still air. A differential automatic pressure recorder may also be used.

Barometric pressure

The barometric pressure should be observed and recorded whenever samples from a sealed-off area are collected. Knowledge of the barometric pressure may help in explaining the make of gases, particularly oxygen and firedamp, in the sealed-off area.

Air quantity

Measurement of air quantity flowing past a sampling place assists in interpretation of the results of sampling. Where there is measurable air movement, an anemometer or other air-velocity measuring instrument may be used. In nearly-stagnant or slowly-moving air, a chemically-produced smoke may be used to estimate air-flow rate.

Tables 5.1 and 5.2 show specimen cards or pages of a Mine Atmosphere Sample Record and Mine Atmosphere Sample Analysis Record, respectively, that should be maintained at mines.

5.3 Interpretation of Analyses of Mine Atmospheres

The value of sampling of mine atmospheres lies in the correct interpretation of the results of their analyses in terms of the conditions obtained at the time of sampling.

When interpreting the analyses of atmospheres in active mine workings, one ascertains whether the composition of the atmosphere in question conforms to the prescribed values or recognizes if there is any hazard from the presence of firedamp or toxic gases.

The interpretation of the composition of air coming from a suspected heating or of atmospheres in sealed-off areas consists in ascertaining the progress or status of fire, effectiveness of fire-fighting method(s) adopted, and development of flammable atmospheres with a possible explosion hazard during the period of sealing and at the time of recovery operations. The gases of interest are usually O_2, CO, CO_2, CH_4, H_2, and total hydrocarbons, and the decision on when to reventilate is governed by the gas concentration data collected throughout the period of sealing. As the gas concentrations are affected by the intensity of combustion, closeness of the sampling points to the fire seat, movement of the gases in the fire zone, gassiness of the mine, impossibility of completely sealing the area, and time, they may not accurately reflect the conditions inside the fire area.

5.3.1 Status of fire

The following gas concentration ratios that are unaffected by dilution have found widespread acceptance over the years as criteria of the state of heatings and fires in their early as well as in the later stages of development:

$$\text{CO index } \frac{\text{CO}}{\Delta \text{O}_2} = \frac{100\ \text{CO}}{0.265\ \text{N}_2 - \text{O}_2}$$

Jones–Trickett (JT) ratio [77]

$$\text{JT ratio } = \frac{\text{CO}_2 + 0.75\ \text{CO} - 0.25\ \text{H}_2}{0.265\ \text{N}_2 - \text{O}_2}$$

It should be pointed out that the CO index is not to be completely relied upon as the absence of CO is not a safe criterion that the fire has been extinguished but rather

Table 5.1 Mine atmosphere sample record

						Ventilating air		Meteorological data					
								Underground		Surface		Sampler	
Sl. No.	Date	Time	No.of sample container	Place of sampling	Kind of Sample†	Kind*	Quantity m^3/min	Temp. °C	Barom. pressure Torr/mbar	Temp. °C	Pressure Torr/mbar	Name & Designation	Remarks

† Point sample (P), cross-section sample (A), sampling pipe sample (SP)
* Intake, return, still atmosphere

Table 5.2 Mine atmosphere sample analysis record

Sl. no.	Specific data				Meteorological data						Initials of sampler	Results of Analysis													Re-marks
	Sampling		No.of sample container	Kind of samples †	Underground				Surface																
	Date	Time			Kind of Air*	Air Quantity m^3/min.	Temp-erature	Barom press Torr/ mbar	Temp-erature	Barom press Torr/ mbar		Date of ana-lysis	CH_4 %	CO ppm	H_2 %	C_nH_n	CO_2 %	O_2 %	N_2	% total	CO index	Ini-tials	Ini-tials	Ini-tials	

† point sample (P), cross-section sample (A), sampling pipe sample (SP)
* Intake, return, still atmosphere

that active combustion has ceased. When the area sealed off is large, CO may be lost due to oxidation by wet coal or bacteria, or it may not diffuse throughout the entire area. Also, in some seams, the CO produced by normal oxidation in goaves or wastes may not disappear at all or may fall at a very slow rate. A CO index less than 0.4 generally indicates that there is no fire. Where airflows are steady and CO is monitored in them, the index will be of limited additional value.

The JT ratio will not work if the air reaching a fire is oxygen-deficient through injection of nitrogen or carbon dioxide, or through a high make of methane. For such conditions:

$$\text{JT ratio} = \frac{(CO_2^a - CO_2^b) + 0.75(CO^a - CO^b) - 0.25(H_2^a - H_2^b)}{(O_2^a - O_2^b)}$$

where a and b refer to the downwind and upwind samples respectively. When the JT ratio

< 0.4	no fire;
$= 0.5$ to 1.0	if the fuel is coal, oil, conveyor belting, insulation;
$= 0.9$ to 1.6	if the fuel is wood;
> 1.6	not possible; the sample does not represent the atmosphere from a mine fire.

5.3.2 Flammability of atmosphere in sealed-off areas

In gassy mines, it is important to know before attempting recovery of a sealed-off area whether the firegases in the area would form a flammable mixture when admixed with air. The composition of the firegases which depends, within limits, upon the development, extent, and intensity of fire at the time of sealing as well as upon dilution through methane and leakage air, consists in general of CO, O_2, CO_2, N_2, CH_4, seldom H_2, H_2S, and C_nH_{2n}. Table 5.3 gives the range of composition of mine firegases [78].

A given mixture of firegases can be considered as consisting of combustibles, suppressors of combustion, and oxygen. It is the combustible constituents of the firegases, notably methane, that combined represent an explosion hazard in a fire area during its sealing or unsealing. The presence of small quantities of the combustible gases CO, H_2 and C_nH_{2n}, has the effect of reducing the lower limit of flammability of methane–air mixtures. Table 5.4 gives the flammable limits of the combustible gases mixed with air [78].

Table 5.3 Composition of mine firegases

Constituent	From about Vol. %	to about Vol %
Methane (CH_4)	0.2	80
Carbon monoxide (CO)	0.001	2
Hydrogen (H_2)	–	2
Unsaturated hydrocarbons (C_nH_{2n})	–	2
Nitrogen (N_2)	10.0	85
Carbon dioxide (CO_2)	0.2	20
Oxygen (O_2)	0.2	20

Table 5.4 Flammable limits of combustible gases

Combustible gas	Flammable limits	
	Lower Vol.%	Upper Vol.%
Methane (CH_4)	5.0	14.0
Carbon monoxide (CO)	13.0	72.0
Hydrogen (H_2)	4.0	72.0
Unsaturated, hydrocarbons (C_nH_{2n})	3.0	14.7

5.3.2.1 Coward method

Coward was the first to represent graphically the relationship between the quantitative composition and the flammability of mixtures of methane and air. In the diagram (Fig. 5.7) one distinguishes the following four areas:

(1) An area above the line AD in which no mixture of methane and air is possible impossible mixtures range). The point A represents the normal air of 20.93 per cent O_2 and 79.07 per cent N_2 and CO_2.
(2) An area to the left of the line BEF in which methane does not form any flammable mixture with air at all (non-flammable or safe range). The line BE represents the lower limits of flammability of methane–air mixtures.
(3) An area to the right of the line CEF in which too rich methane can form flammable mixtures when mixed with air in suitable proportions (possible flammable range). The line CE represents the upper limits of flammability of methane air mixtures. As the oxygen content of the mixture decreases, BE and CE approach each other and meet at, E which is called the 'nose flammability limit'.
(4) A triangular area BEC known as the Coward triangle, in which any methane–air mixture is flammable *per se* (flammable range). The shape of the Coward triangle does not alter with the percentage of CH_4 in the sample.

It can be seen from the diagram that no mixture that contains less than about 12.1 per cent oxygen is explosive by itself.

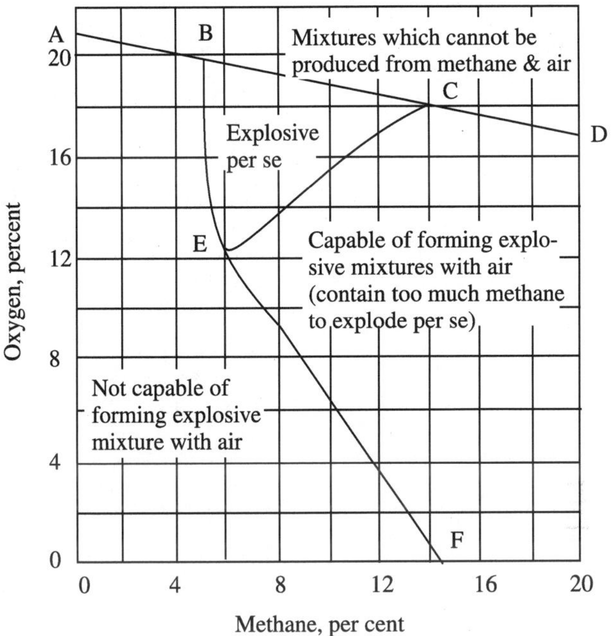

Figure 5.7 Coward flammability diagram for CH_4.

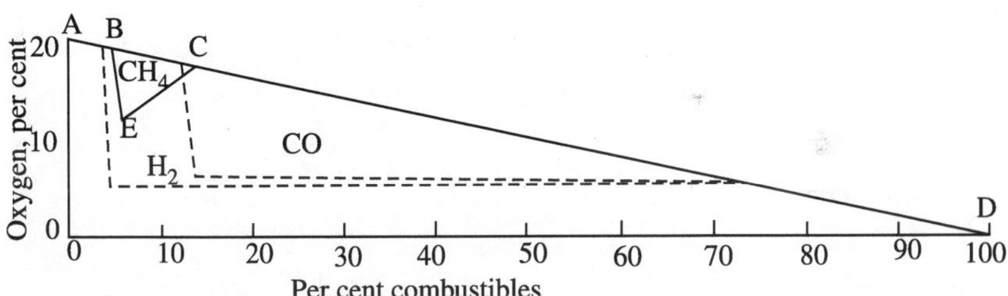

Figure 5.8 Flammability triangles for CH_4, CO, and H_2.

Coward triangles for gases other than methane can also be drawn. Figure 5.8 shows the diagram with flammability triangles for CH_4, CO, and H_2.

5.3.2.2 Drekopf Method

Drekopf [78] reduces the composition of mine firegases as found from chemical analysis to form combustible constituents, air, and excess nitrogen and uses the explosion-suppressing excess nitrogen as a measure of determining the flammability of a given mixture of firegas.

Drekopf represents graphically:

(1) the flammability of mixtures consisting of one combustible gas, air and excess nitrogen;
(2) the flammability of mixtures consisting of two combustible gases and air;

(3) the flammability of mixtures consisting of two combustible gases, air and excess nitrogen;
(4) the flammability indices for mixtures consisting of two combustible gases, air, and excess nitrogen; and
(5) the flammability indices for mixtures consisting of four combustible gases, air, and excess nitrogen.

The method of calculation of the excess nitrogen from a chemical analysis of mine firegases is illustrated by the following example:

A sample contains

Methane	11.0 Vol.%
Oxygen	16.0
Nitrogen	68.0
Carbon dioxide	5.0
	100.0

The above composition may be expressed as:

Methane	11.0 Vol. %
Air 16 × 4.79 =	76.6
Excess nitrogen 68–16 × 3.79 =	7.4
Carbon dioxide	5.0
	100.0

Assuming the extinctive effect of carbon dioxide in suppressing gas explosions to be equivalent to that of nitrogen, the above composition can further be reduced to

Methane	11.0%
Air	76.6
Excess nitrogen	12.4
	100.0

Flammability of mixtures of one combustible gas, air, and excess nitrogen (Fig. 5.9)

The diagrams are explosive triangles drawn for the gases, methane, carbon monoxide, hydrogen, and unsaturated hydrocarbons from experimental results. The tip of an explosive triangle (though actually round) gives the percentage of the combustible gas and the excess nitrogen at the nose limit. The nose limit represents the most dangerous mixture as this mixture requires the largest amount of excess nitrogen to render it non-flammable. The ratio of the percentage of excess nitrogen to the percentage of a combustible gas at the nose limit is called the 'inert factor'. Table 5.5 gives the percentages of the combustible gases and the excess nitrogen at the nose limits and the inert factors.

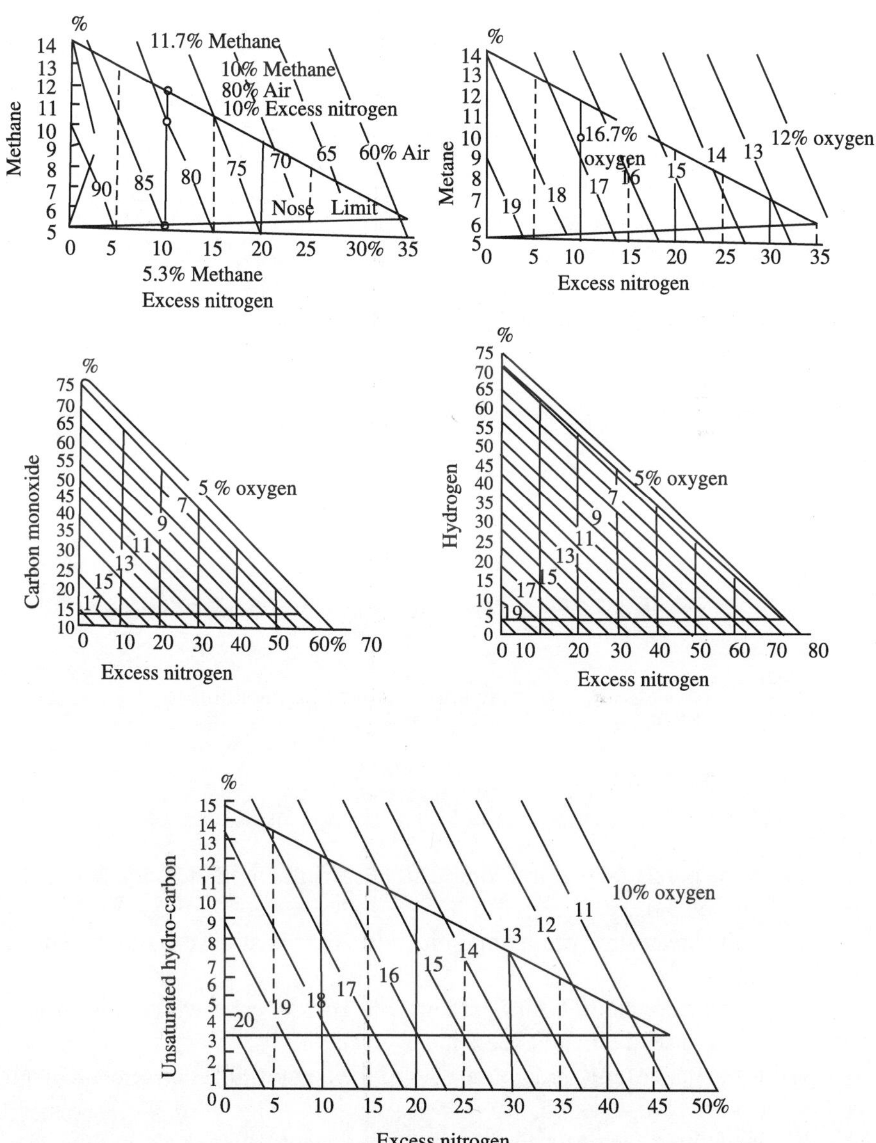

Figure 5.9 Flammability of mixtures of one combustible gas, air, and excess nitrogen.

Table 5.5 Nose limits of gases, excess nitrogen and inert factor

Combustible Gas	Nose Limit of gas. Vol.%	Excess nitrogen Vol. –%	Inert factor
Methane (CH_4)	5.93	36.6	6.00
Carbon monoxide (CO)	13.78	57.2	4.15
Hydrogen (H_2)	4.30	71.2	16.55
Unsat. hydrocarbons (C_nH_{2n})	3.10	47.7	15.40

Flammability of mixture of two combustible gases and air (Fig.5.10)
The different diagrams for mixtures of firegases in which two or more combustible gases are present are drawn by using the following general relations using the Le Chatelier principle:

$$\frac{p_1}{l_1} + \frac{p_2}{l_2} + \ldots \frac{p_i}{l_i} \ldots = K_l \quad \text{(for the lower limit of flammability)}$$

$$\frac{p_1}{s_1} + \frac{p_2}{s_2} + \ldots \frac{p_i}{s_i} \ldots = K_s \quad \text{(for the nose limit)}$$

$$p_1 f_1 + p_2 f_2 + \cdots + p_i f_i \cdots = K_n \text{ (for excess nitrogen at nose limits)}$$

$$\frac{p_1}{u_1} + \frac{p_2}{u_2} + \ldots \frac{p_i}{u_i} \ldots = K_u \quad \text{(for the upper limit of flammability)}$$

$$100 - p_{O_2} \times 4.79 - (p_1 + p_2 + \cdots p_i + \cdots) = N_e$$

where

- p_i is the percentage of the combustible constituent in the firegases (in Vol. %)
- l_i is the lower limit of flammability of the combustible constituent *i* in air (in Vol. %)
- s_i is the nose limit of the combustible constituent *i* when present in a mixture with air and excess nitrogen (in Vol.%)
- u_i is the upper limit of flammability of the combustible constituent *i* in air (in Vol. %)
- f_i is the inert factor for the combustible constituents *i*
- K is the flammability index
- N_e is the percentage of excess nitrogen
- p_{O_2} is the percentage of oxygen.

When $K_l < 1$, the mixture of firegases lies below the lower limit of flammability and is not dangerous even without excess nitrogen. For $K_l = 1$, the mixture is flammable. When $K_l \leq 1$, $K_u < 1$.

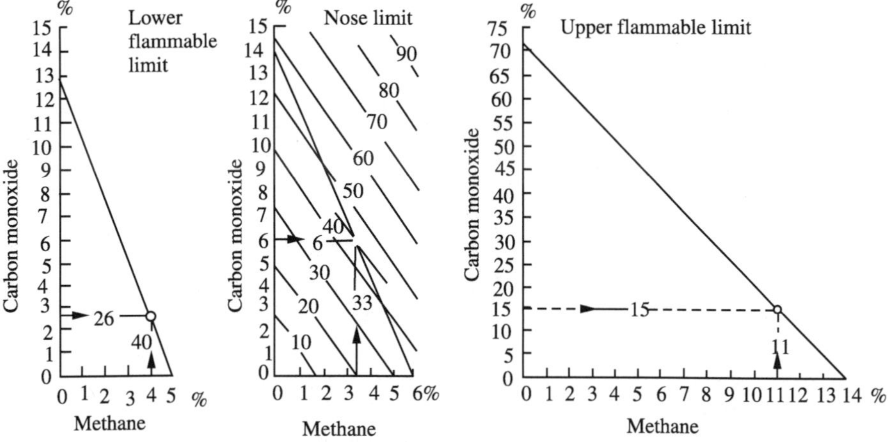

Figure 5.10 Flammability of mixtures consisting of two combustible gases and air.

When $K_u > 1$, the mixture lies above the upper limit of flammability and is not dangerous even without excess nitrogen. On dilution with air, the mixture gradually moves towards the upper limit of flammability, and when the dilution is sufficiently large, it becomes flammable. When $K_u = 1$, the mixture lies at the upper limit of flammability when $K_u \geq 1$, $K_l > 1$.

When $K_l \geq 1$ an $K_u \leq 1$, the mixture is flammable without excess nitrogen but can be rendered non-flammable with sufficient excess nitrogen. The minimum content of excess nitrogen which must be present to render the mixture just non-flammable at the lower and upper limits of flammability can be obtained from the relations:

$$n = \frac{K_l - 1}{K_l - K_s} \cdot K_n \quad (\text{for } K_s \leq 1)$$

$$n = \frac{1 - K_u}{K_s - K_u} \cdot K_n \quad (\text{for } K_s \geq 1)$$

The diagrams representing the flammability of mixtures comprising two combustible gases and air are drawn by using the relations:

$$\frac{p_1}{5} + \frac{p_2}{13} = 1 \text{ (at the lower limit of flammability)}$$

$$\frac{p_1}{5.93} + \frac{p_2}{13.75} = 1 \text{ (at the nose limit)}$$

$$n_2 = 6.00\, p_1 + 4.15\, p_2 \text{ (at the nose limit)}$$

$$\frac{p_1}{14} + \frac{p_2}{72} = 1 \text{ (at the upper limit of flammability)}$$

where $p_1$and p_2 are the percentages of methane and carbon monoxide in the mixture respectively.

Flammability of mixtures of two combustible gases, air, and excess nitrogen. The graphs (Fig. 5.11) are drawn by using the relations

$$l_m = \frac{p_1 + p_2}{\frac{p_1}{l_1} + \frac{p_2}{l_2}} = \frac{\frac{p_1}{p_2} + 1}{\frac{1}{l_1} \cdot \frac{p_1}{p_1} + \frac{1}{l_2}}$$

$$s_m = \frac{p_1 + p_2}{\frac{p_1}{s_1} + \frac{p_2}{s_2}} = \frac{\frac{p_1}{p_2} + 1}{\frac{1}{s_1} \cdot \frac{p_1}{p_2} + \frac{1}{s}}$$

$$n_s = \frac{p_1 f_1 + p_2 f_2}{\frac{p_1}{s_1} + \frac{p_2}{s_2}} = \frac{\frac{p_1}{p_2} . f_1 + f_2}{\frac{p_1}{p_2} \cdot \frac{1}{s_1} + \frac{1}{s_2}}$$

$$u_m = \frac{p_1 + p_2}{\frac{p_1}{u_1} + \frac{p_2}{u_2}} = \frac{\frac{p_1}{p_2} + 1}{\frac{1}{u_1} \cdot \frac{p_1}{p_2} + \frac{1}{u_2}}$$

If, in a mixture of two combustible gases, air, and excess nitrogen, the ratio between the combustible gases is known, the lower and upper limits of flammability, the nose limit, and the content of excess nitrogen can be calculated.

In Fig. 5.11 the flammability indices are also graphically represented.

Flammability of mixtures off our combustible gases, air, and excess nitrogen For representing such mixtures graphically, the following relations are used:

$$\frac{p_1}{l_1} + \frac{p_2}{l_2} + \frac{p_3}{l_3} + \frac{p_4}{l_4} = K_l$$

$$\frac{p_1}{s_1} + \frac{p_2}{s_2} + \frac{p_3}{s_3} + \frac{p_4}{s_4} = K_s$$

$$p_1 f_1 + p_2 f_2 + p_3 f_3 + p_4 f_4 = K_n$$

$$\frac{p_1}{u_1} + \frac{p_2}{u_2} + \frac{p_3}{u_3} + \frac{p_4}{u_4} = K_u$$

These relation can be expressed as

$$A_l + B_l = K_l \quad \text{where } A_l = \frac{p_1}{l_1} + \frac{p_2}{l_2},$$

$$\text{and } B_l = \frac{p_3}{l_3} + \frac{p_4}{l_4},$$

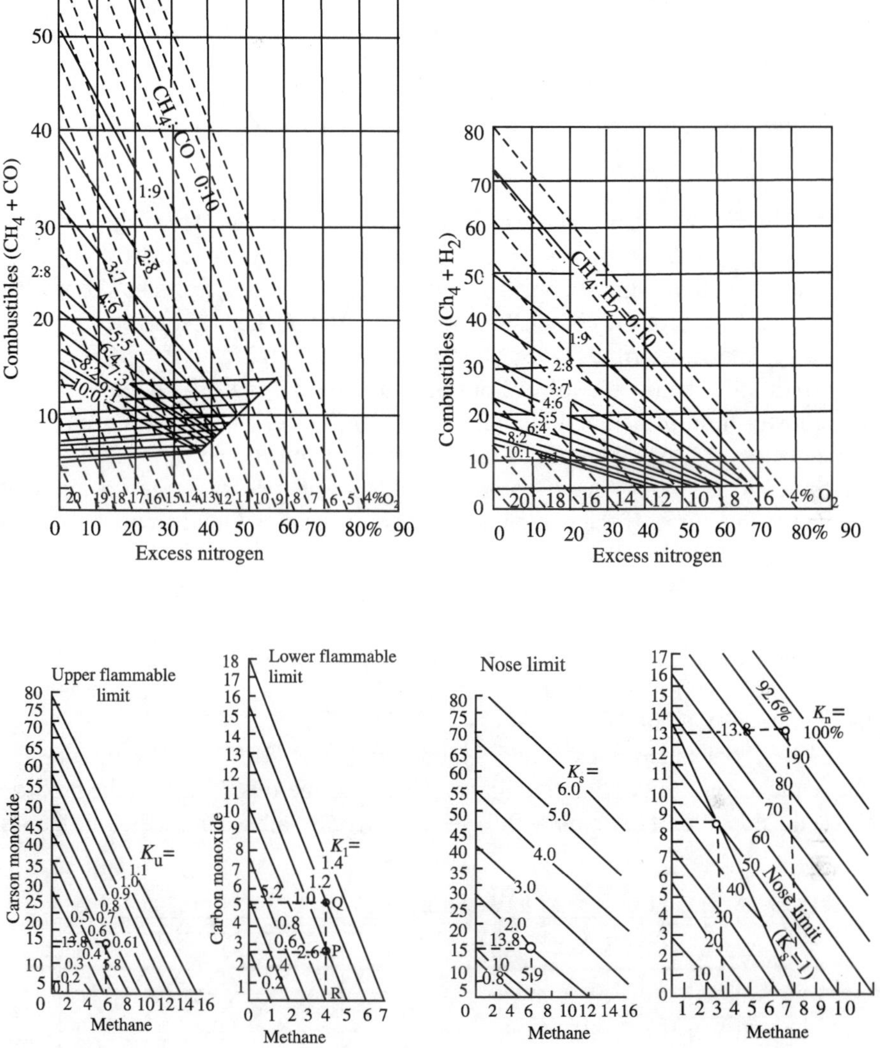

Figure 5.11 Flammability of mixtures consisting of two combustible gases, air, and excess nitrogen.

$$A_s + B_s = K_s \quad \text{where } A_s = \frac{p_1}{s_1} + \frac{p_2}{s_2},$$

$$\text{and} \quad B_s = \frac{p_3}{s_3} + \frac{p_4}{s_4}.$$

$$A_n + B_n = K_n \quad \text{where } A_n = p_1 f_1 + p_2 f_2,$$

$$\text{and} \quad B_n = p_3 f_3 + p_4 f_4.$$

$$A_u + B_u = K_u \text{ where } A_u = \frac{p_1}{u_1} + \frac{p_2}{u_2},$$

$$\text{and } B_u = \frac{p_3}{u_3} + \frac{p_4}{u_4}.$$

The A- and B- values for a given result of analysis can be obtained from the diagrams (Figs. 5.12, 5.13, 5.14 and 5.15) prepared by using the above relations.

When using the diagrams, one finds the values of A_s and B_s from the knowledge of the percentages of the combustible gases and the obtains $K_s = A_s + B_s$.

If $K_s < 1$, one determines the values of A_l, and B_l, and $K_l = A_l + B_l$. If $K_l < 1$, the mixture lies below the lower limit of flammability. If K_l=1, the mixture lies at the lower limit of flammability and is then only safe, when excess nitrogen is present. If $K_l > 1$, one determines the values of A_n and B_n and $K_n = A_n + B_n$ and multiplies K_n by $(K_l-1)/(K_l-K_s)$ to get the content of excess nitrogen required at the flammable limit. If the content of excess nitrogen as found from analysis is greater than the calculated value, the mixture is not dangerous, and if it is less than the calculated value, the mixture is flammable or dangerous.

If K_s= 1, one determines A_n and B_n and $K_n = A_n + B_n$. If the content of excess nitrogen as found from analysis is smaller than the calculated value, the mixture is flammable, and if it is greater than the calculated value, the mixture is non-flammable or not dangerous.

If $K_s > 1$, one determines A_u and B_u and $K_u = A_u + B_u$. If $K_u > 1$, the mixture lies above the upper limit of flammability and is not dangerous. If $K_u = 1$, the mixture lies at the upper limit of flammability and is then only safe when excess nitrogen is

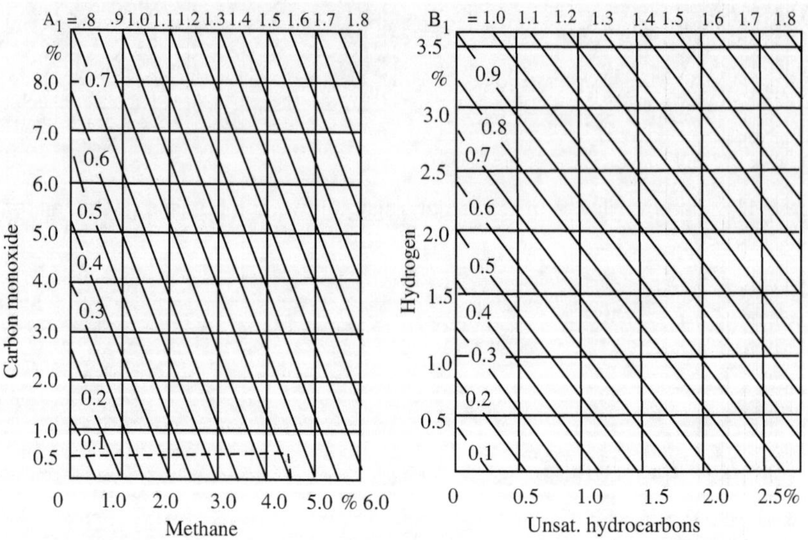

Figure 5.12 Diagrams for determining the flammability indices A_1 and B_1.

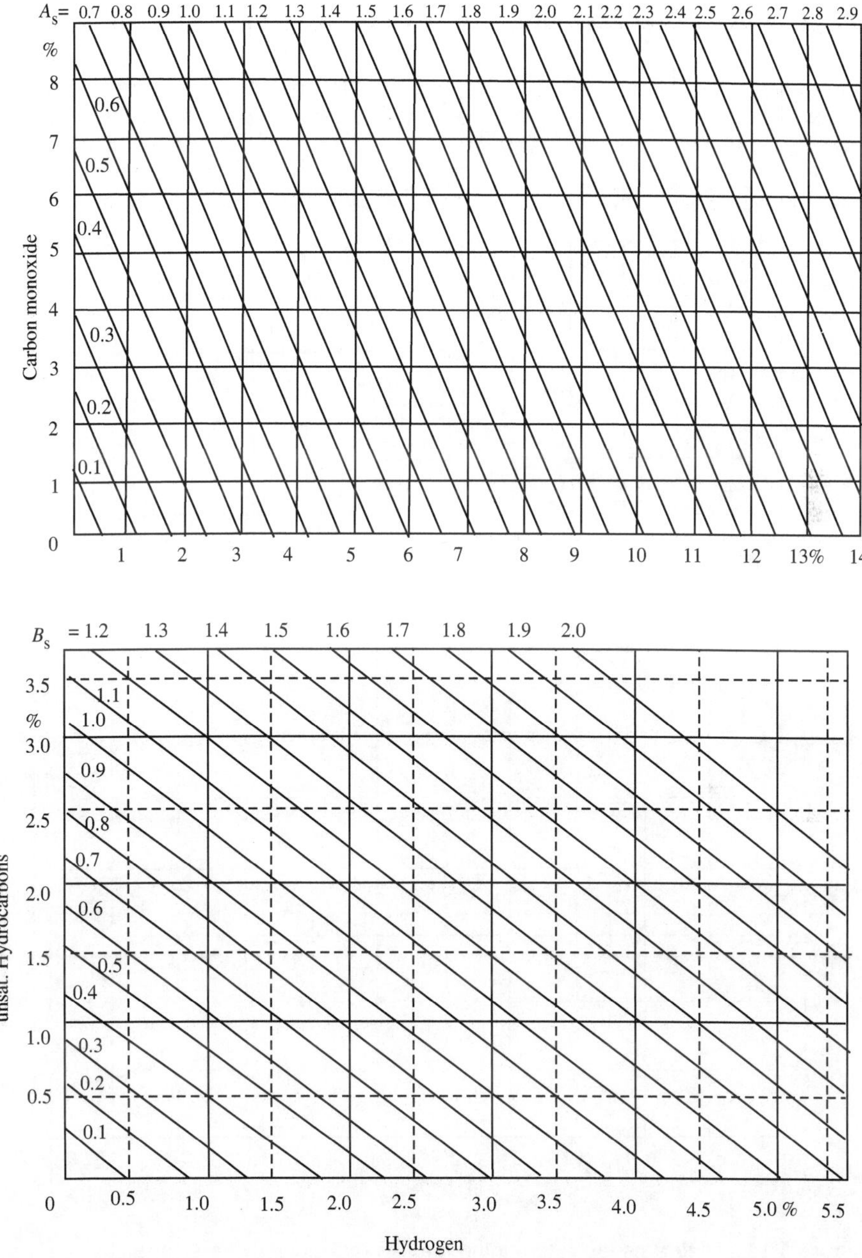

Figure 5.13 Diagrams for determining the flammability indices A_s and B_s.

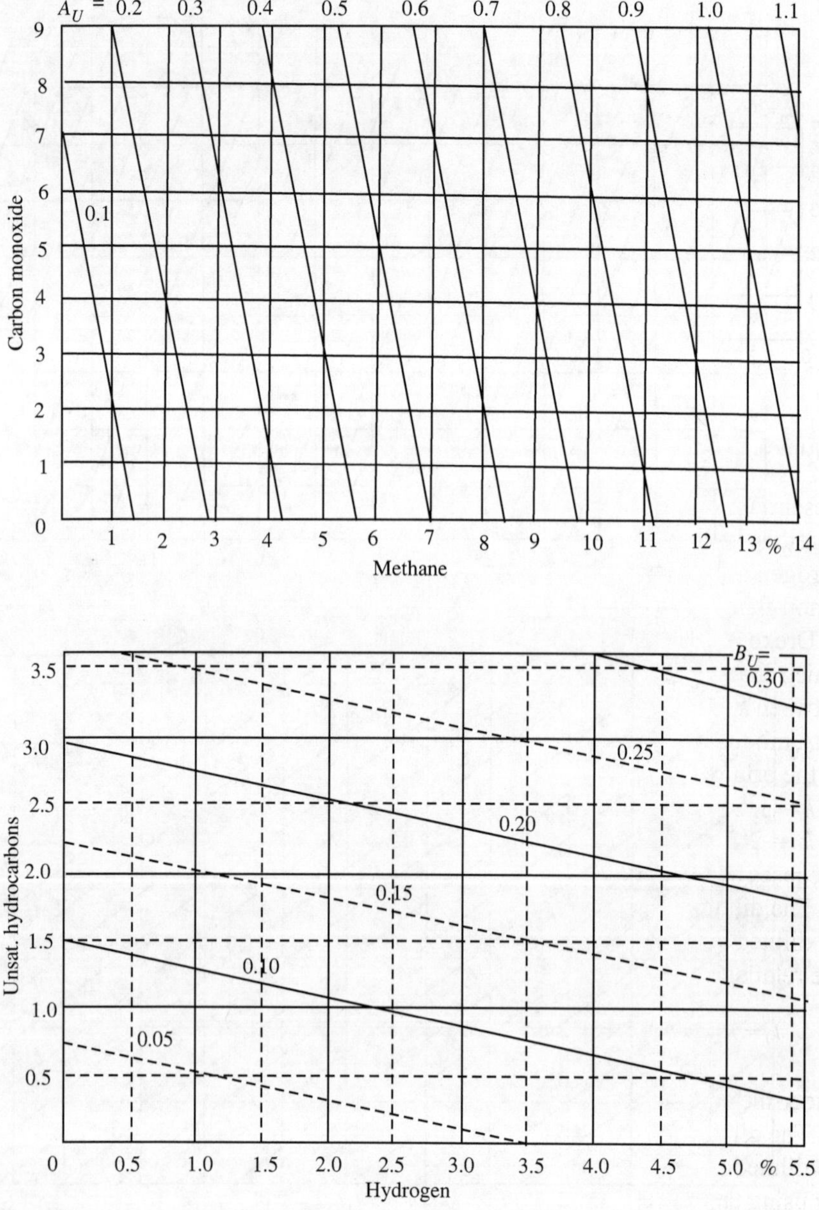

Figure 5.14 Diagrams for determining the flammability indices A_u and B_u.

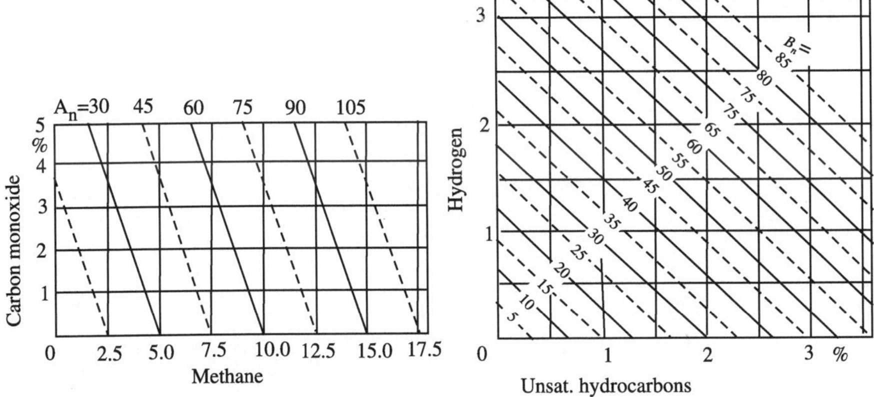

Figure 5.15 Diagrams for determining the flammability indices A_n and B_n.

present. If $K_u < 1$, the value $K_n = A_n + B_n$ should be multiplied by $(1–K_u)/(K_s–K_u)$ to get the excess nitrogen required at the flammable limit. If the content of excess nitrogen as found from analysis is greater than the calculated value, the mixture is non-flammable.

Drekopf [79] developed his method further by introducing a dilution factor k which characterizes the flammability of firegases. There exists a linear relationship between k and N_e, which can be represented graphically.

A mixture of firegases diluted with air has a dilution factor k when one volume of the original mixture is diluted with $(k – 1)$ volume of air.

$k = 1$ for undiluted original mixture of firegases.

$k = 2$ for a diluted mixture comprising volume of the original mixture of firegases and 1 volume of air.

The dilution factor k_l indicates how far the original mixture of firegases must be diluted to bring it to the lower limit of flammability. It is determined by using the relation

$$k_l = K_l - \frac{N_e}{K_n}(K_l - K_s)$$

under the condition $k_l > K_s$.

The dilution factor k_u indicates how far the original mixture of firegases must be diluted in order to bring it to the upper limit of flammability. It is determined by using the relation

$$k_u = K_u + \frac{N_e}{K_n}(K_s - K_u)$$

under the condition $k_u \leq K_s$.

In the above two equations, the dilution factors k_l and k_u as well as the excess nitrogen are variable quantities. These equations represent in rectangular coordinates with the ordinates (K_u, K_s, K_l, k_u, and k_l) and abscissae (N_e, K_n), two straight lines which form a triangle ABC called the Characteristics Triangle

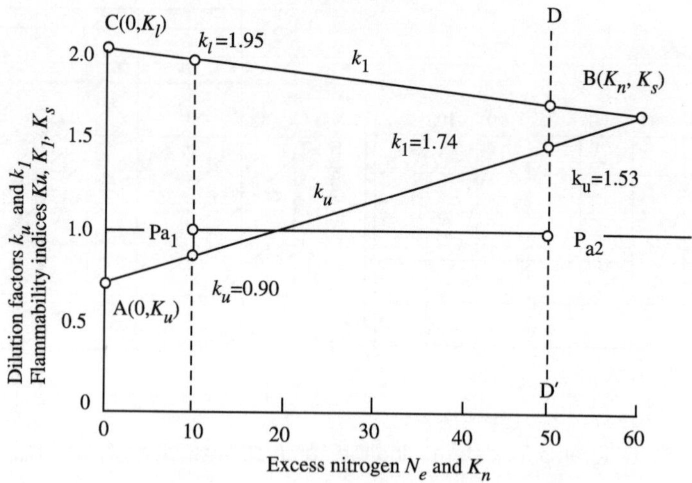

Figure 5.16 Drekopf characteristics triangle.

(Fig. 5.16). The sides AB and CB correspond to the upper and lower limits of flammability of the diluted firegases, respectively.

When using the diagram, the following points must be kept in mind:

When $N_e > K_n$, a parallel drawn to the ordinate from the abscissa value of N_e will not intersect the triangle, in which case the original mixture of firegases on the ordinate so drawn will not intersect the triangle, in which case the mixture is non- flammable even after dilution with air.

When $N_e < K_n$, if the point representing the original mixture of firegases falls inside the triangle or on its sides, the mixture is flammable if $k_l \geq 1$and $k_u \leq 1$. If the point lies outside the triangle, the mixture is non-flammable. A parallel drawn to the ordinate axis intersects the sides CB and AB to give values of k_l, and k_u which indicate how much air will be required to be added to or taken away from the original mixture of firegases in order to bring it to the lower or the upper limit of flammability.

5.3.2.3 Hughes and Raybould method

This method [80]utilizes limit diagrams in order to construct an explosive triangle for a given mixture of mine firegases containing methane, hydrogen, and carbon monoxide. The very small amount of unsaturated hydrocarbons is neglected, and carbon dioxide is equated with nitrogen. The flammability characteristics of the given mixture are then determined by plotting its composition on the explosive triangle.

The limit diagrams for the combustible gases are constructed using the Le Chatelier formula. They represent:

(1) The lower limit of flammability (combustible content) of mixtures, consisting of three combustible gases and air (Fig. 5.17);
(2) The oxygen content at the nose limit of mixtures consisting of three combustible gases, air, and excess nitrogen (Fig. 5.18);

(3) The combustible content at the nose limit of mixtures consisting of three combustible gases, air, and excess nitrogen (Fig. 5.19); and
(4) The upper limit of flammability (combustible content) of mixtures consisting of three combustible gases, and air (Fig. 5.20).

For construction of the diagrams shown in Figs. 5.17 and 5.19,

$$\frac{p_1+p_2+p_3}{\frac{p_1}{l_1}+\frac{p_2}{l_2}+\frac{p_3}{l_3}} = l_m$$

Expressing the percentage of each of the combustible gases in the mixture as the percentage of the total combustible,

$$p_1 + p_2 + p_3 = 100$$

$$\frac{p_1}{l_1}+\frac{p_2}{l_2}+\frac{p_3}{l_3} = \frac{100}{l_m}$$

$$\frac{p_1}{l_1}+\frac{p_2}{l_2}+\frac{100-p_1-p_2}{l_3} = \frac{100}{l_m}$$

$$p_1\left(\frac{1}{l_1}-\frac{1}{l_3}\right)+p_2\left(\frac{1}{l_2}-\frac{1}{l_3}\right)=100\left(\frac{1}{l_m}-\frac{1}{l_3}\right).$$

This is an equation of a straight line,

$Ax + By = C,$

of slope $\left(-\frac{A}{B}\right) = -\dfrac{\frac{1}{l_1}-\frac{1}{l_3}}{\frac{1}{l_2}-\frac{1}{l_3}}$.

Substituting the values for l_1, l_2, and l_3, the slope is equal to –0.732.

The intercept on the p_1 (CH_4) abscissa is (C/A),

$$= \frac{\frac{100}{l_m}-\frac{100}{l_3}}{\frac{1}{l_2}-\frac{1}{l_3}} = \frac{\frac{100}{l_m}-8}{0.12}.$$

The intercept on the p_2 (H_2) ordinate is (C/B)

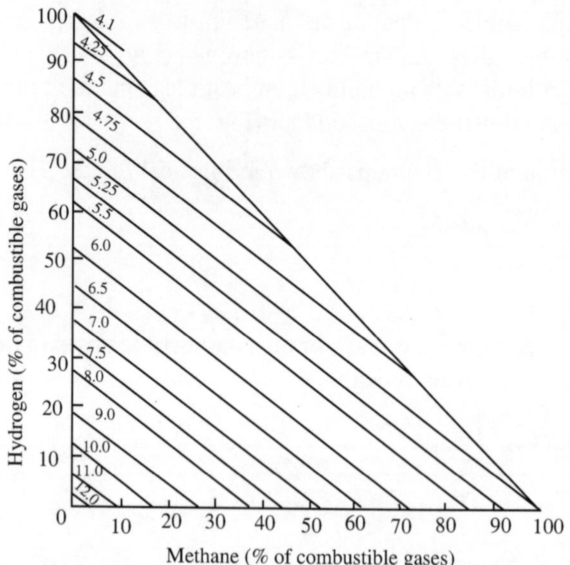

Figure 5.17 Diagram for determining the LFL of mixtures consisting of three combustible gases and air.

$$= \frac{\frac{100}{l_m} - \frac{100}{l_3}}{\frac{1}{l_2} - \frac{1}{l_3}} = \frac{\frac{100}{l_m} - 8}{0.164}.$$

By choosing a series of values of l_m, a series of parallel straight lines having a slope –0.732 is obtained.

From the knowledge of the proportions of CH_4 and H_2 in a given mixture of combustibles, the lower limit of flammability of the mixture can be obtained.

The above reasoning can be applied to the determination of the combustible content at the nose limit by using the relation

$$\frac{p_1}{s_1} + \frac{p_2}{s_2} + \frac{p_3}{s_3} = \frac{100}{s_m}.$$

Construction of the diagram shown in Fig. 5.18

Percentage of excess nitrogen at nose limit

$$n_s = \frac{p_1 f_1 + p_2 f_2 + p_3 f_3}{\frac{p_1}{s_1} + \frac{p_2}{s_2} + \frac{p_3}{s_3}}.$$

Substituting the values of the inert factors for CH_4, H_2, and CO as well as their nose limits as given by Drekopf,

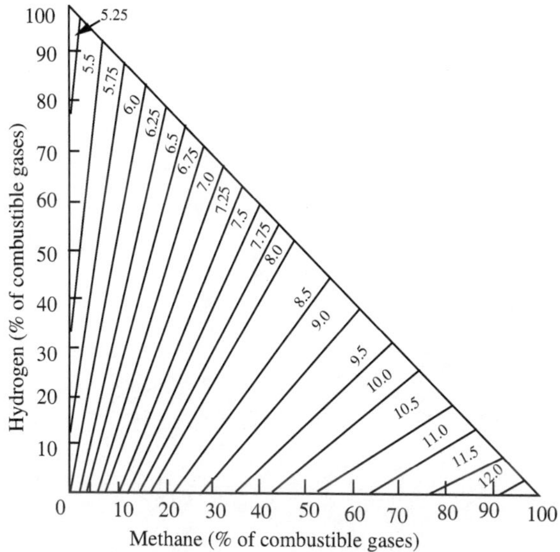

Figure 5.18 Diagram for determining the oxygen content at the nose limit of mixtures consisting of three combustible gases, air, and excess nitrogen.

$$n_s = \frac{6.0\,p_1 + 16.55\,p_2 + 4.15\,(100 - p_1 - p_2)}{\frac{p_1}{5.93} + \frac{p_2}{4.30} + \frac{100 - p_1 - p_2}{13.78}}.$$

Simplifying and rewriting,

$$p_1\left(0.096 - \frac{1.85}{n_s}\right) + p_2\left(0.160 - \frac{12.40}{n_s}\right) = \left(\frac{415}{n_s} - 7.26\right)$$

This is an equation of a straight line of slope

$$= -\left(\frac{0.096n_s - 1.85}{0.160n_s - 12.40}\right)$$

The intercept on the p_1 (CH_4) abscissa is

$$\frac{415 - 7.26n_s}{0.096n_s - 1.85}$$

The intercept on the P_2 (H_2) ordinate is

$$\frac{415 - 7.26n_s}{0.16n_s - 12.40}$$

Therefore, for a series of values of n_s, straight lines of varying slope with intercepts on the axes will be obtained.

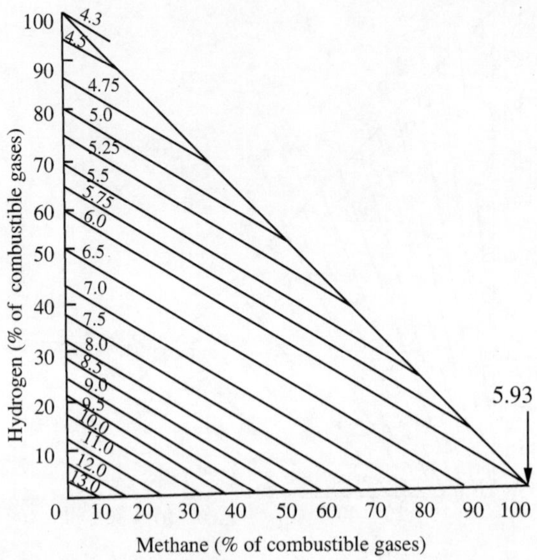

Figure 5.19 Diagram for determining the combustible content at the nose limit of mixtures consisting of three combustible gases, air, and excess nitrogen.

Construction of the diagram shown in Fig. 5.20

As the upper flammable limits of H_2 and CO in air are equal at 74 per cent, they behave at their upper limits as if they were a single constituent.

$$\frac{p_1}{u_1} + \frac{p_2}{u_2} = \frac{100}{u_m}$$

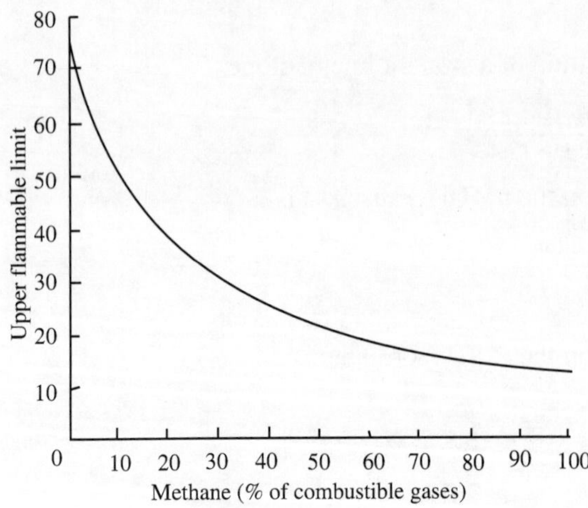

Figure 5.20 Diagram for determining the UFL of mixtures consisting of three combustible gases and air.

$$\frac{p_1}{u_1}+\frac{100-p_2}{u_2}=\frac{100}{u_m}$$

$$p_1\left(\frac{1}{u_1}-\frac{1}{u_2}\right)=\frac{100}{u_m}-\frac{100}{u_2}$$

Substituting $u_1 = 14$, $u_2 = 74$, we get

$$p_1=\frac{1727}{u_m}-23.33$$

This is an equation of an equilateral hyperbola with the p_1 (CH_4) axis displaced by 23.33 units.

5.3.2.4 Jagger and James method

Jagger and James [81] prepared a set of triangular diagrams using experimental values of Coward and Jones for rapid determination of the limits of flammability of mixtures consisting of three combustible gases, air, and excess nitrogen. The basis on which this presentation rests is identical to that used in the method of Hughes and Raybould, and, therefore, within the limits of error of the use of the diagrams, the results obtained are identical to those given by the Hughes and Raybould method.

In this method, the percentages of two of the combustible gases, methane and carbon monoxide, are expressed as percentages of the total combustibles,

$$M=\frac{\%CH_4}{\%CO+\%\,H_2+\%\,CH_4}$$

$$L=\frac{\%CO}{\%CO+\%\,H_2+\%\,CH_4}$$

A set of Coward triangles is constructed for mixtures containing, 0, 10, 20, 30, 40, and 50 per cent CO in the total combustible (L)for a selected range of values of M which will vary from diagram to diagram (Figs. 5.21 to 5.26).

To use the set of diagrams, the ratios L and M, the percentage of total combustibles, and the percentage of oxygen are calculated from the gas analysis. The diagram with the nearest value of L is chosen and the triangles interpolated for the required M value. The point corresponding to the composition of the atmosphere (percentage total combustibles, percentage oxygen) is plotted on the diagram and the line joining the 100 per cent air apex (that is 20.93 per cent O_2) to the point is then drawn. The points where the line would intersect the interpolated triangle give the percentages of combustibles and oxygen at the upper and lower limits of flammability.

Although 10 diagrams are needed to cover all the possible combinations of the three combustible gases, it is found in practise that only six diagrams for 0 to 50 per cent CO are required.

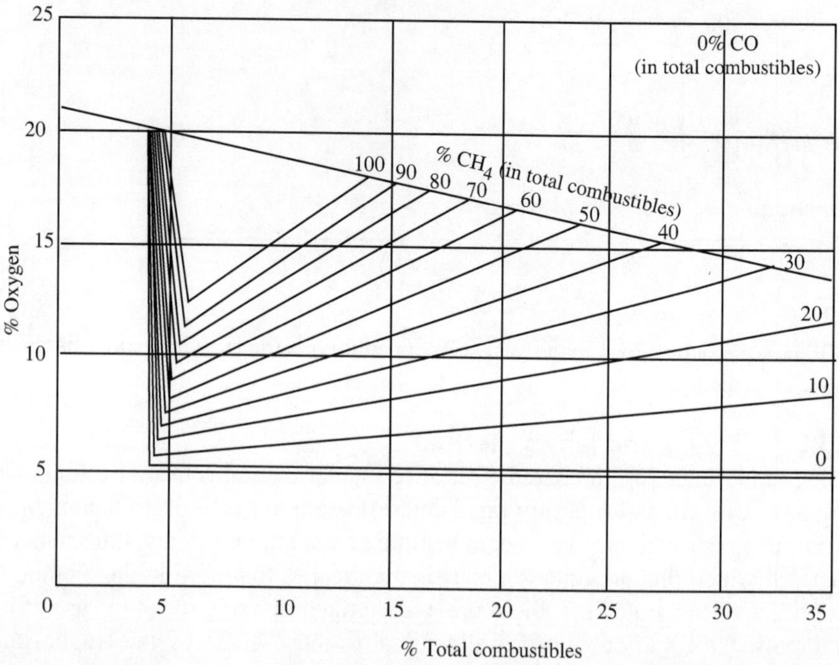

Figure 5.21 Diagram for determining the flammability of mixture of three combustible gases containing 0% CO.

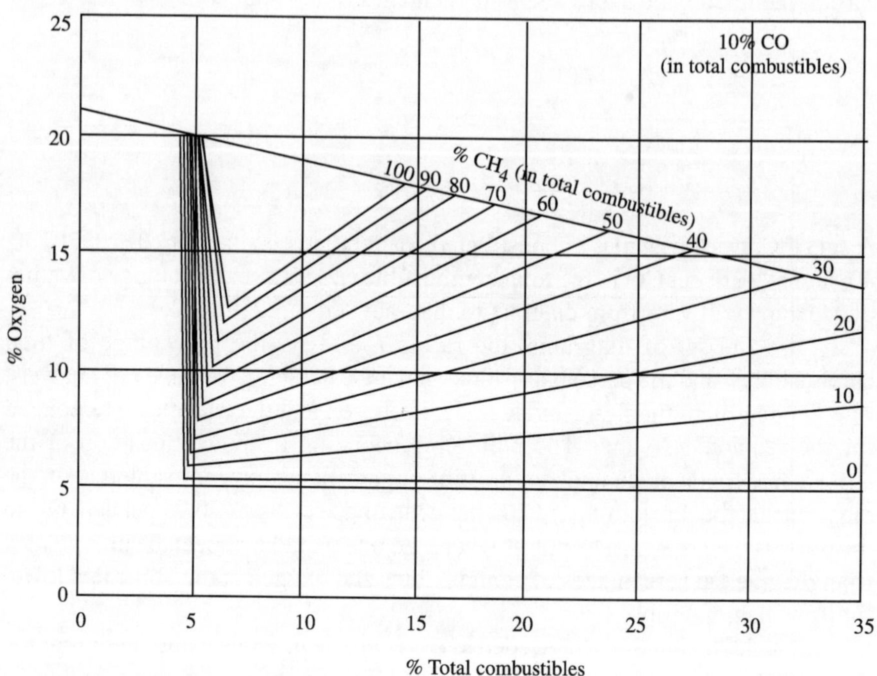

Figure 5.22 Diagram for determining the flammability of mixtures of three combustible gases containing 10% CO.

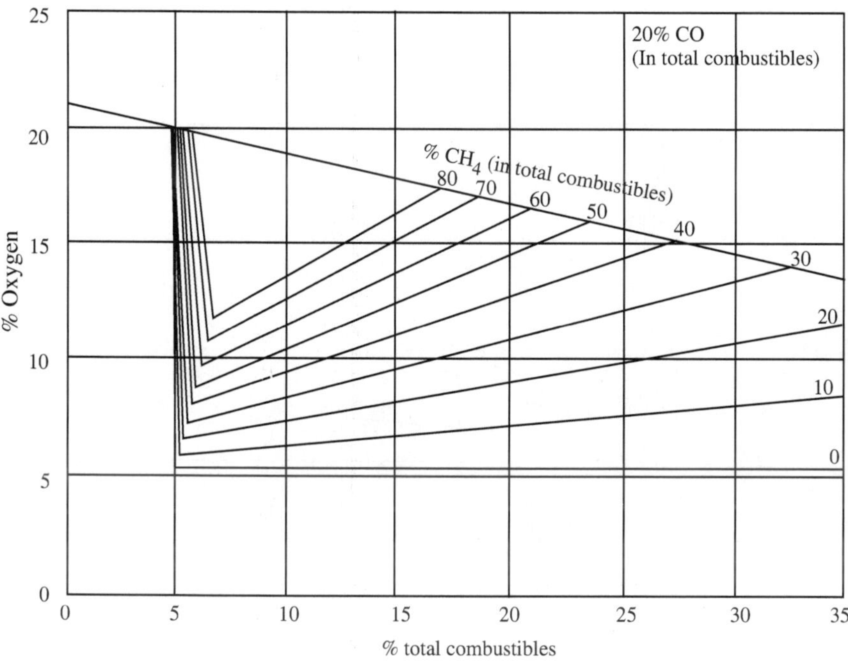

Figure 5.23 Diagram for mixtures containing 20% CO.

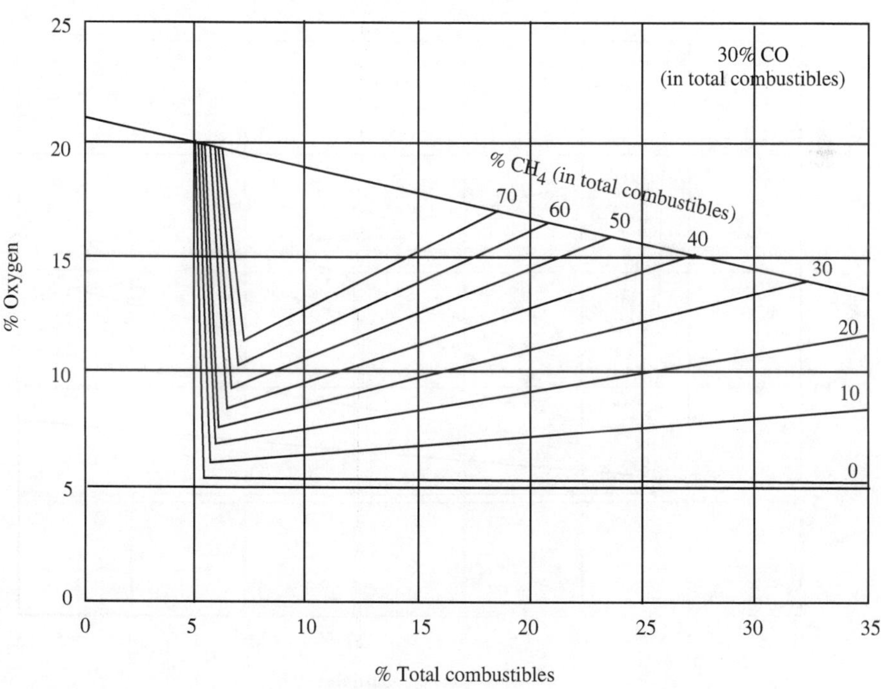

Figure 5.24 Diagram for mixtures containing 30% CO.

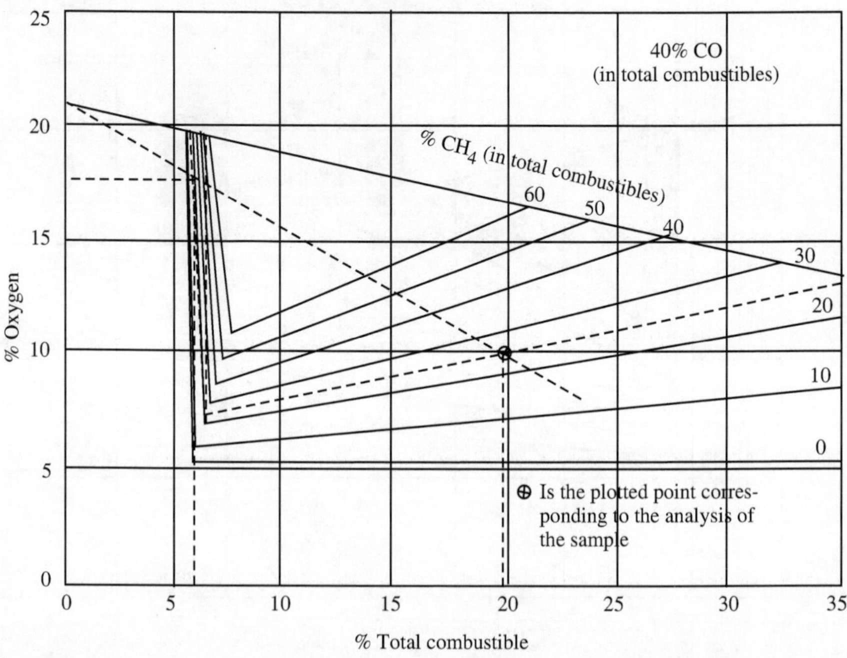

Figure 5.25 Diagram for mixtures containing 40% CO.

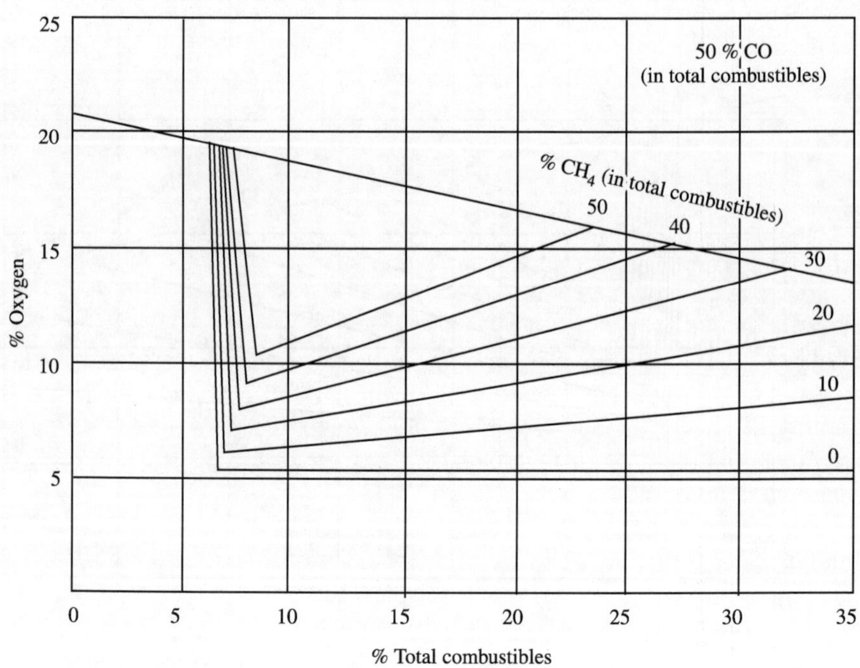

Figure 5.26 Diagram for mixtures containing 50% CO.

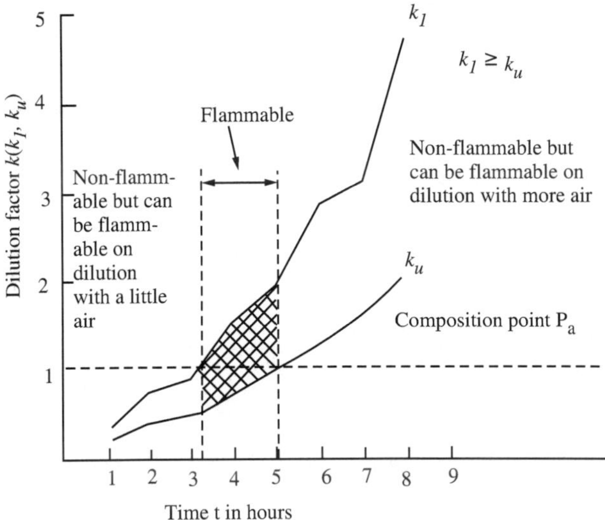

Figure 5.27 Development of flammability of a mixture of firegases with time according to *R*. Müller.

5.3.2.5. Müller method

Müller [82] obtained from the Drekopf characteristic triangle a diagram (Fig. 5.27) showing the variation of the dilution factors, k_1 and k_u, with the time at which the gas samples were collected for the condition k_1 ³ k_u. By drawing a line for the composition point parallel to the abscissa for the dilution factor equal to one, he identified the following three areas:

for $k_u < k_l, < 1$, the firegases are non-flammable, which can, however, become flammable on little a dilution with air;

for $k_u \geq 1 \leq k_l$, the firegases are flammable;

$k_l > k_u > 1$, the firegases are non-flammable, which can, however, become flammable on more dilution with air.

The diagram enables prediction of a trend towards flammability of the firegases.

From Fig.5.27, Müller obtained another diagram (Fig. 5.28) in which the flammability index (EKZ) given by the product $(k_l - 1)(1 - k_u)$ is plotted against time for the condition $k_l \geq k_u$. If the difference $k_l - k_u$ is negative, the firegases are non-flammable, irrespective of whether the dilution is little or more.

Several explosibility diagrams and indices have been further proposed by others, but there is no single ideal method or index for determining the explosibility of mine firegases during reopening of sealed fire areas.

5.3.2.6 U.S.B.M. Method

The U.S.B.M. diagram (Fig. 5.29) represents a series of flammability triangles drawn for various values of % CH_4 to the percentage of total combustibles

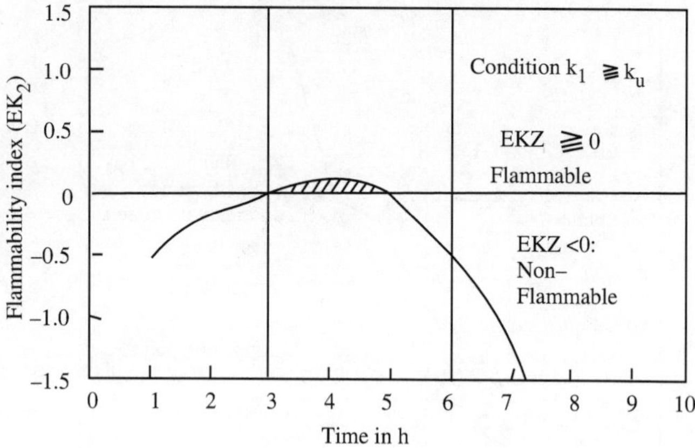

Figure 5.28 Development of flammability index (EK7) according to R. Müller.

(% CH_4 + % H_2 + % CO) called nose flammability limit *R* in the samples taken.

The X-coordinate (effective inert) and the Y-coordinate (effective total cumbustibles) are calculated using the relations given by Zabetakis, Stahl and Watson (1959).

$$\text{X coordinate} = \%\ N_2 + 1.5\ \%\ CO_2$$

$$\text{Y coordinate} = \%\ CH_4 + 1.25\%\ H_2 + \%\ 0.40\ CO$$

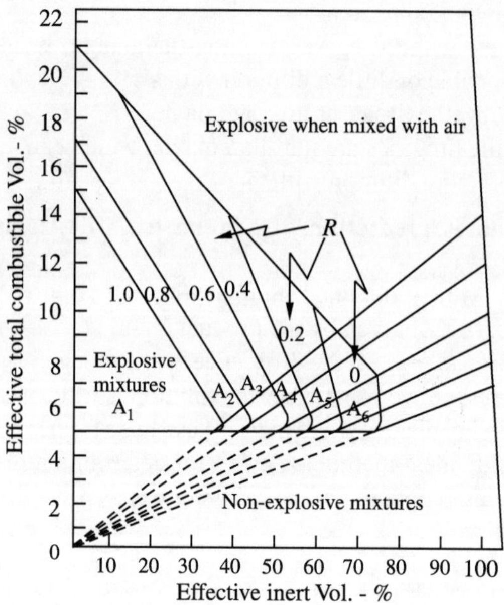

Figure 5.29 U.S.B.M. explosibility diagram.

assuming that hydrogen's contribution to combustibility is 25% higher than that of methane and carbon monoxide's contribution is only 40% of that of methane.

Each flammability triangle has a line which extends from its right-hand bottom corner separating atmospheres which become flammable with the addition of air from those which will not. These lines when extended downwards will converge at the origin of the graph.

CHAPTER 6

Re-opening of Sealed-off Areas in Mines

The re-opening or recovery of a district or an area which has been sealed off on account of spontaneous combustion or fire from other causes poses an arduous and hazardous problem to mine management. There can be no one procedure of recovery which would satisfy all conditions and each case should be considered on its own peculiar conditions.

6.1 Considerations when Re-opening a Sealed-off Area

The re-opening of a sealed-off area should not be undertaken lightly. It should be undertaken only when the conditions ensure the safety of those engaged in the re-opening work and prevent additional damage to property. A certain amount of time must elapse before conditions become favourable for re-opening.

The time of re-opening a fire area is governed by the following factors:

1. *Extent and intensity of fire at the time of sealing*

The extent and intensity of fire at the time of sealing influence the reduction of oxygen inside a sealed-off area (well below 10%) if there is no leakage of air into it. A larger amount of burning material will bring about a quicker reduction of oxygen than a smaller amount but will, at the same time, lengthen the time required for cooling off.

2. *Nature of burning material and adjacent strata*

The nature of the burning material inside a sealed-off area, whether it is timber, coal, or both, and the rate of burning may influence the possibility of rekindling of fire on admission of air. Coals having a higher volatile–combustible ratio burn faster and are more likely to be rekindled than coals having a lower ratio. The nature of the adjacent strata, especially when they are combustible, influences the time of re-opening as they retain heat for a long time even after the oxygen content has fallen below the limit when combustion ceases. Valuable information can be obtained by the use of thermocouple in the sealed area. Sub-micrometre particle concentrations in the sealed area have been found to correlate exceptionally well with the temperatures within the area, independent of the combustibles involved in sharp contrast to the gas concentration data which exhibit no correlation with the temperatures, and their measurement may be used as a more universal technique for determining the status of the underground sealed fire area [83].

3. *Airtightness of stoppings and the sealed-off area*
Airtightness of stoppings and the enclosed area is essential for control of oxygen. A fire is effectively sealed off when there is a constant decrease of oxygen in the samples taken from behind the stoppings. Air may leak through the stoppings and adjacent strata due to barometric and temperature changes or due to differences in ventilation pressure between different parts of the area, thereby prolonging the process of extinguishment of the fire.

4. *Composition of the atmosphere in the sealed-off area*
Knowledge of the composition of the atmosphere obtaining in a sealed area is of vital importance in deciding the reasonably safe time of re-opening the area. The value of the composition lies in its correct interpretation to ascertain the status of fire and possible explosion hazard upon admission of air, which have been discussed in Chapter 5. Samples of atmosphere should be collected through surface boreholes wherever possible. Otherwise, the first trip into the mine after sealing should be for the purpose of collecting samples from the sealed-off area. In interpreting the composition, it should be remembered that active combustion ceases when the percentage of oxygen falls below 12, but that slow combustion with evolution of CO and CO_2 may continue even at oxygen concentrations of 5 per cent or less. The presence of combustible gases other than methane, which reduce the lower flammability of methane, can be disregarded if their total content does not exceed 1 per cent as the amount of oxygen necessary to form an explosive mixture as compared to methane alone is insignificant. With the composition of firegases as is normally found in sealed-off areas, there is less likelihood of any explosion taking place during re-opening if the oxygen content of the gases is reduced to 3 per cent or less. Carbon dioxide, although exerting an extinctive effect upon the mixture of gases, is seldom more than 6 to 8 per cent and, for practical purposes, can also be disregarded except for the information it provides on the depletion of oxygen in the area. The levels of carbon monoxide may never reach zero even though it may be considered safe to re-enter the area.

It should, however, be pointed out that no method of ascertaining the status of fire or evaluating the danger of explosion can offer any guarantee of safety as it is nearly impossible to predict accurately the air leakage, the rate of methane emission, and the reliability of the gas samples as representative of conditions in the vicinity of the fire seat.

5 *Original cause of fire*
If the fire was due to spontaneous combustion, re-kindling of the fire may take place and contingency plans should be drawn up to meet the situation. A fire caused by machinery would be considered in a different light.

6 *Inert gas injection*
The time of re-opening a sealed area can be considerably reduced and the area may be safely entered by injection of an inert gas into it.

6.2 Preparatory Measures for Re-opening

For the successful re-opening of any sealed-off fire area, certain precautionary measures should be undertaken. They are:

1. Assembling rescue and recovery crew;
2. Withdrawal of all men from the mine other than those required in connection with re-opening operations;
3. Stationing a man at the mine main fan to see that the fan continues to run;
4. Cutting off electric power from the part of the mine in which a fire is sealed off as well as in return airways utilized for carrying the firegases;
5. Making necessary adjustments in ventilation so that the return from the fire area can be directed into the main return;
6. Heavily stonedusting all roadways leading to and from the fire area;
7. Establishing telephonic communication between the fresh-air base and the surface; and
8. Preparatory measures for nitrogen flushing during re-opening where it is contemplated.
9. An action plan should be prepared and agreed to by all concerned parties.

6.3 Methods of Re-opening

For re-opening a sealed-off area, one of the following methods may be employed:

1. Re-opening by re-ventilation;
2. Re-opening by air-locking in stages (stage method); and
3. Combination of (1) and (2).

The choice of a particular method depends on the following factors:

1. Type and extent of fire;
2. Size of area sealed off;
3. Time allowed for cooling off;
4. Volume of firedamp enclosed;
5. Probable condition of doors and other ventilation appliances in the area;
6. Inclination of the roadways;
7. Accessibility of roadways;
8. Presence of water in the area;
9. Temperature; and
10. Availability of an inert gas for atmospheric inerting.

6.3.1 Recovery by re-ventilation

There are two variants of this method:

(a) Re-ventilation without inspection by rescue brigades (direct method);
(b) Re-ventilation following inspection by rescue brigades.

The method of direct circulation of air through a fire area without inspection by rescue brigades is employed when a fire in an isolated area in a non-gassy mine is known to be small in extent and when it is definitely known from evidence obtained from a close and thorough inspection made with breathing apparatus that the fire has been extinguished. If it is decided to circulate a large quantity of air in one operation, the return stopping is breached first by men wearing rescue apparatus, followed immediately by breaching of the intake stopping. It is desirable' to take samples at the return stopping by the rescue men. It is preferable to circulate not more than 140 m^3 per minute of air in one operation. If large-diameter ventilation pipes are left in the stoppings, all that is necessary is to open their ends. Air should be circulated for several hours before an inspecting party is admitted into the area.

If a district has been sealed off in a gassy mine on account of spontaneous combustion and there is possibility of heavy falls in roadways or when there is only one communicating roadway, it is preferable to send a rescue brigade into the district to make an inspection of the prevailing conditions therein.

An air-lock is first constructed near the intake stopping and a fresh-air base is established outbye it. A fully-equipped rescue brigade using a lifeline or portable telephones then breaches the intake stopping and enters the area to observe conditions, take hygrometer readings, collect air samples, and then returns to the fresh-air base. If, on the basis of observations thus made and results of analysis of samples taken, it is concluded that conditions are favourable for re-opening by circulation of air, necessary adjustments in ventilation are made. It is advisable that all men are sent out of the mine before the air is actually directed into the sealed area. The return stopping is broken by a rescue brigade and fresh air is coursed through the area by opening the air-lock. The fresh-air current should be sufficiently strong so that no accumulations of firegases are left behind and the content of the combustible gases in the main return as well as in airways carrying the gases to it is kept below the lower flammable limit. A reasonable period should be allowed for the firegases to be removed, during which periodic sampling of the main return air should be carried out. On reaching the fire seat, it should be watered down and the burning coal spread out and transported away. If during re-opening smoke begins to be formed, the fire seat should be closely sealed off by stoppings.

Where an adequate supply of inert nitrogen gas is available, it may be used, instead of air, to flush out the gases.

When in an area being re-opened, there are heavy falls in roadways which cannot be easily cleared and re-ventilation in the normal way is not practicable,

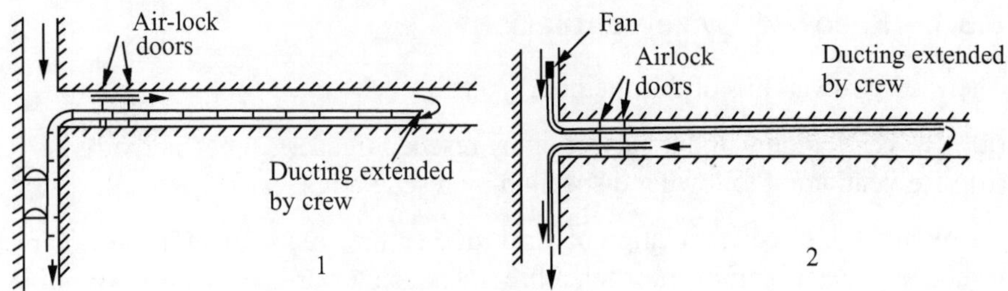

Figure 6.1 Method of ventilating a sealed-off area.

recourse must be taken to auxiliary ventilation using a brattice line or ducting with or without a mechanical ventilator. A fresh-air base is established and the rescue brigade advances systematically away from it by extending the brattice line or ducting.

The methods which have been successfully adopted are shown in Fig. 6.1. Method 1 is adopted where most of the mine water gauge can be utilized for producing the necessary depression. Method 2 requires the use of a forcing fan and gives good service where the ventilating pressure in the vicinity of the stopping is inadequate for adoption of Method 1. Good duct joints are essential for the success of this method. Ducting is extended by men wearing rescue apparatus.

Re-ventilation for re-opening of a sealed-off area must be done according to a definite plan, as far as possible, on a non-working day. The method can always be employed where there is no explosion hazard.

6.3.2 Re-opening by air-locking in stages (Stage method)

This method of re-opening is usually employed where a sealed-off area is extensive, the roadways are highly inclined, the fire seat is inaccessible, there are open break-throughs or connections between the intake and return airways in the area, there is a fairly large influx of water in the area, and the atmosphere in the area is too hot and humid for a rescue team to travel very far. The area is recovered in successive blocks or stages in dead atmospheres by means of air-locks (Fig. 6.2).

An air-lock consists of two brick walls, one-and-a-half to two-bricks thick, 5 m apart, equipped with airtight wooden or steel doors having glass windows for watching the advancing rescue brigade inside. It is erected at a convenient distance outbye the intake stopping. Between the doors of the air-lock, all equipment and materials necessary for the erection of the next air-lock are stored; water and compressed-air lines, if existing, are extended into it. After the air-lock has dried, a rescue brigade, with another fully equipped in reserve at the fresh-air base, enters the area through the air-lock, breaches the stopping, and inspects up to a point where the next air-lock is to be erected, a distance generally lying between 50 and 150 m, depending on the difficulties encountered. The exploring brigade should observe the general conditions, collect air samples, take hygrometer readings, measure for materials required for the inbye stoppings of the next air-lock, and return to

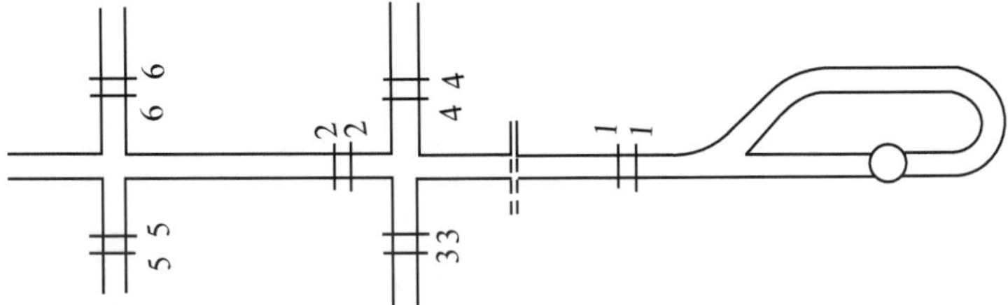

Figure 6.2 Stage method by means of air-locks.

the fresh-air base. After the next air-lock is erected, the one previously erected is broken down and the space between the air-locks is ventilated by auxiliary ventilation, adequately supported, and fitted with necessary fittings. It is only after completion of these auxiliary operations that the rescue brigade advances further and, by making such advances in successive stages, recovers the entire area. It is necessary that during the operations the oxygen-content of the firegases be kept as low as possible at all times by limiting air leakage into the area. As leakage of air through the doors of the air-locks takes place when they are opened, the doors should be opened maximum twice in a period of 4 hours. To keep back gases and heat during the erection of an air-lock, a temporary brattice stopping or screen is erected just beyond the proposed site of an air-lock.

Re-opening by use of air-locks is a very costly operation especially when complicated mine workings exist, as a large number of air-locks required to be constructed with the help of men wearing respiratory protective equipment.

Partial re-opening method

This is the most difficult method of re-opening. In general, it is employed where it is desired to re-open part of a district fairly soon after sealing off on account of spontaneous combustion. Expert advice must be taken and the operations carefully planned before commencement of the task. All general precautions should be taken as for the other methods of re-opening.

The method consists in re-opening the desired part of the district by the stage method and sealing off the remainder of the district by means of inbye stopping sited so that it would be possible to ventilate the face of the stoppings with fresh air and ventilating pressure balanced on them. The inbye stoppings should be extended to 8 m or more in thickness as soon as possible. Sample pipes should be inserted through them.

6.3.3 Other methods

Re-opening of hydraulically-flushed sealed district

When a fire is sealed off with stoppings in the usual manner and the fire seat or the fire area is flushed with sand or clay, the district can be re-opened either by cleaning the mine workings of the flushed material or driving new ones to start a new district (Fig. 6.3). This method is suitable for smaller fires.

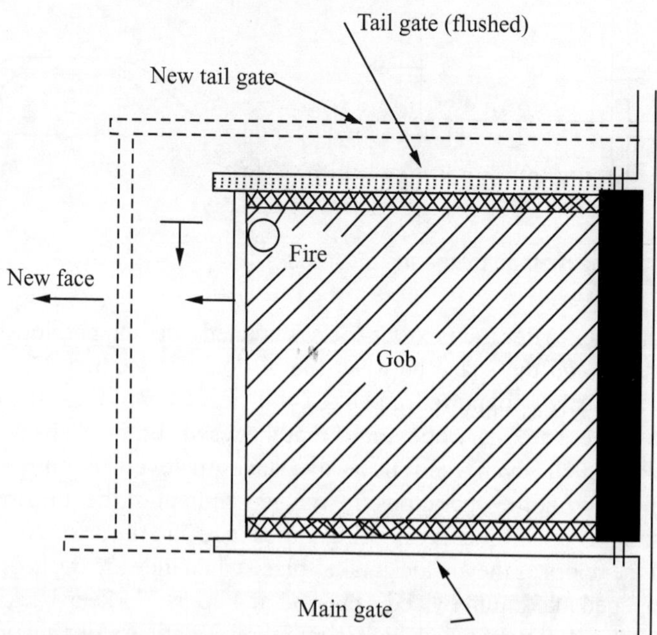

Figure 6.3 Abandoning the old face and opening a new face.

Re-opening of a sealed-off mine

Re-opening of a sealed-off mine with sealed surface shafts should be done according to a carefully worked-out plan. When the two shafts are not far from each other, the seal of the downcast shaft is broken and a rescue brigade goes down the shaft to erect temporary stoppings in dead atmosphere to isolate the rest of the mine from the shafts. A fresh-air base is established between the two shafts by breaking the stopping in the fandrift and operating the fan. The entire mine is then recovered in stages by means of air-locks.

It should be borne in mind that the re-opening with danger of explosion should be carried out when personnel are not in the mine. After re-establishment of the ventilation, none should be allowed to enter the mine for 20 hours.

Approximate calculations may be made for the possible volume of gas entrapped and the time it would take to clear the volume.

CHAPTER 7

Mine Rescue

The subject of mine rescue deals with all measures and devices used for working in irrespirable and toxic atmospheres occurring in mines for the purpose of fire-fighting and sealing off mine fires and rescue and/or recovery operations speedily and safely. The saving of lives of men overcome by toxic gases or oxygen-deficient atmospheres forms the immediate and the most important objective of mine rescue.

7.1 Human Respiratory System

When a person inhales air or oxygen along with nitrogen and carbon dioxide as a result of rhythmical respiratory movements of the chest, the air or oxygen is drawn into the lungs down the windpipe or trachea which divides into the left and right main bronchus supplying the left and right lungs, which then subdivide into a number of smaller and smaller bronchioles to end in multitudes (altogether about six million) of minute air sacs or alveoli which form the ultimate structure of the lungs (Fig. 7.1). The alveoli are lined with a thin membrane over which the circulating blood is spread in a microscopic network of myriad capillaries which, if joined in one tube, would stretch over 3000 km. The red cells in them would have a surface for absorption of oxygen of about 100 m^2 . During the brief exposure in the alveoli, there is an interchange of gases between the air and the blood. The red cells of the venous blood combine with a fraction of the inhaled oxygen depending on the quantity and ability of the contained haemoglobin, while the blood parts with its carbon dioxide and water vapour (respiratory exchange). Under normal conditions, 100 ml of blood carry from the lungs 18.5 to 20 ml of oxygen out of which only 0.36 ml is in solution and the rest is in chemical combination. The oxygen-enriched blood, aided by heart action, supplies the necessary oxygen to the body cells for the combustion of the nutrient material producing, in the biochemical process, water and a small quantity of carbon dioxide which dissolve in the venous blood but diffuse out of it during its transit through the lungs.

The carbon dioxide given out is often less than the oxygen absorbed in the same time. The ratio of these quantities to one another is called the ‘respiratory quotient’ (RQ)

$$\frac{\text{Vol.CO}_2}{\text{Vol.O}_2} = \text{RQ}$$

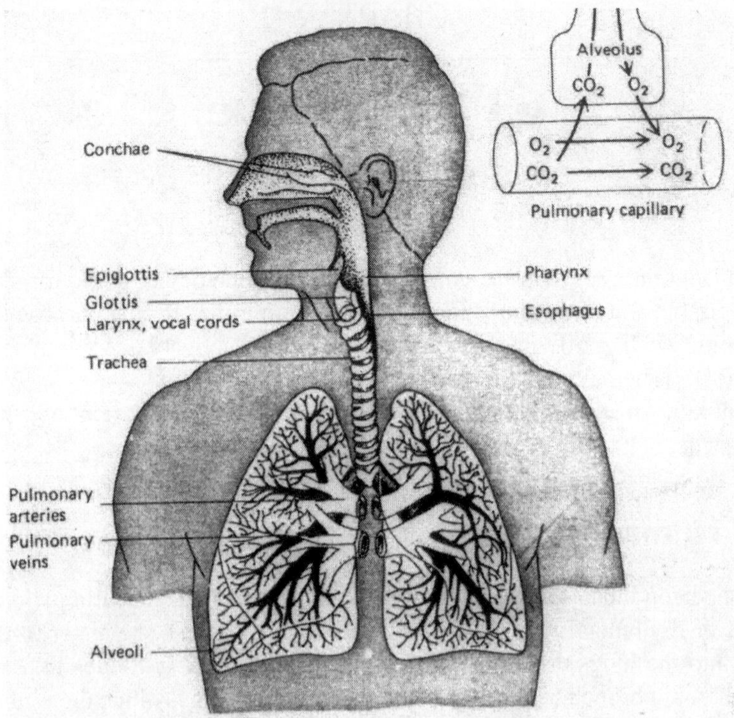

Figure 7.1 The respiratory passages.

The respiratory quotient depends on the type of diet taken. With normal diet, the quotient is equal to 0.85.

The respiratory exchange in the lungs is never complete as the lungs neither empty themselves completely during expiration nor fill completely during inspiration.

7.1.1 The pulmonary volumes and capacities

With quiet respiration, a man inspires or expires about 500 ml of air *(tidal volume,* TV). On a very deep breath, he can take in about another 3000 ml of air over and beyond the normal tidal volume *(inspiratory reserve volume,* IRV). On a subsequent forceful expiration, he can expire about 1100 ml of air after the end of the normal tidal expiration *(expiratory reserve volume,* ERV). The volume of air still remaining in the depth of the lungs in the anatomical dead space after the most forceful expiration is the *residual volume,* RV, which averages about 1200 ml; it is by no means pure air but contains about 5 to 6 per cent CO_2, 13 to 14 per cent O_2, and about 80 percent N_2 and the breathing mechanism maintains these figures constant.

The pulmonary capacities are obtained by combinations of two or more of the above volumes. The *inspiratory capacity* (IC), is the amount of air (about 3500 ml) that a man can breathe at the normal expiratory level by distending the lungs to the maximum extent; it is given by the sum of the tidal volume and the inspiratory reserve volume. The amount of air remaining in the lungs at the end of normal expiration (about 2300 ml) is the *functional residual capacity,* (FRC); it equals the expiratory reserve volume plus the residual volume. The maximum amount of air that a person can expel from the lungs following the deepest inspiration is called the *vital capacity,* VC (about 4600 ml), and is made up of the inspiratory reserve volume, the tidal volume, and the expiratory reserve volume; it varies in different persons depending on the age, health, and respiratory training and is about 3 to 4 litres for rescue-trained men. The *vital capacity* is related to the surface area of the body and amounts to 2.6 litres per m^2 surface area. The *total lung capacity* (TLC), is the maximum volume to which the lungs can be expanded with the deepest inspiration (about 5800 ml); it is equal to the sum of the vital capacity and the residual volume.

The interrelationships between the different pulmonary capacities and volumes can be described as follows:

$$IC = TV + IRV$$

$$FRC = ERV + RV$$

$$VC = IRV + TV + ERV = IC + ERV$$

$$TLC = VC + RV = IC + FRC$$

The *minute respiratory volume* is the total amount of new air moved into the respiratory passages each minute and is equal to the tidal volume times the respiratory rate. With the normal tidal volume of about 500 ml and the normal respiratory rate of approximately 12 breaths per minute, the minute respiratory volume averages about 6 litres per minute. *Alveolar ventilation* per minute is the rate at which new air enters the gas exchange areas of the lungs which include the alveoli, the alveolar sacs, alveolar ducts and the respiratory bronchioles. It is equal to the respiratory rate times the amount of new air entering the alveoli with each breath.

An idea of the relative proportions of air in the lungs is shown in Fig. 7.2 under different conditions of breathing.

For the design of respiratory protective equipment, it is important to know the air and oxygen consumption rates of a normal human being for different degrees of exertion. As a man consumes, due to gaseous exchange in the lungs, an amount of oxygen equal to about 4 to 5 per cent of the inspired air, his oxygen consumption can be approximately calculated from the air inhaled per minute which is given by the product of respirations per minute and air inhaled per respiration, called 'minute respiratory volume' or pulmonary ventilation.

Table 7.1 gives the air inhaled per minute and oxygen consumed per minute during different degrees of effort [76]. A spirometer is used to determine the volume of air breathed per minute.

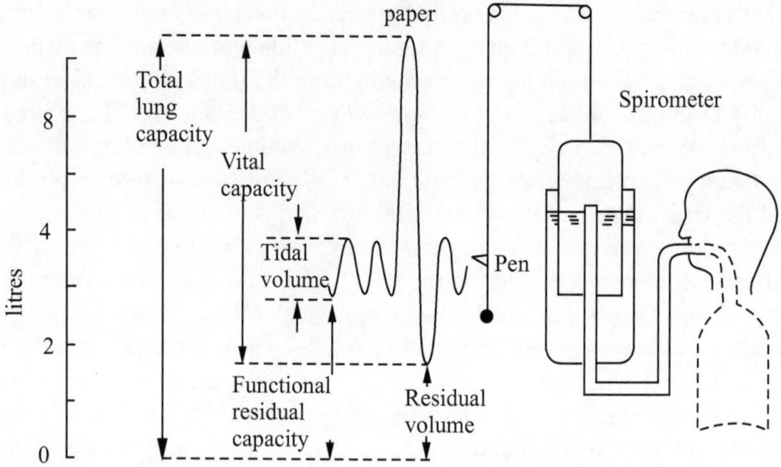

Figure 7.2 Spirogram

Table 7.1 Air and oxygen consumption for different degrees of exertion

Activity	Air inhaled litres/minute	O_2-consumption litres/minute
Resting	8–10	0.3–0.4
Walking with rescue apparatus	15–20	0.6–0.9
Rescue drill	20–30	0.9–1.3
Moderate work with pauses	30–40	1.3–1.8
Hard work with pauses	40–50	1.8–2.3
Very hard work for short duration	60–90	2.7–4.0

7.2 Mine Rescue Apparatus

Mine rescue apparatus, also called respirators or respiratory protective equipment used in mines, includes all types of apparatus that enable a wearer to enter or remain for long or short periods in irrespirable and toxic atmospheres retaining his full physical and mental capacities. They are primarily used for respiratory protection of men employed in fighting mine fires and in rescue and recovery work after explosions. Figure 7.3 gives the classification of the various types of apparatus that have been developed and used in mines today.

The various types of apparatus fall generally into the following three main classes:

(a) Self-contained breathing apparatus (SCBA)
(b) Filter apparatus or filter respirators
(c) Fresh-air tube breathing apparatus or supplied air respirators

Each class of apparatus has more or less a field of its own.

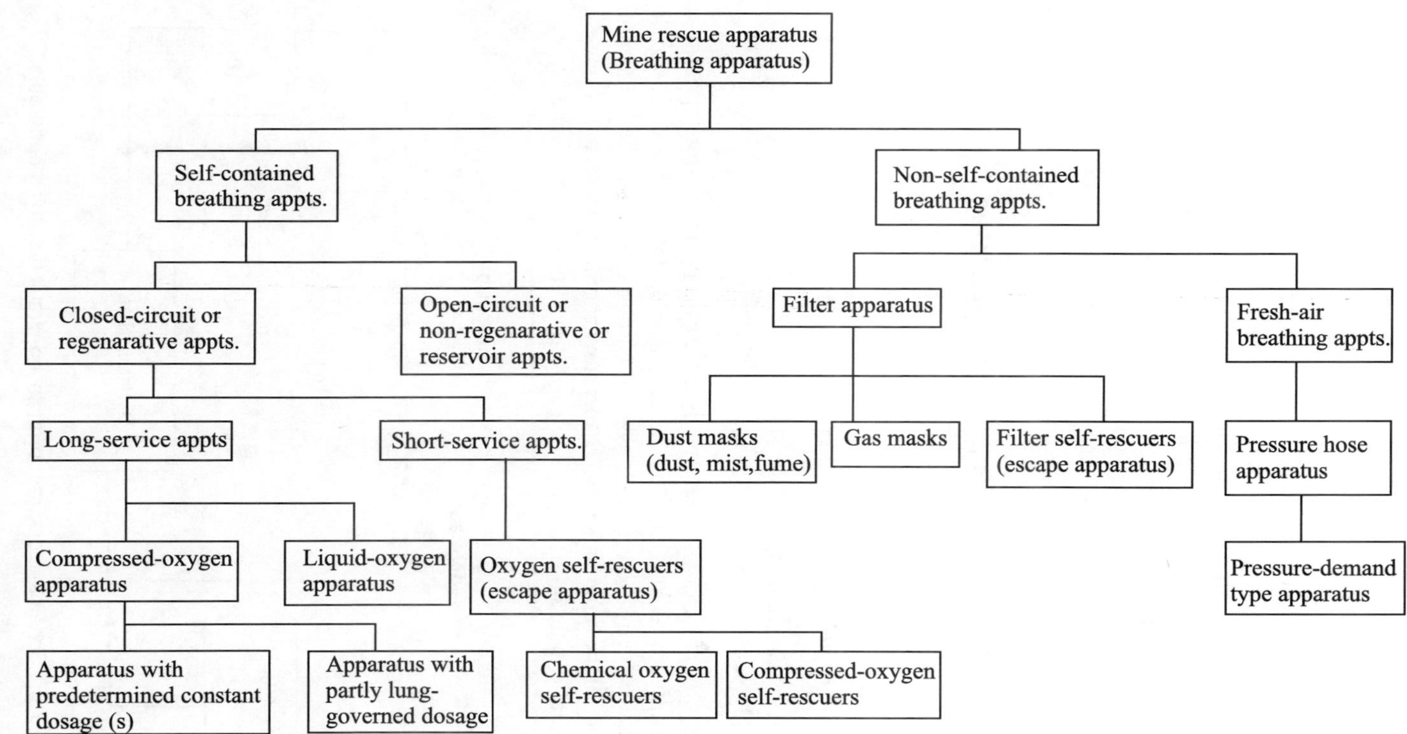

Figure 7.3 Classification of mine rescue apparatus.

The European Committee for Standardization comprising the national standards institutes of eighteen states (Belgium, Denmark, Germany, Finland, France, Greece, Ireland, Iceland, Italy, Luxembourg, Netherland, Norway, Austria, Portugal, Sweden, Spain, and the United Kingdom) laid down stringent European Standards or Norms for compliance in the design and testing of all types of respiratory protective equipment for use in toxic, oxygen-deficient or immediately-dangerous-to-life-or-health atmospheres in mines. The European Standards stipulate the minimum requirements to be fulfilled in the design, materials of construction, and performance testing of not only the whole apparatus but also their component parts. The tests include tests conducted using a breathing machine and man-tests conducted by specially trained personnel under different work load conditions usually encountered in practice. In the USA, the Mine Safety and Health Administration and the National Institute for Occupational Safety and Health jointly approve the design and certification of respirators as a part of product approval.

7.2.1 Self-contained Breathing Apparatus

A self-contained breathing apparatus is an apparatus that supplies all the requirements for respiration by itself and is independent of the surrounding atmosphere.

There are two types of self-contained breathing apparatus:

(1) Closed-circuit apparatus; and
(2) Open-circuit apparatus.

The closed-circuit apparatus is an oxygen-circulating apparatus of the regenerative type in which the oxygen used up by the wearer is supplemented from an oxygen reserve, the unwanted carbon dioxide in the exhaled air being absorbed at the same time by a regenerating chemical absorbent. Figure 7.4 gives a schematic diagram of a typical closed-circuit breathing apparatus.

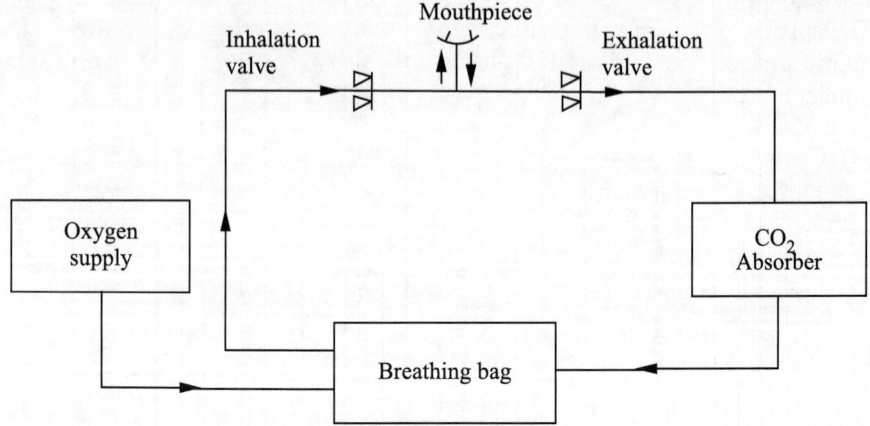

Figure 7.4 Schematic diagram of a closed-circuit breathing apparatus.

Depending on the source of oxygen supply, the apparatus may be divided into:

(1) Compressed-oxygen apparatus;
(2) Self-generating or chemical oxygen apparatus; and
(3) Liquid-oxygen apparatus.

Compressed-oxygen apparatus are the principal equipments used by all mine rescue stations throughout the world.

In the open-circuit apparatus, oxygen or air from a compressed-oxygen or compressed-air reserve is supplied to the wearer and the exhaled oxygen or air is discharged into the open and is put to no further use. They are also called reservoir or non-regenerative apparatus.

All designs of the closed-circuit- type apparatus are essentially the same as those of the open-circuit type. They differ only in construction of the several parts, source of oxygen or air, and the arrangement of the parts and the circulating system.

7.2.1.1 General requirements of self-contained breathing apparatus

Self-contained breathing apparatus are designed with the following objectives which must be kept in mind when making their selection.

(1) *Safety and reliability*
The apparatus must be designed on sound engineering and scientific principles so that it is safe and reliable when used under the most unfavourable and dangerous conditions encountered in mining. It must meet the respiration needs for a period equal to the rated service time plus a reserve period of about 25 per cent of that time. The components and materials used should not cause irritation to skin, should withstand repeated disinfection, and meet the requirements of permissibility.

(2) *Simplicity*
The apparatus should be as simple as possible in design, free from complicated manipulations on the part of the wearer and consistent with safety and efficiency.

(3) *Comfort*
The apparatus should be designed so that it gives maximum possible breathing comfort to the wearer under adverse operating conditions. It should provide as cool an air as is practicable, maintain low levels of CO_2 in the inspired air, offer low resistance to breathing, and have a suitable head harness.

(4) *Weight*
The apparatus should be reasonably light when completely assembled and fully charged, as with lighter apparatus the wearer will be able to perform a larger amount of work.

(5) *Compactness*
The apparatus should be designed to be as compact as possible and unnecessary projections are eliminated so that work in intricate and confined spaces is facilitated. The advantages of a modular component design which facilitates servicing and maintenance should not be lost sight of.

(6) *Durability*
The apparatus should be of robust construction. Before being officially approved for use in mines, all individual parts of the apparatus as well as the assembled apparatus must pass laboratory and practical approval tests which vary in rigorousness from country to country.

(7) *Initial cost and ease and cost of maintenance.*

(8) *Compliance with the country's national standards.*

7.2.1.2 Self-contained closed-circuit compressed-oxygen apparatus for mine rescue and recovery work

This type of apparatus is the first and the most commonly used apparatus in mines. It works on the re-breather principle. With this apparatus, the wearer inhales through a reducing valve oxygen stored at a high pressure in a steel cylinder and exhales into the apparatus where carbon dioxide of the exhaled air is removed by a chemical absorbent. Before the purified exhaled air is rebreathed again by the wearer, it is enriched or regenerated with oxygen from the oxygen cylinder automatically by the reducing valve, the amount of oxygen added to the circuit being equal to that consumed by the wearer. Several types of this form of apparatus were designed and produced ever since the idea of developing portable breathing apparatus was mooted by Alexander von Humboldt in the year 1795. The various apparatus included those of Schwan (1853), Fleuss (1879), Schamrock (1897), Giersberg (1901), Pneumatophor Walcher-Gaertner (1903), Draeger (1904), Meco, Westfalia or Securitas (1906), Fleuss-Davis (1906), Weg (1907), Tisset (1907), Gibbs (1917), Audos (1919), Paul (1920), Fenzy (1921), McCaa (1926), Draeger BG 170/400 (1952), Auer 54/400 (1954), Draeger BG 172 (1956), Auer 56/400 (1954), Auer MR 58/150, Draeger BG 174 (1962), Biopak (1985), Sefa (1987), BG4 (1995).

Depending on service time, approved compressed-oxygen breathing apparatus may be divided into:

(1) Long-service apparatus, and
(2) Short-service apparatus.

The long-service apparatus are used for periods of 2 or more hours by mine rescue crews for long-range rescue and recovery work and has an oxygen reserve of 300 to 400 litres.

The short-service apparatus are used as auxiliary apparatus for short periods of half to three-quarters of an hour for rescuing miners in an emergency when they have to be brought through irrespirable and poisonous atmospheres. They have an oxygen reserve of 120, 150 or 200 litres.

Depending on the type of oxygen feed or dosage, compressed-oxygen apparatus can be classified into the following three groups:

(a) Apparatus with a constant dosage supplemented, when necessary, by manual operation of a bypass valve.
(b) Apparatus in which the dosage is entirely lung-governed.
(c) Apparatus with a constant but small dosage of oxygen supplemented when necessary by a lung-governed oxygen admission valve (partly or semi-lung-governed apparatus).

In apparatus with a constant dosage, oxygen at a definite predetermined rate, 2 litres per minute, is supplied to the wearer when he is working hard but when the wearer is not working hard the excess oxygen is lost. When working very hard, however, more oxygen can be supplied by manual operation of a special valve called the bypass valve. A well-known example is Proto IV 1980.

In purely automatic lung-governed apparatus, the oxygen supply is governed by the movement of the lungs of the wearer. With such apparatus, there is danger of nitrogen narcosis due to enrichment of the circulating air with nitrogen unless means are adopted to remove that danger. Such apparatus (BG 170/400 and McCaa) are no longer in use for mine rescue work.

In apparatus with constant and lung-governed dosages, oxygen is supplied to the wearer at a constant rate of 1.5 litres per minute and, if the wearer requires more, a lung-governed oxygen admission valve provides an additional supply which his exertion may demand. They are widely used throughout the world.

7.2.1.2.1 General design features of closed-circuit modern self-contained compressed-oxygen breathing apparatus

The self-contained compressed-oxygen breathing apparatus consists of the following components and accessories:

A steel cylinder of 1- or 2-litre capacity containing medical oxygen under high pressure not less than 120 bar (g), usually 135, 150, 200 or 300 bar (g), for supplying the wearer with oxygen. Modern designs of steel cylinders are lighter than the older ones. A 2-litre light-weight cylinder weighs only 2.7 kgf. The cylinder is fitted with a main valve which should be opened fully and locked in the open position when the apparatus is being worn.

A pressure reducing valve to reduce the pressure of the oxygen contained in the cylinder and allow it to be supplied to the wearer at a fixed rate and at a pressure slightly higher than the atmospheric. The reducing valves usually operate with spring-loaded rubber diaphragms.

A regenerator purifying canister or purifier cartridge to absorb the carbon dioxide exhaled by the wearer. It is a removable sheet metal container or canister charged or filled with a specially prepared chemical which will completely absorb carbon dioxide over the prescribed wearing period. Exceptions, however, are the Siebe-Gorman Mark IV and Mark V Proto apparatus in which the absorbent is placed at the bottom of the breathing bag. As a regenerating chemical, alkali (anhydrous sodium hydroxide), lithium hydroxide, and soda lime (a mixture of sodium hydroxide and calcium hydroxide) are used. Extensive comparative tests with regenerators filled with alkali and soda-lime conducted by the Draegerwerk, Lübeck [84] showed that, although the efficiency of absorption of carbon dioxide can be considered the same for the two chemicals, alkali has a decisive advantage over soda-lime in that the dry and wet bulb temperatures of the inspired air with apparatus using alkali are significantly lower than with apparatus using soda lime. Investigations by the US Bureau of Mines [85] showed that LiOH has the greatest capacity for CO_2 absorption as compared to NaOH or soda lime.

A breathing bag to serve as an air reservoir from and into which the wearer breathes. The bag also provides flexibility to the circulatory system. It is made of high-grade sheet rubber or rubberized fabric, gas-impervious, and usually has one compartment with a useful capacity of 4 to 6 litres. Exception, however, is the Proto apparatus in which the bag has two compartments which are in communication near the bottom of the bag. In some apparatuses, the bag is fitted with a relief or excess-pressure valve to allow escape of excess air while in some apparatus of the lung-governed type, it operates the oxygen admission lever.

A mouthpiece or facepiece assembly to permit breathing entirely through the mouth or nose. The mouthpiece assembly consists of a soft rubber mouthpiece shaped to fit smugly between the lips and teeth of the wearer, a nose clip, a T shaped connecting piece, two inhalation and exhalation breathing tubes that connect with the rest of the apparatus, and a head harness that holds the mouthpiece in place. The full mask facepiece assembly consists of a moulded silicone rubber facepiece, a connecting piece, and breathing tubes. The all-vision or wide-vision facepiece covering the whole face permits breathing through the nose and also protects the eyes without use of goggles. Impediments to a good face-to-mask seal are facial hair, eye glasses, denture problems, widely varying racial characteristics, and skin irregularities. Full facepieces restrict peripheral vision in varying degrees and preclude the use of normal eye glasses. Half-mask facepieces reduce these problems somewhat. Users should, therefore, be clean-shaven. The effectiveness of the fit of the facepiece must be checked each time the apparatus is worn. In order to have non-zero minimum inhaled CO_2 level, facepieces are sometimes provided with a nose cup, which reduces the facemask deadspace volume thereby reducing the average inhaled CO_2 level.

The *breathing tubes* consist of 25-mm diameter strong highly flexible, deeply corrugated tubes of ageing-resistant rubber with a fabric insert or neoprene. They are long enough to permit the wearer to turn his head without much difficulty. They are fixed so that, when worn, they pass either under the left arm of the wearer before connecting to the mouthpiece or facepiece (Draeger) or over the shoulder (Biopack 240 of Biomarine). When the tubes pass under the left arm, the shoulders are left free to carry materials.

Inhalation (inspiratory) and exhalation (expiratory) valves to compel the circulating air to travel in one direction. The valves are usually of spring-loaded mica-disc type or of neoprene rubber type and are extremely sensitive. They are located in the circulatory system differently by different manufacturers. In the Draeger apparatus, they are located inside the apparatus casing.

A pressure gauge to indicate to the wearer the available supply and duration of oxygen in the oxygen cylinder. It is built into a strong brass case and is mounted on a special flexible high-pressure tube attached to the outlet of a pressure-gauge valve which is provided on the high-pressure fitting of the reducing valve.

A bypass valve to supply oxygen direct to the wearer should the reducing valve or the lung-governed admission valve through any cause fail to act properly. The valve is usually designed as a self-closing push-button valve.

A lung-governed oxygen admission valve or regulator in the case of automatic lung-governed apparatus to supply the wearer with oxygen in the exact quantity which his exertion may demand. There are two types of lung-governed oxygen admission valves: the lever-arm type and the diaphragm type. In the first type, the valve is automatically actuated by the rise and fall of the breathing bag which is in turn controlled by the rate of respiration and oxygen consumption. In the second type, the valve is actuated by the negative pressure produced by the wearer's respiratory effort and is independent of the movement of the breathing bag.

Warning signals or alarms to give a clearly audible whistling or hooting sound in case the reducing valve fails to shut off at the proper pressure or the cylinder is approaching exhaustion.

A relief or excess-pressure valve to release any excess pressure and to avoid accumulation of nitrogen in the respiratory system in the event of the oxygen contained in the cylinder not being perfectly pure. It may be located on the facepiece or on the breathing bag and operated manually or automatically by the breathing bag itself when the latter expands.

A preflushing device incorporated in modern design of the apparatus to automatically flush out the apparatus with 7 to 8 litres of oxygen when the cylinder valve is opened to purge the nitrogen-rich ambient air initially found in the breathing circuit.

A saliva trap to accumulate saliva of the wearer. It may be provided with a release valve to permit discharge of saliva accumulations to the outside as well as release any excess pressure without any external air being drawn into the apparatus. The saliva trap is located either in the inhalation tube or at the base of the mouthpiece or facepiece.

A casing to protect the breathing bag, regenerator, reducing valve, and other vital parts against direct blows and falling material. It is made of light metal of great strength, tough moulded fibre glass, or stainless steel and is designed so that it permits ease of passage through narrow mine workings. The back of the casing (carrying frame) has openings to enable the wearer to reach the handwheel of the cylinder main valve, bypass valve, pressure gauge valve, and for pressure-gauge tube and breathing tube unions.

Carrying harness of nylon designed to wear and remove the apparatus quickly.

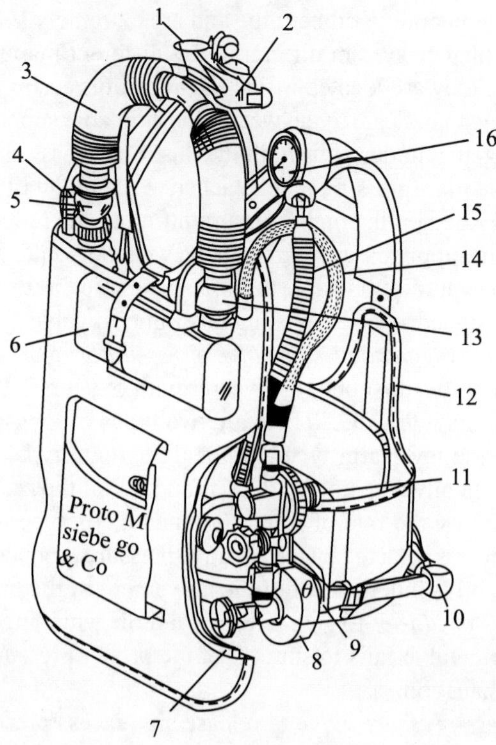

Figure 7.5 Siebe Gorman Proto IV 1980 apparatus.
1: nose clip assembly; 2: mouthpiece assembly; 3: breathing tube; 4: relief valve assembly; 5: exhalation valve; 6: cooler assembly; 7: breathing bag; 8: rubber cushion assembly; 9: fork; 10: cylinder arm with square elbow; 11: reducer valve assembly; 12: saddle assembly; 13: inhalation valve assembly; l4: oxygen supply tube; 15: pressure gauge tube assembly.

7.2.1.2.2 Siebe-Gorman Proto IV-1980 Apparatus (Fig. 7.5)

Proto Mark IV was first approved in the 1930s in the UK and inducted in India in the 1940s and still continues to be used today along with Draeger BG 174.

Specifications

Endurance (nominal)	2 hours
Cylinder capacity, empty	3 litres
Cylinder capacity at 122 bar	382 litres
Breathing bag capacity, full	excess of 5 litres
Mass of apparatus, fully charged	17.27 kg
Oxygen flow rate	2 litres per minute

The special features of the apparatus are:

(1) The moulded rubber breathing bag with integrally moulded ribs is divided into two compartments by a ribbed rubber partition which extends from the top

to a little over the bottom and a charge of 2 kg of carbon dioxide absorbent 'Protosorb' is placed at the bottom of the bag divided equally between the front and rear compartments. It is fitted at the top right-hand corner with a manual relief valve.

(2) A cooler is used to reduce the temperature of the regenerated air before inhalation. The cooler is a two-compartment copper chamber containing 170 g of a chemical di-sodium phosphate which melts at a temperature of 35°C. The melting of the sodium phosphate results in absorption of heat. The chemical resolidifies on cooling and remains permanently in the cooler.

(3) The reducing valve is of the well-proven diaphragm design in which a spring-loaded diaphragm is balanced by the reduced pressure at which the reducer is set so that the diaphragm is continually moving backwards and forwards maintaining a constant flow independent of cylinder pressure.

(4) The apparatus is not mounted in a carrying frame but is worn in front and back of the wearer.

Circulatory system

The exhaled air containing unused oxygen and carbon dioxide enters the breathing bag at the top of the front compartment via the exhalation tube and exhalation valve and passes down this compartment, through the chemical absorbent (soda lime) lying in the bottom of the bag, and up the back compartment as purified air. The purified air mixes with fresh oxygen which is being constantly delivered at the top of the back compartment from the cylinder through the reducing valve, and, on inspiration, the oxygen–air mixture passes through the cooler, inhalation valve, inhalation tube into the wearer's lungs. When the bypass valve is opened, the breathing bag is filled direct from the oxygen cylinder. Excessive pressure build-up is prevented by the manual relief valve.

Figure 7.6 gives a schematic diagram of the Proto breathing apparatus.

The Proto breathing apparatus which had been in use in the Indian mining industry for mine rescue work over six decades has become obsolete and is being

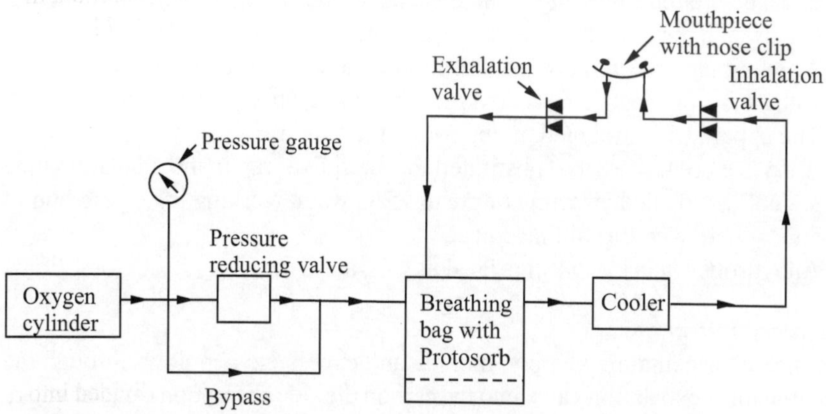

Figure 7.6 Schematic diagram of Proto IV 1980 breathing apparatus.

increasingly replaced by pressure-demand type in which the pressure inside the system in relation to the environment is positive during both inhalation and exhalation.

7.2.1.2.3 Draeger Model BG 174 Apparatus (Fig. 7.7)

This apparatus manufactured by Draegerwerk AG, Lübeck, Germany, is widely used as a standard mine rescue apparatus in many countries of Europe and India. It is of the closed-circuit type with a constant and lung-governed dosages or feeds of oxygen. It was introduced in India in 1992 to replace the Proto Mark IV apparatus.

Specifications

Endurance (nominal)	4 hours hard exertion at a working pressure of 200 bar
Cylinder capacity, empty	2 litres
Cylinder capacity at 200 bar	400 litres
Breathing bag capacity, full	6 litres
Weight of apparatus	12.8 kg
Oxygen flow rate constant dosages	Average 1.5 litres per minute (1.4-1.7 litres per min.)
Lung-governed dosage	As required (min 100 litres per min.)

The special features of the apparatus are:

(1) The oxygen regulator, also referred to as the oxygen distributor, comprises a pressure reducer, an automatic preflushing device, a bypass valve, and a pressure gauge shut-off valve. It has no connection with the breathing bag. The pressure reducer reduces the pressure to 4 bar.
(2) The lung-demand valve is a diaphragm-operated stem valve in a valve box or housing. It is not actuated by the breathing bag which has unrestricted movement but by the control diaphragm responding to small negative pressures resulting from inhalation. The diaphragm also actuates a relief valve to dissipate the excess circuit pressure. The demand valve, the relief valve, a metering nozzle, and the inhalation valve are all contained in the valve box.
(3) A preflushing device is fitted to automatically purge the breathing circuit of nitrogen with a burst of about 7 litres of oxygen when the cylinder valve is opened.
(4) The apparatus is mounted on the back of the wearer.
(5) A dry ice cooler may be substituted for the saliva trap in the inhalation tube to cool the inhaled air temperature to 15°C when working in hot and humid atmosphere wearing full facepiece.
(6) Anhydrous NaOH (1.5 kg) is used as CO_2 absorbent.

Circulatory system

The exhaled air containing carbon dioxide and excess oxygen flows through the exhalation tube, exhalation valve into the carbon dioxide absorption canister where it is freed from carbon dioxide. The air thus purified then flows into the breathing

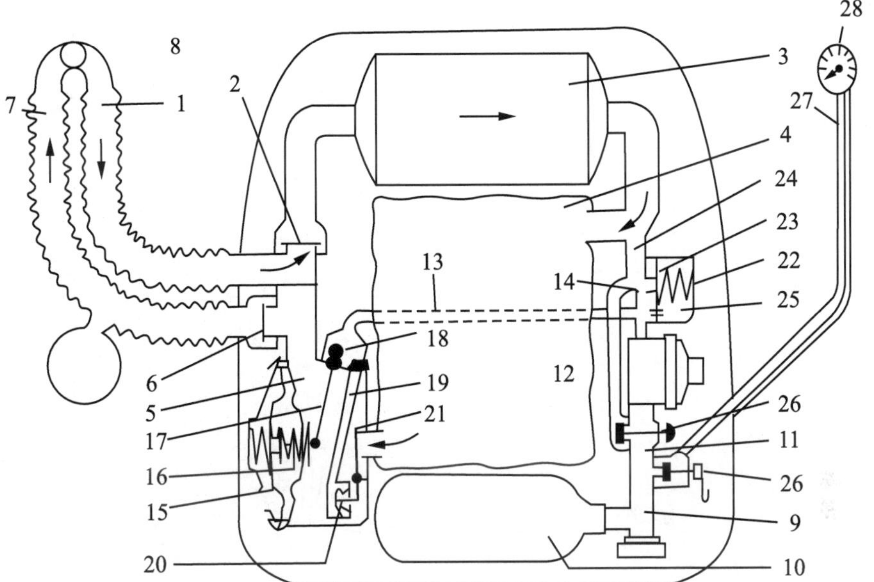

Figure 7.7 Draeger self-contained compressed-oxygen breathing apparatus Model BG 174.
1: exhalation tube; 2: exhalation valve; 3: regenerator; 4: breathing bag; 5: valve assembly; 6: inhalation valve; 7: inhalation tube; 8: connection socket; 9: cylinder valve; 10: oxygen cylinder; 11: oxygen regulator; 12: pressure reducer; 13: oxygen-supply tube; 14: constant-flow dosage valve; 15: control diaphragm; I6: excess pressure valve (cotter pin with sealing gasket); 17: stem/lever of lung-demand valve; 18–lung-demand valve; 19: control line; 20: warning signal control bellows; 21: warning signal flap; 22: pre-flushing device; 23: preflushing valve; 24: preflushing line; 25: control chamber; 26: by-pass valve; 27: high-pressure line; 28: pressure gauge.

bag and, on inhalation, is drawn from the breathing bag into the lung demand valve housing where it gets enriched with oxygen and then flows through the inhalation tube into the wearer's lungs. Excessive pressure build-up is prevented by the automatic relief valve. Additional oxygen, if needed, is provided by the lung-demand valve.

Figure 7.8 shows the construction of the Draeger Model BG 174A apparatus approved in 1975 by the Mine Safety and Health Administration (MSHA) and the National Institute for Occupational Safety and Health (NIOSH), USA, and widely used at present in US mines.

This unit is essentially the same as the Draeger BG 174 except for the following:

(1) It has 3- and 4-hour approval ratings;
(2) The low-oxygen warning device is located in the oxygen regulator instead of in the demand regulator assembly or valve box;
(3) A second pressure gauge is mounted on the oxygen cylinder;
(4) It incorporates a divider in the breathing hose facepiece connector;

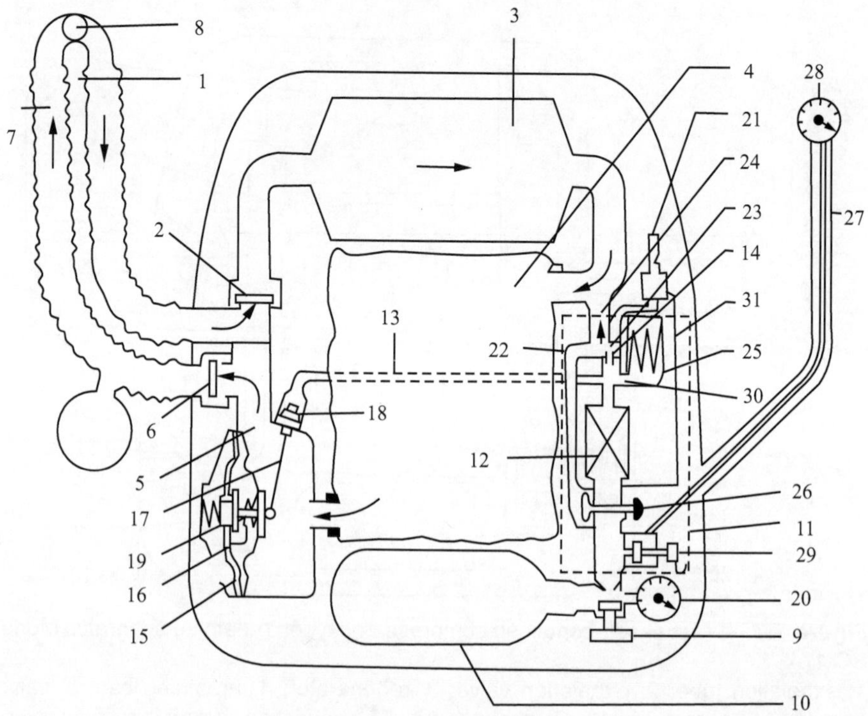

Figure 7.8 Draeger self-contained compressed-oxygen breathing apparatus Model BG 174A.

1: exhalation tube; 2: exhalation valve; 3: regenerator; 4: breathing bag; 5: valve assembly; 6: inhalation valve; 7: inhalation tube; 8: connection socket; 9: cylinder valve; l0: oxygen cylinder; 11: oxygen regulator; 12: pressure reducer; 13:oxygen-supply line of demand valve; 14: constant flow dosage nozzle; 15: control diaphragm; 16: pressure pin with gasket; 17: demand valve stem/lever; 18: lung-demand valve; 19: release valve system; 20: pressure gauge; 21: warning device; 22: preflushing device; 23: preflushing valve; 24: oxygen line; 25: control chamber; 26: bypass valve; 27: high-pressure line; 28: pressure gauge; 29: pressure gauge shut-off valve; 30: preflushing dosage nozzle; 31:control mechanisms for warning device.

(5) The oxygen metering nozzle is located on the oxygen regulator; and
(6) The cylinder valve of 'step clutch' design.
(7) The CO_2 absorbent in the canister consisting mostly of $Ca(OH)_2$ is not of packed-bed design but is suspended in a wire mesh offering low exhalation resistance.

7.2.1.2.4 Drager BG 4 Apparatus (Fig. 7.9)

Draeger BG 4 self-contained compressed-oxygen breathing apparatus (Fig.7.10) is a technically-advanced model of BG 174, which uses a disposable soda lime canister and a water-ice cooling unit to cool the inhaled air. It is approved by NIOSH CFR 30 and EN- 145 European Standard. It was introduced in India in 2002.

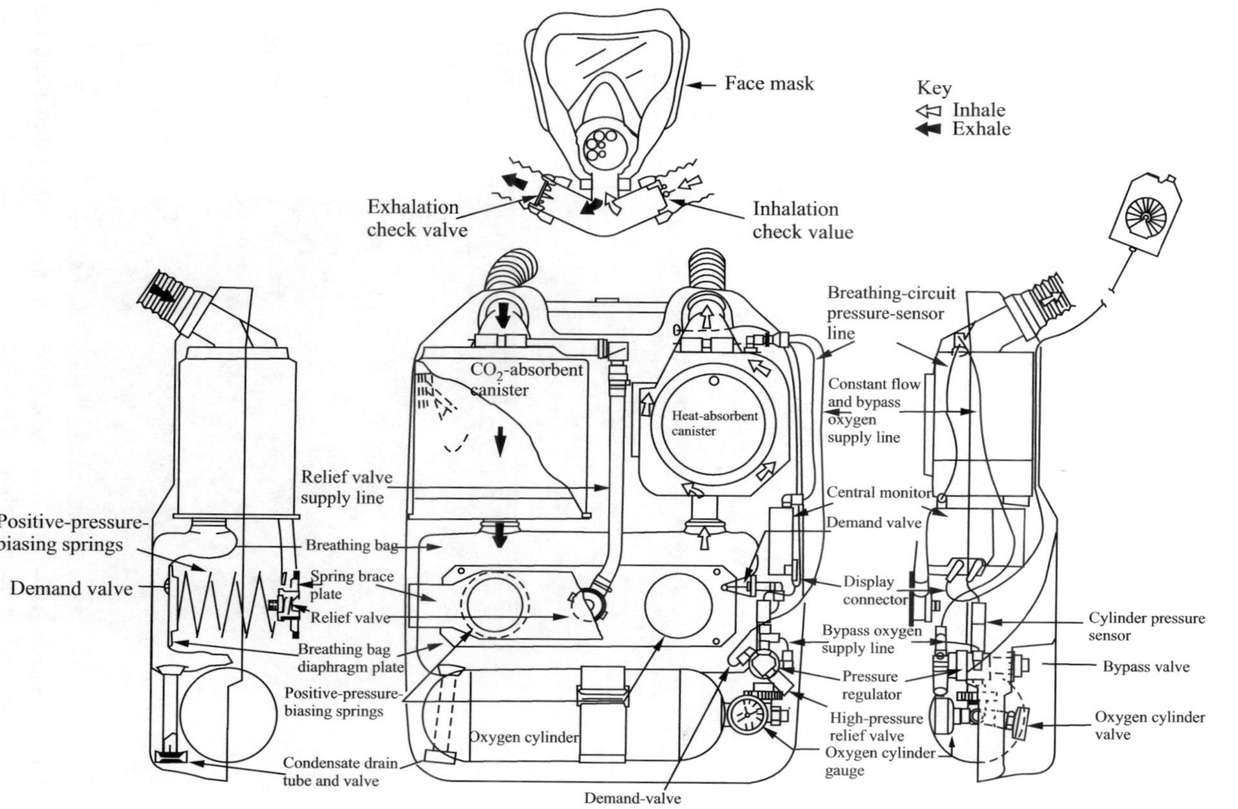

Figure 7.9 Schematic of Draeger BG-4 self -contained compressed-oxygen breathing apparatus

Specification:

Endurance	4 hours hard exertion at a working pressure of 200 bar
Cylinder volume, empty	2 litres
Breathing bag volume	5.5 litres
Oxygen flow rate	
constant dosage	1.5 to 1.8 litres per minute
lung-governed dosage	minimum 80 litres per minute
bypass valve dosage	minimum 50 litres per minute
Dimensions	
length	590 mm
width	450 mm
height	177 mm
Weight in use	13.5 kgf
Temperature	
operating	– 5° to + 30°C
storage	–30° to + 25°C

Reliable information on the status of the apparatus during use is provided by the Monitron which is an electronic pressure monitor with audible and visual alarms. The Monitron is automatically activated as soon as the cylinder valve is opened. It automatically performs a self-test and a battery check. By opening and closing the cylinder valve, the user can perform a high-pressure leak test

Figure 7.10 Draeger BG–4 Self-contained long-duration compressed-oxygen breathing apparatus when donned showing monitron.

in less than 15 seconds. When the pressure falls during operation, it flashes a red warning light. It sounds a residual pressure alarm for 30 seconds when the cylinder oxygen pressure is about 48 bar (700 psi) and again continuously when the pressure is 10 bar (145 psi).

Circulatory System

The exhaled air containing carbon dioxide and excess nitrogen flows through the exhalation valve, exhalation tube into the soda-lime absorption canister or scrubber where it is freed from carbon dioxide generating heat in the process. The air, thus purified, flows into the breathing bag and, on inhalation, flows through the heat-absorbent canister where it gets cooled as well as enriched with a constant feed of oxygen and then flows through the inhalation tube into the wearer's lungs. In the canister, the inhaled air is routed around a chamber containing a large cylinder of ice inserted just before use. Additional oxygen during peak demands of the breathing air is provided by an automatic demand valve. Any excess pressure build-up in the breathing circuit is released through the relief valve. The Monitron digital pressure gauge gives the user the pressure and provides residual pressure alarm.

7.2.1.2.5 Sabre SEFA Apparatus

SEFA, an acronym for Selected Elevation Flow Apparatus has been developed and designed by Sabre Safety Ltd., Aldershot, UK, in close cooperation with British Coal as a new generation of compressed-oxygen breathing apparatus for mine rescue work. It was approved by the UK Safety and Health Executive in 1985 and is being manufactured in the UK since 1986, and now being used in the UK, India, Australia, and Papua New Guinea. The apparatus developed for the Indian market by Vijay Sabre Safety Ltd. is a refinement of this apparatus with a lower mass and smaller size.

Specifications

Endurance:	
Low-flow mode	2 hours + 25 minutes reserve
High-flow mode	1 hour + 15 minutes reserve
Cylinder capacity at 207 bar	750 litres
Breathing bag diaphragm capacity	6 litres
Oxygen flow-rate: Constant dosage	5 litres per minute (low-flow mode) 10 litres per minute (high-flow mode)
Mass of apparatus, fully charged	16 kg

The salient features of the apparatus are:

(1) High- and low-oxygen flow-rates or dosages which can be set at 5 litres per minute for 2-hour duration and at 10 litres per minute for one-hour duration depending on the environmental temperature. The high flow-rates together

with the incorporated evaporative cooling system reduce the inspired air temperature under hard working conditions from the normal 45°–50°C to 39°C at 5 litres per minute flow-rate and to 35°C at 10 litres per minute flow-rate. It has no demand valve.

(2) Elimination of pre-start-up purging of the apparatus by incorporation of a spring-loaded breathing bag diaphragm contained in a gas-tight chamber. When the apparatus is not in use, the breathing bag is held deflated by the spring and, consequently, it is possible to introduce oxygen immediately into the breathing bag and thus to the wearer without any need for purging of the breathing circuit.

(3) The breathing bag diaphragm can be flushed with fresh oxygen by means of a bypass valve fitted on the pressure reducing valve.

(4) A heat exchanger unit containing copper wire windings, which is covered with a wet cloth. The heat exchanger functions in tandem with the ambient-air chamber containing the breathing bag. Ambient air is drawn over the hot wet surface of the cloth through a non-return valve in the exchanger casing by the bellows effect of the breathing bag producing a cooling effect through evaporation of water.

(5) The CO_2 absorbent canister contains 2 kg of soda lime, size 6 to 10 mesh, and is of split-bed design.

(6) Low breathing resistance compared with other self-contained oxygen breathing apparatus.

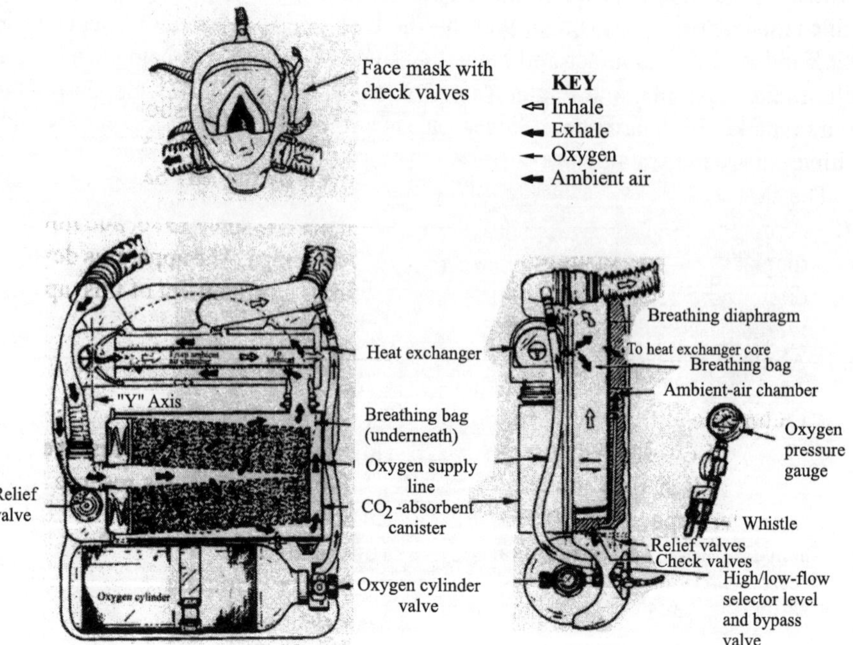

Figure 7.11 Sabre SEFA self-contained compressed-oxygen breathing apparatus schematic.

(7) Simplicity of construction and ease of maintenance.
(8) For high temperature work, the flow of oxygen can be doubled halving the working duration to one hour but cooling the set further.
(9) The apparatus is housed in a stainless steel casing.

Circulatory system
The exhaled air containing unused oxygen, CO_2, and moisture flows through the exhalation valve, corrugated exhalation tube into the purifying canister. The air thus purified but hot then passes through the heat exchanger, breathing bag diaphragm and inhalation valve into the inhalation tube where it gets enriched with fresh oxygen before it is drawn into the wearer's lungs. During inhalation, the breathing bag diaphragm collapses, pressure drops in the surrounding chamber and the non-return valve opens to fill the chamber with the ambient air. On exhalation, the breathing bag diaphragm fills, the pressure inside the chamber rises, the non-return valve closes, the non-return valve in the wetted heat exchanger case opens and the ambient air then passes through the heat exchanger case.

Figure 7.11 gives the schematic diagram of the SEFA apparatus.

7.2.1.2.6 *Biomarine BioPak 240 (Fig. 7.12)*
This is manufactured by Biomarine Inc., a wholly-owned subsidiary of Neutronics Inc., Exton, USA. It is a 4-hour, positive-pressure, ready-for-use long-duration self-contained compressed-oxygen breathing apparatus. In its design, some of the shortcomings of other long-duration apparatuses have been addressed. It is NIOSH/MSHA certified (1985). Besides mine rescue work, BioPak 240 is used in a wide variety of applications such as deep diving, fire-fighting, etc. It is used as a standard mine rescue apparatus in the USA, Canada, Mexico, New Zealand, China, Japan, Australia, and Pakistan.

The special features of the apparatus are:
1. A protected polypropylene breathing chamber with a spring-loaded breathing diaphragm. It supplies a constant flow of 1.7 litre /min oxygen with a safety demand flow of 80–100 litre/min for extreme work conditions. It is fitted with an excess-pressure relief valve.
2. A coolant canister made of spun fibre glass to cool the inspired air to a workable temperature after leaving the breathing chamber prior to being inhaled by the wearer. A replaceable cartridge filled with 'Blue ice' gel is inserted into the canister; the cartridge is kept frozen and inserted immediately prior to use in about 30 seconds. Blue ice gel is chosen by virtue of its superior cooling property compared to water-ice.
3. Carbon dioxide absorption canister with LimePak CO_2-absorbent which considerably reduces the pre-use cost compared with other SCBAs.
4. The facepiece of anti-oxidant silicone rubber has an anti-fog insert, a speaking diaphragm, and a CO_2 build-up prevention nose cup.
5. A high-pitched pressure whistle alarm which sounds for 30 to 60 seconds when 25% of the rated duration remains in the cylinder (approx. 60 min).

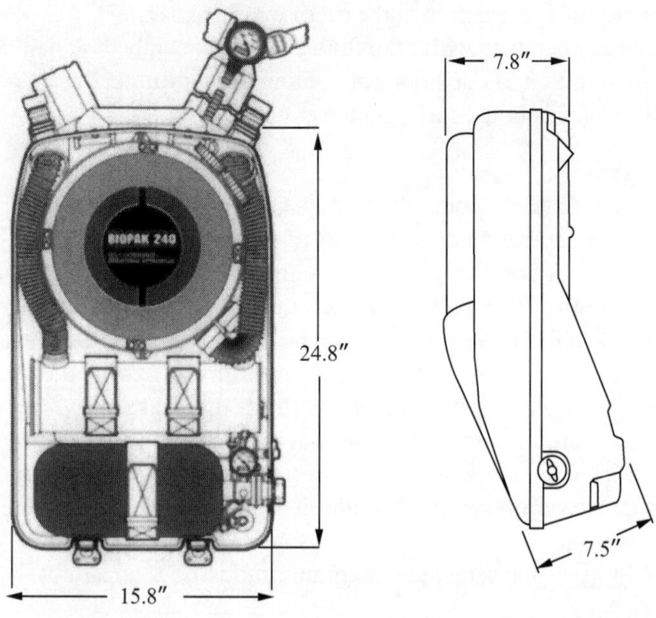

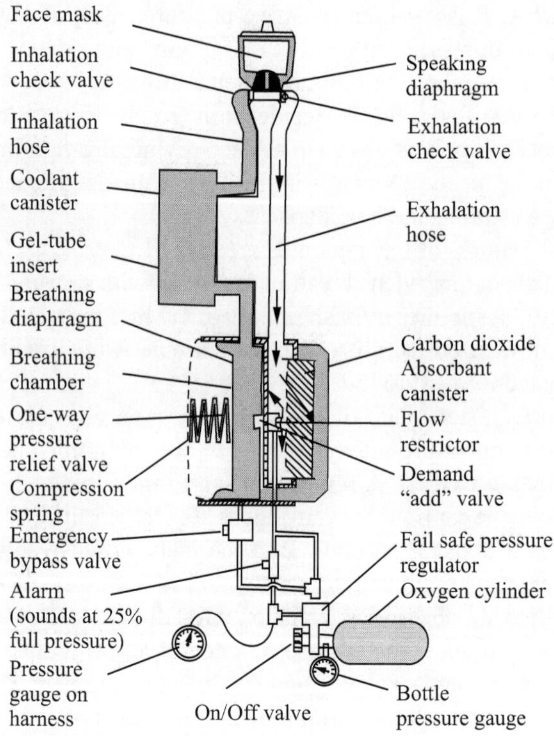

Figure 7.12 Biomarine BioPack 240 apparatus.

6. The weight of the apparatus is carried on the hip. Over-the-shoulder design of neoprene hoses with low breathing resistance reduces wearer fatigue.
7. The oxygen cylinder is fibre glass-wrapped aluminium cylinder.

Specifications:

Endurance	4 h
Cylinder capacity (empty)	2.76 litre
Cylinder capacity at charging pressure (210 bar)	596 litre
Constant oxygen flow rate	1.9 ± 0.3 litres per minute
Bypass/demand valve flow rate	80–100 litres per minute
Usage temperature	–9.4 to + 60°C
Weight	15.8 kgf

Circulatory system

The exhaled air flows through the exhalation tube, exhalation check valve into the carbon dioxide absorbent canister where it is freed from carbon dioxide. The air then flows into the breathing chamber where fresh oxygen is added within the exhalation side of the chamber before flowing into its inhalation side. The replenished air then passes through the cooling chamber prior to being inhaled by the wearer through the inhalation tube.

A spring-loaded diaphragm in the breathing chamber maintains a positive pressure in the system. During inhalation, the diaphragm moves towards the demand valve which is not activated during normal work (Fig. 7.13 a). The constant-flow restrictor permits a flow of 1.78 litre/min throughout the four hours of operation. However, when the breathing bag is fully depleted during periods of high demand, the diaphragm contacts the demand valve activator which opens the demand valve causing flow of additional oxygen into the breathing circuit at a rate of approximately 80 litre/min (Fig. 7.13(b)). During exhalation, the diaphragm moves away from the demand valve as the breathing chamber fills with clean scrubbed breathing air (Fig. 7.13(c)). If the wearer's exhalation causes the diaphragm to fully expand, the excess air is ventilated out of the relief valve. A push-button actuated bypass valve supplies oxygen direct to the breathing chamber in an emergency.

7.2.1.3 Self-contained liquid-oxygen breathing apparatus

In this type of apparatus, the oxygen required by the wearer is stored in a container in a liquid form and is supplied as the liquid vaporizes depending on the wearer's work level. The chief advantages of the apparatus over the compressed-oxygen type are:

(1) It provides cool dry oxygen to the wearer at a temperature below the ambient temperature for full duration of the apparatus;
(2) It removes heat from the wearer's body via respiratory tract;
(3) Breathing resistance with high flow-rate is low so that it is hardly noticeable even under heavy work conditions;

(4) It is free of high-pressure components and requires less maintenance;
(5) It is automatic in use;
(6) It is simple to maintain.

Aerorlox, the liquid oxygen breathing apparatus manufactured by Siebe Gorman, UK, was inducted in the British mining industry in the late 1960s as standard

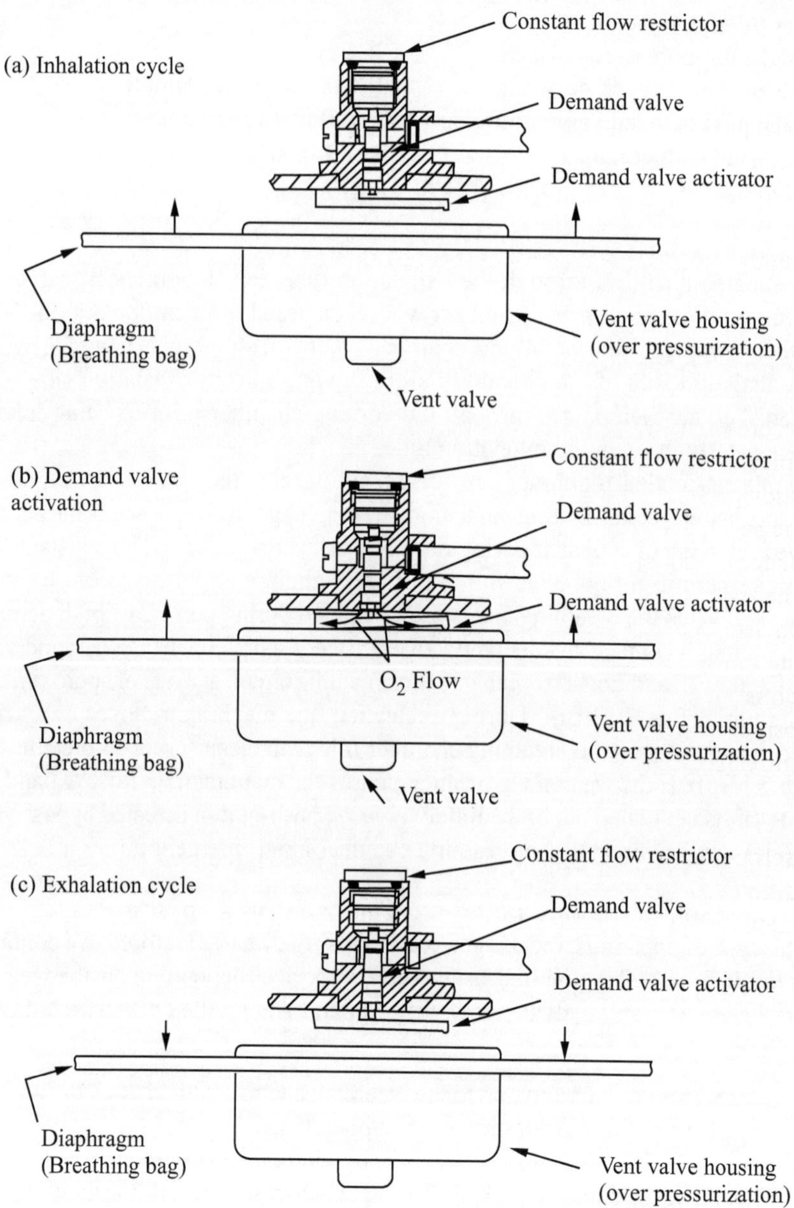

Figure 7.13 Operation of the demand valve of BioPak 240 apparatus.

breathing apparatus for mine rescue stations but it was superseded by SEFA apparatus in 1989 due probably to the dangers and difficulties associated with the handling of the liquid oxygen and lack of flexibility in its use.

7.2.1.4 Self-contained non-regenerative or reservoir apparatus

In this open-circuit-type of apparatus, the inhaled air is supplied from a pressure gas cylinder containing air or oxygen at 200 or 300 bar pressure and the exhaled air passes through an exhalation valve into the outside atmosphere. Such apparatus can be used where breathing emergencies are created by toxic atmospheres immediately dangerous to life or oxygen-deficient atmospheres such as occur in gas, chemical- and metallurgical- works and mines. In mines, they are particularly suitable for use as escape apparatus which may be taken inbye and fitted by trained rescue men to survivors who are found alive and conscious on the inbye side of an irrespirable atmosphere. The well-known apparatus are the MSA Air Mask and Draeger PA 54/1800 (single cylinder) and PA 34/1600 (twin cylinder) apparatus.

All these apparatus essentially consist of a full facepiece, a corrugated rubber breathing tube, a lung demand regulator assembly, air- or oxygen-supply cylinder, and harness. They operate on the demand principle. Pure breathing air from the air-supply flows to the facepiece automatically through the demand regulator in accordance with the wearer's requirements. On exhalation, the flow to the facepiece stops, starting again on the next inhalation. The apparatus have a rated duration of 30 minutes. Draeger apparatus belonging to PA 80 system is based on the positive pressure system with a piston pressure reducer and a lung demand regulator.

The apparatus are also designed as pressure-demand type to provide breathing air on demand, maintaining a positive comfortable pressure within the facepiece during inhalation above that of the outside atmosphere. This positive pressure which is maintained by the facepiece exhalation valve prevents external toxic atmospheres from entering the facepiece if a leak should occur providing an extra margin of safety for users.

7.2.1.5 Tests of self-contained breathing apparatus in use

All self-contained breathing apparatus should be maintained in a safe working condition for use at all times. This is achieved in practice by subjecting the apparatus to the following tests:

(a) An approved full test programme carried out on each component of the apparatus between periods of actual use for air-tightness or air leakage and operation; and
(b) Tests for air-tightness of assembled apparatus before it is worn (wearer's examination and wearer's tests).

The full test programme for self-contained compressed-oxygen breathing apparatus usually comprises:

(1) Leak tests at positive and negative pressures;

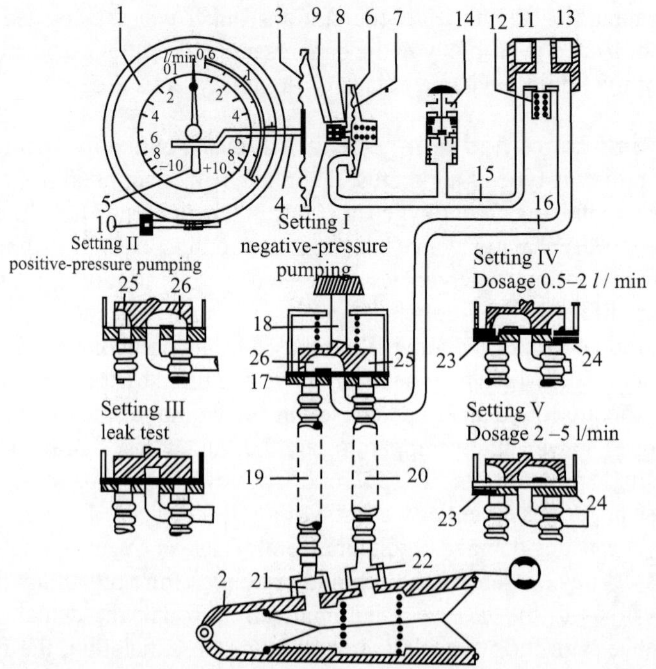

Figure 7.14 Draeger Portable Universal Tester Model Rz 25.
1: Indicator dial; 2: air bellows; 3: diaphragm; 4: transmission rack; 5: pointer; 6: safety protection; 7: diaphragm; 8: valve; 9: cotter pin; 10: zero adjustment; 11: apparatus connector; 12: pressure relief valve; 13: hose socket; 14: air vent valve; 15: connecting line; 16: collecting line; 17: rotary valve casing; 18: multi-channel rotary slide valve; 19: suction line; 20: pressure line; 21: negative pressure control valve; 22: positive pressure control valve; 23: measuring nozzle 0.5-2 litre/mm; 24: measuring nozzle 2-5 litre/min; 25: bore in rotary slide valve; 26: bore in rotary slide valve.

(2) Pre-flush test when a pre-flushing device is provided;
(3) Exhalation valve test;
(4) Inhalation valve test;
(5) Relief valve test for setting pressure;
(6) Pressure gauge equalization test;
(7) Lung demand valve test for response pressure and response volume;
(8) Constant dosage test;
(9) Breathing bag volume test;
(10) Bypass test;
(11) Whistle activation and duration tests; and
(12) High-pressure leak test.

The test programme for self-contained compressed-air breathing apparatus comprises:

(1) Leak tests at positive and negative pressures;

(2) Lung demand valve test for response pressure; and
(3) Exhalation valve test.

The test programme of self-contained chemical oxygen apparatus includes the following:
(1) O_2-content in the inspired air;
(2) Temperature of the inspired air;
(3) Inhalation resistance;
(4) Exhalation resistance; and
(5) CO_2-content of the exhaled air.

All the above tests are conducted as per the approved standards in force.

There are in the market standard portable testing sets manufactured by the Draegerwerk, Auergesellschaft, and others for carrying out prescribed tests on self-contained oxygen- and air-breathing-apparatus, self-rescuers, and facepieces. Figure 7.14 shows the diagrammatic arrangement of the Draeger Portable Universal Trester Model Rz 25.

7.2.1.6 Performance comparison of long-duration self-contained closed-circuit rescue breathing apparatus

A performance comparison of 14 long- and short-duration self-contained closed-circuit breathing apparatus of the US, German, and British manufacture, some of which are in current use in those and other countries, was carried out by the Pittsburg Research Laboratory of the National Institute for Occupational Safety and Health [87]. The long-duration apparatus tested were the Biomarine BioPak 240, Draeger BG 174A, Draeger BG 4, Sabre SEFA, and Scott Rescue-Pak. The tests were conducted on an automatic breathing and metabolic simulator (BMS). The metabolic demand on the apparatus was 1.35 litre O_2/min. for most of the test with two 5-min intervals of 2.5 litre O_2/min, the first beginning 10 min. into the test and the second beginning 10 min. before the end of the rated duration of the apparatus. The physiological parameters measured were the average inhaled concentrations of CO and O_2, the minimum inhaled CO_2, the end-of-breath inhaled wet- and dry- bulb temperatures, and the inhalation and exhalation peak breathing pressures. Test averages were derived from the minute-averages including the two high work-rate periods specified. At least 5 tests were run on each apparatus.

The levels of the physiological parameters considered to be acceptable were:

Average inhaled CO_2	<	4%
Average inhaled O_2	>	15%
Wet-bulb temperature	<	50°C
Exhalation pressure	<	200 mm WG
Inhalation pressure	>	300 mm WG

Comparison of performance test results showed that:

1. The Draeger BG 174A and the BG 4 have the highest durations.

2. The BG 4 has the highest level of positive pressure and the lowest pressure swing (exhalation and inhalation pressures combined) with Sabre SEFA coming a close second.
3. The BG 174A has the lowest exhalation pressures. The Sabre SEFA has the lowest exhalation peak pressures.
4. The BG 4 has the lowest minimum inhaled CO_2 levels attesting to the effectiveness of CO_2 absorbent canister. The Sabre SEFA has the lowest average inhaled CO_2 levels due mostly to the low dead space in the mask and the nose cup.

7.2.1.7 Self-contained closed-circuit oxygen self-rescuers (SCSRs)

Like filter self-rescuers, these are short-duration emergency gas respirators which provide protection against toxic and noxious gases in mine atmospheres and enable the wearer to escape from the danger zone to a place of safety but, unlike in filter self-rescuers, the exhaled air is regenerated and enriched with oxygen for re-breathing so that the wearer is independent of the surrounding atmosphere. They should not be used for entering hazardous atmospheres or for fire-fighting.

The first generation oxygen self-rescuers in 1981, which were bigger and two to four times heavier than the filter self-rescuers, underwent design developments, and the second generation oxygen self-rescuers appeared in early 1990s, which are smaller, lighter and person-wearable on the miner's belt.

Depending on the oxygen source, there are two types of oxygen self-rescuers: chemical-oxygen and compressed-oxygen self-rescuers.

In the chemical-oxygen self-rescuers, a chemical bed is used which, upon contact with the moisture in the exhaled air, evolves a plentiful supply of pure oxygen for meeting the breathing requirements, and, by subsequent reaction, absorbs the exhaled carbon dioxide. The chemical employed is potassium tetroxide (K_2O_4) which liberates oxygen and absorbs carbon dioxide according to the equations:

$$2K_2O_4 + 2CO_2 \rightarrow 2K_2CO_3 + 3O_2$$

$$2K_2O_4 + 2H_2O \rightarrow 4KOH + 3O_2$$

$$2KOH + CO_2 \rightarrow K_2CO_3 + H_2O$$

The rate of liberation of oxygen is governed by the rate of breathing by the wearer under various exertion levels, the degree of training, and the condition of the apparatus. Once the chemical reaction has started, oxygen is liberated faster than it is consumed until the depletion of KO_2 and, in consequence, a pressure is built up in the circulatory system of the apparatus unless the excess oxygen is released by means of a relief valve. The apparatus, when worn, has, therefore, a slight positive pressure in all parts of its circulatory system. All chemical oxygen self-rescuers place some limitations on their use due to increasing breathing resistance and an increase in the temperature of the inhaled air. For this reason it is advisable to limit the level of physical exertion, if possible, when wearing them.

The compressed-oxygen self-rescuers use for the oxygen source an oxygen cylinder or bottle storing oxygen under high pressure with a separate absorbent bed for the removal of CO_2.

All oxygen self-rescuers are normally rated for one hour of service during extreme physical exertion and can provide an emergency oxygen-supply for over 5 to 6 hours if the wearer is at rest waiting for rescue. In Europe, the European Standards demands all new models to be rated for 90 minutes at 35 litres per minute.

All oxygen self-rescuer designs have many parts in common such as the mouthpiece with a nose-clip or full facepiece, breathing hose, CO_2 absorbent bed, breathing bag, heat exchanger and a relief valve. The compressed-oxygen self- rescuers use some additional components not necessary with the chemical-oxygen self-rescuers such as a high-pressure oxygen cylinder, a reducing valve, a constant-dosage valve, and in most cases a demand valve. There are many variations in the size, shape, and placement of the various components.

Well-known examples of chemical-oxygen self-rescuers are the AUER SSR 90 (K 60), MSA Portal-Pack, Draeger Oxyboks K and Oxy K-plus, and CSE SR-100 which have a rated duration of use of 60 min. and approved for use in mines.

7.2.1.7.1 Auer chemical-oxygen self-rescuer SSR 90 (K 60) (Fig. 7.15)

The Auer SSR 90 (K 60) has German mining approval for escape times of maximum 60 minutes. The apparatus is worn on the chest.

The oxygen needed for breathing is produced by KO_2 contained in a replaceable canister. The self-rescuer is rated for 60 minutes when performing medium heavy work but the life-supporting emergency supply will continue for 5 hours when the wearer is at rest. It has a unidirectional flow path through the chemical bed, a volume-activated relief valve, and a 'quick starter' chlorate candle for initial oxygen flow. The breathing bag assembly includes a breathing bag of 6-litre capacity, a breathing tube, and a valve housing incorporating a particulate filter, inhalation and exhalation valves, a heat exchanger, and a relief valve. The heat exchanger maintains the temperature of the inhalation air below 50°C. The oxygen produced by the chemical is inhaled through the breathing bag, filter and heat exchanger.

The technical specifications of the SSR 90 are:

Dimensions (with container):

Height	310 mm
Width	220 mm
Depth	120 mm

Weight:

With container	4.9 kgf
in use	3.4 kgf

Service time:

At a minute volume of

35 litre/min	approx.	70 min

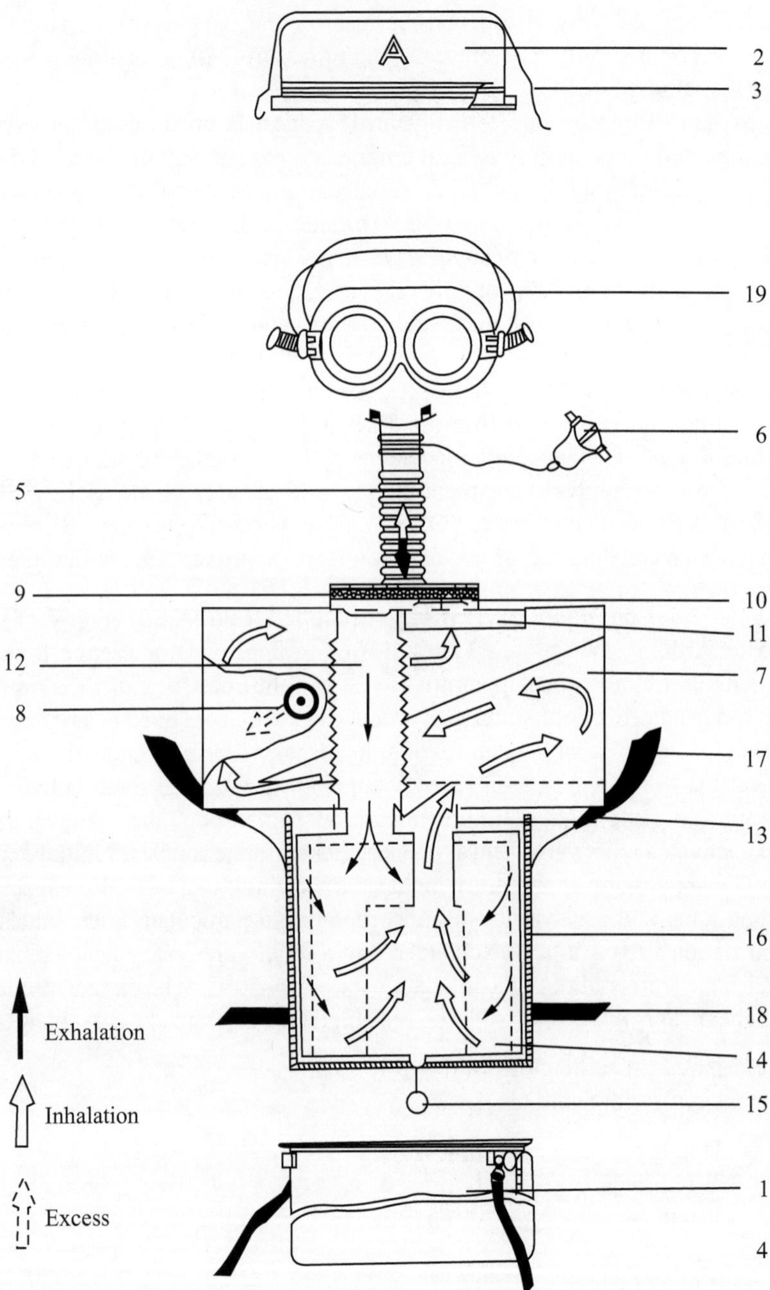

Figure 7.15 Auer chemical-oxygen self-rescuer SSR 90 (K 60).
1: container bottom, 2: cover with gasket, 3: locking assembly 4: carrying strap, 5: breathing tube with mouthpiece, 6: noseclip, 7: breathing bag, 8: pressure relief valve, 9: valve housing, 10: heat exchanger, 11: air filter, 12: corrugated tube, 13: connection canister/breathing bag, 14: chemical canister, 15: quick starter, 16 canister cover, 17neck strap, 18–waist belt, 19–gas protective goggle.

30 litre/min	approx.	90 min
10 litre/min	approx.	300 min

Oxygen content of inhalation air ≥ 21 per cent,
Shelf life of absorbent canister-5 years, if properly stored.

The self-rescuer is housed air-tight in a robust stainless steel case for protection against rough handling.

A further design development of this self-rescuer is the model SSR 30/100 which is 170 mm high and 180 mm wide and weighing just 2 kg with a service life of 30 minutes at an air consumption rate of 30 litres per minute. The container is small and light enough to be carried on the belt.

7.2.1.7.2 CSE SR-100 chemical-oxygen self-rescuer (Fig. 7.16)

The self-contained chemical oxygen self-rescuer is manufactured by the CSE Corporation, Monroeville, USA, where it is jointly approved by the National Institute for Occupational Safety and Health (NIOSH) and the Mine Safety and Health Administration (MSHA). It was developed in 1991 with a rated duration of one hour. The exhaled air passes through a CO_2-absorption cum-O_2 generator canister before the enriched air returns to the wearer. The starting oxygen (7–9 litres) is provided from a small compressed-oxygen steel cylinder which eliminates the uncertainty of initiating oxygen flow. Except for the starter oxygen, the rest of the oxygen is provided chemically. The starter oxygen may not completely fill the bag. Only when the bag is full with air, is the self-rescuer ready for use by the wearer. The bag may not stay full depending on the level of exertion but as long as some air is in the bag, the unit will function properly.

The SR- 100 can supply 3 litres/min on demand. If waiting for rescue, it can provide oxygen for 4–6 hours.
Its technical specifications are:

Height	197 mm
Width	140 mm
Depth	102 mm
Weight	2.6 kg
In use	2.2 kg
Service life	10 years

It is housed in a stainless steel container and, because of its small size, light weight, and rugged construction, it is belt-wearable; it can also be carried on the chest.

The CO_2-absorption-cum-O_2 generating canister utilizes a hybrid bed of KO_2–LiOH to match O_2 produced to CO_2 absorbed. On exhalation, the expired air passes through the canister directly into the breathing bag where it is mixed with freshly generated oxygen. A relief valve actuated by the breathing bag through a wire automatically vents the excess pressure in the breathing bag.

Readiness of the SR-100 for use is indicated at any time by the moisture indicators in the top and bottom covers. They will be blue as long as moisture

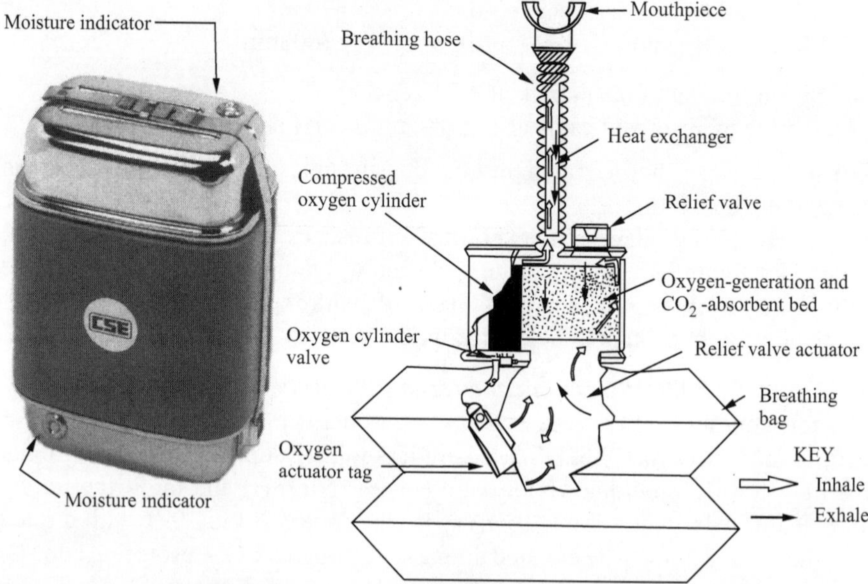

Figure 7.16 Schematic of CSE SR-100 chemical oxygen self-rescuer.

has not entered due to broken or damaged seals. Should the moisture enter the self-rescuer, the blue colour of either indicator changes to pink or white when it should be removed from service. It should not be stored in temperatures greater than 130°F or less than 32°F.

7.2.1.7.3 Draeger Oxy K-Plus chemical-oxygen self-rescuer (Fig. 7.17)

As with other chemical-oxygen self-rescuers, the oxygen needed is produced by a chemical bed of potassium peroxide (KO_2) which reacts with the carbon dioxide and water vapour in the exhaled air absorbing carbon dioxide and liberating chemical oxygen depending on the breathing intensity. The apparatus consists of a mouthpiece with a noseclip, a 6-litre breathing bag with a volume activated relief valve, a starter sodium chlorate candle or cartridge to provide start-up oxygen independent of the wearer's breathing, a metal-mesh heat exchanger contained in a hard plastic housing to which the mouthpiece is attached, and a head harness. Like the SR-100, the relief valve purges breathing circuit gas from the breathing hose before it has entered the chemical bed.

The self-rescuer is rated for 60 min. It is of light-weight design and can be constantly carried in its case on the wearer's belt which allows the wearer to put on or remove the unit without taking off the belt. The carrying case is provided with a colour display which provides a continuous indication of the readiness of the apparatus for use.

The apparatus has NIOSH/MSHA approval for use in the American mines as an escape apparatus.

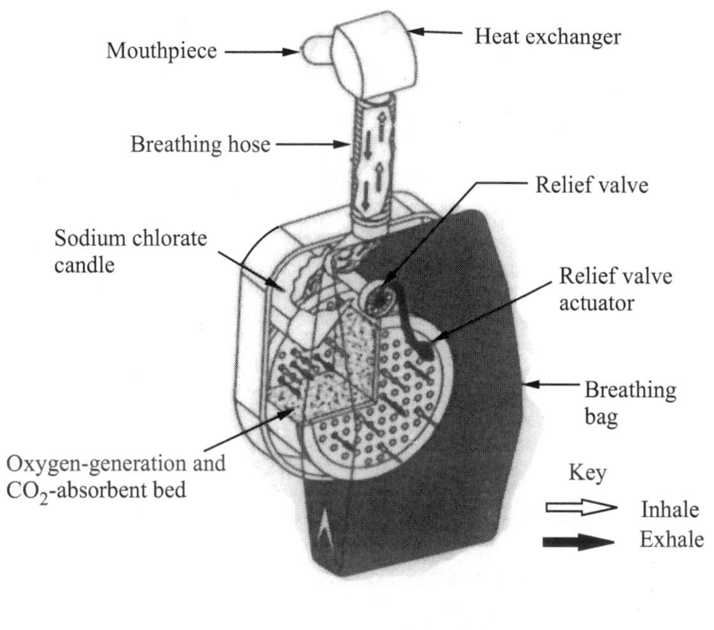

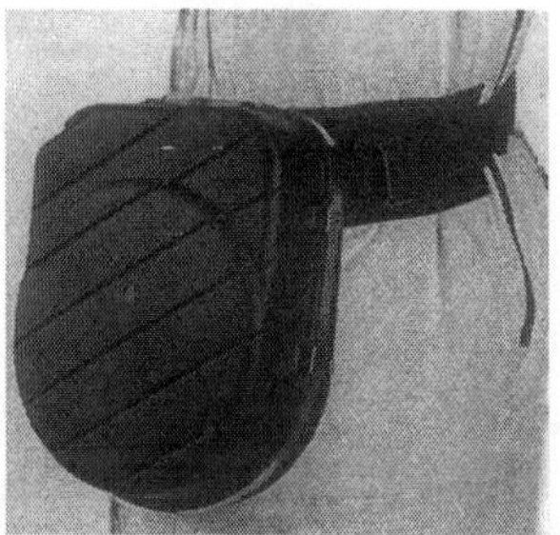

Figure 7.17 Schematic of Draeger oxy K-plus chemical oxygen self-rescuer.

Specifications:

Height	257 mm	
Width	200 mm	
Depth	105 mm	
Weight in case	approx. 2.8 kgf	
Weight in use	approx.2.4 kgf	
Service life		
at minute volume of		
30 litres per minute	approx.	60 min.
10 litres per minute	approx.	180 min.
90 litres per minute	approx	15 min.

Inhalation/exhalation resistance at minute volume of

30 litres per minute	4 mbar
	end of usage period max. 6 mbar

CO_2-content of inhaled air at minute volume of
30 litres per minute less than 1.5%
end of usage period max. 2.5%
Temperature of inhaled air at the end of usage period max. 6 mbar
Minimum usage temperature –5°C
Storage temperature –20°C to +50°C
+70°C for max. 24 hours

7.2.1.7.4 MSA Life-Saver 60 chemical-oxygen self-rescuer (Fig. 7.18)

The MSA Life-Saver 60 is a single-use self-contained close-circuit chemical oxygen self-rescuer, NIOSH/MSHA approved, and rated for 60 min. of use under moderate to heavy workload conditions. It can be belt-worn or stored in a cache for emergency evacuation use in toxic or oxygen-deficient atmospheres.

As with other chemical-oxygen self-rescuers, the initial supply of oxygen (approx. 9 to 10 litres) is generated by a chlorate candle which is automatically activated when the apparatus is donned taking about 45 to 90 seconds to fill the circulating system including the breathing bag when it is extended. The self-rescuer consists of a stainless steel housing enclosed in high impact- and heat-resistant urethane. It contains the primary KO_2 bed and the chlorate candle which is the first and immediate source of oxygen. It has a removable end cap on the top of which is a moisture indicator which indicates readiness for use. In the normal air-tight mode, the indicator shows both pink and blue, but, when contaminated, a solid pink thereby eliminating confusion in times of emergency.

The breathing bag is abrasion-resistant with noseclip, mouthpiece, and relief valve all located on it.

Specifications:

Dimensions-
Height 142 mm
Width 196 mm

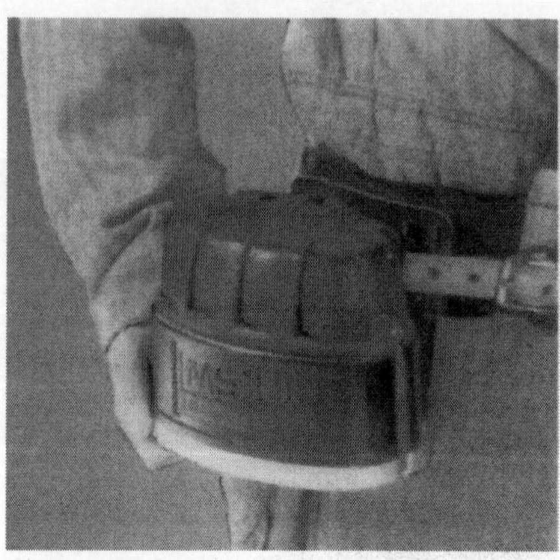

Figure 7.18 MSA Life-Saver 60.

Depth 122 mm
Weight in case 2.27 kgf
Weight in use 2.18 kgf

Breathing bag volume minimum 8.5 litres per minute
Operating temperature range – 2.8°C + 49°C
Storage temperature:
Normal range – 2.8°C + 49°C
Short term (24 h) – 40°C + 54.4°C

Service life:
* 60 min. or more during moderate to heavy use
* 4 to 5 hours under rest or light use
* less than 60 min. under extremely heavy use

Maximum total life from date of manufacture 10 years
Inhalation resistance at minute volume of 40 litres/min. less than 48 mm WG
CO_2 concentration less than 1.5%
O_2 concentration greater than 21%
Temperature of inhaled air at mouthpiece less than 46°C

The apparatus is ergonomically designed to ensure total personal safety with maximum comfort to the wearer.

7.2.1.7.5 Ocenco EBA 6.5 compressed-oxygen self-rescuer (Fig. 7.19)

The Ocenco EBA 6.5 compressed-oxygen self-rescuer manufactured by Ocenco Inc., U.S.A., has been approved by NIOSH/MSHA as a one-hour self-contained compressed-oxygen self-rescuer which will provide the wearer with over 60 minutes of life-saving oxygen during escape under arduous working conditions. It is not designed or approved for use in fire-fighting or underwater rescue. It consists of a light-weight compressed-oxygen fibre glass-wrapped aluminium cylinder, a pressure-reducing valve, a pressure-activated demand regulator and relief valve, a breathing bag constructed of durable urethane-coated nylon, a carbon dioxide scrubber with a lithium hydroxide (LiOH) bed, breathing tubes, and a mouthpiece assembly with directional check valves. It is housed in a rugged transparent polycarbonate case which enables the wearer to inspect the unit easily and quickly and is designed to be hand-carried, shoulder or back-worn, or stored underground.

The circulatory system consists of a compressed-oxygen supply circuit and a closed breathing circuit. When donned, the breathing bag must first be purged of nitrogen by exhaling, holding breath, deflating the bag by pressing on it, deeply inhaling through the mouthpiece, and then breathing normally.

Specifications:

Dimensions
Height 302 mm

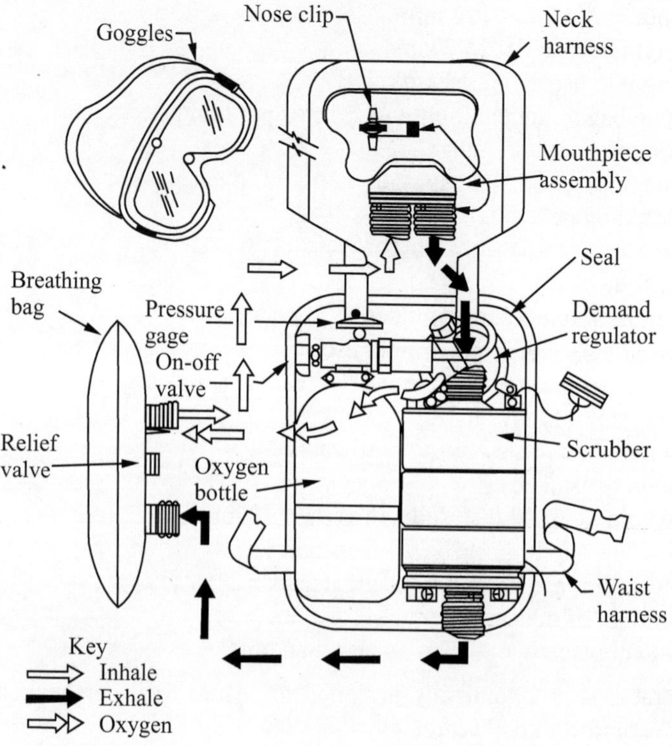

Figure 7.19 Schematic of Ocenco EBA 6.5 compressed-oxygen self-rescuer.

Width	218 mm
Depth	117 mm
Weight in use	2.9 kgf
Cylinder capacity at 200 bar	157 litres
Breathing bag volume	5 litres
Oxygen flow rate:	
constant dosage	1.6 litres per minute
demand flow	minimum 30 litres per minute
Operating temperature	minimum – 12.2°C
Storage temperature range	– 12.2°C + 60°C

Service life:

60 min or more during moderate to heavy use

up to 8 hours under rest

Storage life:

3 years between manufacture inspections if carried

5 years if stored in a cache

Inhalation resistance at minute volume of 30 litres per minute 38 mm WG

Exhalation resistance at minute volume of 30 litres per minute 51 mm WG

Temperature of inhaled air 41°C

Circulatory system

The exhaled air flows through the mouthpiece and the exhalation tube to the CO_2 scrubber which contains lithium hydroxide bed to remove CO_2 from the exhaled air which then enters the breathing bag through a tube connected to the bottom of the scrubber. In the breathing bag, the purified exhaled air is enriched with fresh oxygen supplied from the oxygen cylinder through the pressure-reducing valve and the demand regulator which provides a constant flow of 1.6 litre/min and a pressure-activated demand flow of minimum 30 litre/min. On inhalation, the oxygen-air mixture flows through the inhalation tube into the wearer's lungs. A relief valve located in the centre of the breathing bag releases any excess pressure in order to maintain the exhalation pressure of the breathing circuit within safe limits.

7.2.1.7.6 Use and maintenance of oxygen self-rescuers

The oxygen self-rescuers are carried into the mine each shift by the miners, placed on whatever equipment the miner is operating or hung on pegs near the face, and taken out at the end of the shift. They may also be stored in a readily accessible location in a section not farther than the miners can walk (crawl) in 5 minutes from their workplace under normal circumstances.

Service life might be reduced if the oxygen self-rescuers are exposed to conditions such as excessive heat, cold, water, and vibrations.

Inspection, maintenance and testing procedures are prescribed by the manufacturers and approval sanctioning authorities and every mine should provide for proper inspection, testing, maintenance and repair by trained persons.

7.2.2 Filtered air respirators, air-purifying respirators, or filter masks

These apparatuses are of the open-circuit type and afford respiratory protection for limited periods against carbon monoxide in atmospheres containing not more than 2 per cent carbon monoxide and not less than 16 per cent oxygen needed to sustain life.

There are two main types of air filter masks that are used in mines:

(1) Chemical respirators or filter masks; and
(2) Particulate respirators or mechanical filter respirators.

The chemical respirators can be further divided into:

(1) Canister-type filter masks, gas masks, or gas respirators; and
(2) Self-rescue respirators or filter self-rescuers.

7.2.2.1 Gas masks

These have been adopted widely for mine use. Gas-mask crews carrying a lighted flame safety lamp and carbon monoxide detector have successfully fought mine fires and engaged in rescue and recovery operations following mine disasters, with self-contained breathing apparatus crews in reserve for their protection. The gas masks may be a single-canister or double-canister type. The double-canister type is particularly suitable for arduous and prolonged work. As the gas masks do not defend against oxygen deficiency, one should be careful in using them during fire-fighting operations and their use normally must be discouraged.

7.2.2.1.1 Common features of gas masks

The following are the common features of gas masks which differ only in matters of details of construction but are based on the same basic principles.

A replaceable 'all-service'-type canister of oval cross-section containing mechanical and chemical filters deposed one above the other that remove toxic dusts, fumes, mists and smoke, absorb acid gases and organic vapours, and convert carbon monoxide to carbon dioxide. The canister has openings at the top and at the bottom so that, when the wearer inhales, the external air surrounding him enters the bottom opening, passes upward through the filters arranged in layers, and leaves the canister through the top opening. The elimination of irrespirable or toxic constituents of the air is effected by processes of chemical absorption, physical absorption, catalytic oxidation, and mechanical filtration. The absorbents used for the removal of gases and vapours are in the form of granules.

The various types of filtering layers commonly used in gas-mask canisters are:

(i) Cellulose particulate filter for removing dusts, fumes, mists and smoke;
(ii) Impregnated activated charcoal and caustite for absorbing organic vapours and acid gases;
(iii) Activated charcoal and baryta-charcoal for the removal of acid gases;
(iv) Silica gel or charcoal impregnated with sulphuric acid for the removal of ammonia;
(v) Charcoal impregnated with zinc chloride for removal of the bulk of water vapour; and
(vi) Anhydrous calcium chloride or calcium chloride–zinc chloride for removal of final traces of moisture.

The catalytic oxidation of carbon monoxide at ordinary temperatures to the relatively harmless carbon dioxide is effected by 'hopcalite', an activated granular mixture of manganese peroxide and copper oxide which was developed at the John Hopkins University, USA, in 1919. Hopcalite should be specially prepared so that the granules have immediate 'pick-up' (ability to function as soon as the first traces of carbon monoxide come into contact with them), be hard, and show no tendency to powder. The catalytic granules which are hygroscopic and have a strong tendency to hydration, function indefinitely as long as they are not poisoned by water vapour and the inspired air must, therefore, be effectively dried before coming into contact with them.

The nominal service life of the canister is given by the manufacturers as so many hours of total use, either continuously or intermittently. However, the specified period may be reduced considerably if the canister is used under conditions of high temperature, high humidity, and high carbon monoxide concentration. Canisters should be discarded within one year after the seal is broken. Sealed canisters have a safe 'shelf life' of at least five years and carry a date of four years from the date of manufacture to provide a margin of safety.

A check valve (inhalation valve) provided either at the top opening in the canister (internal check valve) or in a special coupling (external check valve) which connects the canister with a breathing tube, to pass air through the canister in one direction only, thus preventing the exhaled air from entering the canister. It also provides an effective seal against entry of any moisture into the top of the canister during use or storage. It closes automatically after inhalation.

A facepiece assembly to permit the wearer to breathe through his nose or mouth. It consists of a moulded rubber facepiece (full mask) which readily fits any face with minimum dead space, an exhalation valve, a corrugated breathing tube, and a head harness. The facepiece is usually of the wide-vision type with one or two non-fogging large-area lenses. The exhalation valve allows the wearer to exhale to the outside atmosphere. The breathing tube connects the facepiece to the canister. The head harness is made either of rubber bands or terylene elastic straps.

A warning device or built-in indicator to give a positive indication to the wearer when the canister is no longer effective against carbon monoxide.

A canister harness to support and hold the canister securely against the body. The canister may be worn on the front, on the side, or on the back of the wearer. The back-carrying arrangement has the advantage that, when the wearer bends over the source of noxious gas, the canister is not exposed to an unnecessarily high concentration of gas and its life is extended.

M.S.A. all-service gas mask and Draeger gas mask are two well-known examples of gas masks available in the market. Figure 7.20 shows the section of the Draeger canister. The canister incorporates a breathing resistance-warning device which causes resistance to breathing to increase considerably when the normal carbon monoxide protection has begun to reduce. The increase in resistance does not take place suddenly so the wearer has sufficient time to withdraw. The resistance of an unused canister to the passage of inspired air through it is about 18 mm WG (1.8 mbar).

7.2.2.1.2 Limitations and use of gas masks

Although the catalytic oxidation of carbon monoxide can still take place in extremely high carbon monoxide and low oxygen concentrations, there are other reasons that render the filtered air irrespirable. Firstly, the oxidation of carbon monoxide causes destruction of half the volume of oxygen in the inspired air, and as the catalytic granules do not supply any of the oxygen used up, the gas mask does not protect the wearer in atmospheres that do not contain sufficient oxygen to sustain life. Secondly, the heat developed in the catalytic layer would be so great that injury to the canister is likely to occur. Hence, the gas masks should only be used in atmospheres containing not more than 3 per cent volume of carbon

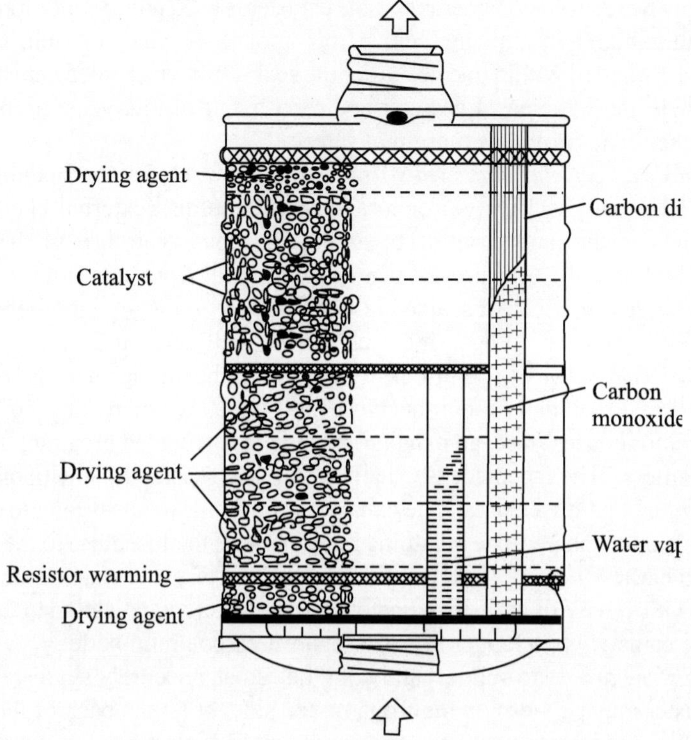

Figure7.20 Section of Draeger gas mask canister 112

monoxide and not less than 16 per cent by volume of oxygen.

The following precautions should be observed when using gas masks in mines:

(1) Only trained men should be allowed to wear the gas mask for entering hazardous atmospheres.
(2) Gas-mask crews should always carry a lighted flame safety lamp or an oxygen meter and a carbon monoxide detector with a measuring range. If it is indicated that the oxygen concentration is less than 16 per cent or carbon monoxide is 2 per cent or more, the crew should immediately return to the fresh-air base.
(3) A man wearing a gas mask should never be allowed to enter a hazardous atmosphere alone without at least one or other man accompanying him.
(4) A crew equipped with a self-contained breathing apparatus should be kept in reserve at the fresh-air base when gas-mask crews advance.
(5) The canister should be changed when its service life has ended or when the wearer notices any gaseous contaminant in the facepiece by odour, taste, breathing resistance or other irritation whichever occurs first.

7.2.2.2 Filter self-rescuers (FSRs)

Filter self-rescuers are emergency gas respirators which provide instant respiratory protection against carbon monoxide gas such as occurs in mines after fires or explosions and thus enable the wearer to escape to a place of safety. They do not generate oxygen.

A filter self-rescuer is small, compact, and light in weight (maximum 100 g and, unlike an oxygen self-rescuer, it is a one-time-use respirator for escape purposes only. It uses the catalyst hopcalite to convert the toxic carbon monoxide to non-toxic carbon dioxide. It is carried by every miner on his body and may be taken off only at the workplace. It does not offer protection in atmospheres containing less than 16 per cent oxygen.

All filter-rescuers are designed on the same principle but differ only in matters of constructional details. A filter self-rescuer consists of a sealed filter canister or cartridge which is drawn over by a flannel filter bag which acts as a coarse dust filter, an exhalation valve, a mouthpiece and chin rest, a nose-clip, head straps, and a carrying case with carrying straps and seal. The canister contains a layer of a highly efficient drying agent to protect the layer of the hopcalite catalyst from moisture. An inner fine-dust filter removes dust particles.

Filter self-rescuers were introduced in the coal mines of Germany in the early 1950s. They are being increasingly replaced by oxygen self-rescuers. They are still required in Germany and in the UK although they are not used in mines subject to gas outbursts. In India, the use of self-rescuers became mandatory in gassy mines of the third degree with effect from 1985.

7.2.2.2.1 Acceptance specifications for filter self-rescuers

All filter self-rescuers must be designed to comply with the specifications laid down in respect of duration of protection, performance characteristics, and construction. They are approved for a minimum duration of one hour. The actual duration may be longer or shorter depending upon CO concentration and other environmental conditions. Their safety and performance have steadily improved over the past four decades and the acceptance specifications today are most stringent. The key element in the approval testing is the mechanical-lung machine. The European Standards, EN 404 Class 4 BR, have laid down design and performance guidelines for filter self-rescuers.

The principal German current acceptance specifications are given below:

Breathing resistance (inhalation resistance)

The initial breathing resistance when tested at a constant air flow-rate of 94 litres per minute shall not exceed 65 mm WG (6.5 mbar). When using a test air containing 0.25 per cent CO by volume, the breathing resistance after 60 test minutes shall not exceed 80 mm WG (8 mbar).

Carbon monoxide slip

Using the lung machine set at 20 strokes per minute, 1.5 litres per stroke, and a test air containing 1.5 per cent CO and 20.7 g water per m^3, the CO-content in the inspired air after 60 test minutes shall not exceed 0.001 per cent and the maximum carbon monoxide slip shall not be greater than 100 ml.

Temperature of the inspired air

Using a test air containing 1.5 per cent CO at body temperature saturated at 37°C saturated, the temperature of the filtered inspired air shall not exceed 65°C.

Exhalation resistance

The exhalation resistance shall not exceed 25 mm WG (2.5 mbar) with a constant air flow-rate of 94 litres per minute.

Duration of protection

Under the test conditions described above, the duration of protection shall be at least 60 minutes with a flow rate of 30 litres per minute.

Mass

The mass of a complete rescuer (without carrying straps) shall not exceed 1000 g.

Size

The height shall not be greater than 160 mm and the area of the cross-section shall not be greater than 95 cm^2.

Jolting test

All self-rescuers shall pass the shock or jolting test of 50,000 jolts with a drop of 20 mm.

7.2.2.2.2 Draeger FSR 850

Figure 7.21 shows the sectional view of the canister of the Draeger filter self-rescuer satisfying the German acceptance specifications. It incorporates a heat exchanger in its mouthpiece assembly, which absorbs heat from inhaled air resulting from the catalytic combustion of CO and gives it off to the exhaled air which passes through it and out through the spring-loaded exhalation valve. The drying agent used is activated charcoal impregnated with lithium bromide and silica gel.

The specifications are:

Height	135 mm
Cross-section	94 cm^2
Mass	1060 g
Maximum CO-slip using test air containing 0.25 per cent CO and 20.7 g water/m^3 air after 60 test minutes	0.001%
Inhalation resistance	
unused	6.0 mbar
under test conditions after 60 test-minutes	8.0 mbar
Temperature of inspired air at 1.5 per cent CO, saturated at body temperature	60°C

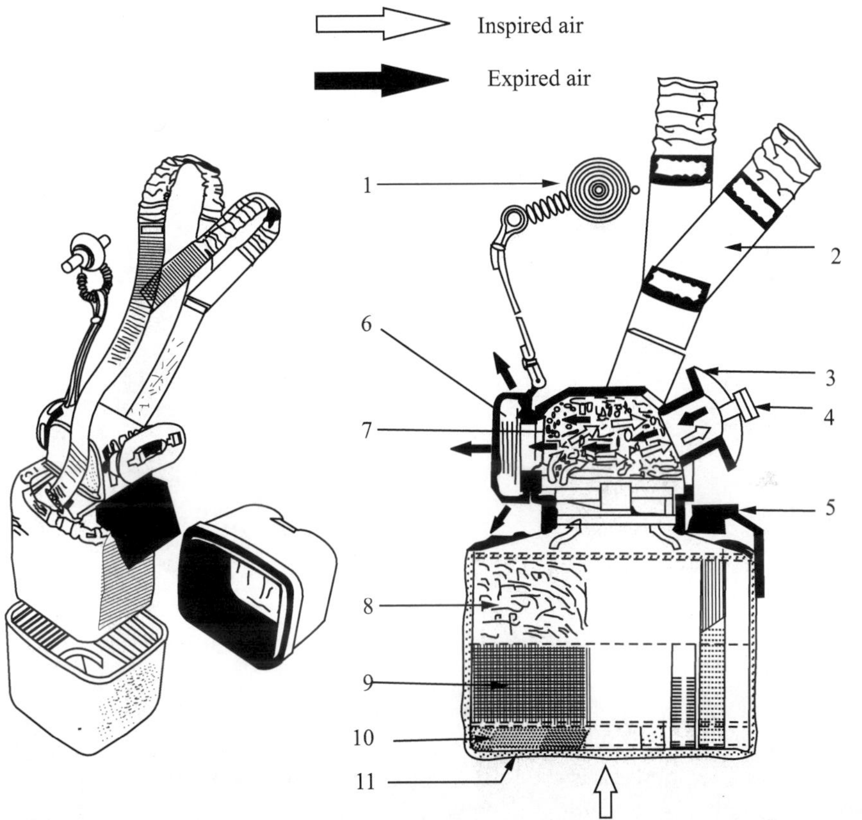

Figure 7.21 Draeger filter self-rescuer FSR850:
1: nose-clip; 2: head straps; 3: mouthpiece; 4: biting lugs; 5: chin rest; 6: Exhalation valve; 7: heat exchanger; 8: hopcalite; 9: drying agent; 10: fine-dust filter; 11: coarse dust filter.

Joseph Leslie Draeger Manufacturing Ltd., a subsidiary of Draegerwerk, introduced a model IFSR 910 of one-hour duration combining the approved features of Draeger FSR 850 and FSR 950. Draegerwerk has now replaced FSR 950 by Draeger FSR 990.

7.2.2.2.3 MSA / Auer FSR W 65 (Fig. 7.22)

Figure 7.23 shows the sectional view of the canister of the MSA./Auer filter-rescuer satisfying the acceptance specifications laid down in the USA. and Germany. It contains an internal heat exchanger in the mouthpiece assembly to reduce the discomfort caused by high concentrations of carbon monoxide. Tests at 1.5 per cent CO showed that the heat exchanger will effectively reduce the temperature of inhaled air from approximately 149° to 65°C. The drying agent is activated charcoal impregnated with a mixture of calcium bromide and lithium chloride in the proportion 10 : 1. The inhalation resistance at 95 litres per minute is approximately 6 mbar while the exhalation resistance is approximately

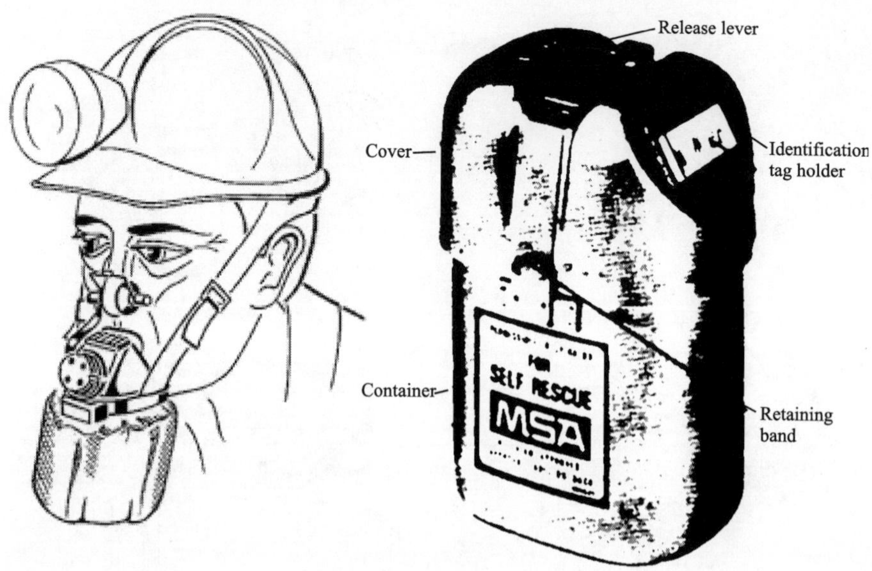

Figure 7.22 MSA/Auer Filter Self-rescuer FSR W65.

1.8 mbar. The increase in inhalation temperature with CO concentration and time is shown in Fig. 7.24.

A further development is the FSR W 65-2.'It has an increased service life of 140 or 180 minutes depending on test conditions. It has also slightly increased height and weight as compared to W 65.

MSA (India) Limited introduced a model IW 65 approved by the Chief Inspector of Mines, India.

A new development is Auer FSR W 95 (Fig. 7.25) which not only meets the European Standard but also the "basic specifications" of German coal mining. Its configuration corresponds to the proven design of the Auer FSR W 65 and W 65-2 but with improved performance as well as breathing and wearing comfort by a new filter design.

The air to be filtered is first drawn through the mechanical filter bag and the dust filter and is then pre-cleaned by a pre-layer of hopcalite before it passes through a noble metal catalyst filter layer which converts carbon monoxide to carbon dioxide. Both hopcalite and the noble metal catalyst filter CO by different properties but complement each other ideally.

This design eliminates the moisture-sensitive pre-layer of drier which had caused heat build-up and breathing resistance.

The technical specifications are:

Dimensions (with case)

Height	approx.	140 mm
Width	approx.	100 mm

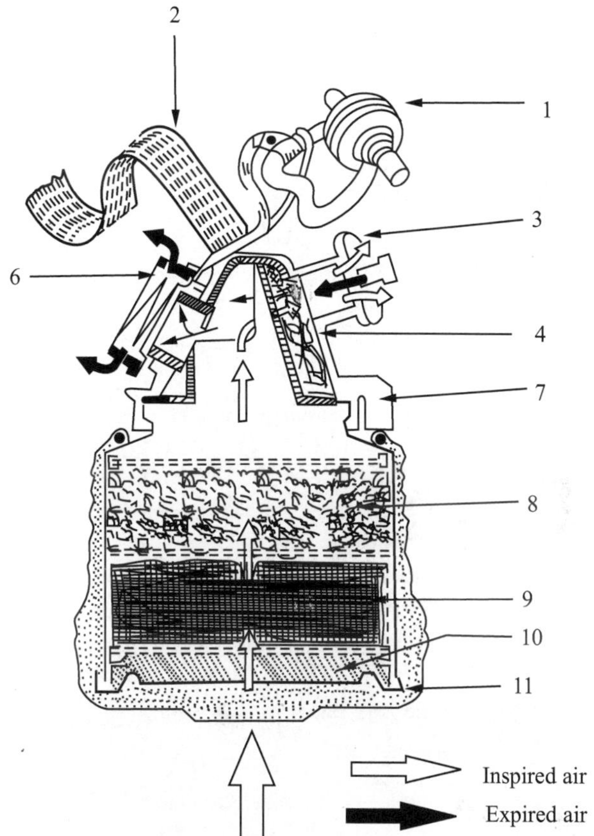

Figure 7.23 Section of the canister FSR W65.
1: nose-clip; 2: head straps; 3: mouthpiece; 4: biting lugs; 5: chin rest; 6: exhalation valve; 7: heat exchanger; 8: hopacalite; 9: drying agent; 10: fine dust filter; 11: coarse dust filter.

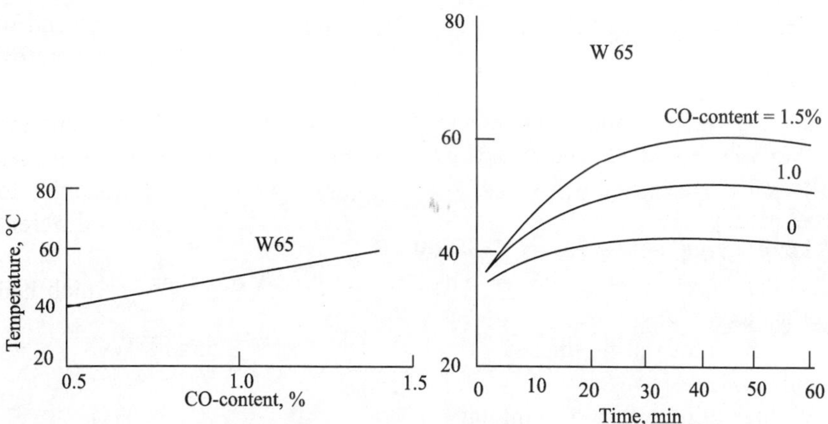

Figure 7.24 Variation of inhalation temperature with CO-concentration and time for FSR W65.

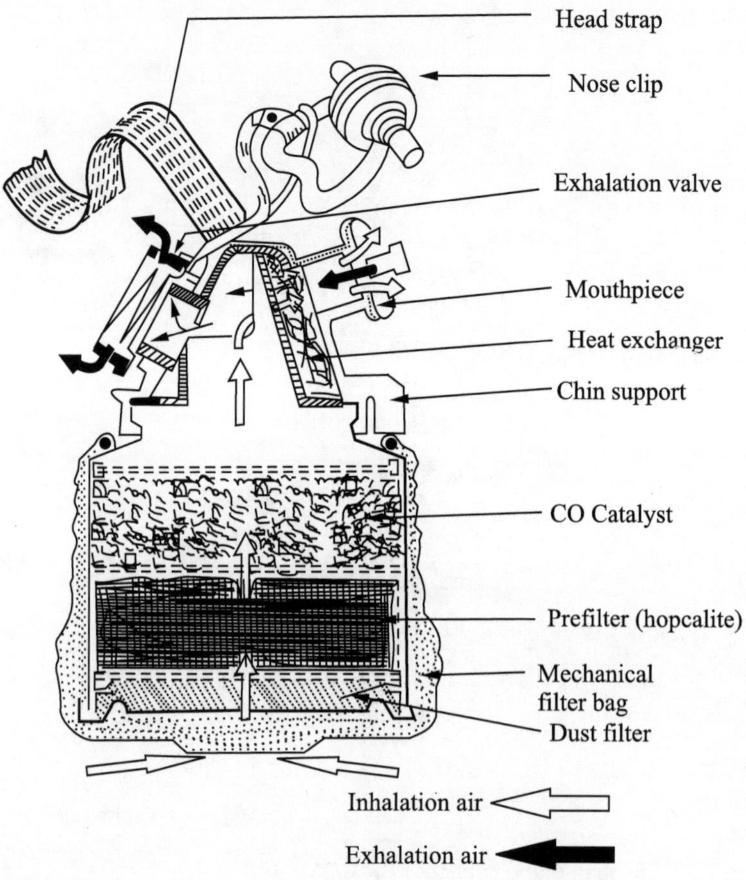

Figure 7.25 Auer filter self-rescuer FSR W 95.

Depth	approx.	80 mm
Weight with case	approx.	900 g
without case	approx.	520 g

Table 7.2 gives the important characteristics of the new filter self-rescuers Auer W 95 and Draeger FSR 990 compared to the European Standard EN 404 Class 4 BR.

7.2.2.2.4 Vijay Sabre Safety VFSR 60

The design of VFSR 60 is similar to that of the MSA W 65. It has the following specifications:

Inhalation resistance, unused	$\leq$	65 mm WG
Inhalation resistance at 85 litres/min. after 60 test minutes	$\leq$	80 mm WG
Maximum CO slip using test air containing 1.0 Vol.-% CO and		

Table 7.2 Important characteristics of the new filter self-rescuers Auer FSR W 95 and Draeger FSR 990 compared with the European Standard EN 404 Class 4 BR [86]

	EN 404 Class 4 BR	Auer FSR W 95	Draeger FSR 990
Dimensions	–	140 mm × 100 mm × 80 mm	151 mm × 138 mm × 90 mm
Weight			
with case		900 g	1450 g
without case	< 800 g	520 g (neck strap)	885 g
Breathing rate (min-vol)	35 litres/min.	40 litres/min.	40 litre/min.
Minimum duration	> 120 min.	240 min.	200 min.
Inhalation resistance at start of use	< 8.0 mbar	4.5 mbar	4.5 mbar
Inhalation resistance at end of use	< 12 mbar	5.0 mbar	6.0 mbar
Exhalation resistance	< 3.5 mbar	2.3 mbar	< 2.5 mbar
Temperature of inhaled air	< 90°C	80°C	80°C

20.7 g/m^3 water content after 60 test minutes	≤	0. 01 Vol.-%
Maximum carbon monoxide slip		100 ml
Temperature of the inspired test air containing 1.5 vol.-% CO saturated at 37°C	≤	650°C
Mass in use	≤	700 g
in case	≤	1200 g
Expected shelf life		5 years

7.2.2.2.5 Testing and maintenance of filter self-rescuers

All filter rescuers should be inspected and tested periodically to determine their reliability. They should be visually inspected for external defects or damage and air-tightness of seal as well as for air-tightness (where possible) and increase in weight. If a self-rescuer gains in weight more than what is laid down by the manufacturer, it should not be reissued. When determining the weight once a month, it is essential that the self-rescuer is free from dust, dirt, etc., and that no parts of it are missing. The results of tests for air-tightness, nature of any repairs made, and any corrections of weight should be entered in a book kept for the purpose.

The filter self-rescuers are carried on the person and taken off only at the workplace. They are stored on the surface in the lamproom or in a self-rescuer room usually located adjacent to the lamproom. In the self-rescuer room, all units are externally cleaned and visually examined each day to ascertain that they are in safe working condition. Experience has shown that the self-issue system is the best.

7.2.3 Fresh-air hose or tube breathing apparatus

These apparatus, also called a supplied-air respirators or hose masks, supply the wearer with fresh air from a source of fresh-air supply through a flexible non-collapsible (crush-and-kink resistant) air tube or air hose so that he is independent of the surrounding irrespirable atmosphere.

These are two types of air hose apparatus:

(i) Suction hose apparatus
(ii) Pressure hose apparatus

7.2.3.1 Suction hose apparatus

These are designed to work at a short distance from fresh air. The wearer sucks or draws fresh air through the hose by the inspiratory effort of his lungs. As the inspiratory resistance increases with increasing length of the hose, the use of suction apparatus is limited to short distances – within 20 m of fresh air.

A suction hose apparatus consists of a full mask (double- or single-lens type), half mask, or a mouthpiece with a nose-clip, a flexible corrugated breathing tube, a 25-mm diameter smooth bore hose of canvas and rubber with embedded spiral wire armouring, a stout leather belt with a rustless connecting socket (coupling) or metal clamp to prevent the hose from dragging on the facepiece, half mask, or mouth piece, and an air filter to prevent entry of dust and foreign matter. An expiratory valve is provided either on the facepiece or on the facepiece/mouthpiece connection, and an inspiratory valve is placed either in the connecting socket or on the facepiece/mouthpiece connector.

The apparatus is available in the lateral or back type. In the lateral-type, the connecting socket or clamp on the belt comes on the left hip so that the shoulders of the wearer are free. The back-type apparatus, on the other hand, has twin corrugated breathing tubes passing over the shoulders and connected to a swivel-type metal Y-connecting socket on the wearer's back. Such apparatus is particularly suited for work in confined spaces into which the wearer enters from above.

For reasons of safety, suction hose apparatus are not approved for use below ground.

7.2.3.2 Pressure hose apparatus or Supplied-air respirators (SAR)

In this type of apparatus, fresh air or breathable air from a clean air source is continuously forced through a hose to the wearer by means of a suitable air-supply device. Such apparatus is used when the distance between the workplace and fresh air is between 20 and 200 in depending on the air-supply means. As the air hose is constantly under a slight positive pressure, there is no danger to the wearer from leakage of outside irrespirable atmosphere into the apparatus around the facepiece.

Pressure hose apparatus is available as lateral- or back-type apparatus. A lateral-type pressure hose apparatus consists of a gas-tight helmet with apron, facepiece (double- or single-lens type), or mouthpiece with nose-clip, a flexible corrugated breathing tube, a breathing bag or equalizer, a belt with a connecting socket containing an inspiratory valve, and shoulder harness.

With a valveless facepiece or mouthpiece, an expiratory valve is provided on the facepiece or mouthpiece connector to which the corrugated breathing tube is attached. The breathing bag serves to maintain a continuous flow in the breathing tube during the inspiration and expiration phases and to smooth down the peak demands.

The back-type apparatus has two corrugated breathing tubes passing over the shoulders. It has one inspiratory and one expiratory valve. Fresh air is supplied to the wearer by using one of the following devices (Fig. 7.26):

(1) Manual bellows;
(2) Centrifugal blower (hand-motor- or motor-hand-operated);
(3) Compressed-air injector (operation from compressed-air storage cylinders).
(4) Waist-mounted air cylinders and mask-mounted air-pressure regulator; and
(5) Compressed-air lines by compressed-air system incorporating a fine filter.

The maximum lengths of air hoses that can be used with pressure hose apparatus are:

With manual bellows ... up to 50 m.
With electric blowers (using a breathing bag and with one apparatus user) ...up to 100 m.
With compressed-air injector ... up to 100 m.

Hand bellows are used for short working periods and where electricity is not available. For long working periods, apparatus with blower or injector unit are used, which are capable of supplying air for two men. With motor-hand-operated blowers, the blowers can be hand-operated where electric current is interrupted or is not available. When using air from permanent compressed-air lines, an oil filter should be used for cleaning the air and making it respirable. The compressed-air supply hose is made from electrically conducting, oil-resistant synthetic rubber for use in areas with explosion hazard.

When using compressed-air pressure hose apparatus, a manually-operated regulator must be used so that the volume of air required may be adjusted. The excess on expired air escapes into the atmosphere through an expiratory valve.

The main advantages of an air hose apparatus are its low breathing resistance, longer duration, and the fact that with waist-mounted air cylinders and a mask mounted air-pressure regulator, it can be used, with approval as a 15-minute stand-alone self-contained breathing apparatus. The disadvantages, however, lie in its heavy large-diameter unwieldy air hoses, restriction of movement, and potential hazard where the hose can come into contact with machinery.

7.2.3.3 Precautions when using fresh-air hose apparatus

The following precautions should be observed when using a fresh-air hose apparatus:

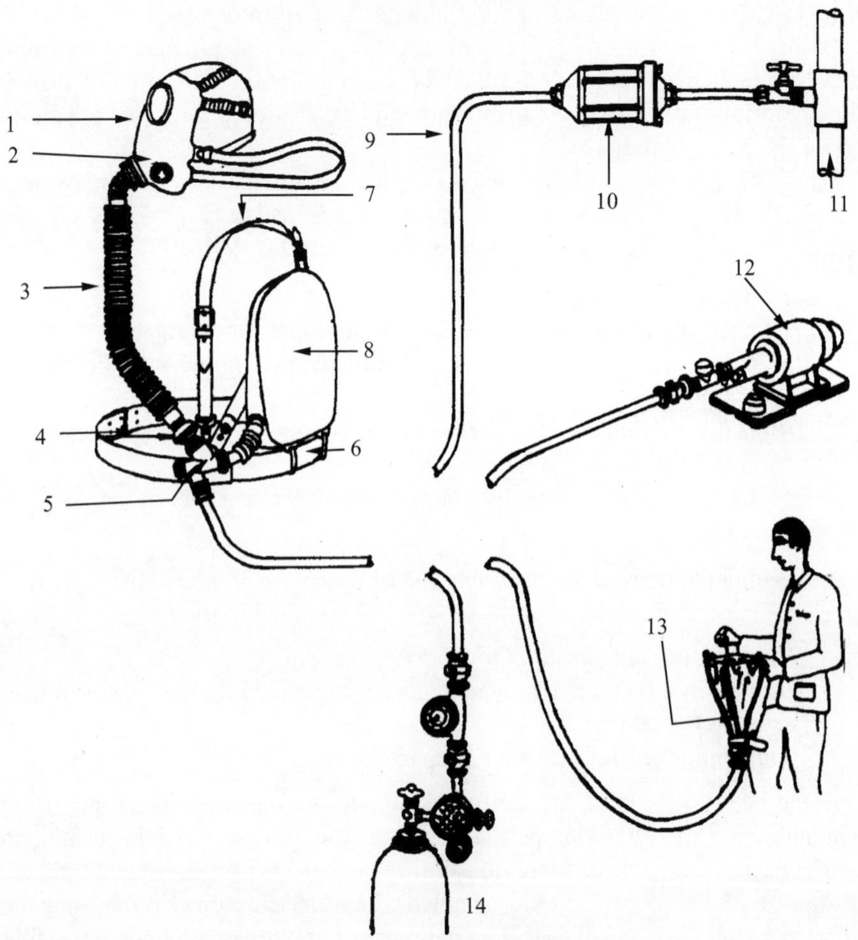

Figure 7.26 Fresh-air supply devices for pressure hose apparatus:
1: facepiece; 2: expiratory valve; 3: breathing tube; 4: inspiratory valve; 5: coupling; 6: waist strap; 7: shoulder strap; 8: breathing bag; 9: air-supply hose; 10: oil filter; 11: compressed-air pipe; 12: motor-driven blower; 13: manual bellows; 14: air injector unit.

(1) The apparatus should be used by trained rescue men;
(2) Before commencing work, the method of signalling should be decided; if a code of signal is laid down by regulations, it should be followed;
(3) One should never work without an observer who should be a trained rescue man in readiness at the fresh-air source or base for help;
(4) The wearer should see that the air hose does not get pinched or jammed;
(5) Full face mask- and half mask-type apparatus should not be used except in conjunction with either a rotary blower or compressed-air injector which are capable of maintaining positive pressure;
(6) When the wearer gives the signal "I require help" the fresh-air supply must be maintained;

(7) The fresh-air supply should not be interrupted before the wearer has removed the facepiece or mouthpiece;
(8) When using an electric blower, the wearer should not make a headlong retreat should the blower cease to function as the pressure hose apparatus then operates as a suction hose apparatus with increased resistance;
(9) When using an injector unit, the wearer should retreat from the danger zone as soon as the pressure gauge on the pressure reducer shows a cylinder pressure of 15 bar (g); and
(10) The wearer shall have attached to his person a lifeline leading from the fresh air

The air hose apparatus should be periodically tested. The test should include visual examination for deterioration of perishable parts, a flow test, and water immersion test of the whole of the air flow circuit. The results of all tests shall be recorded in a book kept for this purpose at the mine.

7.3 Resuscitation or Artificial Ventilation

When a person becomes unconscious, the gas interchange in the alveoli of the lungs is disturbed to an extent that depends on the degree of unconsciousness. Unless the normal gas interchange is immediately restored by resuscitation, death will result. There will be no respiration without heart activity and vice versa. For resuscitation, therefore, the lungs of the patient must be ventilated with adequate quantity of air or oxygen by artificial respiration and the heart muscles and other important nerve centres must be excited or stimulated to restore the normal blood circulation.

The time factor is of greatest importance for the success of resuscitation. Even while rescuing the patient, the rescuers should constantly think of saving time. There is enough oxygen in the blood to keep cells alive for about 10 minutes but the brain cells start dying after being deprived of oxygen for only 4 minutes. It is not always necessary to take the patient to the fresh-air base but a place in fresh air nearest the place of accident will be satisfactory.

When the patient is to be taken to a hospital on the surface, oxygen should be administered on the way to the hospital. An electrocardiogram and chest X-ray should be taken immediately. Serious cases must be admitted in the intensive care unit where specialised treatment measures can be undertaken.

Resuscitation operation must be continued after it is once started until natural breathing is restored or till such time as the doctors decide that further efforts will be of no avail. There are many accidents in mines which require resuscitation operation. The principal causes of such accidents are:

(a) Throttling of the inspired air due to trapment under the fall of debris, crushing of the chest, compression of the windpipe, and drowning.
(b) Inhaling oxygen-deficient atmospheres.

(c) Inhalation of toxic gases. The inhalation of small quantities of toxic gases present in the mine atmosphere may do harm to the supply of oxygen to the body cells. With carbon monoxide poisoning, resuscitation of the patient using large quantities of oxygen must be commenced at the earliest opportunity. With poisoning by nitrous gases, on the other hand, artificial respiration with the application of pressure on the chest and lungs should not be attempted. Only oxygen must be administered and greatest heart activity promoted.

(d) Electric shocks. Electric shocks from voltages greater than 42 V affect the respiratory centre paralysing the oxygen supply to the body cells.

The success of resuscitation can be achieved only after a time elapse of a few hours. Sometimes, the gas-poisoned men are to be rescued with burns, bone fractures and artificial haemorrhage such as after mine explosions. In such cases, the first-aider must be quite clear in his mind as to what help the patient needs foremost. An uncontrolled arterial haemorrhage may make the success of resuscitation quite illusive.

7.3.1 Preparatory measures for resuscitation

Experience has shown that before any resuscitation operation, the following preparatory measures must be carried out:

Proper positioning of patient

In order that the lungs are well ventilated, it is necessary to position the patient in such a posture that his chest cavity expands as much as possible during inhalation but does not remain in the contracted condition during exhalation. The patient must be laid on his back on a flat surface with shoulders raised and supported by a 15-cm thick pad of clothes or folded blanket. All tight clothes around the back, chest, and waist must be loosened.

Ensuring free air passages

In an unconscious person, the mouth is often closed and the tongue falls back and obstructs the air passage. Also, the lower jaw recedes downwards and backwards. To ensure free air passage, therefore, the mouth must be opened by hand or by means of a mouth opener and the pharyngeal cavity cleaned of water, chewing gum, chewing tobacco, mucus, food, blood and also teeth, etc. The tongue must be pulled out either with hand or forceps and held by means of a bandage. In most cases, holding forward of the tongue is not necessary. It is sufficient if the head is tilted backwards and then turned laterally.

Retaining the body heat

In a completely unconscious person (coma), the formation of heat in the body ceases. For maintenance of metabolism in the body cells, it is necessary that whatever heat is in the body must be retained. The patient should, therefore, be laid on a blanket and his body, excepting the upper portion, covered with warmed-up blankets. In every case, wet clothes must be removed. The ventilating current must be prevented from acting on the body by hanging a brattice cloth in the airway.

7.3.2 Methods of artificial ventilation or respiration

The methods of artificial respiration can be divided into the following two groups:

(a) Manual methods using hands
(b) Mechanical methods using resuscitators

7.3.2.1 Manual methods using hands

There are several manual methods of artificial respiration. All the methods are based on the principle of compressing the chest cavity to drive air out of the lungs and relaxing the pressure to let air flow into the lungs. Apart from the differences in hand grips, they differ only in the position of the patient during resuscitation. Every first-aider should employ only that method which he has thoroughly mastered and which is suitable for the case in hand.

A man at rest breathes at a rate of about 15 times per minute. When carrying out manual resuscitation, one must aim at this rhythm but, in practice, from considerations of depth of breathing and the strenuous nature of work on the part of the first-aider, a rate of breathing of 10 to 12 times per minute will be quite satisfactory.

With every resuscitation work, the cycle of operations should begin with expiration. To keep the regular rhythm, a suitable method of counting and timing should be followed. The pressure necessary for respiration should be applied gradually.

Depending on the position in which the patient is laid, manual methods can be further divided into two groups. In one group, the patient is laid on his back (Sylvester and Howard methods) while in the other the patient is laid in the prone position (Holger–Nielsen method).

Sylvester method

It is a two-arm method and is the oldest and the most important method of artificial respiration by hand. It dates back to 1858. It was later modified by Brosch (1896) and Koch (1924) and is also called Sylvester–Brosch–Koch method [76].

The first-aider or operator kneels just above the patient's head and grasps both his arms immediately below the elbows from outside (Fig. 7.27). He then presses the arms steadily and firmly downwards and inwards against the lower portion of the chest cavity with forearms crossed. The applied pressure is maintained steady for 2 seconds. This causes expiration. Next, the operator grasps the upper arms near the elbows from inside, raises and pulls the arms backwards until they are in line with the body and the elbows are just touching the ground. In this movement, the chest cavity is extended and fresh air is inhaled. A short pause of 2 seconds should be allowed before the expiration movement is commenced.

Sylvester method cannot be applied if the casualty has suffered fracture of arms or ribs. It is used when mouth-to-mouth inflation method cannot he applied due to extensive facial injuries.

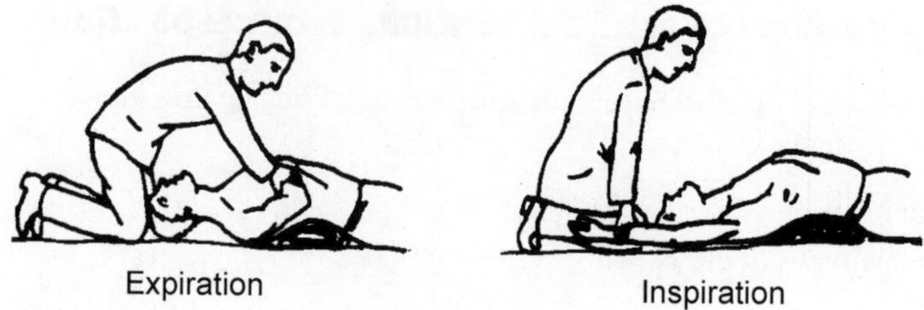

Figure 7.27 Sylvester method of artificial respiration.

Howard method

This method dates back to 1871. The casualty is laid on his back with his arms swung backward until they are in line with the body. After all the preparatory measures have been completed, the operator kneels astride the patient as shown in Fig. 7.28 with his hands on the sides of the lower portion of the chest cavity. He then swings slowly forward so that the sides of chest cavity are compressed under the weight of his body and the muscular force applied. This movement causes expiration.

Next, the operator swings slowly back thus relaxing the pressure. This causes the chest cavity to return back to its normal position due to elasticity and, in consequence, air is drawn into the lungs.

The Howard method cannot be applied with rib fractures. If the arms are fractured, they should be placed by the side of the body.

Holger–Nielsen back-pressure, arm-lift method

This method dates back to 1932. In this method, the patient lies in the prone position, i.e., face downwards on a flat surface with the head resting on his folded hands and turned slightly to one side. Before beginning artificial respiration, the operator, as with the other methods, should see that the air passages are clear. The patient's tongue is made to fall forward by giving several light blows or slaps with the flat hand between the shoulder blades. The tongue need not be fixed in that position.

When resuscitating, the operator kneels over the patient on one or both the knees and places his hands on the shoulder blades of the patient with the thumbs alongside the spine (Fig. 7.29). Keeping his arms straight, he then swings gently

Figure 7.28 Howard method of artificial respiration

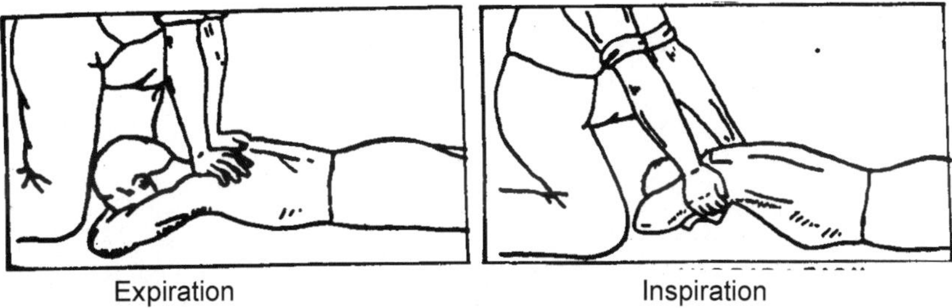

Figure 7.29 Holger–Nielsen method of artificial respiration.

forward until the arms are approximately vertical thereby exerting pressure almost directly downward on the shoulder blades and causing expiration.

To induce inhalation, the operator swings back slowly, grips the upper arms of the patient near the elbows from the outside and raises and pulls on the arms to the extent that the head remains on the folded hands.

After the inspiration movement, the operator lowers the patient's arms gently so that they lie in their original condition and replace his hands on the shoulder blades for expiration movement.

The whole operation occupies 6 seconds which gives a frequency of operation of 10 times per minute. It should be noted that the pressure applied during the expiration movement should be just sufficient to lightly compress the chest. A pressure of 12 to 15 kgf will usually suffice for the average patient.

Inflation method: Expired air resuscitation

This method is also called the Biblical method. It is probably the earliest method of artificial respiration. It was only in recent years that it came to be recognised as an effective method of resuscitation of asphyxiated persons in mines. In this method, the rescuer blows air forcibly into the patient's mouth or nose to inflate his lungs and simulate the act of inspiration. Expiration will automatically occur due to the elastic recoil of the chest walls. Investigations have shown that an oxygen content of 16 per cent in the exhaled air of the first-aider is adequate for successful resuscitation and the carbon dioxide in the expired air helps to simulate the respiratory centre of the patient.

Before applying the mouth for resuscitation, the patient must be laid on his back, his pharyngeal cavity cleaned and his head tilted backwards, so that the air passages are clear. If the patient has dentures or bridges, they must be removed. The first-aider kneels down behind the head of the patient, checks for breathing for at least 5 seconds, and, if the patient is not breathing, covers the face of the patient except the mouth with a handkerchief or a bandage, pinches the nose closed and, after taking in a deep breath, places his mouth over the patient's mouth forming an air-tight seal and blows air into the lungs until the chest rises. After the blowing period, the first-aider raises his head while taking another breath and repeats inflation a total of four times as quickly as possible. If he feels or hears no air exchange, he must clean the mouth of any foreign objects and breathe into the patient again. If there is still no air exchange, he turns the patient on to his side, slaps him on the back between the shoulder blades, and again cleans his mouth to remove any foreign matter and repeats inflation maintaining a rhythm of 12 to 15 operations per minute.

With mouth-to-nose resuscitation which may be practised when mouth cannot be opened due to serious mouth injury or tongue badly swollen, the first-aider kneels on one side of the patient, grasps the chin and the forehead of the patient with his hand and, with the thumb closing the mouth, takes a breath, rounds his lips and applies the mouth round the nose to inflate the lungs of the patient.

During the mouth-to-mouth (nose) resuscitation, the pulse should be checked every two minutes using the carotid artery in the neck. If a pulse is not present, external cardiac compression must be started immediately.

In order that the first-aider does not get into direct contact with the mouth of the patient, a handkerchief or similar cloth may be placed between mouths or an airway 'Orotube or the Orospirator of Draegerwerk' may be used.

Orotube (Fig. 7.30) consists of a sealing plate or shield with two rubber thumb pieces, a short tube, and a nose-clip, all being made of special rubber. The nose of the patient is closed by means of the nose-clip and the short tube which is oval at the bottom is inserted into the mouth. The mouth is then sealed by pressing both the thumbs against the thumb pieces of the shield. The first-aider can then blow the expired air into the lungs of the patient through the tube (Fig. 7.3 1).

If lung ventilation is difficult due to blood, mucus or vomit, the original position of the patient should be changed, who should be turned to one side and placed in a stable lateral position. The mouth should then be cleaned by the forefinger or by using the Draeger Orosucker (Fig. 7.32) which consists of a plastic bottle of about 100 ml capacity with a mouthpiece and a catheter. By applying suction with the mouth (Fig. 7.33), a negative pressure up to 4 m water column can be created in the bottle and maintained by a built-in rubber valve.

With resuscitation using the Orotube, the first-aider has to bend down to the face level of the patient which, at times, may be quite strenuous. By using the Orospirator, he can conveniently carry out resuscitation in narrow places and without coming into contact with the exhaled air of the patient. The Orospirator (Fig. 7.34) consists of a mouthpiece, a 30-cm long corrugated hose, inhalation and exhalation valves, and an Orotube.

The advantages of the inhalation method are that it can be more easily and effectively employed than other methods, gives the greatest ventilation of the lungs, and is less tiring requiring no strength. Workers should be trained in this method by a 3-hour class. If it is impossible to use the method, other manual methods of artificial respiration should be employed.

Cardio-pulmonary resuscitation (CPR)

This is performed in cases of cardiac arrest in which the heart does not beat and pulse is not present. It combines expired air resuscitation and external cardiac

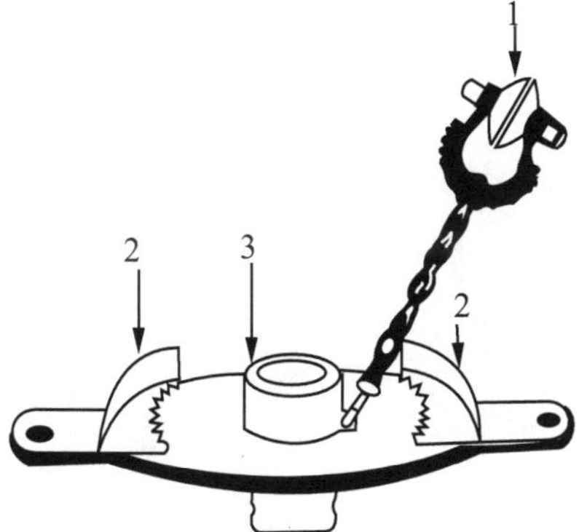

Figure 7.30 Draeger Orotube:
I: nose-clip; 2: rubber thumb pieces; 3: mouthpiece.

Figure 7.31 Mouth-to-mouth resuscitation with Orotube.

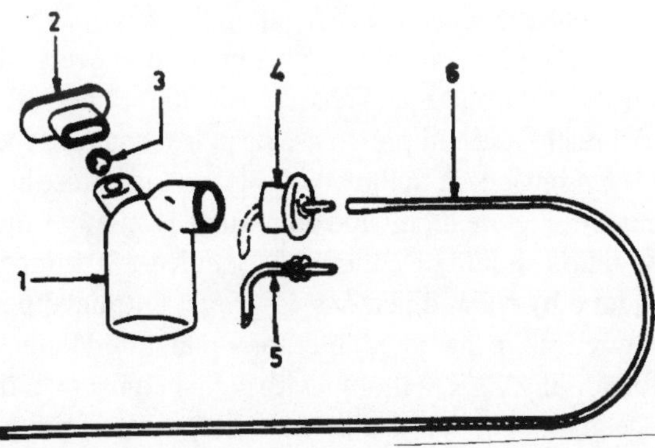

Figure 7.32 Draeger Orosucker.

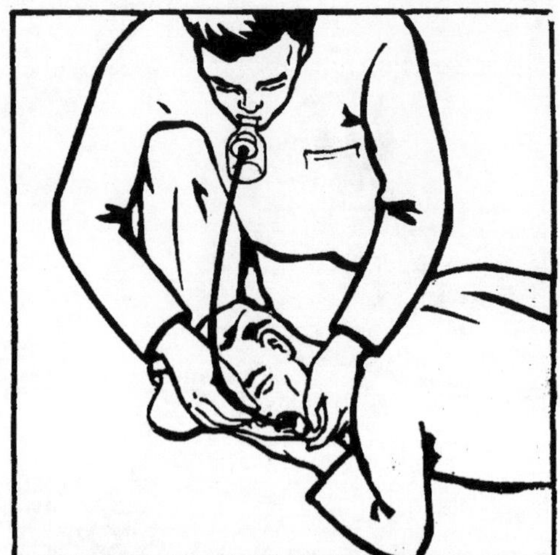

Figure 7.33 Cleaning the mouth with Orosucker.

Figure 7.34 Mouth-to-mouth resuscitation with orospirator

compression. If during expired air resuscitation, a pulse is not present, external cardiac compressions must be started immediately.

The patient is laid on a hard flat surface and the first-aider then determines the pressure point for cardiac compressions by locating the bony tip of the breast bone (sternum) with his ring finger, placing two fingers just above that point. He places the heel of his hand adjacent to the fingers and then places the second hand on top of the first. Positioning his shoulders directly over the patient's breastbone, he presses downwards keeping arms straight so that the sternum is depressed 38 to 50 mm exerting about 40 to 50 kgf of pressure on the breast bone. The time spent in depressing and releasing the sternum must be the same.

If there is one first-aider, one-person CPR, compressions should be carried out at a rate of 60 to 90 per minute with two breaths with the nostrils pinched off (lung ventilation) after each 15 compressions in a row.

If there are two first-aiders, two-person CPR, they should position themselves on opposite sides of the patient. One first-aider should perform compressions at a rate of 60 per minute while the other is inflating the lungs after every fifth compression. Compressions must be continuous and not interrupted for lung inflation. After four complete cycles of breaths and compressions, the pulse should be checked within five seconds and, if it is present, check for breathing. If there is a pulse but no spontaneous breathing, continue rescue breathing and continuously monitor the pulse. Cardio-pulmonary resuscitation should be continued for at least 30 minutes.

CPR must be done by trained persons. With an untrained person, the victim may suffer a fractured rib, a lacerated liver, or a punctured lung. If a heart attack is witnessed before giving CPR, a thump with clenched fist over the breastbone as hard as one can be given, can make the heart start beating and permit the victim to breathe again.

7.3.2.2 Mechanical methods using resuscitators

Although the manual methods of artificial respiration have the advantage that they can be employed immediately, they suffer from an important disadvantage that the first-aider can get quickly fatigued and the resuscitation of the patient may not be carried out uniformly. It is for this reason that resuscitating equipment were developed, which require no manual assistance in their operation and ensure uniform respiration.

Many types of resuscitators are available each with its own characteristic principles of operation. Basically, a resuscitator consists of a supply of oxygen, a mechanism for forced breathing, and a mask that fits over the face of the victim. Depending on the method of operation, the resuscitators can be divided into two groups. To the first group belong equipment which brings about resuscitation in a manner similar to the manual methods. By application of external pressure on the chest cavity, the stomach, and the diaphragm, the air of the lungs is expelled (expiration). For inspiration, the stomach and the chest (biomotor) or the arms are raised. In the second group are included apparatus which provide automatically-controlled forced-breathing resuscitation. An oxygen–air mixture is blown into the lungs during the inspiration phase and sucked out or expelled by recoil of the respiratory muscles and lungs during the expiration phase.

The forced breathing-type resuscitators are of two types: the pressure cycling type and the volume cycling type.

In the pressure cycling–type resuscitators, the apparatus forces oxygen through the mask into the lungs of the victim during the positive pressure cycle and pulls the air out by negative pressure. When oxygen is forced into the lungs under positive pressure, the pressure inside the chest cavity becomes greater than the pressure anywhere else in the body and, in consequence, the flow of blood into the chest from the peripheral veins is impeded thereby reducing the cardiac output sometimes to dangerous levels. A person can usually survive as much as 20 mm Hg continuous positive pressure in the lungs but exposure to pressure greater than 30 mm Hg for more than a few minutes may cause death. It is for this reason that most resuscitators are fitted with safety valves that prevent the positive pressure from rising above + 14 mm Hg and the negative pressure from falling below –9 mm Hg. These pressure limits are adequate to provide excellent artificial respiration of normal lungs without any damage to them. A well-known example of the pressure cycling type of resuscitator is the Draeger Pulmotor.

The volume cycling type resuscitator operates using the lung ventilation technique employed in the intensive care units called mandatory minute volume ventilation which must be supplied to the victim at varying respiratory rates. The concept is that a reservoir is supplied with a pre-set minute volume of oxygen from which the victim breathes spontaneously as much as he is able via a unique demand system. If the actual volume breathed spontaneously is less than the preset minute volume, the difference is automatically delivered by the ventilator fed from the reservoir at pre-set tidal volumes. If there is no spontaneous breathing, then the full minute volume is automatically given by the ventilator. If the victim desires to breathe spontaneously a volume greater than the pre-set minute volume, a supplementary circuit feeds the demand valve accordingly. Once the mask is placed on the victim's face, his volume of spontaneous breathing is continuously monitored and ventilation is switched on or off automatically according to his needs. All this is achieved by reliable pure pneumatic logic housed in module. A well-known example of the volume cycling type of resuscitator is the Siebe Gorman Maxaman Ventilator/Resuscitator Type M which is provided at Indian mine rescue stations.

7.3.2.2.1 Draeger Pulmotor

The apparatus was first constructed by Heinrich Draeger in the year 1906 and in course of time was considerably modified and improved upon to become a well- proven automatic equipment for resuscitation. It provides for automatic cycling of breathing by blowing an oxygen–air mixture into the lungs of the victim and removing the carbon dioxide-charged exhaled air out of the lungs by suction under pre-set positive and negative pressures. With simple adjustments, it can also be used for extraction of secretions from the respiratory tract and for oxygen inhalation.

Figure 7.35 shows the principal parts of the Pulmotor. It essentially consists of one or two 2.5-litre capacity steel oxygen cylinder(s) containing oxygen at a filling pressure of 200 bar, a pressure-reducing valve, a distribution manifold with three shut-off valves and a safety valve, a change-over valve for 50 or 100 per cent O_2, a cycling or switching valve unit, a face mask, an aspirating injector, a secretion bottle, an oxygen economizer breathing bag, an inhalation mask, and four sizes of oral airways. The reducing valve reduces the high-pressure oxygen to a constant operating pressure of 5 bar. Of the three shut-off valves, one is connected to the aspirating injector, another to the oxygen inhalation mask, while the third is connected to the switching unit. The switching unit is the soul of the apparatus. The changeover valve is normally set for 50 per cent O_2, the remaining being atmospheric air sucked by an injector. It is set for 100 per cent O_2 in a toxic atmosphere. Provided that the respiratory tracts are clear and the mask fits tightly, the respiratory air flows into the lungs of the victim producing a clearly visible expansion of the thorax. As soon as the pressure of about + 20 mbar is reached in the lungs, the inspiration phase is completed and the switching unit switches over automatically to the expiration phase and begins to suck air out of the lungs. When the required negative pressure of –10 mbar is reached towards the end of the expiration phase, the appliance switches over to a new inspiration phase.

The switching rate depends on the size of the lungs and on the oxygen flow-rate. If the switching is too fast, the oxygen-supply must be reduced. The negative pressure at the end of expiration assists the blood circulation but in special cases a special attachment is supplied for cutting it out during the expiration phase.

Before resuscitation, it is necessary that the patient is laid flat on his back with his head tilted backwards and turned to one side. After the pharyngeal cavity is cleaned, the lower air passages are cleaned by using the aspirating catheter of the Pulmotor

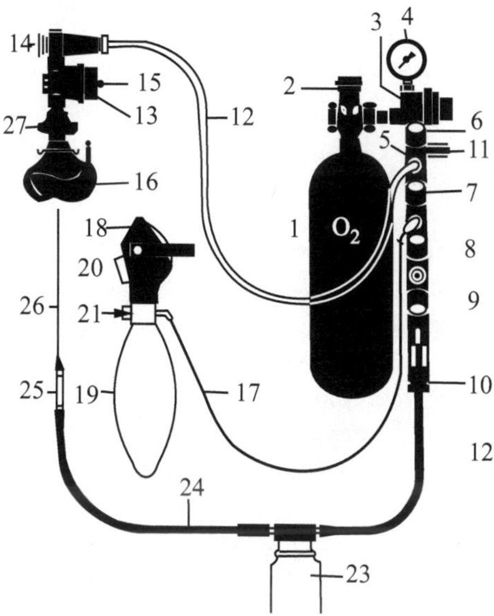

Figure 7.35 Draeger Pulmotor.
I: oxygen cylinder; 2: cylinder valve; 3: reducing valve; 4: pressure gauge; 5: distributor manifold; 6:pulmotor shut-off valve; 7: inhalation shut-off valve; 8: spare valve for connecting other equipment; 9: suction valve; 10: aspirator injector; I I: safety valve; 12: oxygen connecting hose; 13: pulmotor switching unit; 14: changeover valve for 50% or 100% oxygen; 15: selector knob; 16: facepiece; 17: connecting inhalation tube; 18: inhalation facepiece; 19: economizer breathing bag; 20: expiratory valve; 21: air addition valve; 22: connecting hose; 23: secretion bottle; 24: aspirator hose; 25: secretion vision glass; 26: aspirator catheter; 27: respiratory valve (for cutting-off the negative phase), optional.

aspirator. As soon as the air passages are free, an oral airway is inserted into the mouth to prevent the falling back of the tongue. The cylinder valve and the shut-off valve for resuscitation are then opened and the face mask with the switching unit is pressed against the face. If the face mask is fitting tightly, the switching unit will start functioning and automatically change over from inspiration to expiration and vice versa. If the change-over takes place rapidly, it will mean that the air passages are still not free and have to be cleaned again. When the switching unit operates normally, the face mask is fastened to the head band by means of straps.

It is necessary that no air enters the stomach during resuscitation as the diaphragm which is stretched upwards would hinder the expansion of the lungs and circulation of the blood. During the operation of the Pulmotor, the rescuer should always observe that the respiratory rhythm remains constant. If, during resuscitation, the action of the heart can no more be observed, heart massage must be carried out during the expiration phase. Should severe spasms occur as it happens with carbon monoxide poisoning, the tongue should be immediately loosened after lifting the face mask and, if necessary, respiration interrupted.

The Pulmotor should not be used except as an inhalator in cases of poisoning by nitrous fumes. It should, however, be emphasized that the first few minutes after breathing has ceased are the most crucial and that manual respiration must be started at once and continued till the Pulmotor becomes available.

The Pulmotor is no longer being manufactured at present. Three new models of the pulmotor, Pt 60, PT61, PK60 have been developed.

7.3.2.2.2 Siebe Gorman Maxaman resuscitator

The Maxaman resuscitator is a dual-purpose oxygen-powered resuscitator that automatically adjusts from forced to spontaneous breathing, and vice versa according to the victim's demands. It has been specially designed for use in irrespirable atmospheres wherein the victim may or may not be breathing when located or during the rescue operation. The rescuer need not know whether the victim is breathing or not. It is based on the mandatory minute volume lung ventilation technique.

The resuscitator consists of a compressed-oxygen supply cylinder with a pin index cylinder yoke, a first-stage pressure regulator and pressure relief valve, a control module connected to the pin index cylinder yoke by a small-bore tube and to a ori-nasal mask through a non-breathing valve, and a head harness (Fig. 7.36).

The first-stage pressure regulator reduces the oxygen pressure to a value between 4 and 7 bar before it flows to the second-stage pressure regulator in the control module.

The control module is an oxygen-powered automatic ventilator combined with a monitored demand facility. It consists essentially of three chambers. The central stainless steel chamber constitutes the reservoir of the system and contains tubing connecting together the logic units A and D and the demand valve. All the logic units and the second-stage pressure regulator are contained in a plastic covered chamber at one end of the stainless steel chamber while the demand valve, safety relief valve, and an obstruction whistle and indicator are contained in another plastic covered chamber at its other end. The inlet and outlet tubes are connected to the latter end. The outlet tube connects to the victim's non-breathing valve (unidirectional respiratory valve) fitted to the ori-nasal mask. The second-stage pressure regulator is pre-set and fixed at the maximum and oxygen from this regulator passes to the three logic units C and A and, through the minute volume orifice, the logic unit block D. This provides the reference pressure for the cycling pressures of the logic unit C and oxygen supply for the logic unit A setting its cycling pressures. The inlet orifice in the unit D sets the minute volume flow into the reservoir and sets the mandatory minute volume depending on the pressure output of the second-stage regulator.

The victim is free to breathe continuously from the reservoir via the demand valve at any time. If he breathes an amount equal to the minute volume passing to the reservoir, the logic units A and C will not cycle. If he breathes more than the pre-set minute volume, the pressure in the reservoir will fall and the logic

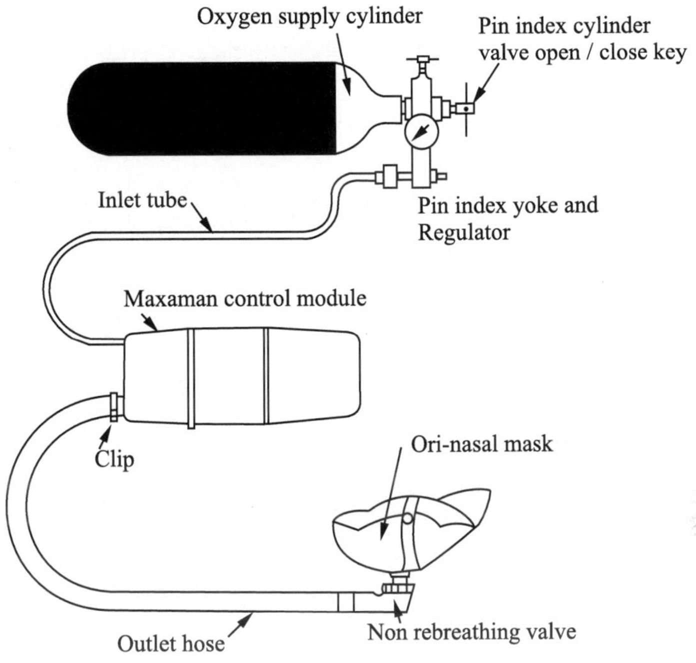

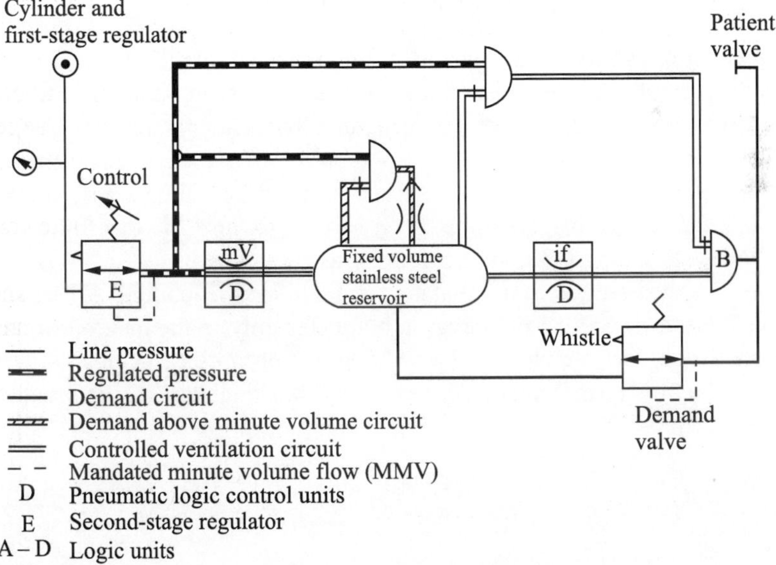

Figure 7.36 Siebe Gorman Maxaman ventilator / resuscitator flow circuit.

unit A will then keep refilling the reservoir so that the victim can breathe freely. If he breathes less than the pre-set minute volume, the pressure in the reservoir will rise and the logic unit C will cycle and open the logic unit B which opens the reservoir to the victim via the outlet orifice in the logic unit block D. The volume of the reservoir and the characteristics of the logic unit C are such that correct tidal volumes are delivered before the logic unit C recycles and closes the logic unit B. The logic unit C is also set to close the logic unit B before the pressure in the reservoir falls enough to open the logic unit A. Under these conditions, the volume of the controlled breaths via the logic unit B will be equal to the mandatory minute volume entering the reservoir minus the volume breathed spontaneously via the demand valve.

In case respiratory obstruction occurs in the victim, the safety relief valve operates with audible alarm and visual indication.

In trials conducted by the erstwhile National Coal Board [88] on healthy subjects breathing normally, the best performance of Maxaman was obtained when the relief valve settings were 250 mm WG, 800/900 for the tidal volume, and 9/10 cycles per minute for the frequency.

The Maxaman set to operate only on demand has a potential application for escape purposes in an emergency.

7.4 Inhalators or Oxygen Reviving Apparatus

Inhalators or oxygen reviving apparatus supply oxygen to the patient in response to his own breathing demands. They are used in cases of asphyxia where the casualty has at least partial control of respiration but is not getting enough oxygen, or where the casualty has ceased to respire but has regained consciousness after successful resuscitation. It must be borne in mind that the quantity of oxygen available with a reviving apparatus is very small, usually 280 to 420 litre which is sufficient only for 20–30 min duration of use.

There are different types of inhalators available in the market. All are similar in construction as well as in operation but differ only in the method of oxygen supply and auxiliary attachment for reviving two or more casualties.

Depending on the method of oxygen supply, the inhalators can be divided into two main groups:

(1) Inhalators with constant dosage,
(2) Inhalators with lung-governed dosage.

7.4.1 Inhalators with constant dosage

These consist of one or two oxygen cylinders, a pressure-reducing valve with a fine adjustment hand-controlled valve, a pressure gauge, an oxygen economizer rubber breathing bag with an excess-pressure valve, a flexible corrugated breathing tube, and a face mask which is designed to cover the mouth and nose only and incorporates inhalation and exhalation valves. A special valve is sometimes provided to admit fresh air to the flow circuit if desired.

The rate of flow of oxygen to the breathing bag is carefully regulated by the control valve to meet the patient's requirements. To eliminate oxygen losses, the pressure in the bag must be adjusted so that it is less than the blow-off pressure of the excess pressure valve. In the inspiration phase, the bag gets emptied and the walls of the bag collapse while, in the expiration phase, the exhaled air escapes out of the face mask through the exhalation valve.

With minor accidents, a rate of feed of 4 to 6 litres per minute oxygen will be sufficient but with serious accidents, especially with carbon monoxide poisoning, the rate of feed should be increased to 6 to 15 litres per minute.

When a patient (casualty) shows definite signs of recovery, it is permissible to partially open the fresh-air valve so that the mixture administered would consist of 50 per cent air and 50 per cent oxygen. A resuscitator with inhalation mask and breathing bag is an ideal appliance for oxygen inhalation.

7.4.2 Inhalators with lung-governed dosage

These are entirely of the lung-governed type available in different models with one, two, or four supply points or outlets. The apparatus with one supply outlet consists of an oxygen cylinder of 2.6-litre capacity charged to 150 bar pressure, a bypass valve, a lung-governed admission valve, a pressure gauge, a flexible breathing tube, and a moulded rubber facepiece with an expiratory valve. The lever(s) of the lung-governed valve is (are) enclosed in or protrudes (protrude) into a flexible bag protected in a protective casing. The lung-governed valve is opened when the bag is emptied by inhalation. The bypass valve enables the oxygen to be delivered as a continuous feed direct to the facepiece in cases of respiratory failure or faint respiration. A well-known inhalator still widely used in the Commonwealth countries is the Siebe Gorman Novox Model 1.

7.5 Rescue Organization

The mining laws of a country prescribe a general organisation of mine rescue for its mines which will secure safe and efficient conduct of such operations for rescue of persons as may be necessary to conduct at mines following an explosion, mine fire, or other accident of whatsoever kind. In particular, the regulations make provision for:

(a) the construction, equipping, maintenance, and control of rescue stations at suitable locations for the purpose of providing facilities common to a number mines for the conduct of first-aid and mine rescue and for training of rescue men, mine fire training and
(b) the establishment and maintenance at mines of such organisations of persons and equipment as may be necessary for rescue purposes.

7.5.1 Rescue stations

One distinguishes between three types of rescue stations:

(1) Central Rescue Stations;
(2) District / Area Rescue Stations;
(3) Rescue Stations/Rescue Rooms at Mines.

The central rescue stations have wider objectives than the district rescue stations and rescue stations at mines.

The objectives of a central rescue station are:

(1) Recommend formulations of mine rescue rules as well as rules for protection against toxic gases in auxiliary plants on the surface of mines;
(2) To draw mutual-aid plans under which neighbouring mines, after occurrence of a major mine disaster, assist each other on a reciprocal basis;
(3) To train directors or in-charges of rescue operations, leaders/captains, and apparatus mechanics or attendants in rescue and disaster techniques for mine rescue brigades, and also to conduct refresher training courses for them;
(4) To supervise the training of mine rescue brigades at mines and, under certain circumstances, even train mine rescue brigades;
(5) To guide and supervise the conduct of rescue and recovery and re-opening operations in mines;
(6) To maintain a permanent rescue corpse in constant readiness where the station is required to help in conducting rescue and recovery operations in mines falling within its radius of action;
(7) To store special types of equipment and apparatus for firefighting and mine rescue work;
(8) To supervise the working of district rescue stations;
(9) To inspect apparatus and equipment for mine rescue work maintained at mines and report defects and shortcomings to the management;
(10) To conduct approval tests and give expert opinion on new designs of equipment and apparatus for mine rescue work;
(11) To initiate development of new apparatus and equipment;
(12) To conduct approval tests of portable fire extinguishers for use in mines; and
(13) To advise on all matters concerning mine rescue, protection against toxic gases; fire protection, and working of seams or deposits liable to spontaneous combustion.
(14) To train specialised rescue teams for underwater rescue and recovery work and surface firefighting on the mine surface.

In some countries, notably on the Continent of Europe, one or two stations are established by their governments in the centre of important coalfields depending on their geographical location while in other countries only district rescue stations are established.

The district rescue stations are established to serve a group of mines in a defined mining region or district / area. They may also be established at isolated mines with special gas outburst- and explosion-hazard. They are fully equipped for rescue work and for training of rescue men. District rescue stations must be equipped with a rescue van or truck.

The mine rescue stations or mine rescue rooms are provided at mines employing 100 or more persons underground on any shift and maintaining rescue brigades. Neighbouring mines belonging to a single large mining company or different mining companies may maintain a joint rescue station at a suitable place. A mine rescue station is equipped with specified breathing apparatus, equipment and supplies which are maintained in good order and ready for immediate use by the mine rescue brigade. It comprises an apparatus room, a maintenance room, a cap lamp charging rack, modern hand-held electronic methanometers, CO monitors and a test room. Figure 7.37 gives a layout of a mine rescue station or rescue room with a workshop for 20 self-containing breathing apparatus [89].

The central and district rescue stations should be located so that the radius of action does not exceed 25 to 35 km. All stations must efficiently cooperate with one another in emergencies.

The establishment, maintenance, and management of the rescue stations other than those at the mines are usually vested in a Rescue Station Committee appointed by the government, which includes representatives of the mines inspectorate, mine operators, mine employees, and miners union. The cost for establishment, equipping, maintenance and control of the rescue stations is met by levying on the mine operators an excise duty per tonne of coal or mineral mined.

The first rescue station is India was established at Oorgaum in the Kolar Goldfield in the year 1923 to serve four gold mines at Kolar. In the coal mining industry, the first rescue stations were established in the year 1941 at Dhansar in the Jharia coalfield and at Sitarampur in the Ranigunj coalfield. After nationalisation in 1971 and 1973, several rescue stations came into existence in mining areas in different geographic regions (45 rescue stations in the coal mining industry and 6 in the metal mining industry). The Mine Rescue Rules 1985 placed all the rescue station under the respective companies in whose areas they existed for their administration, control, and operation for mine rescue coverage.

In some countries, mines may totally rely on state-sponsored rescue teams for mine rescue . For example, in the Pennsylvania coalfields of the USA most of the coal operators rely on state-trained and maintained teams as the costs of provision of mine rescue services are too burdensome to comply with regulations within their resources.

A modern central or district rescue station contains offices, an apparatus room, a repair and maintenance shop with an oxygen pump and cleaning and drying facilities, a dormitory for members of the resident rescue corpse on continuous duty, wash rooms, a store, a gas analysis laboratory, a garage, a drivers' waiting room, a recreation room, and a guest room. The training is carried out in a training gallery under conditions simulating those obtained underground with ladders and

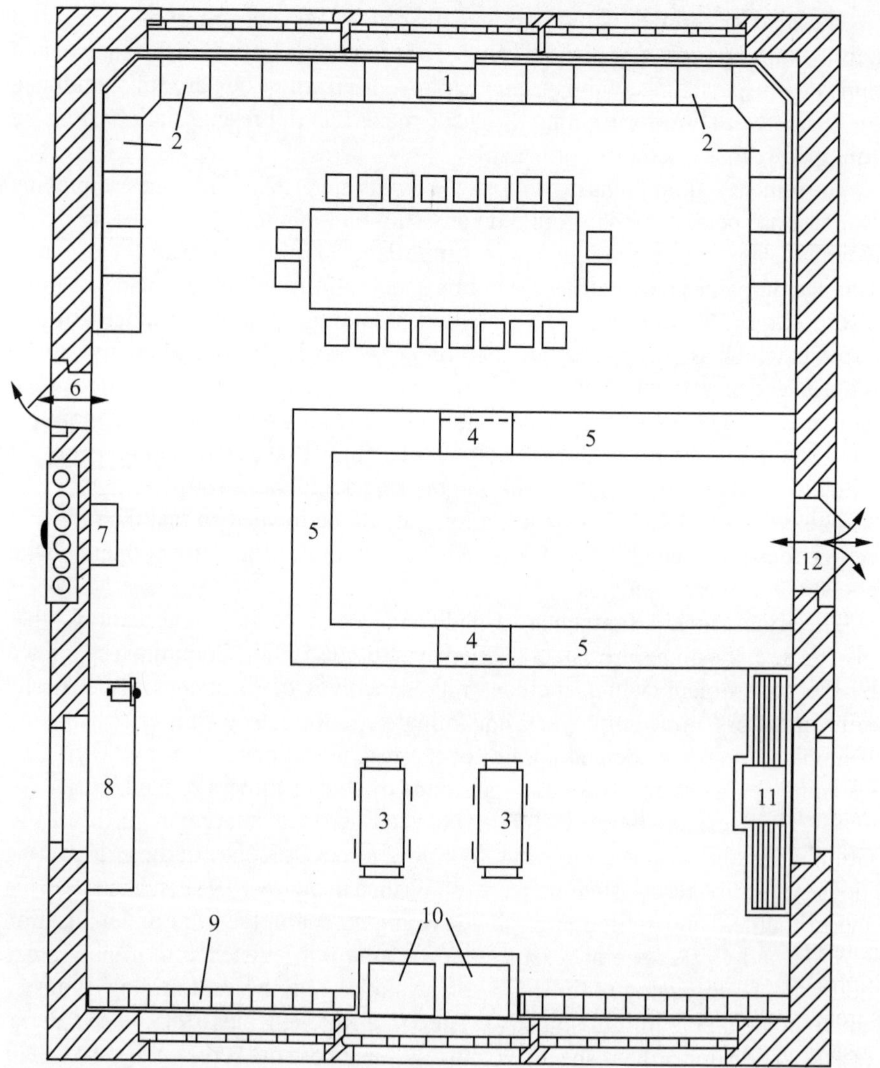

Figure 7.37 Layout of a rescue station (rescue room) at mine:
1: central test desk; 2: apparatus bench; 3: trolley; 4: flap with door; 5: counter; 6: emergency exit; 7: oxygen-filling pump; 8: work bench; 9: gas-mask cupboard; 10: disinfection chamber; 11: apparatus wash basin; 12: main entry and exit.

crawl spaces to negotiate and an environment which can be controlled to create heat, humidity, and visibility conditions as tough as are likely to be encountered during actual rescue operations. It may either form part of the main rescue station building or be constructed outside it. Residential accommodation for the Station Superintendent, instructors, members of the permanent rescue corpse, and other personnel is provided on the large grounds of the rescue station.

Training should include lectures and practicals, use of various types of fire extinguishers, first-aid including CPR, proper use of respirators and breathing apparatus, evacuation procedures, and training for each type of disaster response.

A training video will help in better preparation of mine rescue team members for the arduous situations they will encounter in rescue and recovery work, thereby using available human resource very efficiently..

7.5.1.1 Station personnel

The permanent personnel at every central or district station usually comprise a Superintendent who is a custodian of the station, one or two Assistant Superintendents, at least two instructors, two mechanics, and a rescue corpse of six to nine active trained rescue men.

7.5.1.2 Station apparatus and equipment

The mining regulations specify the minimum safety apparatus and equipment of the officially-approved type that should be kept, and maintained at every rescue station. The equipment of a rescue station comprises the equipment stored at the station and a mine rescue van which is kept fully stocked and ready for use as a mobile rescue station whenever an emergency arises. A rescue station is equipped with self-contained oxygen breathing apparatus and necessary equipment for testing such apparatus, a portable supply of pressurised oxygen, or oxygen-generating chemical as applicable to the supplied breathing apparatus, tins of absorbent chemicals, all-service gas masks, oxygen self-rescuers, gas detectors for CO and CH_4, oxygen indicators, safety lamps, (flame and electrical), bird testers with oxygen cylinders, permissible flashlights, electric cap lamp charging rack, resuscitators and inhalators, first-aid materials, stretchers, portable mine rescue communication system or a sound-powered communication system, a mobile inert gas generator or a mobile nitrogen inertisation plant, a large-diameter hole drill rig, a rescue cage/capsule, a diesel–electric mobile emergency hoist, high-capacity submersible pumps, hydraulic rescue tools consisting of hydraulic spreaders, cutters, combi-cutters, rams, jack sets, pumps, pneumatic lifting bags, hose reels and adequate supply of necessary replacement parts of all apparatus and equipment and other materials necessary to carry out efficiently the function of such a station.

Provision of a gas chromatograph in the mine rescue van for analysis of air samples will be of great help in rescue and recovery operations.

All mine rescue apparatus and equipment must be properly maintained to assure their availability for immediate use. All breathing apparatus must be inspected and tested at intervals not exceeding 30 days and a record of all such inspections and tests must be maintained.

7.5.2 Rescue organisation at mines

Every mine must maintain and organise a sufficient number of volunteer rescue-trained men with training in all types of possible emergencies depending on the size and hazardous character of the mine. The rescue men may be trained to cooperate with the permanent rescue corps of the rescue station to which the mine is affiliated on the basis of the knowledge of the mine, or organised into two or more rescue brigades which will be supplemented by the permanent rescue corps of the rescue station when an emergency arises. Every mine should have a joint scheme of mutual assistance with neighbouring mines whose advice, rescue teams, and rescue equipment can be drawn upon in willing cooperation when coping with underground emergencies.

On the Continent of Europe, the rescue organisation at the mine level comprises one director/commander, one deputy director, two apparatus mechanics, and three competent rescue brigades of five persons each. Each brigade has a captain chosen from among the members for his experience in leading and decision-making, who will be responsible for the safety of the members. The members of the rescue brigades are drawn from both underground supervisory officials (deputies) and reliable workmen (miners and mechanics) who must have been employed underground for a minimum period of one year within the past five years. They are carefully selected on grounds of their coolness of temperament, powers of endurance, general suitability for work, age, and medical fitness as may be prescribed, and are made to undergo a course of instruction and training as prescribed in the regulations. The director and the deputy director are selected from among suitable technical supervisory officials who should have already worked for sometime as members of the mine rescue brigades. They should undergo a prescribed course of training at a central rescue station before they officially head the mine rescue organization. The director has responsible charge and control of the rescue organization and his appointment must be approved by the central rescue station and the mines inspectorate. In the UK, the director of operations may be a senior official on duty or a senior official of the area or central headquarters.

In India, the Superintendent of the rescue station within whose jurisdiction the mine falls shall perform such rescue and recovery work as may be assigned to him by the manager of the mine or in his absence the principal official on duty.

To maintain the rescue organisation at peak efficiency, periodic underground drills and refresher training courses should be conducted for all its members according to a definite schedule which may be prescribed.

All the members of the mine rescue team should be medically examined annually for their physical fitness to perform mine rescue and recovery work for prolonged periods under strenuous conditions of extreme heat and humidity.

At ordinary times, the rescue men should be distributed, as far as practicable, equally over the different shifts on their normal duties. They should be easily identified at all times and should leave their working places for their pre-planned destinations immediately after a mine rescue notification alarm or warning.

All personnel of the rescue organisation of a mine should live at a distance not greater than 4 km from the rescue station/room at the mine. They should preferably be housed as near the mine as practicable and be provided with communication and transport facilities.

7.5.2.1 Mine rescue notification alarm

A mine rescue organisation comprising two or three rescue brigades can only function effectively when arrangements are made to summon its members immediately their services are required. Every mine must perfect its own emergency organisation depending on the type(s) of emergency most likely to occur and the size of the mine, which can be set into action immediately an emergency arises such as after a mine fire or explosion. The emergency organisation includes a plan for notifying mine rescue teams and mine officials likely to be needed and summoning outside help.

For summoning the rescue men employed underground, telephones have proved to be the simplest and quickest means of sending warning messages in emergencies in mines. Fire warning systems may also be used.

For summoning the rescue men on off-duty, telephone, sirens, messengers, amateur radio systems and portable radio-frequency phones may be used. Sirens and messengers as means of communication are seldom used today.

The notification of the on-duty and off-duty rescue men is done according to a pre-planned scheme in which the order or priority of notification and the method of communication are laid down.

7.5.2.2 Mine emergency notification plan

There are two types of messages for notifying officials and summoning help, 'Action Messages' and 'Warning Messages'.

'Action Messages' are addressed to persons whose attendance is required at once or who have to carry out duties immediately as outlined in their 'duty cards'. An action message chart must be prepared indicating the order in which messages are to be transmitted. Action messages must be short, clear and to the point.

Warning Messages are addressed to other key personnel whose attendance is required less urgently or who may have to prepare some action to be taken at a later stage or on receipt of a further message. A Warning Message Chart must be prepared for the mine and the area in which it is located.

Warning messages should indicate clearly what has occurred and what action, if any, the person or organisation is required to prepare for.

Besides informing the mine rescue men, action messages should be sent to the following key persons at the mine:

(1) All mine officials;
(2) Safety Engineer/Safety Officer;
(3) Rescue Room In-charge;
(4) Ventilation Officer;
(5) Chief/Assistant Chief Surveyor/Surveyors;
(6) Surface Manager;
(7) Senior underground mechanical and electrical supervisory officials;
(8) Senior officials on duty in emergency;
(9) Welfare officer;
(10) Medical officer;

(11) First-aid attendants;
(12) Banksman;
(13) Lamproom in-charge;
(14) Timekeeper;
(15) Storekeeper;
(16) Security, Main Gate Office;
(17) Winding Engineman;
(18) Fire Deputy;
(19) Canteen Manager;
(20) Public Telephone Exchange;
(21) Colliery Engineer.

Warning messages should be sent to the following:

(1) Central/District Rescue Station;
(2) Mines Inspectorate;
(3) Adjoining mines for assistance under mutual-aid plan;
(4) Head office of the mine/Area/Headquarters;
(5) Police authorities;
(6) Doctors;
(7) Local hospitals;
(8) Connecting and adjoining mines endangered;
(9) Mine Safety Council/Commission;
(10) Mineworkers' Union;
(11) Overmen and Deputies Union; and
(12) District Magistrate.

The mine telephone system must be examined for its capacity for internal extensions that are likely to be required in an emergency as well as adequacy of telephone communications between the surface and the underground. The telephone operators should be given special instructions for compliance in an emergency. It is essential to request the supervisor/operator of the Public Telephone Exchange to give priority for outgoing calls from the mine and to restrict incoming calls to those concerning the emergency until further notice.

Finally, the emergency plan should be reviewed periodically and updated to maintain its execution at peak efficiency.

Figure 7.38 gives the telephonic connections to the Mine Telephone Exchange/ Fire and Rescue Station.

7.5.3 Rescue and recovery work following mine disasters

The objectives of rescue and recovery operations in a mine following a large fire or explosion are ordinarily as follows:

(1) To ensure safety of the persons involved in rescue/recovery work;
(2) To rescue entombed, asphyxiated and missing men or recover their bodies as soon as practicable;

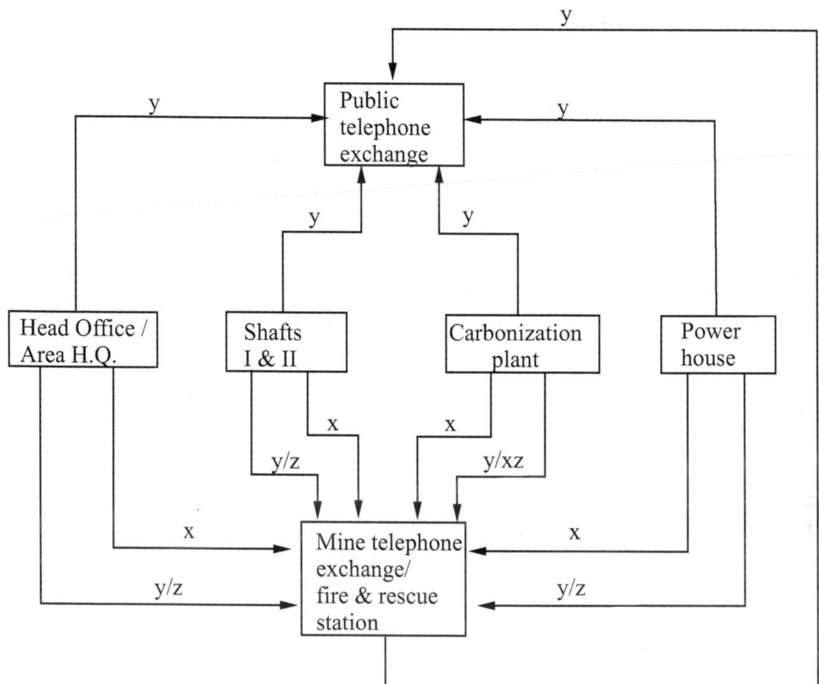

Figure 7.38 Telephonic communication system on surface.

(3) To examine location of fires and fight them effectively before an explosion could occur; and

(4) To restore ventilation throughout the mine and to ensure that the mine is in safe condition for resuming mining operations.

Experience has shown that an efficient organisation, proper and adequate equipment and materials, and a proper procedure are vital in conducting rescue and recovery operations with safety. In the following, organisation for rescue and recovery operations and procedure for rescue brigades will be described.

In any mine emergency, it would be advantageous to designate a room adjacent to the Manager's Office as a conference room in which important decisions on the conduct of exploration, rescue, and other operations are taken by an advisory committee comprising senior officials of the mine management in consultation with the representatives of the mines inspectorate, rescue station, and the employees' unions. The conference room should contain a complete set of accurate plans and sections of the mine including charts showing the compressed air, water and electrical supply systems.

There should also be a sound-proof 'control room' for issue of instructions to under-officials as per decisions taken at the conference of senior officials as well as for interrogation. In the control room a 3-member crisis control or management team continuously assesses the emergency situation and directs the operation as needed to control the situation, recording the actions taken and keeping in constant touch with the company's chief executive officer. A line of command should be established to minimise confusion so that the employees will have no doubt about who has authority to direct the operation.

Rooms should also be provided for accommodation of the director/superintendent or the man in charge of operations, rescue brigades from outside the mine, doctors, the injured, the dead, and for storage of food.

Experience with numerous rescue and recovery operations following mine disasters has shown that temporary underground and surface organisations should be formed as soon as mine rescue men comprising at least one brigade and other local mine officials and selected employees have assembled after their notification of an emergency at the rescue station or rescue room at the mine or surface rescue base, and at the mine office respectively.

If, after a mine rescue alarm underground, the rescue men present in the mine have assembled at a pre-planned central meeting station underground, their services may be utilised, under certain circumstances, to start rescue and recovery operations or to do some exploration work in order to throw some light on the situation. In such a case, breathing apparatus must be transported from the surface to the meeting station by other rescue men and employees. Ordinarily, after the alarm, the rescue man first arriving at the surface rescue base performs the duties of the director or in-charge until the latter's arrival. On his arrival, the director must immediately contact the manager or, in his absence, the principal official present to obtain information on the probable place of occurrence of the disaster, prevailing underground conditions, and the nature of the rescue and recovery manager or, in his absence, the senior official operations to be conducted. The official in-charge must formulate a plan for the safe conduct of work in consultation with the director and his assembled experienced colleagues who are conversant with local conditions, and are well-versed in the procedure following mine disasters. This plan is then discussed at a joint meeting with the representatives of the mines inspectorate, rescue station, and employees' unions, before it is finally approved for execution. The work should be planned to be carried out preferably in four 6-hour shifts per day.

As soon as a brigade is formed out of the assembled rescue men, the apparatus mechanic hands over to them the oxygen breathing apparatus and other accessories. Before the brigade is sent underground, the director and the mine officials should obtain information on the condition of the shafts and the main mine fans and, if they are found to be damaged, make necessary arrangements for their immediate repair or replacement as little or no recovery progress can be made when they are out of commission. Also, power should be cut off from the mine. The mine rescue brigade should be ready for rescue operation within 30 minutes.

Besides the rescue brigades, the temporary organisation should include officials, material crews, track crews, and other men necessary to assist the director or the man in-charge of operations in performing the work safely, rapidly, and efficiently. The temporary organisation includes selected persons who will have responsible charge of important points on the mine surface such as telephones, mine gates, heapstead, main fans, and laboratory (if existing), supervise transport of equipment and materials required underground from the stores to the pitbottom and from the pitbottom to the fresh-air base, look after the injured, dead, and the relatives, and perform such other duties as may be necessary.

When the task is too great for the temporary organisation to handle efficiently or when a devastating explosion occurs, the rescue and recovery operations by the temporary organisation should be continued until the arrival of additional assistance from the neighbouring mines, district and central rescue stations and other agencies when a permanent organization should be formed. The permanent organisation should take over the work started by the temporary organisation underground as well as on the surface, perform any other necessary functions, and complete the rescue and recovery work in the safest and speediest possible manner.

A running record of all important events as they occur should be kept for use as a log.

It is extremely important for the mine management to properly handle the news media and the public during a mine disaster. All facts about the situation at specific points of time, covering important subjects, must be told as fast as they are available through spokespersons from the same platform.

7.5.3.1 Fresh-air base

With the main fan(s) running normally and the shaft in commission, the first rescue brigade and other crews and men whose presence is required underground enter the mine on orders from the director or man in-charge of operations after they are briefed by him on the objectives of the operations. On entering the mine, the rescue brigade and other personnel should advance in fresh-air up to a point beyond which ventilation controls have been destroyed and establish a fresh-air base outbye that point. The exact location of the fresh-air base is determined by the director. For establishing a fresh-air base, a length of a large-section roadway should be selected. The apparatus mechanics lays out the base according to a definite plan. The base is divided into two sections, one for the rescue personnel and the other for first-aid. Figure 7.39 gives the general arrangement of a fresh-air base for extensive rescue and recovery operations. The fresh-air base is advanced as work progresses. With extensive recovery operations involving a large mine or a large area and requiring several rescue brigades, it may become necessary to establish more than one fresh-air base. If possible, a fresh-air base must be in telephonic communication with the pitbottom or surface.

7.5.3.2 First exploration ahead of fresh-air base

Exploration ahead of the fresh-air base is determined by the advisory committee after evaluation of conditions encountered by rescue teams. As the fresh-air base is being set up, each brigade member, on orders from the captain, should carefully

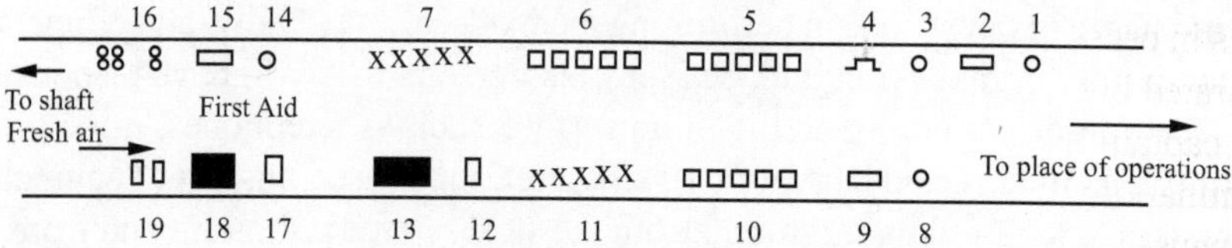

Figure 7.39 General layout of fresh-air base for extensive rescue and recovery operations:
1: director/man in-charge of operations; 2: table; 3: assisting official; 4: telephones; 5: equipped brigade No. 1; 6: apparatus No. 2 brigade; 7: brigade without apparatus; 8: apparatus mechanic; 9: table; I0: used apparatus; 11: resting brigade; 12: beverages; 13: storage space for consumed regenerators and oxygen cylinders; 14: doctor; 15: table; 16: first-aid attendants; 17: mechanical resuscitator; 18: place for resuscitation; 19: stretchers.

inspect and test his apparatus to ensure that the apparatus is air-tight and that its various parts are in safe working condition. After the apparatus is satisfactorily tested, each member reports to his captain who examines each member and his apparatus, opens the cylinder valve and connects the breathing tubes to the facepiece. The captain should have definite understanding with the director or the man in-charge of operations as to the extent of exploration, distance to travel, things to observe, and time to be taken in making the trip before he dons his apparatus aided and examined by one of the brigade members. The captain then makes entries of the names of the brigade members and the condition of their apparatus on a special card which he hands over to the director as he reports to the latter that he is ready to proceed. The director checks the entries, and, after comparing the time of his watch with that of the captain, gives the order for advance. The code of signals as specified by the mining regulations must be used in rescue work.

It is essential that when the rescue brigade is about to make an exploration ahead of the fresh-air base, another brigade fully equipped with apparatus is kept in reserve at the fresh air-base. It is only when lives are to be saved and there is little danger during the rescue operations that a brigade can advance with a reserve brigade on its way to the fresh-air base from the surface.

Under all circumstances, the exploring brigade should carry a watch, a spare oxygen cylinder, chalk, bandages, a flame safety lamp and/or methanometer, a carbon monoxide detector, a tool kit containing apparatus wrenches and screw drivers, writing pads and pencils. With rescue operations, escape apparatus and stretchers should be carried. The equipment should be equally distributed among the team members.

After entering the irrespirable atmosphere a short distance ahead of the fresh-air base, the brigade members should stop for a short time to check that their apparatus are working properly and that they are all in good physical condition without the slightest defect or in any way uncomfortable and then proceed on the trip. They should use a lifeline or battery-less or battery-powered portable telephone and proceed slowly in a single file about 2 m apart in the order: first, second, third and fourth man, captain. When using a lifeline, it must be stretched taut at all times in order to be able to give or receive signals. The brigade must not become separated but maintain the same order during advance, retreat, and during work. The captain is responsible for the safety of his men, assignment of duties, and examination of the apparatus. If the operations are strenuous, he should arrange rest pauses. During the course of operations, he should check at regular intervals the supply of oxygen remaining in each apparatus. In practice, it is a good rule to have, just before retreating, a reserve of oxygen in any apparatus equal to at least twice the maximum quantity of it consumed by any member during advance. This rule must be strictly adhered to even if the given job is not completed or if it is not time to retreat.

During exploration, the brigade members should examine the condition of roadways, mark with chalk their course of travel, location of bodies, and the farthest point of the trip. They should observe conditions and ascertain the extent and violence of the explosion. As an underground explosion drastically alters the prevailing ventilation patterns, new ventilation patterns must be established quickly so that effective rescue and recovery operations may be conducted. This can be done with brattice of impermeable fabric. In US mines, self-sealing brattice and parachute stoppings have been used in coal and non-coal mines with considerable success in rescue and recovery operations as well as in day-to-day ventilation changes during the normal working of the mine. The parachute stopping, like an ordinary parachute, is made of damage-resistant, light-weight fabric with regularly spaced straps around its perimeter that run to a common point. During erection, the common point of straps is attached to a roof bolt or some strongly fixed point and the stoppings is rolled out and lifted so that the ventilating air current inflates it into place sealing the perimeter. The self-sealing brattice is hemispherical and can be effectively used to replace damaged or destroyed stoppings. Such stoppings should be replaced as soon as possible with more substantial ones.

A note of all dead bodies and their positions should be made; if possible, each body should be labelled. The positions of the bodies and other articles give a good indication as to the origin of the explosion and the direction of its travel.

Experience has shown that it is always advisable to make short trips rather than long ones in advance of the fresh-air base. With a fresh brigade in good physical condition wearing self-contained breathing apparatus, exploration in flat coal seams should not exceed about 300 m under favourable conditions. This distance should, however, be reduced when steep inclinations and obstructions are encountered *en route,* roof is dangerous or low, visibility is poor, and wet bulb temperatures are high.

Exploration trips in coal mines should not be undertaken under the following conditions:

(1) In dense smoke except to save life, turn valves, or to open or shut doors essential to recovery operations;
(2) When there is probability of a gas explosion;
(3) When there are heavy falls or serious obstructions;
(4) When it is necessary to wade in more than knee-deep water;

(5) When the atmosphere is hot and humid and high wet bulb temperatures exceeding 34°C are encountered except to save life;
(6) Without a reserve full rescue brigade fully equipped at the fresh-air base except for very short trips; and
(7) With apparatus not adequately charged or in unsafe condition.

If fires are found during exploration work, they should be extinguished with water, stone dust, or fire extinguishers, or sealed off at once if they are inaccessible.

When operating in hot and humid atmospheres, the following precautions should be observed:

(1) Only such rescue persons should be selected as have good physical fitness and temperament for work in hot and humid atmospheres. Prior to undertaking rescue work, they should not have been engaged in hard physical work. Also, they should not have suffered from any organic disease or weakness in the recent past which would reduce their efficiency (for example, influenza, etc.) and their age should not exceed 45 years.
(2) The rescue men should wear minimum of light clothing.
(3) A brigade should not be allowed to operate for more than the safe period which should be decided on the basis of the condition of the atmosphere, travelling conditions in the roadways, and the tasks to be performed.

    Maximum safe periods of operation under specified conditions of temperature and humidity have been recommended in some countries for the guidance of director of rescue operations.

    Table 7.3 gives the maximum safe periods in the range wet bulb temperature 28° to 45°C as determined by tests in a climatic chamber in Germany wearing light clothing, while Table 7.4 gives the periods in the range wet-bulb temperature 31° to 42°C wearing cooling jackets using ordinary ice [90]

    Table 7.5 give the maximum safe periods as recommended for use in the U.K. [91].
(4) If any member of a brigade shows any signs of discomfort, dizziness, nausea, headache, burning sensation of skin, the captain should withdraw the whole of the brigade to the fresh-air base.
(5) There should be a constant telephonic communication between the captain and the fresh-air base. Should the communication system fail, he should withdraw his brigade. The reserve brigade at the fresh-air base should have its own communication equipment.
(6) While returning to the fresh-air base, the rescue men should be adequately protected against the sensation of coldness arising from entering a comparatively cool atmosphere. On return to the fresh-air base, they should, if possible, be provided with dry clothing and served with lukewarm water containing vitamin B1. They can be given hot drinks after 20 minutes have elapsed.
(7) The protective breathing apparatus should be subjected to thorough examination, overhaul, and testing after they have been used. In the case of compressed-oxygen apparatus, both the CO_2 absorbent and the cooler (if provided) must be changed.

(8) After working approximately for the maximum safe period, members of the rescue brigades should normally rest for 4 hours before they are called upon to perform another such period of duty. After two periods of duty in hot and humid atmosphere, they should normally rest for 24 hours.
(9) With extremely arduous rescue and recovery operations, a medical doctor must be in attendance at the fresh-air base.

If the brigade is to look for missing men, all necessary mine workings within the area to be explored should be systematically searched for them, and, if unconscious victims are found, they should be carried out of the irrespirable atmosphere as soon as possible to the nearest point in fresh air or to the first-aid station at the fresh-air base. When transporting dead bodies, it should be remembered that the brigade should not ordinarily exhaust their strength in carrying the dead bodies any great distance in fresh air. 20 m relays is plenty for each pair to carry the loaded stretchers. Special precautions must be taken when handling dead bodies when they are much decomposed.

Table 7.3 Maximum safe periods under difficult working conditions for rescue personnel donning compressed-oxygen breathing apparatus and wearing light clothing

t_w° \ Δt°C	0–2	3–4	5–6	7–8	9–10
		Minutes			
28	95	90	85	80	80
29	80	80	75	70	70
30	70	70	65	60	60
31	60	60	55	50	50
32	50	50	50	45	45
33	45	45	45	40	40
34	40	40	40	35	35
35	35	35	35	35	30
36	30	30	30	30	30
37	30	30	30	25	25
38	25	25	25	25	25
39	25	25	25	20	20
40	20	20	20	20	20
41	20	20	20	20	15
42	20	15	15	15	15
43	15	15	15	15	15
44	15	15	15	15	15
45	15	15	10	10	10

7.5.3.3 Advancing fresh-air base

After returning to the fresh-air base, the captain reports his observations to the director of the rescue operations who, after full discussion with the captain and other members of the brigade, informs the captain of the second brigade in reserve

Table 7.4 Maximum safe periods under difficult working conditions wearing ice-cooled jackets

$t_w°$ \ Δt°C	0–2	3-4	5–6	7–8	9–10
			Minutes		
31	–	60	60	60	60
32	60	60	60	60	60
33	60	60	60	60	60
34	60	60	55	55	50
35	55	50	50	45	45
36	45	45	45	40	40
37	40	40	35	35	35
38	35	35	35	30	30
39	30	30	30	30	25
40	25	25	25	25	25
41	25	25	20	20	20
42	20	20	20	20	20

of the prevailing conditions and orders him to proceed in the same manner as the first exploration if further explorations are indicated before the fresh-air base is advanced. The brigade members hand over the apparatus to the apparatus mechanic, reporting any difficulties met with in their use. The progress of work done in each shift must be shown on a map of the mine showing area recovered, position of bodies, etc.

When it is advisable to shift the fresh-air base to a predetermined point, the reserve brigade proceeds to erect temporary stoppings, ventilate all open accessible workings by suitably conducting the ventilating current along the most direct paths known, and perform other necessary operations.

The above procedure of alternately exploring ahead of the fresh-air base and moving the fresh-air base should be continued until the entire area affected by the fires or explosion has been recovered.

7.5.3.4 Communication in rescue work

The director or man in-charge of operations at the first-air base must be in constant communication with the exploring brigades. The brigade members must also be able to communicate between themselves. A sound-powered telephone system adapted to an all-vision facepiece fitted with a speaking diaphragm was successfully developed by the MSA. Battery-powered telephones can also be used. Where such equipment is not available, lifeline or audible signals may be used and for communication between brigade members Klaxon horn may be used.

7.5.4 Underwater rescue and recovery

To rescue men trapped behind a flooded synclinal roadway, diving apparatus of self-contained compressed-oxygen type must be worn by the rescue men. As it

Table 7.5 Maximum safe periods under difficult working conditions for rescue personnel donning Proto compressed-oxygen breathing apparatus and wearing light clothing as recommended for use in U.K. mines [91]

In fully saturated atmosphere

t_w°C	Minutes
26.7	60
28.1	52
29.4	44
30.8	38
32.2	32
33.0	28
35.0	24
36.4	21
37.8	19

In partly saturated atmosphere

t_w°C t_d°C	26.7	29.4	32.2	35.0	37.8	40.6	43.3	46.1	48.9
				Minutes					
22.5	–	–	–	–	–	–	–	–	59
23.9	–	–	–	–	–	60	59	57	54
25.3	–	–	–	60	56	54	53	52	48
26.7	60	60	56	53	50	48	46	44	41
28.1	–	50	49	46	44	42	40	38	36
29.4	–	44	42	39	38	36	34	33	32
30.8	–	–	37	35	34	32	30	29	28
32.2	–	–	32	31	30	28	27	26	25
33.6	–	–	–	27	26	25	24	24	22
35.0	–	–	–	24	23	22	22	21	20
36.4	–	–	–	–	22	20	19	19	–
37.8	–	–	–	19	–	–	–	–	–

is not possible to bring trapped men through the water, air must be taken to them through the water. As the amount of air that becomes dissolved in the tissues and blood increases with the hydrostatic head above the rescuing diver and the gas comes out of the solution in the form of very fine bubbles which travel with the blood through the body when he surfaces, the diver must ascend at a controlled rate determined by the depth and duration of dive. If he rises to the surface too fast, the gas comes out of the solution too fast causing decompression sickness.

It should be realised that pure oxygen must not be used at depths greater than 10 m but must be diluted with nitrogen which should constitute 60 per cent of the inhaling air up to a depth of 55 m.

The rescue men wearing the diving apparatus must move in a crouching position holding on to rails, etc. As the mine water is usually dirty and lights are reflected back, the rescue men must be trained to work by feel and only men of very calm disposition should be selected. Specialised teams of divers should be employed for rescue and recovery operations.

7.5.5 Mine rescue through large-diameter drillholes

Large-diameter drillholes and bored shafts have been successfully used in Germany, Holland and the USA, for rescuing miners trapped alive underground after a rock/coal outburst or inundation. Special rotary and down-the-hole drills have been developed for the purpose. Rescue drilling may be carried out from suitable underground workings or from the surface depending on the location of the trapped miners. A probe/pilot hole of smaller diameter is first drilled to have access to the trapped men which is then reamed to a large diameter of 500 mm. It is possible today to drill rescue holes or shafts from the surface to a depth of 300 m through hard rock within a week. The trapped miners can be expeditiously and safely rescued through the drillhole by means of a rescue capsule or cage. For the first time in India, 65 miners trapped in Mahavir Colliery, Ranigunj, India, due to sudden irruption of water from water-logged workings in an overlying seam were rescued on November 15, 1989 by means of a rescue capsule through a 600-mm borehole. There must be a plan and strategy.

Rescue of persons trapped underground after a mine disaster requires, in general, careful planning on many fronts so that minimum time is lost in starting rescue operations. The extent of planning required before putting the first probe hole depends on the situation arising out of the peculiar location of the possible site of entombment. While planning for rescue by the conventional methods in the normal way, action should simultaneously be taken to procure a drill rig of proven design for putting boreholes for communication and rescue. For easy availability in an emergency, the drill rig may be located at a Mine Rescue Station or at any notified location and a drilling engineer appointed exclusively for the purpose of putting rescue boreholes.

The detection of trapped men is often difficult and remains somewhat of a guess estimate. Senior mine supervisory officials should jointly assess the probable presence and location of the men and the most likely cause of their entombment. Rapid identification of the noises as signals and locating their source of emission point to the presence of men and their likely position is essential. The surveyor should then pinpoint this location on the mine plan for a probe hole (65, 80 or 100 mm diameter) to be rapidly drilled to make the first contact. Experience has shown that the initial probe drilling may end up in empty cavities or miss the targeted place due to deviation of the hole particularly when traversing through faulted ground or old workings. Once the primary contact is established, the men must be supplied with air, water, food, medicines, telephone and other moral boosting articles. During the probe drilling, it should be foreseen that no further hazards to the trapped men are created. The primary contact borehole should not be disturbed until a rescue hole is drilled and enlarged in stages if a drill rig which will drill 500-mm holes in one stage is not available. When the rescue borehole has made contact, the trapped men can be hoisted by means of a cylindrical rescue capsule with conical ends and a two-wing door, which should also be located at a Mine Rescue Station or at any notified location. A 440-mm diameter capsule is used in 500-mm diameter rescue boreholes.

7.5.6 Barricades

Barricading has proved to be a very useful technique for saving lives of trapped miners after a serious mine fire or explosion. A temporary shelter is constructed by the trapped miners out of available building materials in a nearby dead-end heading or location which is still free of toxic gases and an airtight shelter can be constructed to conserve an adequate amount of air so that they can survive for a few days while awaiting rescue.

The following important guidelines may be followed when barricading:

(1) The trapped miners should collect all tools, timber, boards, brattice, buckets, water, and any other materials which might be useful.
(2) Every effort should be made to erect the barricade as air-tight as practicable. Where compressed-air line is not available, the miners should not unnecessarily move in the enclosed area but should either lie down or sit on the floor to conserve oxygen. Occasionally, one person should slowly walk around the area to mix the air enclosed.
(3) Before barricading, the ventilating current outside the proposed barricade site should be stopped or short-circuited.
(4) The trapped miners should try to send signals at intervals of time by pounding on the water- and compressed air- lines, haulage track rails, and roadway sides and roof so that they can be heard at some distance from the barricade. An emergency communication system must be laid down in such emergencies to locate the miners and to rescue them.
(5) While retreating into an area to be barricaded, the miners should indicate on doors, pipelines, rails, roof and sides of roadways traversed by chalk or other means to indicate the course taken in retreating.

7.5.7 Rescue chambers, refuge stations, or refuge bays

These are an outgrowth of temporary barricades and provide shelter on temporary or permanent basis at predetermined locations in the mine workings in emergencies. Temporary rescue chambers are constructed in underground workings as mining advances in order that workmen from production sections can easily seek safe temporary refuge donning self-contained self-rescuers within their rated duration. In course of time, one of them will become a permanent rescue shelter. The primary function is to sustain life in the event of an underground fire, explosion, or other emergency by preventing ingress of noxious gases and providing a source of respirable air before eventual escape or rescue during an emergency. Difficulty in breathing and sleeping, rapid heart rate, sweating, nausea, dizziness, thirst, and body pains may be experienced by miners while they are enclosed in the rescue chamber. Their provision has over the years become a widely accepted practice as hundreds of lives have been saved in both coal and metal mines for which reason they generally form an integral part of the escape and rescue strategies in underground mines All persons must be explicitly instructed to seek refuge in the rescue chambers in emergencies.

The rescue chambers should be designed keeping in view the following objectives:

(1) withstand low-intensity explosions,
(2) be designed as far as possible with a minimum height of 1.8 m and a floor area and volume adequate for the number of workmen likely to use them,
(3) be constructed of incombustible and heat-resistant materials; with temporary rescue chambers the construction materials should have at least 1-hour fire-resistant rating,
(4) be located at easily accessible places in an area, where possible, free of combustible material in accordance with the maximum safe travelling distance which can be covered with or without the aid of a SCSR but inaccessible to air containing noxious smoke, fumes or gases,
(5) be equipped with a means for maintenance of a healthy respirable atmosphere,
(6) be equipped with a sufficient supply of potable water,
(7) be equipped with a means of communication with surface,
(8) be equipped with first-aid equipment.

The quality of air within a rescue chamber is influenced by the following factors:

(1) the size of the chamber,
(2) the maximum number of workers to be accommodated,
(3) the duration of the occupancy,
(4) the permeability of the surrounding strata and the probable presence of other leakage paths,
(5) the virgin rock temperature,
(6) the temperature and humidity conditions,
(7) the metabolic characteristics of the workers.

Maintenance of safe environmental conditions within the rescue chamber necessitates supply of air or oxygen for replenishment of the oxygen consumed and dilution or removal of exhaled carbon dioxide and other gases emitted from the surrounding strata into the chamber.

The various methods that can be used for adequate ventilation of refuge chambers are:

(1) Use of compressed air from compressed-air pipelines,
(2) Use of boreholes and fans to supply fresh air from the surface,
(3) Use of compressed-air steel cylinders,

(4) Use of life support or environmental control systems.

The use of compressed air for ventilation of refuge chambers is possible in metal and coal mines laid out on the horizon system of mining where compressed-air lines are provided in main development roadways.

The use of boreholes to supply fresh air from the surface is costly and is often not feasible.

In mines which do not have compressed air underground, a mine environmental control system Survivair-E has recently been developed by Naschem, a division of Denel (Pty) Ltd, Rep. of South Africa, which will provide an alternative method of ventilating reclaimable rescue chamber [92].

Survivair-E combines two integrated systems comprising the replenishment of oxygen consumed by means of six oxygen-generating-units and the removal of metabolically produced carbon dioxide by means of two separate carbon dioxide scrubbing units.

The oxygen-generating system releases oxygen through thermal decomposition of sodium chlorate chemical by an ignition device. Six generating units are used, each generating 2900 litres of oxygen of 99.5% purity within 45 min after activation. The oxygen generators comply with intrinsic safety standards set out by the South African Bureau of Standards and certified for use in fiery mines.

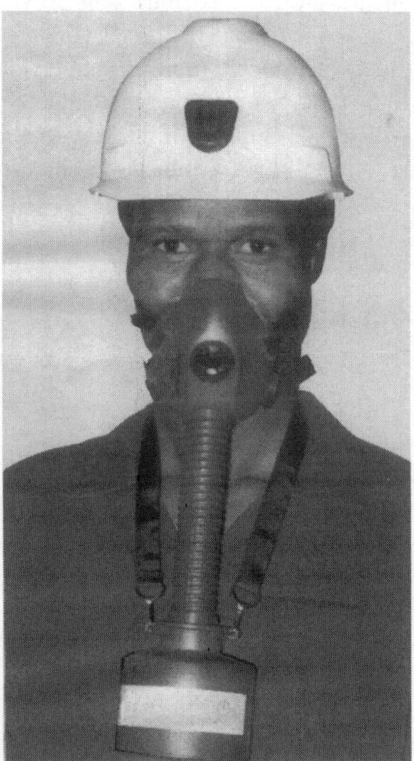

Figure 7.40 Dioxcrub-P™ carbon dioxide filter respirator

Another solution to carbon dioxide scrubbing was obtained by the development of personal respirator (DIOXSCRUB-P^{TM}) with a replaceable filter canister with 90% scrubbing efficiency and weighing 650 g also manufactured by Naschem (Fig. 7.40).

Appendix 2 gives Mines Rescue Rules, 1985 which apply to underground mines in India.

7.5.8 Accidents to mine rescue brigade members

The causes of accidents to rescue brigade members are:

1. Faulty mouthpiece breathing, facemask not properly sealed;
2. Faulty breathing equipment and accessories;
3. Incorrect handling of equipment and accessories;
4. Carelessness in performance of tasks assigned;
5. Overexertion by making long trips rather than short ones, etc.;
6. Undertaking work without specific orders; and
7. Not heeding difficult climatic conditions in the area to be recovered.

7.5.9 International mines rescue competitions

A few coal mining companies around the world organize every year an international mines rescue competition at one of the coal mines with a dedicated mines rescue station equipped with adequate modern mine rescue facilities. The rescue teams from the participating mines compete with one another demonstrating their specific strengths and skills, which will improve mine rescue organization and rescue techniques that may be followed by the industry in emergencies.

CHAPTER 8

Water Inundations

Ever since mining began, most of the mines throughout the world had always to contend with water problems which often assumed serious proportions.

One distinguishes between two types of water influx in mines: the normal influx and the sudden inrush, irruption or inundation.

The normal influx can be attributed to several sources such as stream bed seepage, general surface seepage, and barrier pillar seepage. For a given mine, it varies within a certain range depending on the amount and intensity of rainfall, intersection of faults and fissures by mine workings, and the condition of strata as affected by the progress of extraction. The amount of water pumped out of mines may be up to 20 or more times the r.o.m output.

An inrush or irruption of water is a sudden inflow of large quantities of water into mine workings causing their inundation. It may take place from the surface, overlying strata, or water-logged workings in the same mine or neighbouring mines. Inundations of mine workings are dangerous as they are sometimes unpredictable in their occurrence and often result in loss of life and property. In hot deep mines, an inrush of water may create such adverse humidity conditions that it may become almost impossible to erect a dam.

The danger of inundations is especially great in potash and salt mines as well as in metal mines with overlying salt, limestone, or dolomite beds which develop sink holes. When planning a new mine, therefore, local geographical, geotectonic, and hydrogeological conditions of the deposit in which the mine is to be opened up must be accurately known to determine the possible sources of water so that the method of shaft sinking, layout of the mine, method of extraction, and measures for control of water irruptions may be decided upon. The control of water irruptions has, as its objectives, their elimination, prevention, and delay of outbreak and it is necessary that one must have a knowledge of the different circumstances under which inundation of mine workings may occur. The fatalities from inundations are only next to those from mine explosions. In India, between 1912 and 1976, there were 12 mine disasters due to inundations, the worst disaster being that in Chasnalla (1975) when 375 miners were killed.

8.1 Causes of Inundations in Mines

8.1.1 Inundations by surface waters

Inundations by surface waters may occur after sudden and abnormally heavy rains when the surface mine outlets such as shafts, inclines, and adits may get flooded or subsidence fractures reaching the surface get submerged. They are very dangerous as large quantities of water break into the mine within a short time preventing escape of workmen. Surface drainage must be designed to cope with storm rainfall run-off conditions.

8.1.2 Inundations from overlying strata

Inundations from the overlying strata can occur under one or more of the following conditions:

(1) When impervious strata are pierced by mine workings;
(2) When fissures or fracture planes develop in impervious strata due to subsidence communicating with water-bearing strata above;
(3) Where faults, fissures or fracture planes in communication with a water-bearing bed are intersected by mine workings;
(4) Where the deposit occurs under a water-bearing bed, lying uncomformably on the eroded surface of the deposit;
(5) When a mine working is too near to the surface and accidental holing has taken place into a pond, stream bed, or outcrop workings;
(6) Where boreholes drilled for prospecting have not been sealed-off; and
(7) Mining coal from beneath the seabed as at Ellington mine, UK Coal.

8.1.3 Inundations from water-logged workings

Inundations from water-logged workings occur when they are accidentally holed or when barrier pillars fail due to inadequate design. They are not easily predictable and the danger from them is especially great in semi-steep and steep formations.

8.2 Measures Against Inundations

These measures can be divided into: surface measures and underground measures.

The surface measures aim at preventing dangerous accumulations of water on the mine surface.

The underground measures offer protection against inundations.

Both surface and underground measures may be adopted to control inundations with varying degrees of effectiveness depending largely upon geological and hydrological conditions.

Before mining, a suspected water-rich area could be drained by drilling or building a reliable drainage system.

8.2.1 Surface measures

They can be further divided into:

(a) measures against flooding of mine main entries or outlets; and
(b) measures against seepage of surface waters.

The selection of one or more remedial measures is governed by the cost–benefit ratio and the method of financing.

8.2.1.1 Measures against flooding of mine main entries

These consist of the following:

(1) Locating shaft sites away from faults especially formed by major tensional stresses;
(2) Laying mouths of shafts, inclines, and adits above the high-water mark and lining them for the first 20 m with watertight lining.
(3) Filling up with debris and other sealing materials all abandoned shafts and boreholes which have ceased to serve any purpose with the existing mine;
(4) Cutting diversion drains or ditches or erecting embankments or concrete walls on the surface to intercept and conduct the surface run-off water away; and
(5) Constructing dams and reservoirs in the upper reaches of rivers to prevent their flooding.

8.2.1.2 Measures against seepage of surface waters

Depending on the nature of the bed(s), surface water (streams, ponds, tanks, lakes) lose considerable quantities of water which may enter mine workings or form water pools in the strata. The infiltration of surface waters can be controlled by one or more of the following measures:

(1) Straightening, cleaning, widening, and grading stream channels to provide free flow of water especially in areas with vertical fractures, subsidence, or high-permeability rocks;
(2) Silting or lining stream beds with concrete or rubble masonry;
(3) Grouting the river bed with cement to stabilise and seal it;
(4) In the case of near-surface mines, laying ponds and tanks dry if they form a cause of water influx in mines;
(5) Diverting streams/rivers, if technically and economically feasible, with safety to new and safe channels;
(6) Back-filling surface excavations or subsided areas with impervious materials to an established hydraulic gradient that will ensure natural drainage;
(7) Diverting run-off to prevent its infiltration into fissures on subsided areas;
(8) Conducting run-off across pervious or subsided areas of the mining property by means of flumes;
(9) Grouting overlying strata to reduce permeability and the flow; a seismic reflection survey on the surface will reveal the location of subsurface anomalous structures such as fractures, joints or faults for the drilling and grouting programme.
(10) Leaving outcrop barrier pillars of adequate size;
(11) Selecting a method of extraction, especially of thick seams, by which the strata subside uniformly without fracturing. For extraction under important waterways, hydraulic stowing is the best method of roof control; and
(12) Afforestation along river banks.

8.2.2 Underground measures

These protect life and property against inundations. They consist of the following measures:

1. General lowering of the water table to below the level of the workings by borehole pumps was extensively applied for a long time for opencast mines but it suffers from the disadvantage that a stage might be reached when further de-watering would severely interfere with water resources, wells, etc.
2. Avoiding blasting and drilling operations near suspected water-logged workings.
3. Leaving safety water pillars or barriers. A safety water pillar is that portion of the bed that is left unmined:
   (i) below an overlying water formation along boundary line or lines of adjoining properties;
   (ii) between parts of a mine;
   (iii) below surface streams, tanks and lakes;
   (iv) around shafts; or
   (v) along major faults.

Its principal function is to act as a dam to prevent water accumulations from suddenly breaking into mine workings. Lack of maintenance of dependable pillars by depending on old surveys and incorrect old plans had resulted in several mine disasters in the past.

The vertical thickness of the safety pillar against water-bearing strata overlying a bed is generally prescribed by the mining regulations. In coal mines, it should not be less than 20 m.

The width of a safety pillar between adjacent mines is usually prescribed by the mining regulations. In coal mines, it should be at least 20 m on either side of the boundary line at right-angles to it.

If possible, a mine should be laid out in districts or panels according to their hydrology. The panels should have substantial safety barriers on three sides with a minimum number of entries or drivages through them so that, after mining, each panel can be isolated from the others.

The width of a safety pillar-barrier to be maintained against abandoned water-logged workings depends on the following factors:

(1) The degree of uncertainty regarding the exact location of the old workings;
(2) The thickness of the bed;
(3) The nature of the bed whether it is friable, contains dirt partings, or has been crushed and fractured by folding;
(4) The inclination of the bed and the direction of the pillars in relation to the line of full dip;
(5) The maximum hydrostatic head;
(6) The nature and condition of the adjacent strata whether pervious or broken;

(7) The method of extraction and roof control on the side of the pillar;
(8) The presence of faults, their throw and direction; and
(9) Effect of mining other beds.

The geophysical electrical resistivity determination method can be used with reasonable certainty for determination of coal barrier thickness against water logged workings or delineation of hidden water-filled galleries within the barriers. There is, however, no general rule or formula for determining the size of safety pillars as no rule can possibly serve all cases.

4. Supporting roadways not coming under the influence of mining operations with water-tight lining.
5. Cementation of fractured strata in the roof containing water in fissures.
6. Driving drainage tunnels or adits to de-water the property. This method had been practised in certain metalliferous mines in the early days of mining.
7. When driving through hard ground traversed by water-bearing fissures, adopting a technique of diamond drilling cover ahead of the advancing face in which long holes (100 m) are drilled ahead of the face from bays (40 m apart) excavated on alternate sides of the roadway (Fig. 8. 1);
8. Providing adequate sump and pumping capacities at predetermined points for dealing with inrushes of water even where safety pillars are provided.
9. Erecting water dams or hydraulic seals to seal abandoned sections of the mine.
10. Erecting bulkhead doors in mine workings with immediate danger of inundation.
11. Providing additional lodgement capacity in worked-out area(s) to which sudden inrushes of water may be directed in an emergency.

8.2.2.1 Mine sumps

Every mine should have adequate sump and pumping capacities to deal not only with the normal water influx but also with any sudden inflows or irruptions of water, or powerful feeders that may be encountered so that mine safety is assured. There should be sufficient power available to pump out all the water inflow to the surface.

Pumping systems vary from mine to mine depending on the rate of water influx, depth of mine, mine layout, and whether hydraulic winning and /or hydraulic stowing is practised. A mine may have a main pumping station at a deep level

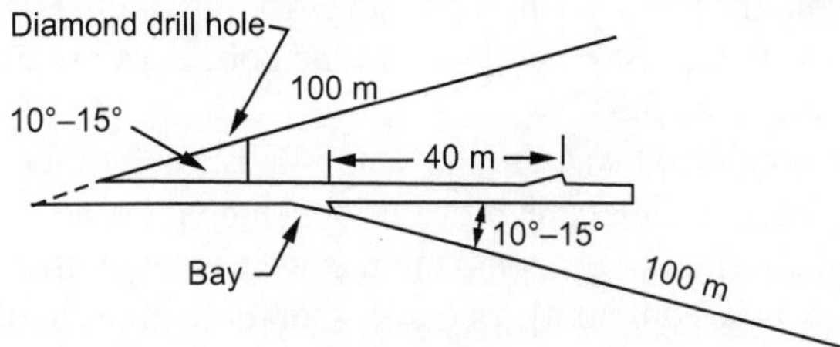

Figure 8.1 Cover drilling for advancing heading.

and water from upper levels may be allowed to gravitate to the main sump for pumping to the surface. Water may also be intercepted at various levels and pumped either direct to the surface from each level or between one or more levels to a main pumping station at the upper level. One characteristic feature of the main pumping station is that the main pumps and main sump are located near the pitbottom of a main surface shaft. In hydraulic-stowing mines, small pumping stations are established with settlers/settling tanks, which pump water to the main pumping station.

The capacity of a mine sump constructed near the pitbottom is provided by the sump roads of uniform cross-section which should be fundamentally driven below the main haulage level (about 4 m) in order to offer maximum storage volume or lodgement capacity as well as ensure safety of the pitbottom against drowning or flooding. The sump roads must be laid in water-impervious rocks. Sump roads are preferable to settling tanks of very deep construction designed to settle the solids against a vertical flow.

The necessity for support and the type of support for sump roads depend on their expected life, nature of the strata, and rock pressure conditions. For roads needed for a short life and built on strong ground, they may be left unsupported or lightly supported with timber sets, but for life long and on weak ground, they may be supported with brickwork, concrete, or concrete blocks. Timber and steel should not be used.

For a given cross-sectional area, the total length of the sump roads is determined by the degree of wetness of mine, acidity of mine water, manual or automatic operation of pumps, capacity and daily operational time of pumps, and possible future extension of capacity due to expansion of mine. In general, the sump capacity must be planned for a water influx over a period of 24 to 48 hours to take care of power failures, major pump breakdowns, and possible future extension of capacity. In mines with acid mine water problem, as the water must be removed rapidly and continuously by pumping, the sump capacity should be held to a minimum needed for pump operation. Furthermore, the sump roads must be laid so that one half of them can be laid still for purposes of cleaning while the other half is in commission.

Sump roads are connected with the pump chamber through suction pits in which pump suctions are placed to give flooded pump suctions. There should be at least two suction pits accessible either through shallow vertical pits or through inclines driven from the main roads (Fig. 8.2). To prevent water from rising up the suction pits into the pump chamber in the event of flooding of the main level, regulators/check valves must be provided in the portion of the sump road that is near the suction pits (Fig. 8.3).

As the drains which feed water to the sump roads carry a lot of solid particles and suspended dirt, a settling gallery or settling sump must be provided to settle out most of the sediments so that pump maintenance is minimised. Long shallow settling sumps are more commonly used than short deep ones. To facilitate sludge removal, they must be divided into two parts so that cleaning can go on in one

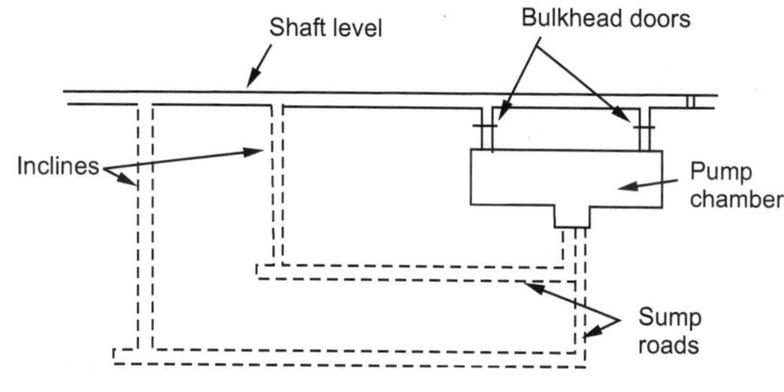

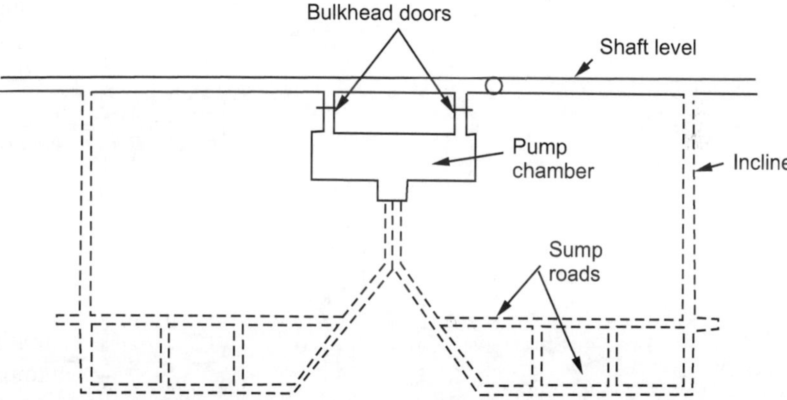

Figure 8.2 Layouts of pitbottom main sump with inclines connecting sump roads.

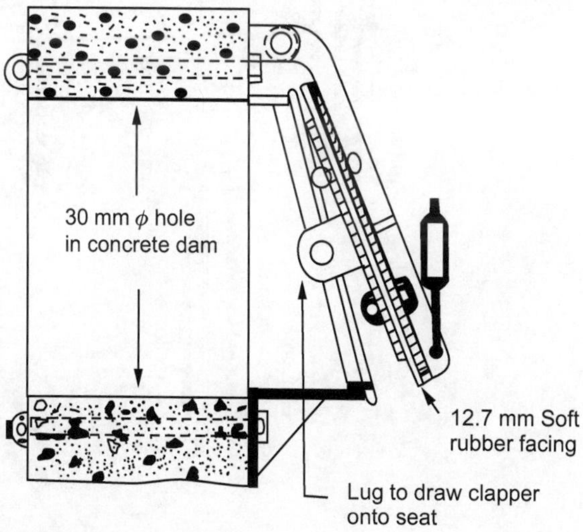

Figure 8.3 Sump check valve.

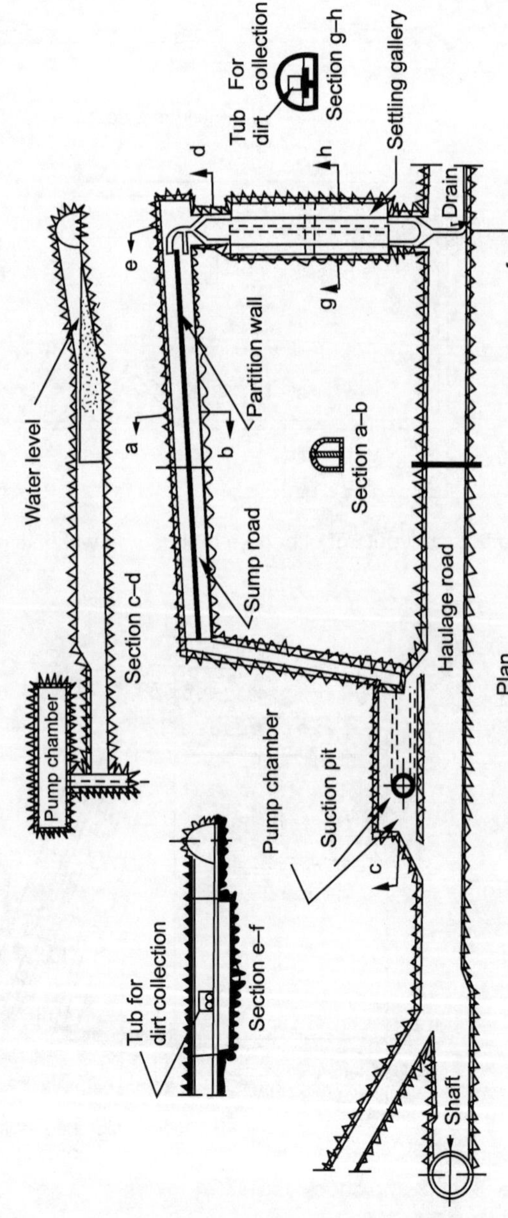

Figure 8.4 Pitbottom sump layout with small water influx.

while the other receives the inflow. If the pumps are well designed, comparatively little sludge will settle in suction pits in which the pump suctions are placed.

A convenient method of cleaning the sump is by means of a scraper which drags the dirt up an incline. Or a track can be laid on the bottom of the sump or above it if the sump is deepened below all along the track, the sludge can be shovelled into a car by hand. The car is then hauled up an incline to the level.

Only electrically-driven conventional horizontal multi-stage turbine pumps having motors of high voltage, 3000 V, 50 cycles, must be used at the main sump in deep mines. Where two pumps are installed, each pump should be of such a capacity that it can deal with water influx over a period of 24 hours in 20 operating hours if pumping is to be done in all the three shifts. Where the sump capacity is large, large-capacity pumps may be used to operate on night shifts, week-ends, and holidays when tariff is low as an energy conservation measure. It is a good rule to provide as many pumps in reserve as are normally required. With uncertain power supply, diesel-powered pumps may also be provided besides electric pumps. The pumping installation may be laid out for a fully automatic operation.

In recent years, with larger and more powerful submersible pumps on the market, mine de-watering pumps can be based entirely on heavy-duty, high-head submersibles unless the mines are very deep.

The pump chamber which should be of fireproof construction must be connected to the pitbottom by means of at least two connections which can be hermetically closed with strong bulkhead doors or stoppings in an emergency. It must also be connected by a raise to the pumping shaft which will ensure minimum numbers of bends with least possible interference with any of the activities at the shaft. The raise will serve not only to conduct the delivery range or ranges to the shaft but also serves as an escapeway. Such a design will enable the pumps to function even when the whole level they serve is flooded and filled with water.

The dimensions of the pump chamber depend on the size of the equipment to be accommodated and the arrangement of the pumps. Its shape is governed by the magnitude of the rock pressure acting. Widths up to 4.75 m, heights up to 4.5 m and lengths up to 30 m are not uncommon.

The pump foundation usually of concrete should be kept at a level of 200 to 250 mm above the pump chamber floor level which is usually at the same elevation as the level or 1.5 to 2.5 m above it. Where bulkhead doors are not installed for isolation of the pump chamber, placing the pumps above the level prevents them from being drowned until a large part of the level has been filled.

The distance between the individual pump foundations should be at least 1.5 to 2 m; the distance between the pump foundation and the pump chamber side walls should be at least 1 m on the suction side and 1.5 to 2 m on the other side. The vertical distance between the pump shaft and the strainer of the suction pipe in the suction pit must not be greater than 5.5 m.

It is recommended to have two delivery ranges leaving the pump chamber to which the delivery pipes of all the pump units are connected through valves.

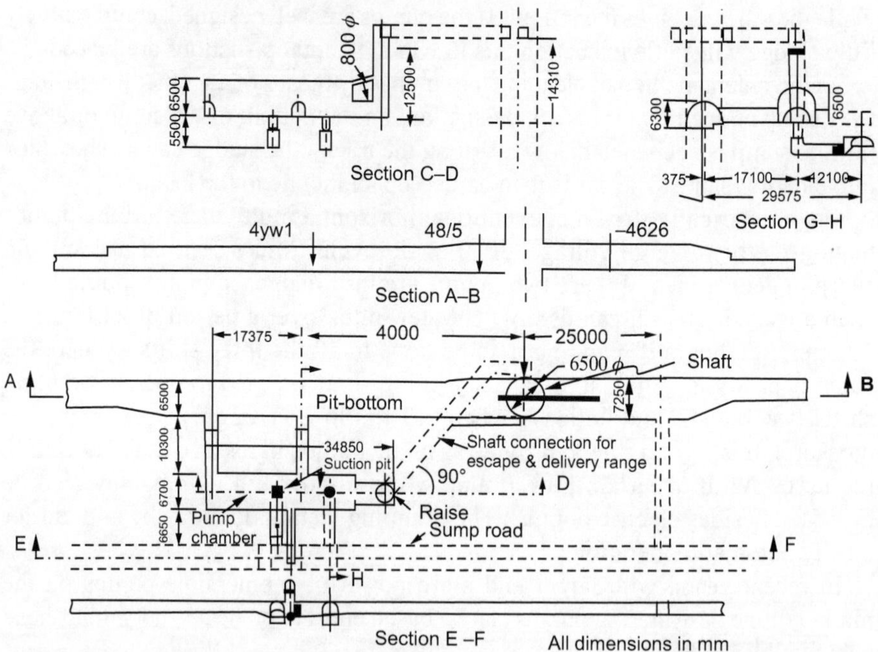

Figure 8.5 Pitbottom sump layout with large water influx.

Figures 8.4 and 8.5 give real-life pitbottom main sump layouts real-life illustrating the afore-mentioned principles. For pumping between levels or between a level and the main pumping station, submersible wear-resistant pumps as feeder pumps with heads of 180 m can be advantageously used as they have no priming problem, are level-regulated, can handle unsedimented water, and are not too unwieldy for easy maintenance.

8.2.2.2 Water dams (hydraulic seals)

Water dams are permanent artificial barriers or seals built in mine workings including shafts, slopes, drifts and adits under any one of the following circumstances:

(1) To guard against irruptions of water from adjacent water-bearing strata;
(2) To guard against irruptions of water from adjacent old workings;
(3) When approaching water-logged workings and draining off the water by means of boreholes;
(4) To limit the amount of pumping by allowing water in worked-out areas to accumulate behind the dams;
(5) To reduce or eliminate acid water being discharged in mines with the acid mine drainage problem;
(6) To seal off operating mines that will close in the future;
(7) To isolate acid-producing zones in a mine where they can be identified from active mine workings where natural barriers cannot be provided; and

(8) In most cases, to withstand the maximum hydrostatic pressure that may develop.

The problem of sealing off with dams can be minimized or avoided by proper mine planning which would minimise water pressures so that less expensive dam constructions would be required.

When selecting a suitable site for a dam, the purpose of the dam and the hydrological conditions must be taken into consideration.

The following points must be borne in mind:

(1) The ground must be strong, sound and solid; shaly sandstones are most suitable while sandstones, conglomerates, and clayey shale are unsuitable. In most coal mines, supplemental roof supports should be installed at the site.
(2) If a dam is to be erected in a pervious or fissured ground, the ground should first be injected with liquid cement (cementation) or polyurethane.
(3) The head of water to be withstood by the dam should be as small as possible.
(4) The site should be easily accessible.
(5) The site should be self-draining, if possible, to facilitate inspection and erection.
(6) The site should be carefully prepared by cutting into the sides, roof, and floor so that the dam has a firm grip with the surrounding ground and the risk of its displacement and shearing of the strata at abutments are obviated. A continuous miner/roadheading machine may be used if the ground permits and the number of dams to be erected is more. This will also eliminate the slow and tedious hand-cutting. Blasting should be avoided as much as possible.
(7) Potential success of the dam.
(8) Effect on ventilation.

Dams may lose effectiveness with time depending on the method of construction employed and strata changes. They may either fail or cause seepage around them.

8.2.2.2.1 Types of dams

According to design or shape, underground dams can be classified into straight (or flat), cylindrical (or arched), and spherical dams.

The selection of a type of dam is governed by the physical characteristics of the site and its preparation time, safety, availability of finances, and practical considerations.

Depending on the materials used in their construction, the dams may also be classified into clay, timber, brick, brick-and-concrete, and concrete dams. Brick-and-concrete, and concrete dams are most commonly constructed in mines because of their reliability and the small space required for dams of great strength.

8.2.2.2.2 Design of dams

The factors governing the design of a dam are:

(1) Size of roadway;
(2) Nature of the adjacent strata;
(3) Estimated water pressure;
(4) Materials used in construction; and
(5) Form of dam.

The size of the roadway in which a dam is to be constructed is a determining factor in dam design. For the same head of water, a dam built in a larger roadway cross-section will be required to withstand greater total pressure than when it is erected in a smaller roadway cross-section (total pressure = water pressure × area of dam).

Dams built in weak ground (low compressive and shear strengths) must be of greater dimensions than those built for the same head of water in strong ground in order that the ground does not fail in shear.

The estimated head of water in a dam is an important factor in determining its size. The permissible compressive strength of the materials used in the construction of a dam influences the size of the dam.

The dams should be constructed from a material such as concrete that will resist deterioration by water.

The form of the dam selected is a determining factor in dam design. The size of a dam is usually expressed by its thickness or length as it is called in some countries. Formulae have been given for determining the thickness of certain forms of dams but they cannot be entirely relied upon due to the varying conditions obtained in mines. Extreme caution should, therefore, be exercised in determining the thickness of a dam. In all the designs, the stress on the dam decreases along its thickness as the load is transferred to the rock (ground).

Anchorage of the dam to mine roof, sides and floor for given strata type and condition is important when designing dams.

Flat dams
For small water pressures, a brick or concrete dam, 1 to 2 m thick, hitched into the sides, roof, and floor of the roadway, will be adequate (Fig. 8.6). With larger pressures, two or more single bricks or a solid plug of mass concrete built into the roadway which has been only dressed will serve the purpose (Figs. 8.7 and 8.8).

The bricks used must be hard burnt with a compressive strength of 15 to 18 MN/m^2 (150 to 180 kgf/cm^2). For concrete dams, blast furnace slag cement or Portland cement may be used. The proportion of cement must be 20 per cent and that of the aggregate 65 per cent of the concrete mass. The ratio of the sand to aggregate must be 2:3.

The total length of a plug dam based on the shear strength of the construction material used or of the ground whichever is less is calculated from the formula:

$$t = \frac{pbh}{2(b+h)\tau_s}$$

where

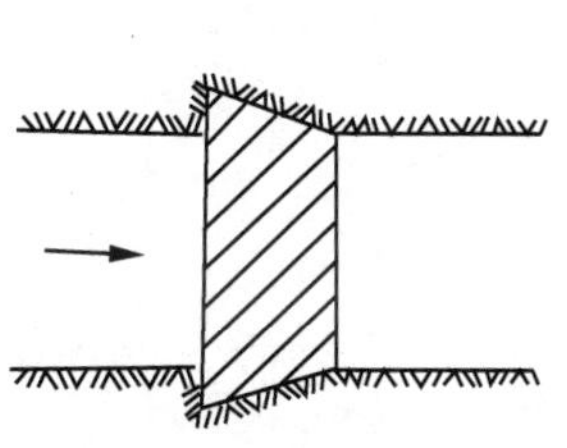

Figure 8.6 Brick dam.

Concrete or grouted crushed mine rock

Figure 8.7 Brick dam for larger pressures.

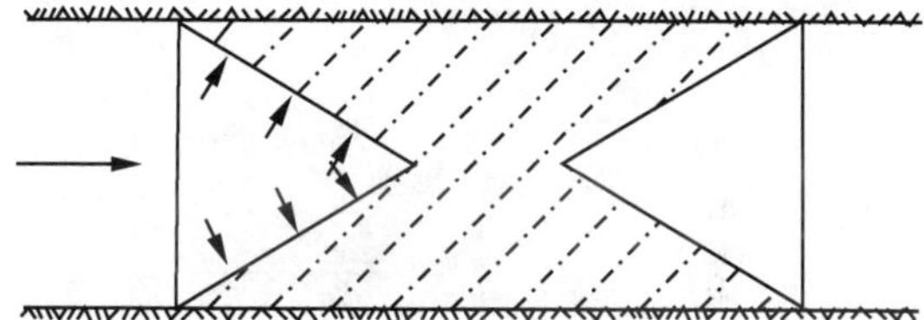

Figure 8.8 Parallel plug dam.

- t is the length of the plug (m)
- p is the maximum water pressure (N/m^2)
- b is the width of the roadway (m)
- h is the height of the roadway (m)
- τ_s is the safe shearing stress of the material used or the ground, whichever is less (N/m^2)

The total length of the plug is also given by the relation [93].

$$t = \frac{pa}{4\tau}$$

where

- t is the length of plug (m)
- p is the water pressure (tf/m^2, N/m^2)
- a is the length of the longest side of the roadway cross-section (m),
- τ is the strength of the construction material used or ground, whichever is less (tf/m^2, N/m^2)

The minimum length in the middle of the plug with hollowed out ends is given as t/4.

Concrete plug dams are successfully used in South African gold mines.

Arch dams (Figs. 8.9 and 8.10)

An arch dam distributes the thrust acting on it by arch action to the abutments in the ground containing it. It may be designed as one or more arch rings each of which is considered to be subjected to a constant radial hydrostatic pressure.

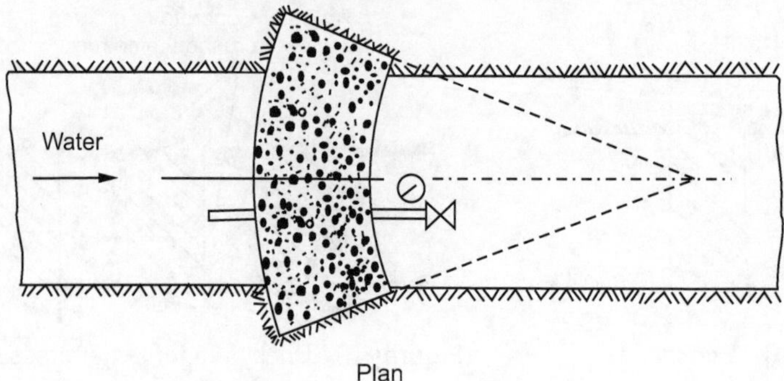

Figure 8.9 Concrete arch dam.

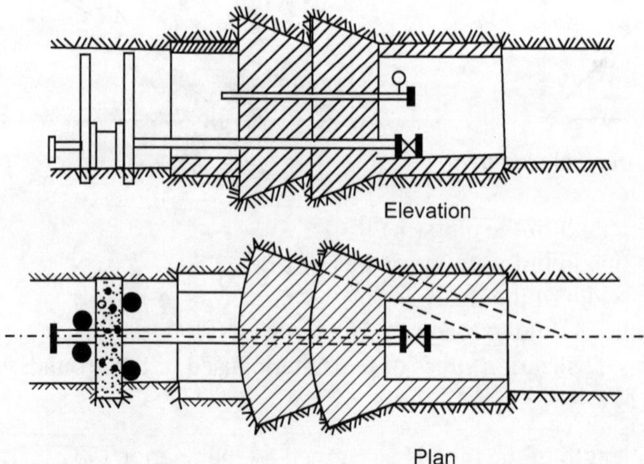

Figure 8.10 Brick arch dam.

The radial thickness of an arch ring may be approximately determined by using the cylinder formula and by considering the dam to be a segment of a thin cylinder subjected to an external water pressure.

$$t = \frac{pr_e}{\sigma_s} = \frac{pr_i}{\sigma_s - p} \text{ (m)}$$

where p is the maximum water pressure (N/m^2)

r_e is the external radius of the arch ring (m)

r_i is the internal radius of the arch ring (m)

σ_s is the safe compressive stress of the material used (N/m^2).

When the safe compressive stress of the material used in construction is exceeded by the water pressure, a series of independent arch rings (usually two to four) will be necessary, each ring being designed for a water pressure of p/n, where n is the number of rings.

$$t = \frac{r_i}{\frac{n\sigma_s}{p} - 1}$$

the internal radius, r_i can be deduced from the relation:

$$r_i = \frac{b}{2\sin\frac{\alpha}{2}}$$

where b is the width of the roadway (m) and $\alpha/2$, the half central angle of the arch

= 20° to 30° in strong ground
= 15° to 20° in moderately strong ground
= 15° in weak ground

To avoid bending stresses in the dam, $\alpha/2$ should not normally exceed 20°.

As a rough guide, one may take the inner radius of the dam as equal to the width of the roadway in strong ground and as one-and-a-half times the width in moderately strong ground [94].

When the safe compressive stress of the surrounding ground is less than that of the material used for dam construction, its value should be used instead of the material in calculating the dam thickness.

The safe compressive stress of hard rocks is usually taken as one-sixth to one-tenth of their ultimate compressive strengths. In other types of rocks, the following values may be taken [95]

Soft sandstone, limestone	20 to 30 kgf/cm^2 (2 to 3 MN/m^2)
Clayey shale	8 to 25 kgf/cm^2
Very hard coal	20 to 25 kgf/cm^2
Friable coal	3 to 10 kgf/ cm^2

Concrete is the best material for dam construction. The main disadvantage of the use of bricks lies in the difficulty of establishing watertight contact with the surrounding ground.

The safe compressive stress of concrete and bricks may be calculated by using the relations [96]

Concrete:

$$\sigma_s = \frac{\sigma_{28}.\lg n}{v.\lg 28}$$

Bricks:

$$\sigma_s = \frac{\sigma_{\text{ult}}}{v}$$

where

σ_{28} is the 28-day compressive strength of concrete (N/m^2)
n is the time between completion of dam and application of full load on the dam (days)
σ_{ult} is the ultimate compressive strength of bricks (N/m^2)
v is the factor of safety which may be taken as 1.5 to 2 for bricks and 2 to 3 for concrete.

The grade of the cement and strength of the bricks to be used must be properly selected. Aldis derived the following formula for determining the thickness of an arch dam:

$$t = r_i \left[\frac{1}{\sqrt{1 - \frac{2h}{\sigma_s}}} - 1 \right] \quad \text{(m)}$$

where

r_i is the internal radius of the dam (m)
h is the maximum head of water (m WG, N/m^2)
σ_s is the safe compressive stress of the material used (tf/m^2 , N/M^2).

The factor $2h/\sigma_s$ must be less than unity if the expression under the root is not to be imaginary. It is greater than unity when the building material is not strong enough.

Spherical dams
These consist of two or more spherical rings with abutments in the surrounding ground. They are difficult to build although their thickness is less than that of the arch dams for the same head of water.

Aldis derived the following relationship for determining the thickness of a spherical dam:

$$t = r_e \left(1 - \sqrt[3]{1 - \frac{1.5h}{\sigma_s}} \right)$$

where

r_e is the external radius of the dam.

8.2.2.2.3 Construction of a dam

Before commencing work on the dam proper, a stank of brick in cement, concrete, or clay rammed between two board walls is built across the roadway on the inbye side of the dam site to a height of 0.6 to 1 m and a pipe 75 to 200 mm or more in diameter, depending on the rate of water overflow, passed through it (Fig. 8.11) This is necessary in order to keep the actual site of the dam as dry as possible. Next, the sides, roof, and floor of the roadway at the dam site are

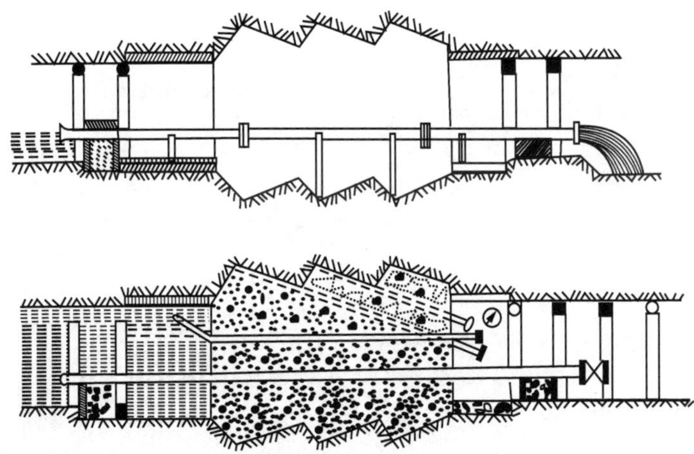

Figure 8.11 Construction of flat concrete dam.

cut to form suitable abutments for the type of the dam chosen and the dam then erected. In order that the pipe is firmly embedded in the dam, it is provided with several flanges. A pipe 20 to 25 mm in diameter is also brought through the dam near the roof to vent air from the back of the dam as the water fills the roadway as well as to measure the water pressure. Owing to the difficulty of making the dam watertight at the abutments, pipes 30 to 50 mm in diameter, are also left in the dam for cement injections. Figure 8.11 gives the construction of a simple flat concrete dam [97].

Figure 8.12 gives the construction of a flat concrete dam suitable for water pressures of 12 to 15 bar (g) [98]. Steel anchors are inserted into the four sides of the roadway which are also injected with cement.

Figure 8.13 shows the construction of brick-and-concrete dam used in British mines. It consists of two 0.9-m thick brickwalls in cement mortar, about 3.6 m apart, with the space between filled with broken rock. Pipes of varying length are laid through the front wall as it is built up to inject cement into the loose rock to

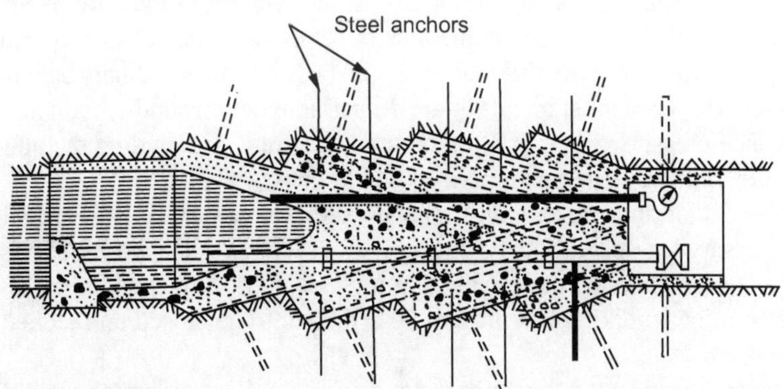

Figure 8.12 Flat concrete dam for water pressures [12 to 15 bar.]

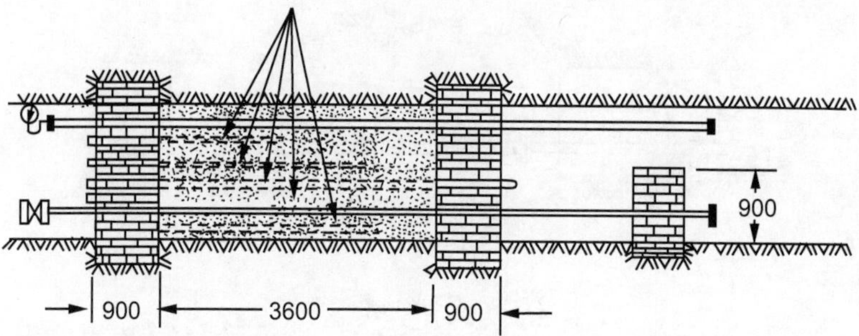

Figure 8.13 Brick-and-concrete dam.

render it watertight.

8.2.2.2.4 *Bulkhead doors or emergency dams*

A bulkhead door is a watertight dam containing a strong steel door which is quickly closed in the event of a sudden water inrush or when there is an immediate danger of inundation. They are often used in development workings which are driven under constant fear of heavy inflows of water or for protection of underground districts against sudden inrushes of water.

A bulkhead door consists of a solid abutment, a door frame, and a door (single or two-wing type). The abutment is of concrete formed in the same way as with normal dams. The door frame is of cast iron or cast steel having a conical seating on the abutment (Fig. 8.14) [94], in order that the pressure acting on the door is transferred to the abutment. It is usually made, depending on the size and weight, in several segments which can be bolted to one another watertight by means of packing. The door which must always close quickly and reliably in the direction of water pressure is made of cast steel or thick boiler plate 30 to 60 mm in thickness. It may be flat, cambered or hemispherical depending on the water pressure. A rubber, leather, or felt gasket between it and the frame provides an effective hydraulic seal. The door may be hung up next to the roof or carried on substantial side hinges. Rusting and corrosion of bolts and other vital parts must be prevented. Rail track(s) should be of folding type, or, if they are fixed, tools for their removal should be available on site. Only first-class cement capable of withstanding attack by corrosive waters should be used. As in ordinary dams, water and air-release pipes must be left in the door frame or surrounding concrete.

Adequate pressure grouting of the immediate strata surrounding the bulkhead will ensure its long-term performance.

Bulkhead doors must be carefully maintained so that they close easily and reliably. Tools necessary for closing and locking the door as well as spare parts must be stored in a special room near the door. The door must be lighted by fixed lights.

In deep mines, bulkhead doors can be arranged to be closed and locked with remote control.

Figure 8.15 shows a bulkhead door in a parallel-sided concrete plug experimented in a deep gold mine of South Africa.

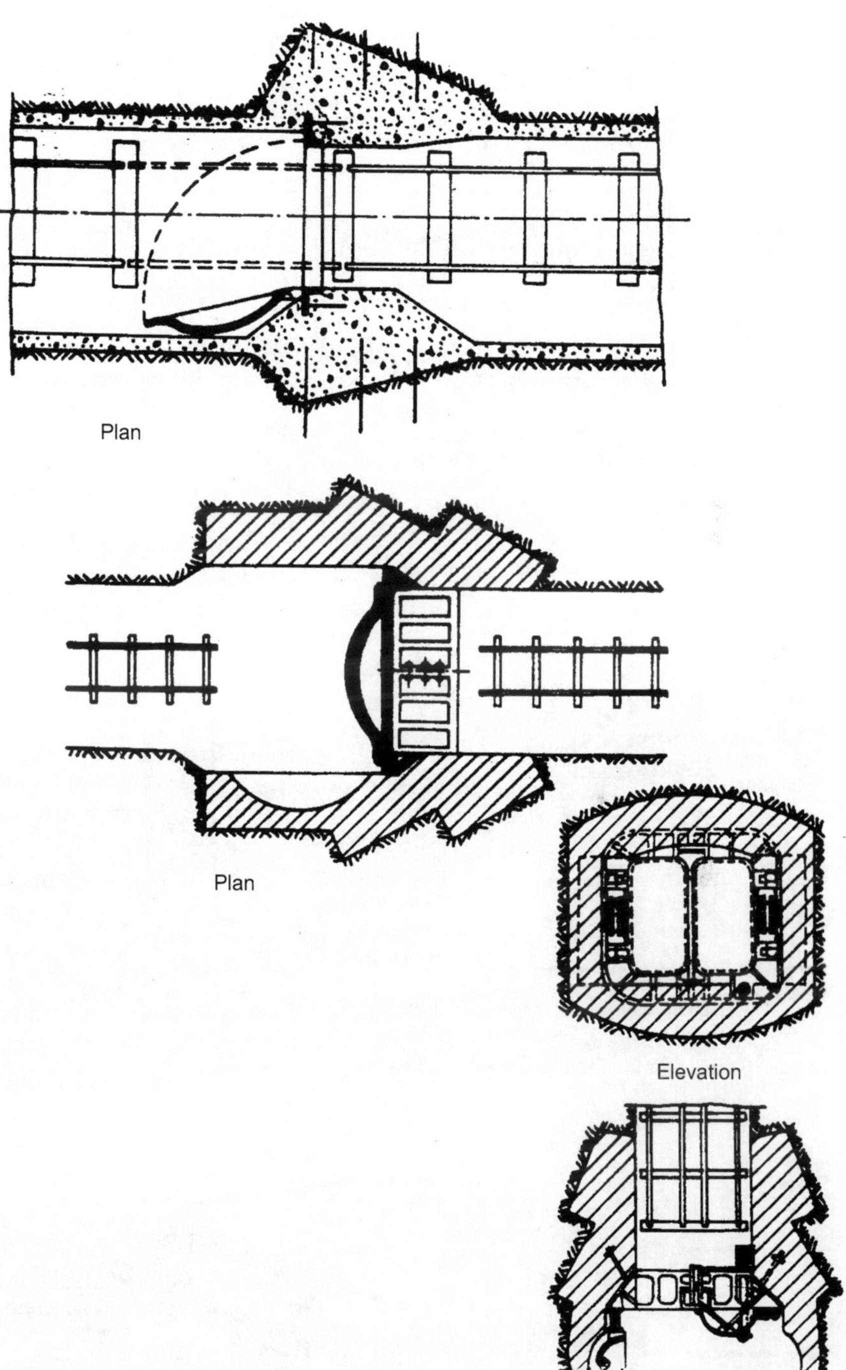

Figure 8.14 Bulkhead doors

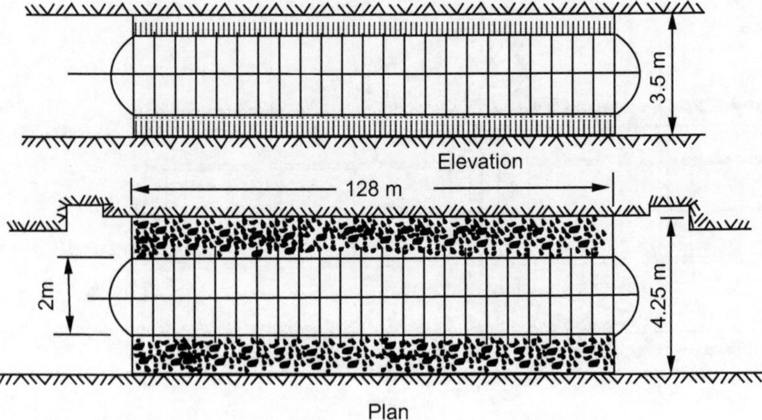

Figure 8.15 Bulkhead door in concrete plug.

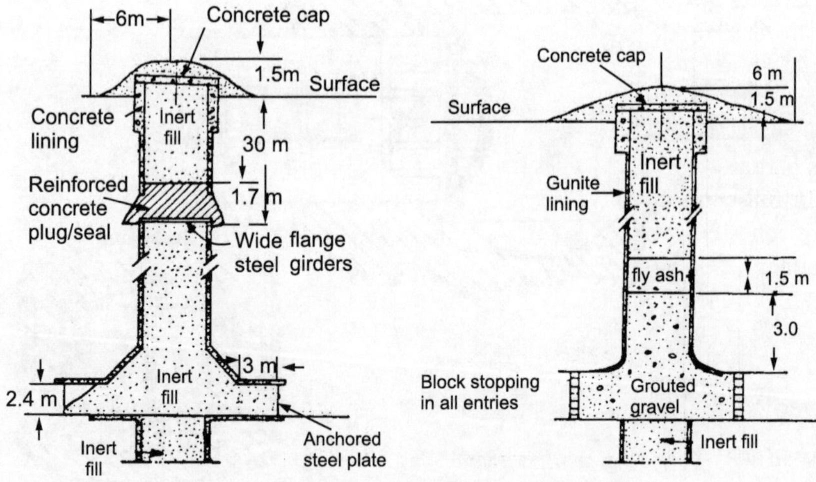

Figure 8.16 Hydraulic sealing of vertical shafts.

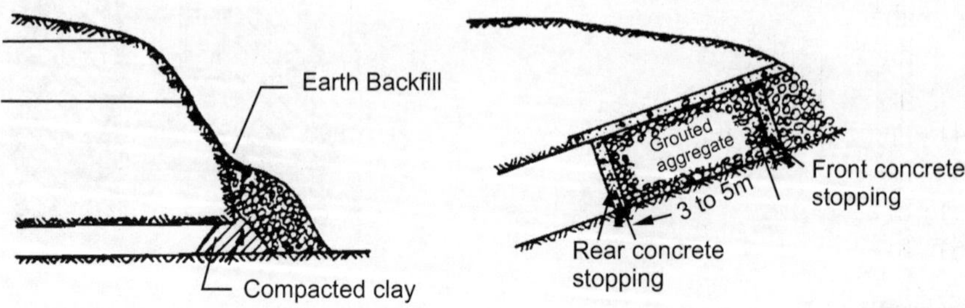

Figure 8.17 Hydraulic sealing of adit and incline mouths.

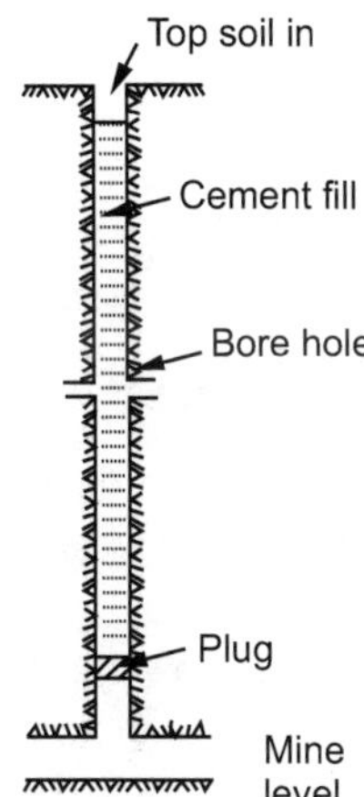

Figure 8.18 Hydraulic sealing of borehole.

8.2.2.2.5 Hydraulic sealing of shafts, adits, inclines, and boreholes

Figure 8.16, 8.17 and 8.18 show the methods of hydraulic sealing of vertical shafts, adits and incline mouths, and boreholes. In old coalfields, the problem of filling of many abandoned mine shafts arises. Different filling methods are used depending on the future requirement the shafts may have to meet. Both full-column and partial-column filling methods are used.

In full-column filling, a permanent void-free column of fill is achieved by filling with cohesive building material. In partial filling, the column of fill is set on an abutment structure erected at depths determined by geotechnical considerations.

8.3 Water-Logged Workings or Water Pools in Mines

Water-logged workings in mines are formed under the following circumstances:

(1) In abandoned mines that have no reserves, the water has accumulated because pumping has stopped;
(2) In inactive mine workings of active mines where the inflow of water exceeds the pumping capacity;
(3) Purposely in parts of active mines which are separated from adjacent abandoned mines filled with water by means of barriers of insufficient thickness; these pools have a stabilizing effect and reduce the hydrostatic pressure exerted on the barrier by the water in the abandoned mines;
(4) Purposely in inactive dip-side workings of an active mine, so that there is no fire hazard, and no pumping, ventilation, and inspection of the workings are necessary;
(5) In abandoned mines opened from the outcrop; and
(6) In active mine workings due to an inrush of water.

The extent of known and supposed water-logged workings in each seam must be shown on separate plans and the year when the workings have been abandoned must be indicated on them. Water under pressure must be specially indicated.

In the Jharia and Raniganj Coalfields, India, there are a number of seams occurring at shallow depths with water-logged workings which pose problems for safe and economic exploitation of seams occurring below them.

8.3.1 De-watering of water-logged workings

The necessity of de-watering water-logged workings arises:

(a) When a safety barrier between an active and an inactive mine is considered unsafe as a protection against a hydrostatic head that is more than a definite value;
(b) When it becomes necessary to drain water from an abandoned mine or mines into an adjacent active mine to operate with safety;
(c) When it is desired to extract reserves left in an abandoned mine filled with water from an adjacent active mine by draining water out of the abandoned mine into the active mine and utilising the surface shafts of the abandoned mine for ventilation and manriding; and
(d) When an active mine or part thereof is inundated and the mine is to be quickly brought into production.

Besides ensuring complete safety, de-watering obviates the necessity of leaving barriers or providing dams for the protection of new mine workings.

When considering de-watering of old workings or goaves, one should determine whether the workings to be de-watered are likely to be fed after their de-watering

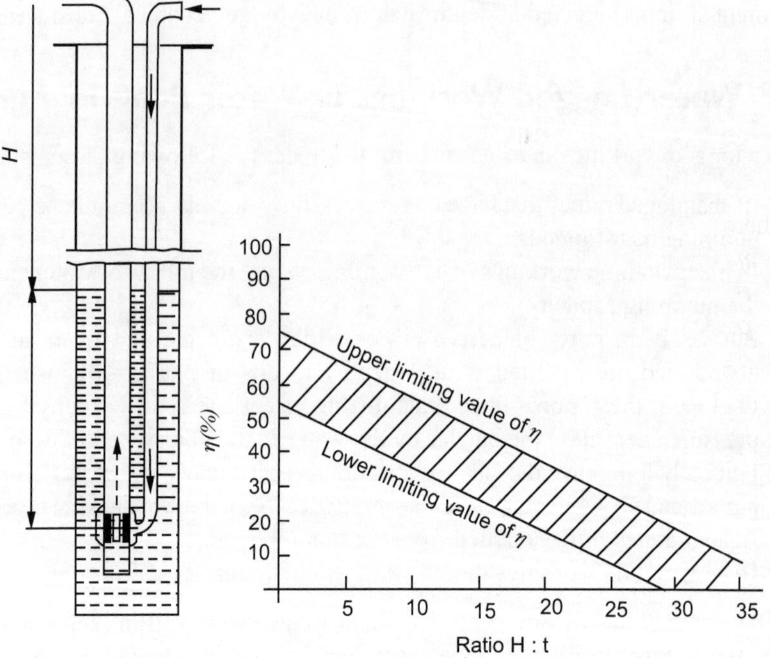

Figure 8.19 Air-lift pump.

by surface and ground waters. All old plans and records should be carefully checked to determine the possible number and size of water feeders. Where the workings are directly fed from the surface and the inflow is considerable, de-watering may be inadvisable unless the country's economy demands it. This is because an expensive pumping plant may be required and the pumping cost over a long period may make mining unprofitable.

8.3. 1.1 Methods of de-watering

The method of de-watering to be adopted depends on whether an entire mine (active or inactive) is flooded, layout of the mine (in-the-seam or horizon mining), location and extant of water-logged workings, time available for de-watering operation, available power supplies, and physical condition of the shaft(s) and mine.

De-watering of a flooded mine in which water has risen into the shaft(s) may be done by suspended electrical vertical centrifugal/turbine pumps, air-lift pumps, or electrical submersible pumps installed in the shaft.

Where a standard vertical pump is used as de-watering pump, it is lowered as the water recedes, the discharge being connected to the pump column by a flexible rubber hose. In another approach, when the de-watering pump lowers the water to a predetermined level, a permanent pump with a sump is installed on that level so that the de-watering pump is used to lower the water to the next predetermined level.

In the air-lift pump (Fig. 8.19), compressed air produced by an efficient compressor is used for pumping out water. The compressed air is fed through a pipe to the bottom end of a larger pipe immersed in water where it forms a mixture with water having a density less than that of water so that it rises upwards through the larger pipe constituting the rising main.

The actual head of an air -lift pump is given by

$$H = \frac{\eta . t . (\rho_w - \rho_m)}{\rho_m} \text{ (m)}$$

where

η	=	efficiency which depends on the ratio H: t
t	=	immersion depth (m)
ρ_w	=	density of water to be pumped (kg/m^3)
ρ_m	=	density of compressed air–water mixture (kg/m^3)

Generally, the immersion depth is made 1.5 to 2 times the lift head.

The main advantages of the air-lift pumps are: (a) there are no wearing parts, (b) fabrication is simple, (c) any kind of pipes can be used, and (d) water containing mud and sand can be pumped. The disadvantages, however, are that an efficient compressor must be available and the efficiency in normal operation is not higher than 0.2 to 0.3. They can be used only in emergencies as at low t: H ratios which are usually encountered in mines, the high cost on compressed air does not play an important role. Air-lift pumps had been used in the past for raising water from flooded shafts.

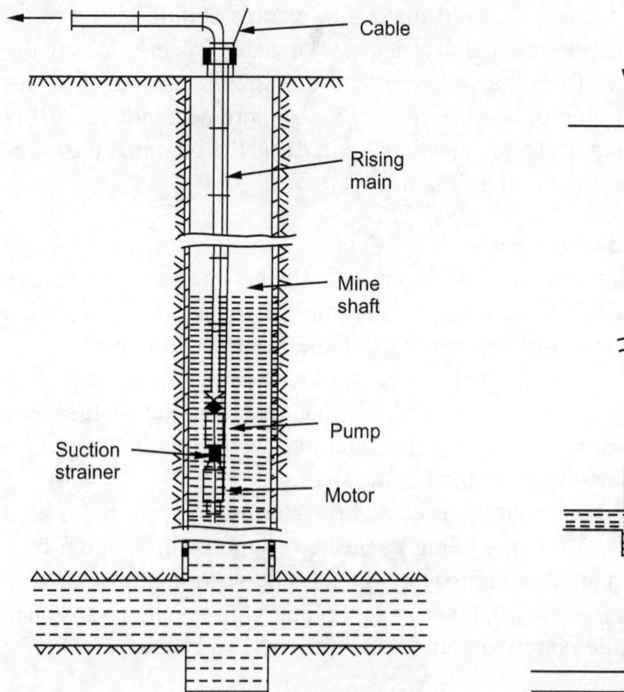

Figure 8.20 Electric submersible pump.

Figure 8.21 De-watering mine by means of a borehole from a working below the adjacent mine.

Where electricity is available, submersible pumps offer the easiest means of de-watering mine shafts. The submersible pump is of the multi-stage centrifugal type with a motor coupled to it and the drive is from below (Fig. 8.20). The squirrel cage motor is of the completely 'wet' type in which the motor is cooled and lubricated by water which circulates vigorously between the rotor and the stator and throughout the windings. The circulation ensures efficient cooling of the conductors and enables a high horsepower output to be obtained from a small frame size motor.

A flooded mine can also be de-watered from an adjacent mine by driving a narrow roadway from the adjacent mine to a point below the lowest level flooded and boring up to tap off the water (Fig. 8.21).

De-watering of a known or suspected water-logged area in a mine may be done by one of the following two methods:

(1) By approaching the water-logged area up to a suitable point with one or two narrow mine roadways in order to bore and tap off the water.
(2) By putting long boreholes.

8.3.1.1.1 De-watering by means of narrow mine roadways

This method is feasible only when it is possible to approach a water-logged area sufficiently near to it and when the water pressure is less. The safe distance up to which the workings may be driven depends on the water pressure and the nature of ground. It can be determined by using the formula [94]:

$$s = \frac{pb}{4\tau}$$

where

- b is the length of the longest side of the roadway section (m)
- p is the water pressure at the floor level of the approaching working (tf/m^2 or m WG)
- s is the shortest distance between the approaching mine working and the water-logged area. It must be at least equal to the longest side of the roadway section when the direction of force is acting against the face, and equal to the roadway height when the direction of force is acting against the roadway side.
- τ is the shear strength of the ground (tf/m^2)

The value of τ for different rocks is given as follows:

(i) Very hard rocks (quartzite, conglomerate, granite, basalt, porphyry, etc.,) free from fissures	300 tf/m^2
(ii) Very hard rocks with developed joints	100 tf/m^2
(iii) Hard rocks (shale, sandstone, limestone, etc.) free from fissures, less developed joints	50 tf/m^2
(iv) Hard rocks with developed joints, coals with less developed cleavage; clayey shale	30 tf/m^2
(v) Hard rocks under ground movement; coals with well-developed cleavage	20 tf/m^2
(vi) Coals under effects due to mining	15 tf/m^2

(1 tf/m^2 ≈ 1 m WG ≈ 1000 kgf/m^2 ≈ 10^4 N/m^2)

When approaching a water-logged area from its bottom side, the determined value of s should be increased by 50 per cent. A further 25 m should be added to it if the exact location of the area is not known.

The drivage of the de-watering workings must take place with simultaneous boring to avoid being too near to the water. The holes must be bored in all directions in which water accumulation is expected, with at least one hole (better two holes) bored straight ahead of face. Their minimum length is calculated from the relation

$$L_{min} = s + l$$

where

- s is the shortest safe distance between the approaching working and the water-logged area calculated as indicated above.
- l is the expected length of pull.

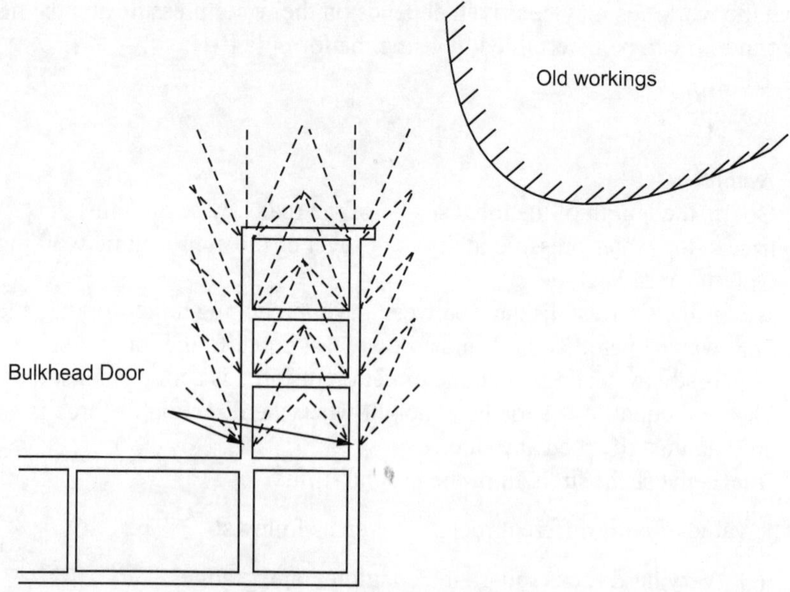

Figure 8.22 De-watering water-logged old workings by means of narrow mine workings and advance boreholes.

The holes should be at least 4 m long in hard rock and 10 m long in coal. A record of the number, direction, and depth of holes should be maintained. The drivage of the workings must be stopped at the first appearance of water coming out of the borehole, fine cracks and cleavage planes becoming moist, and 'sweating' of the place. The pillar between the faces of the workings and water-logged area will then be bored with a single borehole for tapping water.

Figure 8.22 shows a method of approaching and de-watering water-logged workings in a coal seam.

8.3.1.1.2 De-watering by means of long boreholes

This method of de-watering is adopted when the water pressure is great and boring and tapping must be done from great distances by using special safety boring apparatus. One may have to drive narrow roadway(s) in order to have a suitable location with respect to the water pool. For the success of the method, an exact knowledge of location of the water-logged area is necessary.

8.3.1.1.3 Precautions when approaching water-logged workings

During drivage of de-watering mine workings and tapping of water, a number of precautionary measures must be adopted. These include the following:

(1) For the safety of men engaged in de-watering operations, an escapeway, preferably a level one, must be provided. The escapeway must be properly supported, be free from obstructions, and be electrically lighted. If an

escapeway is steeper than 3°, it must be provided with a water drain, a raised travelling way, and a rope railing.

(2) The de-watering mine workings must be well-ventilated to remove any noxious gases such as carbon dioxide and hydrogen sulphide that may occur. If through ventilation is not possible, provision for auxiliary ventilation must be made. Forcing ventilation system must be preferred.
(3) Open lights should not be used. Only electric safety lamps should be used.
(4) Only experienced miners should be employed who should be equipped with self-rescuers.
(5) For rescue of men overcome with gases, a rescue team equipped with respiratory protective apparatus should be stationed near the place of work. The final boring and tapping of water should be done by the rescue men only.
(6) During tapping, workers from adjacent mine workings should be withdrawn.
(7) Necessary materials for erection of a dam should be stored at a suitable place and the dam site prepared. A bulkhead door must be built if high-pressure water is expected.
(8) All de-watering operations must be done according to a definite plan prepared by the mine management.
(9) All operations must be done under the supervision of an experienced supervisory official. The actual tapping operation must take place in the immediate presence of the official. In difficult cases, the presence of the mine manager is recommended.

Regulations 126 to 129 of Coal Mines Regulation, 1957(Appendix 1) give precautions against danger of inundation for surface waters and underground water bodies.

8.3.1.1.4 Safety boring machines

For tapping off old water-logged workings by means of long boreholes or for putting advance boreholes when driving exploratory headings in anticipation of danger from accumulations of water or gas, rotary core boring machines equipped with a special safety boring outfit or apparatus is used. Among the well-known equipment are the Craelius, Longyear, and Burnside boring machine with which holes can be bored at any desired angle safely and easily under heavy pressures of water.

The Burnside safety boring apparatus of British manufacture (Fig. 8.23) consists of a boring tube, a mild steel sleeve tube, fixed and loose cross-heads with rubber seal, expansion bolts, a debris cock, a cross-piece with rubber clamps, a fullway control cock, and a stuffing box and gland. The boring rods have a diameter of 38 mm (heavy type) or 33.3 mm (light type) and are made in the lengths of 1.52 m (5 ft) and 3 m (10 ft). The boring bits are tungsten-tipped wet drilling bits of 56 mm (2.19 inches), 73 mm (2.88 inches) and 95 mm (3.75 inches) diameter. The

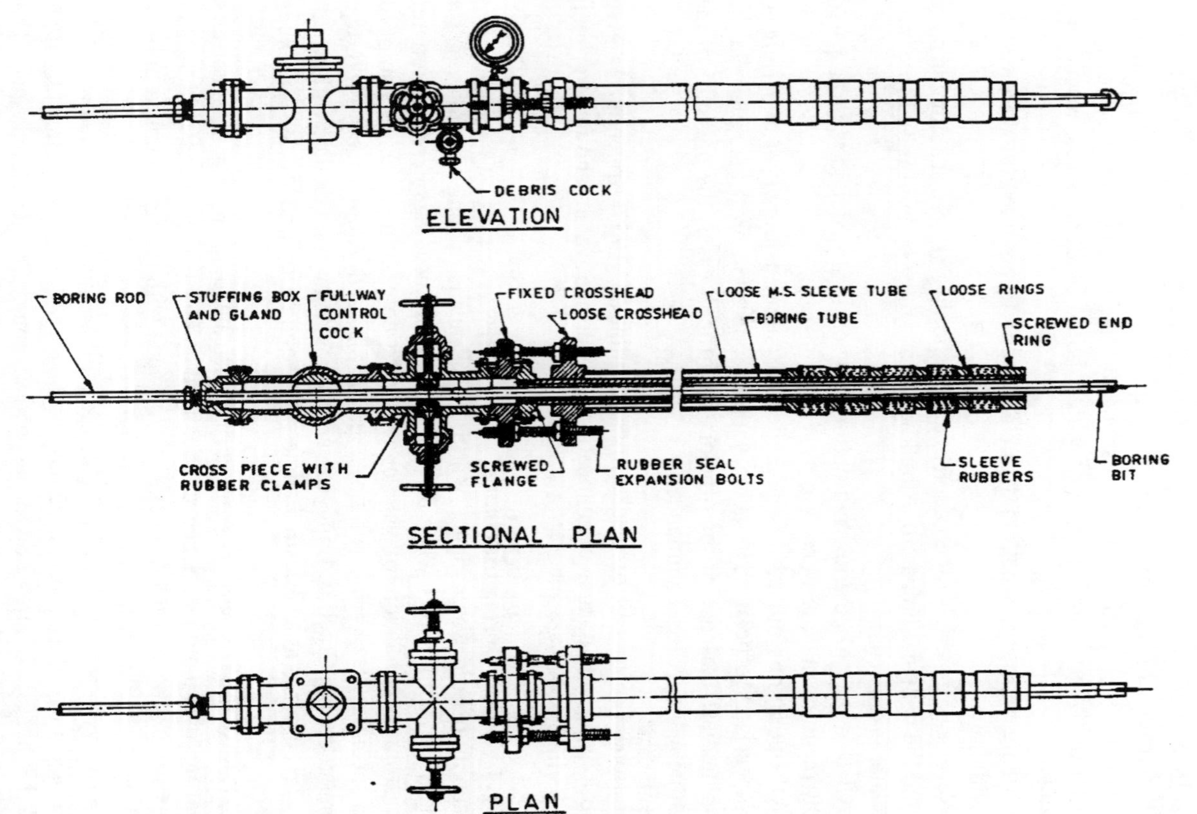

Figure 8.23 Burnside safety boring apparatus.

tungsten carbide-tipped reamers have diameters of 111 mm (4.38 inches), 121 mm (4.75 inches), 146 mm (5.75 inches), and 222 mm (8.75 inches). This machine has been in successful operation in the UK and India.

Mine waters have to be treated to meet the discharge standards by dosing with electrolyte and lime sedimentation in two lagoons.

Discharge standards: 5 ppm iron and 60 ppm suspended solids.

When discharging to river system, quality of the final discharge to be within permitted limits.

8.4 Acid Mine Drainage (AMD)

Acid mine drainage is the outflow of acidic mine waters from active and inactive abandoned underground coal and metal mine workings as well as from the immense volumes of surface mining waste dumps, open coal-stack piles, coal refuse and dirt from beneficiation plants, tailings piles and ponds, and large construction activities. The acidic water generated from surface sources is termed acid rock drainage (ARD), a term preferred over acid mine drainage to emphasize the general nature of the problem.

Acidic drainage has an adverse impact on the health and environment due to pollution of surface streams and ground water and is a continuing problem for government entities, private industry and the general public. This problem is as old as the beginning of mining activities. It is generated by the atmospheric oxidation of associated reactive sulphide rock (often iron sulphide) present in the deposit or surrounding rocks in the presence of percolating waters and air. The sulphide minarels which under oxidation are: pyrrhotite (FeS), chalcocite (Cu_2S), pyrite (FeS_2), arsenopyrite (FeAsS), covellite (CuS), chalcopyrite (Cu FeS_2), sphalerite (ZnS), and borrite (Cu_2FeS_4). Bacteria naturally occurring in the rock accelerate the decomposition of the metal ions. Thiobacillus ferro-oxidants and thiobacillus thio-oxidants are key contributors to oxidation of sulphide minerals at approximate operating temperatures of 25–45°C.

In the case of iron sulphide (pyrite/marcasite), the chemical reaction from dissolution can be simplified to

$$FeS_2 + (15/4)\,O_2 + (7/2)\,H_2O \rightarrow Fe(OH)_3 + 2SO_4 + 4H$$

In the presence of oxygen and water, pyrite oxidizes to form a ferric oxide called yellow boy, and hydrogen ions which lower the pH and causes increased acidity in water passing over the rock, which is capable of dissolving heavy metals contained in the waste material with precipitation of metal hydroxides. The various stages in acid generation may last for weeks, months or centuries until control actions are taken. Acid neutralization is often related to the calcareous material contained in the rock.

There are thousands of acid mine drainage sites world over.

8.4.1 Prevention and control of acid mine drainage

Acidic mine drainage from active mines must have a pH 6 to 9 before being discharged into a stream. Prevention and control of acid generation can be achieved by limiting the availability of at least one of the three essential components of the acid generating process i.e., sulphide mineral, air, or water.

Conducting proper predictive tests for sulphide mine waste rock is of paramount importance in developing a successful waste management plan which will save millions rupees in preventing and control of AMD.

Methods that can be used to control AMD are:

Wastage segregation and blending: By thoroughly blending the acid generating waste rock with enough carbonate rock with net neutralizing potential.

Treatment of acid mine drainage with base additives: Treating with alkaline materials such as limestone, lime and soda ash to increase the water pH; remove the settled sludge and discharge the purified water.

Construction of impervious covers and caps: Soil, clay, and synthetic cover over acid generating rock will minimize air or water access to it.

Wet disposal of thickened tailings: Depositing tailings with a solid content of 50% is considered the best practice to reduce the oxidation of the sulphide mineral, and biotechnological treatment of AMD best for the recovery of zinc, copper, gold, and uranium. Biological treatment of systems cuts down infrastructural costs and is simple to operate.

Use of bactericides: The introduction of bactericides, which are chemicals that reduce the activity of the catalyzing bacteria, has been effective in controlling the problem.

Prevention of AMD at the source: The techniques that may be used for this include modified mining methods, mine sealing, surface reclamation, drainage diversions, and the control of the groundwater flow system to minimize its recharge into the vicinity of the mine.

Bacterial treatment in wetlands, natural or constructed, has been found to be effective in the treatment of contaminated drainage water over a wide range.

APPENDIX 1

Coalmines Regulations, 1957

Precautions Against Dangers from Fire, Dust, Gas and Water

[116] Classification of coal seams according to their degree of gassiness[1]

(1) After the coming into force of this regulation, all the coal seams shall be classified into different degrees of gassiness by the Chief Inspector or an Inspector assisted by such assistants and after such investigation as he may consider necessary.

(2) If, in a gassy seam, the percentage of flammable gas in the general body of air or the rate of emission of such gas increases so as to bring that seam into a higher degree of gassiness, the Owner, Agent or Manager shall, within 24 hours from his knowledge of such increase, inform the Regional Inspector and also observe all the precautions required to be taken under these regulations in respect of a gassy seam of that degree. The Regional Inspector shall, within 30 days of the receipt of such information, verify the degree of gassiness by suitable investigation and classify the seam into the appropriate degree of gassiness.

Provided that, if it is not practicable to observe all the precautions required to be taken under these regulations within 24 hours as stipulated in the subregulation, the Regional Inspector, on a request in writing by the Owner, Agent or Manager, may defer the observance of the required precautions, subject to such conditions as he may specify for a period not exceeding sixty days.

(3) If, in a gassy seam, the percentage of flammable gas in the general body of air or the rate of emission of flammable gas decreases so to bring that seam to a lower degree of gassiness, the Owner, Agent or Manager may inform the Regional Inspector of the same. The Regional Inspector shall, within 30 days from the receipt of such information, verify the degree of gassiness by suitable investigations and classify the same into appropriate degree of gassiness. Till such time as the Regional Inspector so classifies, all the precautions required to be observed previously shall be observed.

(4) Notwithstanding anything contained in sub-regulation (2) or (3), the Regional Inspector may, at any time, make investigations and reclassify gassy seam into the appropriate degree of gassiness.

---

[1] Inserted vide Notification No. GSR 359 dated 25th March 1972.

(5) The Owner, Agent or Manager shall, at least once in every 30 days, examine the rate of emission of flammable gas in cubic meters per tonne of coal raised and the percentage of flammable gas in the general body of air as laid down in regulation 145. The results of every such examination shall be recorded in a bound-paged book kept for the purpose.

[116-A] General precautions against fire[1]

(1) No oil, grease, canvas. or other flammable materials shall be stored in any mine in a fireproof receptacle. In case of workings below ground, greasy or oily waste shall be regularly removed to the surface.
(2) No person shall place or throw, or cause or permit to be placed or thrown any naked light or lamp on or near any timber, wooden structure, or other combustible material.

117 Surface precautions against fire

(1) All surface structures and supports within a horizontal distance of 10 metres from all entrances to a mine shall be of fire-proof material: Provided that this sub-regulation shall not apply to temporary structures, supports and coverings at the top of a shaft which is in the course of being sunk and to the small lid of a shaft covering operated by the rope cappel.
(2) Shale or other carbonaceous material shall not be heaped or dumped and dead leaves or dry vegetation shall not be allowed to accumulate or remain, and combustible materials other than materials required for use within a period of 24 hours and flammable materials shall not be stored within a distance of 15 metres from any entrance to a mine, which is not effectively sealed off from the workings below ground: Provided that nothing in this sub-regulation shall prevent the dumping of coal, raised from the mine, near the entrance to the mine.
(3) In opencast workings and, where possible, in any ground broken by extraction of coal, wild or herbaceous plants shall be removed and all dead leaves and dry vegetation cleared as often as may be necessary to prevent an outbreak of fire.
(4) No person shall deposit any heated material or ashes on any outcrop of coal or in any opencast working or on any ground broken by extraction of coal.
(5) No person shall light a fire or permit a fire to be lighted in any opencast working or within a distance of 15 metres from any entrance to a mine, except by the permission in writing of the Manager and only for a special purpose specified therein. All such permissions shall be recorded in a bound-paged book kept for the purpose: Provided that this sub-regulation shall not apply to boilers other than vertical boilers.

---

[1] Renumbered vide Notification No. GSR 359, (E) dated 25th March 1972.

(6) A competent person shall, once at least in every seven days, inspect the top of all entrances to a mine, all opencast workings and any ground broken by extraction of coal in order to ascertain whether the precautions laid down under the regulation have been complied with, and for the presence of any fire that may have broken out or any indications thereof. A record of every such inspection shall be maintained in a bound-paged book kept for the purpose, and shall be signed and dated by the person making the inspection.

118 Underground precautions against fire

(1) (a) No timber or other combustible material shall be used in the construction of, or in connection with, any shaft-lining or room housing any machinery or apparatus below ground.

(b) Wood cuttings shall not be left in any working below ground but shall be regularly removed to the surface.

(2) No person shall light a fire or permit a fire to be lighted in any workings below ground:

provided that:

[(i) in the case of a gassy seam of first degree, flame or electric welding or repairing apparatus may be used belowground if permitted by an order in writing of the Manager. Every such order shall specify the person who shall be in charge of the apparatus and it shall be the duty of such person to bring the apparatus back to the surface when no longer required belowground; and

(ii) in the case of a gassy mine of the second or third degree, a flame or electric welding or repairing apparatus may be used belowground if prior permission in writing has been obtained from the Regional Inspector and subject to such conditions as he may specify therein.][1]

(3) (a) No person shall leave a portable light or lamp belowground unless he has placed it in charge of some other person remaining therein.

(b) At the end of shift, unless the mine is worked by a succession of shifts, after all persons have left the mine, all lights shall be extinguished and all power cut off.

[(4) Proper provisions shall be made to prevent an outbreak of fire belowground or the spread of fire from any part of the mine or from any adjoining mine, and adequate steps shall be taken to control or isolate any such fire or heating that may occur.

(5) All unused workings connected to the surface through a walkable entrance which is not permanently closed, shall once at least in every 30 days be inspected by a competent person for signs of illicit distillation of liquor. A report of every such inspection shall be recorded in a bound-paged book kept for the purpose, and shall be signed and dated by the person making the inspection.][2]

---

1 Substituted vide Notification No. GSR 359, dated 25th March 1972.

2 Inserted vide Notification No. GSR 568, dated 17th April 1971.

118-A Further precautions against spontaneous heating[1]

The following further precautions shall be taken against the danger of spontaneous heating:

(1)

(a) The seam or section shall be worked in panels having independent ventilation in such a manner that it is possible to isolate one from another easily, if necessary. Where development has already been made without regard to this factor, artificial panels should be created by the construction of stoppings. In determining the size of the panel, due consideration shall be given to the desirability of enabling complete extraction of the pillars therein within the incubation period of the coal.

(b) No coal, shale or other carbonaceous material shall be left or stacked belowground. Where removal of fallen coal out of the mine is not practicable, the area shall be effectively sealed off.

(c) Except where, otherwise permitted by the Chief Inspector by an order in writing and subject to such conditions as he may specify therein, no extraction of pillars in any seam or section shall be commenced until fire dams or stoppings have been provided in all entrances to the panel, except that in the fire dams or stoppings built in entrances which are to be kept open for ventilation or haulage, suitable doors or openings may be left and bricks and other suitable materials shall be kept readily available in their vicinity. Shale or other carbonaceous material shall not be used in the construction of fire dams or stoppings.

(d) A panel shall be isolated by adequate stoppings as soon as it has been goaved out.

(2) Sufficient material for dealing with fire shall be kept in readiness at suitable places belowground for transport and use. A sufficient number of persons shall be trained in the use of this material.

(3)

(a) In order that spontaneous heating is detected in early stages, the air in the return airway of every depillaring district, and of every goaf which has not been isolated shall be:

(i) tested for percentage of carbon monoxide once at least in every seven days with an automatic detector of a type approved by the Chief Inspector; and

(ii) completely analysed once at least in every 30 days with a view to determining the ratio CO formed/O_2 absorbed. The result of every such test shall be recorded in a bound-paged book kept for the purpose and shall be signed and dated by the person carrying out the test.

---

[1] Inserted vide Notification No. GSR 568, dated 17th April 1971.

(b) If successive tests show any steady increase in the CO formed/O_2 absorbed ratio, suitable measures shall be taken to determine the site of the heating and to deal with it.

(c) Every depillaring district shall be inspected on every idle day, and all unused workings which have not been sealed off shall be inspected once at least in every seven days, by a competent person for any fire risk. The isolation stoppings built around goaved out areas [and unused workings] shall be inspected at similar intervals. A report of every such inspection shall be recorded in a bound-paged book kept for the purpose, and shall be signed and dated by the person making the inspection.

(4) Where at any mine or part special conditions exist which make compliance with any of the provisions of this regulation not necessary or reasonably practicable, the Regional Inspector may, by an order in writing and subject to such conditions as he may specify therein, grant a relaxation from the provision:

[(4)][2]

(5) If any dispute arises as to the provisions of this regulation, it shall be referred to the Chief Inspector for decision which shall be final.

119 Precautions after a fire has broken out

(1) (a) On the appearance in any part of a mine, of smoke or other signs indicating that a fire or spontaneous heating has or may have broken out, [effective steps shall be taken, without delay, to deal with the fire or heating and][3] all persons other than those whose presence in the mine is deemed necessary for dealing with the fire or heating shall be immediately withdrawn from the mine. No person, other than those required for dealing with or sealing off the fire or heating, shall be readmitted in the mine until the fire or heating has been extinguished or effectively sealed off and an examination has been made by the Manager or by the Under Manager or Assistant Manager and the mine has been declared to be safe. A report of every such examination shall be recorded in a bound-paged book kept for the purpose and shall be signed and dated by the person making the examination: Provided that the Regional Inspector may, by an order in writing and subject to such conditions as he may specify therein, permit the employment in the mine of persons other than those required to deal with the fire of heating.

(b) The examination required by Clause (a) shall be made with an approved flame safety lamp and a cage containing suitable birds or other means of detecting carbon monoxide gas approved by the Chief Inspector. No additional light shall be used other than an approved safety lamp or torch.

---

1 Inserted vide Notification No GSR 550 (E) dated 6th June 1990.

2 Omitted vide *ibid.*

3 Inserted vide *ibid.*

(2) During the whole time that any work of dealing with or sealing off a fire or heating below ground is in progress:[1]
   (a) a competent person shall be present on the spot throughout; and
   (b) adequate precautions shall be taken to prevent danger to persons from asphyxiating or flammable gases, flame, steam and ejected or rolling down hot material, explosion of water gas, and falling into crevices or potholes that may occur in the area on fire;
   (c) there shall be kept available at or near all places below-ground-
      (i) adequate number of self-rescuers and at least two smoke helmets or other suitable apparatus for use in emergency;
      (ii) a cage containing suitable birds or other means of detecting carbon monoxide gas approved by the Chief Inspector; and
      (iii) a flame safety lamp or other means of detecting, carbon dioxide gas and oxygen- deficiency, approved by the Chief Inspector.

(3) The Manager of every mine shall prepare and establish a detailed scheme for the provision and maintenance of suitable fire-fighting arrangements for the prevention, detection, dealing and control of any heating or fire; for the examination and maintenance of the protective measures taken to control or isolate a fire or heating and for ensuring safety of persons engaged in the said operations. The scheme shall be suitably modified and kept updated as the situation warrants.

120 Equipment and organisation for fire-fighting[1]

(1) In every mine
   (a) unless expressly exempted in writing by the Regional Inspector, effective means of delivering to all working places below ground and all other places of fire risk such as coal stacks, spoil heaps containing carbonaceous material and exposed coal surfaces liable to heating, an adequate quantity of water at sufficient pressure for the purpose of efficient fire-fighting shall be provided and kept maintained;
   (b) fire stations with a suitable supply of fire-fighting equipment shall be established and kept maintained at convenient points, both on surface and belowground; and
   (c) sufficient supply of sand or incombustible dust or suitable portable fire-extinguishers shall be provided at:
      (i) every entrance to a mine or district and at every landing and shaft bottom in use;
      (ii) every place where timber, grease, oil or other flammable material is stored;
      (iii) every engine room, electrical gear, driving unit of roadway conveyor, diesel engine, maintenance workshop and filling station, storage battery charging station; and

---

[1] Substituted vide Notification No. GSR 550 (E), dated 6th June 1990.

(iv) such other special places of fire risk as may be specified by the Manager.

(d) an up-to-date fire-fighting plan showing the water mains, taps, firestations, pumping stations, ventilation system, escape routes, etc., shall be kept maintained and a copy thereof posted in the mine office and at convenient places belowground. Adequate number of persons shall also be trained in the use of fire-extinguishers and in fire-fighting. All such persons shall be made familiar with the position of all fire-fighting equipments provided in the mine.

(2) (a) Soda-acid-type extinguishers or water shall not be used for fighting oil or electrical fires.

(b) Foam-type extinguishers shall not be used for fighting electrical fires. Substituted vide Notification No. G.S.R. 550 (E), dated 6th June, 1990.

(c) Fire-extinguishers containing chemicals which are liable, when operated, to give off poisonous or noxious gases, shall not be provided or used belowground. Provided that nothing in this clause shall be deemed to prohibit the use belowground of fire-extinguishers giving off carbon dioxide when operated.

(3) (a) A competent person shall, once at least in every month, examine all the equipment, materials and arrangements provided for fire-fighting and shall discharge and re-fill fire-extinguishers as often as may be necessary to ensure that these are in proper working order.

(b) Any deficiency found during such examination or otherwise shall be immediately remedied.

(c) A report of every such examination including discharge and re-filling of fire-extinguishers shall be made in a bound-paged book kept for the purpose and shall be signed and dated by the person making the examination.

[121 Apparatus for testing for carbon monoxide

In every fiery seam, there shall be kept at the mine constantly available for use two or more suitable birds or other means of detecting carbon monoxide gas approved by the Chief Inspector: Provided that the Regional Inspector may, by an order in writing require compliance with this regulation in the case of any other mine also.][1]

[122 Precautions when a fire exists

(1) No person shall be employed in any seam:

(a) where a fire or spontaneous heating exists in a lower seam whether such fire has been sealed off by means of fire-stoppings or not; or

(b) where the seam has a common ventilation system with another seam on fire; or

---

1 Substituted vide Notification No. GSR 359, dated 25th March, 1972.

(c) where the outlets or openings of the seam are within 60 metres of an active fire or spontaneous heating in a higher seam or on the surface in any ash heap or spoil heap or in any other heap or place or any other fire or spontaneous heating which cannot be controlled immediately; or

(d) where the outlets or openings of the seam are within 60 metres of such fire or spontaneous heating; or

(e) where the parting with an overlying seam on fire or in which spontaneous heating has taken place or with surface containing an active fire or spontaneous heating in any spoil heap or ash heap or in any other heap or place or any other fire or spontaneous heating which cannot be controlled immediately consists of less than 10 metres of hard rock; except with permission in writing of the Chief Inspector and subject to such conditions as he may specify therein.][1]

[(2) In any working mine, in which a fire is known or believed to exist-

(a) adequate precautions shall be taken to prevent the passage of air from any part of the mine or from the surface to the fire area through any broken strata; and

(b) no work other than the precautions required by clause (a) shall be done in any part of the mine which is not effectively sealed off from any such goaf or broken strata.

(3) In every fiery seam or gassy seam of the second or third degree, arrangements shall be made once at least in every 30 days to ascertain the atmospheric condition behind the stoppings built to seal off the area of old workings or such goaf or a fire or spontaneous heating unless such stoppings are capable of resisting the force of an explosion.][2]

(4)

(a) Every stopping erected to isolate or control a fire or spontaneous heating belowground [or to seal off goaf or an area of old workings][3] shall be numbered, and shall be of adequate strength and so maintained as to prevent any leakage of air or gas through it. Where water is likely to accumulate behind any such stopping, there shall be provided in the stopping a suitable pipe or other device to drain away the water without permitting any leakage of air or gas etc.

(b) Where in any mine or part thereof the provisions of clause (a) have not been complied with or where, in the opinion of the Regional Inspector, the steps so taken are inadequate, he may give notice in writing to the Owner, Agent or Manager, requiring him to take such protective measures, within such time, as he may specify therein. In case of non-compliance with the requirements of the notice, the Regional Inspector may, by an order in writing, prohibit until the requirements of the notice have been complied with, the employment in the mine or part, of any

---

1 Substituted vide Notification No. GSR 1558, dated the 31st August 1968.

2 Substituted vide Notification No. GSR 359, dated 25th March 1972.

3 Inserted vide Notification No. 550 (E), dated 6th June, 1990.

person whose employment is not necessary for the purpose of complying with the requirements aforesaid.

(5) A competent person shall, once at least in every seven days, inspect all stoppings erected to isolate or control a fire or spontaneous heating belowground. During every such inspection, he shall ascertain the general condition of every stopping, check it for leakage and presence of gas, and ascertain the temperature and humidity of the atmosphere outside the stopping. For every stopping, he shall place his signature, with date, on a check-board provided for the purpose at a suitable position on the stopping and this record shall be maintained for a period of not less than three months. A report of every such inspection shall also be recorded in a bound-paged book kept for the purpose and shall also be signed and dated by the person making the inspection: Provided that the Regional Inspector may, by an order in writing, require such inspection to be made at such shorter intervals as he may specify therein.

[123 Precautions against dust

(1) The Owner, Agent or Manager of every mine shall take such steps as are necessary for the minimising of emissions of dust and for the suppression of dust which enters the air at any workplace belowground or on surface and for ensuring that the exposure of workers to respirable dust is limited to an extent that is reasonably practicable but in any case not exceeding the limits that are harmful to the health of persons.

(2) For the purpose of this regulation, a place shall not be deemed to be in a harmless state for persons to work or be therein if the 8-hour time-weighted average concentration of airborne respirable dust in milligrams per cubic metre of air sampled by a gravimetric dust sampler of a type approved by and determined in accordance with the procedure as specified by the Chief Inspector by a general or special order exceeds 3 where working is being made wholly in a coal seam or where free respirable silica present is less than 5 per cent and the value arrived at by dividing the figure of fifteen with the percentage of free respirable silica present in other cases.

(3) (a) The Owner, Agent or Manager of every mine shall, within six months of the coming into force of this regulation and once at least every six months thereafter or whenever the Regional Inspector so requires by an order in writing, cause the air at every work place where respirable dust is evolved to be sampled and the concentration of respirable dust therein determined: Provided that, if any measurement of any work place shows the concentration in excess of fifty per cent or seventyfive per cent of the allowable concentration specified in sub-regulation (2) (hereinafter referred to as "permissible limit") the subsequent measurements shall be carried on at intervals not exceeding three months or one month respectively. Provided further that such measurements shall also be carried on immediately upon the commissioning of any plant, equipment

or machinery or upon the introduction of any new work practice or upon any alteration therein that is likely to bring about any substantial change in the levels of airborne respirable dust.

(b) The samples shall, as far as practicable, be representative of the levels of dust exposure of work-persons. For this purpose, the sampler shall be positioned on the return side of the point of dust generation and within 1 metre of the normal working position of but not behind the operator or other worker whose exposure is deemed to be maximum in his working group.

(c) Based on the results of fixed-point sampling, the representative dust exposure profiles for different categories of workers shall be estimated and as a measure of cross-check the "static monitoring" shall be duly supplemented by "portal to portal personal monitoring" of selected workers whose exposure is deemed to be representative of their working groups.

(d) Samples shall be taken by a person who has been specially trained for the purpose in the sampling equipment and accessories that have been checked to ensure correct maintenance and efficient operation thereof and examined, treated and calibrated on a date which is not earlier than one year.

(e) Respirable dust content of the samples and in case of samples collected from a working other than the working being made wholly in a coal seam, quartz content shall be determined as soon as practicable at a properly equipped laboratory approved in writing by the Chief Inspector in that behalf.

(f) All results of measurements of airborne respirable dust and all other relevant particulars shall be systematically recorded within fourteen days of the date of collection of samples, in a bound-paged book kept for the purpose, and every entry in the book aforesaid shall be countersigned and dated by the Manager within twenty four hours.

(4) When the dust-monitoring results have established that the permissible limit of dust concentration is being exceeded at any place, immediate steps shall be taken to minimise the emission of dust and to notify the Regional Inspector. If however, the average concentration of respirable dust in a series of 5 samples taken in 7 successive normal working shifts during the subsequent month exceeds one- and-a-half times the "permissible limits", the relevant operation or operations causing excessive dust shall cease. The operation or operations shall not be resumed and allowed to be carried on until improvements have been made in the prevention and suppression of dust and fresh sampling carried out immediately on resumption of the said operation or operations has established that such improvements have reduced the dust concentration below the "permissible limit".

Provided that, if the dust prevention and suppression device of any machinery or equipment fails to operate efficiently, the operation of the said machinery or equipment shall likewise cease and shall not be resumed until the defect therein has been rectified:

Provided further that, purely as a contingency measure or as secondary means of protection in a work situation wherein it is technically not feasible to reduce the respirable dust concentration below "permissible limit" or during the time period necessary to install and commission any device or to institute any new workpractice for dust prevention or suppression, compliance with the permissible limit of dust may be achieved by remote operation or by a job rotation and failing which by the use of suitable dust respirator.

(5) The Owner, Agent or Manager of every mine where need of dust respirators might arise, shall provide dust respirators in sufficient number and at no cost to the concerned workpersons for their use; for the dust respirators to be regularly cleaned, disinfected and maintained in efficient working order, and for the proper fitting of and for thorough training of the concerned workers in the need for and correct use of respirators.

(6) To prevent the liberation and accumulation of dust and the propagation of airborne dust, the following provisions shall have effect, namely:

- (a) dust shall be suppressed as close as possible to its source of formation;
- (b) during any operation of drilling or boring in stone on surface or below-ground:
  - (i) the production of dust shall be reduced by using bits which are sharp and of proper shape, by keeping suitable pressure on the bits and by keeping the holes clear of the cuttings:
  - (ii) except in naturally-wet ground, a jet of water shall be directed on to the cutting edge to wet the cuttings or other equally efficient device approved by the Chief Inspector shall be provided and kept in operation to prevent the atmosphere being charged with dust. Where pneumatic drilling is performed, water shall be turned on before turning on compressed air to the drill. When however, drilling is done by hand, it shall be sufficient if holes are kept constantly moist during such drilling;
- (c) every roadway on surface or belowground, where mobile mining machinery ply, shall be regularly wetted or shall be effectively treated with some other equally efficient agent to reduce dust being raised in the atmosphere to a minimum;
- (d) no plant for the screening or sorting of coal and, as far as practicable, no heap of cinder, cement, sand, mortar or other dry and fine material, shall be placed within 80 metres of the top of downcast shaft or intake airway nor shall any such material be so handled as to make it air-borne and drawn into any such shaft or such airway;
- (e) in every mine belowground-
  - (i) no machinery or equipment which is likely to emit dust in excess of "permissible limit" shall be operated unless it is equipped with

a suitable dust prevention and suppression device and unless such device is operating efficiently;

(ii) the design, arrangement, materials and condition of picks on every mechanical coal cutter shall be such as to reduce the formation of dust to minimum and no mechanical coal cutter shall be operated unless suitable water sprays or jets of water are directed on the cutting edges thereof so as to damp the cuttings as they are formed;

(iii) every working face and the floor, roof and sides of every roadway or airway within 50 metres thereof shall be, unless naturally wet throughout, regularly washed down to prevent accumulation of dust and shall be kept throughout wetted during work shifts;

(iv) a cur-rent of air sufficient to clear away the dust emitted by any machinery or operation and to dilute the dust concentration below the "permissible limit", shall be maintained by means of general ventilation and if necessary, by local ventilation, so however, that, as far as practicable, the velocity of air in any roadway or workplace shall not be such as to raise dust in the atmosphere;

(v) after blasting, working places shall not be entered unless sufficient time has elapsed for dust, smoke and fumes to be cleared by a current of air and the broken material shall not be moved unless it has been thoroughly wetted with water;

(vi) vehicles, tubs, and conveyors used for transport of coal shall be maintained in good condition so as to minimise spillage or leakage. Chutes, spiral conveyors, bins, tipplers, conveyor discharge points, and skip loading and unloading installations shall be so controlled as to reduce the formation of dust to the minimum. Such material shall be also thoroughly wetted with water unless it is already wet or other effective means of dust suppression are used; and

(vii) unless, owing to special difficulties, exempted in writing by Regional Inspector in that behalf and subject to such conditions as he may specify therein, water in pipes, in sufficient quantity and under adequate pressure and independent of any pumping system, shall be provided and maintained so as to get maximum efficiency in the allaying of dust.

(f) no process of crushing, breaking, disintegrating, dressing sorting, grinding, screening or sieving of coal, or any operation incidental thereto, shall be carried out at any mine unless efficient watering or other appropriate and effective dust control measures such as, but not limited to isolation, enclosure, exhaust ventilation and dust collection are designed, provided, maintained and used.

(g) the exhausted air belowground, which contains dust in excess of the "permissible limit" shall be efficiently diluted and if necessary filtered so as to reduce the concentration of respirable dust therein below ten per cent of the "permissible limit" before being recirculated into workplaces.

(h) every device used for the prevention and suppression of dust produced by any machinery, equipment or process as also for the filtering of the exhausted air and every dust respirator shall be inspected once at least in every seven days and shall be thoroughly examined and tested at least once in every period of six months and the results of every such inspection and test shall be recorded in the register maintained under clause (f) of the sub-regulation (3).

(7) The Manager of every mine where airborne dust is generated shall formulate and implement a scheme specifying-

(a) the location, frequency, timing, duration and pattern of sampling;

(b) the instruments and accessories to be used for sampling;

(c) the laboratory at which respirable dust content of samples and quartz content shall be determined;

(d) the format in which the results of measurements of dust concentration and other particulars are to be recorded;

(e) the Organisation for dust monitoring and for the examination and other particulars are to be recorded; and

(f) the manner of making all persons concerned with the implementation of the dust control measures fully conversant with the nature of work to be performed by each in that behalf.

(8) The Regional Inspector may, where special conditions exist, permit or require by an order in writing and subject to such conditions as he may specify therein, any variation in the foregoing provisions or in the Manager's scheme.

(9) If any doubt arises to any matter referred to in this regulation, it shall be referred to the Chief Inspector for decision.][1]

[123A Execution of measures for dust control[2]

(1) (a) There shall be maintained at every mine having workings belowground a *dust plan* on a scale having representative factor of not less than 1:2400. The dust plan shall clearly show (by distinctive colours, code letters and/ or numbers) the separate areas

(i) which are naturally wet;

(ii) which require treatment with water indicating the system of water pipelines laid down for the purpose; and

(iii) which require treatment with incombustible dust at such intervals of 24 hours, 7 days, 14 days, 30 days or three months or other specified period as the case may be. (The intervals aforesaid shall be based on the results of analysis of routine mine dust samples collected from the areas concerned.)

---

1 Substituted vide Notification No. 650 (E), dated 6th June 1990.

2 Inserted vide Notification No. GSR 568, dated 17th April 1971.

(b) The areas aforesaid shall be clearly demarcated in the workings belowground by means of suitable notice boards or by other suitable means. '[(IA) (a) Every part of a mine which is not naturally-wet throughout or which is not isolated by explosion-proof stoppings shall be treated-

(i) with fine incombustible dust in such manner and at such intervals as will ensure that the dust on the floor, roof and sides and any support or structure shall always consist of a mixture containing not less than 75% of incombustible matter in case of coal seams containing less than 30% volatile matter (on dry ash-free-basis) and 85% of incombustible matter in case of coal seams containing more than 30% of such volatile matter; or

(ii) with water in such manner and at such intervals as will ensure that the dust on the floor, roof and sides and on any support or structure is always combined with not less than 30% by weight of water in intimate mixture; or

(iii) In such manner as the Regional Inspector may approve by an order in writing.

(b) The incombustible dust used for the purpose of this sub-regulation shall be:

(i) such that it does not contain more than 5% of free silica;

(ii) of such fineness and character, that it is readily dispersible into the air and that, when used in places which are not directly wetted by water from the strata, it does not cake but it is dispersed into air when blown upon with mouth or by a suitable appliance; and

(iii) as far as practicable light in colour.

(c) No such incombustible dust shall continue to be used if it is found by tests which shall be carried out once at least every three months, not to comply with the foregoing requirements:

Provided that when the supply of incombustible dust used in a mine is not from a regular source, these tests shall be carried out whenever a fresh supply of incombustible dust is received.

(d) Where any place or part of the mine is to be treated with incombustible dust:

(i) before treating with incombustible dust, all coal dust shall be cleaned, as far as practicable, from the roof, sides, floor, props, cogs, bars, brattice cloth or any other objects or structure or place on which coal dust may deposit, and all dust so collected shall be removed to the surface within 24 hours;

(ii) incombustible dust shall be spread on the objects, structure and places aforesaid in adequate quantity and at such intervals as may be necessary to ensure compliance with the provisions of this sub-regulation;

(iii) The cleaning of coal dust and spreading of incombustible dust shall be carried out in the direction of the flow of the air;

(iv) a sufficient supply of incombustible dust shall be kept readily available at suitable places in the mine, and any deficiency in the supply of dust underground shall immediately be brought to the notice of the Manager; and

(v) incombustible dust stocked at different places and kept on pans or on dust barriers in the mine shall be changed whenever it is no longer readily dispersible or whenever it becomes coated with coal dust.][1]

(2) A daily record of the areas cleaned of coal dust and of the areas treated with incombustible dust or with water and the amount of incombustible dust used shall be maintained in a bound-paged book kept for the purpose. Every entry in this book shall be signed and dated by the Dust Incharge, and countersigned by the Manager or the Ventilation Officer.

(3) The dust control measures aforesaid shall be carried out under the supervision of a competent person holding a Manager's or Overman's Certificate or a degree or diploma in mining or mining engineering from a university or institution approved by the Central Government for the purpose of provision to Regulation 16(l). No duties with respect to sampling of dust under Regulation 123B shall be entrusted to this person who may be designated as the "Dust Incharge" nor any other duties shall be entrusted to such person except with the previous permission of Regional Inspector:

Provided that in the case of a mine having an average monthly output of less than 5000 tonnes, the Dust Incharge referred to in this regulation can act as the Sampling Incharge referred to in regulation 123B.

(4) The Dust Incharge shall also see:

(a) that every part of the mine which, under these regulations, requires treatment with water, is thoroughly drenched or sprayed with water immediately before firing shots and also at intervals during the working hours so as to strictly comply with the provisions of regulation 123 (5)(b) (ii);

(b) that every part of the mine which, under these regulations can be treated with incombustible dust, is so treated as to strictly comply with the provisions of regulation 123 (i) (b) (i); and

(c) that the arrangements for treating with water or incombustible dust as aforesaid are maintained in good order][2]

---

1 Substituted vide Notification No. GSR 550 (E), dated 6th June 1990.

2 Inserted vide Notification No. GSR 550 (E), dated 6th June 1990.

[123B Check on measures for dust control[1]

(1) For the purpose of ensuring adequate treatment of coal dust as required under [regulation 123 and 123A][2], systematic samples of mine dust shall be collected, tested, and analysed at intervals and in the manner specified in this regulation.

(2) (a) Every return airway as lies within two hundred metres of the last working face and every haulage, tramming or conveyor roadway which is not naturally-wet throughout, shall be divided into zones not longer than one hundred and fifty metres each: Provided that where in a mine some parts are being treated with water and others with incombustible dust, zones shall be so formed that in each zone only one system of treating coal dust is being followed.

(b) Every zone formed as aforesaid shall be divided into three equal sections each not exceeding 50 metres in length.

(3) (a) Every zone shall be given a distinct number and every section the code letters a, b or c in a systematic manner. The zones and sections, with their numbers and code letters, shall be clearly marked on a plan prepared on a scale having a representative factor of not less than 1:2400 hereinafter called 11 sampling plan." The sampling plan shall clearly show the areas of the mine that are naturally-wet throughout.

(b) Every zone and section shall also be distinctly demarcated in the working belowground by means of suitable notice boards or by other suitable means.

(4) (a) Representative sample of dust shall be collected once in every 30 days from every zone, and for this purpose samples may be collected from different sections a, b or c in rotation such that during every such period of 30 days, all samples are collected from the section a or section b or section c.

(b) Representative samples aforesaid shall be collected in a systematic manner irrespective of the cleaning and treating operations but shall in no case be collected within [20 hours][3] of cleaning and treating of any zone, section, or part thereof.

(c) If the representative sample of mine dust from any particular zone shows that the provisions of [regulation 123A (IA) (a)][4] have not been complied with, immediate steps shall be taken to clean and treat whole of the zone so as to comply with the provision of [regulation 123A (A) (a)][5].

(5) In every travelling roadway and in every airway other than those specified in sub-regulation (2) (a), samples shall be taken in such systematic manner and at such intervals (not exceeding three months) that proper check is maintained on the efficiency of the treatment thereof in terms of [regulation 123 (lA) (c)][6].

---

1 Inserted vide Notification No. GSR 568, dated 17th April 1971.

2 Substituted vide Notification No. GSR 550 (E) dated 6th June 1990.

3 Substituted vide *ibid.*

4 Substituted vide *ibid.*

5 Substituted vide *ibid.*

6 Substituted vide *ibid.*

(6) (a) Samples of dust shall be collected from roof, sides and floor, and shall comprise dust collected to a depth not exceeding five millimetres on the roof and to a depth not exceeding two millimetres on the floor.

(b) Where a zone is treated with incombustible dust, the samples shall be collected by a method of 'strip sampling', the strips being as near as possible of equal width of not less than 10 centimetres and at uniform intervals not exceeding five metres.

(c) Where a zone is treated with water, the samples shall be collected by a method of 'spot sampling' such that a spot-collection of dust is made for every metre of the length sampled, as nearly as possible at regularly spaced intervals along a zig-zag path.

(d) In collecting the samples aforesaid, the strips shall be extended into or spot collections made from any cross-galleries up to the air-stoppings, if any.

(e) Each sample shall be well-mixed and then reduced in bulk (by quartering) to a weight of not less than 30 grammes. Each sample so reduced shall be picked in a moisture-proof container which shall be suitable labelled or marked.

(7) The sampling operations aforesaid shall be carried out under the supervision of a competent person holding a Manager's or Overman's Certificate or degree or diploma in mining or mining engineering from a university or institution approved for the purpose of regulation 16. He shall be designated as the "Sampling In charge" and shall be different from "Dust In charge 11 appointed under regulation 123A. No other duties shall be entrusted to this person except with the previous permission of the Regional Inspector.

(8) Within seven days of taking of each sample, it shall be sent for analysis and the result of such analysis, immediately on its receipt, shall be recorded in a bound-paged book kept for the purpose. Every entry in the book aforesaid shall be signed and dated by the Sampling In charge and be countersigned and dated by the Manager.

Explanation: A place in a mine is considered "Naturally wet throughout" if it is moist enough to keep the coal dust present at any time, on the roof, sides and floor and other objects at that place so that it is always combined with not less than 30% by weight of water in intimate mixture.]"

123C Stone-dust barriers[1]

(1) In every gassy seam of the second or third degree [or in the development workings in a gassy seam of the first degree in which there is likelihood of occurrence of flammable gas in dangerous quantities][2], additional precautions shall be taken by providing stone-dust barriers to prevent an ignition of explosion from extending from one part of the mine to the other.

---

[1] Inserted vide Notification No. GSR 369 dated 25th March 1972.

[2] Inserted vide Notification No. GSR 32, dated 16th December 1978.

(2) Every such stone-dust barrier shall be of such a type as may be approved by the Chief Inspector by a general or special order in writing and shall be maintained in such manner as may be specified in the said order:
Provided that the Chief Inspector may permit in any mine or part thereof alternative precautionary measures to be taken in lieu of stone-dust barriers.

(3) [If any dispute arises as to whether stone-dust barriers or other alternative precautionary measures are required to be provided in any part of a gassy seam of the first degree under sub-regulation (1), the question shall be referred to the Chief Inspector who shall decide the same.][1]

124. Precautions against irruption of gas

(I)[2]

(2)[3] Where any working is extended to within 30 metres of any goaf or disused workings containing or likely to contain an accumulation of flammable or noxious gases, there shall be maintained at least one borehole not less than 1.5 metres deep in advance of the working. The operation of drilling the borehole shall be carried out under the supervision of a competent person, and no lamp or light other than approved safety lamp or torch shall be used in any such working.

125 Recovery and exploratory work

(1) After an explosion of flammable gas or coal dust has occurred in a mine, only such persons as are authorised by the Manager or by the principal official present at surface, shall be allowed to enter the mine.

(2) When it is intended or proposed to re-open a mine or part thereof, which has been isolated, sealed off or flooded with water to deal with a fire or spontaneous heating, the Owner, Agent or Manager shall, not less than 14 days before the commencement of such work, give notice in writing of such intention or proposal to the Regional Inspector and the Chief Inspector.

(3) Where it is intended to carry on any exploratory work in a mine or part belowground likely to contain irrespirable atmosphere:
   (a) party of less than three persons shall be allowed to proceed to carry out such work; and
   (b) every such party shall carry a cage containing suitable birds or other means of detecting carbon monoxide gas approved by the Chief Inspector and also an approved flame safety lamp. No other lamp or light other than an approved lamp or torch shall be used during such exploratory work.

---

[1] Inserted vide Notification No. GSR 32, dated 16th December 1978.
[2&3] Omitted vide Notification No. GSR 359, dated 25th March 1972.

126. Danger from surface water

[(I) (a) Where any mine or part thereof is so situated that there is any danger or inrush of surface water into the mine or part, adequate protection against such inrush shall be provided and maintained [whether such protection is adequate or not can be determined by the Chief Inspector whose decision shall be final,][1]

[(b) Except with the permission of the Chief Inspector in writing and subject to such conditions as he may specify therein and subject to the provisions of clause (a), every entrance into a mine shall be so designed, constructed and maintained that its lowest point (which means the point at which a body of rising water on surface can enter mine) shall be not less than 1.5 metres above the highest flood level at that point."][2]

(2) No workings shall be made in any mine vertically below

(a) any part of any river, canal, lake, tank or other surface reservoir, or Inserted vide Notification No. G.S.R. 32 dated 16th Dec. 1978. 2 (3) Omitted vide Notification No. G.S.R. 359 dated 25th March 1972. (4) Renumbered vide Notification No. G.S.R. 568, dated 17th April, 1971.

(b) any spot lying within a horizontal distance of 15 metres from either bank of a river or canal or from the boundary of a lake, tank or other surface reservoir, except with the permission in writing of the Chief Inspector and subject to such conditions as he may specify therein.

(3) Every application for permission under sub-regulation (2) shall be accompanied by two copies of a plan and section showing the existing position of the working of the mine, the proposed layout of workings, the depth of the workings from the surface, the position and depth of any goaves in every seam in the neighbourhood, all faults, dykes and other geological disturbances and such other particulars as may affect the safety of the mine or of the persons employed therein.

Explanation-Where sand or alluvium are lying in the course of a river, canal, lake, tank or reservoir, the depth from the surface shall be reckoned from the surface of the hard ground underlying such sand or alluvium.

[(4) All workings made under sub-regulation (2) shall be clearly demarcated below ground][3].

(5) (a) A competent person shall, once at least in every 14 days during the rainy season and once at least in every 30 days during other periods of the year, examine every protective measure provided under sub-regulation (1), whether in use or not, for their stability. A report of every such examination shall be recorded in a bound-paged book kept for the purpose and shall be signed and dated by the person making the examination and countersigned by the Manager.

---

1 Submitted vide *ibid.*

2 Submitted vide *ibid.*

3 Inserted vide Notification No. GSR 568, dated 17th April 1971.

(b) The protective measure and workings aforesaid shall also be inspected, once at least in every quarter by the Manager personally."]

127 Danger from underground inundation

[1](1) Proper provision shall be made in every mine to prevent irruption of water or other liquid matter or any material that is likely to flow when wet from the workings of the same mine or of an adjoining mine and to prevent accidents while drilling boreholes for probe or release of a body of water or other liquid matter.

(2) Where work is being done in-

(a) (i) any seam or section below another seam or section; or

(ii) any place in a seam or section, which is at a lower level than any other place in a lower seam or section; or

(iii) any place in a seam approaching a fault through an upper seam or section, which contains or may contain an accumulation of water or other liquid matter of any material that is likely to flow when wet; or

(b) any water-bearing strata, all useful information including the position, extent and depth of the abovementioned features shall be acquired and kept recorded and a scheme of working designed to prevent irruption of water or other liquid matter or any material which flows when wet shall be prepared and put into operation.

(3) Without prejudice to the requirements of sub-regulation (1) and subregulation (2), no working which has approached within a distance of 60 metres of any other working (not being the working which has been physically examined and found to be free from accumulation of water or other liquid matter or any material that is likely to flow when wet) and whether in the same mine or in an adjoining mine, shall be extended further except with the prior permission in writing of the Regional Inspector and subject to such conditions as he may specify therein.]

Explanation-For the purpose of this sub-regulation, the distance between the said workings shall mean the shortest distance between the workings of the same seam or between any two seams or sections, as the case may be, measured in any direction whether horizontal, vertical or inclined.]

(4) [(a) Every application for permission to extend any working referred to in sub-regulation (3) shall be accompanied by two copies of the plan and section showing:

(i) The outlines of all such disused or abandoned workings in relation to the working approaching them and also the depth of such disused or abandoned workings from the surface.

(ii) The outlines, the layout and the method of the proposed working for which permission is sought.

---

1 Substituted vide Notification No. GSR 550(E), dated 6th June 1990.

(iii) The faults, dykes, and other geological disturbances in relation to working specified in clause (i) or (ii) of the sub regulation, and

(iv) Any other information that is available with the management and other particulars or information that may be required by the Chief Inspector.

(b) When permission is granted to extend any working referred to in subregulation (3) or sub-regulation (5), it shall be extended strictly in accordance with the plan and the method approved under, and the conditions specified in such permission; and there shall be no variation therefrom unless such variation is again approved by the Chief Inspector.][1]

(5) Whenever seepage of water, which is not normal to the seam, is noticed at any place in any working, or if there be any such suspicion or doubt, such working shall immediately be stopped and the Chief Inspector and the Regional Inspector shall forthwith be informed of such seepage. Such working shall not be extended further except with the prior permission in writing of the Chief Inspector and subject to such conditions as he may specify therein.

(6) (a) The height of any working referred to in sub-regulation (3) or subregulation (5) shall not exceed 2.4 metres and there shall be maintained at least one borehole near the centre of the working face and sufficient flank boreholes on each side where necessary, boreholes above and below the workings at intervals of not more than five metres. All such boreholes[2] [drilled sufficiently close to each other to ensure that the advancing face will not accidentally hole through into a working containing water or liquid matter or any material that is likely to flow when wet and shall be] maintained and shall be constantly maintained at sufficient distance in advance of the working and such distance shall in no case be less than three metres. These precautions shall be carried out under the direct supervision of an official, having Manager's or Overman's Certificate specially authorised for the purpose.

(b) A record showing the exact height and width of such working, the number of boreholes driven, the length of each borehole, the places at which and the direction in which each borehole was driven, shall be maintained by the official referred to in clause (a) in a bound-paged book kept for the purpose and the entries made therein shall be signed and dated by such competent person and shall be countersigned by the Manager every day. Also, a plan and section of such working showing the above particulars shall be prepared and maintained and they shall be brought up-to-date at least once in every fifteen days.

(7) Unless specific relaxation is granted by the Chief Inspector in writing under sub-regulation (8), all the provisions of sub-regulation (6) shall be strictly complied with while extending any working referred to in sub-regulation

[1] Inserted vide Notification No. GSR 875, dated 19th March 1980.

[2] Inserted vide Notification No. GSR 550(E), dated 6th June 1990.

(3) or sub-regulation (5) whether or not the permission granted to extend such workings requires compliance with all or any of the provisions of sub-regulation (6).

(8) If the Chief Inspector is satisfied that the conditions in any mine or part thereof are such as to render compliance with all or any of the provisions specified in sub-regulation (6) unnecessary or impracticable, he may, by an order in writing and subject to such conditions as may be specified therein, relax, vary or dispense with all or any of the conditions and requirements contained in subregulation (6) and if he is of the opinion that the conditions at any mine or part thereof are such as to require additional precautions to be taken, he may, by an order in writing, require that such additional precautions besides those specified in sub-regulation (6) shall be taken.]

128 Intentional flooding

(1) When the Owner, Agent or Manager intends or proposes, by introducing water from the surface or from any other part of the mine, or from an adjacent mine, to flood any part of the workings of his mine, he shall give, in writing, not less than 14 days' notice of such intention or proposal, to the Chief Inspector and the Regional Inspector and to the management of all adjoining mines and of such other mines as might be affected by such flooding:

Provided that the Regional Inspector may, by an order in writing and subject to such conditions as he may specify therein, permit such operation to be commenced on any day prior to the expiry of the said 14 days:

Provided further that the Regional Inspector may, by an order in writing, either prohibit any such operation or require that such operation shall not be commenced until such precautions, as he may specify, have been taken to his satisfaction.

Explanation-For the purposes of this sub-regulation, a mine shall have the meaning assigned to it under regulation 30.

(2) If the operations in respect of which notice is given under sub-regulation (1) are not commenced within 60 days from the expiry of the said 14 days, the notice shall be deemed to have lapsed and the provisions of sub-regulation (1) shall apply as if no such notice had been given.

129. Construction of water dam, etc.

(1) Where in any mine it is intended to construct a reservoir, dam or other structure to withstand a pressure of water or other material which will flow when wet, or to control an inrush water, the Owner, Agent or Manager shall give in writing not less than 14 days' notice to such intention to the Regional Inspector. Every such notice shall be accompanied by two copies of plans and sections showing the design and other details of the proposed construction:

Provided that where the safety of the mine or of the person employed therein is seriously threatened, the provisions of this regulation shall be deemed to have been complied with if the said notice is given to the Regional Inspector as soon as the work of construction is commenced:

Provided further that, where such a reservoir, dam or other structure was constructed before the coming into force of these regulations, the said copies of the plans and sections shall be submitted to the Regional Inspector within three months of the coming into force of these regulations. Where these details are not available, the Regional inspector shall be informed of the fact within the aforesaid period.

(2) The Regional Inspector may, by an order in writing, require such modification or alteration to be made in the design of any such reservoir, dam or structure, as he may specify therein.

APPENDIX 2

Mines Rescue Rules, 1985

Chapter I Preliminary

1. Short title, application and commencement

(1) These Rules may be called the Mines Rescue Rules, 1985.

(2) They shall apply to below/ground mines.

(3) They shall come into force on the 2nd April, 1985.

2. Definitions. In these rules, unless there is anything repugnant to the subject or context,

(a) "Act" means the Mines Act, 1952;

(b) *"Belowlground mine"* means any excavation which extends below superjacent ground;

(c) *"Board of Mining Examinations"* means the Board of Mining Examinations constituted under the Coal Mines Regulations, 1957, or the Metalliferous Mines Regulations, 1961, as the case may be;

(d) *"Chief Inspector"* means the Chief Inspector of Mines appointed under Sec. 5 of the Act;

(e) *"Foreman's Certificate"* means the Foreman's Certificate granted by the Board of Mining Examinations;

(f) *"Inspector"* means an Inspector of Mines appointed under the Act, and includes a District Magistrate when exercising any power or performing any duty of an Inspector which he is empowered by the Act to exercise or perform;

(g) *"Instructor"* means a person appointed as such under sub-rule (2) of Rule 3;

(h) *"Manager"* means a person appointed under Sec. 17 of the Act;

(i) *"Manager's Certificate"* means the Manager's Certificate granted by the Board of Mining Examinations;

"Ordinarily employed" with reference to any mine or part thereof means the average number of persons employed per day in the mine or part of mine during the preceding calendar year (obtained by dividing the number of mandays worked by the number of working days excluding rest days and other non-working days);

(k) *"Overiman's Certificate"* means the Overman's Certificate granted by the Board of Mining Examinations;

(1) **"Owner"** means a person who is the immediate proprietor or lessee or occupier of the mine or of any part thereof and in the case of a mine the business whereof

is being carried on by a liquidator or receiver, such liquidator or receiver, but does not include a person who merely receives a royalty, rent or fine from the mine, or is merely the proprietor of the mine, subject to any lease, grant or licence for working thereof, or is merely the owner of the soil and not interested in the minerals of the mine; but any contractor or sub-lessee for the working of a mine or part thereof shall be subject to the Act in like manner as if he were an owner, but not so as to exempt the owner from any liability;

(m) *"Principal Official"* means the senior-most mine official in mining discipline on duty in the mine;

(n) *"Qualified Medical Practitioner"* means a medical practitioner who possesses any recognised medical qualification as defined in clause (h) of Sec. 2 ' of the Indian Medical Council Act, 1956 and who is enrolled on a State medical register as defined in clause (k) of that section;

(o) *"Rescue Room"* means a rescue room as established and maintained under Rules;

(p) *"Rescue Station"* means a rescue station established and maintained under Rule 3;

(q) *"Rescue-trained person"* means a person certified by the Superintendent to be rescue-trained person under sub-rule (1) of Rule 21];

(r) *"Schedule"* means a Schedule appended to these rules;

(s) *"Superintendent"* means a Superintendent of Rescue Station appointed under sub-rule (2) of Rule 3.

Chapter 2 Rescue Stations and Rescue Rooms

3. **Establishment and Location of Rescue Station. (1)** The Chief Inspector may permit or require the Owner of a below/ground mine or a group of below/ground mines to establish and maintain rescue station/stations with such designs and specifications and at such place/places as may be considered necessary in consultation with the owner; Provided that, where there are below/ground mines belonging to more than one Owner, the Chief Inspector may permit or require two or more Owners to jointly establish a common rescue station; Provided further that all the existing rescue stations as on the date of coming into force of these Rules, shall continue to function for a period of three years from that date.

(2) At every rescue station, there shall be appointed one Superintendent and at least two Instructors and also, there shall be maintained a rescue brigade of not less than eighteen rescue-trained persons.

(3) In case, where the absence of the Superintendent at a rescue station exceeds 60 days, the Owner shall appoint another Superintendent.

(4) The Owner shall, within seven days from the date of assumption or relinquishment of charge by the Superintendent, inform the Chief Inspector and the Inspector in-charge of the region where the mine is situated (hereinafter referred to as Regional Inspector) in Form 1.

4. **Functions of Rescue Stations** The functions of rescue stations shall include:
   (i) imparting initial training in rescue and recovery work;
   (ii) imparting refresher training to rescue-trained persons;
   (iii) providing support by its own rescue teams and equipment in case of major accidents or long-lasting rescue and recovery operations; and
   (iv) carrying out the functions of rescue room in respect of these belowground mines where there is no rescue room.

5. **Establishment and Location of Rescue Rooms**
   (1) At every below-ground mine where more than 100 persons are ordinarily employed below,-round and there is no rescue station within a radius of 35 km, the Owner shall establish and maintain on surface close to the mine entrance a rescue room: Provided that it may be sufficient to provide one rescue room for a number of mines belonging to the same Owner where:
   (a) the total number of persons ordinarily employed in below-ground workings of all such mines does not exceed 5,000; and
   (b) the mines are situated within a radius of 35 km from and connected by road with the rescue room;

   Provided further that the Chief Inspector may permit the Owner of a group of mines having the total number of persons ordinarily employed below-ground and in excess of 5,000, to use the rescue room as a rescue station excepting the functions of imparting initial training in rescue work, if such rescue room is:
   (a) equipped with requisite additional rescue apparatus including at least 15 extra sets of two-hour self-contained breathing apparatus; and
   (b) placed under the charge of a person holding the qualifications prescribed under Rule 8 and a minimum of five rescue-trained persons of whom at least one shall hold the qualifications prescribed under Rule 10 are posted thereat.
   (2) Notwithstanding anything contained in sub-rule (1), in the case of below-ground coal mines having a fiery seam or gassy seam of second or third degree, the Chief Inspector may, for reasons to be recorded in writing, require the owner to establish and maintain a rescue room irrespective of the number of persons ordinarily employed below ground therein.
   (3) At each rescue room, there shall be appointed such number of rescue trained persons as may be necessary and one of them possessing the qualifications specified in Rule 10 shall be made in-charge of the rescue room. At least one rescue-trained person shall always be in attendance at the rescue room.

6. **Functions of Rescue Rooms**

   A rescue room shall provide facilities for the storage, assembly, testing, and adjustments of breathing apparatus and other rescue equipment and apparatus and for their speedy transport to mines.

7. Qualifications, Experience, etc., of Superintendent
After coming into force of these Rules, no person shall be appointed as Superintendent unless he
(i) is a rescue-trained person;
(ii) has 5 years practical experience of below ground work in mines; and
(iii) holds a First Class Manager's Certificate of a type not restricted to opencast workings.

8. Qualifications, Experience, etc., of Instructors After the coming into force of these rules, no person shall be appointed as Instructor unless he
(i) is a rescue-trained person;
(ii) has 3 years practical experience of below-ground work in mines; and
(iii) holds a Manager's Certificate of type not restricted to opencast workings.

9. Selection of rescue-trained Persons for posting at Rescue Stations
(1) After coming into force of these rules, the rescue-trained persons for posting at a rescue station shall be selected from amongst the rescue-trained persons employed in mines served by the rescue station by the Superintendent in consultation with the Managers of such mines.
(2) A person selected under sub-rule (1) shall be posted for not less than one year and not more than five years at a rescue station at any one time.

10. Qualifications, Experience, etc., of Rescue Room In-charge
No person shall be appointed as rescue room in-charge unless he-
(i) is a rescue-trained person;
(ii) has 3 years practical experience of below-ground work in mines; and
(iii) holds a Manager's Overman's or Foreman's Certificate of a type not restricted to opencast workings.

11. **Equipment.**
(1) At every rescue station, there shall be provided and maintained for immediate use, apparatus and equipment as specified in Sch. I.
(2) At every rescue room, there shall be provided and maintained for immediate use apparatus and equipment as specified in Sch. II.
(3) At a below ground mine, where rescue room is located, apparatus and equipment as specified in Sch. III, shall be maintained at the entrance of such mine.
(4) Self-contained breathing apparatus shall be provided at a rescue station and that at rescue rooms under it, shall be of the same type and make.
(5) The following apparatus and equipments provided in pursuance of subrules (1), (2) and (3), shall be of a type or standard approved by the Chief Inspector, namely
  (a) breathing apparatus;
  (b) smoke helmets and apparatus serving the same purpose;
  (c) reviving apparatus;
  (d) electric safety lamps and flame safety lamps,
  (e) gas detectors; and

(f) self-rescuers.

(6) All breathing apparatus and every flowmeter shall be adjusted and tested and the purity of oxygen for use in breathing apparatus shall be tested in such manner as are laid down in Sch. IV.

(7) In case of an accident in a below-ground mine arising out of the use of any rescue apparatus, a written report thereof shall be sent, within 24 hours of such accident, by the Manager of the mine to the Chief Inspector and Regional Inspector in Form II appended to the Mines Rules.

(8) In case of an accident in a rescue station or rescue room arising out of the use of any rescue apparatus, a written report thereof shall be sent, within 24 hours of such accident, by the Superintendent to the Chief Inspector and Regional Inspector in Form II aforesaid.

(9) No absorbent charges, chemicals, self-rescuers and gas detector tubes shall be kept at a rescue station, rescue room, or below-ground mine for use beyond the expiry date, which shall be legibly marked on the boxes thereof.

Chapter 3 Duties and Responsibilities of Superintendent, etc.

12. Duties and Responsibilities of Superintendent, etc.

(1) The Superintendent shall be in overall control of the rescue station and the rescue rooms served by such rescue station.

(2) The Superintendent shall ensure that all the rescue equipment and apparatus kept at the rescue station, rescue rooms, and at the entrance of the below ground mines under his control are-

(a) maintained in perfect working order;

(b) inspected by instructors at specified intervals; and

(c) tests are conducted and adjustments are made.

(3) The Superintendent shall ensure that adequate stock of spare parts and supplies are kept for maintaining rescue equipment and apparatus in perfect working order.

(4) The Superintendent shall countersign the records maintained under sub-rule (1) of Rule 13.

(5) The Superintendent shall ensure the persons selected for initial training and those undergoing refresher training receive the prescribed course of instructions and practices and are issued the certificates for the same.

(6) The Superintendent shall make periodical inspection of rescue rooms and the apparatus and equipment under his control.

(7) In the event of an emergency at a below-ground mine, the Superintendent shall perform such rescue and recovery work as may be assigned to him by the Manager or, in his absence, by the principal official present at the surface. He shall, within three days of completion of the rescue or recovery work, send a report thereof to the Regional Inspector or the Chief Inspector.

(8) The Superintendent shall maintain in a bound-paged book, a diary and shall record therein the results of each of his inspections and also the action taken by him to rectify the defects observed during Inspection.

(9) The Superintendent shall submit to the Chief Inspector and to the Regional Inspector a detailed report on the functioning of the rescue station and rescue rooms under his control in the preceding year on or before the 20th day of February of the succeeding year with particular reference to-

(a) type and number of equipment and apparatus provided and maintained;

(b) Superintendent, instructors, rescue room in-charge and rescue brigades in position as on the 31st December;

(c) number of rescue-trained persons at each below-ground mine served by the rescue station and number of such persons given refresher practices and medically examined, with results thereof;

(d) particulars of emergencies attended;

(e) any other relevant matter.

13. Duties of Instructors

(i) Under the direction of Superintendent, the instructor shall-

(a) impart course of instructions and practices to persons selected for training in rescue and recovery work as well as to rescue-trained persons and maintain a record thereof; and

(b) make inspection, test and adjustment of rescue equipment and apparatus and maintain a record thereof.

(2) In the event of an emergency at a below-ground mine. The Instructor shall perform such rescue and recovery work as may be assigned to him by the Manager or in his absence by the principal official present at the surface.

(3) The Instructor shall not leave the rescue station without prior permission of the Superintendent.

(4) In the absence of the Superintendent, the Instructor shall be incharge of the rescue station.

14. Duties and Responsibilities of Rescue Room In-charge

Every rescue room in-charge shall

(a) display prominently a list of mines served by his rescue room;

(b) maintain the equipment and apparatus kept at the rescue room in perfect order;

(c) maintain a proper record of all rescue equipment and apparatus kept at the rescue room and inspections thereof; and

(d) not allow any unauthorised person to enter into, or permit any unauthorised person to take out any apparatus or equipment from the rescue room.

15. Duties of rescue-trained Persons posted at Rescue Stations

The rescue-trained persons shall

(a) obey order of the Superintendent and Instructor and assist them in discharge of their functions;

(b) attend to messages, telephone calls, wireless and maintain a record thereof;
(c) maintain the rescue station in neat and tidy condition;
(d) maintain the equipment and apparatus kept at the rescue station in perfect order;
(e) perform rescue and recovery work in mines; and
(f) not leave rescue station without obtaining permission from the Superintendent.

16. Duties of Rescue Room Attendant

Every rescue room attendant shall-

(a) not leave the rescue room until relieved by a substitute;
(b) not allow any unauthorised person to enter in or to take out any apparatus or equipment from the rescue room;
(c) attend to telephone calls and maintain a record thereof;
(d) maintain the rescue room in neat and tidy condition; and
(e) obey orders of the rescue room in-charge and assist him in discharge of his functions.

Chapter 4 Organisation and Equipment in Mines

17. Telephone Communication

Every mine shall be connected telephonically with the rescue room and rescue station serving the mine. Wherever practicable, wireless communication shall also be provided:

Provided that where there is no telephonic communication system, the Chief Inspector may by an order in writing and subject to such condition as he may specify therein, approve any other means of communication.

18. Rescue Tracings

There shall be kept at a below-ground mine, more than three legible tracings of the workings of the mine up to a date not before three preceding months. The tracings shall show the system of ventilation in the mine, and, in particular, the general direction of air current, every point where the quantity of air is measured, every air-crossing, ventilation door, stopping, booster fan, and any other principal device for regulation and distribution of air, firedams, preparatory stoppings, every fire-fighting equipment, every water dam with dimensions and other particulars of construction, every pumping, telephone, and ambulance station, every room used for storing flammable material, reserve stations and every haulage and travelling roadway. The signs specified in Sch. V shall be used in the said tracings.

19. Appointment of rescue-trained Persons in Mines, their Disposition and Accommodation

(1) The Manager of a below-ground mine, where more than 100 persons are ordinarily employed below ground, shall ensure that at least 5 rescue-trained persons are readily available at surface at any time.

(2) The Manager of a below-ground mine, where more than 500 persons are ordinarily employed below ground, shall also ensure that persons on a scale of one man for every 100 persons or part thereof are rescue-trained persons.

(3) It shall be the responsibility of the Owner to provide suitable accommodation-

(i) close to the rescue station to the Superintendent, Instructor, and members of rescue brigade;

(ii) close to rescue room to rescue room in-charge, rescue-trained persons, and attendants attached to it; and

(iii) close to below ground mine entrance to rescue-trained persons other than those specified in (i) and (ii).

(4) There shall be provided at a below ground mine effective bell or other arrangements, as may be approved by the Regional Inspector, for immediate summoning of rescue-trained persons.

20. Selection of Persons for training in Rescue Work

No person shall be selected for training in rescue work, unless-

(i) he is between 21 and 30 years of age and holds a valid First-Aid Certificate of the standard of the St. John Ambulance Association (India);

(ii) he is certified by the Manager that he has sufficient underground experience for the purpose of rescue work;

(iii) he is certified by a qualified medical practitioner, as may be designated by the Manager after examination in accordance with Sch. VI, to be free from any organic disease or weakness and to be fit for undertaking rescue work; and

(iv) he is considered by the Superintendent of Rescue Station, after such examination and interview as he considers necessary, to be suitable for rescue work with breathing apparatus.

21. Instructions and Practices, etc.

(1) Every person selected for training in rescue work shall undergo the course of instructions and practices as set out in Part I of Sch. VII, until he has passed and has been certified as efficient by the Superintendent.

(2) Rescue-trained person shall undergo practices and receive instructions as set out in Part II of Sch. VII.

(3) A record shall be kept at every rescue station of all persons undergoing practices and receiving instructions. Such record shall contain-

(i) the date and the character of each practice;

(ii) the condition of each person after the practice, and if anything abnormal was observed in his condition, whether it was due to a defect of the apparatus or of that person; and

(iii) any other relevant information.

22. Medical Examination, etc. of rescue-trained Persons

Every rescue-trained person shall be re-examined once at least every twelve months by a qualified medical practitioner as may be designated by the Manager in accordance with Sch. VI, and, in case he is declared medically **unfit,** he shall cease to be a rescue-trained person with effect from the date he has been so declared.

23. Suspension of rescue-trained Persons

If, in the opinion of the Owner, Agent, Manager or an Inspector, a rescue-trained person is incompetent or is guilty of negligence or misconduct in the performance of his duties, the Owner, Agent, Manager or Inspector, as the case may be, after giving such person an opportunity to give a written explanation, suspend him from or debar him for undertaking any rescue and recovery work.

Chapter 5 Conduct of Rescue Work

24. Duties of Manager, etc., in Emergency

(1) On receiving information of any emergency likely to require the services of a rescue team, the Manager, or in his absence, the principal official present at the surface, shall immediately-

(a) inform the rescue room or the rescue stations serving the mine for necessary assistance;

(b) summon rescue-trained persons employed in the mine;

(c) inform the Owner, Agent or Manager of nearby mines to make available the services of rescue-trained persons employed therein, if so required;

(d) inform the rescue station about the nature of the occurrence stating whether assistance would be needed from the rescue station;

(e) summon medical assistance; and

(f) send information of the occurrence to the Regional Inspector.

(2) All rescue and recovery work at a below-ground mine shall be conducted under the control, direction and supervision of the Manager of the mine or in his absence the principal official present at the surface.

Provided that in the event of a major emergency, such as ignition, explosion, big underground fire, or an accident involving a number of persons, the Manager or the principal official shall, in taking decisions regarding rescue and recovery operations, take guidance from a group consisting of a senior official of the management, a representative each from the Director General of Mines Safety, concerned rescue station, and the recognised union of the workers, so however, that he must take necessary decisions and direct the operations as the situation warrants without waiting for the constitution or deliberations of the said group.

25. Accommodation at the below-ground Mine for Persons engaged in Rescue Work.

Whenever rescue-trained persons are engaged in rescue or recovery work at a below-ground mine, there shall be provided at such mine suitable accommodation for storage and charging of apparatus required for that work.

Such accommodation shall be situated at convenient place near the entrance in use, and shall be properly ventilated and lighted. Adequate quantity of cool and wholesome drinking water shall be provided at such accommodation, and proper canteen facilities shall also be provided for the rescue workers.

26. Entry into below-ground Mines for Rescue or Recovery Work.

(1) No person shall be allowed to enter a below-ground mine or part thereof which is unsafe for the purpose of engaging in rescue or recovery work, unless authorised by the Manager or in his absence by the principal official of the mine present at the surface. Only rescue-trained persons shall be permitted to enter the mine for the purpose of using self-contained breathing apparatus.

(2) During the course of rescue or recovery work, person or persons shall be stationed at the entrances to the below-ground mine and shall keep a written record of all persons entering and leaving such mine, and the time thereof.

27. Fresh-air Bases.

(1) As soon as possible, base or bases shall be established in fresh air as near to the irrespirable zone or zones as safety permits. Every such base shall, if possible, be connected by telephone:

(i) if the base is below ground, to the surface; or

(ii) if the base is on the surface, to the shaft bottom.

(2) Except in cases where the delay involved may result in danger to life, rescue-trained persons shall not proceed beyond any place where a base is to be established until there have been provided at such base:

(a) two persons, of whom one shall be a qualified medical practitioner, if practicable, and other shall be a rescue-trained person;

(b) a spare team with rescue apparatus, ready for immediate service;

(c) one or more reviving apparatus, oxygen revivers, etc.;

(d) first-aid box and stretcher;

(e) means of testing for carbon monoxide;

(f) hygrometer; and

(g) two flame safety lamps.

(3) Whenever men are already at work beyond the fresh-air base, there shall be provided at the base, as soon as possible, the persons, apparatus and equipment specified in sub-rule (2).

28. Leader

Every rescue team engaged in work with breathing apparatus in a mine shall be under a Leader who shall be appointed by the Superintendent.

29. Instructions to Leader

Prior to sending a rescue team underground, the Superintendent or a person authorised by him shall give clear instructions to the Leader of the team as to where it shall go and what it shall attempt.

30. Test of Apparatus

Before proceeding below ground, the Leader shall test or witness the testing of self-contained breathing apparatus of the team for leakage. No such apparatus shall be used unless it is found safe. He shall check the equipment of his party and, immediately, before entering irrespirable atmosphere, shall make sure that all breathing apparatus are working properly.

31. Duties of Leader below Ground.

(1) The Leader shall not engage in manual work. He shall give his attention solely to directing the team and to maintaining its safety. He shall examine the roof and supports during the journey, and, if there is any likelihood of fall at any place along the roadways, shall not proceed further until the team has made the place secure.

(2) The Leader shall keep the team together and shall not allow any member of the team to stray.

(3) If the atmosphere is clear, the Leader shall, when passing the junction of two or more roadways, clearly indicate the route by means of arrow marks in chalk. If the atmosphere is obscure, the Leader shall see that a lifeline is laid from the fresh-air base, and shall not allow any member of the team to move out of reach of that line; or, if that course is impracticable, he shall not proceed until every roadway branching of from the route is fenced across the whole opening.

(4) When using rescue apparatus, the Leader shall carry a watch, shall record the pressure of the compressed oxygen at intervals of 20 minutes or so, and shall commence the return journey in ample time. During travelling, he shall adopt the pace of slowest member and, if any member of the team is in distress, he shall immediately return to the fresh-air base with the whole team.

(5) The Leader shall not permit any member of the team using breathing apparatus in a mine to remain at work at any one time for a period longer than one-and-a half hours or such other period as may be specified by the Chief Inspector in respect of the breathing apparatus being used.

32. Rescue Team Members and their Duties.

(1) The number of persons in any rescue team using breathing apparatus in a mine shall not be less than five and not more than six including the Leader.

(2) In case there is no provision in any of the breathing apparatus carried by the rescue team for an extension for supply of oxygen to another person in an emergency, the team shall carry a self-rescuer.

(3) Members of rescue team shall, in general, use the signals prescribed in Sch. VIII in communicating to one another.

(4) In travelling with rescue apparatus on, every member of the team shall keep the place given to him when numbering off. If the pace is too quick or if distress is felt, the member shall at one call attention to the fact.

(5) Every member of a rescue team engaged in work with breathing apparatus in a mine shall obey the orders of the Leader of the team.

33. Restriction of second Spell of Work.

No person shall commence a second or subsequent spell of work in irrespirable atmosphere without being examined and found fit by a qualified medical practitioner.

Chapter 6 Miscellaneous

34. Obligation of Owner, Agent and Manager in a certain Situation

Whenever emergency arises at a below-ground mine, whether served by a rescue room or rescue station or not, the Owner, Agent or Manager may seek assistance or additional assistance, as the case may be, from the nearest rescue room or rescue station and in such an event:

(a) all possible assistance shall be promptly rendered by the rescue room or rescue station; and

(b) the Owner of the mine shall pay to the owner of the rescue station or rescue room rendering such assistance, the full cost of rescue services and facilities borrowed.

35. General Management

It shall be the responsibility of the Owner to establish, maintain, and ensure proper functioning of rescue room or rescue station as required under these rules, to appoint Superintendent, Instructors, rescue room in-charge, rescue-trained persons, and to provide necessary rescue equipment and apparatus as may be necessary for compliance with the provisions of these Rules.

36. Inspections

(1) The Chief Inspector or other Inspector, authorised by him in his behalf or the Regional Inspector may enter, inspect and examine any rescue station and rescue room and make such examination or inquiry as he thinks fit in order to ascertain whether the provisions of these Rules and of any orders made thereunder are being complied with.

(2) When the below-ground mines served by a rescue station or rescue room fall under the jurisdiction of two or more Regional Inspectors, the Chief Inspector may authorise any one of them for enforcement of these Rules.

37. Power to relax

Where in the opinion of the Chief Inspector, the conditions pertaining to a mine or rescue station or rescue room are such as to render compliance with any provisions contained in these rules, unnecessary or impracticable, he may, by an order in writing and subject to such conditions as he may specify therein, grant exemption from the said provisions.

38. Repeal and Saving

(1) The Coal Mines Rescue Rules, 1959, are hereby repealed.

(2) Notwithstanding such repeal, anything done or any action taken under the said Rules shall be deemed to have been done or taken under the corresponding provisions of these Rules.

Schedule I

[See Rule II (1)]

Equipment to be Kept at Rescue Room

		Nos.
A.	**Breathing Apparatus**	
	1. Two-hour self-contained breathing apparatus	54
	2. Short-duration self-contained breathing apparatus	6
	3. Absorbent charges	2,000
B.	**Resuscitating Apparatus**	
	1. Resuscitating apparatus	12
	2. Spare cylinders	8
C.	**Tube Apparatus**	
	(a) Pressure-type with bellows	2
	(b) Spare helmets	2
	(c) Pressure-type with fan	I
D.	**Ancillary Equipment**	
	1. Oxygen cylinders	12
	2. (a) oxygen pump (hand-driven)	4
	(b) oxygen pump (power-driven)	2
	3. Bobin meter	3
	4. Flow meter	2
	5. Universal tester	2
	6. Pressure gauge testing device	2
	7. Oxygen testing apparatus	1
	8. Apparatus testing tool kit	8
E.	**Lamps, Etc., and Gas Testing Device**	
	1. Flame safety lamps with maintenance kit	8
	2. Electric safety lamps	
	(a) Cap lamps with belt	60
	(b) charging rack for cap lamp with charger	
F.	**Gas Detectors**	
	1. Methane detector with battery charger, if required	3
	2. CO-detector	3
	3. CO-tube	30
	4. Multi-gas detector	2
	5. Multi-gas detector tubes for each of the noxious gases likely to be found in mines	20
G.	**Air-and Temperature-measuring Instruments**	
	1. Vane anemometer	1
	2. Velometer	1
	3. Clinical thermometer	2
	4. Whirling hygrometer or psychrometer	2

H.	**Telephone**	
	1. Genophone-Portable Telephone sets	2
1.	**Safety-and First-Aid Equipment**	
	1. Safety helmets	60
	2. Safety belts	6
	3. First-aid boxes	10
	4. Blankets	15
	5. Folding stretchers	12
	6. Self-rescuers	12
J.	**Fire-fighting Equipment**	
	1. CO_2 fire-extinguishers	4
	2. Foam-type fire-extinguishers	10
	3. Foam charges	50
	4. Dry powder-type extinguishers	15
	5. Trailer pump	1
	6. Trailer for carrying goods	1
	7. Hose pipe	300 metres
K.	**Miscellaneous Equipment**	
	1. Charging rack for car batteries	1
	2. Stop watches	3
	3. Rain gauge	1
	4. Lifeline	1 roll
	5. Guide line	1000 m
	6. (a) Evacuated sampling tubes	10
	(b) Two-line capacity stoppered sampling bottles	6
	7. Siren (hand-operated)	1
	8. Siren (Power-operated)	1
	9. Barometer	1
	10.VHF Equipment	2
	11. Rescue vans	2
	12. Station wagons	2

Schedule 2

[See Rule 1](2)]

Equipment to be Kept at Rescue Room

A.	**Breathing Apparatus**	
	1. Two-hour self-contained breathing apparatus	15
	2. Short-duration self-contained breathing apparatus	2
	3. Absorbent charges	50
B.	**Resuscitating Apparatus**	
	1. Resuscitating apparatus	3
	2. Spare cylinders	5
C.	**Tube Apparatus**	
	(a) Pressure-type with bellows	

	Item	Quantity
	(b) Spare helmets	
	(c) Pressure-type with fan	
D.	**Ancillary Equipment**	
	1. Oxygen cylinders	3
	2. Oxygen pump (hand-driven)	2
	3. Bobin meter	2
	4. Universal tester (where necessary)	1
	5. Pressure gauge testing device	1
	6. Apparatus testing tool kit	2
	7. Oxygen testing apparatus	1
E.	**Lamps, Etc., and Gas-testing Device**	
	1. Flame safety lamps (re-lighter type) with maintenance tool kit	4
	2. Electric safety lamps	
	(a) Cap lamps with belts	20
	(b) Charging rack for cap lamps with charger	
F.	**Gas Detectors**	
	1. Methane detector with battery charger, if required	2
	2. CO-detectors	2
	3. CO-tubes	10
	4. Multi-gas detector	1
5.	Multi-gas detector tubes for each of the noxious gases likely to be found in mines	10
G.	**Air- and Temperature-measuring Instruments**	
	1. Clinical thermometer	1
	2. Sling whirling hygrometer or psychrometer	I
H.	**Telephone**	
	1. Genophone-Portable telephone sets	I
I.	**Safety- and First-Aid Equipment**	
	1. Safety helmets	20
	2. Safety belts	2
	3. First-aid box	4
	4. Blankets	4
	5. Folding stretchers	4
	6. Self-rescuers	4
J.	**Fire-fighting Equipment**	
	1 CO_2 fire-extinguisher	2
	2. Foam-type fire-extinguisher	2
	3. Foam charges	20
	4. Dry powder-type extinguisher	5
K.	**Miscellaneous**	
	1. Stop watch	1
	2. Rain gauge	1
	3 . Lifeline	I roll
	4. Guide line	1000 m

5. (a) Evacuated sampling tubes	5
(b) Two-litre capacity stoppered sampling bottles	2
6. Siren (hand-operated)	1
7. Siren (power-operated)	1
8. Barometer	1*
9. Rescue van	

Schedule III

[See Rule 11(3)]

Minimum Equipment to be Kept at the Surface of Mine where no Rescue Room is Located Close to Mine Entrance

1.	Pressure-type tube apparatus with bellows	1
2.	Flame safety lamp with maintenance tool kit.	1
3.	(a) CO-detector	1
	(b) CO-tubes	10
4.	Whirling hygrometer	1
5.	Safety belt	1
6.	Resuscitating apparatus	10
7.	First-aid box	1
8.	Blankets	2
9.	Folding stretcher	1

Schedule IV

[See Rule 11(6)]

Adjustments and Tests of Breathing Apparatus, Flowmeter, Bobinmeter, Oxygen, etc.

1. Every breathing apparatus shall be thoroughly tested once at least every month or at such shorter interval as may be recommended by the manufacturers of the breathing apparatus in a manner specified in para 2.

2.
   (i) The apparatus shall be examined in respect of its general condition and particular attention shall be given to every delicate and perishable part.

   (ii) The apparatus shall be tested for leakage. If any leakage is observed, the apparatus shall be deemed unsafe for use.

   (iii) The pressure at which any automatic relief-valve discharges shall be measured and, if required, so adjusted as to operate within the limits recommended by the manufacturers.

   (iv) The pressure in the oxygen cylinder shall be measured.

   (v) The rate of delivery of oxygen shall be measured by a flowmeter, bobinmeter, universal tester. If required, the reducing valve shall be adjusted to supply oxygen at a rate of flow specified by the manufacturers. A record of such measurements and adjustments shall be kept in a bound-paged register.

---

* Not necessary if the rescue room is situated close to mine entrance or serve only one mine.

(vi) If an apparatus has been provided with an automatic demand valve, the pressure at which it operates shall be measured and, if required, adjusted so as to operate within the limits recommended by the manufacturer.

(vii) Other tests and adjustments, if any, as recommended by the manufacturers shall be performed and a record thereof kept in a bound-paged register.

3. The purity of oxygen supplied for use in breathing apparatus shall be tested. No oxygen which is found to contain more than one per cent of impurities shall be used.
4. Flowmeters shall be tested for accuracy at least once every six months and the results of every text shall be recorded.
5. Where by this schedule any particulars are required to be recorded, they shall be recorded forthwith in a bound-paged register kept at rescue room or rescue station, as the case may be, and shall be signed and dated by the person making the tests and shall be countersigned by the Superintendent.

Schedule V

[See Rule 18]

Code of Signs

Name	Symbol	Remark

Schedule VI

(See Rules 20 and 22)

Medical Examination

1. Every person selected for undergoing training in rescue and recovery work and every rescue-trained person shall be thoroughly examined medically. Particular attention shall be paid to the following requirements:
   (1) The person shall be in good mental and bodily health and free from any physical defect.
   (2) The limbs shall be well formed and developed and the function of all limbs shall be within normal limits.
   (3) (a) The standard of distant vision without glasses shall not be less than the following:
       (i) Better eye 6/6
       (ii) Worse eye 6/12
     (b) There shall be no squint in the eyes
     (c) There shall not be any organic disease of the eyes, which is likely to affect distant vision within a period of one year.
     (d) The person shall not be suffering from nystagmus or colour blindness.
   (4) Hearing shall be good. Person shall be able to hear conversational voice from a distance of 3 metres.

(5) (a) Respiratory system shall be sound and free from any chronic laryngeal, bronchial and pulmonary disease.

(b) An X-ray examination shall be made once in two years and there shall not be any evidence of any pulmonary disease.

(c) The difference of chest measurements taken after full inspiration and full expiration shall not be less than 5 cm.

(6) (a) There shall be no evidence of cardiac or vascular disease.

(b) Normal heart rate shall not be above 90 or less than 60 beats per minute. The person shall be free from dyspnoea on light exertion.

(c) Blood pressure shall not exceed 140 mm of mercury, systolic, and 80 mm of mercury, diastolic.

(7) Person shall not have hernia.

(8) Person shall not have hydrocele.

(9) The nervous system shall be sound and there shall not be any history of epilepsy or any other organic or hysterical fits or vertigo.

(10) The gums and teeth shall be healthy and free from any infection. Persons with artificial denture shall be declared unfit.

(11) Weight of person shall be in accordance with the Table given below:

Height in cm	Age in years											
	18 to 22		23 to 27		28 to 32		33 to 37		38 to 42		43 to 45	
	(1)	(2)	(1)	(2)	(1)	(2)	(1)	(2)	(1)	(2)	(1)	(2)
140–145	41	52	41	53	43	56	43	57	43	58	43	59
146–150	43	54	43	56	44	59	45	60	45	60	45	61
151–155	45	56	46	58	46	62	47	63	47	64	47	64
156–160	48	59	48	61	48	65	50	67	50	67	50	68
161–165	51	62	51	65	51	69	53	70	53	71	53	72
166–170	54	66	54	68	55	73	55	75	56	75	56	76
171–175	58	71	58	73	58	78	60	80	60	80	60	81
176–180	61	75	62	78	62	83	64	85	64	86	64	87
181–185	65	80	65	83	66	88	68	90	68	92	68	93
186–190	69	85	69	89	70	94	72	96	72	97	72	98

(1) Minimum weight in kilogram.

(2) Maximum weight in kilogram.

N.B.: In case of 12-monthly re-examination of rescue-trained person, variation up to 10% in the fitness standards may be accepted and the standard of distance vision under Cl. 3(a) may be accepted even with glasses.

Schedule VII

(See Rule 21)

Courses of Instructions and Practices

Part I-Initial Course

The course of instructions and practices shall be as follows:-

A. **Instructions:** Instructions in the following subjects-

(i) the general methods of dealing with fires below ground and the recovery of mines after fires and explosions;

(ii) the construction, use, repair, maintenance, and testing of the type or types of breathing apparatus provided, and the smoke helmets or other apparatus serving the same purpose;

(iii) the use of methods and apparatus for reviving persons;

(iv) the properties, and the methods of detection of noxious and flammable gases which may be found in mines;

(v) the taking of gas samples in irrespirable atmospheres;

(vi) the reading of mine plans;

(vii) the requirements contained in Chapter V and Sch. VII to these rules.

B. Practices

Not less than twelve practices with breathing apparatus and not less than two practices with smoke helmets or other apparatus serving the same purpose. The practices in each case shall be carried out under conditions devised to resemble those likely to be encountered in operations below/ground and requiring the use of such apparatus and shall be carried out as follows—

(a) Not more than eight and not less than five men shall take part in any practice.

(b) The practices with breathing apparatus shall commence in ordinary air, and shall progress gradually until practices can be carried out in hot and irrespirable atmosphere.

(c) The practices with breathing apparatus shall comprise the following operations:

(i) repeatedly raising and lowering of a weight of 25 kilogram to and from a height of 1.8 metres by means of a rope and pulley;

(ii) Walking continuously at a fair pace for half an hour;

(iii) building and removing temporary stoppings of stone, brick, sand bags, brattice cloth, or other materials, and carrying the materials required for such operations over a distance of at least ten metres;

(iv) removing debris in confined space as representing the clearing of a fall of roof;

(v) setting timber or other roof supports;

(vi) carrying, pulling or pushing on a stretcher a live person or dummy body weighting 70 kilogram along the length of the gallery;

(vii) the rapid establishment of communication.

Part II-Practices and instructions after becoming competent

A. Instructions

Revision of all subjects included in Part 1.

B. Practices

At least eight practices with breathing apparatus in every calendar year of which at least four months shall take place in mines and the remainder in hot and irrespirable atmosphere in the Training Gallery at rescue station. As far as practicable, these practices shall be evenly distributed, so, however, that the gap between two consecutive practices shall not exceed four months:

Provided that, if a rescue-trained person fails to undergo a refresher practice over a period exceeding four months, the Chairman, Board of Mining Examinations may, on being satisfied that the discontinuance was on valid reasons, permit him subject to the provisions contained in Rule 21, to undergo a special course of refresher practices and instructions extending over five consecutive days, whereupon he shall again become active.

Notes:

(i) All practices shall last at least two hours except on occasions when, in the opinion of Instructor, it is desirable in the interest of safety to curtail the period of practice. At some of the practices, breathing apparatus shall be worn continuously for a period of two hours.

(ii) The code of signals set out in Sch. VIII shall be used in training.

Schedule VIII

[See Rule 32(3)]

Code of Signals

A. Between members of rescue tea

One hoot	"Distress" or "Help wanted" (If no answer given to a call, "Distress" to be understood).
Two hoots	Halt
Three hoots	Retire
Four hoots	Advance
Five hoots	To call attention

E. *Between tube apparatus operator and user*

One tug	More air required
Two tugs	Give less air
Three tugs	Help me out

References

1. Peters W.: Methanausgasung und Selbstentzündung als Beispiele chemisch-physikalischer Grundlagenforschung, *Glückauf* 101 (1965), Heft 26.
2. Münzner, H. and W. Peter: Selbstentzündlichkeitsverhalten von Steinkohlen, *Erdöl und Kohle-Erdgas-Petrochemie* 19(1966), Heft 6.
3. Kuchta J.M., V.R. Rowe, and D.S. Burgess: Spontaneous Combustion Susceptibility of U.S. Coals, RI 8474, U.S. Bureau of Mines.
4. Sondreal, E.A. and H.C. Ellman: Laboratory Determination of Factors Affecting Storage of North Dakota Lignite, RI 7887, U.S. Bureau of Mines.
5. Münzner, H.: Der Einfluss von Fremdstoffen auf das Selbstentzündungsverhalten von Steinkohlen, *Glückauf Forschungshefte* 33(1972).
6. Harasta, M: Concentration of Oxygen in the goaves of longwalls, *Proceedings of the First Czechoslovak Conference on Spontaneous Combustionof Coal in Theory and practice*, Pribram, Czech, June 11-13, 1986.
7. Vinogradova, L.P., B.A. Surnatchev and E.A. Terpigorava: How Gas in Seams Affects Heatings and Susceptibility to Spontaneous Combustion, Ugol 1972 No. 9.
8. Münzner, H. and W. Peters: Adiabatische Oxidation von Steinkohlen zur Charakterisierung ihres Selbstentzündungsverhaltens, *Brenstoff-Chemie* 50(1969) No. 8.
9. Olpinski, W.: Die Bedeutung der Untersuchungen über die Selbstentzündlichkeit von Kohlen für die Prophylaxis von Grubenbränden, *Freiberger Forschungshefte* A II 5(1959), Akademie Verlag, Berlin.
10. Raju, G.S.N., V. Mahadevan, and M.A. Ramlu: Some Studies on Spontaneous Combustion of Indian Coals, *Proceedings of the Seminar on Combating Coal Fires*, Dhanbad, 1980.
11. Feng, K.K., R.N. Chakravorty and T.S. Cochrane: Spontaneous Combustion-A Coal Mining Hazard, *Can. Min., and Met. Bulletin* 66 (1973).
12. Mahadevan, V. and M.A. Ramlu: Fire-Risk Rating of Coal Mines due to Spontaneous Heating, *Journal of Mines, Metals and Fuels*, August 1985.
13. Banerjee, S.C.: A Theoretical Design to the Determination of Risk Index of Spontaneous Fires in Coal Mines, *Journal of Mines, Metals and Fuels*, 1982, Vol. 30, No. 8.
14. Beurteilung der Analysenergebnisse Grubenbrandgasproben, *Steinkohlenbergbauverein, Verlag Glückauf GmbH*, Essen, 198 1.
15. Thorp, P.: Report on Frictional Ignition at Face Power-Loaders, April 1969.

16. Report on the Use of Inertisation for Fire-fighting at Coal Mines in the European Community Adopted by the Safety and Health Commission for the Mining and Other Extractive Industries on 7.11.1985.
17. Sebor, G., and 1. Hofbauer: Chemische Verfahren zur Verhütung und Bekämpfung von Grubenbränden, VEB Deutscher Verlag fur Grundstoffindustrie, Leipzig, 1962.
18. Bureau of Mines Research: Compiled and edited by Pederson, J.R., 1983.
19. Hjelmstad, K.E. and W. H. Pomroy : Fire Warning Alarm for Underground Mines, *CIM Bulletin*, May 1964.
20. Maneval, D.R.: Assessment of Latest Technology in Coal Refuse Fire Extinguishment, *Mining Congress Journal*, May 1976.
1 . Wilson, H.S.: An Update on Coal Storage Technology, *Combustion*, August 19.
2. Mahadevan, V., and M. A. Ramlu, : Project Report on Spontaneous Combustion in Large-scale Coal Stacks, 1985, Sponsored by the Department of Science and Technology, Govt. of India.
23. Ninteman, J. Donald : Spontaneous Oxidation and Combustion of Sulphide Ores in Underground Mines, A Literature Survey, U.S.B.M Inf. Circular 8775, 1978.
24. Cameron, A.M.: *Chemistry in Relation to Fire Risk and Fire Extinction*, Sir Isaac Pitman & Sons Ltd., 1944.
25. Skotschinski, A.A., and W.B. Komarow : Grubenbewetterung, VEB Verlag Technik, Berlin, 1956.
26. Freytag, H.H.: *Handbuch der Raum Explosionen,* Verlag Chemie GmbH, Weinheim, 1965.
27. Nagy, **J.,** and D.W. Mitchell: Gas Explosion Phenomena. *Mechanization*, 1963, Vol. 27, No. 9.
28. Cashdollar, K.L., and Herzberg M.: 20-1 Explosibility Test Chamber for Dusts and Gases, *Rev. Sci. Instrum.*, 56(4), April 1985.
29. Herzberg, M., K.L. Cashdollar, C.P. Lazzara and A.C. Smith: Inhibition and Extinction of Coal Dust and Methane' Explosions RI 8708, 1982, U.S. Bureau of Mines.
30. Maskow, H. and W. Bartknecht: Zündung explosibler Gemische durch bewegliche heisse Metallteilchen, *Glückauf* 91 (1955) Heft 1/2.
31. Phillips, H.R.: Frictional Ignition Hazards Associated with the Continuous Miners, *Proceedings of the 27th International Conference of Safety in Mines Research Institutions,* New Delhi, February 20-22, 1997.
32. Thomas, V.M.: Design of Intrinsically Safe Apparatus for Use in Coal Mines, A Review of Data and Techniques, *The Min. Elect. and Mechanical Engineer*, 44(1964), No. 523.
33. Middendorf, H.: Methanschichten und Möglichkeiten zu ihrer Beseitigung, *Glückauf* 101(1965), Heft 3.
34. Skow, M.L., A.G. Kim and M. Deul: Creating a Safer Environment in U.S. Coal Mines, Methane Control Program 1964–1979.

35. Meerbach, H.: Entstehung und Verlauf von Kohlenstaubexplosionen, In-house Notes of Versuchsgrubengesellshaft, Dortmund-Tremonia.
36. Herzberg, M., K.L. Cashdollar, D.L. Ng and R.S. Conti: Domains of Flammability and Thermal Ignitability for Pulverized Coals and Other Dusts-Particle Size Dependences and Microscopic Residue Analyses, *19th Symposium (International) on Combustion*, The Combustion Institute, 1982.
37. Herzberg, M., K.L. Cashdollar, J. Opferman: The Flammability of Coal-Dust-Air Mixtures, RI 8360, 1979, U.S. Bureau of Mines.
38. Hartmann, I., M. Jacobson and R.P. Williams: Laboratory Study of American Coals, RI 5052, 1954, U.S. Bureau of Mines.
39. Hartmann, I.: Studies on the Development of Coal-Dust Explosions in Mines IC 7785, 1957, U.S. Bureau of Mines.
40. Fritzsche, C.H., and S. Rhonhof: Explosionsunglück auf der Grube Luisenthal, *Glückauf* 101 (1965), Heft 1.
41. *Fire Protection Handbook*, 14th Edition, National Fire Protection Association, Boston, 1976.
42. Nagy, J., and D. Mitchell: Coal-Dust Explosions–Interpreting the Evidence, *Coal Age* 69 (1964), No. I 1.
43. von Königslow: Der Bergbau stellt der Technik verpflichtende Aufgaben, *VDI Nachrichten*, No. 27, 1962.
44. Reeh, D.: Explosionsgeführlichkeit von Kohlenstäuben, *VGB Kraftwerkstechnik* 59 (1979), Heft 4.
45. Extembrink, W.: Experience in Dust Suppression with Solid Hygroscopic Salts (English Translation), *Glückauf* 106(1970), Heft 2 1.
46. Hartmann, 1. and J. Westfield: Rockdusting and Sampling, IC 7755, 1956, U.S. Bureau of Mines.
47. American Standard Practice for Rockdusting Underground Bituminous Coal and Lignite Mines to Prevent Coal-Dust Explosions, IC 8001, 1960, U.S. Bureau of Mines.
48. Schuhknecht, W. and H. Kunz: Ein Verfahren zur Prüfung der Flugfähigkeit von Gesteinstaub, *Glückauf* 100(1964), Heft 16.
4 9. Hartmann, I., J. Nagy and J.K. Rauschenberger: Lessons from Intensive Dust Sampling of a Coal Mine, RI 5054,1954, U.S. Bureau of Mines.
50. Terence, C.: *Introduction to Mining Chemistry*, Leonard Hill (Book) Ltd., London,1963.
51. 25 Jahre Versuchsgrube, Versuchsgubengesllschaft mbH, Dortmund.
52. Proempeler, O., H. Hobrecker and J. Epping: *Taschenkalender für Grubenbeamte des Steinkohlenbergbaus*, Karl Marklein Verlag, GmbH, Düsseldorf, 1958.
53. Externbrink, W. and H. Lewer: Das Neue Chlorkalzium-Pulver fahren, *Glückauf* 102 (1966), Heft 10.
54. Schulze-Rhonhof, H.: Versuche über die Wirksamkeit des Chlorkalzium-pastenverfahren als Explosionsshützmittel, *Glückauf* 90(1954), Heft 13/14.

55. Hamm, E.: Untersuchungen des Staubbindevermogens hygroskopischer Salzpasten zur Staubbekampfung im Steinkohlenbergbau, *Glükauf-Forschungshefte* 31(1970), Heft 3.
56. Steffenhagen, A. and H. Merbach: Wassersperren-ein wesentlicher Fortschritt in der Grubensicherheit?, *Glüickauf* 100(1964), Heft 17.
5 7. Liebman, 1. and J.K. Richmond: Suppression of Coal-dust Explosions by Water Barrier in a Conveyor Belt Entry, RI 8538, 1981, U.S. Bureau of Mines.
58. Liebman, 1. and J.K. Richmond: Suppression of Coal-dust Explosions by Passive Water Barriers in a Single Entry Mine, RI 7815, 1974, U.S. Bureau of Mines.
59. Liebman, I., J.K. Richmond, R. Pro, R. Conti and J. Corry: Triggered Barriers for the Suppression of Coal-Dust Explosions, RI 8389, 1979, U.S. Bureau of Mines.
60. Katsabanis, P.D. and Liu, Q.: Ignition of Sulphide Dust Clouds by Explosives, *CIM Bulletin*, February 1993.
61. Rispin, M. and J.R. Dalton: Sulphide Dust Ignition-resistant Explosives, CIM Bulletin, May 1994.
62. Gimm, W., H. Brenn, and P. Marggraf: Organization eines ökonomischen effectiven Betriebablaufes in Kaligruben der DDR unter schwierigen geologischen Bedingungen, *Neue Bergbautechnik*, 2(1972), Heft 8.
63. Zabetakis, M.G.: Mine Gases, Safety Manual No. 2, Mining Enforcement and Safety Administration, U.S.A.
64. *Draeger Detector Tube Handbook*, 3rd Edition, 1976.
65. Richtlinien für die Verhütung und Bekämpfung von Grubenbränden auf den Steinkohlenbergwerken im Verwaltungsbezirk des Ober-bergamts Dortmund, 1951.
66. Fires, Gases and Ventilation in Metal Mines, Miner's Circular 55, U.S. Bureau of Mines, 1946.
67. Tröstel, H.: Ein Handgerät zur Methanmessung im Wetterstrom und in Absaugeleitungen, *Glückauf* 100 (1964), Heft 3.
68. Diel, Peter, Uranium mining in Eastern Germany: The Wismut legacy. On the Internet. updated 2 Sept 2003.
69. Mesagi, F.L. The Radiation Hazard in Mining. Safety Manual No. 7. US Department of the Interior.
70. Gudelines for Drinking Water Quality. World Health Organization Draft. Third Edition 2003.
71. Bräuner, G.: Gebirgsdruck und Gebirgsshläge, *Verlag Glückauf* GmbH, Essen, 1981.
72. Hargraves, A.J.: Instantaneous Outbursts of Coal and Gas – A Review, *Proc. Australas. Inst. Min. Metall.*, No. 285, 1983.
73. Report of the Working Party on Outbursts of Firedamp from the Floor of Coal Seams, Coal Industry National Consultative Council of Safety and Health Committee, Ministry of Power, U.K., 1965.

74. Ujihira, M. and K. Hashimoto: Memoirs of Faculty of Engineering, Hokkaido University, 14(1976), No. 3.
75. Patteisky, K.: Gebirgsshläge beim Abbau von Stenkohlenflözen (11 Teil), Bergfreiheit 21 (1956), Heft 6.
76. Leitfaden für das Grubenrettungswesen, *Verlag Glückauf* GmbH, Essen, 1958.
77. Mitchell, D.W. and F.A. Burns: Interpreting the State of a Mine Fire, RI 1103, 1979, U.S. Bureau of Mines.
78. Drekopf, K.: Die Explosionsfdhigkeit von Grubenbrandgasen, *Glückauf* 89(1953), Heft 29/30.
79. Drekopf, K.: Die Bestimmung der Explosionsfähigkeit von Grubenbrandgasen, Bergbau-Archiv 24(1963).
80. Hughes, A.J. and W.E. Raybould: The Rapid Determination of the Explosibility of Mine Fire Gases, *The Mining Engineer*, 1960, No. 1.
81. Jagger, J.B. and T.E. James: a Simplified Graphical Method for Determining the Flammability of Mine Fire Gases, *The Mining Engineer*, 1963, No. 29.
82. Müller, R.: Ermittlung und Beurteilung der Explosionsfähigkeit von Grubenbrandgasen, *Glückauf-Forschungshefte*, Dec. 1977.
83. Litton, C.D., M. Herzberg, A.L. Furno and J.M. Kuchta: Monitoring Submicrometer Particles in Sealed Fire Areas, RI 8586, 1981 U.S. Bureau of Mines.
84. Hollmann, F.: Alkali or Lime for Regenerator Cartidge for Self-Contained Oxygen Breathing Apparatus? *Draeger Review*, No. 2, 1960.
85. Bernard, T. E., N. Kyriazi and R.L. Stein: CO-Absorption Characteristics of Mine Rescue Breathing Apparatus, RI 8342, 1979, U.S. Bureau of Mines.
86. A Report prepared by Hauptstelle fur das Grubenrettungswesen, Ruhrkhle Bergbau AG on behalf the International Energy Agency.
87. Kyriazi, Nicholas: Performance Comparison of Rescue Breathing Apparatus, Report of Investigations 9650, NIOSH, Pittsburgh, October 1999.
88. Thorp, P: A Note on the Maxaman Ventilator/Resuscitator with Special Reference to the Mines Rescue Application, H.O. Mines Rescue, National Coal Board, April 1983.
89. Gasschützgerdteraüme, Austrüstung Draeger, 1943.
90. Mitteilungen für Oberftihrer von Grubenwehren, Hauptstelle für das Grubenrettungswesen, Essen, 1987.
91. Rescue Workers Instruction Manual, Mines Rescue Service, Yorkshire District, National Coal Board, U.K.
92. Venter, J.M., C.J.H. Oosthuizen *et al:* An Alternative Method to supply Respirable Air in Refuge Bays of Collieries, *Journal of the Mine ion Society of South Africa*, October/December 1997.
93. Fritzsche, C. H.: *Lehrbuch der Bergbaukunde*, Springer Verlag Berlin, Gottingen, Heidelberg (I 95 8).

94. Potsch, H.: Wasserhaltung und Laugenwirtschaft, Taschenbuch für den Bergmann Band III-Tiefbau, VEB Deutscher Verlag für Grundstoffindustie, Leipzig, 1962.
95. Trupak, N.G.: *Special Methods of Driving Mine Entries* (Russian Text), Publishing House Nedra Moscow, 1964.
96. Baltaitis, V.A.: *Fighting Fires in Coal Mines* (Russian Text), 1961.
97 Fjodorow, S.A.: *Hauptgrubenbaue*, VEB Verlag Technik Berlin, 1954.

Index